GENDER

THIRD EDITION

LISA WADE

Tulane University

MYRA MARX FERREE

University of Wisconsin–Madison

W. W. NORTON & COMPANY

Celebrating a Century of Independent Publishing

W. W. Norton & Company has been independent since its founding in 1923, when William Warder Norton and Mary D. Herter Norton first published lectures delivered at the People's Institute, the adult education division of New York City's Cooper Union. The firm soon expanded its program beyond the Institute, publishing books by celebrated academics from America and abroad. By midcentury, the two major pillars of Norton's publishing program—trade books and college texts—were firmly established. In the 1950s, the Norton family transferred control of the company to its employees, and today—with a staff of five hundred and hundreds of trade, college, and professional titles published each year—W. W. Norton & Company stands as the largest and oldest publishing house owned wholly by its employees.

Editor: Sasha Levitt
Assistant Editor: Erika Nakagawa
Project Editor: Maura Gaughan
Managing Editor, College: Marian Johnson
Managing Editor, College Digital Media: Kim Yi
Production Manager: Brenda Manzanedo
Media Editor: Eileen Connell
Associate Media Editor: Alexandra Park
Media Editorial Assistant: Caleb Wertz
Marketing Director, Sociology: Julia Hall
Design Director: Jillian Burr
Director of College Permissions: Megan Schindel
Permissions Specialist: Josh Garvin
Photo Editor: Amla Sanghvi
Composition: Achorn International, Inc.
Manufacturing: Core Publishing Solutions

Permission to use copyrighted material is included in the Credits, which begin on page 465.

Library of Congress Cataloging-in-Publication Data

Names: Wade, Lisa (Professor), author. | Ferree, Myra Marx, author.
Title: Gender : ideas, interactions, institutions / Lisa Wade, Tulane University,
    Myra Marx Ferree, University of Wisconsin, Madison.
Description: Third Edition. | New York, NY : W. W. Norton & Company, Inc., [2023] |
    Revised edition of the authors' Gender : ideas, interactions, institutions, [2019] |
    Includes bibliographical references and index.
Identifiers: LCCN 2022036320 | ISBN 9780393892864 (paperback) |
    ISBN 9781324044055 (ebook other)
Subjects: LCSH: Sex role. | Sex differences. | Feminist theory.
Classification: LCC HQ1075 .W33 2023 | DDC 305.3—dc23
LC record available at https://lccn.loc.gov/2022036320

ISBN: 978-0-393-89286-4 (pbk.)

W. W. Norton & Company, Inc., 500 Fifth Avenue, New York, N.Y. 10110
www.wwnorton.com
W. W. Norton & Company Ltd., 15 Carlisle Street, London W1D 3BS
1 2 3 4 5 6 7 8 9 0

ABOUT THE AUTHORS

LISA WADE is an Associate Professor at Tulane University with appointments in Sociology, the Gender and Sexuality Studies Program, and the Newcomb Institute. She is the author of *American Hookup: The New Culture of Sex on Campus* (2017); the author of *Terrible Magnificent Sociology* (2022), an introduction to sociology; and the co-editor of *Assigned: Life with Gender*, with Chris Uggen and Douglas Hartmann. She is also the author of numerous academic journal articles and other professional publications. As a public-facing scholar, Dr. Wade enjoys working to make her and others' scholarship engaging to a public audience, frequently appearing in news and opinion outlets. You can find her online at lisa-wade.com and on Twitter @lisawade.

MYRA MARX FERREE retired in 2019 as the Alice H. Cook Professor of Sociology at the University of Wisconsin-Madison and is currently affiliated with the Minda de Gunzberg Center for European Studies at Harvard University. She is the author of *Varieties of Feminism: German Gender Politics in Global Perspective* (2012) as well as numerous articles and book chapters; the co-author of *Shaping Abortion Discourse* (2002) and *Controversy and Coalition* (2000); and a co-editor of *Gender, Violence, and Human Security* (2013), *Global Feminism* (2006), and *Revisioning Gender* (1998). Dr. Ferree is the recipient of various prizes for contributions to gender studies, including the Jessie Bernard Award from the American Sociological Association, the Victoria Schuck Award from the American Political Science Association, and the Distinguished Career Award from the American Sociological Association Section on Race, Gender, and Class. Her post-retirement research has focused on the contentious gender politics that contribute to polarization and to anti-democratic mobilizations from the populist right in both Germany and the United States.

CONTENTS

PREFACE

We would never have dared to take on the challenge of writing a textbook without Karl Bakeman's initial encouragement. His confidence in our initial vision was inspiring and kept us going until the project could be placed into the very capable hands of Sasha Levitt. Sasha ushered the first edition to completion with her meticulous reading, thoughtful suggestions, and words of encouragement.

During the revision processes, Sasha has come to be an invaluable member of the team, with a perfect mix of stewardship, cheerleading, careful decision-making, and collaborative data-wrangling and fact-checking. She has kept us on target conceptually as well as chronologically, helping us to think hard about points raised by reviewers, and yet kept the revision process smoothly moving forward to meet our deadlines. Without her firm hand on the tiller, our occasional excursions into the weeds might have swamped new revisions with unnecessary changes or ballooned them with new material. Her editorial eye has kept us within our word limits, focused on key points, and true to our vision, all without too much sacrifice. Sasha has become a true partner in the difficult process of adding the new without losing the old, and we could not have pulled off either revision without her.

Indeed, the revision for the third edition was far more challenging than any of us anticipated. World-shattering events, political upheavals, and ideological schisms came one after the other in the past few years: war, illness, and natural disaster, to name but three. Meanwhile, the further rise of authoritarianism in the United States and elsewhere has led to heightened conflict between movements and countermovements of all kinds, including efforts to roll back reproductive rights.

Good things are happening, too, and we tried hard to capture these positive changes. Since the second edition, intersectionality has become a household word. Trans women and men and nonbinary people have achieved an impressive amount of visibility. The Black Lives Matter and Stop Asian Hate movements have raised awareness of both interpersonal and institutionalized forms of racism. As usual, advances must be fought for. We had the opportunity to celebrate when Ketanji Brown Jackson and Kamala Harris rose to positions of leadership in the United States.

It was dizzying to try to capture how much the world had changed since the second edition went to print. We are ever grateful to our reviewers, whose suggestions helped us know how to respond to these roiling changes. Within the social sciences, expectations to be intersectional have rightfully intensified. Myra, especially, held our collective feet to the fire to do justice to the importance of intersectionality. Heightened attention to the experiences of gender minorities has raised the bar for inclusive, responsible, and respectful language. Even we had to work hard to catch up to the new and better ways of talking about bodies, identities, and relationships. Our own standards for readability have also risen. Lisa had written an entire introductory textbook since the second revision had gone to print, leaving her with higher expectations for clarity, prose, and material that truly captures the imagination.

We hope the balances we struck between new insights, continuing concerns, and accessibility will prove satisfying, but we also recognize that the challenges and changes in understanding of inequalities are ongoing. We expect that the future will continue to demand reconsideration of things we think we know now. We are always open to further criticism and grateful for specific suggestions.

Of course, we could have done none of this without the mountain of support that Norton has offered from beginning to end. Although Sasha has been our visible director, the many hands behind the scenes include project editor Maura Gaughan, who kept us on schedule and collated our changes, and production manager Brenda Manzanedo, who turned our manuscript into the pages you hold now. We also thank assistant editor Erika Nakagawa for her logistical help in preparing that manuscript as well as her thoughtful suggestions for ways to improve the book, designer Jillian Burr for her keen graphic eye, and our copyeditor, Jude Grant, for crossing our t's and dotting our i's. The many images that enrich this book are thanks to photo editors Amla Sanghvi and photo researcher Jane Miller. We are also grateful to have discovered Leland Bobbé, the artist whose half-drag portraits fascinated us. Selecting the individuals to feature on each edition is a collaborative process aided by the further creative work of Jillian Burr and Debra Morton Hoyt. We're grateful for the result: striking covers that we hope catch the eye and spark conversation.

We would also like to thank the reviewers who commented on drafts of the book and its revision in various stages: Rachel Allison, Shayna Asher-Shapiro, Phyllis L. Baker, Kristen Barber, Anne Barrett, Miriam Barcus, Shira Barlas, Bernadette Barton, Sarah Becker, Dana Berkowitz, Maura Ryan Bernales, Emily Birnbaum, Natalie Boero, Catherine Bolzendahl, Valerie Chepp, Nancy Dess, Lisa Dilks, Mischa DiBattiste, Erica Dixon, Mary Donaghy, Michelle Durden, Julia Eriksen, Jennifer Fagen, Angela Frederick, Jessica Greenebaum, Nona Gronert, Lee Harrington, Jennifer Haskin, Sarah Hayford, Alexandra Hendley, Penelope Herideen, Melanie Hughes, Miho Iwata, Jennifer Jacobson, Rachel Kaplan, Madeline Kiefer, Linda Kim, Rachel Kraus, Carrie Lacy, Thomas J. Linneman, Caitlin Maher, Gul Aldikacti Marshall, Janice McCabe, Karyn McKinney, Carly Mee, Jennifer Bickham

Mendez, Beth Mintz, Joya Misra, Beth Montemurro, Christine Mowery, Stephanie Nawyn, Madeleine Pape, Lisa Pellerin, Anna Penner, Sarah Prior, Megan Reid, Mahua Sarkar, Rachel M. Schmitz, Gwen Sharp, Mimi Schippers, Emily Fitzgibbons Shafer, Kazuko Suzuki, Jaita Talukdar, Rachel Terman, Mieke Beth Thomeer, Ashley Vancil-Leap, Kristen Williams, and Kersti Alice Yllo, as well as the students at Babson College, Occidental College, Nevada State College, and the University of Wisconsin-Madison who agreed to be test subjects. Our gratitude goes also to the users of the first edition who offered us valuable feedback on what they enjoyed and what they found missing, either directly or through Norton. We've tried to take up their suggestions by not merely squeezing in occasional new material but by rethinking the perspectives and priorities that might have left such concerns on the cutting room floor the first time around.

Most of all, the two of us are happy to discover that we could collaborate in being creative over the long term of this project, contributing different talents at different times, and jumping the inevitable hurdles without tripping each other up. In fact, we were each other's toughest critic and warmest supporter. Once upon a time, Lisa was Myra's student, but in finding ways to communicate our interest and enthusiasm to students, we became a team. In the course of each revision, we came to appreciate each other's strengths more and more. We rejoice in the collegial relationship we have constructed and how we relied on it in making this revision happen. We hope you enjoy reading this book as much as we enjoyed making it.

Lisa Wade
Myra Marx Ferree

GENDER

IDEAS, INTERACTIONS, INSTITUTIONS

THIRD EDITION

Introduction

Some of the most vicious killers who ever lived served in the Persian army. In the late 1500s, under the reign of Abbas I, these soldiers defeated the Uzbeks and the Ottomans and reconquered provinces lost to India and Portugal, earning the admiration of all of Europe. Their most lethal advantage was the high heel.[1] Being on horseback, heels kept their feet in the stirrups when they rose up to shoot their muskets. It gave them deadly aim. The first high-heeled shoe, it turns out, was a weapon of war.

Enthralled by the military men's prowess, aristocratic men in Europe began wearing high heels in their daily lives of leisure, using the shoe to borrow some of the Persian army's masculine mystique. In a way, they were like today's basketball fans wearing Air Jordans. The aristocrats weren't any better on the battlefield than your average basketball fan is on the court, but the shoes symbolically linked them to the soldiers' extraordinary achievements. The shoes invoked a distinctly *manly* power related to victory in battle, just as the basketball shoes link the contemporary wearer to the amazing athleticism of Michael Jordan.

As with most fashions, there was trickle down. Soon men of all classes were donning high heels, stumbling around the cobblestone streets of Europe feeling pretty suave. And then women decided they wanted a piece of the action too. In the 1630s, masculine

Abbas King of Persia

Shah Abbas I, who ruled Persia between 1588 and 1629, shows off not only his scimitar but also his high heels.

fashions were "in" for ladies. They cut their hair, smoked pipes, and added military decorations to their dresses. For women, high heels were nothing short of masculine mimicry.

These early fashionistas irked the aristocrats who first borrowed the style. The whole point of nobility, after all, was to be *above* everyone else. In response, the elites started wearing higher and higher heels. France's King Louis XIV even decreed that no one was allowed to wear heels higher than his.[2] In the New World, the Massachusetts Bay Colony passed a law saying any woman caught wearing heels would incur the same penalty as a witch.[3]

But the masses persisted. And so the aristocrats shifted strategies: They dropped high heels altogether. With the Enlightenment had come a shift toward logic and reason. Adopting the philosophy that it was intelligence—not heel height—that bestowed superiority, aristocrats donned flats and began mocking people who wore high heels, suggesting that wearing such impractical shoes was the height of stupidity.

Ever since, the shoe has remained mostly out of fashion for men—cowboys excluded, of course, and disco notwithstanding—but it's continued to tweak the toes of women in every possible situation, from weddings to the workplace. No longer at risk of being burned at the stake, women are allowed to wear high heels, now fully associated with femininity in the American imagination. Some women even feel pressure to do so, particularly if they're trying to look pretty or professional. And there remains the sense that the right pair brings a touch of class.

The attempts by aristocrats to keep high heels to themselves are part of a phenomenon that sociologists call **distinction**, a word used to describe efforts to differentiate one's own group from others. In this historical example, we see elite men working hard to make a simultaneously class- and gender-based distinction. If the aristocrats had had their way, only rich men would have ever worn high heels. Today, high heels continue to serve as a marker of gender distinction. With few exceptions, only women (and people doing femininity) wear high heels.

Distinction is a main theme of this book. The word *gender* exists only because we distinguish between people in this particular way. If we didn't care about distinguishing men from women, the whole concept would be utterly unnecessary. We don't, after all, tend to have words for physical differences that don't have meaning to us. For example, we don't make a big deal out of the fact that some people have the gene that allows them to curl their tongue and some people don't. There's no concept of "tongueability" that refers to the separation of people into the curly tongued and the flat tongued. Why would we need such a thing? The vast majority of us just don't care. Likewise, the ability to focus one's eyes on a close or distant object isn't used to signify status and being right handed is no longer considered better than being left handed.

Gender, then, is about distinction. Like tongueability, vision, and handedness, it is a biological reality. We are a species that reproduces sexually. We come, roughly, in two body types: one built to gestate new life and one made to mix up the genes of the species. The word **sex** is used to refer to these physical differences in primary sexual characteristics (the presence of organs directly involved in reproduction) and secondary sexual characteristics (such as patterns of hair growth, the amount of breast tissue, and distribution of body fat).

We usually use the words **male** and **female** to refer to sex. Often, this book will instead refer to

Louis XIV, king of France from 1643 to 1715, gives himself a boost with big hair and high heels.

male and female as one's **assigned sex**, an outcome of the interpretation of known sex-related characteristics before and at birth. Recognizing that sex is assigned acknowledges that features of our bodies do not determine who we are and also that not every body fits neatly into one category or the other.

Unlike tongueability, vision, and handedness, we make the biology of sex socially significant. When we differentiate between men and women, for example, we also invoke blue and pink baby blankets, suits and dresses, and action movies and chick flicks. These are all examples of the world divided up into the **masculine** and the **feminine**, into things we associate with men and women. The word **gender** primarily refers to the symbolism of masculinity and femininity that we connect to bodies assigned male and female at birth. *Gendering* is an active process that connects physical bodies, meaningful identities, and symbolic representations and then translates them into distinctions.

Symbols matter because they shape our sense of self. They push us to try to fit our bodies into constraints that "pinch" both physically and symbolically, as high heels do. They prompt us to invent ways around bodily limitations, as eyeglasses do. They inform how our bodies are interpreted; we form

One of these people is not like the others. We perform gendered distinctions like the one shown here every day, often simply out of habit.

self-concepts based on the categories our society finds meaningful: Black or Hispanic, able or disabled, men or women, old or young. Symbols are part of our collective imaginations and, accordingly, the stuff out of which we create human reality. Gender symbolism shapes not just our identities and the ideas in our heads but also our workplaces, families, and schools, and our options for navigating through them.

This is why the concept of distinction is so important. Much of what we believe about men and women—even much of what we imagine is strictly biological—is not naturally occurring difference that emerges from our bodies. Instead, it's an outcome of active efforts to produce and maintain difference: a sea of people working together to make men masculine and women feminine (and to erase people who are neither) and to signify the relative importance of masculinity and femininity in every domain and for every body.

Commonly held ideas, and the behaviors that both uphold and challenge them, are part of **culture**: a group's shared beliefs and the practices and material things that reflect them. Human lives are wrapped in cultural meaning, like the powerful masculinity once ascribed to high heels. So gender isn't merely biological; it's cultural. It's the result of a great deal of human effort guided by shared cultural ideas.

Why would people put so much effort into maintaining this illusion of distinction?

Imagine those aristocratic tantrums: pampered, wig-wearing, face-powdered men stomping their high-heeled feet in frustration with the lowly copycats. *How dare the masses blur the line between us*, they may have cried. Today it might sound silly, ridiculous even, to care about who does and doesn't wear high heels. But at the time it was a very serious matter. Successful efforts at distinction ensured that these elite men really *seemed* different and, more importantly, *better than* women and other types of men. This was at the very core of the aristocracy: the idea that some people truly are superior and, by virtue of their superiority, entitled to hoard wealth and monopolize power. They had no superpowers with which to claim superiority, no actual proof that God wanted things that way, no biological trait that gave them an obvious advantage. What *did* they have to distinguish themselves? High heels.

Without high heels and other symbols of superiority, aristocrats couldn't make a claim to the right to rule. Without difference, in other words, there could be no hierarchy. This is still true today. If one wants to argue that Group A is superior to Group B, these must be distinguishable groups. We can't think more highly of one type of person than another unless we have at least two types. Distinction, then, must be maintained if we're going to value certain types of people more than others, allowing them to demand more power, attract more prestige, and claim the right to extreme wealth.

Wealth and power continue to be hoarded and monopolized. These inequalities continue to be justified—made to seem normal and natural—by producing differences that make group membership seem meaningful and inequality inevitable or right. We all engage in actions designed to align ourselves with some people and differentiate ourselves from others. Thus, we see the persistence of social classes, racial and ethnic categories, the urban-rural divide, queer and heterosexual identities, liberal and conserva-tive parties, and various sects of religions, among other distinctions. These categories aren't all bad; they give us a sense of belonging and bring joy and pleasure into our lives. But they also serve as classifications by which societies unevenly distribute power and privilege.

Gender is no different in this regard. There's a story to tell about both difference and hierarchy, and it involves both pleasure and pain. We'll wait a bit before we seriously tackle the problem of gender inequality, spending several chapters first learning just how enjoyable studying gender can be. There'll be funny parts and fascinating parts. You'll meet figure skaters and football players, fish and flight attendants, and, yes, feminists too. Even-tually we'll get to the part that makes you want to throw the book across the room. We won't take it personally. For now, let's pick up right where we started, with distinction.

> THE ONES WITH EYELASHES ARE GIRLS;
> BOYS DON'T HAVE EYELASHES.
>
> —FOUR-YEAR-OLD ERIN DESCRIBING HER DRAWING[1]

1

Ideas

In 2014, when the first edition of this textbook was published, most people had very little exposure to the idea that gender could be expressed in many different ways. This was still largely true in 2018, when the second edition was released. In the few years since, awareness of gender diversity has increased dramatically. As a result, young people in the United States today are growing up with a language for gender diversity—and, often, an appreciation of it—that previous generations lacked. You may already be a part of this broader conversation. Or you may be relatively new to it. This chapter aims to provide a shared foundation so that the conversation can continue, in class and beyond.

Central to this discussion is the notion of the **gender binary**, a phrase that refers to the idea that there are only two types of people: masculine men assigned male at birth and feminine women assigned female at birth. Invoking the gender binary, we often cast men and women as "opposite sexes"—a striking phrase that suggests that whatever men are, women are not, and vice versa. The gender binary is also reflected in the tendency to talk about men and women as if those in each group are all alike. The nervous father might warn his thirteen-year-old daughter, for example, "Boys only want one thing," while the Valentine's Day commercial insists all women love chocolate. We might say "I'm such a girl!" when we confess we love romantic comedies or repeat the refrain "Boys will be boys" when observing the antics of a young cousin. If we're feeling hurt, we might even comfort ourselves by saying "Men suck" or "Women are crazy."

These are gender **stereotypes**: fixed, oversimplified, and distorted ideas about categories of people. When push comes to shove, we know that these stereotypes are untrue. Most people we know well defy such stereotypes. And we know that we personally don't conform to stereotypical versions of men or women. Some of us may not even be men or women. Almost all of us are a mishmash of characteristics, some of which are deemed feminine and some masculine. In other words, we contain multitudes, with the capacity to like both romantic comedies *and* superhero movies. Why would it be otherwise? This leads us to the first of many probing questions this book will attempt to answer:

> Q+A   **If we don't learn the idea of the gender binary by observing the people around us, where does the idea come from?**

This chapter will show that even as we've become more sophisticated about gender diversity, we still often use the gender binary as a scaffold for understanding the world. Being part of our culture means that most of us will put people and things into masculine and feminine categories and subcategories out of habit. We apply the binary to human bodies, usually assuming that the people we know can be divided into two categories with different, nonoverlapping anatomies, physiologies, and identities. We also apply the gender binary to objects, places, activities, talents, and ideas.

We become so skilled at layering ideas about gender onto the world that we have a hard time seeing gender for what it really is. We don't notice when gender stereotypes don't make sense. Even more, we tend to see and remember things consistent with gender stereotypes while forgetting or misremembering things inconsistent with them. In other words, gender is a logic that we are talented at manipulating, but it's manipulating us too.

In this, we are not alone. Essentially all societies notice and interpret sex-related differences in our bodies, so we're no different in that sense. In fact, in a later section this chapter will explore some of the other ways that people have thought about gender. But first, let's take a closer look at the gender binary itself and examine whether our bodies support the idea that there are two and only two sexes.

THE BINARY AND OUR BODIES

At fertilization, a sperm meets an ovum. If that sperm carries an X chromosome, the fertilization prompts the development of a female fetus; if the sperm carries a Y chromosome, it prompts the development of a male fetus. This, however, is just the beginning of a complex process involving at least eight steps, as shown in Table 1.1. It's a process, too, that involves many biological twists and turns, naturally producing many different kinds of bodies and leaving room for a variety of gender identities. Our **gender identity** is our subjective sense of our own gender.

The gender binary presumes that we are all **cisgender**. The term refers to people who are assigned male at birth who identify as men and to people who are assigned female at birth who identify as women. In other words, a cisgender person's gender identity aligns with the sex they were assigned at birth. Column 1 describes the pathway followed by a typical cisgender man. In this case, a fertilized egg carries an X and a Y chromosome. A gene on the latter will interact with several genes on the former and dozens of other genes located on yet other chromosomes, triggering the development of testes.[2] If testes develop, they begin producing a mix of androgens and estrogens. These usually guide the body to develop internal and external genitalia typical of males. At puberty, XY males will experience a deepening of their voice. They'll also probably have less breast tissue and different patterns of pubic hair than XX females. People on this pathway will likely identify as men.

Column 2 illustrates the pathway followed by a typical cisgender woman. Without the intervention of a Y chromosome, an XX fertilized egg will usually develop ovaries that produce a mix of androgens and estrogens that prompt the development of internal and external genitalia typical of females. At puberty, XX females may develop breasts that are, on average, larger than those developed by XY males and grow pubic hair in a slightly different pattern. Typically, XX females will begin menstruating. People on this pathway will likely identify as women.

Many people grow up with bodies that follow these pathways, comfortably identifying with the gender category that is culturally associated with the sex they were assigned at birth. However, this isn't true for everyone.

Intersexuality

Apart from columns 1 and 2, dozens of conditions can result in a body defined as **intersex**, with a reproductive or sexual anatomy that doesn't fit the typical definitions of female or male.[3] The sociologist Georgiann Davis is open about being

TABLE 1.1 | EXAMPLES OF SEX/GENDER PATHWAYS

Step	Cisgender Men	Cisgender Women
Chromosomes	XY	XX
Gonads	Testes	Ovaries
Hormones	Androgens/estrogens	Estrogens/androgens
External Genitalia	Penis, scrotum	Clitoris, labia
Internal Genitalia	Seminal vesicles, prostate, epididymis, vas deferens	Vagina, uterus, fallopian tubes
Examination at Birth	Assigned male	Assigned female
Secondary Sex Characteristics	Pubic hair, deep voice, Adam's apple	Pubic hair, breasts, menstruation
Gender Identity	Boy/man	Girl/woman

intersex.[4] At thirteen years old, she began complaining of abdominal pain. Her parents brought her to the doctor. After extensive examination and testing, she was told she had "underdeveloped ovaries" that had a high chance of becoming cancerous. Her parents consented to surgery to remove them. Six years later, she requested her medical records in the routine process of acquiring a new doctor, only to learn she'd never had ovaries at all.

Georgiann was diagnosed with what physicians call complete androgen insensitivity syndrome.[5] The pathway is captured in the third column of Table 1.1. At fertilization, a Y sperm combined with an X egg, putting her on the biological path to becoming male. She developed testes, not ovaries. Her testes produced a specific mix of hormones intended to instruct her body to produce external genitalia typical of males, but because her cells lacked the ability to detect these hormones, her testes remained in her abdomen and her external genitalia developed such that doctors assigned her female at birth.

Georgiann's condition is a hormone-based departure from the path to unambiguous male and female bodies. Other intersex conditions are also caused by such differences. Sometimes an XX fetus has a hyperactive adrenal gland, for example. That gland may produce hormones that press the body to develop a clitoris that resembles a small-to-medium-size penis. Most babies born with this condition are comfortable as women when they grow older and are perfectly healthy, as it's not a medical problem to have a slightly large clitoris.

Woman with Complete Androgen Insensitivity	Man with Klinefelter Syndrome	Trans Man
XY	XXY	XX
Testes	Testes	Ovaries
Estrogens/androgens	Androgens/estrogens	Estrogens/androgens
Clitoris, labia	Penis, scrotum	Clitoris, labia (unless changed via surgery)
A vagina that is shallow in depth	Seminal vesicles, prostate, epididymis, vas deferens	Vagina, uterus, fallopian tubes (unless changed via surgery)
Assigned female	Assigned male	Assigned female
Pubic hair, breast tissue (will likely have testes removed and begin hormone therapy)	Pubic hair, deep voice, Adam's apple; some develop breast tissue	Pubic hair, breast tissue, menstruation (unless hormones are blocked)
Girl/woman	Boy/man	Boy/man

Another potential intersex pathway is illustrated in the fourth column of Table 1.1. This one is produced by chromosomal instead of hormonal differences. The column follows the path of a typical man who carries XXY chromosomes, a condition called Klinefelter syndrome.[6] Compared to people with XY chromosomes, people with Klinefelter syndrome may be especially tall, with broader hips and less body hair. They generally identify as men and develop internal and external genitalia typical of XY males.

Other chromosomal differences occur in nature too. Some of us carry XXXY, XXX, or XYY chromosomes. Some people are born with only one chromosome, an X (a person can't be born with only a Y). These conditions are caused by an anomaly in the cell division that make eggs and sperm. Sometimes sex chromosomes "stick" to each other and resist dividing with the rest of our chromosomes. In other cases, variations in development can produce individuals with XX chromosomes that carry some genes from a Y (who are assigned male at birth) or individuals carrying XY chromosomes in which essential genes are damaged or deleted (who are assigned female at birth).

It's estimated that at least one out of every hundred people is to some degree intersex.[7] Some people with these differences face trouble with fertility (but not always); some (but not all) will face specific health problems or developmental differences. Most have gender identities that match their assigned sex. Such individuals often easily blend in with non-intersex people. We all almost certainly know people who are intersex—and we likely don't know who they are. While some of us are diagnosed at birth, other times it's discovered later in life; sometimes we never learn of it at all.

If a child's intersexuality is discovered, parents often face pressure to consent to surgery to bring their children's bodies into alignment with the gender binary. This occurs even when that surgery is medically unnecessary.[8] More often than not, doctors default to female assignment.[9]

Upon adulthood, many of these children have questioned the necessity of these procedures, noting pain and suffering, the frequent loss of physical function, the inability of infants or small children to give consent, and the presumption involved in choosing a side of the binary on behalf of someone else. The work of intersex activists—those who, like Georgiann, have been trying to draw attention to the problems with medically unnecessary surgery before the age of consent—has influenced many doctors to delay surgery until people with intersex bodies can make informed decisions, but surgeries on infants have not ended. In fact, in 2020 California rejected what would have been the first state ban on such procedures in the United States.

Trans and Nonbinary Identities

Distinct from bodies that follow intersex biological paths, there are people whose internal sense of self emerges as inconsistent with the sex they were assigned at birth. Some of us are **transgender**, or **trans**, a term that refers to people whose gender identity is different from the sex they were assigned at birth. Trans people can be women, men, or nonbinary. **Nonbinary** is a gender category that encompasses people who are either both man and woman or neither man nor woman. People may also be **gender fluid**, or without a fixed gender identity. To be gender fluid is to adopt different gender identities and expressions over time. About 1 out of every 250 people in the United States is trans, inclusive of nonbinary and gender-fluid people, and young people are more likely to be trans than older people.[10]

The last table column illustrates the path for a trans man. In this case, he carries XX chromosomes and follows the biological pathway typical of XX females, yet during childhood he develops a sense of self as a boy. This was the experience, for example, of a boy named Benjamin.[11] Though he was assigned female at birth, Ben consistently expressed preferences for boys' clothes and games. He made friends primarily with other boys. He liked hockey and martial arts. His parents saw him as a boyish girl, but he saw himself as a boy.

One day during his teen years, Ben found himself arguing with his mother about what to wear to a formal occasion. She expressed exasperation at his insistence on wearing a tuxedo instead of something more feminine. "Why is it so difficult for you?" she asked. And Ben replied: "Because when I wear girls' clothes, I feel like I'm cross-dressing!" Ben had always felt this way, and suddenly his mother was able to see him as a boy, not just a tomboy. New research suggests that trans identities emerge at about the same time as cis identities, prompting scientists to explore whether our gender identities—cis, trans, and otherwise—have biological bases.[12]

Some trans people opt for **gender-affirming care**, medical procedures and treatments that help people physically embody their gender. Trans teenagers may opt to take hormone-blocking drugs to prevent puberty from changing their bodies in ways they don't want. This buys them time to consider what bodily changes feel right to them. As they grow older, they may take hormones to change the appearance of their bodies. Surgeries can also help trans people make or remake their bodies into ones with which they feel more comfortable. Reflecting a commitment to the gender binary, doctors are often quick to perform surgery on intersex children but slow to do so on trans adults who are actively seeking it.[13]

Any given trans person may or may not seek out gender-affirming care, and the procedures and treatments they choose will vary. Thomas Beatie, for example, made headlines when he became pregnant with the first of his three children. Thomas was assigned female at birth but realized he was a boy during

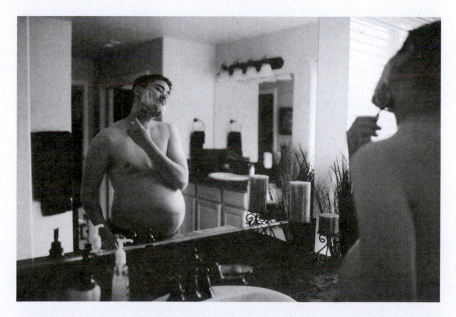

Thomas Beatie was assigned female at birth but chose to live his adult life as a man. Because he opted not to undergo a hysterectomy, he was able to give birth to three children.

Actor Elliot Page (right) knew he was a boy from age nine but didn't transition until age thirty-four. Children today may feel more comfortable revealing their true selves earlier. Zaya Wade (left), daughter of retired NBA player Dwayne Wade, announced her identity at just twelve years old.

childhood. He started gender-affirming care beginning at age twenty-three, but he chose not to undergo a hysterectomy, preserving his ability to get pregnant and bear children.

In the United States, trans people have recently gained much greater visibility. For example, Laverne Cox, a trans woman, starred in the television show *Orange Is the New Black*, appeared on the cover of *Time* magazine, and was named Woman of the Year by *Glamour* magazine in 2014. In 2019, Victoria's Secret featured Valentina Sampaio as its first-ever openly trans model; in 2020, *Sports Illustrated* decided to feature her in its swimsuit issue. That same year, retired professional basketball player Dwayne Wade announced his support for his trans daughter, Zaya. And Elliot Page—an actor known for his role in *The Umbrella Academy* and *X-Men*—came out as a trans man.

Singers Demi Lovato and Janelle Monáe are nonbinary. So is actor Amandla Stenberg (Rue in *The Hunger Games*) and *Queer Eye* star Jonathan Van Ness. "I think my energies are really all over the place," explained Van Ness in an interview. "Any opportunity I have to break down stereotypes of the binary, I am down for it."[14] Pop icon Miley Cyrus is gender fluid, as is Australian model and actress Ruby Rose. In 2020, *RuPaul's Drag Race* star Gigi Goode expressed their fluid identity this way: "Sometimes I identify as more male and sometimes I identify as more feminine. I think that I'm both . . . and I'm neither. . . . I've kind of always teetered between male and female throughout my whole life."[15]

The rising visibility of trans people is not limited to the arena of celebrity. In 2017, Danica Roem became the first openly trans person elected to a state legislature; she defeated the incumbent, a man who had introduced a bill that would have restricted trans rights. And Jennifer Finney Boylan is a longtime columnist for the *New York Times*, where she frequently writes about her continuing relationship with her wife, whom she married before she transitioned.

Some of us who are trans use the pronouns *he/him* and *she/her*. Others prefer gender-neutral pronouns like the singular *they/them* or an alternative like *ze/zir*. Some mix their pronouns; others make a single choice. Some may choose the honorific Mx. instead of Ms. or Mr., while others will resist any of these. Some people in the United States have replaced the binary terms *Latino* and *Latina* with the gender-neutral Latinx (pronounced "Latin-ex"), but across Latin America the emerging preference is for *Latine* (pronounced "lah-TEE-nay").[16]

Increasingly, media outlets are responding to this diversity. Facebook now offers dozens of gender-identity labels as well as a free-form field. It also allows people to choose up to ten identities and decide which friends see which, allowing users to control how they present themselves to different audiences. Most dating apps now allow users to choose from a large list of gender identities or write in their own.

Businesses are responding to gender diversity too. In 2018, Coca-Cola's Super Bowl commercial used the pronoun *them* to refer to a face on-screen. In 2019, United Airlines started giving customers the option of choosing "nonbinary" when they book tickets. Nike, Converse, and other shoemakers are offering unisex size charts for adults (as they had for kids), and Uniqlo and others offer size charts for clothing that show "chest/bust" measurements to choose unisex styles. Responding to student demand, over 270 colleges now have gender-inclusive housing.[17] Many more have nondiscrimination clauses. And all-gender restrooms on campuses are now commonplace, if not as universal or ubiquitous as is necessary.

Governments are coming around too. A Washington, DC, resident named Shige Sakurai was the

Danica Roem is a singer in a death metal band and the first openly trans person to be elected and serve in a US state legislature.

first American to be issued a gender-neutral driver's license. That was in 2017. Today, almost half of US states legally recognize people who are nonbinary on their driver's license, birth certificate, or both.[18] As of 2021, twelve countries allow citizens to choose a third option on their passports.[19]

These new products and shifting policies are increasingly inclusive of those of us who don't—or don't want to—fit into a rigid gender binary. And it's becoming clearer, as we learn more about both biology and identity, that there's no obvious way we *could* place everyone into the binary. How would we decide where those of us with intersex bodies go? To qualify as male or female, do our bodies have to match every criterion, from chromosomes to hormones to genitals to identity to expression? If so, what do we call those of us who can't claim a "perfectly" male or "perfectly" female body? Would it be better to pick just one criterion as the determinant of sex? Which one? Should genitals trump chromosomes? Or are chromosomes more "fundamental"?

World Athletics has tried heartily to figure out a definitive way to differentiate male from female athletes.[20] Over the decades, it has struggled to determine a single criterion. In the 1960s, athletes were subjected to physical examinations of their genitals, but World Athletics soon discovered that genitals didn't always align with chromosomes. So it pivoted to chromosomes in the 1970s. In the 2010s, it fixated on testosterone levels as the ultimate criterion. That didn't work either. Today, World Athletics considers a set of traits, including chromosomes, hormones, and genitals. Tomorrow, it may be something else.

The truth is, there are no correct criteria because sex is not binary. In fact, late in 2021, the International Olympic Committee formally recommended that the international federations that govern sport pivot away from biology and toward a human rights approach.[21] This new framework emphasizes freedom from discrimination, prevention of harm, and the right to privacy. It also supports sport-specific restrictions on competition only when based in scientific evidence. The hope is that this new framework will be widely applied, meaning that fewer athletes will be arbitrarily denied access to elite sport.

Above and beyond making the gender binary less rigid, there are ways to organize sport that make the gender binary entirely irrelevant; Chapter 7 will discuss this in some depth. Meanwhile, it's important to ask why establishing a rigid gender binary is so important, and to whom. If our bodies function but don't fit into the gender binary, is that a problem? Who gets to decide? And where do we draw the line? How many millimeters separate a boy with a small penis at birth and a child diagnosed as intersex? And if our body does fit all the criteria but our gender identity and assigned sex diverge, why not give us tools that allow us to better fit our bodies to identities, just as we provide eyeglasses or allow surgery for people with limited vision? How much body manipulation is "good," and how much is "bad"? And who gets to decide what to demand or allow?

Questions abound. And the truth is, we can't answer them satisfactorily. We can't because we're trying to impose a false binary on reality. Our bodies just don't come in the neat packages it assumes. This is true, in fact, even when we're thinking solely about cisgender men and women. It turns out, those of us who are cisgender don't conform well to the binary either.

Cisgender Men and Women

Remember that the gender binary allows for only two sexes while also making the much stronger claim that we're "opposite sexes." The idea of "oppositeness" presses us to behave in ways that shore up the binary. This gives the illusion that the gender binary is more real than it is while also—paradoxically—exposing the fact that men's and women's bodies do not form a biological binary at all. If they did, we wouldn't have to work so hard to affirm it.

The truth is that our bodies are much more alike than different. We have livers, hearts, arms, legs, eyes, ears, and so much more in common. Even characteristics strongly associated with sex, like height, are not binary. The average man is five and a half inches taller than the average woman.[22] But it's false to

FIGURE 1.1 | THE RANGE AND OVERLAP IN HEIGHT AMONG AMERICAN MEN AND WOMEN

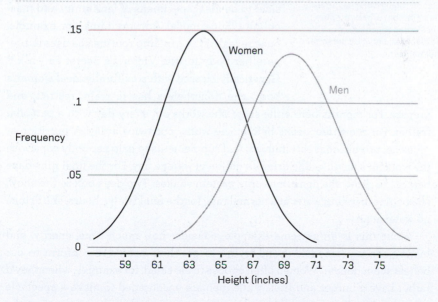

Source: Cheryl D. Fryar, Qiuping Gu, and Cynthia L. Ogden, "Anthropometric Reference Data for Children and Adults: United States, 2007–2010," National Center for Health Statistics, *Vital and Health Statistics* 1, no. 252 (October 2012).

Victoria's Secret model Adriana Lima struts her stuff on the runway, displaying a body bestowed to her by nature and painstakingly sculpted by personal trainers and dietitians.

state that men are taller than women. There is an *average* difference, not a *binary* one—a measure of tendency, not absolutes (Figure 1.1). So some women are taller than many men, and some men are shorter than most women.

We see this type of overlap in all sex-related traits. There are hairy women and men who can't grow a mustache, men with breasts and women with flat chests, women with strong bodies and broad shoulders and slender men who lift weights with little result. The truth is that our physical traits—height, hairiness, shape, strength, agility, flexibility, and bone structure—overlap far more than they diverge and vary widely over the course of our lives.

But many of us are *committed* to the idea of a gender binary, and this requires that we maintain noticeable differences between people perceived as men and people perceived as women. Consequently, we work to minimize any overlap, pressing our bodies into ideal manly or womanly shapes. This work is needed even by the people many consider to be ideal specimens of femininity and masculinity. Supermodel Adriana Lima, for example, once revealed the grueling routine she uses to prepare her body for the Victoria's Secret catwalk.[23] Genetically blessed with a culturally ideal woman's body, she nonetheless has to train, restrict, and prepare. For months before the show, she works out every day with a personal trainer. For the three weeks before, she works out twice a day. A nutritionist gives her protein shakes, vitamins, and supplements to help her body cope with the workout schedule. She drinks a gallon of water a day. For the final nine days before the show, she consumes only protein shakes. Two days before the show, she begins drinking water at a normal rate; for the final twelve hours, she drinks no water at all.

While this is an extreme example, consider how much time, energy, and money non-supermodels spend trying to get their bodies to conform to our beliefs about gender. Women often choose to eat salad, for example, when they'd rather have a burger and fries, while men are encouraged to make a spectacle of overeating. Gyms are effectively gender segregated, with most men at the weight machines trying to build muscles and most women on the exercise machines trying to lose weight. Women try to tone their bodies by building lean but not overly noticeable muscles with yoga and Pilates; men drink protein shakes and try to bulk up. Gender differences in size and strength aren't very pronounced naturally, but we sure do work hard to make them appear that way.

Similarly, many women take pains to keep their faces, legs, and armpits free of hair, often shaving or waxing their entire pubic area too. The body hair on men, in contrast, is seen as naturally masculine; men have the option to let it all hang out. By removing hair, women preserve the binary idea that men are hairy and women are not.

We gender the hair on our heads too. Long hair and certain short styles signify femininity. Cropped hair is more masculine. Women bleach their hair blond, sometimes platinum blond, a hair color that is natural almost exclusively to children. Men almost never choose this color. When women go gray, they often cover it for fear of looking old. On men, in contrast, gray hair is a mark of acquired wisdom, and the salt-and-pepper look is thought to be sexy.

People also tend to wear clothes that preserve the illusion of the gender binary. This starts when we're children, partly because clothes for kids are designed to emphasize gender difference.[24] Reds, grays, blacks, and dark blues are for boys. Pinks, purples, turquoises, and pale blues are for girls. Boys' clothes are decorated with trucks, trains, and airplanes; girls' are adorned with sparkly stars, hearts, and flowers. Even the animals decorating children's clothes are gendered, with lions and dinosaurs for boys, and kittens and bunnies for girls. Girls' clothes are tighter and are cut to emphasize curves that they don't yet have—shirts for girls, for example, sometimes cinch at the waist or include lower necklines—whereas boys' clothes, even in the exact same sizes, are looser, boxier, and show off less skin. Clothes for boys are even made with stronger fabrics and more robust stitching than those for girls. The assumption is that boys will be active in their clothes, but girls will not.

As adults, these trends in color, cut, and quality continue. Meanwhile, many women wear padded or push-up bras to lift and enhance their breasts and wear low-cut tops that emphasize and display cleavage. High heels create an artificially arched spine that pushes out the breasts and buttocks. Form-fitting clothes reveal women's curves, while looser or even baggy clothes make men's bodies appear more linear and squared off. Fitted clothes also help women appear smaller, while baggier clothes make men seem larger. (Putting on clothes designed for the other gender is a quick and easy way to test how much they contribute to our masculine and feminine appearances.)

When diet, exercise, and dress don't shape our bodies into so-called opposite ideal forms, some men and women resort to chemicals and cosmetic surgeries. Men are more likely than women to take steroids to increase their muscle mass or get bicep, tricep, chin, and calf implants that make their bodies appear more muscular and formidable. Women are more likely to take diet pills. Some undergo liposuction. If they don't think they're curvy enough, women may choose to get buttock implants or a breast augmentation. Conversely, breast *reduction* surgeries are a common plastic surgery performed on boys and men, who are often horrified by the slightest suggestion of a breast.

In addition to working on the shape of our bodies, we learn how to *move* our bodies in ways that conform to the idea that men are big and muscular and women are delicate and small. Masculine movements tend to take up space, whereas feminine movements minimize the space women inhabit. A masculine walk is wide, with the arms held slightly away from the body and the elbows pointed out. A feminine walk, in contrast, involves placing one foot in front of the other, swinging the arms in front of the body, and tucking the elbows for a narrower stride. A masculine seated position is spread out, disparagingly referred to as "manspreading." A man might open his shoulders and put his arms out to either side and spread his legs or rest an ankle on a knee, creating a wide lap. Women, in contrast, are taught to contain their bodies when seated. Women often sit with their legs crossed at the knees or the ankles, with their hands in their lap and their shoulders turned gently in. Both cis and trans men and women learn how to embody their identities in these ways.

The sheer power we have over our bodies is illustrated by **drag queens** and **drag kings**, usually cisgender men and women who dress and behave like members of the other gender. Some make a hobby, or even a career, of perfecting gender display, manipulating their bodies to signify either masculinity or femininity at will.

Drag queens and kings are excellent examples of how physical characteristics can be manipulated, but we all do drag when we use our bodies to display an artificial gender binary. None of the tools used by drag queens to make their bodies look feminine is unfamiliar to a culturally competent woman. Makeup, fitted clothes, high heels, jewelry, and carefully styled hair are everyday tools of femininity. The queen may wear heavier makeup, higher heels, and more ostentatious jewelry than the average woman, but it's not really different, just exaggerated.

Working out, dieting, and push-up bras are tools many of us use to try to respond to a gender binary that makes *all* our bodies problematic. The cumulative effect of this collective everyday drag show is a set of people who act and look like "women" and a set who act and look like "men." If male and female bodies *were* naturally "opposite," as the binary suggests, we wouldn't need to work so hard to make them appear that way. Instead, much of the difference we see doesn't emanate from our bodies themselves; it's the result of how we adorn, manipulate, use, and alter our bodies.

In sum, the logic behind the gender binary—that people come in two strongly distinct types—doesn't account for those of us whose biological markers aren't clearly in the male or female category, those whose identity doesn't match their assigned sex, those whose preferred expression is more fluid than fixed, or even those of us who are cisgender. Whatever our gender identities, we are either actively struggling to force our bodies into the binary or actively trying to reject it. Without efforts to make the binary a reality, some of us would still appear manly or womanly according to convention, since some of our bodies naturally conform to those types. But collectively, we wouldn't look *as* different as we do.

We do this work, though, or are forced to resist it, because we live in a society that still believes in the gender binary. Not all societies do. The next section takes a quick tour through a few examples of societies that think about the relationship between sex and gender in significantly different ways. It reveals that gender may be universal, but how we think about it is not.

GENDER IDEOLOGIES

The gender binary is an **ideology**, a set of ideas widely shared by members of a society that guides identities, behaviors, and institutions. **Gender ideologies** are widely shared beliefs about how men and women are and should be. The gender binary presumes not only that chromosomes, hormones, and genitals are consistent as markers of sex, which we saw is untrue, but also that all XY males will grow up to be men and all XX females will grow up to be women. When we look around the world and backward through history, however, we see that the gender binary is far from universal. Instead, there is a dizzying array of different gender ideologies, ones that show that the gender binary is just one of many ways of thinking about gender.

Seventeenth-century Europeans, for example—the same ones fighting over high heels—didn't believe in "opposite" sexes; they didn't even believe in *two* sexes.[25] They believed men and women were better and worse versions of the same sex, with differently arranged but identical reproductive organs: Men's genitals were pushed out of the body, while women's remained inside. As Figure 1.2 shows, they saw the vagina as simply a penis that hadn't emerged from the body; the womb as a scrotum in the belly; the ovaries just internal testes. As the lyrics to one early song put it: "Women are but men turned outside in."[26]

In the 1500s, when those same Europeans began colonizing what would become the United States, more than one hundred Native groups recognized third and fourth genders, described collectively today as *two-spirit*.[27] Charlie Ballard, a two-spirit who lives in Oakland and is a descendant of the Anishinaabe, Sac, and Fox, explains that a "two-spirit is a whole person that embodies feminine and masculine traits."[28]

The Diné (Navajo) also recognize a fifth category for a person whose gender is constantly changing, a *nádleehí*: sometimes a man, sometimes a woman,

FIGURE 1.2 | SEVENTEENTH-CENTURY ILLUSTRATION OF THE VAGINA AND UTERUS

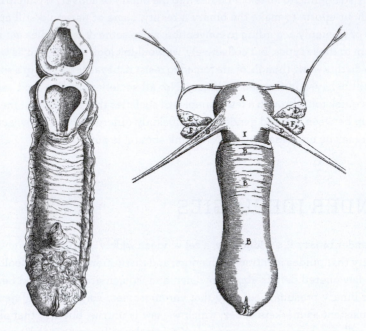

This anatomical illustration from 1611 of the interior of a vagina (left) and the exterior of a vagina and uterus (right) shows the Renaissance idea of female genitalia—an internal phallus.

and sometimes a two-spirit. If a person is a nádleehì, no one is surprised by these changes, which can occur monthly, daily, hourly, or even by the minute. In Indonesia, the Bugis also recognize a fifth gender.[29] The *bissu* are a combination of the other four genders (which include, roughly, masculine men, feminine women, feminine men, and masculine women).

In Hawaii, individuals whom mainlanders might describe as two-spirit are called *māhū*. Kaumakaiwa Kanaka'ole, a Native Hawaiian recording artist who is māhū, describes it as "the expression of the third self."[30] In the Cook Islands, a similar category of people are *akava'ine*. In Tonga, they use the word *fakaleiti*. And in Samoa, they say *fa'afafine*.[31]

In Oaxaca, Mexico, people assigned male at birth who adopt a feminine gender expression are called *muxe*; in Brazil, *travesti*; and in India and Bangladesh, *hijra*, a third gender that is recognized by both governments and used in official documents.[32] Unlike two-spirits and the third genders of Polynesia, who adopt the everyday behaviors and typical appearance of men or women, hijras, muxes, and travestis perform a different and sometimes exaggerated femininity. Laxmi

Narayan Tripathi, who uses the pronoun *she*, is a hijra who lives in Maharashtra, India. She explains her hijra identity this way:

> *Being called gay or a man really upsets me. . . . A hijra is [someone who has transi-*
> *tioned from] male to female, but we don't consider ourselves female because cul-*
> *turally we belong to a completely different section of society. . . . They say it's the*
> *soul which is hijra. We feel we are neither man nor woman, but we enjoy femininity.*
> *I enjoy womanhood, but I am not a woman.*[33]

A muxe interviewed for the documentary *Beyond Gender*, who uses the pronoun *they*, had something similar to say about identity: "There are men, women, and muxes," they said. "I am so comfortable being in between two. I myself represent duality of two things because I have the strength of a male and the sensitivity of a female."[34] Another interviewee explained that they thought that generally people were fearful of the space in between masculinity and femininity, but that "being a muxe allows you to defeat that fear so that you can be your own self."[35]

Both hijras and muxes represent a third gender in their own culture, and yet each is cross-culturally distinct from the other. They reveal that there is no universal, or natural, set of gender identities. Gender identities are specific to cultures and places, such that how a person comes to see gender depends on where

Cultures across the globe recognize more than just two genders. For example, in the southern Mexican state of Oaxaca, people assigned male at birth who adopt a feminine gender expression are known as muxes (pronounced MOO-shays).

and when they grow up. "I don't think that anywhere else it could be the exact same," says a muxe in Oaxaca, "because clearly the Istmo region is a thing of its own with a history of years and years. It's not a recent thing and this is what makes it unique. Obviously you cannot export it or replicate it."[36]

Genders other than man and woman are part of traditions all over the world: Pakistan, Thailand, Indonesia, Italy, Kenya, Tanzania, the Philippines, Nepal, Oman, Benin, Myanmar, Madagascar, Siberia, New Zealand, Australia, Peru, Ethiopia, Egypt, the Congo, and likely more.[37] Each of these cultures differs in how it conceptualizes the categories it recognizes and what role nonbinary people play. Sometimes they are expected to "prove" their membership by changing their bodies. Travestis, for example, are expected to feminize their bodies and hijras traditionally must show erectile dysfunction. Other times the only requirement is community acknowledgment, as is the case for two-spirits.

In other words, genitals don't determine one's gender. This is the case for the Gerai in West Borneo. The anthropologist Christine Helliwell spent time living with this group of subsistence farmers, immersing herself in the Dayak culture. They were studying her, too, and she discovered that her gender was uncertain to them for some time. This was despite the fact that she defecated and urinated in full view, as was customary. "Literally dozens of people," Helliwell explained, "would line the banks to observe whether I performed these functions differently from them."[38] From her Western point of view, her genitalia counted as strong evidence that she was a woman, but not to the Gerai. "Yes, I saw that you had a vulva," said a member of the community when she inquired, "but I thought that Western men might be different."

For the Dayak, being a man or woman is not tied to genitals. It is tied to expertise. A "woman" is a person who knows how to distinguish types of rice, store them correctly, and choose among them for different uses. As Helliwell learned more about rice and gained practice in preparing and cooking it, she became "more and more of a woman" in their eyes. Still, her gender remained at least a little ambiguous to the Dayak because she "never achieved anything approaching the level of knowledge concerning rice-seed selection held by even a girl child in Gerai."

The Dayak are not unique in divorcing gender from genitals. The Hau in New Guinea do this too. They see masculinity and femininity as parts of the character that grow and fade with age and experience. For the Hau, children become boys or girls at puberty, and then, over the life course, men lose masculinity with every son they father and women gain masculinity with each son they bear, until elders are again genderless. In pre-1900s Japan, in the years after puberty but before boys became full-fledged adults, they could occupy the status of another age-constrained gender: *wakashu*, a third gender permitted to have sex with both men and women.[39]

Among the Lovedu in Zambia, gender is assigned neither by genitals nor by age but by status.[40] A high-ranking woman can occupy the social position of a man. She might marry a young woman and be the socially recognized father to their children (who are biologically fathered by the young woman's socially endorsed lover). A similar system has been documented among the Nnobi in Nigeria.[41]

In the Netherlands, children are taught that men and women are different but overlapping categories.[42] Dutch schools do not teach children that men have "male" hormones and women have "female" hormones, as US schools typically, and mistakenly, do. Instead, they teach them that all people have a mix of hormones, just in somewhat different proportions on average, which is true.[43] Further, they also emphasize that hormone levels vary among men and among women (not just between them) and that these levels rise and fall in response to different situations and as people of both sexes age.

Sometimes the biological quirks of a community shape its gender ideology. In an isolated village in the Dominican Republic, it is not uncommon for girls to become boys at puberty. A rare genetic condition called 5-alpha-reductase deficiency is concentrated in the community. The condition makes genetically male children appear to be female until puberty, at which time the organ thought to be a clitoris grows into a penis and their testes suddenly descend from their abdomen. Many of these children simply adopt male identities and live as boys and then men. The villagers experience this as a completely routine event, calling such boys *guevedoces*, or "eggs at twelve." A similar phenomenon happens among the Simbari in Papua New Guinea. They name the girls who grow up to be men *kwolu-aatmwol*, or "female thing transforming into male thing."

In some places, strict social rules lead to the acceptance of temporary or permanent gender-switching. In Afghanistan, girls are not allowed to obtain an extensive education, appear in public without a man to chaperone, or work outside the home. These restrictions are typically discussed as a burden for girls and women, but they can also be a burden on families. Daughters can go out in public only if they are chaperoned by a brother. Having a brother gives girls freedom and parents more flexibility; they can send their children on errands, to school, or on social visits without their supervision. Since boys can also work outside the home, sons can be a source of extra income. Families without sons can't do any of these things, so some will pick a daughter to be a boy. They cut her hair, change her name, and put her in boys' clothes. This type of child is called a *bacha posh*, or "dressed up as a boy." One father of a bacha posh explains:

> It's a privilege for me, that she is in boys' clothing.... It's a help for me with the shopping. And she can go in and out of the house without a problem.[44]

Mehran Rafaat, a six-year-old bacha posh in Afghanistan, poses cheekily with her twin sisters. After puberty, she will stop playing the part of a boy and be considered a girl again.

Gender-switched children are accepted in Afghanistan. In fact, the phenomenon is common enough that most people are unsurprised when a child assigned female at birth later emerges as a boy. Relatives, friends, and acquaintances accept and participate in the transformation. Still later, when the child reaches puberty, she becomes a young woman. Meanwhile, the family might choose a younger daughter to take over her role as a boy.

Unlike a bacha posh in Afghanistan, girls in Albania can live as boys *and* grow up to be socially recognized men.[45] To do so, girls have to publicly promise they'll remain virgins. The role of the *virgjinesha*, or "sworn virgins," emerged in the early 1400s when war left a dearth of men in many communities. Since only men had certain rights—to buy land, for example, or pass down wealth—all families needed either a man or someone who could stand in for one. Many girls would take the oath after their father or brother died. A similar identity emerged in the African Dahomey Kingdom in the 1700s; when the male population was decimated by war, women were allowed to become warriors but only if they promised to remain childless.[46]

"It was my decision as well as the family's," explained Nadire Xhixha, who uses *she/her* pronouns. Xhixha became a virgjinesha at thirteen years old when the only boy among her eight siblings tragically died. Speaking of her young adulthood, she said: "I lived freely, like all men back then. I smoked, I drank rakia [fruit brandy] and did many other things that were characteristic of men at the time." Xhixha has lived nearly her whole life as a man: "I've never done women's domestic chores such as cleaning and cooking. I lived in the village and worked alongside men. I worked hard. I worked like a man and lived like one."[47] Xhixha is one of a dwindling group of sworn virgins who still live in Albania today. As women gain more rights, fewer girls feel the need to adopt an identity as a man for themselves or their families.[48]

In the eighteenth and nineteenth centuries, American and European people who were assigned female also found ways to live as men.[49] For example, in 1929, a London laborer named James Allen, who was married to housemaid Abigail Naylor, was fatally crushed by falling timber. In examining the body, the coroner discovered that Allen physically presented as female. Incidents of so-called female husbands were widely documented during this era, and responses varied. In this case, the coroner persisted in referring to Allen with male pronouns, arguing: "I call the deceased a 'he,' because I considered it impossible for him to be a woman, as he had a wife."[50]

Haki is one of the remaining "sworn virgins" of Albania. Born female, Haki has lived her entire adult life as a man.

How many genders are there? Is gender fluid? Does it have anything to do with genitals? Can it change over the life course? Can we adopt a gender identity for strictly practical reasons? The answers to all these questions make sense only in specific times and places. We might have felt differently about ourselves if we had grown up with different opportunities or faced different demands. This isn't to say that our experiences here and now aren't authentic; it's to suggest only that how we interpret our feelings about our bodies will vary depending on the cultural resources we have for thinking about gender.

The ideology that dominates in the United States today—the gender binary—is somewhat unusual in requiring all bodies to fit into two and only two categories. This ideology not only ignores the problems of categorization that arise from variation in chromosomes, hormones, and genitals but also expects that certain traits and talents will align with sex assignments and remain stable throughout our lifetimes. The ideology of the gender binary presumes that our sex determines our personalities, drowning out other influences and generating two distinct social groups: men and women. Although nonbinary options are increasingly available, they are still often treated as controversial choices rather than as cultural facts.

Thus far, this chapter has argued that the gender binary is not derived from our bodies but rather is *imposed* upon our bodies. But this is merely the beginning. In fact, we impose the gender binary on just about everything.

THE BINARY AND EVERYTHING ELSE

Because gender varies across cultures and through time, it's correct to say that gender is a **social construct**, an arbitrary but influential shared interpretation of reality.[51] Social constructs are the outcome of **social construction**, the process by which we layer objects with ideas, fold concepts into one another, and build connections between them. The metaphor of "construction" draws attention to the fact that we are *making* something. This construction is "social" because, to be influential in society, the meaning ascribed to something must be shared.

Most of our daily lives are governed by an elaborate series of social constructs. We generally start every morning, for example, with a social construct: breakfast. In the United States, people sometimes call breakfast the "most important meal of the day." In parts of Eastern Europe, like Poland and Hungary, they double down on this idea, enjoying a traditional "second breakfast" (as do the Hobbits of Middle Earth). During the Middle Ages in Europe, people skipped breakfast altogether. The influential thirteenth-century Dominican priest Thomas Aquinas called breakfast *praepropere*, roughly translated as "the sin of eating too soon." It was allowed only for children, the elderly, the weak, and hard laborers.[52]

Whether one eats in the morning, and how often, is a social construct; so is *what* one eats. In the United States, it's traditional to eat either bacon and eggs or something sweet, like cereal or pancakes, but breakfast varies around the world. In Korea, a traditional breakfast includes a savory broth-based soup with vegetables, something most Americans would recognize as lunch. In Japan, breakfast is often a rice stir-fry with dried fish in soy sauce. In Istanbul, it includes a healthy serving of olives. In Iceland, a slurp of cod liver oil. In Egypt, fava beans and a tomato-cucumber salad.[53] Such variation in traditions reveals that "breakfast food" is a social construct.

We gender sweet and savory foods as feminine and masculine, respectively, too. Women can and do eat bacon and eggs for breakfast, but shoveling in a good, hearty portion of salty, fatty protein is a manly way to eat breakfast. And while men often have a sweet tooth, a waffle drenched in syrup or covered in strawberries with a dollop of whip cream is a meal generally associated with women. This gendering of breakfast food is an example of the social construction of gender.

The Social Construction of Gender

In the process of socially constructing the world, we often layer objects, characteristics, behaviors, activities, and ideas with notions of masculinity or femininity. Sociologists use *gender* as a verb when talking about the *process* by which something becomes coded as masculine or feminine. So we will sometimes say something is "gendered" or that we "gender" or are "gendering" things.

We gender just about everything. Ask yourself: Who, stereotypically, is a sports fan? Who do we expect to play rugby? Volleyball? How much opportunity do women have to play American football? Men are allowed to figure skate, but when they do, are they "masculine"? Are women basketball players feminine? Is it manly to watch basketball? Is it less so if the athletes are women?

Who, stereotypically, drinks Diet Coke? Coke Zero? Monster energy drinks? Who do we think is more likely to become a vegetarian? At a bar who, stereotypically, orders beer? A cosmopolitan? Whiskey? White wine?

Who, stereotypically, plays the drums? The flute? Who DJs? Who dances? Who sings? Which teenagers, typically, babysit, and which mow lawns? Who do you expect to major in computer science, engineering, or physics? How about nursing or elementary education? After college, who, stereotypically, becomes a therapist? An investment banker? For those who do not go to college, who do we expect will become a construction worker? A receptionist?

Even animals are divided by gender. In children's books, mice and rabbits are usually female, while wolves and bears are male. Are men, in their heart of hearts, allowed to love unicorns? Are women expected to have a pet snake?

Dogs, physics, energy drinks, and bacon and eggs. All these things are associated with masculinity, thrown together in a senseless pile. Whiskey and lawn-mowing share little in common, except that we associate them with men. Likewise with femininity. Nothing connects Diet Coke, ice skating, and being a therapist except the cultural prescriptions tying them all to women. Our social constructs, then—the collection of things we lump together as masculine or feminine—don't rely on logical connections between and among them. Instead, they are a jumble of unrelated ideas.

Not only are these things mostly unrelated, but they're also often contradictory. Consider how women are believed to be naturally inclined to do the most selfless job in the world (raising children) at the same time they're stereotyped as vain and overly concerned with superficial things (like fashion and makeup). If the latter is true, do women really make good parents? Likewise, men are believed to be especially capable of running factory equipment but dopes at running a washing machine. Are men mechanically inclined or not? Likewise, men are stereotyped as excellent at running companies but ill-suited for running households. Are they leaders or not?

The gender binary also causes us to falsely *disconnect* masculine ideas from feminine ones, making it harder to form connections between these ideas. For example, even though we're taught that women have small hands and good coordination, giving them aptitudes for needlework and sewing, we rarely notice that such characteristics would also make them excellent surgeons. The ways in which sewing and surgery are alike tends to escape our notice because they've been socially connected to femininity and masculinity, respectively, which we culturally expect to be opposites. Likewise, because we imagine men to be rational and women emotional, we think that the opposite of rational is emotional. But this isn't true. When people suffer brain trauma that interferes with their ability to feel emotions, their decision-making powers are inhibited because emotion is a key part of careful decision-making, not its antithesis.[54] Our association of emotion with women and rationality with men, however, falsely presents them as opposites.

Seeing Gender

We've grown up learning to see gender in the world and, sometimes frustratingly, we see it whether we like it or not. Metaphorically, this is because we wear **gender binary glasses**—a pair of lenses that separates everything we see into masculine and feminine categories. We acquire prescriptions for our gender binary glasses as we learn the ways of our culture. As we grow up, our prescriptions get tweaked as ideas about gender change around us. Some of us may even have weaker prescriptions than others. We all, however, own a pair.

If we belong to multiple subcultures, as most of us do, we may even have several pairs of glasses. Sometimes we'll disagree about gendered meanings because someone else sees things differently. A guy who grew up in Taos, New Mexico, with a father who sells healing crystals may have a different idea about what counts as masculine than his college roommate whose dad is the football coach. But when they argue, they'll likely still argue about what is and isn't within the category of masculine. In other words, they may have different prescriptions, but they are both wearing glasses.

Because reality doesn't conform to a simple pink and blue vision of the world, our glasses encourage us to engage in progressive **gender binary subdivision**, the practice by which we divide and redivide by gender again and again, adding finer and finer *degrees* of masculinity and femininity to the world. We do this progressive subdivision with just about anything. Dogs are masculine, for example (when opposed to the feminized cat), but poodles are feminine (as opposed to a pit bull). Among poodles, though, the large standard poodle is a more masculine sort, while the teensy toy poodle is more feminine. Similarly, most people agree that cooking dinner is a feminine task, unless dinner involves grilling steak in the backyard or is done for pay at a fancy restaurant. Housework is feminized and yard work is masculinized, unless we're talking about flower gardening, a subcategory of yard work associated with women. You can even make a unicorn masculine. In one study, boys showed little interest in My Little Pony toys until a researcher painted one black, gave it a mohawk, and added spiky teeth.[55]

Subdivision is necessary for the gender binary to survive. Any time a challenge arises, as with the poodle, we can protect the binary by dismissing deviations from it with reference back to it. If the guitar is a masculine instrument, how do we explain the pretty girl singing a love song while gently strumming a guitar cradled in her lap? We subdivide the guitar into electric (more masculine) and

Because we both divide and subdivide in accordance with the gender binary, we can think of dogs as masculine but poodles as feminine.

acoustic (more feminine) and further subdivide playing styles such that strumming is feminized and louder playing is seen as more appropriate for a man.

Likewise, if emotion is coded feminine, then what is anger? The masculinization of anger is a result of subdividing emotions in order to preserve the idea that women are more sensitive than men. Somehow our belief that men are prone to anger coexists with our belief that they rationally control their emotions. We don't resolve the contradiction by admitting the stereotype is false. Instead, we resolve it by subdividing emotions into masculine and feminine types. Because of the gender binary, men can be angry without being labeled "emotional."

Subdivision allows us to dismiss the toy poodle, pretty strummer, and emotional man as exceptions and not question the rule. In this way, we can maintain the illusion that the gender binary occurs naturally. Divisions of gender also make the gender binary appear to be timeless, even as cultures are constantly changing and the rules are rewritten. When women began wearing pants in the 1940s, for example, their choice of attire was viewed as breaking the rule that men wore pants and women wore skirts. By the 1960s, tight jeans and hip-hugging slacks feminized pants, subdividing that category of clothing to reaffirm the binary. Today, the binary persists despite women's ubiquitous adoption of pants. It just looks a little different: Men wear "men's pants," and women wear "women's pants." Subdivision makes the gender binary endlessly flexible, able to accommodate whatever challenges and changes emerge over time.

Thanks to our gender binary glasses, gender becomes part of how our brain learns to organize the world. Cells in our brains that process and transmit information make literal connections, so some ideas are associated with other ideas in our minds. This phenomenon, called **associative memory**, is a very useful human adaptation. It's how our ancestors learned to think "big mouth, sharp teeth" and then "danger!" It's why we couldn't separate the idea "red" from "stop" even if we tried. Associative memory latches on to gender, too, so when we grow up with gender binary glasses, our brain forms clusters of ideas revolving around the concepts of masculinity and femininity. Our brains, in other words, encode the gender binary.

Researchers can tap into our subconscious brain organization with the Implicit Association Test (IAT).[56] The IAT measures subconscious beliefs by comparing how quickly we can make connections between items. We are faster to connect associated items than nonassociated ones, a fact discovered in speed tests for arbitrary associations like the ones on playing cards: red with hearts and black with spades. In one study, gender-stereotyped words like *mechanic* and *secretary* were flashed on a computer screen, followed by a common man's or woman's name.[57] The viewer's task was to identify the gender of the name as quickly as possible. Results showed that, on average, it takes longer for a person to identify a name as a man's if it was preceded by a feminized word like *secretary* than with a masculinized word like *mechanic*. Viewers have to cognitively "shift gears." Many studies have confirmed this experiment, showing that we unconsciously associate feminine things with one another and masculine things with one another. (You can take the IAT yourself online at www.implicit.harvard.edu/.)

People who explicitly endorse gender stereotypes tend to show the strongest unconscious associations, but even those of us who refute stereotypes test "positive" for them on the IAT. Stereotypes are a natural way for human brains to work, and it may be impossible to rid ourselves of them. Still, it's useful to be aware of how they distort our perception of reality. If we choose to, we can learn to *think about our thinking* and thus counter our brains' automatic stereotyping.

When we are distracted or asked to respond quickly, however, essentially all of us revert to stereotypical thinking.[58] For instance, when asked to perform the challenging task of recalling a series of random words, study respondents often use the gender binary as a scaffold on which to structure their recollections. In one such study, people were offered a set of masculine, feminine, and neutral words like *wrestling, yogurt, bubble bath, ant, pickup truck, shirt, water, steak,* and *flower.* When asked to recall the words later, respondents would cluster the words by gender, saying *wrestling, pickup truck,* and *steak* in a row, then *yogurt, bubble bath,* and *flower.*[59] Sometimes they even added gendered words that weren't on the original list, adding *beer,* perhaps, or *perfume* because they fit so nicely with the concepts of steak and flower, respectively. Somehow they just seemed to belong.

Having a brain organized by the gender binary helps us get along with others whose brains are similarly trained. In other words, our gender binary glasses give us **cultural competence**, a familiarity and facility with how the members of a society typically think and behave. It's how we know *most people* think unicorns are supposed to appeal only to girls, even if we personally believe that the love of unicorns should know no bounds. This knowledge is important. To interact with others in a meaningful way, we need a shared understanding of the world.

Whether out of conviction, mere habit, or the desire to see the world in the same way as people around us, we routinely apply a gender binary to characteristics, activities, objects, and people. This isn't reality; it's ideology. Our culture posits a gender binary, and we apply that binary to our world by peering at it through gender binary glasses. And those glasses, it turns out, bring the world into false focus.

Blurred Vision and Blind Spots

While gender binary glasses help us see the world the way other people do, the glasses also distort our vision.[60] Our lenses warp reality, causing us to dismiss, forget, and misremember the exceptions to the gendered rules that we encounter daily. Without this distortion, this constant *inattention* to deviations from the gender binary, it would appear patently false. The gender binary is preserved not because it's real, then, and not even merely because we often act in ways that affirm it, but because we learn to ignore or unsee evidence that falsifies it.

In a classic study, for example, five- and six-year-olds were shown both stereotypical pictures (e.g., a boy playing with a train) and counterstereotypical pictures, ones that violated stereotypes (e.g., a boy cooking on a stove).[61] One week later, asked to recall what they had seen, children had more difficulty remembering the nonstereotypical pictures than the stereotypical ones. They also sometimes reversed the gender of the person in the picture (e.g., they remembered a *girl* cooking) or changed the activity (e.g., they remembered a boy *fixing* a stove). Many later studies have confirmed that children are more likely to forget an experience that deviates from stereotypes—skateboarding girls or belly-dancing boys—than one that fits in.[62]

This is true of adults too. Stereotype-consistent experiences are more likely to be remembered and remembered correctly than stereotype-inconsistent ones.[63] We pay less attention to nonstereotypical information and are quicker to forget it. When it's ambiguous as to whether what we are observing is stereotypical or counterstereotypical, we tend to assume the former, strengthening our preconceived notions. We may assume, for example, that a man who shoves a woman is attacking her but that a woman who shoves a man is defending herself, using gender stereotypes to interpret the encounter. Further, when we actively seek information, we tend to seek that which affirms our beliefs. Whenever stereotypes are activated, those stereotypes influence our attention, thinking, and memory, and they do so in their own favor.

Stereotypes are so powerful, in fact, that they are a source of false memories. In one study, people were asked to watch a dramatized account of a bicycle theft.[64] The actors playing the thieves varied. In some videos, the criminal was a masculine man, in others a feminine man, a feminine woman, or a masculine woman. Study subjects could remember more about the theft if the criminal conformed to gender stereotypes. This is because, just as with the words *yogurt*, *bubble bath*, and *flower*, it is easier to remember a set of ideas if they conform to a preexisting schema (in this case, criminal behavior = masculine = men). The authors write, "When eyewitnesses are exposed to a theft, gender schemas will enhance recall," but only if the criminal fits gender expectations.[65]

This phenomenon applies even to memories we think would be impervious to such effects. In one surprising study, French high school students were asked to fill out a quick survey about whether men or women were better at math and art.[66] Reminded of gender stereotypes, they were then asked to report their own scores on a national standardized test they'd taken two years prior. Girls underestimated their own performance on the math portion of the test and overestimated their performance on the art portion. Boys misremembered in the opposite direction.

In these ways, and in many others, our gender binary glasses distort what we see. They often bring things into false focus and affect our cognition and memory. Even when we're conscious that stereotypes are wrong, our brains make gender-stereotypical associations. When we see counterevidence, it tends not to enter into our daily interpretation of the world. We may soon misremember it as having confirmed our preexisting beliefs.

Revisiting the Question

Q+A   **If we don't learn the idea of the gender binary by observing the people around us, where does the idea come from?**

Everywhere!

Humans socially construct their worlds and gender is one way we do so. We apply the binary to our bodies, treating bodies that don't fit as in need of fixing. Many other cultures offer more space between and outside of male and female gender categories. This is changing in the United States, as all cultures change. Still, many Americans remain uncomfortable with those of us who are intersex, trans, nonbinary, or gender fluid. And even cisgender people are encouraged to embody the gender binary much more fully than they naturally do.

Meanwhile, we apply a binary gender ideology to the world. We look through gender binary glasses. What we then perceive and remember is often false on many fronts. When the binary fails to reflect reality, we subdivide our gender categories to reaffirm it. All this makes it more difficult to notice that masculinity and femininity are jumbled and often contradictory categories. And it obscures the fact that gender stereotypes fail to describe most people we know well, including ourselves.

Next . . .

The idea that gender is socially constructed bumps up against things we hear about blue and pink brains, the male sex drive, or mothers' intuition. Each of these is frequently named as a seemingly irrefutable biological difference between men and women. With this in mind, we'll tackle this question next:

 The gender binary might be an ideology, but there are real differences between men and women, right?

This question is so much harder to answer than you might think.

FOR FURTHER READING

Aggleton, Peter, Paul Boyce, Henrietta L. Moore, and Richard Parker. *Understanding Global Sexualities: New Frontiers*. New York: Routledge, 2012.

Barbee, Harry, and Douglas Schrock. "Un/gendering Social Selves: How Nonbinary People Navigate and Experience a Binarily Gendered World." *Sociological Forum* 34, no. 3 (2019): 572–93.

Fausto-Sterling, Anne. "Gender/Sex, Sexual Orientation, and Identity Are in the Body: How Did They Get There?" *Journal of Sex Research* 56, nos. 4–5 (2019): 529–55.

Meadow, Tey. *Trans Kids: Being Gendered in the Twenty-First Century*. Berkeley: University of California Press, 2018.

Paoletti, Jo. *Pink and Blue: Telling the Boys from the Girls in America*. Bloomington: Indiana University Press, 2012.

Risman, Barbara. *Where the Millennials Will Take Us: A New Generation Wrestles with the Gender Structure*. New York: Oxford University Press, 2018.

Schilt, Kristen, and Danya Lagos. "The Development of Transgender Studies in Sociology." *Annual Review of Sociology* 43 (July 2017): 425–43.

MEN ARE FROM NORTH DAKOTA,
WOMEN ARE FROM SOUTH DAKOTA.

—KATHRYN DINDIA[1]

2

Bodies

In a part of the ocean so deep no light can reach, an anglerfish hunts. She attracts prey with a glowing lure that springs from her forehead and looks suspiciously like something other creatures would like to eat. No matter if they are bigger than she, as she can swallow prey up to twice her body size.

She pays no attention to her male counterpart, who is tiny in comparison. Females can grow over three feet long, but males are never longer than a few centimeters. He, in contrast, needs her desperately. Born without a lure, a male anglerfish can't catch prey, and without a stomach, he couldn't digest it if he did. A male's only chance at survival is finding a female before he dies of starvation. If he's so lucky, he'll latch on to her with his mouth, initiating a chemical reaction that slowly dissolves his face into her body. Eventually he will lose all his organs; his entire body will waste away, except his testicles. A healthy female anglerfish will carry many pairs of testicles on her body, all that is left of the males who found their fate with her.

This is high **sexual dimorphism**. The phrase refers to typical differences in body type and behavior between males and females of a species. Across the range of species on Earth, some are highly sexually dimorphic and others are less so. The high end includes the green spoonworm (the male lives its entire adult life inside the

In some species, males and females appear very different from each other; in other species less so. Elephant seals, lions, and anglerfish are all species that are more sexually dimorphic than humans.

female's digestive tract), peacocks (males carry a resplendent half-moon of a tail with which to dazzle relatively drab females), and elephant seals (males outweigh females by about 4,600 pounds).

Other species have much lower sexual dimorphism. The male and female Fischer's lovebird look so much alike that even ornithologists (professional bird-folk) can't tell by looking. They have identical plumage and near-identical behavior, and their genitals are inside their bodies. Very experienced bird handlers might be able to tell based on feeling the width of a bird's pelvis (the females' are wider to allow egg-laying), but most people have to resort to genetic testing to know for sure.

Considering the range of sexual dimorphism among animals helps us put human sex difference in perspective. Given some of the extremes, we should be rather impressed by how obviously similar we are. If humans were as dimorphic by size as elephant seals, for example, the average male would tower six feet above the average female. If we were as sexually dimorphic as the blanket octopus, human males would be no bigger than walnuts. Human males don't have appendages that human females do not (beyond their genitals, of course), like the horns of the Alaskan moose or the rhinoceros beetle, the mane of the lion, the poisonous claw of the platypus, or the bulging cheek flaps or bulbous nose of the orangutan and the proboscis monkey, respectively. Nor do human males come in pretty colors like the male species of many birds. If we were like northern cardinals, males would be bright red with a black mask around their eyes and throat, and human females would look more or less as they do now.

Male and female humans are not *that* different. We're not peacocks. Yet we're more different than your average pair of lovebirds. That's why we posed the question we did at the end of the last chapter:

Q+A **The gender binary might be an ideology, but there are real differences between men and women, right?**

Whoa whoa whoa . . . Now *there* is a question that prompts some further questions. First, what do "men" and "women" mean in this context? And what do they have to do with the ideas of maleness and femaleness captured in the concept of sexual dimorphism? Chapter 1 argued that men and women are diverse categories, including cis, trans, and intersex people. And not all the people in them are biologically male or female on each and every measure from genes to genitals.

Second, what is meant by "differences"? Are the differences we're looking for strictly dimorphic sex categories, such that all males are one way and all females another, like anglerfish or sea lions? Or can they merely be the average differences we observe when studying people who identify as men or women? And how much overlap can there be before we dismiss an average difference as trivial?

And, finally, who's asking? And why? Recall that sociologists use the word *distinction* to describe efforts to differentiate one's own group from those of others. Efforts to answer this chapter's driving question are, in essence, acts of distinction. They're efforts to prove definitively that there are categorical differences between men and women. And why? Surely partly out of scientific curiosity. But the origin of that curiosity is not neutral.

Scientific thinking emerged as a socially important force in the 1600s in Europe, a time when most people already believed it was obvious that women were an inferior category of human and relied on their religious texts for evidence. So when scientists, nearly all men, posed research questions, they almost exclusively posed variants of the one with which we began this chapter. They did so because finding evidence of difference enabled them to continue to justify elevating men above women, even when scientific evidence was shaking other religious beliefs, like creationism.

Scientists have now been asking versions of this question for more than four hundred years. They've measured, weighed, poked, prodded, imaged, and assayed the human body, asking it to provide the proof that men and women are *really* different. As a result of this ideological project, most Americans today believe that people who fall into the category "men" are fundamentally different from people who fall into the category "women" and that biology explains much of this difference.[2]

This chapter doesn't dismiss this idea out of hand. It takes the science seriously, sincerely trying to answer this question: What are the real differences between men and women? In doing so, it asks the other questions too: What do we mean by those terms? What is meant by *difference*? And, especially, what makes a difference real?

Prepare to be confused. These questions are much more difficult to answer than you might think. They involve a far more complex relationship between biology and society than even scientists once imagined. And they're complicated by new research driven by curiosity about a previously overlooked question: What are the real *similarities* between men and women?

RESEARCH ON GENDER DIFFERENCES AND SIMILARITIES

Getting a clear understanding of how men and women are alike and different is more challenging than pinpointing the differences between, say, male and female baboons or birds. Measured differences in humans vary over time and across cultures, and they respond to psychological manipulation and practice and training. They're also sensitive to how we design studies and define measurements. Usually researchers assume that the people they're studying are straightforwardly male or female and presenting as men or women, respectively, an assumption we know is faulty. Accordingly, we would have to amass a lot of evidence and consider all possible influences in order to determine which differences we find consistently and which we don't. And that's just what a team of psychologists led by Ethan Zell did.

Zell and his colleagues combined more than twenty thousand individual studies with a combined sample size of more than twelve million people.[3] The study included more than 21,000 measures of 386 traits: data on differences between (mostly self-identified) men and women in thoughts, feelings, behaviors, intellectual abilities, communication styles and skills, personality traits, measures of happiness and well-being, physical abilities, and more. They separated the variables into ones for which there appeared to be negligible to no difference between men and women, and those for which there was evidence for small, medium, large, or very large differences. Table 2.1 shows the results: 39 percent of possible differences were negligible to nonexistent, 46 percent

TABLE 2.1 | THE SIZE OF OBSERVED GENDER DIFFERENCES

Size of the Difference	% of Variables in Each Category
Negligible to nonexistent	39
Small	46
Medium	12
Large	2
Very large	1

were small, 12 percent were medium, 2 percent were large, and 1 percent were very large.

The average difference between men and women—on all traits included in the study—fell into the small category, illustrated by the bell curve in Figure 2.1. The graph represents levels of self-esteem (from low on the left to high on the right), and the height of the curve represents the number of people who reported each level. Few people have very low self-esteem (far left) or very high self-esteem (far right). While Zell and his colleagues' analysis offered good evidence for a statistically significant difference between men and women, it's not a large one.

Other variables that fell into the categories of small to negligible or nonexistent included reading comprehension and abstract reasoning; talkativeness, likelihood of self-disclosing to friends and strangers, tendency to interrupt others, and assertiveness of speech; willingness to help others; negotiation style and approach to leadership; degree of impulsiveness; symptoms of depression, coping strategies, life satisfaction, and happiness; vertical jumping ability, overall activity levels, balance, and flexibility; willingness to delay gratification and attitudes about cheating; likelihood of wanting a career that makes money, offers security, is challenging, and brings prestige; and some measures of sexual attitudes and experiences (e.g., disapproval of extramarital sex, levels of sexual arousal, and sexual satisfaction).

FIGURE 2.1 | AN ILLUSTRATION OF A "SMALL" DIFFERENCE BETWEEN MEN AND WOMEN

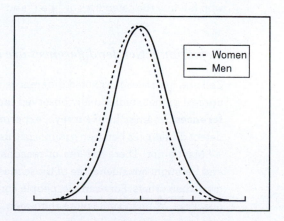

Source: Kristen C. Kling, Janet S. Hyde, Carolin J. Showers, and Brenda N. Buswell, "Gender Differences in Self-Esteem: A Meta-Analysis," *Psychological Bulletin*, 125, no. 4 (1999): 484.

Medium-size differences included physical aggression and visual-spatial abilities (turning a two- or three-dimensional object around in one's head), while large gender differences were found on some measures of physical ability, especially throwing (because these differences are related to size, they are particularly pronounced after puberty). Large differences were also found in some measures of sexuality: frequency of masturbation and approval of casual sex.[4] Two traits show especially strong sexual dimorphism: gender identity (most people assigned male at birth identify as men and most people assigned female at birth identify as women) and sexual identity (most men are sexually interested in women and most women in men).

Are these, then, the "real differences" our opening question asked about?

It depends on how you define "real."

DEFINING DIFFERENCE

When we wonder about the real differences between men and women, it's helpful to consider what evidence we would need in order to conclude that we've discovered them. Is it enough just to be able to measure differences, like Zell and his colleagues did? Is it important that those differences be stable—that is, relatively unchanged across an individual's life or, even more, true throughout human history? To count as real, do they need to be found in all or most societies? Would finding a biological cause make a difference *more* real? And if we do find a biological cause, does it count as real only if it resists cultural influences? The following sections explore these questions by considering different definitions of the word "real" when describing average differences between people who fall into the categories of "men" and "women."

Definition 1: Gender differences are real if we can measure them

Zell and his colleagues noted differences on 61 percent of characteristics. These are real in that studies really observed them in real life. They are **observed differences**: findings from surveys, experiments, and other types of studies that detect differences between groups. Is this what we mean by "real"?

Maybe not. There are lots of reasons why differences might be observed, and we might consider some of those reasons more indicative of an underlying truth than others. For example, people sometimes act differently if they're being observed. Women smile more than men, and men are more likely than women to engage in heroic helping behavior—in both cases, though, only if they know they're being watched.[5] Men are just as likely as women to offer emotional support to friends on social media via a private message but are less likely to do so publicly.[6] When people think they're alone or acting without an audience, gender differences can fade or disappear.

People also lie. Men typically report higher rates of masturbation than women, but when scientists attach them to fake lie detectors or offer them anonymity, men's rates drop to the same level as women's. We see similar patterns in reported number of sexual partners and age at first intercourse.

In other cases, psychologists have discovered they can manipulate study results quite easily. If you remind study subjects of a stereotype right before the test, in a trick called **priming**, test scores will reflect that stereotype. For example, if women are asked to report their gender immediately before a test of empathy (the ability to understand and sympathize with others' feelings), they'll do better than those who weren't asked about gender.[7] Because Americans tend to associate empathy with women, priming women to think of themselves as women encourages them to focus on these capacities and may motivate them to try to do better. Conversely, priming men with gender lowers their scores.

You can also depress women's scores on empathy tests simply by asking them to imagine themselves as men for a few moments before they begin the experiment. In one study, women were asked to write a fictional story about a day in the life of a person named Paul.[8] Half were asked to write *about* Paul and half *as* Paul. Women who wrote about Paul did better on the empathy test than the men in the study, but women who wrote as Paul did just as badly.

Does this mean that women are on average more empathetic than men but only if they're motivated to be so? Nope. Men can be motivated to score higher on tests of empathy too. Psychologists only need to trick them into thinking that the task they're performing is one that men are stereotypically good at (perhaps telling them that they're testing leadership ability) or by offering a social or financial reward for doing well.[9] Similarly, men (presumably hetero-sexual ones) will get higher average scores on tests of empathy if they're told that women really like sensitive guys.[10]

Sometimes observed differences are simply the result of social and cultural conditions. We might observe that women are more likely to carry a purse and men are more likely to carry a wallet. That's real, but these are simply **learned differences**, ones that are a result of how we grow up (with certain parents or peers) or our sociocultural environment (like religion, education, or media). We know, for example, that parents tend to see their sons as big, strong, and active and their daughters as little, pretty, and cute, then treat them accordingly.[11] Girl babies are more likely to be talked to; boy babies are more likely to be handled. Accordingly, girls may develop quicker and stronger language skills than boys, while boys might outpace girls on motor skills.

Is that what we're getting at when we're asking the question about real differences? Probably not. Some differences are simply a result of how we're treated and what we're taught to do.

The average differences Zell and his colleagues observed, then, are real in that we really observed them, but they don't necessarily stand up when we poke and prod at them. Some are quite obviously just norms, unrelated to anything but culture. Others can shift, reverse, and disappear when we manipulate the conditions of the data collection. Perhaps what we need is a definition that carries more heft and stands up under such examination.

Definition 2: Gender differences are real if they are observed in all or most contemporary and historical cultures

Questions like the one this chapter is exploring—regarding the "real" differences between men and women—imply that we're interested in universal human truths, ones that are true around the world and throughout history. If we could find such a difference, we would have a compelling reason to think it was real. The majority of research on gender differences, however—in fact, the majority of research on behavioral differences of all kinds—uses subjects only from societies that are Western, educated, industrialized, rich, and democratic, five words that add up to the acronym WEIRD.[12]

It turns out these samples really are weird. Only 12 percent of the world's population lives in such a country and the people who do are quite unusual. So research done in WEIRD countries often comes to different conclusions than research done elsewhere.[13]

Let's take math ability as an example.

In 1992, the toy company Mattel released a talking Barbie doll that said, among other things, "Math class is tough!" Many Americans still believe that girls and women struggle with mathematics more than boys and men.[14] At the time Barbie was making her confession, it was true. Starting in high school, boys scored slightly higher than girls on the math portion of the SAT, the standardized test for college admissions.[15] In the intervening twenty years, however, the gap narrowed as girls started taking math classes at the same rate as boys. This suggests that the difference in performance in the 1990s had less to do with gender and more to do with training, practice, and the messages sent by Barbie.[16]

The same conclusion appears true if we look at average differences cross-culturally. Across developed nations, girls do about as well as boys in about half the countries.[17] In the other half, boys outperform girls. In a few outlier countries, such as Iceland, girls outshine boys significantly. So whether men or women appear to be better at math depends on what country you're looking at. Still, boys do better than girls more often than girls do better than boys, so maybe that's evidence that boys are slightly better than girls at math on average.

If you look a bit closer at the data, though, you'll also discover that boys do better than girls on average only if you compare boys to the girls *in their own country*. Math ability varies so widely across societies that sometimes girls who underperform boys in their own country significantly outperform boys in other countries. For instance, though Japanese girls do less well than Japanese boys, they generally do better than American boys by a considerable margin.[18]

How we measure math ability also matters. Even if men and women are equally capable on average, men are more likely to be math geniuses.[19] Boys outnumber girls in the top 1 percent of math ability. But boys are also more likely than girls to struggle with math.[20] On average, they're a bit more likely than girls to get nearly all the answers on a math test right, but they're also more likely to get nearly all the answers wrong. So when boys do better, they're usually also doing worse.

But this, of course, also varies by country, over time, and across subgroups. Even among those whose math scores are in the top 1 percent, boys outperform girls among only some parts of the US population. White boys are more likely than White girls to perform at this high level of ability, but among Asians in the United States, girls outperform boys. Looking cross-culturally, girls also dominate the top 1 percent in Iceland, Thailand, and the United Kingdom. Boys, then, don't always outnumber girls when we look at the highest-scoring students. And in the United States, as girls and women have closed the average gap, they've also been closing it at the highest levels of mathematical ability.[21] Today, boys outnumber girls at the genius level 3:1; in the 1980s, the ratio was 13:1.[22] That's quite a remarkable catch-up.

In any case, performance on standardized tests doesn't predict grades students get in math classes. Girls in US high schools and colleges get higher grades in math classes than boys.[23] Only a few decades ago, most math majors were men; today, nearly half are women. Six times as many women get PhDs in mathematics today as they did in 1976.[24] And neither high scores on the SAT nor high grades in math classes predict who will opt for math-related careers. Many high-scoring girls don't go into these careers, and many poorly scoring boys do.

So are men better at math than women? In part, it depends on how we test for aptitude. If you go by standardized tests, sometimes boys outperform girls, but if you go by grades, girls outperform boys. If you test for genius-level math ability, boys outperform girls, but if you test for average level, girls and boys come out about even. And lastly, if you look at the most poorly performing students, girls come off looking much more capable than boys. But none of these generalizations about difference is consistent among groups in any given country, across countries, or even over time in a single population.

In fact, the best predictor of whether boys or girls do better in math is *belief*. Gender differences in math ability are highest in countries whose citizens most

FIGURE 2.2 | GENDER GAP IN MATH ACROSS COUNTRIES

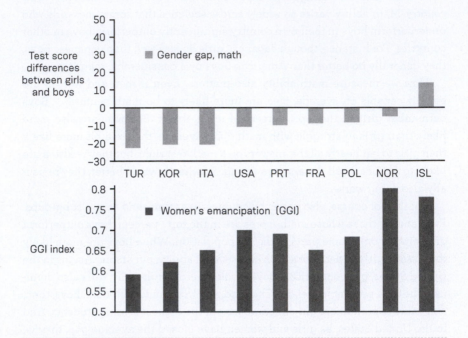

Note: With the exception of PRT (Portugal) and Iceland (ISL), the countries are abbreviated as their first three letters.
Source: Guiso Luigi, Fernando Monte, Paola Sapienza, and Luigi Zingales, "Culture, Gender, and Math." *Science* 320, no. 5880 (2009): 1164–65.

strongly endorse the idea that men are naturally better at math than women.[25] Overall, there is a strong correlation between gender differences in math ability and the level of gender inequality in a country (Figure 2.2).[26] The differences diminish, and then disappear, as men and women become more equal.

It turns out that mathematical ability is mostly about practice. When girls are required and encouraged to take the same classes as boys and have the opportunity to go into math-based careers, we see the lowest gender difference on tests of math aptitude. All this suggests that the gender difference in math performance has more to do with training and opportunity than with aptitude.[27]

This complex story is just one example of how observed gender differences in humans often vary over time and across cultures. This variation suggests that many observed differences are not inevitable and universal. When we see less variation, assuming the differences are "real" is more plausible. Indeed, it's a hint that they're not merely related to gendered stereotypes and opportunities but are part of being biologically human. That's our next definition.

Definition 3: Gender differences are real if they are biological

Biological differences include ones caused by our genes, hormones, and our brains. Let's review what scientists know about our bodies and how they do, don't, or might contribute to gender difference and similarity.

GENES   Our **genes** are a set of instructions for building and maintaining our bodies. Each of us has a unique set of genes, our *genotype*, and an observable set of physical and behavioral traits, our *phenotype*. By our current working definition, the differences described by Zell and his colleagues are biological if they are phenotypes produced by our genes.

Genetic females carry two X chromosomes and genetic males carry an X and a Y. Is the Y a significant source of gender differences? In fact, it's not.[28] At least, not directly. As the image below shows, the X chromosome is far larger than the Y chromosome; it has ten times the genetic material. Research is still ongoing, but so far it seems that the Y chromosome doesn't do much other than contribute some of the genes that give XY fetuses functioning testes and help facilitate male fertility. Weirdly, it also causes hairy ears.[29]

Once a body is set on the path to being male, other genetic consequences may follow. Some genes are expressed only if they're in a male or female body, such as the genes that allow a person to breastfeed. The expression of others is influenced by their hormonal environment. The baldness gene, for instance, thins hair on the head only in the presence of high levels of testosterone, so most women who carry the gene don't show signs of baldness. Curiously, the same gene that produces high voices in female bodies also produces low voices in male bodies.

Counterintuitively, the fact that most women have two X chromosomes and most men have only one is more significant than the presence or absence of a Y. Human beings need only one X chromosome to survive, so two Xs are redundant. XX bodies respond by using only one at a time. Which one they use, though, is random. In some cells, the X chromosome they received from their biological father actively provides genes, and in others the one they received from their biological mother is the source.[30] This means that people with two Xs can put a more diverse set of genes to work than people with an X and a Y. Twice as much. And that has some interesting effects.

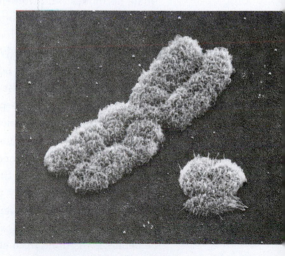

Despite its mighty reputation, the Y chromosome contains substantially less genetic material than the X chromosome.

A single X chromosome, for example, is why genetic males are more suscep-
tible to recessive traits, ones that aren't expressed in the presence of a gene for
a dominant trait. If a trait carried by a gene on the X chromosome is recessive,
XY males are more likely to show that trait, since they don't have a backup gene.
The inability to see the difference between red and green is an example. People
who carry XY chromosomes are fifteen times more likely than people who carry
XX chromosomes to be red-green color-blind. If their single X has the gene for
color blindness, the cells in their eyes won't be able to detect the difference. No
backup. People who carry XX chromosomes, on the other hand, have to inherit
two copies of the gene to be functionally color-blind.

It's a shocker, we know, but sex chromosomes themselves don't cause all that
many differences of interest. However, they do contribute the genes for whether
we develop ovaries or testes, potentially producing differences in our hormonal
profiles that may affect our personalities, abilities, and traits.

HORMONES Our **hormones** are messengers in a chemical communication
system. Released by glands or cells in one part of the body, hormones carry
instructions to the rest of it. They put our bodies on the path to being male or
female and, later, trigger puberty. They regulate basic physiological processes,
like hunger and the reproductive cycle. And they influence our moods: feelings
of happiness, confidence, and contentment. They are part of what inspires us to
have sex, get into (or run away from) fights, and settle down and raise a baby.

Importantly, it's a mistake to use binary language and say that men have
"male hormones" and women have "female hormones." All human hormones
circulate in essentially all bodies, but some of them do so in different proportions. Male bodies tend to have higher levels of androgens and female bodies
higher levels of estrogens. While these hormones do contribute to producing
noticeably female or male bodies, that is far from the only thing they do. In
fact, estrogen sometimes has the same effects in females that testosterone has
in males. And testosterone plays essential functions in female bodies, while
estrogen plays essential functions in male bodies.[31] Testosterone, for example,
helps facilitate ovulation. Just as we're not "opposite sexes," our hormones are
far from opposite in their chemical structure, presence, or function.

Still, differing levels of these hormones might contribute to gender differences. Testosterone usually gets the most attention. In pop culture, it is the
King Hormone[32]—the one most strongly associated with masculinity. A singular substance given an almost mythological power, testosterone is assumed to
be behind everything from athletic ability to aggression to risk-taking. In fact,
there isn't very strong evidence for any of this.

Why? Well, for one, there isn't a straightforward way to measure testosterone.[33] First, study results are affected by whether we collect testosterone from
samples of blood, plasma, saliva, muscle, or urine. Some testosterone is nonre-

active because it's bound to other chemical compounds. So scientists have to decide whether to measure "total" testosterone or just the amount of the hormone that's "free."

Second, in any given person, cells in some parts of the body will respond more strongly to testosterone than cells in other parts, and which parts of the body are most sensitive vary from person to person. This makes the amount of testosterone—free or not—sometimes a less significant factor than the level of sensitivity, which depends on the part of the body under investigation.

Third, naturally occurring testosterone levels vary throughout the day, year, and on idiosyncratic schedules particular to individual people. So it matters *when* our level of testosterone is measured. Levels are also affected by the intake of substances like caffeine and alcohol. Testosterone also interacts in complicated ways with other hormones in the body, such that it may have effects but only under certain chemical conditions.

Finally, female bodies on average are sensitive to lower levels of testosterone than male bodies and are more responsive to swings in those levels. Male bodies respond similarly to hormone levels ranging anywhere from 20 percent to 200 percent of normal. This means we should expect most disparities in men's levels of testosterone to have zero effect, with the exception of cases in which levels are exceedingly high or exceedingly low.

So what do we know? Well, the hormone does appear to help stimulate sex drive in most people, and people in female bodies need less of the hormone to experience a significant effect.[34] Testosterone levels also correlate with visual-spatial ability, such as mental rotation, but not in the way people usually assume.[35] Very high levels of testosterone correlate with poor visual-spatial ability. So do very low levels. The sweet spot is in the middle. So it's high-testosterone women and low-testosterone men who do best on visual-spatial tests. The advantages of having even those Goldilocks-level testosterone levels aren't large enough, however, to correlate with work performance, even in jobs like engineering or architecture.[36]

There is also good evidence that the hormone cycles that regulate menstruation correspond to mild changes in mood, sexual interest, and partner choice (though we see no changes across the menstrual cycle in memory, creativity, problem-solving ability, or athletic, intellectual, or academic performance).[37] People in male bodies experience hormone fluctuations as well, and their moods are also somewhat affected by their personal chemistry.[38] That is, men get "hormonal" sometimes too. In any case, hormonal fluctuations that regulate mood are a relatively minor influence compared to, say, whether it's Monday morning or Friday afternoon.[39]

Contrary to popular belief, testosterone does not correlate well with elite athletic performance. One large comparative study of Olympic athletes found low testosterone concentrations in fully a quarter of the male competitors across twelve of the fifteen sports studied and high testosterone concentrations in only 5 percent of female elite athletes, and only in three sports. Counterstereotypically, male powerlifters were one of the groups of elite athletes with below-average testosterone levels.[40]

In sum, we find differing levels of androgens and estrogens in bodies, and those hormones have been linked to a limited number of observed differences, especially sex drive and visual-spatial ability, as well as when (but not whether) we experience changes in mood. All the effects are small, with the possible exception of sex drive.

Although hormones do not place people unambiguously into the categories of woman or man, they may be good candidates for the "real" differences we're after. But that's not all. Hormones may also indirectly produce average differences between male and female brains.

BRAINS Scientists have documented average gender differences in brain anatomy (the size and shape of its parts), composition (characteristics of the tissue), and function (rate of blood flow, metabolism of glucose, and neurotransmitter levels).[41] Women have smaller brains on average (mostly explained by their overall smaller size), and men and women have different ratios of gray matter to white matter in some regions. None of these differences is particularly pronounced, and all are average differences with significant overlap (like the bell curve illustrating differences in self-esteem in Figure 2.1).

When we look at these differences all at once, though, we discover that female-typical structures in a single brain often coexist with male-typical structures. One study, for example, examined 625 brains, measuring the ten regions with the strongest evidence for sexual dimorphism.[42] Only 2.4 percent of the brains were internally consistent: all male-typical or all female-typical. This means that 97.6 percent of us have "gender nonconforming" brains.

To complicate things further, scientists have struggled to tie these anatomical and physiological differences to observed differences in traits or abilities.[43] In other words, we don't know what any of these differences actually *do*. One intriguing theory is that some differences may compensate for others, producing similarity from difference.[44] That is, our bodies may be evolved to enable *sex difference* for the purposes of reproduction but reduce *other biological differences* that arise in the process of building male and female people. So, counterintuitively, some differences might cause sameness. That's not the kind of "real" difference we're after either.

Some research does suggest that gender identity, gender expression, and sexual orientation could be shaped in part by hormonally caused brain differences, though the evidence is not especially clear or strong.[45] The genitals develop earlier in pregnancy than the brain, so it's possible that the hormonal environment of the developing brain could be different from that of the devel-

FIGURE 2.3 | EXAMPLE OF A MENTAL ROTATION TASK

(a)   (b)

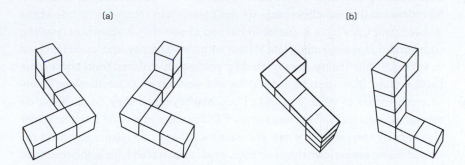

Mental rotation tasks like this one measure how easily and accurately you can determine whether two figures are identical except for their orientation. Assembling jigsaw puzzles is one use of this skill.

oping genitals, creating discrepancies between the two. This might explain why some people experience same-sex desire or strongly feel that their assigned sex and gender identity don't match.[46] However, most neurologists believe that hormonal influence on the brain during fetal development plays at most a small role.

If we could definitively prove a biological origin for a significant difference between men and women, would *that* make it real? Well, only if we assume that biological differences are permanent. Some biological features are, in fact, mutable. That is, they change in response to people's experiences. If biologically based differences can be decreased in size, erased, or reversed quite easily, do they still count as real?

Consider mental rotation, our very best candidate for a large biological cognitive gender difference (Figure 2.3). It turns out that mental rotation can be taught, quickly and easily.[47] One study found that assigning women to a semester of *Tetris* (a simple video game that involves rotating and fitting various geometric shapes into one another) almost closed the preexisting gap between men's and women's scores.[48] In another study, just ten hours of video-game play reduced the gap to statistical insignificance.[49] In a third study, five and a half hours of play erased the gender difference.[50] And in a fourth experiment, just two minutes of practice right before the test did the same.[51] Further studies reveal that playing *Tetris* heightens blood flow to the parts of the brain used for mental rotation and thickens the cerebral cortex.[52]

It turns out that whatever natural ability an individual has for mental rotation, everyone can improve with a little bit of practice.[53] Indeed, the difference between the scores of people with training and people without training is larger than the difference between men and women.[54]

While this finding doesn't rule out an inborn biological advantage for males, neuroscientist Lise Eliot argues that we probably see gender difference in mental rotation ability mostly because we don't teach it in school (so no one learns it there), and boys have a greater likelihood of learning it elsewhere (playing with building toys, spending lots of time with video games, and being involved in sports).[55] This theory is supported by studies on children from low-income backgrounds. Boys growing up in poor and working-class families don't have as much access to video games and building toys, and they do no better on mental rotation tasks than their sisters.[56] Differences in mental rotation ability also vary by race, ethnicity, age, and country.[57] Black and Hispanic girls in the United States outperform their boy counterparts; in Iceland, girls do better than boys. In Korea, the gender difference shrinks as kids get older; in Ireland and Spain, it increases. This gender difference may also be shrinking over time.[58]

In sum, even mental rotation—the most robust cognitive gender difference we've ever measured—is mutable, minimizable, and even erasable by instruction and practice, undone with just a few minutes of *Minecraft*.[59] As two prominent scientists explained, "Simply put, your brain is what you do with it."[60] In fact, lots of observed differences respond to intervention (and we will discuss more examples in the next section). For now, let's consider one final definition of real—the most strict of all.

Definition 4: Gender differences are real if they are biological and immutable

Perhaps a gender difference could count as real if it were observed, had a known biological cause, and could not easily be overcome by social interventions like practice and priming. Differences in size and, by extension, throwing ability and some other physical differences would qualify. Gender and sexual identity may be good candidates. There might be others, possibly different levels of sexual desire and empathy. And, of course, there are the hairy ears.

But the majority of gender differences documented by Zell and his colleagues would not qualify under this definition. This is a good time to remember the anglerfish. We're sexually dimorphic in that we reproduce sexually, and the process of making us reproductively male and female appears to lead to some other average differences. But on the spectrum of high-to-low sexual dimorphism, we're on the low side. We're of a similar size and weight, we have (almost) all the same appendages, and we have the same desires, traits, and physical and cognitive abilities, even if there are some average differences here and there. We're quite clearly not "opposites."

But . . . why not? Why *aren't* we more different? Well, that's another kind of question altogether.

SIMILARITIES BETWEEN MEN AND WOMEN

What are the real similarities between men and women? If it seems odd to ask this question, it's because it is. Scientists have looked so hard for differences, and for so long, that it never occurred to them to flip their research question on its head. In recent decades, however, more and more women have become scientists. Some scientists have adopted feminist and queer points of view. Resisting the assumption of inferiority and thinking outside the binary prompted new and different research questions, like the surprisingly obvious one, "What explains our similarities?" To close out this chapter, then, let's explore some of the theories for why we are so much alike. We'll examine three: biosocial interaction, intersectionality, and evolution.

Biosocial Interaction: The Natural Power of Human Culture

One of the things that makes humans stand out from all other animals is the extent to which we wrap ourselves in culture. We live in a natural environment, but we live, simultaneously, in our collective imaginations, in a world that we invent, one with things that don't exist in nature: corporations, wedding vows, holidays.

By virtue of being cultural, we're also diverse. Take any two human societies and you'll find countless differences in their cultural practices and ideas. As a species, in fact, our ways of life are not just more varied than those of any other primate on earth; they are more varied than those of every other primate *combined*.[61] That is why reality shows like *Wife Swap*—in which women from different backgrounds swap families for the purpose of producing mayhem—can run for sixteen years. Commenting on this, psychologist Cordelia Fine observed: "Other animals are fascinating, to be sure. Many are highly flexible and adaptable. But there just aren't that many ways to *be* a female baboon."[62] Not so for female humans.

This diversity is not merely cultural, though; it's *natural*. That is, human biology makes it possible for us to be culturally different from one another. Understanding this helps us avoid the discredited and fruitless argument referred to as the **nature/nurture debate**. The "nature" side is premised on the idea that men and women are *born* different, and the "nurture" side presupposes that we *become* different through socialization alone. Both sides are wrong.

Scholars from all disciplines now overwhelmingly reject the ideology of **naturalism**, the idea that biology affects our behavior independently of our environment. Likewise, they reject **culturalism**, the idea that we're "blank slates" who become who we are purely through learning and socialization. This should make sense. Any given gender difference can't be purely a result of "nurture" (a culturalist assumption) because it's only through our bodies that we encounter our social world. Nor can it be purely "nature" (a naturalist assumption), because our bodies don't exist in a cultural vacuum. Accordingly, both sex and gender are products of the interaction between nature and nurture.

The phrase **biocultural interaction** refers to the process by which our bodies respond to our cultural environment and vice versa (Figure 2.4).[63] To describe our species with only nature or only culture is like describing a rectangle with reference to only its length or width. Without both pieces of information, there *is* no rectangle.[64] Likewise, without both biology and culture, it's impossible to understand what it is to be human. (In fact, some scholars use the term *gender*sex* to draw attention to the social construction of the sexed body, as discussed in Chapter 1.) The evidence for this is so overwhelming that scientists now agree that it makes no sense to talk about "human nature" except insofar as "the social *is* the natural."[65]

One example of biocultural interaction involves physical characteristics like flexibility, strength, and speed. Within biological limits, our bodies react to use by developing the capacities we ask of them. We can get faster if we train, stronger if we lift, and more flexible if we stretch. In societies that ask people to develop these capacities, they will. And in ones that ask women and men to develop different capacities, men's and women's bodies will be more different than they would be otherwise.

Consider marathons. Women in Western societies were discouraged from running for centuries and formally excluded from competing in marathons until the 1970s. In that time, men got much faster. When women were first allowed to compete, they were much slower than men, but since then, they've gotten faster too. In fact, they've gotten faster much more quickly than men ever did. It took approximately thirty years for men to shave thirty minutes off their best time; it took women only five.[66] Today, the men's record is still faster than the women's record but by less than ten minutes (Figure 2.5). What we are allowed and encouraged to do shapes what our bodies are capable of doing.

This is true of our brains too.[67] Remember those kids playing *Tetris*? Changes in the brain have been documented in response to a wide range of other activities too: juggling, dancing, singing, meditating, and even driving a taxi.[68]

FIGURE 2.4 | BIOCULTURAL INTERACTION

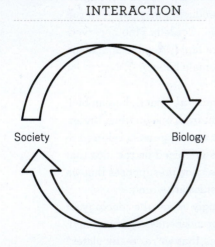

Society   Biology

FIGURE 2.5 | MARATHON WORLD RECORDS BY GENDER

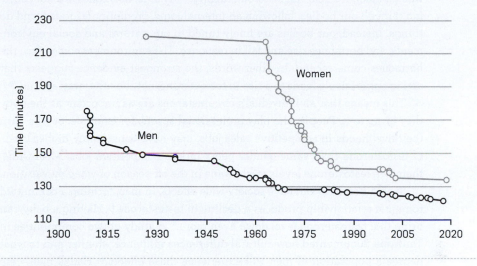

Source: World Athletics.

Of course they have. Our brain is a cultural organ, responding to our social environment.

Even our hormones and genes respond to culture.[69] When we experience a culturally defined "win," for example, our bodies cooperate by using hormones to make us feel good about it.[70] A study of men, for example, found that anticipating a competition caused testosterone levels to rise. If they won the contest, their testosterone levels went up further. If they lost, their testosterone levels went down.[71] Hormones respond to social settings not only in sports but in games like chess too.[72] Another study found this phenomenon among men just sitting on the couch watching their favorite team.[73] When men do something they think is cool—like drive a sports car—their testosterone gets a bump; if they do it in front of other people, their levels jump even higher.[74] In the immediate aftermath of the 2008 presidential election, men who supported the losing candidate saw a drop in their testosterone levels; those who supported the winning candidate did not.[75]

Emerging evidence suggests that this is true for women too.[76] In one study, for example, women who exerted power over others under experimental conditions saw their testosterone levels rise.[77] The authors suggest that gender differences in who is expected and allowed to exert power may shape the average hormonal profiles of men and women. "A lifetime of gender socialization," they write, "could contribute to 'sex differences' in testosterone."

This is important. We tend to think of behavior as being "testosterone fueled" when, in fact, it's also "testosterone fueling."[78] That is, hormones are not coursing through our bodies, following an internal logic, prompting us to feel and do things. Instead, our bodies are finely tuned to our natural and social environments, and hormones rise and fall in response. The environment comes *first*; the hormones come *second*. In other words, the strongest evidence suggests that acting aggressively leads to a rise in testosterone, not the other way around.[79]

This means that an individual's circumstances are as important as the body they bring to it. People who play professional sports, for example, or who earn their livelihoods in competitive sales jobs, may have consistently higher levels of testosterone than same-gender peers in less competitive jobs. Meanwhile, their own testosterone levels might wane in the off-season or when on vacation.

Such differences can have society-wide effects. In men, forming a committed romantic relationship produces a decline in testosterone.[80] Having a baby can bring that testosterone level down even more.[81] A study of two communities in Tanzania documented how cultural differences influence whether and to what degree a population of men will experience these effects.[82] Hadza men were involved fathers, taking care of children alongside women. Datoga men did not parent, leaving the work to mothers. The difference in behavior was reflected in their testosterone levels: On average, Datoga men had higher levels than Hadza men.

Our genes also respond to the environment in a process called gene-environment interaction. Instead of dictating our phenotype in a simple one-directional way, our genotype is flexible.[83] Each gene can express itself in many, sometimes thousands of, different ways. Our bodies adapt on the fly, smartly designing and redesigning themselves in response to the challenges of their environment. Even identical twins become genotypically different over time.[84]

Highly aggressive people, for example, often carry genes for aggression, but having those genes does not, in itself, make a person violent. The genes need to be triggered by trauma.[85] Living in a happy home with loving parents decreases the likelihood that a person with genes for aggression will become aggressive. In contrast, poverty, a dysfunctional family life, and abuse all increase the chances that the genes for aggression will be "turned on" and lead to violent behavior. Genes matter. A person without a genetic predisposition for violence probably won't grow up to be violent, even if they suffer trauma.[86] But genes don't work in a vacuum. A person with the genetic predisposition may never become violent at all; it depends on the quality of their life.

In some cultures, men are nurturing; in others, they are less so. In some environments, people genetically primed to be aggressive become aggressive; in others, they don't. Why? Because humans are not evolved to be either nurturers *or* warriors. Instead, human biology has given people the potential to be either, and more. Our brains, our bodies, the chemicals that circulate within them, and

If fathers are actively involved with their children, their bodies respond in ways that help them be good dads.

the genes that build them are all prepared to respond to our cultural environment. What have we evolved to be? Flexible!

So, in societies in which men and women are pressed into very different social roles, we might see them developing quite different strengths and weaknesses. But these aren't necessarily "real," even if they're biological. They come to be embodied only through a process of gender socialization. In other words, they are **deceptive differences**: ones that, by being observed, make it seem like groups are more different than they really are. When studying gender, deceptive differences are those that make it seem as if men and women are more sexually dimorphic than they really are.[87]

Alternatively, when societies put all of us on similar paths, we might look more alike than different. US society is probably somewhere in the middle. There are many ways in which Americans raise girls and boys very similarly: they live in the same houses, have access to the same foods, go to the same types of schools, and so on. Then again, they're dressed differently, given different toys, and encouraged to do different activities, on average. Based on these facts, we should expect some differences (in sportiness, for example, or interest in dance) but also quite a lot of similarities (like an increasingly equal aptitude for math). If human bodies are designed to rise to the cultural occasion, some occasions will evoke difference, while others will evoke sameness. So gender similarity is as much part of human biology as gender difference.

Intersectionality: Putting Gender in Context

When asked to imagine a "man" or a "woman," most Americans don't at first envision a man who is a professional ballet dancer, a Sikh engineer who wears a turban, or a Mexican immigrant couple who co-own a food truck. Instead, the mythical inhabitants of the gender binary—the prototypical man and woman who usually come to mind—fit into a rather narrow slice of reality. Do a Google image search for "man and woman" and it will return dozens of images that feature people who appear White, cisgender, middle or upper class, heterosexual, able bodied, urban or suburban, and native-born.

Men and women like these fall within what sociologists call the **normative standard**, the example against which people tend to measure themselves and others. The centering of people who conform to the normative standard preserves the plausibility of the gender binary, because it presses us to forget all the people who fall outside it. The gender binary centers people who have the privilege of being defined as the norm, casting everyone else as exceptions to the rule.

When we consider the whole array of people in our societies, however, another reason for similarities among the genders becomes clear: the *many* other identities, experiences, and social positions we have in common. Bodies may be partly designed biologically to play different roles in reproduction, but people with different genders often share a race, class, nationality, religion, age, or other identity. These also are sources of experience that can shape how bodies behave. People seen as Black in the United States, for example, have higher levels of the stress hormone cortisol, which contributes to racial disparities in health.[88] This affects the health of Black people of all genders. Social positions—like class, occupation, and immigration status—are shared by people of all genders. The manifestation of gender differences, then, may be muted by the things we have in common: national, regional, and local cultures; the quality of our educations; our diet and health; our family structures; and our social networks.

Gender diversity complicates this picture, too, as some of us identify and express ourselves as trans, nonbinary, or gender fluid. This is disruptive of the gender binary, almost by definition. Increasingly, cisgender people are also grasping for greater freedom from rigid gender expectations.[89] For centuries, women have sought the privileges reserved for men by claiming identities like tomboy.[90] Many people of all genders find increasing freedom in older age, when retirement from work and reproduction make gender less all-encompassing.

Sometimes men and women have more in common with each other than they do with others of their own gender.

Differences and similarities between women and men are filtered through cultural categories and diverse life experiences. Men, for example, have greater bone mass and strength than women, making women twice as likely to break a bone and four times as likely to be diagnosed with osteoporosis.[91] Genes and hormones contribute to this discrepancy, but an individual's bone health is also strongly affected by diet, leisure activities, and type of work.[92] Accordingly, among ultra-Orthodox Jewish adolescent boys, the gender pattern is reversed.[93] Boys in these communities begin intensive study of religious documents at a young age, so they spend much less time exercising and more time indoors than other boys. As a result, their bones never grow as strong as those of their sisters, who have lighter study loads, do more physical chores, and get more sunlight. Both the biological and the cultural influence of gender on bone mass and strength, then, is mediated by the power of religion.

The idea that gender is not an isolated social fact about us but instead intersects with our other social positions and identities is called **intersectionality**.[94]

We are not just men, women, trans, nonbinary, or two-spirit. A woman might be a White, middle-class Christian who votes Democratic and parents a two-year-old with her heterosexual husband. Or she might be a gender-fluid jazz-loving Eastern European immigrant to Milwaukee who plays rugby. Or perhaps a child-free Texan who works for the Girl Scouts, manages her epilepsy, and collects Legos. Some of these other features of our lives are distinctions that place us in hierarchies, like gender. Others are merely differences without great social significance, like tongue-rolling ability.

We're going to talk a lot more about intersectionality throughout this book, starting with Chapter 4. For now, just notice that *all* the things that make us who we are shape our individual personality traits, emotional tendencies, cognitive abilities, and physical potential. When people of different genders share other identities and life experiences, those things produce physical similarities as our complex bodies respond to shared cultural environments.

Evolution: Similarity as an Adaptation

Human males and females evolved to have different roles in reproduction. One sex carries, delivers, and nurses babies. The other contributes new genetic material. Given this, it's tempting to argue that because we've evolved to have bodies that play different roles in *reproduction*, we've also evolved to have different roles in *life*. This, however, doesn't stand up to the facts.

To start, evolution-based thinking about humans often assumes that humans naturally form **nuclear families**—ones in which a mother and father with children live together without extended kin. But this family form didn't exist until very recently and is still far from universal. Instead, for most of our species' existence, humans lived together in **kin groups**, culturally variable collections of people considered family.

In **forager societies**, people migrate seasonally, following crops and game across the landscape. Because everyone travels together, evolution would have selected for similarity in walking speeds. Foraging groups are relatively egalitarian, and people live similar lives.[95] They have the same acquaintances, eat the same foods, travel the same territory, share the same beliefs, and raise the same kids.

Given these conditions, there are good reasons we might have evolved to be similar. It makes sense for everyone to be well suited for important activities, as cooperation in nonreproductive matters is essential for human survival. In other words, if it's evolutionarily adaptive for half the population to be good at something (like remembering where the bison graze or designing houses and tools), it hardly makes sense for the other half of the population to be bad at it.

Insurmountable differences are arguably deeply *mal*adaptive. In a crisis it could be fatal for a social group to consist of two types of people, both incapable of taking on the work assigned to the other. Sudden shortages of men or women—not to mention third, fourth, or fifth genders—would require that group members be able to substitute for one another. Think of the families that needed to turn daughters into sons in Albania, those that still do so in Afghanistan today, and the millions of single fathers across the United States and elsewhere. Being able to share responsibilities is incredibly useful. Adaptive, even. So there were (and are) strong evolutionary pressures toward biological sameness.

This is true even in terms of sexuality. Instead of being a strictly biological behavior, humans have always made sexual decisions in response to cultural rules.[96] Given this, we should expect to see more differences across cultures than we do between people of different genders in any given culture. And that is what we see. Some cultures depict men as more sexual than women; others have cast women as more sexual than men. Some offer substantial tolerance of homosexual behavior and room for additional genders (like the māhū of Hawaii, the muxe of Mexico, and the hijra of India discussed in Chapter 1).[97] In fact, in some cultures, same-gender sex may have been expected, often to cement alliances and enhance one's access to reproductive sex.[98] Moreover, the exchanges of intimacy and pleasure in same-gender relationships may have fostered more cooperative behavior of all kinds in humans.[99]

The notion that men have evolved to be more promiscuous than women is another common myth. For men to "sow their seed" (to impregnate as many women as they can), there must be an endless field of fertile women to plow.[100] This was almost never the case. At any given time, the majority of women in a kin group were too young or too old to get pregnant; already pregnant; with reduced fertility due to breastfeeding; or infertile for unknown reasons. Even sex between two healthy fertile individuals results in a pregnancy only 3 percent of the time. And another guy's sperm might get to the egg first. Most men would have been lucky to sire twelve to sixteen children in their lifetime, not so many more than women's birthing

Women warriors are not just the stuff of mythology. DNA evidence has recently confirmed the existence of high-ranking women Viking warriors.

nine to twelve. Instead of sowing seeds, a man's reproduction was probably maximized by having regular sex with one or just a small number of women.

Since sexual reproduction has mattered to all human groups, we've almost certainly evolved to notice and care about differences between males and females. This, however, does not translate into universal evolutionary pressures that differ by sex. Most kin-based communities gendered their tasks, but *how* they gendered them varied. Some forms of provision (gathering, farming, and hunting smaller animals) were more likely to be women's than men's work.[101] Still other tasks, like building houses, were sometimes considered feminine and sometimes masculine work.[102] And the mythic status accorded to men as hunters overlooks substantial variation in how hunting roles were divided by gender.

In other words, the social construction of gender among early human groups was just as cross-culturally variable, historically dependent, and ideologically jumbled as it is today for us. None of this was consistent enough to account for an evolution into an "oppositeness" that spans the whole human species. Instead, our current ideas about the "real" differences between men and women are based on what we see today in WEIRD societies, which are just our new ways of organizing our gendered social life.[103]

To summarize, the idea that males and females in all parts of the world evolved to have the same contrasting traits doesn't do justice to the diversity of our ancestral environments, the power of our cultures, or our actual evolved biology. Societies need to ensure biological reproduction, but they respond to other equally pressing demands too: for food and shelter, love and care, and the need to make sense of the natural world. All these competing needs mean that, for humans, sexual dimorphism in nonreproductive biological capacities would not be particularly advantageous. We shouldn't be so surprised, then, to discover that research on gender differences has detected much more overlap than the gender binary predicts. There may be ways in which we are different, and in some cultures those differences may be quite pronounced, but we also have the biological capacity to be quite alike.

Revisiting the Question

Q+A **The gender binary might be an ideology, but there are real differences between men and women, right?**

Well, sure. But it's not nearly as simple as it sounds. As H. L. Mencken famously observed: "There is always an easy solution to every human problem—neat, plausible, and wrong."[104] The gender binary that characterizes men and women as "opposite sexes" doesn't reflect reality but instead an ongoing search among scientists to justify gender difference and therefore gender inequality. Even so, all the gathered evidence points to a more complex picture. Human biology, evolution, and the diversity of our embodied experiences work together to make us the people we are.

For the remainder of this book, then, it's important not to fall back on explanations that offer simple answers. Biology matters, gender matters, society matters, and they all work together to make us the people we are. That's our true nature. We're an extraordinary species with a rich sociocultural life, one that we all share, and our bodies express that flexibility.

Next . . .

OK, fine, so establishing that men and women are substantially different from each other isn't as easy as pop culture leads us to believe. But it still *seems* like men and women are different. They move differently, decorate themselves differently, choose different college majors and careers. If these differences aren't biological and immutable, then what are they? It's a good question:

 If men and women aren't naturally opposite, then why do they act so differently so much of the time?

It's time to put the "social" in social theory.

FOR FURTHER READING

Browning, Frank. *The Fate of Gender: Nature, Nurture and the Human Future*. New York: Bloomsbury, 2016.

Charles, Maria, and Sarah Thébaud, eds. "Gender and STEM: Understanding Segregation in Science, Technology, Engineering and Mathematics." Special issue, *Social Sciences* 7, no. 7 (2018). Basel, Switzerland: MDPI, 2018.

Eliot, Lise. "You Don't Have a Male or Female Brain: The More Brains Scientists Study, the Weaker the Evidence for Sex Differences." *The Conversation*, April 22, 2021. https://theconversation.com/you-dont-have-a-male-or-female-brain-the-more-brains-scientists-study-the-weaker-the-evidence-for-sex-differences-158005.

Jordan-Young, Rebecca, and Katrina Karkazis. *Testosterone: An Unauthorized Biography*. Cambridge, MA: Harvard University Press, 2019.

Wade, Lisa. "The New Science of Sex Difference." *Sociology Compass* 7, no. 4 (2013): 278–93.

Zell, Ethan, Zlatan Krizan, and Sabrina Teeter. "Evaluating Gender Similarities and Differences Using Metasynthesis." *American Psychologist* 70, no. 1 (2015): 10–20.

3

Performances

In 2015, an unknown singer and songwriter named Billie Eilish uploaded a song to SoundCloud. "Ocean Eyes" went triple platinum. Five years later, Eilish became only the second person in history to win all four main Grammy categories in one year: Best New Artist, Song of the Year, Record of the Year, and Album of the Year. She was still a teenager.

In addition to Eilish's "whispery goth pop" sound, her clothes rocketed her to stardom.[1] Borrowing from decades of Black music culture, Eilish's style relied on baggy crew-neck T-shirts or sweatshirts and equally loose-fitting sweatpants or board shorts, paired with sneakers and athletic socks. Her clothes were often cartoonishly oversized, so much so that one commentator called her look "bloblike."[2] If she showed any skin below the neck, it was likely a shin, maybe a knee. She preferred to maintain privacy about the exact shape and size of her body and its parts. Her fans *adored* this about her.

What made Eilish remarkable, however, wasn't her decision to dress as she preferred; it was the context in which she made this decision. Female pop stars—like young women more generally—are *supposed* to make a spectacle of their bodies. It's an unwritten rule of celebrity. And yet Eilish broke this unwritten rule. In a sea

As a breakout star, Billie Eilish became as famous for her shape-concealing clothes as her unusual sound. Boldly and unapologetically, she flouted the rule that women pop stars show off their bodies.

of crop tops, miniskirts, leotards, catsuits, and form-fitting evening gowns, Eilish stood out.

This chapter is about the gendered expectations that we each confront in our daily lives. That is, it's about **gender rules**, or instructions for how to appear and behave as a man or a woman, such as the rule that young women give visual access to the curves and contours of their bodies, at least under certain circumstances. The chapter is also about our ability to break these rules, as Eilish did, and the circumstances that allow us to get away with breaking them. Gender rules explain what centuries of research into the biology of gender cannot: the many differences between how men and women live their daily lives. Gender rules, in other words, are the central answer to this chapter's question:

Q+A **If men and women aren't naturally opposite, then why do they act so differently so much of the time?**

Indeed, men and women *do* behave quite differently. Women are four times as likely to major in education as men, while men are more than three times more likely to major in engineering.[3] Compared to women, men prefer to play sports for exercise; women prefer Pilates, yoga, or dance.[4] Women are also more likely than men to say that religion is "very important" to them.[5]

Women and men use their bodies differently too. And this goes far beyond whether we show it off. Consider how we inspect our fingernails. Women tend to hold their hand out in front of them with fingers splayed. Men tend to turn the palm toward themselves and curl their fingers down. Gender informs how we hold a cigarette. The masculine way is to hold it between the thumb and forefinger with the palm facing to the side. The feminine way is to hold it between two forefingers with the palm facing in. There is a gendered way to hold hands. Men's palms usually face backward and women's forward, such that her body is placed just slightly behind his as they walk. Heck, gender even influences how we take off our clothes. Women tend to put their arms inside their T-shirt, then glide it over their head. Men tend to grab it at the back of the neck and tug it off.

The reasons for these differences are not biological. They're social. Across a lifetime of interacting with others, we absorb complex sets of gendered expectations. We learn to act in gendered ways out of habit and for fun, but we also learn that if we fail to do so, others may tease, hassle, or hurt us.

None of us, however, simply follows gendered expectations thoughtlessly. Like Eilish, we're crafty manipulators. We make exceptions (for ourselves and others), and we apply different standards depending on the situation and the person. In response, most of us develop ways of managing gendered expectations that work for us as unique individuals, if imperfectly. Others of us find that these expectations are painful, even intolerable.

If we can manage it, most of us tend to behave in gendered ways most of the time. Eilish aside, it's easier to obey gender rules than to break them—and life is challenging enough as it is. So we make choices that contribute to the gendered patterns that we see around us. This is true of most of us, even those of us who are trans, nonbinary, or gender fluid. These collective decisions sustain the illusion that the gender binary is natural and inevitable, even biological.

For this reason, sociologists generally describe gender not as something we *are* but as something we *do*.

HOW TO DO GENDER

One day a four-year-old boy named Jeremy decided to wear a hair clip to preschool.[6] "Several times that day," his mother said, "another little boy insisted that Jeremy must be a girl because 'only girls wear barrettes.'" Jeremy protested, refusing to acknowledge the rule. He repeated what he'd been told by his mother, that anyone can wear barrettes and "being a boy means having a penis." His protestations fell on deaf ears, and eventually his mom recalled: "Jeremy finally pulled down his pants to make his point more convincingly." The other boy was unfazed. "Everybody has a penis," he insisted. "Only girls wear barrettes."

Jeremy's schoolmate stated his objection in the form of a general rule. It wasn't that *he* didn't like it when boys wore barrettes, or that *Jeremy* specifically didn't look fetching in a barrette, it was that only girls and no boys under any circumstances should wear one. Jeremy's schoolmate articulated a rule for all boys that Jeremy had broken: *Only girls wear barrettes.*

You could likely brainstorm hundreds of such rules if you tried. They apply to every area of our lives, specifying how we should dress and decorate our bodies and homes, what hobbies and careers we should pursue, with whom we should socialize and how, and much more. Most of us do gender when we stand, sit, and walk. We do gender when we talk, laugh, and curate our personalities. Gender inflects routine activities like eating, bathing, and driving.

Sociologists use the phrase **doing gender** to describe the ways in which we actively obey and break gender rules. According to his classmate, Jeremy was doing gender wrong. *Only girls wear barrettes!* A penis was irrelevant. This response is not merely childhood naivete about bodies; it highlights how gender operates as a social construct enforced in social interaction.

Every day we do thousands of things that signal masculinity or femininity, and we do them according to gender rules. When using social media, for example, women's choices tend to reflect the rules that they're supposed to be attractive, social, and sweet.[7] They're more likely than men to feature friends and family members and to try to look pretty in their pictures. Women also post more pictures overall. When they offer reactions, they're more likely to express congratulations or give compliments and encouragement.

Men, in contrast, respond to gender rules that dictate they be active, independent, and anti-authority. Their profile pictures often include images of them playing sports, looking tough, and taking risks. When men offer reactions, they're more likely than women to be argumentative, insulting, or ironic. Many of us infer the gender rule *Only men troll.*

We learn gender rules like these implicitly, gradually absorbing them as we become increasingly acculturated into our families, communities, and societies. Some rules are relatively rigid, like *Men don't wear eyeshadow.* Other rules are more flexible and negotiable, like *Only women have long hair.* We tend to become most aware of the rules when we are trying to master new ones, as we pass through puberty, for example, and start to practice looking and acting like an adult.[8]

Cross-Cultural Variation in Gender Rules

Gender rules exist everywhere, but the rules themselves vary tremendously. In France and Argentina, for example, men exchange kisses on the cheek when

President George W. Bush welcomes Saudi Crown Prince Abdullah to his Texas ranch. Holding hands is not an accepted way for two adult men to touch in the United States but is a common practice in some Middle Eastern cultures.

they greet one another. Traditionally, in Scotland, men wear skirts called kilts. In Arab countries, men don white robes, often with pink-and-white head coverings. The color pink is gender neutral there. In Belgium, pink is for boys. Certain floral patterns on a kimono signal masculinity in Japan. In some Middle Eastern societies, men who are colleagues and friends hold hands. All these examples violate gender rules for men in America.

Many South Korean men today wholeheartedly embrace skin care and cosmetics. Men living there consume more beauty products than men from any other country.[9] Three-quarters receive beauty treatments at least weekly.[10] They do so, according to one makeup artist, because it makes them look "cool" and "confident."[11] In South Korea, said one K-pop star, "makeup is not just for women or necessarily feminine. It's for everyone."[12] "Men can feel more masculine in their own way by wearing it," explained another.

This new ideal version of masculinity was introduced by K-pop stars in the 1990s.[13] And they still epitomize this ideal today. Members of the South Korean boy band BTS, for example, wholly embrace symbols Americans would characterize as feminine. They dye their hair platinum blond or bright colors like pink and turquoise. They're frequently photographed wearing lipstick and eye makeup. They maintain the slight frames typical of adolescents. They wear dangly earrings and other delicate jewelry. They embrace pastels, dressing in soft

The Korean members of the internationally beloved boy band BTS are mainstreaming a new version of masculinity, one that celebrates slim bodies, longer hair, pastel colors, and lots of accessories.

colors. In their choreography, they touch themselves provocatively, make elegant gestures, and give the audience "come hither" looks.

Notably, BTS is not doing what Billie Eilish is doing. They're not breaking gender rules. Their style is not alternative or transgressive. The masculinity they're performing has become a new norm for young men. Nor do they interpret their performance as a mixture of masculinity and femininity. In South Korea, BTS is what youthful masculinity looks like. It dominates Korean popular culture, from fashion to photography to advertising and television.

As this example illustrates, different cultures have different ideas about what men and women should be like. We tend to take the rules we know for granted and find ourselves surprised, even shocked, when we run up against unfamiliar ones. In the United States, for example, women are not supposed to expose their breasts in public. We take this gender rule so seriously that whether people can breastfeed in public is hotly debated. This discomfort with breasts seems bizarre in the parts of Europe where women sunbathe topless. In turn, many Americans and Europeans condemn the modesty practices associated with Islam, like wearing a head scarf. Some Europeans think it's irrationally prudish to cover one's breasts; many Americans think it's irrationally prudish to cover one's hair. It can seem obvious that women should cover some parts of their bodies but not others, but these opinions simply reflect the idiosyncrasies of each culture.

Once we realize that the gender rules we live with are not universal, we may begin to see them as socially constructed. Until we read about, travel to, or move to a different country, we may not notice this process at all. A study of Japanese women who went to work at firms abroad, for instance, found that carrying a briefcase or drinking beer with colleagues was initially alien to their idea of femininity.[14] After becoming more comfortable in their new environment, however, many did not want to be assigned back to Japan, where this would have been unacceptable behavior for a woman. Realizing that gender rules vary from place to place can draw our attention to the fact that there are options.

Gender Rules and Change over Time

The masculinity epitomized by South Korean pop stars is relatively new. Before the 1990s, most recording artists portrayed themselves as tough guys. Borrowing from Japanese manga, K-pop changed the version of masculinity that Koreans held up as ideal. For example, one observer notes:

> What might be called the "cult of male beauty" is clearly observable in the Japanese youth culture of the past decade or so, not only on TV screens and in men's magazines but on every city street, standing and sitting right next to you at cafeterias, CD shops and inside subways. These young men sport colourfully dyed hair, neatly coordinated outfits, and display a fashion sense that is well-learned and skillfully represented on their slim bodies.[15]

The K-pop version of masculinity is also making inroads in China, upsetting men politicians who prefer a more militarized masculinity.[16] Some even say that K-pop is changing ideas about masculinity worldwide.[17]

Gender rules are constantly changing in all societies. As a fun example, consider the earring.[18] In the United States in the 1920s, only women of Italian and Spanish descent and sailors pierced their ears. For the women, it was an ethnic practice, similar to the small dot, or *bindi*, that Hindu women wear on their foreheads. Sailors wore them in the hope that a gold earring might serve as payment for a proper burial should they die at sea, wash ashore, and be found by strangers.

Michael B. Jordan, villain of the megahit superhero movie *Black Panther*, wearing his earrings. Or, to protect the gender binary, we might say "studs."

Pierced ears went mainstream in the 1960s, but only for girls and women. Men who wore earrings were called hippies or were assumed to be gay. Twenty years later, male musicians and athletes popularized wearing earrings but only in one ear. Men who wanted to be recognized as gay got their right earlobe pierced; men who wanted to be seen as heterosexual would pierce their left ear. A few decades after that, the side of the head would be irrelevant. Today, many men pierce both ears, and it signifies nothing.

Whether and which ear is pierced is no longer culturally meaningful, but earring *style* remains so (consistent with the practice of further subdividing masculine or feminine things to uphold the gender binary). Today, women are most likely to wear elaborate or dainty earrings, while men typically wear simple studs or small hoops. And now we pierce other things in gendered ways. Belly-button piercings are found almost exclusively on women, whereas men are more likely to stretch their earlobes with plugs.

Gender rules vary. They change across time. They're different across cultures. They also fluctuate as we go from one context to another, even within a single culture and time.

Gender Rules across Contexts

Any given country is home not to one culture but to a turbulent mixture of subcultures. Accordingly, doing gender, even in our daily lives, requires that we simultaneously know the rules of the cultural mainstream as well as those of the alternative cultures that we live in or visit.

Multiple pairs of gender binary glasses enable **cultural traveling**, or moving from one cultural or subcultural context to another and sometimes back. A newly out lesbian named Belinda, for example, joined a queer community. There, she encountered people who pushed her to follow a new set of gender rules. She was teased, she explained, for "carrying a purse and looking 'too girly.'" This hurt because she was excited about her new identity and eager to be taken seriously. "So, my response to that," she continued, "was to kind of change to become less feminine, change my body posturing and the way that I dress and cut off all my hair and that kind of stuff."[19]

Like Belinda, many of us adapt our gender presentation for the audiences we value most. We also make cultural adjustments throughout our day and week. A guy can knock back beers with his friends and yell at his team on TV, then present himself professionally at work the next day. Both these self-presentations are versions of masculinity. Likewise, a college student may comfort crying children at her job at a day-care center, hook up at a party that night, and be attentive in class the next morning. In each context—the nurturer, the flirt, and the student—she does femininity differently.

The gender rules that apply to varying contexts are complex and nuanced. Knowing exactly what is appropriate for a wedding (is it a day or night wedding?), a first date (is it coffee or dinner?), and a job interview (do you want to seem creative or reliable?) requires sophisticated calculations. Most of us culturally travel rather easily, often flawlessly. And thank goodness. People who can't tune their behavior to the social context risk coming off as psychologically disturbed or willfully deviant. The same glowing, silver gown that makes an actress seem glamorous on the red carpet, for example, would make her look drunk or deranged if she wore it at the grocery store the next morning.

In sum, we learn a set of contemporary gender rules specific to our societies. We also learn how that set of gender rules varies by age and context and how to adjust to those variations. We don't get just one pair of gender binary glasses when we're kids; we get many pairs. And we're constantly getting new prescriptions as needed.

LEARNING THE RULES

Children begin to learn gender in infancy.[20] They can tell the difference between men's and women's voices by six months old and between men and women in photographs by nine months old. By the time they're one, they learn to associate deep voices with men and high voices with women. By two and a half, most children know their own gender.[21] This includes trans children, who follow the same gendered developmental trajectory as cis children.[22] That is, cis and trans kids typically begin identifying as their gender at about the same age, even though trans children's genders don't align conventionally with their assigned sex.

As children absorb the social significance of gender, they're often eager to learn the rules that apply. They find lessons everywhere. Most toy stores still sell "boy toys" and "girl toys," categorized in binary ways and coded with gendered messages about which gender is caring, pretty, physically active, or tough. Community and school sports are usually gender segregated, such that girls and boys rarely play alongside or against each other. More often than not, children's television and books tell gender-stereotypical stories. By the age of five, kids have absorbed a great deal of complex and even contradictory information about gender.[23] These are a child's first pairs of gender binary glasses.

Once children have gender binary glasses, they usually begin to act in ways that reflect them, especially if their parents or peers reward or display gender-stereotypical behavior.[24] Most children orient themselves to toys they believe are gender appropriate and begin to make assumptions about other people based on their gender. In preschool, many will use gender as a criterion for whom to befriend and play with.

Developmentally, gender rules are absorbed just like all the other rules kids are busy learning, like how to cross the street safely, what's fair between siblings, and how to eat politely. Learning gender rules is part of growing up. Children sometimes even invent gendered beliefs based on their observations, like one four-year-old who announced confidently to his parents on the way home from an Italian restaurant: "Men eat pizza and women don't."[25] Kids are often pretty rigid about doing things "right," and this applies to doing gender as well. Rigidity peaks around age six, which is exactly when lots of parents throw up their hands and give their sons toy guns and their daughters Barbie dolls.

Children also actively resist others' gender expectations, and as the story of Jeremy and his barrette suggests, they teach one another the rules (they think) they know. Children, then, are participants in their own and others' socialization. They, like us, are negotiating gender rules from the get-go and setting up consequences for both one another and the adults around them. Some kids resist the lessons they learn, even those they receive from their parents.

Parents have to decide how to respond.[26] Many parents actively intervene to ensure that their children follow gender rules. This is especially common among parents who believe that gender is purely and straightforwardly biological.[27] Other parents may encourage conformity primarily to shield their children from policing. "It's not that I don't want him to wear a skirt," they may say. "I just don't want him to be picked on by the other kids."

Increasingly, however, parents are supporting their children's desire to resist gender rules. "If [my kids] want to wear, say, a Batman T-shirt with a rainbow tutu," said one such parent, "they're more than welcome to. . . . It's just very open."[28] Of course, parents who embrace gender nonconformity in their children may themselves face policing.

Given the ubiquity of gendered ideas and interactions, however, there is only so much even parents can do to shield their children from rules about how to do gender. Sociologist Emily Kane, for example, describes reluctantly buying a set of trading cards that glamorized violent combat.[29] She didn't want to encourage her five-year-old to identify with this version of masculinity, but one day her husband found him quietly crying after school. "*All* the boys had these cards," her son explained, and not having them meant he couldn't play with them.[30] It was a choice between buying him a toy she didn't like and watching him feel lonely and isolated. She gave in.

Notably, Kane's son's desire for violent trading cards is *not* a sign that gender is biological. Instead, it's a side effect of the fact that children aren't yet capable of absorbing and negotiating gender rules *in their full complexity*.[31] Childhood rigidity is a learning phase, one that most of us grow out of.[32] As we learn that gender norms are not quite so strict, some of us become much more flexible about our own and others' conformity.

Children today may face less pressure from both their parents and their peers to follow strictly binary gender rules. But rule breakers, both parents and kids, still may be policed by those intolerant of nonconformity.

Peer pressure to follow binary gender rules may be less intense today, both for children and adults. Kids today may be less prone to bullying peers who break gender rules than their parents were at their age.[33] Indeed, young people are themselves pushing these boundaries. In 2016, for example, at the age of eighteen, Jaden Smith became the first man to model womenswear for Louis Vuitton. Already known for blurring gendered fashion boundaries, he explained that he hoped his choices opened up options for the kids coming up below him. "I'm taking the brunt of it," he told *Cosmopolitan*. "So, you know, in five years when a kid goes to school wearing a skirt, he won't get beat up and kids won't get mad at him."

When we're exposed to children and adults who resist gender rules, like Jaden Smith, we begin to see more flexible possibilities for ourselves.[34] We also learn to navigate gender rules in more sophisticated ways. Most of us become more tolerant of ambiguity and contradictions. And we learn and adjust to new sets of gender rules that we encounter as we interact with new people, new places, and a changing social terrain.

Learning the rules, then, is a lifelong process. We're socialized continually as we grow up but also as we grow old. Gender rules change around us, forcing us to adapt. We also act in ways that shift gender rules. A **learning model of socialization** adopted by sociologists posits that socialization is a lifelong process of learning and relearning social expectations as well as how to negotiate them. We aren't socialized once and for all to the gender rules we're exposed to as children; rather, we are constantly being socialized throughout our life course.

Moreover, parents don't just socialize children but are socialized by them. Children and grandchildren are often important sources of learning for adults. This is true for things like hairstyles, tattoos, and jewelry, which are gendered differently from generation to generation, but also for things like identities. As young people are increasingly identifying as trans, gender fluid, pansexual, or otherwise, many "grown-ups" are learning to adapt. Listening to their kids' experiences of gender, and hearing from trans and nonbinary adults, for example, has led many parents to find ways to support their children, whatever their gender identity or expression.[35]

A learning model of socialization also recognizes us as *savvy* members of our culture. We aren't cultural dupes; we're cultural experts. In negotiation with others, we consciously and strategically adjust our behavior to changes in our social environments. We learn to manage conflict and discomfort, usually without resorting to dropping our pants or quietly crying after school. We absorb gendered meanings from the time we're small children, and we never stop. How we respond to and manipulate those meanings is partly up to us.

WHY WE FOLLOW THE RULES

Though we become more sophisticated about the nature of gender rules, many of us follow them most of the time. We may stop noticing gender rules altogether and follow them unconsciously, merely out of habit. Or we may do so because we come to enjoy doing gender. In other cases, we follow gender rules because others are watching us and expecting us to do so. Finally, we sometimes follow gender rules because others can make doing otherwise uncomfortable, even dangerous.

Doing Gender out of Habit

Often we follow gender rules because we're habituated to them. We get used to walking and sitting in a certain way, own a wardrobe of already appropriately gendered clothes, and have experiences in rewarding gender-conforming activities.

All this repeated practice allows us to do gender without really thinking about it. Psychologists call such frequently repeated behaviors "overlearned"; that is, they're learned not only by our minds but also by our bodies, so we no longer need to think about them.[36] Think riding a bike or typing on a keyboard. Men's shirts, for example, are typically made so that the buttons are along the right and the buttonholes along the left; women's shirts are typically made the opposite way. When was the last time you had to stop and think about the relative location of the buttons and buttonholes on your clothes while getting dressed? Your hands just automatically go to the right places.

Once we've overlearned a rule, it's usually easy to follow; we mostly do so unconsciously. American men don't often deliberate, for instance, about whether to pee sitting down or standing up. Conversely, it never occurs to most American women to pee standing up, even though with a little practice the majority could probably do so with little mess (or at least no more mess than frequently left behind by men). In some parts of the world, such as Ghana and China, women do stand up to pee, whereas men in Germany and Japan often do not.

Many of the gender rules that we follow, then, are simply a matter of habit, overlearned and followed unconsciously.

Doing Gender for Pleasure

More than simply being habitual, following gender rules can be quite pleasurable. It can be fun for a group of guys to enact masculinity together while watching a game. They know the script, the beer tastes great, and their team might win. Likewise, many women enjoy dressing up and looking nice in a specifically feminine way. Doing things well is intrinsically rewarding. It feels great to master a new language, improve on guitar, or hone home improvement skills. The same is true for doing gender well. Performing gender is a skill, and it can be rewarding to acquire it.

For just this reason, we may especially enjoy opportunities to do gender elaborately. We may relish formal events like quinceañeras, bar and bat mitzvahs, high school proms, and weddings. These events typically call for strongly gendered displays: suits or tuxedos for men, dresses or gowns for women. It can be fun to pamper ourselves at the salon, bring flowers to our dates, and open doors or have them opened for us. It feels great to know that we look especially beautiful in our dress or unusually dashing in our tux.

Even Billie Eilish ultimately found pleasure in doing gender in a conventional way. In June 2021, she chose a "classic, old-timey pin-up" look for her appearance on the cover of British *Vogue*.[37] She dyed her edgy black and neon-green hair platinum blond and swapped her baggy getup for pink lingerie. Alongside her image was a quote: "It's all about what makes you feel good."

Doing Gender for Others

Sometimes we follow the rules simply because we're under observation. Consider flatulence. In a study of 172 college students, more than half of heterosexual

At the 2021 Met Gala, Billie Eilish shocked audiences by donning a platinum blond bob and a glamorous peach ball gown. She explained her sudden adoption of a hyperfeminine aesthetic by saying it made her "feel good."

women but only a quarter of heterosexual men reported being anxious about the possibility that someone might hear them fart.[38] Almost a quarter of heterosexual men said they sometimes farted in front of people on purpose. For men, a good fart can be a source of pride. "Because if it's strong," said one, "it's more manly." Only 7 percent of heterosexual women thought the same. Nonheterosexual men, interestingly, were the least comfortable with public flatulence, and nonheterosexual women sat squarely between heterosexual men and women.

Of course, the nature of the audience matters too. If observation changes what we do, then who is doing the observing is part of why. A study of women eating in restaurants found that women dining with male companions took smaller bites and ate more slowly than women dining with other women.[39] They were also more likely to sit still, maintain good posture, and use their napkins more delicately. The author of the study, sociology major Kate Handley, described the careful precision with which such women used their napkins:

> In some cases, the woman would fold her napkin into fourths before using it so that she could press the straight edge of the napkin to the corners of her mouth. Other times, the woman would wrap the napkin around her finger to create a point, then dab it across her mouth or use the point to press into the corners of her mouth.

Women dining with other women used their napkins more casually:

> These women did not carefully designate a specific area of the napkin to use, and instead bunched up a portion of it in one hand and rubbed the napkin across their mouths indiscriminately.

Both farting and eating patterns reveal that gender isn't necessarily a part of who we are but rather something we perform when others are listening or watching.

Reflecting the power of an audience, many gendered routines fell by the wayside when the Covid-19 pandemic pushed some of us into quarantine. Stuck at home, men stopped shaving their faces and grew the hair on their heads long. Women stopped shaving their legs and armpits and chose to wear less or no makeup. Some Black women let their hair go natural.[40] Headlines pronounced the death of the bra.[41] (Prior to the pandemic, it was cliché to say that women performed beauty rituals for themselves, not for others, but our collective behavior during the crisis suggests otherwise.)

For some, removing the gaze of others allowed for more freedom to experiment. Rebecca Minor, a licensed clinical social worker, reported that the first phase of the pandemic brought some relief to trans youth (as long as they had supportive parents). It's not that the "peer gaze" disappeared entirely, but its impact was reduced. Being online for school, for example, "removes that feeling that someone sitting in the row behind me might be snickering or looking at what I'm wearing."[42]

Others, like writer Alex Marzano-Lesnevich, found lockdown disconcerting. Suddenly there was no one around to either question or validate their transgender-nonbinary identity. "Devoid of anyone to signal my gender to," they wrote, "I felt, suddenly, amorphous and undefined."[43] When the social part of life disappeared, the social construction of gender seemed to as well. "How do I define my gender," they asked, "when I . . . am no longer being watched?"

When pandemic lockdowns lifted, many of us found ourselves back in the public eye, for better or worse. We may have reveled in returning to our gendered routines, or we may have resisted doing so. As one fashion reporter observed, "A considerable number of us apparently used the time in confinement to rethink some shibboleths about who gets to wear what."[44] Regardless of how our feelings about the rules changed, venturing back out into the world meant that others could passively observe, and actively influence, our gender performances.

Doing Gender to Avoid the Gender Police

Some of us bristle at demands for conventional displays of gender, and this can be true of cis people as well as those who are nonbinary or trans. A girl confident in her girlhood but with the style preferences of a classic "tomboy," for example, may refuse the ruffled dress her mother wants her to wear to her brother's wedding. Her choice, however, may come with consequences.

Remember Jeremy and his barrette? Jeremy's indignant schoolmate felt entitled to enforce the unwritten rule that boys don't wear barrettes. Despite Jeremy's protestations, his schoolmate remained insistent, pushing Jeremy to defend his decision to wear one. In other words, he held Jeremy accountable for doing gender in the way he wanted. Sociologists call this **accountability**, an obligation to explain why we don't follow social rules that other people think we should know and obey.

We're reminded of our accountability to gender rules when people quiz us on our decision-making or offer mild disapproval, as Jeremy's schoolmate did. Calls for accounts can also be friendly, humorous, or take the form of gentle teasing. A raised eyebrow, a derisive laugh, or a comment like "Are you sure you want to do that?" may make us think twice about our choices.

When we're held accountable, we are being asked to provide an **account**, or an explanation for rule breaking that works to excuse our behavior. These stories from our students illustrate some of the ways people can be pressed for accounts:

- James sits down with a cafeteria tray on which he has only a Diet Coke, a slice of quiche, and a side salad. His friends at the table take note and ask, "Why are you eating like a girl?"
- Chandra goes to her economics class wearing sweats, a ponytail, and no makeup. A guy with whom she's been flirting all semester says to her, humorously, "Aw! What's with the sweats?! I thought you liked me!"
- Sun is waiting in line to use a single-stall bathroom. She sees that the men's bathroom is open and starts toward it. As she walks in, her friend says, "You're not going to use the *men's* bathroom, are you?!"

In each of these stories, a person is called out for breaking a gender rule. In the first example, James broke the rule that men are to eat food dense in calories, like meat and potatoes, and lots of it: *Men should take every opportunity to eat heartily.* When Chandra's guy friend used her appearance to suggest she wasn't interested in him, he affirmed the following rule: *Women should dress up for men they like.* Sun's friend expressed surprise that Sun would dare to use a restroom labeled "Men." The rule is clear: *Use the appropriate gender-designated bathroom.* Over time, the pressure to offer accounts can make a big difference in how we choose to do gender.

Examples like these, though, are fairly gentle ways to induce conformity. Requests for accounts sometimes can be forceful demands for compliance. When demands for accounts escalate to include harmful sanctions, sociologists describe them as **gender policing**: negative responses to the violation of gender rules aimed at promoting conformity. When we're policed by others, we learn that we'll face negative consequences if we fail to follow the rules, at least when other people are watching. Gender policing happens every day. It comes from our friends, our love interests, our parents, bosses, and mentors. It's part of our daily lives. Some of it can be brutal and painful, especially for people who don't fit in binary boxes.

When women are called "dyke," "bitch," or "cunt," they're often being policed for displaying characteristics deemed unacceptable for women. Conversely, when men are called "pussy" or "girl," they're being policed for not acting sufficiently masculine. The accusation that a woman is being "bossy" or the put-down phrase "Nice guys finish last" are examples of gender policing. So is the question "What *are* you?" to someone who presents as outside the binary.

We often anticipate and try to avoid this kind of policing of our gender performances. This is because the risks of nonconformity can include losing our friends or the support of our parents. Those of us who refuse to obey the gender police may be rejected, even harshly or violently, by potential sexual or romantic partners. We may even be fired or passed over for jobs or promotions because our gender display doesn't please clients, coworkers, or fans.

Gender policing was part of the narrative of pop star Britney Spears's mental health crisis in the mid-2000s, which ultimately led to her involuntary placement into a conservatorship that gave her father control over her life. In 2007, she made international news when she walked into a salon and asked to have her head shaved. After the hairdresser refused, Spears grabbed the shears and shaved her head herself. This was an in-your-face rejection of a gender rule: *White women should not choose a shaved head.* Notably, if she'd been a man, or possibly a Black woman, shaving her head could have been read as a fashion choice. Because she was a White woman, however, it added to the growing perception that she was incapable of caring for herself. She ended up losing her legal rights to self-determination for thirteen years, only regaining control in 2021.[45]

Other gender policing is physically violent. Sexual and gender minorities are especially vulnerable to the harshest forms of gender policing. In 2020, nearly a quarter of all hate crime victims were targeted because of their sexual orientation or gender identity.[46] Sexual minorities break the rule that *men should only have sex with women and women should only have sex with men.* Trans, nonbinary, and gender-fluid people break the rule that *people's gender identity and performance should match their apparent sex.* Sometimes the consequences for breaking these gender rules is living with other people's discomfort; sometimes it's violence.

The kind of policing we receive will depend on the situation. It's certainly dangerous to be queer in some contexts, for instance, but it can be quite fun at

Halloween, at raves, or at gay-friendly bars. In contexts antagonistic to queer identities and expression, sexual and gender minorities may feel that their safety depends on hyperconforming.

Some of us are more heavily or lightly policed, or otherwise held accountable to gender rules, than others. Generally, people who have bodies that naturally fit gendered expectations have more freedom to act as they please. So do people who hold privileged identities.[47] A less obviously male or female person can threaten others' sense of right and wrong, making policers feel entitled to push that person to "prove" who they are by adorning themselves in signs of masculinity or femininity, like gendered jewelry, clothes, shoes, and hairstyles.[48]

We're also all policed into multiple and even contradictory gender displays by people with various, often clashing, agendas. Middle school boys who show they enjoy school may be chastised by their peers for being overly obedient; but if they adopt a tough-guy performance to avoid this, they may be policed by their teachers and parents for trying to look and act "hard," especially if they're not White. Women athletes may be told by their coach to be more aggressive when they play but policed by their parents or peers if they aren't "ladylike" off the court or field.

Calls for gender accountability are most influential when they come from someone we care for (like a romantic partner) or who has power over us (such as our boss). We also hold *ourselves* accountable, both kindly and cruelly. We watch TV and scroll Instagram to learn how, and how not, to dress. We search YouTube for fitness advice so that we can tailor our workouts to produce the desired gendered results. We stand in front of the mirror and inspect our faces, scrutinize our bodies for too much or not enough hair, and hope for bumps and bulges in gender-appropriate places. We anticipate not just questions but also consequences if we fail to meet gender standards.

We inspect our behavior no less than our bodies: Were we too loud or forward in that last interaction? Too meek or agreeable? Sometimes we call ourselves ugly names or feel shame or envy. We punish our bodies with overexercise or starvation. We review our words and our tone of voice, watching to ensure we don't sound too opinionated or emotional. We may force ourselves to major in engineering when we really prefer English literature because we know we'll later be judged by the size of our paycheck; or we may stay closeted about being nonbinary because we know our parents won't understand; or we may not tell a love interest that we like them because we fear being seen as clingy.

We even recruit others to help keep us accountable. We ask each other to evaluate our bodies, our clothes, and our interactions. We also turn to the media to teach us what others expect. We follow influencers and scrutinize our favorite celebrities. We get together to watch the Oscars and judge people's outfits or watch *The Bachelorette* to evaluate each man's worthiness. In doing so, we communicate to one another what makes a person likable, good looking, or deserving of respect. Through these routines, we learn what our friends think is ugly, slutty, sloppy, gay, bitchy, weak, and gross and, accordingly, how we should and shouldn't dress and act around them. Collective reactions to celebrity fashions and personalities, then, can serve to clarify and affirm rules, giving us resources to avoid being policed.

And, of course, we also ask people for accounts. Sometimes we kindly prompt our friends to follow the gender rules we like. Other times we want to warn our friends and family members that they're at risk of being policed by someone less benevolent than we are. Sometimes we even participate in policing others by creating negative consequences for them, intentionally or not. If we ourselves are committed to a rule, we may be tempted to be mean spirited to those who violate it. We may even feel a sense of injustice or unfairness if the rules we follow—sometimes at a sacrifice—are broken by others.

By holding one another accountable to gender rules, and at times policing one another when we break those rules, we collectively ensure that our choices about whether and how to follow gender rules have real social consequences. Some are mild and some are severe, but they all shape the distribution of rewards and punishments. Facing this, we have three choices: Follow the rules, break the rules and face the penalties, or persuade others to let us get away with breaking them.

HOW TO BREAK THE RULES

Breaking gender rules is routine. Sometimes we break the rules because it's impossible to follow them, no matter how badly we'd like to. The mother undergoing chemotherapy, for example, may not be able to care for her partner and children the way she feels she should. The aging man may not be able to perform sexually the way men are told they must. Likewise, the guy who is five foot three simply can't be taller than most women.

Other times, rules are downright contradictory, like the one that says that men should drink heavily but stay in control. Maybe we're part of a subculture that requires breaking gender rules endorsed by the mainstream, like the female rancher whose daily life involves tromping through manure. Sometimes we don't have the resources to follow a rule, like women who can't afford professional skin care. At times, we break a particular rule because we've concluded that following it is personally undesirable or socially wrong.

All of us break some of the rules some of the time. So it's useful for us to have a way to break rules that staves off harsh policing. Remember the three stories discussed earlier in this chapter? In each case, it turns out that the rule breaker got away with breaking the rule by offering an acceptable account.

Let's revisit the stories, this time following them through to the end:

- James sits down with a cafeteria tray on which he has only a Diet Coke, a slice of quiche, and a side salad. His friends at the table take note and ask, "Why are you eating like a girl?" James says regretfully, "I have to make weight for the wrestling team." His friends commiserate with him and wish him luck at the match.
- Chandra goes to her economics class wearing sweats, a ponytail, and no makeup. A guy with whom she has been flirting all semester says to her, humorously, "Aw! What's with the sweats?! I thought you liked me!" She smiles and replies, "Hey! I just came from the gym." He reassures her, "I figured. I was just kidding."
- Sun's waiting in line to use a single-stall bathroom. She sees that the men's bathroom is open and starts toward it. As she walks in, her friend says, "You're not going to use the *men's* bathroom, are you?!" Sun says, "I wouldn't, but I really have to go!" Her friend nods sympathetically.

As these stories illustrate, we can get away with breaking gender rules if we have a good excuse. When the characters above say, "I have to make weight," "I just came from the gym," or "I really have to go," they're offering an account to justify why they are breaking the rule.

These accounts may or may not be true, but they offer an explanation to others that makes gender nonconformity *incidental* rather than *intentional*. That is, the rule breaking is interpreted as unavoidable and not an attack on the rule itself. In this way, accounting does more than excuse one's behavior; it affirms the rule. So James *really* is saying: "[Of course I would prefer to eat a big sandwich, but] I have to make weight for the wrestling team." Chandra is saying: "I [would have dressed up for you, but I] just came from the gym." And Sun is saying: "I wouldn't [use the men's bathroom], but I really have to go!"

These speakers didn't respond, "Actually, I do like quiche" or "Who says I have to dress up for you?" or "It's stupid that I can't use the men's bathroom!" Such responses reject the rule altogether. This is actually quite rare; defying gender rules outright can cause conflict. To avoid this, the rule breaker needs only to affirm the legitimacy of the rule. This usually satisfies the person asking for an account, and conflict is avoided.

Interestingly, such verbal affirmations of the rule often work just as well as a change in behavior; infractions are punished only when they aren't excused. That is why, for example, trans women are more likely to be victims of hate crimes than guys who dress up like women for Halloween. Halloween is an account. It is a way for men to say, "[I would never dress like a woman, but] it's Halloween!" A trans person has no such excuse. The Halloween reveler is an exception that proves the rule; being trans is an attack on the rule itself.

In addition to learning the rules in all their variety, then, part of gender social-ization is learning what accounts will resonate in different social circles. Four-year-old Jeremy had not yet mastered the art of accounting. He wasn't sophis-ticated enough to negotiate rule breaking with his schoolmate and resorted to a primitive way of proving he was a boy: dropping his pants. Explicit conflict over gender rule breaking is typical of younger kids who've just begun to learn the rules and are less adept at explaining away violations. In contrast, adults tend to be quite good at offering accounts, though some of us are better at it than others.

But there is always the risk that our accounts will fail. Our student Jeff told us a story of a failed account. His guy friends invited him to come over and hang out, but he was going to watch a movie with his girlfriend. "What movie?" they asked, and he replied sheepishly, *The Notebook*. "They laughed hysterically," Jeff recalled, "because I was going to see a 'chick flick.'" So Jeff attempted to offer an account:

> *Even though I really did want to see the movie, I said: "Because [my girlfriend] wants to see it, and if she's not happy, then I'm not happy." This just made them laugh at me more. "You're totally whipped!" they cried.*

In this case, Jeff's account failed to excuse his rule breaking (seeing a chick flick) because it broke another gender rule about heterosexual relationships: *Men don't submit to their girlfriends' desires.* While Jeff's account might have worked in an all-girl or mixed-gender group, it was rejected by this particu-lar group of young single men, who responded with ridicule. Despite his best efforts, his gender performance was policed.

We make strategic decisions as to when and how often to test the limits of our rule breaking. We tend to overconform when we're in unfamiliar settings but break lots of rules in familiar ones. We may even provide accounts on behalf of others when we know them or the setting well. "Janice is taking up trumpet just like her big brother," we might comment. "I suppose the family can't afford another instrument." Or "John is being so quiet and self-effacing; he must be nervous around his new father-in-law."

Higher social status usually provides greater immunity from others' polic-ing. For example, rap and hip-hop stars can get away with blurring gender lines with fashion. Young Thug posed in a dress of periwinkle ruffles on the cover of his *Jeffery* mixtape and A$AP Rocky donned a babushka on the red carpet. Recently, Lil Uzi Vert started wearing women's clothes, but he offered an account: [I wouldn't buy women's clothes, but I already] "bought everything in the Men's Section."[49] In some ways, fame itself is an account: *I wouldn't normally break the rules of gender performance, but pushing boundaries is what artists do.*

Like fame, in gay-friendly contexts, being queer can be a blanket excuse, let-ting people off the hook for lots of rules: *I wouldn't normally break the rules of*

For stars like Billy Porter, celebrity status may act as a built-in "account," giving them more leeway to break gender rules.

gender performance, but I'm gay! This applies even to those rules that have nothing to do with signaling sexual attraction. (For example, some people even expect a love for fashion and interior design among gay men.) So if you happen to be out as a gay man, you may experience less policing for your interests or clothing choices than a heterosexual man might.

Paradoxically, people known to be queer might also get less credit for breaking gender rules. In 2021, for example, *Kinky Boots* and *Pose* star Billy Porter expressed frustration when the media swooned over singer Harry Styles on the cover of *Vogue*.[50] In a first for the magazine, Styles had posed in a dress. Porter, who is Black and gay, had embraced gender-blending styles long before Styles. But it was Styles, who is White and dates women, who landed the cover of *Vogue*. Porter later apologized to Styles for naming him, clarifying that his frustration wasn't with the singer but with the larger "systems of oppression" that erase the cultural contributions of people like him.[51]

Most of us don't have a built-in account in our repertoire. Still, within our own social groups, some of us have more leeway to break rules than others. If we can think quickly on our feet and serve up good accounts, we tend to get away with more rule breaking. If others look up to us, our choices can look cool instead of queer. And if we're exceptionally well liked or charismatic, others may be more likely to give us a free pass. You probably know someone who gets a pass on rules. And you probably also know some people who like to test the rules more than others.

All of us break the rules at least a little bit. This can be scary, but it can also be fun and rewarding. For some of us, the risks of breaking a rule may be outweighed by the value of being who we want to be. Whoever we are, it can be satisfying to nudge the world toward a future we'd like to see. This is true for people of all genders, including cis people. When a cis woman wears sweats and a baggy T-shirt to class, for instance, she sends the message that she doesn't care what anyone else thinks, and that can be empowering.

But breaking rules doesn't mean we're free from them. Wearing sweats and a baggy T-shirt is defiant only in the context of a rule against doing so. It's as much a reaction to the rules as following them. The form of our rebellion, then, is shaped by the gender binary and its dictates. From there, we have agency to follow or break the rules in the ways we desire as long as we're willing to live with the potential consequences.

In sum, sometimes we can't or don't want to follow gender rules. So we break them. We do this quite frequently. We can do so fairly easily, too, if we're willing to offer a "good" excuse: one that affirms the rule being broken. All this affirmation makes the rules seem legitimate and true. In this way, the rules can persist even in the face of frequent rule breaking.

But what if we want more than to just get away with rule breaking? What if we want to break the rules and, in so doing, change how people in our societies do gender? This is what the men of K-pop seem to have succeeded in doing. Alternatively, what if we want to do more than break rules? What if we want to break the gender binary? Let's turn now to consider how some nonbinary people are doing gender.

DOING NONBINARY

Not all of us who are nonbinary want to be read as nonbinary all the time, but many of us want to be read that way at least some of the time. In a gender binary world, this is a real challenge. "There's no foolproof way . . . ," observed Ally, a twenty-one-year-old nonbinary college student, "because you can't pass as something that people don't recognize."[52] There are no tried-and-true symbols for nonbinary people to adopt. There is no color, cut of clothes, or length or style of hair that indicates *neither man nor woman*. Accordingly, Ally continued, "The closest you can come to passing [as nonbinary] is making people unable to classify you."

Some nonbinary people do this by sending mixed signals.[53] They blend masculine and feminine styles and self-presentation, using whatever tools are at their disposal: clothes, hairstyles, makeup, accessories, and even their own bodies, including the pitch of their voices, the way they talk and laugh, and their postures and mannerisms. Interviewed alongside Ally for a research project on nonbinary gender performances, Kline explained why they like pairing their beard with skirts: "I want people to look at me and not think that I'm a man or woman. If they're confused, that's the point."[54] Jesse, who's often read as a woman, prefers short hair because it "adds a masculine touch." Rosi, who is often read as a man, prefers long hair and tweezed eyebrows.

The need to deftly present these mixed messages means that nonbinary people are, ironically, often experts in the very gender binary that they reject. To put together their own brand of ambiguity, they need to know what signifies masculinity and femininity in multiple and evolving contexts. Subject to policing, they also need a keen sense of when they can safely get away with breaking gender rules and around whom, and also when they need to make their nonbinary identity invisible.

Actor Asia Kate Dillon is out as nonbinary, perhaps serving as a role model for people who want to be seen as neither men nor women or as a combination of both.

Unlike many cisgender men and women, nonbinary people can't just simply offer an account. Remember that accounts facilitate rule breaking by *affirming* the rules. For nonbinary people, rejecting the rules is the point. So when they feel they can, many people who are nonbinary police the policers. When misgendered with *he* or *she* pronouns, for example, Emory will speak up: "I will say, 'No, you're wrong. Stop doing that; stop saying that.'"[55] Nonbinary folk often need to assert their gender identity to doctors, family members, coworkers, and others. "I get policed daily," said Lana, "so I police back."[56]

Still, in certain circumstances, some nonbinary people find that the costs of doing their identities is too high. Though it didn't feel natural, Ally performed a binary gender when working at a bagel shop. "I needed to get a job and make money," Ally said, offering an account. When applying for a job in construction, Les checked "man" on the application. They were sure the company "wouldn't give that job to someone nonconforming." Logan worked at a university, and while they felt comfortable performing gender "ambiguousness" around their colleagues, they didn't feel the same around higher-level administrators. Chris found it easier to pass as a trans man at work than as a woman, despite being assigned female at birth. Being read as trans and binary felt safer than being read as nonbinary.

Still, nonbinary people find pleasure in performing gender. They enjoy mixing and matching gender signals and take pride in their self-presentations. Just like cisgender folks, they post selfies when they feel cute. When Shay first started presenting as nonbinary, they felt wonderful: "It felt really good! I just don't think I've ever felt this liberated."[57] "It's awesome," said Adrian when asked about how it felt to present as simultaneously masculine and feminine. "I love being able to occupy my body the way I want to."[58] And when nonbinary people feel safe, some find pleasure in stretching other people's imaginations. "Every day someone can't tell what I am," explained one person, "is a good day."[59]

Because most Americans are unfamiliar with or resistant to nonbinary identities, adopting one is inherently political, which means presenting as nonbinary contributes to shifting others' gender expectations. That can be rewarding too. "I'm glad my identity might lead people to question their preconceptions of gender and might provoke people to think about their own gender identity or expression," said Ally.[60]

Notably, being nonbinary doesn't necessarily mean rejecting gender altogether; it merely means rejecting the rule that we rigidly sit on one side of an artificial divide. As sociologist Tey Meadow argues, the embrace of nonbinary, fluid, trans, and genderqueer identities may not represent the end of gender so much as its expansion. "Atypical gender," they write, "was once considered . . . a failure of gender. Now, for the first time, it's understood . . . as *a form* of gender."[61] With new gender identities being claimed and recognized, there is now more gender, not less. Rejecting the gender binary, in other words, isn't a rejection of gender so much as a remixing.

The fact that we do gender even if we're nonbinary or gender fluid tells us something fascinating. It is evidence for the idea that there's only one gender rule that's nonnegotiable.

THE NUMBER ONE GENDER RULE

Gender rules vary across cultures, subcultures, and history. They intersect with other identities. And they vary in strength. But one rule transcends all identities and is true across cultures and subcultures and throughout recent history. That rule is *do gender.*[62]

If you want to be treated like a true member of society—a person whom others want to know, work with, play with, and love—doing gender in some recognizable way is compulsory. In the West, this (still) generally means that you must identify as a man or a woman, not both, and not something else. And you should perform a culturally recognizable form of masculinity or femininity, especially if you naturally look a little androgynous. As we have seen, that form may include the feminized style of masculinity adopted by male K-pop stars or the masculinized styles of femininity recognized as "tomboy" or "butch." But in each case, the range of performance has limits, even if those limits are widening.

Usually our performance is expected to match our genitals. But even when it isn't—in places, for example, that are welcoming of trans people—everyone is typically expected to do some recognizable version of masculinity or femininity. Being trans is less acceptable, in other words, when the transition is to a nonbinary identity instead of a binary one. Likewise, cultures with more than two genders also expect the members of third, fourth, and fifth gender categories to be recognizable as such. As we've seen, even nonbinary people resort to doing gender—in many cases, *both* masculinity and femininity—in order to be perceived as such.

As nonbinary people know all too well, if we do not do gender in a binary way, we risk becoming **culturally unintelligible**. We'll fall so outside the symbolic meaning system that people won't know how to interact with us. This is the experience of one sociologist, Betsy Lucal, an androgynous-looking woman who doesn't do femininity. "Using my credit cards sometimes is a challenge," she writes:

Some clerks subtly indicate their disbelief, looking from the card to me and back at the card and checking my signature carefully. Others challenge my use of the card, asking whose it is or demanding identification. One cashier asked to see my driver's license and then asked me whether I was the son of the card-holder. Another clerk told me that my signature on the receipt "had better match" the one on the card.[63]

Lucal's experience demonstrates that if we really don't or can't do gender, it can be a serious communicative crisis for people interacting with us. Consequently, most of us do gender at least a little—and usually more than a little. Presenting clearly as either men or women preserves our membership in our cultural community and ensures that those around us treat us with a modicum of benevolence.

This need to be culturally intelligible is why we see gendered social patterns. We see them because everyone is doing gender. We may not do it all the time, we may not do it enthusiastically, and we will not all do it in the same way. We may not even do it in accordance with our assigned sex, but we do it. And while we don't hesitate to provide accounts in order to break the weaker rules, the strong rules are followed by almost everyone, lest we face truly harmful and dangerous levels of policing. The strongest rule of all—the rule to do gender—has nearly 100 percent compliance.

Thus, while the contents of the gender binary are constantly shifting as we move across time and space, the binary itself persists. It persists in our minds (because we fashion our perception of the world to match it). It persists in our bodies (because we adorn and manipulate them to reflect it). And it persists in our society (because we perform it in interaction with others).

Revisiting the Question

Q+A   **If men and women aren't naturally opposite, then why do they act so differently so much of the time?**

We see gendered patterns in society because we learn rules for gendered performances through lifelong processes of socialization. We adjust our gendered performances, often seamlessly and unconsciously, as we encounter different situations and audiences. Sometimes we follow gender rules because it can be enjoyable to do gender well. Much of the time, though, we follow them out of habit. At other times, we quite consciously follow rules. We may do so because we feel accountable to ourselves and others.

Accountability, accounting, and policing all function to produce and protect the gender binary in the face of bodies, personalities, interests, and inclinations that are diverse, regardless of the gender label we hang on ourselves. If we were all naturally feminine or masculine in a binary way, there would be no need to police gender performances. The fact that we can know, follow, and justify different sets of rules for different contexts is another sign that our gender is not simply an unalterable feature of our biology but a social effort to make our identities legible to others.

Most of us develop a way of doing gender that works for us, given our opportunities and constraints. We grow up into culturally adept, gendered adults and leave some of the rigidities of childhood behind.

Next . . .

Our strategy for managing gendered expectations is also shaped by other personal characteristics, such as our social class and residential location, race and ethnicity, immigration status, sexual orientation, age and attractiveness, and our physical abilities and disabilities. We consider this fact next, asking:

 If gender is just one part of who we are, why isn't it crowded out by all the other things about us that are meaningful and consequential?

The answer will add many more layers of complexity to our theory of gender.

FOR FURTHER READING

Barbee, Harry, and Douglas Schrock. "Un/gendering Social Selves: How Nonbinary People Navigate and Experience a Binarily Gendered World." *Sociological Forum* 34, no. 3 (2019): 572–93.

Davis, Lisa. *Tomboy: The Surprising History and Future of Girls Who Dare to Be Different.* New York: Hachette Go, 2020.

Iida, Yumiko. "Beyond the 'Feminization of Masculinity': Transforming Patriarchy with the 'Feminine' in Contemporary Japanese Youth Culture." *Inter-Asia Cultural Studies* 6, no. 1 (2005): 56–74.

Kane, Emily W. *The Gender Trap: Parenting and the Pitfalls of Raising Boys and Girls.* New York: New York University Press, 2012.

Martin, Karin. "Giving Birth Like a Girl." *Gender & Society* 17, no. 1 (2003): 54–72.

Mishna, Faye, Kaitlin J. Schwan, Arija Birze, Melissa Van Wert, Ashley Lacombe-Duncan, Lauren McInroy, and Shalhevet Attar-Schwartz. "Gendered and Sexualized Bullying and Cyber Bullying: Spotlighting Girls and Making Boys Invisible." *Youth & Society* 52, no. 3 (2018): 403–26.

West, Candace, and Don Zimmerman. "Doing Gender." *Gender & Society* 1, no. 2 (1987): 125–51.

Yu, Chunyan, Zuo Xiayun, Robert W. Blum, Deborah L. Tolman, Anna Kågesten, Kristin Mmari, Sara De Meyer, et al. "Marching to a Different Drummer: A Cross-Cultural Comparison of Young Adolescents Who Challenge Gender Norms." *Adolescent Health* 61, no. 4 (2017): S48–S54.

> EVER SINCE
> I'VE BEEN IN A
> WHEELCHAIR, I'VE
> STOPPED GETTING
> CATCALLED.
> —FEM KORSTEN[1]

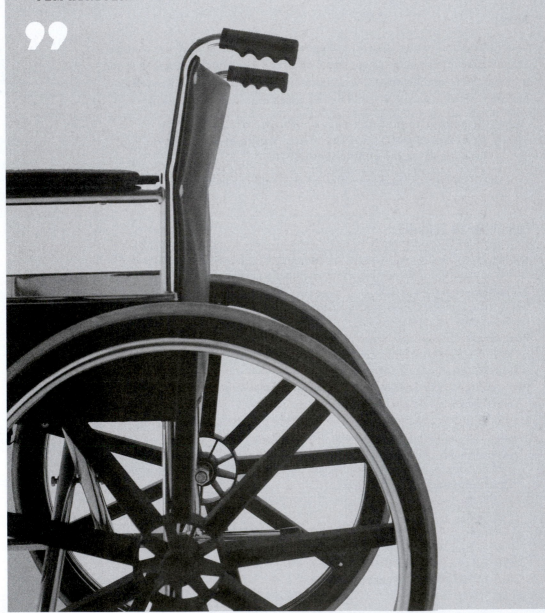

4

Intersections

By now you've been introduced to the idea that gender isn't something we are but something we do. We do gender according to gender rules that offer guidance on how to act. We often follow them voluntarily, though other people push us to follow gender rules too. When we break them, we usually do so in ways that affirm the rule itself. As a result, gendered patterns emerge.

One might observe, however, that gender is just one of the many things about us we're taught to care about. Our racial and ethnic identities are also socially salient, as are our sexual orientations. Certain features of our bodies are made relevant by our societies, such as our disability status and whether we are fat or thin. Various social positions are also consequential, like whether we're born into a wealthy or working-class family and whether we immigrated to the country we live in. Our gender, then, sits alongside many other social facts about us. Accordingly, we asked:

Q+A

If gender is just one part of who we are, why isn't it crowded out by all the other things about us that are meaningful and consequential?

Other things don't crowd out gender, nor does gender crowd out those other things. Instead, gender *inflects* how we experience all our other identities, and those identities equally inflect how we experience gender. Gender isn't more important than age, for example, nor is age more important than gender. Instead, there is a gendered way to age.

Gender and age are **social identities**, culturally available and socially constructed categories of people in which we place ourselves or are placed by others.[2] Sociologists are especially interested in social identities that are the bases of social hierarchies. These identities are enforced through the process of *distinction*, or active efforts to differentiate one's own group from others. Socially enforced distinctions—between Black and White, dark and light, native and foreign, cis and trans, for example—make these social identities about inequality as well as difference.

Identities like these matter. We read other peoples' appearances, body language, accents, turns of phrase, and fashion choices for signs of these identities. We also tend to filter information about people through them. Because they are arrayed in hierarchies, some social identities bring us **privilege**, unearned social and economic advantages based on our location in a social hierarchy. Most of us carry some identities that bring us privileges and some that do not.

All our identities together shape our lived experience. The word that captures this idea, introduced in Chapter 2, is *intersectionality*. In the United States today, the word is well on its way to being part of everyday language.[3] Along the way, it's become a layered concept. First, it's *descriptive*; that is, it accurately describes our lived realities as people with multiple intersecting identities. It's also a *perspective* on difference that stresses that all socially relevant distinctions are always simultaneously at play. Finally, it's a *commitment* to seeing one another as full, multidimensional human beings. Intersectionality is an embrace of our uniqueness and complexity, one that reveals important things about our lives. It shows us how our characteristics combine, sometimes in surprising ways.

It would be impossible to do justice to *every* possible intersection of identities. Rather than trying to be exhaustive, then, this chapter serves as a model for how to adopt intersectionality as a perspective. To do so, it offers examples of the kinds of things we can learn when we think intersectionally, with brief discussions of the intersection of gender with race, sexuality, migration, age, and ability. We begin, however, with a quick history of this important word.

INTERSECTIONALITY: A QUICK HISTORY

The social theorist Anna Julia Cooper was arguably the first person to write a book that was intentionally intersectional. She was born in 1858 to an enslaved mother in Raleigh, North Carolina.[4] Her father, she believed, was the man who enslaved them both, or perhaps his brother.[5] In this way, her very entrance into the world revealed the absolute necessity of intersectionality as a perspective. During slavery, free White women, enslaved Black women, and enslaved Black men were all vulnerable to sexual assault, but only Black women carried and birthed enslaved children.

Slavery was deemed unconstitutional when Cooper was five years old. Given the opportunity to pursue education, she shone. She became only the fourth Black American woman to earn a PhD. Along the way, she wrote a book inspired by the circumstances of her birth, titled *A Voice from the South: By a Black Woman of the South*.[6] In it, she argued that neither women's experiences nor Black people's experiences could be understood without a consideration of the unique lives of Black women. Her argument was so original that some consider her the mother of Black feminism.

Eighty or so years later, during the 1960s and '70s, the White women at the helm of the US women's movement had yet to learn this lesson. They often analyzed gender in isolation, seeing the world as one in which men were empowered over women and ending the story there. In doing so, they often wrongly generalized their conclusions about White women to all women, neglecting to notice that women's experiences of gender are shaped by race.

A civil rights movement was also afoot, this one led by Black men. If White women were largely failing to take their race into account, Black men were largely failing to consider their gender. They extrapolated their own experiences to Black people of all genders, overlooking the way that gender shaped what it was like to be Black in America.

Responding to this dual invisibility, in 1982 three Black women—Akasha Gloria Hull, Patricia Bell Scott, and Barbara Smith—coedited a book titled *All the Women Are White, All the Blacks Are*

While many Black women participated in the US women's movement of the 1960s and '70s, they often had to fight to be seen and heard.

Men, but Some of Us Are Brave: Black Women's Studies.[7] In the book, a diverse group of Black women theorized Black womanhood and wrote about the experiences of Black women in religion, higher education, health care, and more. The book powerfully demonstrated how gender and race operated inseparably.

It wasn't until 1991, however, that another Black feminist—the law professor Kimberlé Crenshaw—introduced the word *intersectionality*.[8] She did so in the context of describing an ill-fated lawsuit against General Motors, filed in 1972.[9] In the lawsuit, five Black women alleged that the company was discriminating against people who shared their race and gender. Lawyers for the defense countered that General Motors employed White women, which it did, and that it also employed Black men, which was true. So, the lawyers concluded, it was nonsense to suggest they were discriminating against either women or Black people.

There was (and is) no law forbidding discrimination against Black women. So the court decided they had no case. This, Crenshaw argued, was why we needed to think intersectionally. Until the law was concerned with how identities intersected as well as the identities themselves, justice for all would remain elusive.

At about the same time as Crenshaw coined the word *intersectionality*, the sociologist Patricia Hill Collins published the influential book *Black Feminist Thought*.[10] In it, she further theorized intersectionality, introducing the idea of the coexistence of multiple *axes of inequality*, or relations of advantage and disadvantage. Scholars have been expanding and refining the concept of intersectionality ever since.

The remainder of this chapter explores how our intersecting social identities and positions shape our opportunities for doing gender. It posits that we all juggle a complex tangle of distinctions as we try to build lives that are consistent with our values and goals. This juggling act is always difficult, but more for some than others.

INTERSECTIONAL GENDER STRATEGIES

Our opportunities for doing gender are affected by both the cultural ideas about us and the material realities of our lives. Given these constraints, we all try to find ways to do gender that work for us. These are our **gender strategies**.[11] There are as many gender strategies as there are people, but many can be roughly captured by familiar archetypes. There is the Girly Girl who emphasizes her femininity most of the time, the Tomboy who rejects many feminine characteristics, the Jock whose identity revolves around sports, the Nerd who prefers *World of Warcraft* to football, and so many more.

When we see them as positive, these archetypes (no less socially constructed, of course, than "man" and "woman") can guide us in carving out an identity that we like and can feel good about. When they're presented as negative, they warn us of the dangers of embodying a disliked or disparaged identity. Navigating others' expectations, we try to be ourselves. We try to put our own spin on Party Girl, Farm Boy, or Science Geek, or whatever archetype we are approximating.

The rest of this chapter adopts an intersectional perspective to describe how different kinds of people develop gender strategies. In doing so, it scratches only the surface of the ways even a handful of identities intersect. Understand, then, that this chapter is simply an introduction to intersectionality, one that hopefully invites you to think about your own intersecting identities.

RACE

Race—like gender—is a social construction: a socially meaningful set of distinctions based on superficial and imagined biological differences.[12] Humans vary by skin color, hair texture, the shape of facial features, and more, but these differences don't map onto distinct human types.[13] The familiar set of racial categories in the United States, for example, is not reflected in meaningful genetic differences. Instead, almost all genetic variation is found within sub-Saharan Africa, where our species originated.

Neither are the racial categories recognized by the United States recognized elsewhere. Other countries have different categories entirely or none at all. When immigrants come to the United States, they can be surprised that they're perceived as members of races rather than members of their national or ethnic communities. Upon immigration, Kenyans, Jamaicans, and Luo people become "Black"; Koreans, Vietnamese, and Bangladeshis become "Asian"; Chileans, Cubans, and Guatemalans become "Hispanic." This sorting reflects a uniquely American way of thinking about the relationships among these various groups, one that is not universal.

The role race plays in our societies, however, reveals the power of socially constructed distinctions. We learn to behave *as if* race were real, producing very real effects. And because some racial groups are denigrated and others are valorized, we reap advantages or suffer disadvantages depending on the racial categories we're placed in. **Racism** refers specifically to the social arrangements designed to systematically advantage one race over others.

The following sections offer three examples of how racial distinctions intersect with gender to shape gender strategies in the United States, considering how some Black, Asian, and White people might experience the intersection of their identities.

Black Americans

For nearly 250 years, men and women were violently abducted from Africa and enslaved by European immigrants and their descendants in what is now known as the United States. Captors exploited the people they enslaved to build personal fortunes and regional power.[14] They protected the institution of slavery with brutal violence and oppression. And they justified it in part by spreading lies about Black people.

One of these lies was that enslavers weren't captors but caretakers. Proponents of slavery argued that Black people were too simpleminded for the complicated responsibilities of freedom.[15] Black men were stereotyped as jolly buffoons unable to take care of themselves, let alone anyone else. Like women and children, it was argued, Black men needed a master to take care of them.

After slavery was abolished in 1865, the stereotype of Black men as weak and ineffectual was no longer useful to White supremacists who were actively terrorizing the Black community in a vicious, violent, and often deadly campaign to keep Black people "in their place."[16] To help justify this violence, White supremacists restereotyped Black men, this time as aggressive, prone to criminality, and sexually dangerous.

Stereotypes in the United States today still reflect these ideas. Black people are stereotyped as tougher than White people, and as more athletic, aggressive, criminal, and sexually promiscuous too.[17] These characteristics, notably, are also associated with masculinity. Black men, then, are frequently described as *hyper-masculine*: super aggressive (as athletes or criminals) and super sexual (as players, cheaters, and potential rapists). In other words, for Black men of all classes, being Black *intensifies* expectations based on their gender.[18]

This stereotyping starts in childhood. While boys of all races sometimes adopt a gender strategy of Bad Boy—a dashing, daring rule breaker—Black boys are more likely to suffer for making this choice. The "boys will be boys" excuse is more available to White boys than it is to Black ones. Research shows that teachers in the United States tend to see White boys as inherently innocent: misbehaved, perhaps, but not malicious.[19] Black boys, in contrast, are seen as always potentially guilty, so their misbehavior is often read as intentional. As a result, Black boys are more likely than White boys to be punished or suspended from school.[20]

As early as kindergarten, people who care for Black boys start teaching their sons how to manage these stereotypes.[21] Some boys are taught to perform an unusual degree of deference, one that White boys almost never have to perform. Black boys may be instructed to avoid even entirely neutral behaviors, with the understanding that completely innocent activities can be read as threatening when a Black boy does them. Trayvon Martin, for example, was killed while walking home from a convenience store. The man who killed Martin described the seventeen-year-old Black boy as threatening, in part because he was wearing a "dark hoodie."

Learning to manage the fear of White people is preparation for adulthood.[22] Indeed, some adult Black men adopt gender strategies designed to manage hypermasculine stereotypes. Some take care never to raise their voice in certain company. Others make a point to dress professionally even in nonprofessional settings. Some report never jogging in White neighborhoods, lest it look like they're running away from or toward something or someone.[23] The journalist Brent Staples, a six-foot-two Black man, whistles classical music when he walks on dark streets late at night. "Everybody seems to sense that a mugger wouldn't be warbling bright, sunny selections from Vivaldi's *Four Seasons*," he writes wryly.[24] This Dapper Black Man strategy is a way of doing masculinity that some Black men use to avoid being seen as a Dangerous Black Man.

This does more than just interrupt racist narratives; it's a survival strategy. Young Black men, even teenagers and young boys, are three times more likely to die at the hands of police than their White counterparts are.[25] In the majority of cases, Black men who die at the hands of police are unarmed and nonviolent (Figure 4.1). In fact, they're more likely to be unarmed and nonviolent than men of other races killed by police, suggesting that in many cases the *only* thing threatening about a Black man is the combination of his race and gender.

FIGURE 4.1 | POLICE KILLINGS BY RACE AND CIRCUMSTANCE

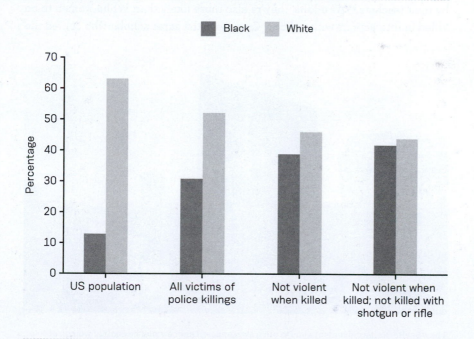

Source: US Department of Justice, Federal Bureau of Investigation, Uniform Crime Reporting Program Data: Supplementary Homicide Reports, 2012.

These are the facts that inspired the hashtag #BlackLivesMatter. It's why people in more than two thousand US cities protested for months in the aftermath of George Floyd's murder in 2020.[26]

Black women are also attributed traits associated with masculinity, and for parallel historical reasons.[27] During slavery, White captors required Black women to do the same hard labor as Black men and suffer the same harsh punishments. Enslaved women were often raped by their enslavers and forcibly paired with enslaved men to produce the next generation of enslaved people. To protect both the institution of slavery and the ideology of gender, White elites portrayed Black women as more like Black men than White women: masculine instead of feminine.

Black women, then, were portrayed in ways that *impeded* others' perception of them as feminine. This is still the case. The contemporary image of the Strong Black Woman—a Black woman who can supposedly withstand any amount of disappointment, deprivation, and mistreatment—has its roots in this stereotype.[28] So does the stereotype of the Angry Black Woman, which suggests Black women are louder, pushier, and more demanding than other women.[29] Research on health care suggests that this stereotype leads physicians to take Black women's pain and suffering less seriously.[30] These same stereotypes in part explain why reports of sexual assault or of missing women are less often investigated when the victim is Black rather than White.[31]

And, like Black boys, Black girls are punished more severely than White girls by their teachers.[32] As adults, they're also more likely than White women to be killed in interactions with police.[33] Crenshaw, the same scholar who coined the

The #SayHerName movement aims to raise awareness of police violence against women of color, including Breonna Taylor, who was shot and killed by police officers while sleeping in her own home.

word *intersectionality*, jump-started the #sayhername campaign to draw attention to how responses to police violence assumed "all the Blacks were men," though Black women face disproportionate violence too.[34]

Because Black girls and women are often perceived as less feminine than White women, a Girly Girl strategy is much harder for Black Women to pull off.[35] To counter such stereotypical beliefs, and the accompanying risks, some adults who care for Black girls actively teach them how to present as a Black Lady, one who appropriates feminine dress to convey respectability.[36] The Black women who adopt this strategy may avoid being seen as angry or dangerous by doing a version of femininity that is prim or pious.

Being a Black Lady may mean doing more femininity than a Black woman would otherwise do.[37] This is especially true for Black girls and women with darker skin. The Nigerian writer Hannah Eko, for example, is a tall, dark-skinned Black woman who is frequently misgendered. When this happens, Eko is left wondering whether it's her height, deep voice, androgynous outfit, or short haircut that is to blame. One thing, though, is for sure: her race plays a role. "I have lived long enough in the world to notice," she writes, "that black women are rarely allowed full access to their femininity."[38] On White women, she notes, androgynous clothes and very short haircuts are seen as playfully "boyish"; on Black women, they're intimidatingly "manly."

Because femininity is implicitly White, doing femininity can sometimes feel like doing Whiteness. "Our oppression has been so well done," said a Black teenager named Nia, "we don't even see that our own values in terms of beauty are very skewed. The contact lenses, lighter eyes. Not just the straight hair, but the longer the better."[39] Nia opted instead to embrace a Black Is Beautiful strategy. This strategy encourages selecting African-inspired clothing styles and colors, wearing headwraps or hairstyles like braids or dreadlocks, and reframing characteristically Black features as both feminine and beautiful.

Those of us who are Black women must find a gender strategy that works for us as individuals, given the facts of our lives. Depending on our age, the Girly Girl, Strong Black Woman, or Black Lady may be archetypes we can try to approximate. In this way, Black women are like all women: All are trying to find a way to be some version of themselves in light of the way their gender intersects with other things about them. In the next section, the experience of Asian Americans offers another example of the intersection of race and gender.

East Asian and Southeast Asian Americans

East Asian and Southeast Asian Americans face a predicament precisely opposite that of Black Americans. While Black people are stereotyped as too masculine, members of these Asian communities are stereotyped as too feminine.[40] Asian people are assumed to be smaller, lighter, and less muscular than people of other races. Such Asian women, then, are stereotyped as quiet, deferential, and shy, while Asian men are often depicted as nerdy, not brawny; passive and reserved; even deficiently sexual. Notably, despite facing similar stereotypes, East Asian and Southeast Asian Americans are diverse, hailing from countries with unique histories and cultures.

These stereotypes didn't come out of thin air. Like the stereotypes applied to Black Americans, they're rooted in history.[41] During the gold rush of the 1800s, Chinese men, largely peasants, came to the United States to work as miners. Without women around, these tens of thousands of men had to learn how to perform domestic tasks for themselves, like cooking and cleaning. When these men had the opportunity to open businesses, they often started restaurants and laundries. In other words, they did "women's work." And so Asian men were feminized in the cultural imagination.

Today, some Asian Americans adopt a gender strategy designed specifically to counter this stereotype. A Chinese American lawyer named Gary who describes himself as "jockish," for example, explains: "Well, I think the stereotype is that Asian men are docile. . . . That is the reason I decided to be a trial attorney—to cut against that." Gary's gender strategy is Assertive Asian, and it's translated into a successful career. But it's also a daily battle. Most of his potential clients, he explains, have never encountered a Chinese American lawyer. "Do I have to overcome [the stereotype] every day?" Gary asks himself out loud. "Yes, I do."[42]

Asian American women are also stereotyped as quiet and polite, even submissive. They are expected to be feminine both because they're women and because they're Asian. Karen Eng, a Chinese American, describes the stereotype this way:

> *The fantasy Asian is intelligent yet pliable, mysterious yet ornamental. She's also perpetually prepubescent—ageless and petite, hairless, high-pitched, girly. . . . As I once overheard someone saying, she's "tuckable" under the arm.*[43]

This fantasy Asian girl appeals particularly to men who want a submissive girlfriend or wife, but Eng has no interest in being "tuckable." She doesn't want to be anyone's geisha or China doll, but some men assume that she will be: "No matter how many combinations of combat boots, 501s, and ratty Goodwill coats you wear," she writes, "they still see a little Oriental flower."[44]

Eng resists others' attempts to make her into an Oriental Flower or, as it's often referred to today, a Lotus Blossom. Instead, she uses a Tough Chick strategy akin to Gary's Assertive Asian. Lisa, an eighteen-year-old Korean American, has adopted this strategy too:

I feel like I have to prove myself to everybody and maybe that's why I'm always vocal. I'm quite aware of that stereotype of Asian women all being taught to be submissive.... I don't want that to be labeled on me.[45]

But while Gary can use his identity as a man to account for behavior inconsistent with the feminized Asian stereotype, Asian women can't account for their counterstereotypical behavior that way. Accordingly, some Asian women use different strategies for different audiences. Andrea, a twenty-three-year-old Vietnamese American, reported her strategy switching:

When I'm with my boyfriend and we're over at his family's house or at a church function, I tend to find myself being a little submissive.... But I know that when I get home, he and I have that understanding that I'm not a submissive person. I speak my own mind and he likes the fact that I'm strong.[46]

In addition to being hyperfeminized, Asian women are hypersexualized, especially by White men. This, too, has a history. In the mid-1800s, thousands of Chinese and Japanese women were trafficked to the United States against their will to work as sex workers.[47] In the next century, during the Korean and Vietnam Wars, American military men sought out

Shang-Chi and the Legend of the Ten Rings was the first big-budget American action film to feature an Asian superhero, challenging stereotypes of Asian men as deficiently masculine.

local women as sex workers. Even today, large red-light districts surround most US military bases, including ones in Thailand and the Philippines. A history in which men have sought out Asian women for sexual release has produced a stereotype of Asian women as submissive sexual partners to White men.

Asian American women today have to live with that stereotype. A study of Filipino American families, for example, found that both mothers and daughters worried that being sexually active would trigger the stereotype of the sexually available Asian girl. As a result, parents encouraged their daughters to show sexual restraint relative to their White peers. "I found that a lot of the Asian American friends of mine, we don't date like white girls date," said one young woman.[48] Adopting a Good Girl strategy is a way of managing the stereotypes that she knows apply to her.

East and Southeast Asian women and men, then, like Black men and women, face challenges because of the specific way gender intersects with race, giving them different choices for personally satisfying gender strategies.

White Americans

Living in the United States, it's common to hear people talk about "African Americans" and "Asian Americans." We hear "White Americans" or "European Americans" far less often. Instead, when people refer to Americans who happen to be White, they often simply say "Americans." This is why politicians can refer to "real Americans" or "working families," for instance, and expect people to know that they're really referring to White native-born Americans, not immigrants, people of color, or Muslims. Whiteness is so normalized that it's even sometimes used as a metaphor for normal. Nonexperimental sex, for example, is described as "vanilla" (just *regular* sex), and clean-cut people are "white bread" (*nothing unusual* about them).

Whiteness, in other words, usually goes unmarked in America. **Marking** is the act of applying a label meant to highlight an exception. Black Americans and East Asian Americans are marked; the modifiers "Black" and "Asian" name them as not just an American but as a specific kind of American. People can be marked by gender too. When women enter men's spaces, or vice versa, the person who crosses the boundary often finds themselves marked. To refer to "women doctors" and "male nurses" is to mark them, highlighting their presumed exceptionality. Likewise, referring to parents as "single fathers" and "lesbian moms" highlights both as notably different from the norm: married heterosexual mothers.

Because White Americans usually go unmarked, White people are never perceived as too masculine or feminine (or not masculine or feminine enough) because of their race alone. Nor is their race an obstacle to their adoption of the most widely prized and rewarded gender strategies. So a young woman born into the middle class with genes that give her light skin and a petite, thin body type can be an All-American Girl. Similarly, the young man who is sufficiently athletic, racially White, and class privileged can be an All-American Guy. These are the Taylor Swifts and Ryan Reynolds of the world (no matter that he's Canadian).

Because Whiteness is bland by definition, White people sometimes try to put distance between themselves and the respectable but boring image it conveys. One striking example is the style of people who take part in Goth or Emo subcultures. Most people in these communities are White and middle class, yet they strive to attain a distinctive, even frightening, appearance. They embody a dark freakiness, employing piercings, hair dye, and strange makeup, even bondage wear and medieval fashion. "Doing" freakiness is a way for them to "become a little cooler" and "differentiate themselves from the mainstream."[49] They enjoy the disconcerting effect their appearance has on others, but this is a choice. Black men, for instance, don't have to try to unsettle others; they may do so merely because of the skin they're in.

Remember, though, that White people are not privileged in every way. When being White intersects with being poor and living in an urban neighborhood, for example, all these distinctions together matter. One study found that low-income White women often identified more with their Black and Puerto Rican neighbors than with the middle-class White women with whom they shared a race but not a class.[50] Many of these women adopted the fashion, mannerisms, and speech style of their neighbors. This gave them some freedom from the more restrictive gender rules for middle- and upper-class White women—they could be assertive, outspoken, and openly sexual—but it also came with certain costs. They faced mockery from the women of color they emulated, who called them Wannabes. And they faced judgment from their White peers, who saw them as White Trash.

Our description of these specific intersections of race and gender shows that these distinctions not only interact with each other but also rely on other aspects of the self. We turn next to sexuality.

SEXUALITY

Just as most tools are designed for right-handed people and most homes for the able-bodied, contemporary Western societies are organized primarily around heterosexuality. They are, in other words, strongly **heteronormative**, or designed on the assumption that everyone is heterosexual. The most commonly used marked categories in the United States are *gay, lesbian,* and *bisexual*. Increasingly, some of us also refer to ourselves as *pansexual*, meaning that we're potentially attracted to all genders. And there is rising awareness that some of us are *asexual*, experiencing little or no sexual attraction or otherwise being uninterested in engaging in sexual activity with others. Together, people in these categories, and others, are considered **sexual minorities**. In this context, the term *minority* is not a numerical term but points to how heterosexuality remains the unmarked case.

Reflecting heteronormativity, individuals are generally presumed to be heterosexual unless they display culturally recognizable signs indicating otherwise. In the United States, some of these signs are directly related to sexuality (for example, displaying a "gay wedding" photo at work), but many are related to gender expression. Effeminate men are often read as gay, while masculine women are often assumed to be lesbians. Indeed, some people claim to have "gaydar," or the ability to detect, radar-like, sexual minorities. What we are usually

Musicians Frank Ocean (left) and Lil Nas X (right) both identify as gay but have adopted very different gender strategies.

looking for is neither the presence nor the absence of same-gender desire but rather gender deviance: "swishy" men and "manly" women. We're looking for people who are breaking gender rules.

This tendency to expect gay men to act feminine and lesbians to act masculine may motivate heterosexual Americans to adopt conventional gender strategies. A White heterosexual woman who performs "too much" masculinity, for example, may be suspected to be gay. If she wants to attract men's sexual attention, she may feel compelled to do a certain amount of femininity. Likewise, men interested in women may avoid feminine styles and interests for the same reason. Societies that conflate gender performance with same-gender attraction create incentives for heterosexual people to conform to gender norms.

How sexual minorities do gender will depend in part on whether they want to "pass" as heterosexual. Many want to keep their sexuality a secret because of **heterosexism**, individual and institutional bias against sexual minorities. Since gaydar is tuned to detect gender deviance, gender conformity is a way to hide in plain sight. A White nonbinary writer named Maya Strong, for example, describes their queerness as "cloaked in girlish garb":

I match my skinny jeans with loose sweaters (never graphic tees), tasteful pairings of necklaces that shouldn't match but do, and booties with a pointed toe and slight heel. My curtain of hair is twisted into a messy bun like every other basic white chick. . . . There are no flannels in my closet, no practical shoes. . . . An inspector would conclude that my closet was that of a decidedly heteronormative, straight girly girl who does not like girls.[51]

Strong describes their wardrobe as "camouflage." It's an approach that would sound familiar to Brandon, a White gay man in rural Colorado. He uses more than just fashion to pass: "I try to live as straight a life as possible. Whether it's dressing, the car I drive, the area I'm in. When I fill up at a gas station, my greatest fear is to look at another guy the wrong way."[52]

Maya and Brandon feel compelled to hide their sexuality behind conventional gender performances because of **compulsory heterosexuality**, the gender rule that men be attracted only to women and women only to men. In some cases, breaking this rule can attract vicious or violent policing.[53] Even for sexual minorities living in places where being "out" isn't dangerous, following gender rules can be advantageous. Many people are more tolerant of sexual minorities who are gender conforming than they are of those who aren't. Asked how she would feel about having a lesbian roommate, for example, a college student expressed just this sentiment:

If my roommate was a lesbian and she was more feminine, I think I would be more comfortable. . . . [If she was] like me—she looked girly—it wouldn't matter if she liked guys or girls. But if it was someone that was really boyish, I think it would be hard for me to feel comfortable.[54]

Likewise, a gay Latino man reported: "I could never bring home someone that was the stereotype of a *joto* or *maricón*," using derogatory Spanish words for feminine-acting gay men.[55] Among gay men generally, those who *masc*, or perform masculinity, tend to be accorded higher status compared to those who don't.[56] Sexual minorities of color who don't come off as *queer* are sometimes more accepted, both in their own communities and in the wider society.

Because sexual minorities face prejudice based on their sexuality as well as their gender performance, some sexual minorities adopt a Not Too Queer strategy. Some lesbians do this because femininity suits them. Others do so because—as with Black women—presenting the conventional femininity associated with White heterosexuality brings rewards, while not doing so has costs. One tall forty-one-year-old White lesbian copywriter named Rebecca, for example, explained that she uses makeup to mute her "difference" from heterosexual coworkers and clients.[57] Some gay men also adopt the Not Too Queer strategy.[58]

This overall strategy of minimizing difference is also called **homonormativity**, a practice of obeying most gender rules with the noted exception of the one that says we must sexually desire and partner with someone of the other sex.

One challenge for women and men who adopt a Not Too Queer strategy is recognizability. In a heteronormative society, gender conformity may make same-gender desire invisible.[59] But sexual minorities of all kinds may want to be visible for multiple reasons: They may want to upset heteronormativity, find people to date or marry, or ward off unwanted attention from the other sex. With this in mind, they might adopt a Recognizably Queer strategy.[60] One forty-year-old White woman explained:

> I have a dyke look that I assume when I want to fit in more with lesbian social set-tings, and I think I've been more careful about keeping my haircut very crisp and clean so I can look more dyke-y when I want to.[61]

For lesbian women, a Recognizably Queer strategy might involve adopting more masculine clothes and mannerisms and avoiding makeup and long hair.

Doing gender in a way that communicates our sexual identity can be especially tricky for people who are bisexual or pansexual. If gender nonconformity marks one as gay or lesbian, and conformity marks one as heterosexual, what is a person who is attracted to both or all sexes to do? In one study, bisexual women suggested that a bisexual "look" was a hybrid between a stereotypically lesbian and stereotypically heterosexual style. "Semibutchy," one called it, or "feminine butch," according to another.[62] "Like mixing it up," said a respondent named Sydney. "Like you're not in the dyke uniform but you're not in the straight uniform. So kind of a playfulness." Several interviewees reported using buttons, pins, stickers, and T-shirts to try to communicate their bisexual identity. Others suggested the look had less to do with what women wear and more to do with how women literally *look* at other women. Sydney said that she suspects a woman is bisexual when "you don't have any reason to think [she] is a lesbian but [she] makes eye contact with you."

Race affects how people perform sexuality too.[63] Because they're hyperfeminized, Asian lesbians may not need to work as hard as Black and even White lesbians to blend in with their heterosexual peers. But doing femininity may make them extra invisible to other women interested in women. One Cambodian American lesbian, for example, explained that she felt she had to adopt a combination of Recognizably Butch and Assertive Asian to get people to truly see her:

> I guess that's one reason why I'm so in your face and out about being a dyke. . . . I'm invisible as a lesbian because I look [Asian] in a cultural way—that is, where I have long hair, you know—and I despise that invisibility.[64]

Conversely, to be seen as feminine, gay Black women have to confront stereotypes applied to Black people and queer women, both of which masculinize them.[65] Accordingly, they may face more pressure than either White or Asian women to perform femininity. In a study of Black lesbian women in New York City, for example, about half chose to dress in a more feminine way to avoid policing; a fifth described choosing to dress somewhat masculine; and the rest adopted a variety of gender-blending styles. Those who didn't adopt a masculine look risked being invisible as queer in the predominantly White lesbian feminist community. However, even Black women who did adopt more masculine styles often went unnoticed by White lesbians, who may have attributed their masculinity to their race rather than their sexuality.

In some parts of the West today, sexual minorities are embraced. In others, they're stigmatized. This affects whether we choose a gender strategy that potentially outs us. Our options depend, too, on our particular set of intersecting identities. Whatever the case, our gender performances are read as signs of our sexual identity. How all this works, of course, can change when we cross borders.

IMMIGRATION AND NATIONALITY

When people move from one country to another, the gender strategies they employed in their place of origin may suddenly be impossible or undesirable. Immigrants may find themselves in an entirely different social class or strange new living environment. They may struggle to learn a new language. In some cases, they may be newly positioned as a racial or ethnic minority. If so, they may face an unfamiliar mix of racism and xenophobia.

When sexual minorities migrate from one country to another, they also encounter new rules about how to do gender and sexuality. Americans, for example, tend to endorse group identities based on interests or membership in political, religious, and ethnic groups. Accordingly, many believe that people have a right to express their sexuality and be "out" to others. In France, though, sexuality is considered a marginal part of one's self-concept, eclipsed by a generic Frenchness. What's important, one man explained, "is that you're French before anything and we don't care if you're anything else."[66] Wearing your identity on your sleeve is considered distasteful and making a big deal about coming out is seen as overly theatrical.

When Xavier moved to the United States, he welcomed the opportunity to adopt a gay identity. "I don't feel there is one way to be an American," he explained. "You can hyphenate your identity in the U.S. while you can't really in France." Danielle, who immigrated to France, enjoys her new country for just

Members of Trans Queer Pueblo, a group that advocates for the rights of LGBT undocumented immigrants, participate in the Phoenix Pride Parade. People of color who are also sexual minorities and immigrants face harsh policing across all their intersectional identities.

the opposite reason: "In the U.S., people want to know your label immediately," she explained. She prefers things the French way.[67]

Some immigrants have a harder time finding strategies that connect their gender identities, sexual desires, and national, racial, and ethnic backgrounds. A study of men who immigrated to London from sub-Saharan Africa found that many were happy to be living in a society that was more accepting of homosexuality, but they still resisted identifying as "gay."[68] The term implied a lifestyle they didn't embrace. One African immigrant explained:

> *If I say gay, it comes with lots of associations and ideas in terms of how you live your life, what kind of culture you are into, what kind of music and kind of the whole construct around that label that most of us, even me, I don't associate myself with.*[69]

This man was still trying to find a gender strategy that bridged the gap between his cultural background and the gay culture he encountered in London.

Similarly, men and women who migrate as married couples may begin rethinking what it means to be a husband and wife.[70] Their skills and educational degrees may not translate into the same privileges in their new country, while smaller social networks and language barriers limit job choices. Some immigrants adjust their ideas of masculinity and femininity accordingly, replacing an emphasis on men as Breadwinners with a value on economic and domestic interdependence.

Wives who migrate without their husbands often feel great pride in taking on a Breadwinner role and helping support their families back home.[71] Wives who stay home may discover that an absent husband requires them to take on tasks previously ruled unsuitable for women. One woman who stayed in Mexico while her husband went to the United States, for example, remarked on her responsibilities for taking care of both the feminine and masculine tasks of the home and joked: "Now I am a man and a woman!"[72]

On the flip side, husbands who migrate without their wives may also develop skills they were able to avoid learning in their home countries. A migrant to the United States named Marcelino, for example, explained how his circumstances required him to adjust his gender strategy:

> Back in Mexico, I didn't know how to prepare food, iron a shirt or wash my clothes. I only knew how to work, how to harvest. But . . . [here] I learned how to do everything that a woman can do to keep a man comfortable. . . . Necessity forced me to do things which I had previously ignored.[73]

Ironically, some men who migrate to be better breadwinners end up acquiring feminine skills in the process.

In response to their experiences, some migrants change their mind as to who they want to be and what kind of spouse they prefer. Rosa, an interviewee from El Salvador, explained:

> Maybe it's the lifestyle. Here [in the U.S.], the man and the woman, both have to work to be able to pay the rent, the food, the clothes, a lot of expenses. Probably that . . . makes us, the women, a little freer in the United States. . . . In this country if you are courageous and have strength, you can get ahead by yourself, with or without [a husband].[74]

When women like Rosa embrace a new gender strategy in response to new cultural and economic realities, they often ask their husbands to embrace a new gender strategy too. Ricardo talked about the adjustment. Referring to his wife, Maya, he said:

> Here we both work equally, we both work full-time. . . . If she is asked to stay at work late, I have to stay with the children. . . . In El Salvador it was different. I never touched a broom there [laughing]. . . . Here, no. If she quits, we don't eat. It's equal.[75]

These examples strongly suggest that a central factor shaping migrant gender strategies is class. This is the intersecting identity the chapter takes up next.

SOCIOECONOMIC CLASS

Many countries are characterized by significant inequalities between the richest and poorest members of society. In the United States, these inequalities are especially extreme. Middle- and upper-class families tend to live in cities and suburbs surrounded by social services, educational opportunities, and employment options. In contrast, many poor and working-class people live in modest suburban developments, inner-city neighborhoods, or small communities in rural America, including on land reserved for American Indian nations, most of which have few resources and opportunities.

In modern societies, though, social class is not just about money. It's also about the social status that money brings. People with money are assumed to have *class*, a word that refers not just to the economic strata they inhabit but to *how* they inhabit it. People carry their wealth in how they move their bodies, what they wear, how they speak, what they talk about, and the food, music, and vacations they like. That's why we use the word *classy* when referring not to people who have money but to those who move through the world the way we imagine rich people do.

Rich people are also more likely than others to know people with connections to other rich people who themselves have connections and investments and the capacity to offer endorsements and introductions. The social networks of the wealthy make it easier for rich people to win awards, get jobs, attract investment, and influence politics, among other things. Everyone has a social network, but rich people have elite social networks.

Our economic resources, our ability to claim to be "high class," and the nature of our social networks all shape the gender strategies available to us. For example, working-class men usually try to carve out a masculinity that both feels good and is possible given their circumstances. They may push back against **classism**, or prejudice against people of lower socioeconomic status. Construction workers, for instance, sometimes adopt this gender strategy.[76] Their bosses may be Breadwinners, but because managers stay in air-conditioned trailers in front of computers all day, the workers can claim to be Blue-Collar Guys: "real men" who do "real work." They may "not know what fork is used for salad," like their bosses do, but they know "which drill bit is used for different forms of masonry under different and varying conditions."[77]

Similarly, women who grow up on farms or ranches may embrace a Country Girl strategy.[78] Ester, for example, enjoyed physical and often dirty work: "I helped my dad a lot on the farm, raising . . . livestock," she said. "I really enjoyed driving the farm machinery! It just empowered me, driving a tractor or truck."[79] Teresa, who grew up in a similarly rural town, said of her high school: "There were farm girls [who] might dress up for the prom, but they also could slaughter a

Men in physically demanding occupations such as construction and truck driving may opt to adopt a Blue-Collar Guy gender strategy that emphasizes the physicality of their work.

hog."[80] Country Girls may take pride in their ability to do things associated with boys and men while also disdaining the Girly Girl as overly soft or dependent. Like Blue-Collar Guys, they may contrast their own femininity with that of different kinds of women in ways that make them feel good about who they are.

Those of us with higher incomes and greater wealth have more resources to shape our lives to match our ideals. Many men in high-pay, high-status occupations, for instance—men who work as lawyers, doctors, and account executives— invest heavily in their career and identify strongly with their job. A senior personnel manager named Bill, a participant in a study on workplace norms, revealed that his life was focused almost exclusively on work.[81] He argued that no one in his line of work could get ahead without putting in at least fifty or sixty hours per week. Emily, his wife, stayed home and took care of their house and four children. Of his marriage, Bill said,

> We made a bargain. If I was going to be as successful as we both wanted, I was going to have to spend tremendous amounts of time at it. Her end of the bargain was that she wouldn't go out to work. So I was able to take the good stuff and she did the hard work—the car pools, dinner, gymnastics lessons.[82]

Earning more than enough money to support his family on one income, and married to a woman who seemed happy to manage things at home, Bill's gender strategy was to excel in the masculine pursuit of extraordinary career success. For him, being the sole Breadwinner was central to his masculinity.

Today, many women who marry men may reject this binary division of labor from the start. Instead, they may propose a Dual Career strategy in which couples share both breadwinning and caregiving. These couples are pressed to find the resources to replace the work that a Family Focused spouse like Emily would have done. When their combined incomes allow it, hiring others to do housework and childcare allows both parents to invest in a Dual Career strategy in which both partners are heavily focused on work. This is what Seth and Jessica did. Both were lawyers who identified strongly with their jobs. By hiring a nanny, a housekeeper, a gardener, a driver, and a neighborhood boy to play with their son, they were able to put in a combined 120 hours of work each week.[83]

Our economic resources shape the gender strategies available to us, and our gender strategies shape the ways we experience our social class. As a source of status, many of us aim to be "classy" rather than "trashy." Whether we can achieve this, and the costs of failing, will vary according to the other identities we hold. Among our resources for doing gender are our physical bodies, which are intricately intersectional. Together with our race, sexuality, and class, our bodies shape our gender strategies.

ABILITY

Ability and disability are relative concepts, not absolutes. That is, none of our bodies is able to do everything we might ask. We vary, for example, in our flexibility, visual acuity, strength, and endurance. But society's failure to respond to these variations in ability produces its own limits on us. This is **ableism**, individual and institutional biases that deny critical resources to differently abled bodies.

Our bodies' abilities, and whether our environments accommodate us, also affect how we do gender. When asked to describe what it means to be a man, for example, a sixteen-year-old wheelchair user named Jerry emphasized self-reliance. A man, he explained, is "fairly self-sufficient. . . . You don't need a lot of help." Growing up with juvenile rheumatoid arthritis, Jerry did often have to ask for help, and this meant struggling to live up to his idea of manliness: "If I ever have to ask someone for help, it really makes me feel like less of a man."[84]

A man with quadriplegia named Damon also conflated masculinity and independence. Unlike Jerry, though, he was grown and commanded a high salary. He used that salary to exert control over his daily life. He was able to pay for renovations to his home, technologies that enhanced his abilities, and twenty-four-hour personal care. He emphasized that he has help, but *he* is in charge, "directing" both people and activities:

Wheelchair rugby allows disabled men to reclaim their masculinity by proving that they are just as assertive and competitive as they were before their injury.

I direct all of my activities around my home where people have to help me to maintain my apartment, my transportation, which I own, and direction in where I go. I direct people how to get there, and I tell them what my needs will be when I am going and coming, and when to get where I am going. . . . I don't see any reason why [I can't] get my life on just as I was having it before.[85]

For Damon, regaining independence was an Able Disabled strategy that preserved his sense of masculinity. It may even have enhanced it, given that he had to overcome great obstacles to have what other men may take for granted.

Few men, however, have Damon's resources. A study of young Black and Latino men from impoverished inner cities found that adapting to paralysis left them feeling like "half a man."[86] They pointed to the inability to enact the same highly physical masculine Tough Guy strategy that their neighborhoods encouraged and they once enjoyed. "No longer could the men walk with a swagger and stand tall in a way that emanated power; no longer could they have sex anywhere at any time; no longer could the men physically fight a potential threat."[87]

Jerry, the teenager with juvenile rheumatoid arthritis, also felt that his disability undermined his claim to a healthy masculine sexuality. His friends who were girls, he explained, didn't seem to see him as a "guy." "I might be a 'really nice person' [to them], but not like a guy per se. I think to some extent that you're sort of genderless to them."[88]

Facing this, some men may adopt an Emphatically Hetero strategy.[89] A man named Roger who lived with a brain injury, for example, embraced the sexual objectification of women. He plastered his living space with images of "bikini-clad women lying on cars and motorbikes."[90] When the sociologist who interviewed him entered his home, Roger immediately winked at her and asked her to do his dishes. His behavior emphasized the fact that, ability and disability aside, he was still a man and she was still a woman.

If men's identities are troubled by an inability to be *assertive* with their bodies, women's identities are more often tied up with being physically *attractive*. All women learn the cultural rule that it's important to be sexy. Yet stereotypes of women with disabilities portray them as unsexy.[91] Beth, a woman with multiple sclerosis, writes: "I am sure that other people see a wheelchair first, me second, and a woman third, if at all."[92] Disability rights activist Judy Heumann explained:

> *You know, I use a wheelchair, and when I go down the street I do not get to be sexually harassed. I hear nondisabled women complaining about it, but I don't ever get treated as a sexual object.*[93]

Some women respond to this degendering and desexualization by trying to conform to gendered expectations as much as possible. Harilyn Rousso was one of these women. She writes:

> *I was determined to prove I was a "normal" woman. I deliberately sought the most handsome man to parade around. . . . One of my proud moments was parading around the supermarket with my [pregnant] belly sticking out for all to see.*[94]

Occupying a position in "no-woman's-land" can inspire women to hyperconform, as Rousso did, but it can also give them permission to resist cultural definitions of femininity.[95] Some women find that their injury or illness frees them from rigid standards of beauty. As one woman with some difficulty with motor control explained: "If I tried to put on mascara, I'd put my eye out, you know; I could never physically do it."[96] For her, being unable to enact the Girly Girl strategy has been liberating:

> *It's meant that I'm dealing with having a better balance in life as a person, not just as a person with a disability. So I think that we're able to be who we are as women 'cause we don't fit the stereotype maybe.*[97]

Disability interacts with masculinity and femininity, as well as other things about us, making the transition to a life with a disability different for men and women. Age is another life transition, one that we all face, and one that intersects with attractiveness in racially specific gendered ways.

AGE AND ATTRACTIVENESS

Society has strict age-related rules that pressure us to "act our age."[98] If we do not, we face policing. Sociologist Cheryl Laz explains:

> "Act your age. You're a big kid now," we say to children to encourage independence (or obedience). "Act your age. Stop being so childish," we say to other adults when we think they are being irresponsible. "Act your age; you're not as young as you used to be," we say to an old person pursuing "youthful" activities.[99]

We must not only act our age but constantly adjust to the fact that we're aging as well. As we grow older, our ability to "pull off" different gender strategies changes. Staying up all night at the club is typically seen as fun loving for young adults, for example, but among forty-somethings, it's a sign that someone is failing to "settle down." Becoming a parent is believed to be a blessing at thirty, a curse at thirteen. Learning to snowboard seems good fun for a twenty-eight-year-old but risky for a fifty-eight-year-old. Just as there are gender rules, then, there are age rules. These rules press us to "do" our age by doing things that are judged as neither "too immature" nor "too old" for the number of candles on our birthday cake.

People learn early on that age matters for how they do gender. Consider Anna-Clara, Fanny, and Angelica, three eleven-year-olds already well versed in these rules. According to Anna-Clara:

> Frankly it's ridiculous to wear thongs [underwear] at our age. 8th, 9th grade, that's when girls start to be mature enough for it. When you are, like, in the 5th grade, it looks ridiculous if you walk around with thongs.[100]

High heels were also off-limits for now. Angelica recalled a pair of high-heeled boots she admired but wasn't ready to wear. Fanny added: "If Angelica wears such shoes I tell her that they're adults' shoes."[101]

Juliet Jacques, a trans woman, writes about figuring out which dresses, skirts, and blouses are right for her, given her age, on any given occasion. She made enough errors in her twenties, she explains, that she learned to rely on the knowledge acquired by cisgender friends. "I was cautious," she writes, "doing most clothes shopping with friends who I knew would tell me if I fell into the trap of dressing too young or too old for my age."[102]

As Jacques gains more experience as a woman, and as Anna-Clara grows up, they'll encounter new expectations for how to perform femininity. Anna-Clara will eventually age into thongs and high heels, but she will also age back out again. Sooner or later, Jacques will have to learn how to do Older Woman.

Everyone who lives long enough will also face physical limitations to doing gender. Our physiologies don't support certain strategies forever (like long days in fashionable shoes) and our limitations usually increase over time. We'll also come to face **ageism**, an institutionalized preference for the young and the cultural association of aging with decreased social value.[103]

Everyone who ages will experience ageism, but because more emphasis is placed on women's physical attractiveness than men's, women lose more esteem as they age.[104] For women, writer Susan Sontag explains, beauty is tightly tied to youth: "Only one standard of female beauty is sanctioned: the girl."[105] Hence, for many women, preserving youthfulness and preserving attractiveness are one and the same. For men, she argues, there are two standards of beauty: the boy and the man. This allows men to transition to a different attractiveness as they age. Sontag writes:

> The beauty of a boy resembles the beauty of a girl. In both sexes it is a fragile kind of beauty and flourishes naturally only in the early part of the life-cycle. Happily, men are able to accept themselves under another standard of good looks—heavier, rougher, more thickly built. A man does not grieve when he loses the smooth, unlined, hairless skin of a boy. For he has only exchanged one form of attractiveness for another.... There is no equivalent of this second standard for women.[106]

Compared to women with low incomes, wealthier women can look younger longer with well-balanced nutrition, good medical care, expensive beauty products, well-made and well-fitting clothes, gym memberships, personal trainers, and even cosmetic procedures.

Generally, once a woman's youthful beauty fades, she's expected to adopt a strategy of invisibility, aging into the asexual and maternal grandma. Duncan Kennedy, who studied fashion-advice TV shows, explains:

> Old women . . . are expected to accept the conventional social assessment that they are sexually unattractive, and dress so as to minimize their sexuality. If they dress sexily . . . [they] are likely to be interpreted as rebels or eccentrics or "desperate," and sanctioned accordingly.[107]

Women especially have to get the timing just right. If they adopt this strategy too early, they'll be accused of "letting themselves go." If they wait too long, they'll fail to "age gracefully."

Aging takes more of a toll on some groups than others. Class-privileged White All-American Boys may grow up to be Breadwinners and then Distinguished Gentlemen, replacing the admiration they enjoyed for their looks and physical fitness with the admiration that comes with building a successful career.

Grande Dame, a gender strategy exemplified by country icon Dolly Parton, is one of the few distinguished archetypes available to older women.

Similarly privileged women may be able to skirt Grandma and become, instead, Grande Dames like Meryl Streep or Dolly Parton.

Aging is typically harder on working-class men and women of all races. Blue-Collar Guys rely on their body's ability to do a demanding job on which their sense of masculinity rests. With time, their physical strength may drop along with their employability. Working-class women also work in physically demanding jobs, ones that often reward beauty. In jobs that trade on femininity, such as waitresses or receptionists, some workers may see their employability, raises, and tips decline sharply as they age. Because of issues with access to health care, exercise, and healthy food, both men and women who work hard jobs for low wages are likely to incur more age-related impairments than their wealthier counterparts. People of color will also experience the cumulative costs of racism on their bodies, aging them more quickly and contributing to stress-related illnesses.[108]

Revisiting the Question

 If gender is just one part of who we are, why isn't it crowded out by all the other things about us that are meaningful and consequential?

Gender isn't crowded out by other aspects of our identities because it doesn't compete with them; it colludes with them. Gender is just one of many socially constructed distinctions that intersect to shape our lives. We draw on such distinctions to construct our identities, inflecting them with gendered meaning; each social position we occupy allows for different short- and long-term gender strategies. These strategies all have their own costs and rewards.

Most of us choose the least-stigmatizing identity strategies available to us, like the working-class White women who choose Wannabe over White Trash. Some of us reject mainstream ideals, like those who choose Black Is Beautiful and Recognizably Queer. And some of us negotiate for more esteem in subcultures of our own, like the Blue-Collar Guys or Assertive Asian. We also experiment with multiple strategies across different situations, like the women who oscillate between Lotus Blossom and Tough Chick. Or we use positive elements of masculinity or femininity to push away stigma, like the Able-Disabled and the Not Too Queer strategies. Not everyone will like the choices we make, but we can't be everything to everyone. Picking our environments and using our accounts, we manage whatever social disapproval we face as best we can.

Next . . .

We are all complex people who use our free will and cultural competence to manage others' expectations of us. This is much easier for some of us than others. Yet, on average, men tend to find the gender binary, and the social rules that enforce it, less objectionable than do women and people of other genders. And men have a much weaker tradition of protesting the way things are and asking for change. This seems like a good time to pose the question:

> Q+A
>
> **If both men and women are constrained by a binary gender system, why is it that more women than men find this system unfair?**

This question brings us to the part of the book where we directly tackle the issue of inequality.

FOR FURTHER READING

Åberg, Erica, Iida Kukkonen, and Outi Sarpila. "From Double to Triple Standards of Ageing: Perceptions of Physical Appearance at the Intersections of Age, Gender and Class." *Journal of Aging Studies* 55 (2020), https://doi.org/10.1016/j.jaging.2020.100876.

Alemán, Sonya M. "Mapping Intersectionality and Latina/o and Chicana/o Students along Educational Frameworks of Power." *Review of Education Research* 42, no. 1 (2018): 177–202.

Brown-Saracino, Japonica. *How Places Make Us: Novel LBQ Identities in Four Small Cities*. Chicago: University of Chicago Press, 2018.

Collins, Patricia Hill, and Sirma Bilge. *Intersectionality*. Malden, MA: Polity, 2016.

Hoang, Kimberly. "Transnational Gender Vertigo." *Contexts* 12, no. 2 (2013): 22–26.

Keating, AnaLouise, Walter D. Mignolo, Irene Silverblatt, and Sonia Saldívar-Hull (eds). *The Gloria Anzaldúa Reader*. Durham, NC: Duke University Press, 2009.

Moore, Mignon R. *Invisible Families: Gay Identities, Relationships, and Motherhood among Black Women*. Berkeley: University of California Press, 2011.

> WHAT PIECE OF WORK IS A MAN!
>
> —WILLIAM SHAKESPEARE[1]

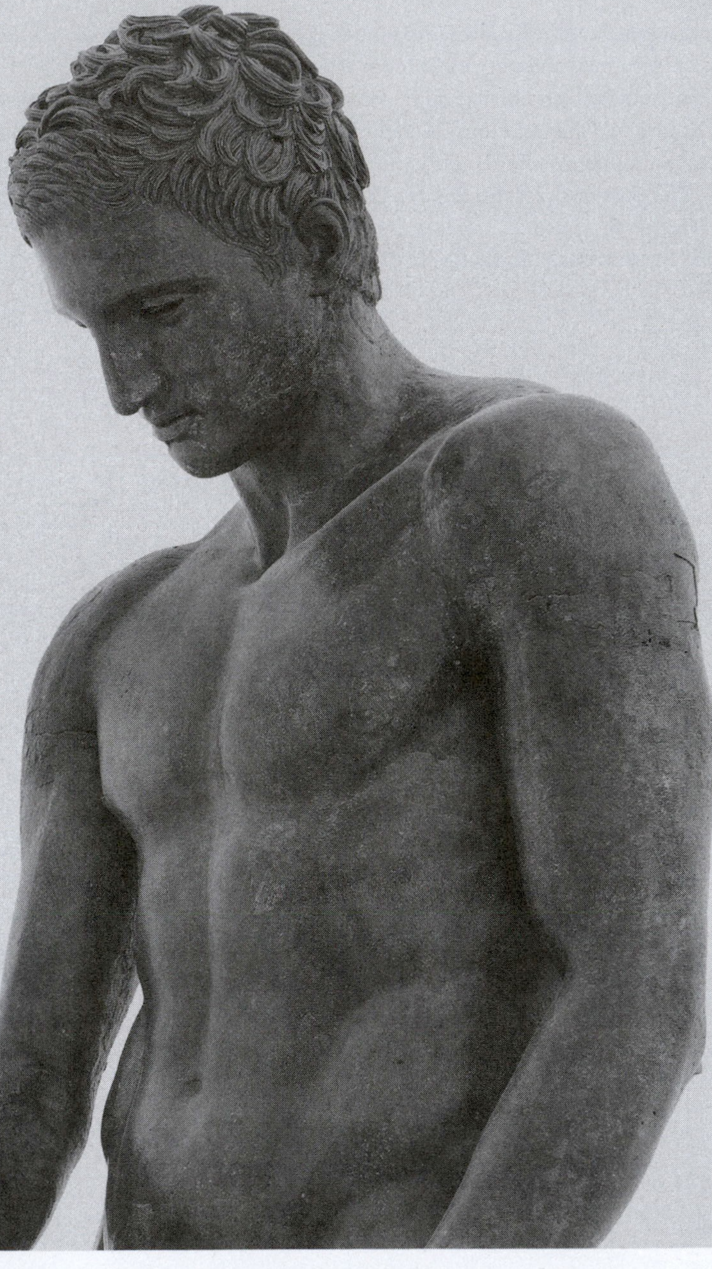

5

Inequality:

MASCULINITIES

For hundreds of years, political activism aimed at changing gender relations has been primarily led by women. Today, the so-called women's movement is most strongly supported by women. In contrast, men, especially ones who are White, heterosexual, and cisgender, are less likely to be avid supporters of gender equality. This is true even though these men are constrained by the gender binary and its rules, just like everyone else.

A young man named Reid was asked to reflect on the impact gender rules had on him—specifically, the rules that a man should be emotionally and physically strong, at the top of his game professionally, and sexually successful with women. He responded by saying that aligning those expectations with his real self was a type of work: "Reconciling the expectations that other people in my life may have of what a man should be," he said, was something he had to actively do.[2] Finding a gender strategy that felt right to him didn't come entirely naturally. He didn't find the work especially onerous—"It's pretty easy for me," he explained—but he acknowledged that it wasn't so easy for others.

The last chapter discussed how living in a gendered society requires people to develop culturally recognizable gender strategies. This chapter explores, in more detail, what living with the gender binary looks like for men. Examining men's experiences helps explain why men haven't been at the forefront of movements against gender inequality. For some men, like Reid, changing gender relations isn't a priority because following gender rules is merely annoying. Other men benefit from gender hierarchies, motivating them to support the status quo. Still others are harmed tremendously yet still feel moved to defend men's superiority over women. Understanding this range of reactions helps us answer this chapter's question:

 If everyone is constrained by a binary gender system, why do many more women than men find this system unfair?

While we all do gender, the costs and rewards of doing gender are not distributed equally. Instead, gender rules demand performances of gender that are asymmetrical. The gender binary is hierarchical. It places men above women, values masculinity above femininity, and routinely positions women as helpers to men.

This is bad for both men and women of all kinds, but in different ways. For men more than women, it narrows the range of life experiences that seem acceptable and right. For women more than men, it results in reduced social status, lower financial rewards, and an expectation that men's needs and interests should take priority. Gender inequality, then, isn't just about preferring men over women. It involves a far more complex calculus. Let's begin with an example.

THE GENDER OF CHEERLEADING

At its inception in the mid-1800s, cheerleading at historically White colleges was only for men. Characterized by gymnastics, stunts, and crowd leadership, it was considered equivalent in prestige to that flagship of American masculinity: football. As the editors of the *Nation* saw it in 1911:

> *The reputation of having been a valiant "cheer-leader" is one of the most valuable things a boy can take away from college. As a title to promotion in professional or public life, it ranks hardly second to that of having been a quarterback.*[3]

Comparing cheerleaders to Pericles—a statesman, orator, and military general in ancient Athens—the *New York Times* in 1924 described Stanford University's men cheerleaders as "lithe, white-sweatered and flannel-trousered youth" projecting "mingled force and grace" and a "locomotive cheer."[4] Cheerleading helped launch the political careers of three US presidents: Dwight D. Eisenhower, Frank-

The men of the Yale University cheerleading team stand proud in 1927.

lin Roosevelt, and Ronald Reagan.[5] Actor Jimmy Stewart was head cheerleader at Princeton. Republicans Rick Perry, Tom DeLay, and Mitt Romney all led cheers for their schools' teams.

As late as 1927, cheerleading manuals still referred to the reader exclusively as a "man," "chap," or "fellow."[6] Women were first given the opportunity to join squads when large numbers of young men were deployed to fight World War I, leaving open spots that women were happy to fill. The entrance of women into the activity, though, was considered unnatural and even inappropriate. Argued one opponent in 1938:

> [Women cheerleaders] frequently became too masculine for their own good. We find the development of loud, raucous voices . . . and the consequent development of slang and profanity by their necessary association with [men] squad members.[7]

Cheerleading was too masculine for women.

When the men returned from the war, there was an effort to push women back out of cheerleading. Some schools even banned women cheerleaders. In the 1930s, Gamma Sigma, the national college cheerleaders' fraternity, refused to include women cheerleaders or recognize squads that did.[8] Ultimately, of course, the effort to preserve cheer as an activity exclusively for men was unsuccessful. With a second mass deployment of men during World War II, women cheerleaders were here to stay.

By the 1950s and 1960s, cheerleaders were primarily women, and the activity became less about leadership and more about support and sexiness.

But that wasn't the end of the story. Instead of changing how we thought about women, the presence of women changed how we thought about cheer. Women were stereotyped as cute instead of "valiant," and soon so was cheerleading. By the 1950s, the ideal cheerleader was no longer a man with leadership skills; it was someone with "manners, cheerfulness, and good disposition." In response, boys pretty much turned away from cheerleading altogether. By the early 1960s, mighty men with megaphones had been replaced by perky girls with pom-poms:

> *Cheerleading in the sixties consisted of cutesy chants, big smiles and revealing uniforms. There were no gymnastic tumbling runs. No complicated stunting. Never any injuries. About the most athletic thing sixties cheerleaders did was a cartwheel followed by the splits.*[9]

In the span of a hundred years, cheerleading evolved from a respected pursuit to a silly show on the sidelines. As women joined the activity, its value and prestige declined. By 1974, the Stanford cheerleaders were described as "simple creatures" who needed only two things: "blondeness, congenital or acquired, and a compulsively cute, nonstop bottom."[10]

We've seen similar changes repeatedly in American society, not only in leisure activities like cheer but also in occupations like secretary and in literature and the arts. We may even be seeing such changes right now, as women are increasingly declaring college majors like biology and entering careers like law. What is going on?

GENDERED POWER

Time and again, adding women to an arena translates into a loss of status. Understanding why requires looking at the relationship between gender and power to see what has—and hasn't—changed.

Patriarchy: Then and Now

The literal meaning of the word **patriarchy** is "the rule of the father." It refers to a practice in which select adult men, or *patriarchs*, control women, children, and other men. Many European societies were patriarchies well into the 1800s and, in some cases, the 1900s. The United States was too.

In fully patriarchal societies, only patriarchs have rights. Women have no right to their own bodies and no right to the children they bear. Patriarchs decide where the family lives and whom their children marry. Women work outside the home only with the permission of the head of household (a father, brother, or husband), and her earnings are given to him. A patriarch may have permission to punish his wife or wives and children, brutally if he chooses. He is "the king of his castle," so his word is law at home.

Meanwhile, because men alone have legal and civil rights in a patriarchy, only men are entitled to act freely in the outside world. In societies like these, women cannot vote, serve on juries, use birth control, work after marriage, keep their own wages, attain a divorce, have custody of their children, enlist in the military, own property, hold political office, or sue for discrimination, among many other restrictions.

Life really was like this for a long time. But then democracies replaced monarchies. Patriarchy was slowly replaced by a **democratic brotherhood**, the distribution of citizenship rights to certain sorts of men. This happened first among White men with wealth. But slowly the brotherhood grew, as poor men, men of color, immigrants, and Indigenous men fought for the rights of citizenship.

Women had to fight too. Only gradually, in struggle after struggle, did they see victories, earning one hard-fought right at a time.[11] These struggles have changed both laws and customs such that today most Western countries have **formal gender equality**: the requirement that laws treat men and women as equal citizens. Incredibly, though the idea is rather new and was once considered absurd, equal rights for women is now common sense. Most people in most countries today see both classic patriarchies and democratic brotherhoods as unacceptably unfair.

However, even as patriarchy has steadily declined as a principle of law, its underlying way of *thinking* about gender has persisted. First, even though women now count as full citizens, men continue to be conceived of as the generic human, with women as a deviation from the norm. Consider how the symbol on a door for a men's bathroom is the same one used for a person on "Walk" traffic lights and elsewhere. The man image can stand in for human; the woman image cannot. Similarly, classes like the Sociology of Gender are often assumed to be primarily about women, as if only women have gender. Cartoon animals are assumed to be male unless they're given hair bows or long eyelashes.[12] And political concerns are generally separated into "issues" and "*women's* issues." Men, in other words, are people, but women are women.

Second, patriarchal thinking persists in the continued equation of power with masculinity.[13] In contemporary American English, synonyms for the word *power* include *male, manful, manlike, manly,* and *masculine,* while synonyms for *weakness* include *effeminate, effete, emasculate,* and *womanly.*[14] Likewise, the word *femininity* is said to be synonymous with the terms *docility, delicacy,* and *softness,* whereas *masculine* is taken as synonymous with *courageous, hardy, muscular, potent, robust,* and *strong.*[15]

These synonyms reveal that gender is a metaphor for power.[16] To be seen as less masculine is to be seen as less powerful, even feminine. Conversely, to be powerful is to invoke the aura of masculinity. If we want to tell someone to stop being weak, we tell them to "man up." If we want to communicate strength, we often do so with gendered language: Powerful cars are "testosterone-charged," aggressive rock music is "cock rock," and finding one's courage is "growing a pair."

In the media, for example, men are more likely than women to be portrayed as aggressive, brave, and physically strong.[17] An analysis of 34,476 comic book characters, for example, found that superheroes were more likely than superheroines to have super strength, stamina, and invulnerability.[18] In contrast, superheroines specialized in mental instead of physical powers, like empathy,

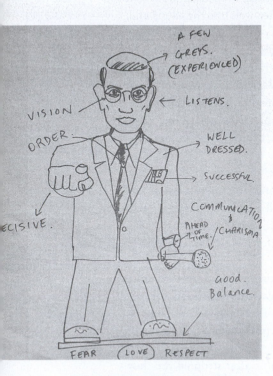

A FEW GREYS. (EXPERIENCED)
← LISTENS.
VISION
ORDER
WELL DRESSED.
SUCCESSFUL
COMMUNICATION & CHARISMA
AHEAD OF TIME.
DECISIVE.
Good. Balance.
FEAR (LOVE) RESPECT

This drawing of an ideal leader assumes a male body and masculine demeanor are essential.

precognition, or seduction. Some of the central superpowers of Marvel's Emma Frost, for example, are telepathy, astral projection, and inducing psychic pain in others. Even among superhumans, then, masculinity is closely tied to strength and invulnerability, with feminine powers more mental and manipulative.

Many societies today are no longer either classic patriarchies (where fathers were little kings) or democratic brotherhoods (where men closed ranks to exclude women). But neither is patriarchy wholly gone. Instead, the United States and like-minded societies are characterized by both some degree of formal gender equality *and* persistent patriarchal ideas. We call these modern societies **modified patriarchies**, societies in which women have been granted formal gender equality but where the patriarchal conflation of power with men and masculinity remains a central part of daily life.

Most of us live in societies like these, ones that are widely, even if unofficially, characterized by patriarchal relations. Even our fantasy worlds, like the Marvel Universe or Wakanda, are modified patriarchies. To help us understand these dynamics more clearly, the next section spells out three relations of gender inequality: sexism, androcentrism, and subordination.

Because power is still conflated with masculinity, women superheroes such as Emma Frost, played here by January Jones, often have powers that are reliant on physical beauty rather than physical strength.

Relations of Inequality

Sexism is the favoring of men over women. It's the best word to describe valuing boy over girl children, the belief that women are less rational than men, or the conviction that men are better suited for public office.[19] Evidence of sexism is ubiquitous. In a recent study, for example, 127 professors of biology, chemistry, and physics were asked to evaluate the application materials of a fictional person seeking a laboratory manager position.[20] Half the professors received a résumé with a woman's name; the other half received the exact same résumé with a man's name. On average, compared to men applicants, women were rated as less competent, less hirable, and deserving of less mentorship and a lower salary. Both men and women professors showed this bias.

Psychologist Janet Swim and her colleagues reviewed 123 experimental studies like this. The researchers conducting these studies asked their subjects to evaluate writing, artwork, behavior, job applications, or biographies attributed to fictional men or women.[21] The aggregated study results showed that holding everything else constant, women are evaluated less positively than men. The same résumé, piece of art, or life's work is seen as less impressive if the evaluator thinks it was created by a woman instead of a man. The legacy of patriarchy tilts people's preferences toward men, putting a thumb on the scale in their favor.

If sexism is prejudice that favors men over women, **androcentrism** is prejudice favoring masculinity over femininity. Androcentrism is different from sexism because it doesn't put men before women; instead, rewards accrue to *anyone* who can do masculinity. This is why women wear pants more readily than men wear skirts; why women are increasingly becoming surgeons, but men have largely abandoned pediatrics; and why women have pushed their way into soccer and ski jumping, but men leave synchronized swimming and softball to the ladies. It's why girls who are boyish are affectionately called tomboys, but boys who act girlish are derisively called sissies.

The pattern is clear, for example, with first names.[22] Once a name given traditionally to boys starts being given to girls, the rate at which parents give it to boys starts to decline. The name Leslie, for example, was almost exclusively for boys until the 1940s.[23] As it rose in popularity for girls in the 1970s, it fell in popularity for boys. A selection of names that have hopped the gender binary are listed in Table 5.1. Notice that such changes are one directional: Names leave the masculine side and join the feminine one, never the other way around. Parents sense that a touch of masculinity is considered advantageous for girls, but femininity does not do the same for boys.

The third relation of inequality describes how men and women are brought together into hierarchical roles. The placing of women into positions that make them subservient to or dependent on men is called **subordination**. By virtue of its association with caring, for instance, nursing is seen as both feminine and

TABLE 5.1 | US NAMES GIVEN PRIMARILY TO GIRLS THAT WERE ONCE GIVEN EXCLUSIVELY TO BOYS

Addison	Bailey	Hadley	Lindsay	Monroe	Shelby
Allison	Beverly	Haven	Madison	Paris	Stevie
Ashley	Blair	Kelsey	McKenzie	Peyton	Sydney
Aubrey	Cassidy	Kennedy	McKinley	Presley	Taylor
Avery	Dana	Lauren	Meredith	Reagan	Whitney

Source: NameTrends.net, accessed Jan. 28, 2022, https://nametrends.net/.

for women. Nurses are also in a subordinate relationship with doctors. Doctors tell nurses what to do; nurses "help" doctors do their job.

The same is true for the gendered relationships between managers and their assistants, dentists and dental hygienists, and lawyers and paralegals.[24] These occupational roles are gendered. In the United States, women represent 95 percent of dental hygienists, 93 percent of administrative assistants, 90 percent of receptionists, 87 percent of registered nurses, and 85 percent of paralegals.[25] Some men become receptionists and paralegals, of course, but this doesn't change the underlying understanding that it's "women's work." Likewise, women become managers and dentists, but typically the support they receive from subordinates is still provided by women.

Because the subordination of women to men is normalized, it even occurs between men and women in formally equal roles.[26] A study of interactions between men and women in Fortune 500 companies found that women were often expected to help or support men colleagues, even when they had the same job title.[27] Women were more likely than men to be asked, or silently expected, to answer phones, make coffee, plan parties, take notes, order food, and clean up after meetings, as well as attend to clients or colleagues having emotional breakdowns.

When roles are gendered, then, they often place women in subordinate positions, helping men (and cheering them on) as they do the high-profile, exciting, well-rewarded work. The supporting role is a distinctly feminine one, and it brings men and women—and masculine and feminine activities—into a distinctly close yet unmistakably hierarchical relationship.

In sum, we do not live in a world that simply insists on gender distinction. We live in one that imbues men, masculine people, and masculinized activities with more visibility, status, and value than women, feminine people, and feminized activities. This is what makes gender about power, not just about difference. These asymmetries make doing gender a *different* challenge for cis men and cis women, and a different challenge still for people who are trans or nonbinary.

GENDER FOR MEN

Though the rules for how to do masculinity are not uniform across the United States, in general men are confronted with expectations to perform masculinity and avoid femininity. The ideal man is nearly superhuman, and men are often evaluated according to how well they live up to this ideal. Men who fail are at risk of being cast as lesser men, the kind that populate the lower rungs of a masculine hierarchy. This makes the performance of masculinity high stakes for men, motivating many to obey gender rules to preserve their standing.

Doing Masculinity, Avoiding Femininity

Sociologist Emily Kane interviewed parents about their children's performance of gender.[28] She found that parents of boys expressed near universal distress over boys' interest in "icons of femininity": girly clothes and nail polish, for example, dance (especially ballet), and Barbie dolls. The parents interpreted this interest as a sign that something was *wrong*. Kane argued that this reaction was evidence of androcentrism: the stigma of femininity.

Kane's research was conducted in the early 2000s, so it best describes the childhood environment of today's young adults. Newer data show that about 68 percent of Americans believe that it's a "good thing" for parents to encourage children to explore the toys and activities typically associated with the other gender. But a gender difference remains: 76 percent of people think this is a good idea for girls, while 64 percent think it's a good idea for boys.[29] We still feel somewhat more comfortable when girls do masculine stuff than when boys do feminine things.

Because of this, boys grow up learning to avoid femininity. A whole host of slurs reflect this imperative: like *sissy* or *soft*, used to suggest that a boy is not boy enough, and *cuck* or *pussy-whipped*, applied to men who are perceived to be overly deferential to women. Likewise, the words *girl* and *woman*, when used as slurs, literally turn the identity into an insult. Other common slurs reference women or femininity, like *bitch* and *douche*. These words tell both boys and girls, in no uncertain terms, that being feminine makes you a girl and being a girl is worse than being a boy or man.

The slurs related to homosexuality—*fag, homo, gay*—send the same message. Being gay is actually incidental.[30] Any man or boy perceived to be feminine attracts these slurs. In one study of college athletes, "everything was fag this and fag that," but after some of their teammates revealed they were gay, the athletes stopped using it in reference to them.[31] "They say, 'this is gay,' and 'that's gay,'" one gay athlete explained, "but they don't mean it like that."[32] In other words, they don't mean "gay" as in *gay*; they mean "gay" as in *feminine*. Accusations of homosexuality are forms of gender policing. This is true, also, of slurs like *cocksucker* and the phrase *suck my dick*; each denigrates someone of any gender who sexually services a man and thereby inhabits the feminine side of the binary.

The chorus of slurs stigmatizing men who perform femininity sends a consistent message, a rule designed to guide all men's behavior: *Guys, whatever you do, avoid acting like a girl.* Today, only 24 percent of young American men describe themselves as "very masculine," but many more report feeling pressure to avoid femininity and do masculinity.[33] More than two-thirds of young men say that they feel at least some pressure to be ready to throw a punch if provoked, 61 percent say they feel pressure to have a lot of sexual partners, and 57 percent say they feel pressure to talk about women in a hypersexual way.[34]

In US culture, being a masculine man involves not just doing masculinity but also avoiding femininity. Because of androcentrism, *anything* a woman does can become off-limits for men concerned with protecting their masculinity. As a result, we see **male flight**, a phenomenon in which men abandon feminizing arenas of life. This is what happened with cheerleading as well as many boys' names. We see the same phenomenon in professional occupations.[35] A study of veterinary school applications, for example, found that for every 1 percent increase in the proportion of women in the student body, 1.7 fewer men applied.[36] One more woman was a greater deterrent than $1,000 in extra tuition.

Men will even flee quite valuable arenas to avoid femininity. Consider education. As girls and women have come to excel in school, many boys and men increasingly associate education with femininity.[37] They may think studiousness is for girls, so they don't study. Or, if they do study, they may pretend they don't. Among young men, underachievement is sometimes seen as cool. Or, at least, liking one's teachers, being interested in lessons, and caring about grades may seem decidedly *uncool*.

As a result, girls and women are now dominating all levels of schooling (Figure 5.1).[38] They're more likely to be identified as "gifted and talented" in elementary

FIGURE 5.1 | BACHELOR'S DEGREES BY RACE/ETHNICITY AND SEX

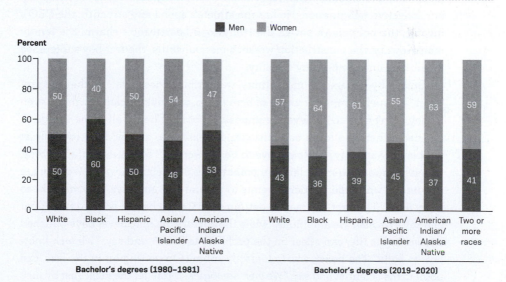

Source: US Department of Education, National Center for Education Statistics, Table 322.20 "Bachelor's Degrees Conferred by Race/Ethnicity and Sex of Student: Selected Years, 1976–77 through 2019–2020," October 2021. Accessed March 14, 2022, https://nces.ed.gov/programs/digest/d21/tables/dt21_322.20.asp.

school, half as likely to be held back in middle school, and less likely to drop out of high school.[39] They get higher grades in high school and take more advanced classes.[40] Women earn 61 percent of associate's degrees, 57 percent of bachelor's degrees, and 61 percent of master's degrees. They even earn 54 percent of PhDs.

In spring 2021, 60 percent of undergraduate students were women.[41] That's almost two women for every man. What the heck!? Are men abandoning education because women are getting too good at it? If so, what else will they let go? Why are so many men doing this to themselves?

Hegemonic Masculinity

Hegemony is a concept used to help us understand the persistence of social inequality. It refers to a state of collective consent to inequality secured by the idea that it's inevitable, natural, or desirable. An idea is hegemonic only when it's widely endorsed by both those who benefit from the social conditions it supports and those who do not. Hegemony, then, means widespread consent to relations of systematic social disadvantage.

The phrase **hegemonic masculinity** refers to a type of masculine performance, idealized by the majority, that functions to justify and naturalize gender inequality, assuring widespread consent to the social disadvantage of most women and some men.[42] Hegemonic masculinity creates the "real man" in our collective imagination. He has the athlete's speed and strength, the CEO's income, the politician's power, the Hollywood heartthrob's charm, the family man's loyalty, the construction worker's manual skills, the frat boy's tolerance for alcohol, and the playboy's virility.

Guided by hegemonic masculinity, we attribute these traits to the category "man." All men, simply by virtue of being men, can make a claim to them, even if they aren't able to achieve the impossible goal of being all those things. A married father who loves only his wife, for example, may nod approvingly at the playboy and say, "*We men* love to chase women." Meanwhile, the playboy, who is a struggling musician, can point to the politician and say, "*We men* are in control," while the politician points to the frat boy and says, "*We men* like to party hard." That frat boy may be getting solid Cs, but he can point to the doctor and say, "*We men* are ambitious," while the doctor, who may never have punched anyone in his life, can cheer on the professional boxer and say, "*We men* know how to fight." The boxer, who voluntarily submits to getting hit in the face, can point to the scientist and say, "*We men* are logical." You get the idea. Just by having membership in the category, all men get to identify with the characteristics we attribute to men in general. In this way, men benefit from the hegemony of

Fit, tall, White, able-bodied, and seemingly heterosexual men such as actor Chris Hemsworth sit atop a hierarchy of men, representing a hegemonic masculinity.

masculinity. They can lay a socially valid claim to advantage by virtue of the traits attributed to their gender.

Interestingly, not all traits believed to be typical of men are good. In fact, many are negative.[43] Television shows and commercials often show men as bumbling parents, perpetual adolescents, and sex-crazed losers. They drink too much and fight too easily. Because masculinity is hegemonic, though, men's bad behavior is either excused (with the typical "boys will be boys" account) or used to excuse them from feminized roles and responsibilities.

One negative stereotype, for example, is that men don't care about cleanliness. If so, who can blame them if they don't help keep the house clean? "It is not that it is women's work," said one husband, "women . . . are [just] far more particular about cleanliness than men."[44] Aw shucks, this guy is saying, women just happen to have higher standards of cleanliness, so I guess my wife will have to do the cleaning.

Similarly, the stereotype that men are bad with kids can be used to excuse men—even dads—from having to take care of them. The idea that men are competitive gives them a pass for being uncomfortable if their wives make more money. And the notion that they're naturally aggressive gives them permission to lose their temper. Commenting on the stereotype that men are sexually insatiable, one man said, "It don't matter how much a man loves his wife and kids, he's gonna keep on chasing other women."[45]

Such accounts are illustrations of **exculpatory chauvinism**, a phenomenon in which negative characteristics ascribed to men are offered as acceptable justifications of men's dominance over women.[46] *Exculpatory* means "to free someone from blame," while the word *chauvinism* refers, in this context, to bias in favor of men. Exculpatory chauvinism, then, refers to the tendency to absolve men of responsibility for embodying negative stereotypes, while simultaneously offering social rewards for such behavior, such as time free from family demands, success at work, and a license to enjoy dominating others.

Men, in this logic, aren't all good. They're not even *better* than women. They're just *better suited* to lead, score, decide, and defend. Exculpatory chauvinism doesn't say that men are superior human beings, just that they're "designed for dominance."[47] So, for men to be seen as rightly in charge, it's not necessary for stereotypes of men to be positive; they need only to validate men's reaping of life's rewards.

Importantly, however, the benefits of masculinity are not awarded equally to all men. Some men are able to enact more of the features of hegemonic masculinity. And some men are able to get away with more "bad" behavior than others. Hegemonic masculinity helps men, but it also hurts them, and it does so in unequal ways.

The Measure of Men

The failure to embody hegemonic masculinity can cause some men to be seen as lesser men. It may even cause some men to see themselves this way. These judgments establish a **hierarchy of masculinity**, a rough ranking of men from most to least masculine. Along the hierarchy we find multiple **masculinities** that vary in their distance from the hegemonic ideal, the nature of the deviation, and their intersections with other identities. The plural *masculinities* highlights that men do masculinity differently given their social positions, intersectional identities, and highly variable contexts.

Because hegemonic masculinity draws on values associated with the privileged ends of *all* hierarchies in a society, not just the gender hierarchy, the ability to embody this ideal is greater for men in the United States who are college educated, tall, affluent, White, heterosexual, able bodied, fit, Christian, and native born. In other countries, hegemonic masculinity may look different. In China, for example, the hegemonic ideal of masculinity is ethnically Han, English speaking, technologically adept, a graduate of an elite university, and personally connected to ruling elites.[48] Men in either country may be judged as failing to embody masculinity and, therefore, less deserving of respect and advancement.

Hegemonic masculinity is why Asian men in the United States (but not in China) are stereotyped as not manly enough and why disabled and aging men sometimes feel like they're losing their masculinity. Society defines "real men" as something they're not. White and Black working-class men are often portrayed as particularly strong but lacking the economic power that a real man must command.

Men who are physically weak, emotional, uncool, or who break important gender rules are also vulnerable to being defined as lesser men. American boys and men report that being chubby makes them look weak, while lean bodies with large muscles communicate confidence, power, and mental strength.[49] Beginning in earnest in the 1980s, the mass media in the United States started subjecting men's bodies to greater scrutiny, often idealizing hard-bodied, bulging physiques that are unattainable for most men.[50] As a result, negative body image is increasing among men and boys, particularly among sexual minority men.[51]

Trans men face unique challenges in doing masculinity.[52] Some grew up learning how to perform femininity; throwing off this habit (if they choose to do so) is easier said than done. It takes practice. So does learning how to do masculinity in ways that others recognize as appropriate. In deciding how to do masculinity, trans men are as aware of the hegemonic ideal as cis men are, maybe even more so.

Like some cis men, some trans men resist performing versions of masculinity aimed at exercising power over women and other men.[53] Other trans men, however, may attempt to embody hegemonic masculinity, whether to validate their identity, soak up some of its privileges, or access the relative safety of the gender binary.[54] A young hotel bartender named Max, for example, explained how his job shaped how he performed masculinity:

> *You . . . have to change the way you banter. . . . You kind of have to be a bit more laddish. . . . Quite a lot of workmen will stay at the hotel. . . . You . . . have to pull pints like a man, and it's, you know, all those manly things like, I'll be like uber macho about it.*[55]

As Max's comment suggests, people around trans men—of all genders and transition statuses—may encourage or press trans men to perform a certain version of masculinity.[56] Trans men themselves can be pretty harsh policers of the masculine performances of other trans men, all too often condemning those they see as "not manly enough."[57] Depending on trans men's circumstances and characteristics, including how well they pass as men, the risks and rewards of doing masculinity may vary.[58]

Some men—mostly cis but sometimes trans—are blessed with the ability to approximate hegemonic masculinity. But even these men can't rest easy. Men's ability to meet these standards is limited by the inherent contradictions of the ideal. Consequently, all men—no matter how privileged they seem—are at risk of losing social status.

Sooner or later, all men will fall in the hierarchy of masculinity. They will fall, first, because the hegemonic man is an impossible fiction: a jumble of idealized, contradictory elements. A person can't be both a perfect husband and a playboy, a team player and an aggressive egotist, or hard bodied and hard drinking. No single man will ever be able to approximate the full scope of hegemonic masculinity.

Meanwhile, as contexts change, the masculinities men are expected to perform often shift around them, making for situational social traps into which men can fall. For example, considering the rules of "guy talk," Evan put it this way:

> There is . . . your kind of dodgy uncle who takes you to the pub or you're out with the boys and that [locker-room talk is] just a normal common talk. . . . So you're under pressure to express masculinity at the pub, but then once everyone's around, you're expected to invert that, that's where the conflict is. And then there's corporate pressure and societal pressure basically to suppress it, but there is this kind of masculine pressure to exaggerate it.[59]

Evan is aware that a crass sort of guy talk is demanded in some contexts and punished in others. While he has agency to choose what types of masculinity to do and knows the rules about when and where to deploy each type, he's also sensitive to the constant possibility that he might misjudge a situation and perform the wrong masculinity at the wrong time.

Second, men will fail to live up to hegemonic masculinity because real men *never* lose. Yet no one can win all the time. Racial minority men are by definition lacking Whiteness and its rewards. Rising economic inequality in the United States leaves a tiny group of multibillionaires to claim success. All men's masculinity is potentially undermined by competitive losses, disability, and age. Inevitably, every man will "view himself—during moments at least—as unworthy, incomplete, and inferior."[60] As Michael Kaufman, a scholar of masculinities, explained:

> Whatever power might be associated with dominant masculinities, they also can be the source of enormous pain. Because the images are, ultimately, childhood pictures of omnipotence, they are impossible to obtain. Surface appearances aside, no man is completely able to live up to these ideas and images.[61]

But many men try. For some men, manliness is a crucial part of their self-image. They try hard to "stay in control," "conquer," and "call the shots"; to "tough it out, provide, and achieve"—and, in the meantime, they have to repress the things about them that conflict with this ideal.[62] They try not to feel, need, or desire things they're not supposed to. To do otherwise is to face **emasculation,** a loss of masculinity.

"Fragile" Masculinity

Men's calculated and even exaggerated avoidance of femininity is described in pop culture as a type of fragility. Men, for example, are more likely than women to respond to gender cues on products, avoiding those that signal femininity.[63] As a result, some companies design products intended to reassure men of their manliness. Often this is subtle, but sometimes it's not. Products like Brogurt (a yogurt brand for men), "brogamats" (yoga mats for men), and "mandles" (candles for men) are tongue in cheek. Or are they? They certainly offer explicit reassurance to nervous men that dabbling in femininity won't diminish them. When we spy the sleek, dark-gray line of Dove Men Care personal grooming products, or others like it, we're seeing the same phenomenon.

Fragile masculinity is premised on the notion of **precarious masculinity,** the idea that manhood is more difficult to earn and easier to lose than womanhood.[64] It is as if a woman is something one *is,* while a man is something one *does.* In other words, womanhood is bestowed at birth, but manhood is attained and sustained through action. Testing this idea, psychologist Jennifer Bosson and her colleagues asked people to finish the sentences beginning "A real man . . ." and "A real woman . . ."[65] The study participants usually completed the first sentence with an action (for example, "A real man works hard") and the latter with a trait ("A real woman is honest"). Our culture asserts that women just *are* women, but men have to prove they're men every day.

Because masculinity is so precarious, it can lead to **compensatory masculinity,** acts undertaken to reassert one's manliness in the face of a threat. In a subsequent study, Bosson and her colleagues randomly assigned college student men to either braid ropes or braid hair. After five minutes of braiding, the men were told that they could choose their next activity: hitting a punching bag or doing a puzzle.[66] The men who braided hair were twice as likely to choose boxing as the men who braided rope. Braiding hair, in other words, was emasculating enough that these men sought out an activity that allowed them to reestablish a sufficient level of masculinity.

Other scholars doing similar studies get the same results. American men whose masculinity is threatened do more push-ups, consume more energy drinks, and report an increased likelihood of buying an SUV.[67] They're more likely to exhibit homophobia, endorse sexism, excuse violence, and support war.[68] Researchers have also found that expressing care for the health of the earth is considered feminine.[69] In response, men litter more than women, recycle less, eat less sustainably, and use more energy. Some men even avoid ecofriendly branded colors. The future of life on our planet, in other words, is in the hands of men who are made nervous by the color green.

Importantly, it's not necessarily women who are making men nervous. Much of the policing of men is done by men themselves. In a series of interviews with college students, for example, American men talked about the importance of seeming masculine in front of their guy friends. Chauncey described putting his "man face" on.[70] Jason reported that he listened to R&B music only when he was alone. Kumar would do "stupid hook-up things . . . just to kind of prove [him]self."[71] Chet talked about how hard it was to be open with even his closest friends: "If a guy starts opening up to another guy, he will joke around like, 'You look like you are ready to make out with me.'"[72] Men must do masculinity in order to avoid policing, much of which comes from other men.

Classic patriarchies and democratic brotherhoods were always as much about relations among men as they were about relations between women and men; modified patriarchal relations still are. Hegemonic masculinity arranges men in a hierarchy all their own. This hierarchy grants men the privilege of looking down on women, but it also arranges them in such a way that other men may be looking down on them.

Because many men are, were, or will be toward the bottom of this hierarchy, it's simply not true to say that all men have more power than all women. Being a man is an advantage, yes, and being a masculine man is a greater advantage, for sure. But men who can't or won't do masculinity, or whose masculinity is stigmatized, find themselves near the bottom of the hierarchy. Women with other kinds of privilege may enjoy greater overall social esteem.

Because gender is not the only game in town, men's disadvantages can significantly outweigh the advantage of being a man. Because of **colorism**, for example—a racist preference for light over dark skin—a light-skinned Latina woman may have more social power than a dark-skinned Latino man. A man who is a gardener has significantly less esteem and opportunity than the rich woman whose flowers he cultivates. An able-bodied woman may be taken more seriously than a man in a wheelchair. A Christian woman may pass through airports with more ease than a Muslim man. It's important to remember that some women have significantly more power, resources, and status than some men do.

In fact, many individual men do not *feel* particularly powerful at all. Many feel downright powerless in certain areas of their lives: at work, in their relationships, and in relation to other men on whom their status in the hierarchy of masculinity depends. Actual men, it turns out, often feel a disconnect between who they are and the power men are said to have.

There is a good reason for this, but it's not that we no longer live in a society characterized by gender inequality. It's that being invested in masculinity is a risky business. Hegemonic masculinity affirms men's power over other men as well as men's power over women, but men pay significant costs in upholding this arrangement. And because gendered hierarchies are strongly and even violently policed, both conformity and resistance to masculinity can be dangerous.

The Danger of Masculinity

"It's become increasingly hard," writes Thomas Edsall, "for [men] to feel good about themselves."[73] Relative to women, men's educational levels are on the decline, while well-paying jobs for non-college-educated workers are disappearing. As the distance between the haves and have-nots in American society grows, the hierarchy of men is stretching out too. White, working-class, native-born men may experience this loss of opportunity as an illegitimate denial of a power that is their birthright.[74] Black, Hispanic, and Indigenous men have long had less access to a wide range of masculine achievements.

In response, some men enact **hypermasculinity**, or an extreme conformity to the more aggressive rules of masculinity. Hypermasculinity is glorified in many corners of American culture.[75] We particularly idealize it in some music genres (such as drill, rap, and heavy metal) and in action movies and video games that glamorize men's violence. We also see hypermasculine performances in sports (especially in highly masculinized ones like football and hockey). These performances naturalize men's violence, aggression, and anger. They also erase its real-life consequences. Meanwhile, men's violence is sometimes justified in the name of protection or defense (see, for example, the good guy with a gun in countless Hollywood movies every year or the armed vigilantes clustering at the US border with Mexico).[76]

Despite the prevalence of hypermasculinity, men are *not* naturally violent. Instead, men must be trained to resist the sensation of empathy and encouraged to enter dangerous situations enthusiastically.[77] Hypermasculinity is nurtured by design in some fraternities, occupations, military units, police squads, neighborhoods, gangs, and prisons. Men in these situations may avoid demonstrating feminized qualities like compassion, nurturance, kindness, and conflict avoidance.

Suppression of empathy often starts sometime around middle school. This is, for example,

The movie poster for *300: Rise of the Empire* glamorizes hypermasculine violence.

the age when the nature of boys' friendships change. To be close friends, men need to be willing to confess their insecurities, be kind to each other, and sometimes sacrifice their own self-interest—a description of friendship that men themselves articulate and say they want.[78] This, though, is incompatible with the rules of masculinity. So as boys grow up to be men, avoiding girlishness can translate into less intimate friendships.

Psychologist Niobe Way interviewed boys about their friendships in each year of high school. She found that younger boys spoke eloquently about their love for their guy friends, but at about age fifteen this began to change. One boy, for example, said this as a freshman:

> [My best friend and I] love each other . . . that's it . . . you have this thing that is deep, so deep, it's within you, you can't explain it. It's just a thing that you know that person is that person. . . . I guess in life, sometimes two people can really, really understand each other and really have a trust, respect and love for each other.[79]

By his senior year, he had changed his mind:

> [My friend and I,] we mostly joke around. It's not like really anything serious or whatever. . . . I don't talk to nobody about serious stuff. . . . I don't share my feelings really. Not that kind of person or whatever.

These efforts to embody masculinity partly explain why men—especially White, heterosexual men—have fewer friends than women do.[80] Since friendship strongly correlates with physical and mental health, this is one way in which closely following the rules of masculinity is bad for men.[81] There are many others.

HARM TO THE SELF Taking masculinity to an extreme makes men dangerous to others, but it also threatens to make men dangerous to themselves. Men are significantly more likely than women to break seat belt laws, drive dangerously, smoke cigarettes, take sexual risks, and abuse drugs and alcohol. Men represent 75 percent of those arrested for drunken driving and 78 percent of those arrested for public drunkenness.[82] Men under twenty-five are almost three times more likely to die in car accidents.[83] They go into dangerous jobs and may resist safety rules, accounting for 92 percent of occupational deaths.[84] Among teens who help their families with farm work, boys are less likely than girls to take safety precautions.[85]

Some argue that being a man is the strongest predictor of whether a person will take risks with their health.[86] Men are less likely than women to undergo health screenings, get regular exercise, see a doctor if they feel sick, and treat existing illnesses and injuries.[87] Being able to function on too little sleep is

Professional bodybuilder Ronnie Coleman breathes pure oxygen immediately after competing in Mr. Olympia. Organizers make oxygen available backstage because contestants are frequently light-headed after their performance.

framed as masculine, leading men to get less sleep than they need.[88] Nearly twice as many men as women died of skin cancer in 2021.[89] The association of lotion with women leads men to resist wearing sunscreen.

Likewise, high school and college athletes sometimes overheat and collapse on the field, while bodybuilders can die from the damage done to their bodies with steroids and diuretics. The image above shows Ronnie Coleman breathing through an oxygen mask, immediately after walking off the stage at the Mr. Olympia competition. He would take first place. Photographer Zed Nelson explains that oxygen is frequently administered to contestants: "The strain of intense dieting, dehydration, and muscle-flexing places high levels of strain on the heart and lungs, rendering many contestants dizzy, light-headed, and weak."[90]

American men even resisted safety precautions during the Covid-19 pandemic. During the early phases of the pandemic, men were about half as likely as women to wash their hands, wear face masks, and comply with social distancing guidelines.[91] When vaccines became available, men were 10 percent less likely to seek out vaccination.[92] Partly as a result, significantly more men have died from Covid-19 than women.[93]

Men's reluctance to take care of themselves extends to their emotional needs, as illustrated by the quality of their friendships. Men are also more likely than women to avoid seeking help for depression. Tragically, they're three and a half times more likely than women to die by suicide.[94]

HARMING OTHERS   Men are also more likely than women to commit violent acts against others. Men account for 88 percent of those charged with murder and nonnegligent manslaughter, 77 percent of those charged with aggravated assault, 68 percent of those charged with family violence, 79 percent of those charged with arson, 85 percent of those charged with robbery, and 91 percent of those charged with unlawful carrying of weapons (Table 5.2).[95] The gendered nature of this violence goes largely unnoted. Likewise, the fact that gang violence, suicide bombings, and serial killings are all overwhelmingly perpetrated by men seems normal, as does the fact that of the 125 mass shootings in the United States between 1982 and 2021, only five involved women perpetrators.[96]

Men are more likely to join White supremacist gangs, neo-Nazi groups, and Islamist jihadist collectives.[97] Women join these groups, too, but they're a minority and less likely than men to physically fight, train for violent conflict, or enact terrorist plots. Research on what attracts men to these groups reveals that many are not particularly drawn to the hateful ideology so much as the promise of a connection to especially masculine men who affirm their own manliness.[98]

TABLE 5.2 | ARRESTS BY GENDER, 2020

Offense Charged	Percent Male
Murder and nonnegligent manslaughter	88
Rape	97
Robbery	85
Aggravated assault	77
Burglary	81
Arson	79
Larceny-theft	61
Motor vehicle theft	78
Fraud	65
Embezzlement	51
Vandalism	77
Weapons (carrying, possessing, etc.)	91
Drug abuse violations	75
Driving under the influence	75

Source: US Federal Bureau of Investigation, Crime Data Explorer, "Arrests in the United States by Offense," accessed Dec. 20, 2021, https://crime-data-explorer.app.cloud.gov/pages/explorer/crime/arrest.

Young boys are often targeted as recruits. Many are at the bottom end of the masculine hierarchy: bullied and made to feel small and weak. Hate groups promise them "an alternate route to proving manhood."[99] Tore Bjørgo, for example, a former skinhead from Sweden, described the appeal of the hate group this way:

> *When I was 14, I had been bullied a lot by classmates and others. By coincidence, I got to know an older guy who was a skinhead. He was really cool, so I decided to become a skinhead myself, cutting off my hair, and donning a black Bomber jacket and Doc Martens boots. The next morning, I turned up at school in my new outfit. In the gate, I met one of my worst tormentors. When he saw me, he was stunned, pressing his back against the wall, with fear shining out of his eyes. I was stunned as well—by the powerful effect my new image had on him and others. Being that intimidating—boy, that was a great feeling![100]*

The attraction of hate groups can't be explained by masculinity alone, but we can't explain their appeal without it either.

Hegemonic masculinity—this single standard of esteem for men—makes the position of even advantaged men feel perilous. Meanwhile, it sometimes presses them to put themselves or others in danger, or to actively harm even the people they profess to care about, whether these are their brothers in a fraternity, fellow soldiers in the army, or romantic partners. This is what is called **toxic masculinity**, enactments of masculinities that are harmful to both the men who enact them and the people around them.

So why don't men just say no to hegemonic masculinity?

Bargaining with Patriarchy

Instead of repudiating hegemonic masculinity, many men embrace strategies that allow them to benefit from being men, even if it simultaneously gives other men status over them. In other words, being *girly* places one at the bottom of the hierarchy of men, and that's bad, but being *a girl* is even worse. Accordingly, many men, even those who populate the bottom rungs of this hierarchy, will defend hegemonic masculinity.

This is called a **patriarchal bargain**—a deal in which an individual or group accepts or even legitimates some of the costs of patriarchy in exchange for receiving some of its rewards.[101] Both men and women make patriarchal bargains. When men do so, they accept some degree of subordination on the hierarchy of masculinity in exchange for the right to claim a higher status than women and some other men.

Few men make these bargains out of a simple desire to exert power over others. Instead, they make them because manliness translates into job opportunities, romantic partners, and social respect. Patriarchal bargains, then, are about figuring out how to thrive in a patriarchal society. We make them to maximize our autonomy, safety, and life satisfaction.

Sociologist Michael Messner described a moment during his boyhood when he made such a bargain.[102] He sensed early on that being a boy and not a girl was important and that being a boyish boy was important too. It was easy to figure out that sports were a "proving ground for masculinity" and that excelling would bring approval. Attracting this esteem, however, also meant enforcing the hierarchy as he ascended it. In particular, he recounts teasing and bullying a nonathletic boy. This, he explains, was "a moment of engagement with hegemonic masculinity" where he acquiesced to patriarchy, agreeing to uphold a masculine hierarchy that empowered him but disempowered others.

All along the hierarchy of masculinity, men make patriarchal bargains. Men often rise to the top by making these bargains and, once they're there, their privileged status depends on enforcing the hierarchy. At the highest levels of large, powerful corporations, for example—where 86 percent of CEOs are White men—these high-status men often close their networks and hoard information and opportunities.[103] Women and men of color are often excluded from these "old boys' clubs."

Men even leave women out of their networks when they're committing fraud.[104] A study of corporate conspiracies in the early 2000s found that a whopping 92 percent of the people indicted for corporate fraud were men. Why? Not because women are so squeaky clean, but because the men didn't include women in their inner circles. A full three-quarters of conspiracies include no women at all. When women were included, it was because the crime was impossible to pull off without them. Or they were the men's wives or girlfriends.

Men lower on the masculine hierarchy also make patriarchal bargains. A study of a group of gay men who formed a college fraternity, for example, found that they chose to emphasize their masculinity and align themselves with other men rather than emphasize their queerness and align themselves primarily with other queer people. Seeking to highlight their more valuable identity, they allowed heterosexual men to be members but not gay women.[105] They also welcomed heterosexual women in the supportive role of "little sister." One brother explained:

> I would prefer straight women because the lesbians would try and take over. A straight woman might enjoy being a little sister and attending functions and hanging out, while a lesbian would consider the role subordinate and get tired of it quickly, trying to dominate and manipulate the program.[106]

As this quote illustrates, these gay men welcomed women into their fraternity but only as subordinates. Meanwhile, they were enthusiastic about making alliances with men of all sexual orientations.

Fans in Tokyo line up to play the new *Grand Theft Auto* video game. The game's advertising prominently features a buxom blond in a bikini.

Nerds, dorks, and geeks also make patriarchal bargains. Characterized by social awkwardness, a lack of athleticism, and a penchant for video and role-playing games, these men are often near the bottom of the hierarchy of masculinity (despite often being White, heterosexual, and middle class). Some bargain with patriarchy by excelling in highly technical and decidedly masculine occupations.[107] Though still notably nerdy, men like Mark Zuckerberg and Elon Musk can point to their success in tech and the size of their bank accounts.

Nerdy men who don't have access to this bargain, however, may stay at the bottom of the hierarchy, embracing it in exchange for the right to exclude, subordinate, and sexually objectify women.[108] Research has found that women and femme-presenting people who play online games regularly encounter sexist harassment.[109] That harassment is more likely to come from low-status men, ones who have, on average, lower scores in the game than men who do not.[110] This patriarchal bargain was also behind the controversy now known as #gamergate.[111] In 2014 and 2015, a group of gamer-identified men mobilized to defend gaming culture from feminist critics, subjecting them to rape and death threats, hacking their accounts, and releasing their personal information.

The White rapper Eminem illustrates yet another patriarchal bargain. Throughout his career, Eminem has aligned himself with Black men while espousing misogyny and homophobia.[112] In his 2017 album, for example, he compared then President Trump with Nazis and White supremacists. On other tracks, though, he raps graphically about women's body parts and makes gendered insults and sexual demands. In one song, he takes the perspective of a serial killer who targets young, beautiful women. Eminem's patriarchal bargain is to identify with men across race and class while distancing himself from women and queer men.

Paradoxically, the men who most ardently defend hegemonic masculinity are likely the ones at the top *and* the bottom of the hierarchy of masculinity.[113] Men at the bottom can claim masculinity to secure at least some privileges, while men at the top may resist any change to the hierarchy on which they're so comfortably perched. All men, however, are pressed to bargain with patriarchy, one way or another, to squeeze some benefit from the system. When they do, they affirm hegemonic masculinity rather than attack it, aiming to improve their position, not tear the whole thing down.

CAN MASCULINITY BE GOOD?

Around the world today, there are men who are actively trying to find new ways of being men: ways that resist patriarchy, eschew hypermasculinity, and avoid oppressing women or other men. They are acting to distance themselves from sexist, androcentric, subordinating forms of masculinity. In doing so, they're trying to do masculinity in ways that are better for them and the people around them.

Men who are rethinking masculinity include the K-pop stars in South Korea and the Black American fashion icons we discussed in Chapter 3. Fathers who are finding ways to be more involved parents are rethinking masculinity, as are men who enter caring professions. These men may be looking for a somewhat softer ideal that is still "masculine enough." A new androgynous masculinity has arisen in China, too, characterized by slender frames, gender-neutral clothing, and a 44 percent increase in men's consumption of beauty products.[114]

Challenges to how masculinity is practiced are not new. Back in the 1970s, wearing flowered shirts and donning long hair was a way for young White men to signal their opposition to the war in Vietnam and differentiate their masculinity from that of their fathers. In the 1980s, pop stars like Prince and Boy George embodied a more colorful way of being a man. Throughout the decades, men have always pushed the boundaries of masculinity, sometimes innovating in ways that undermine masculinity's hegemony.

Today sociologists call these innovations **hybrid masculinities**, versions of masculinity that selectively incorporate symbols, performances, and identi-

While men such as actor Timothée Chalamet may adopt a softer version of masculinity, donning jewelry and sparkly clothing, research suggests these hybrid masculinities do little to undermine gender inequality.

ties that society associates with women or low-status men.[115] Men with hybrid masculinities may mix aspects of femininity into their personalities, "queer" their lifestyles, and resist the impulse to climb the masculine hierarchy. In so doing, these men could potentially undermine the importance of gender distinction, give femininity value, see women as equals, and deconstruct hegemonic masculinity.[116] Hybrid masculinities, then, could be an exciting step toward a more gender-equal society.

There is considerable academic study left to do and much more everyday experimentation left to try, but the existing research doesn't yet support the idea that men with hybrid masculinities are substantially undermining gender inequality. Instead, research suggests that existing forms of hybridity do more to obscure practices of subordination. Hybrid masculinities may feminize or queer styles of expression but fail to challenge men's hold on powerful positions.[117]

An example, to start: For over a decade, and on four continents, an anti-rape campaign that used the slogan "My Strength Is Not for Hurting" aimed to teach young men not to sexually exploit others.[118] The campaign emphasized men's responsibility to protect women, reinforcing the idea that women are weak and in need of protection (as opposed, for instance, to the idea that women have rights to their own bodies that deserve to be respected). The campaign tried to persuade men to be chivalrous instead of exploitative but didn't challenge the underlying unequal relationship between men and women or the stereotypes on which it rests.

Scholars argue that hybrid masculinities aren't living up to their potential for several reasons. First, some hybrid masculinities are largely symbolic. A corporate boss, for example, may endorse the formation of a support group for his women employees but resist investing resources into helping them succeed. A married man may identify as a feminist but neglect to do his fair share of the housework and childcare. Or a heterosexual man may befriend gay men but vote for politicians who are anti-gay because they promise to keep his taxes low. Supporting women, identifying as gender egalitarian, and embracing sexual minorities help move our societies toward greater equality, but more concrete changes—shifts in our laws, how we spend money, and how we organize families—are needed to realize it.

Second, men who adopt hybrid masculinities sometimes ask for extra credit for being "good." The forty-year-old faith-based organization Promise Keepers, for example, is dedicated to spreading the idea that men should be good caretakers of their family.[119] In doing so, the organization naturalizes men's role as the head of the household. Like the "Strength" campaign, the Keepers movement encourages men to adopt a hybrid masculinity that incorporates a feminine ethic of care, but it also positions men's power over women as inevitable. In the anti-rape campaign, it's inevitable because men's ability to overpower women is unquestioned (though fighting back is a proven way to stop a rape attempt).[120] In the case of Keepers, men's control of women remains legitimate as long as men exercise that control kindly.

The final problem with hybrid masculinities is the tendency for men who adopt them to use them to claim status. When men claim to be "good," they're often also claiming to be "better" than the men they identify as "bad," and those men are usually ones who are already on the lower end of the masculine hierarchy as well as other hierarchies. In this case, differentiating between "good" and "bad" men just becomes another way to affirm, not break down, both hegemonic masculinity and the hierarchy of men.

One study, for example, examined the ideals adopted by rich young men attending a therapeutic boarding school: a rehabilitation-focused school serving high school–age boys with drug and alcohol problems, with tuitions ranging between $4,500 and $9,500 a month.[121] Most boys initially resisted the idea that they needed to be open about their personal pain, share their emotions, and develop expressive communication styles. As they adjusted to their new school's expectations, however, they reframed these typically feminized traits as characteristic of a secure and healthy masculinity, contrasting themselves with boys and men whose masculinity was fragile, compensatory, or toxic.

These young men then felt entitled to the class privileges they experienced upon graduation. School administrators taught them to lead offsite Alcoholics Anonymous meetings and sponsor community members, thus putting teenagers in charge of men of all ages, from varied backgrounds, with substantially more experience with both addiction and recovery. Nonetheless, the school encouraged the young men to see themselves as "leaders" of these "lesser" men, thanks to their enlightened masculinities. This further prepared them to go on as privileged adults. "My dad and I used to have major trust issues," said one of the boys:

> [He] used to threaten to kick me out, take me out of the will, all that. Now that we've worked through our issues and actually talk and trust each other with things, he's talking about putting me in charge of one of the divisions of his company after I get a degree.[122]

As this quote shows, these young men may have redefined their masculinity, but they've used that redefinition to justify their class and race privileges. Moreover, by adopting a hybrid masculinity, they now thought that they weren't just *lucky* to have dads who could launch their careers but genuinely *deserving* of that advantage.

Men who adopt hybrid masculinities often see themselves as the good guys, but they still value the fact that they're *guys*. Continuing to embrace an idealized masculinity that differentiates them in important ways from women, they remain invested in gender distinction and resist giving up the substantive advantages that being men affords them.[123]

So *can* masculinity be good?

We don't know. Gender scholars—including many, many men—have spent a lot of time trying to answer that question.[124]

The trouble is that masculinity has been used to symbolize and represent men's superiority over women and lesser men for more than four thousand years. Masculinity has always been about power. Today, it's still synonymous with strength, dominance, and high status. And its meaning is gained in contrast with a femininity that is weak, subordinate, and low status.

If we somehow excised the dominating, toxic, and compensatory behaviors from masculinity, alongside all the other bad things (like being afraid to wear sunscreen), then what's left is a series of *wonderful* traits: duty, honor, hard work, sacrifice, leadership, and the like. And that's lovely. But for these to be traits of men, we must also say that women are not these things. And is that true? Are women not dutiful, honorable, and hard working? Do they not sacrifice? Can they not lead? The truth is that "good men" aren't good *men*; they're good *people*, and they share good traits with women, who are good people too.

Can masculinity be good? We don't know. We know that *men* can be good. But whether they need masculinity to do it is an open question.

We also need to ask: Is masculinity good for men? On that, we have stronger data. Masculinity can make men feel good about themselves, but it hurts men too. It hurts some men a lot. It hurts men who disinvest in masculinity and pay the price. It also hurts many men who embrace it; the belief that they *should* be better than women and other men is at the root of much of men's sadness, self-loathing, and silent suffering.

Revisiting the Question

 If everyone is constrained by a binary gender system, why do many more women than men find this system unfair?

There are good reasons for men to find the system unfair. Because gender rules make femininity only for women, men must avoid performing it. Their daily lives and social interactions are constrained by this imperative. As a result, men may repress the parts of themselves that don't reflect hegemonic masculinity and emphasize those that do, sticking only to man-approved masculinity, at least in public or around certain kinds of people.

It's no surprise, then, that men sometimes find the rules of masculinity to be strict, arbitrary, and even painful. Many men, though, follow gender rules, and press others to do so, because upholding the hierarchical gender binary means preserving at least some privileges for themselves. This often means rough policing of the boundaries of masculinity. This can make masculinity dangerous, creating circumstances in which men are pushed to make unsafe choices, exposed to violence, or incited to harm others.

Under these conditions, men make strategic choices. Sometimes they have to choose between following the rules or being seen as a failure; other times, masculine privilege may feel like the only advantage they have. Men also may think brushes with femininity carry too high a cost. Accordingly, most men make patriarchal bargains in at least parts of their lives. Ironically, men harmed the most by hegemonic masculinity are among its most ardent defenders. At the very least, it guarantees them superiority over women.

This helps explain why so few men actively challenge gender inequality, but we have yet to tackle why so many women do. The next chapter rounds out the answer to our guiding question.

FOR FURTHER READING

Bridges, Tristan, and C. J. Pascoe. "On the Elasticity of Gender Hegemony: Why Hybrid Masculinities Fail to Undermine Gender and Sexual Inequality." In James Messerschmidt, Patricia Yancey Martin, Michael A. Messner, and Raewyn Connell, eds. *Gender Reckonings: New Social Theory and Research*, 254–74. New York: New York University Press, 2018.

Connell, Raewyn W. *Masculinities*. 2nd ed. Berkeley: University of California Press, 2005.

Iida, Yumiko. "Beyond the 'Feminization of Masculinity': Transforming Patriarchy with the 'Feminine' in Contemporary Japanese Youth Culture." *Inter-Asia Cultural Studies* 6, no. 1 (2005): 56–74.

Pugh, Allison. "Men at Work." *Aeon*, December 4, 2015. https://aeon.co/essays/what-does-it-mean-to-be-a-man-in-the-age-of-austerity.

Ridgeway, Cecilia L. *Framed by Gender: How Gender Inequality Persists in the Modern World*. New York: Oxford University Press, 2011.

Walker, Alicia. *Chasing Masculinity: Men, Validation, and Infidelity*. London: Palgrave Macmillan, 2020.

Way, Niobe. *Deep Secrets*. Cambridge, MA: Harvard University Press, 2011.

> SOME OF US ARE
> BECOMING THE
> MEN WE WANTED
> TO MARRY.
> —GLORIA STEINEM

6

Inequality:

FEMININITIES

The last chapter focused on how gendered power shapes men's experiences. This chapter discusses the lives of women. It argues that, on the one hand, women have a lot more freedom than men to enjoy both masculine- and feminine-coded parts of life, a freedom that offers women many exciting opportunities and simple pleasures. On the other hand, because doing femininity is compulsory, and we live in an androcentric society, women are pressed to adopt gender performances that harm them. After reviewing the realities facing different women, the chapter concludes with an intersectional overview of gender inequality. But first, the chapter starts the way the last one did: with cheerleading.

CHEERLEADING TODAY

As you now know, in the 1800s men cheerleaders were respected for their ability to lead a crowd. Women joined teams during World War II, eventually prompting men to abandon the activity. By the 1960s, essentially all cheerleaders were women. No longer equivalent to being a quarterback, cheerleading was now a cute sideshow to the main event.

Cheerleaders at a University of Nevada, Las Vegas, basketball game blend feminine grace, peppy enthusiasm, and impressive athleticism.

It wouldn't stay this way. Eventually, cheerleading would be remasculinized—by women. By the 1990s, cheer involved intense athleticism. Gymnastics were back and stunts became increasingly difficult and dangerous. An entire industry was built around cheer competition.[1] Between 1990 and 2012, injuries among cheerleaders increased almost twofold; concussions almost tripled.[2]

For some time now, men have slowly been returning to cheerleading. Today, recruitment aimed at men appeals to their masculinity, emphasizing physical strength and, this time, access to women. "Want strong muscles? Want to toss girls? Our Cheer Team needs stunt men!!" encouraged a university recruitment poster.[3] "In cheerleading," echoed a football player turned cheerleader, "you get to be around all these beautiful women."[4]

Despite these changes, cheer retains feminine dimensions. Women cheerleaders wear sexy outfits that offer their bodies as spectacles. A cheerleader's primary job still is to root for football and basketball teams. That is, it remains largely a "feminine auxiliary to sport," not the serious main event.[5] Cheer also retains a performative aspect that seems unsuited to men. Sociologists Laura Grindstaff and Emily West explain:

Appearing before a crowd requires that cheerleaders be enthusiastic, energetic, and entertaining. This is accomplished not just through dancing, tumbling, or eye-catching stunts, but also through the bubbly, peppy, performance of "spirit." . . . It includes smiling, "facials" (exaggerated facial expressions), being in constant motion, jumping, and executing dynamic arm, hand, and head motions—all considered feminine terrain.[6]

As one man said, somewhat embarrassedly, "A game face for a cheerleader is a big smile," not exactly the threatening grimace or strained expression associated with "real" sports.[7]

Most people still associate cheerleading with femininity, and as a result, they continue to take it less seriously than other physical activities. Despite the high-impact athleticism of cheer, only about half of US high school athletic associations define cheerleading as a sport, and neither the US Department of Education nor the National Collegiate Athletic Association (NCAA) categorizes it as one.[8] Instead, cheerleading is frequently labeled an "activity" akin to the chess club. Accordingly, cheerleading remains unregulated by organizations responsible for ensuring the safety of athletes, leading to higher rates of catastrophic injury in cheerleading than in any other sport, including American football.[9]

Cheerleading is somehow simultaneously masculine and feminine, hardcore and cute, athletic and aesthetic, admired and belittled. It also sexualizes femininity, making women's ability to appeal to assumed-heterosexual men centrally important even while pulling off impressive feats of skill. It is, in other words, very much like what being a woman can feel like today. Unlike men, who are encouraged to avoid femininity and do masculinity, women are strongly encouraged to embrace *both*.

GENDER FOR WOMEN

In many ways, the daily lives of women are much less constrained than those of men. Men risk policing when they do femininity, but women's performances of masculinity are often regarded positively, such that women today are doing almost everything men do. People are starting to notice that girls are pretty great. In fact, in a dramatic change from the past, most American parents no longer prefer having sons to daughters.[10]

Emily Kane, the sociologist who documented parents' unease about their sons' performances of femininity, found that parents weren't at all troubled by their girls' gender nonconformity.[11] In fact, they were downright tickled if their daughters wanted to wear a dinosaur backpack, collect bugs in the backyard, or dress up like a superhero. They favorably described their daughters as "rough and tumble," even endorsing their girls' interest in icons of masculinity like trucks and tools.[12] And while they felt a need to uncover a reason for their sons' preference for girly things, their daughters' interest in masculine things needed

no such explanation. Since masculine activities are highly valued, it makes perfect sense that girls would be drawn to them and parents would be proud.

A study of trans children found a similar pattern.[13] Children assigned male
at birth who act feminine strike most parents as more concerning and confusing than children assigned female at birth who act masculine. As a result, the
study found that, on average, parents sought help for feminine-acting children
at around five years of age, whereas they sought help for masculine-acting children at age ten. This large discrepancy reflects how androcentrism provides a
built-in explanation for why *anyone* would do masculinity, making that kind of
gender transgression understandable. It's also further evidence that masculinity is particularly precarious, easily undermined by brushes with femininity.

Cis and trans girls and women both benefit greatly from this new freedom to
mix masculinity into their performances of gender. They now have the freedom
to enjoy the complex flavors of scotch, the rigorous training of law school or
the military, the risks and rewards of casual sex, and the thrill of competing in
extreme sports. They can become construction workers or architects and feel
the deep satisfaction of watching one's work materialize; they can become surgeons or CEOs and choose to take responsibility for human life and corporate
profits. As of 2016, women can assume combat roles in the military, breaching
the last occupational barrier America put in their path.

Many people admire women who enter masculine occupations, not only because they are defying stereotypes but also because, by virtue of being associated with men, such occupations are
more esteemed than feminine ones.

These developments are all rightly interpreted as signs that women have much more opportunity than in the past, a state of affairs most Americans endorse. Measured by the scope of gender rules, then, options for women in many contemporary societies are undoubtedly more open than men's. It's a good time to be a woman. But there's a catch.

The Importance of Balance

While women are allowed and even encouraged to do masculinity, a woman who performs *too much* masculinity attracts the same policing as a man who does just *some* femininity. Women who perform too much masculinity violate the gender binary and break the number one gender rule, the rule that one has to identify as a man or woman and perform gender in a way that's consistent with their identity. In other words, if women want to do masculinity, they have to balance it with femininity.

Women who do this, who carefully walk a line between masculinity and femininity, are the new ideal. Only 32 percent of Americans say that people look up to "womanly women."[14] Not surprisingly then, only 19 percent of young adult women today describe themselves as "very feminine," compared to about a third of Gen Xers and baby boomers and the majority of those in the generation before. While men still resist describing themselves as "nurturing" and "sensitive," women are about as likely or even more likely than men to describe themselves as "physically strong," "assertive," and "intelligent." The model woman, the one all women are supposed to try to be these days, is *not* the perfect picture of femininity; she is both feminine and masculine.

Reflecting this change in the ideal woman, media coverage often fawns over women who do both masculinity and femininity gracefully. Christmas Abbott, for example, is a CrossFit competitor, a nationally ranked weightlifter, and the first woman to serve in a NASCAR pit. Media profiles of Abbott highlight her achievements in these masculine-coded arenas, but they often also balance their glowing accounts with references to her femininity.

Presenting oneself as a sex object is one way for women who do masculinity, like CrossFit competitor and weightlifter Christmas Abbott, to balance their gender performance.

Cosmopolitan, for example, emphasized that Abbott "doesn't have to choose between being strong and beautiful."[15] She replied: "You can be a gym rat and turn around and be a hot little minx." In the tattoo-focused *Inked* magazine, where she is profiled and photographed naked, it's remarked that her tattoos include everything from butterflies to pistols and a figure holding both a flower and a sword.[16] In an interview with CNN, Abbott explained:

> *The ongoing joke is, if I'm not in tennis shoes, I'm in pumps. And I love wearing dresses and curling my hair. But that doesn't mean that I don't like to get dirty. You know, I like to work. I like to be physical in my work. And I think that it's been over-looked that women can do both.*[17]

Abbott asserts that doing both is an overlooked possibility for women, but it's not. In fact, it's a widely endorsed ideal. It's exactly what people find so impressive about her: not simply that she excels in masculine arenas but also that she balances both masculinity and femininity. She's strong *and* beautiful, in sneakers *and* heels, in dresses *and* dirty. And the beauty, heels, and dresses aren't incidental; they're a critical part of her self-presentation.

As Abbott illustrates, women have the opportunity to do masculinity, but there are limits to how much masculinity will be tolerated by others. Being intelligent, ambitious, outspoken, and sporty is great, but being properly feminine is essential. In this way, doing femininity can be understood as an account for breaking the rule that requires women to leave the guy stuff to guys. It's a way of saying: "I know it looks like I'm encroaching on men's territory but be assured I know my place as a woman." When women perform femininity, it lets the men around them know that *they know* that they're still, first and foremost, women. Presenting themselves as sexual objects for heterosexual men's sexual imagination, as Abbott does, is one very effective way to do this.

The requirement that women balance masculine interests, traits, and activities with conventional femininity is called the **feminine apologetic**. The term points to how a woman's performance of femininity can be a way to soothe others' concerns about her appropriation of masculinity. Abbott gets away with being masculine by also performing a conventional feminine sexual attractiveness. She, like other women in the United States today, can do "anything she wants to do," as long as she also sends clear signals that she cares what men think of her.

This is the lesson Barbie teaches us so well: Barbie can do anything—she can be a doctor, an astronaut, an athlete, or a presidential candidate—but the important thing is that she look good while doing it. Barbie's relentless takeover of so many masculine arenas would be quite a bit more threatening if she weren't doing a bang-up job of performing femininity too.

Like Christmas Abbott, the character of Wonder Woman, played by Gal Gadot, is both sexy and strong. A male love interest affirms that she's still feminine enough to fall in love.

Abbott has an advantage in this regard. She was born blond into a society that privileges Whiteness, with features considered conventionally pretty. Women who are ascribed masculinity by American culture—like queer and Black women—have fewer options for mixing in masculinity. Instead, they may be forced to perform a feminine apologetic regardless of whether they deliberately mix masculinity into their personas.

A Black lesbian named Zoe invoked Barbie when explaining her struggles with femininity: "I never felt like a girl," she said. "There weren't even black people on TV when I was growing up. The white people were Barbie, and I am not Barbie."[18] Zoe couldn't identify with Barbie's All-American Girl Whiteness, so it was more challenging for her to strike a balance between masculinity and femininity that others would approve of.

For Black women, this is often a question of hair.[19] Femininity is implicitly White, so light-colored, long, straight, or gently wavy hair is associated with femininity. Accordingly, Black women with curly or kinky dark hair have to decide whether to leave it natural, wear wigs, or try to force it to resemble a White aesthetic. Many high-profile Black women do the latter, including women as powerful as Michelle Obama and Beyoncé. Others choose to stay natural much of the time, like Beyoncé's sister, Solange Knowles. Sometimes they do so

Regardless of their personal preferences, both Beyoncé and Solange Knowles must make strategic decisions about what to do with their hair, knowing that others will evaluate them based on their choices.

because it fits with their identity and politics. This was certainly true for Jenny. She explained her decision to wear hers in dreadlocks:

> *I consider myself in a constant state of protest about the realities of cultural alienation, cultural marginalization, cultural invisibility, discrimination, injustice, all of that. And I feel that my hairstyle has always allowed me, since I started wearing it in a natural, to voice that nonverbally.*[20]

While Black women can choose to wear their hair in ways that reflect their own personal values and aesthetics, they must also contend with the way others respond to them. As Jenny knows very well, on Black women in America, hairstyles aren't personal; they're political. Black women's hair has been the subject of decades of lawsuits.[21] Natural hairstyles like twists and braids were not allowed for women in the military until 2014.[22] In 2016, a US federal court held that it is legal for an employer to fire a person for their hairstyle; in the case at hand, a woman wore her hair in dreadlocks.[23]

By forgoing the natural, Black women can offer a feminine apologetic, and possibly a race apologetic, too, one that can help them succeed in White-dominated spaces. Making their hair look less "Black" is a way of saying: "I'm not *that* kind of Black woman." The kind, that is, that doesn't know her place.

In the voiceover for a Nike commercial, the tennis champion Serena Williams states matter of factly, "I've never been the right kind of woman. Oversized and overconfident. Too mean if I don't smile. Too Black for my tennis whites. Too motivated for motherhood."[24] The visuals show her, victorious on the tennis court, with natural hair, and the narration takes a turn: "But I am proving, time and time again," she says, "there's no wrong way to be a woman."

Serena is indisputably one of the greatest athletes—of any gender—of all time. If anyone is proof that women can do and be anything, she is it. But her claim that there is no wrong way to be a woman is aspirational. We're not there yet.

Right Balances and Wrong Ones

Women sometimes refuse or fail to perform enough conventional femininity to soothe the concerns of the people around them. In practice, then, there *are* wrong ways to be a woman. Sociologists call them **pariah femininities**: ways of being a woman that, by virtue of directly challenging men's dominance, are widely and aggressively policed.[25] Women who perform pariah femininities are ones who don't defer to men (*bitches, ballbusters, cunts,* and *nags*), who don't seem to care if men find them attractive (*dykes* and *hags*), who have or withhold sex without concern for whether men approve (*sluts, whores, teases,* and *prudes*), or who do not form households with men (*spinsters* and *old maids*).

Such women don't balance; they *defy*. They refuse to perform a femininity that complements hegemonic masculinity. Or they simply cannot do conventional femininity. They have too little money, the wrong mix of identities, or the wrong bodies: ones that are overweight, disabled, old, or otherwise not amenable to a sexualized gaze.

These femininities are described as *pariah* because they're stigmatizing to the women who adopt or are ascribed them. To do them is to risk rejection, verbal attack, violence, and even ostracism. Choosing these identities can be exhilarating, because defiance is a thrill, but doing so puts women at risk of attracting the familiar slurs, and worse.

The punishments doled out to women who embody pariah femininities reveal that women are afforded opportunities to balance masculinity and femininity, but not exactly as they like and not in any proportion they please. Women must do *enough* femininity and the *right kind* of femininity, given their subcultural environment and mix of identities. A woman working on a construction site, for example, might talk dirty and wear coveralls like her men colleagues, but she may also need to prove her femininity by regularly going on dates with men. An out lesbian working as an aggressive prosecutor at a law firm may be expected to wear a pencil skirt, heels, and blouse to court. A woman from a conservative religious background may be allowed to pursue a high-powered career as long as she demonstrates that motherhood remains her number one priority. What mix of femininity and masculinity women choose to perform depends on their particular intersection of identities and context, but one thing is for sure: If you're a woman, your gender presentation needs to be carefully balanced.

In sum, the requirement that women do femininity, combined with the more recent option to add in masculinity, gives women a great deal more behavioral freedom than men have today. Women can adopt a wider range of interests, activities, and styles, while men are mostly constrained by the imperative to avoid femininity. Women, of course, also face constraints related to their gender performance, but women's constraint is of a different sort than men's: She can do (almost) anything she likes as long as she also acts to affirm the hierarchical gender binary on which men's privilege and power depend.

The constraints women face, though, extend further. Not only are they required to do specific amounts and kinds of difference *from* men; they're required to do inferiority *to* men. Femininity, by definition, is disempowering. So, when people perform it, part of what they're performing is subordination.

Doing More, Winning Less

Recall that we live in a modified patriarchy, one that associates power with men and masculinity and powerlessness with women and femininity. Whatever personality traits, styles, activities, and spheres of life are deemed feminine, then, are subject to all three relations of gender inequality: sexism, androcentrism, and subordination.

SEXISM Because of enduring sexism, the perception of femaleness is always a possible source of prejudice. As we discussed in the last chapter, this means that whatever women do, they have to do it better than men if they want to be evaluated as equally good. One well-documented case of such prejudice is the orchestral audition.[26] Beginning in the 1970s, some orchestras switched to "blind" auditions. The hiring committee would sit in the theater and see only a large blind or screen. The musician would walk forward from the back of the stage, sit behind the screen, play, and leave. They would be heard but not seen. The hope was that the process would result in the committee hiring the best musician, without regard to gender, race, or any other prejudicial factor.

At first, there was no change in the proportion of women hired, suggesting that sexism was not to blame for the low numbers of women in orchestras. But then someone noticed a sound: footsteps. When a woman walked across the stage, the click-clack of her high heels, compared to the clop-clop of men's flats, was giving her away. When they required all musicians to take off their shoes before they walked across the stage, the likelihood that a woman would advance to the final rounds rose by about 50 percent.

For better or worse, life isn't a barefooted, blind audition. In most circumstances, all other things being equal, a woman can be as good as a man and she'll be evaluated as less than. Even when she does more, when she outperforms her men counterparts, she's likely to win less.

ANDROCENTRISM Women must also contend with androcentrism. Because femininity is disparaged relative to masculinity, the gender rules that require a feminine apologetic also require women to perform a devalued identity.[27] Some think, for example, that focusing on the feminized task of raising children makes women boring or unambitious. A feminized occupation, teachers are given lip service but are otherwise poorly paid and underappreciated. The requirement that women be skilled with makeup and interested in fashion threatens to mark them as "shallow." Many traits associated with femininity are quite actively disparaged in our societies.

Sometimes androcentric disparagement of people who do femininity is shrouded in what sounds like a compliment. Social psychologists call this **benevolent sexism**: the attribution of positive traits to women that nonetheless justify women's subordination to men.[28] We put women on pedestals for being supportive, loving, patient, and kind, but this respect is a double-edged sword in societies that revere and reward competition. Women's ability to love others is cast as a weakness that threatens their ability to compete in work, sports, or politics.

Likewise, conventionally feminine women are admired for their graceful and small bodies, but it's also believed that these bodies make them incapable of strenuous physical tasks and vulnerable to attack. This leaves them in need of assistance and protection from stronger, more physically powerful people (that is, men). By making women more dependent on men by virtue of the positive characteristics attributed to femininity, benevolent sexism ultimately positions women as inferior. In this way, it is the inverse of exculpatory chauvinism. While the latter uses negative stereotypes about men to justify their dominance, the former uses positive stereotypes about women to justify their domination.

SUBORDINATION Finally, because power is gendered, the requirement to do femininity is also a requirement to do subordination. The areas in which women are seen as naturally superior to men, for example, are often self-sacrificial. Women are believed to be better suited than men to forgo their leisure time, educations, and career aspirations to help others. The icons of femininity—mother, nurse, secretary, teacher—are supportive, not leading roles (and the efforts of women in these roles are often taken for granted).[29] Most high-powered jobs still assume married men have wives at home to manage the household and care for the children.

Especially when mixing with men, women are encouraged to be unselfish, noncompetitive, and actively supportive. Someone doing femininity well smiles at others sweetly, keeps her voice melodic, and asks questions instead of making declarations. A conventionally feminine person lets others take care of her: open her door, order her meal, and pay her tab. A feminine sexuality is one that waits and responds, never acts or initiates. A feminine body is small and contained: "Massiveness, power, or abundance in a woman's body is met with distaste."[30] Subordination is about never bothering others with one's own discomfort or concerns.

Women can feel the need to demonstrate selflessness even in extreme circumstances.[31] A study of White, middle-class, midwestern American mothers revealed that many of them tried to be nice even while giving birth. They showed interest in others, tried to be gracious, and avoided raising their voices or making demands. If they failed, they apologized, to their husbands, the staff, and anyone they might have bothered. One of these mothers, Valerie, recalled her experience:

> I remember between contractions here, I could hear the other people in the next room, and I remember thinking—'cause I was very loud at this point—and I remember thinking I felt bad because I was being so loud and this poor woman [giving birth] in the next room must be thinking awful thoughts about me.[32]

Being considerate of others in the middle of giving birth is very nice indeed, but it may come at the cost of one's own well-being. It's hard work to try to be lovely while undergoing one of the most demanding and painful experiences of any human's life. And withholding information or not standing up for oneself under such circumstances can be dangerous. Many women learn to put others first, even when it's difficult or dangerous to do so. That is the very definition of subordination.

All this is, truly, about power. Femininity, the philosopher Sandra Lee Bartky writes, is "a language of subordination."[33] So much so that the performance of femininity overlaps with the performances of others who are in subordinate positions: job applicants with their interviewers, enlisted soldiers with their superiors, and students in the offices of their professors. Bartky explains:

> In groups of men, those with higher status typically assume looser and more relaxed postures; the boss lounges comfortably behind the desk while the applicant sits tense and rigid on the edge of his seat. Higher-status individuals may touch

their subordinates more than they themselves get touched; they initiate more eye contact and are smiled at by their inferiors more than they are observed to smile in return. What is announced in the comportment of superiors is confidence and ease.[34]

Likewise, speech forms associated with women—hedging ("It seems like"), hyper-politeness ("I'd really appreciate it if"), and questions in response to questions (like answering "When would you like to eat dinner?" with "Around seven o'clock?")—are actually typical of not just women but all people in weaker positions.[35] To do femininity is to do deference, and to do deference is to do femininity. That's why even computerized assistants like Siri and Alexa default to feminine-sounding voices.[36]

When women refuse to do subordination, they stray into pariah territory. And that makes them a target of **hostile sexism**, the use of harassment, threats, and violence to enforce women's subservience to men. Hostile sexism is rooted in some men's feelings of entitlement to having women in the roles of carers, helpers, sex partners, or admirers. When women don't accept these roles, some men feel **aggrieved entitlement**, anger over something men feel they rightfully own or deserve that is being unjustly taken or withheld from them.[37]

Compared to hostile sexism, benevolent sexism can seem woman-friendly, but that's not how it works. They are two sides of the same coin: Benevolent sexism rewards women's subservience with men's approval, protection, and support (sometimes called "chivalry"), but if women fall or jump from this pedestal, hostile sexism takes its place. Protection and support are revoked in favor of verbal or physical assault. Benevolent sexism is plan A. Hostile sexism is plan B. Reflecting this, societies typically have consistently low or high rates of both hostile and benevolent sexism. The two types of sexism rise and fall together.[38]

Take street harassment as an example. Often the things men say to unfamiliar women in public oscillate between niceties and hostility. Compliments can quickly turn into insults and threats if they're not met with the response men think they deserve: a feminine apologetic in the form of a smile, a thank-you, or another polite response. Likewise, in intimate relationships, attention and flattery can quickly turn to control and coercion.[39] And women who become the targets of men's hostility are often blamed for it on the assumption that they could have, and should have, appeased their partners.

Benevolent sexism isn't a kindness; it's a trap. If both the risk and protection are in the hands of men—that is, if *men* are the problem and *gentlemen* are the solution—then women are always positioned such that they need men in order to stay safe. Moreover, it's difficult to know which men are threats and which are protectors. Should a woman accept this man's offer to walk her home? Who is more dangerous to her: the man in the alley or the man she's suddenly alone with on the street at night? The latter she thinks of as a friend, but 92 percent of

Cartoonist B. Deutsch illustrates what it feels like to be sandwiched between both hostile and benevolent sexism.

women who are raped are assaulted by someone they know.[40] What to do? This is the type of difficult calculation women make routinely.

In this sense, hostile sexism is a measure of the cracks in the system. If women never challenged men's authority, there would be no need to reassert patriarchy by force. Sexually charged taunts, insults, pranks, and violence are about gender policing: putting "uppity" women back "in their place" to preserve the gender binary and the illusion of men's superiority. Policing men who do femininity, trans people who cross the line between man and woman, and nonbinary folks who defy binary gender rules serves this same function.

Women today may have more freedom than men to do gender as they please, but balancing masculinity with femininity requires them to adopt features and behaviors that are actively disparaged, indicate weakness, or place them in service to others. And if they don't want to do these things, there is a carrot and a stick—a benevolent and a hostile sexism. At its extreme, hostile sexism takes the form of violence, making women's choices about how to do femininity, at times, a matter of life or death.

When Being a Woman Gets Dangerous

HARM FROM OTHERS   In 2014, at the University of California, Santa Barbara (UCSB), a college student named Elliot Rodger murdered three Asian men before setting out to get revenge on women. Rodger was a self-described "incel," a term used to refer to men who are involuntarily celibate: desirous of a sexual partner but unable to find one. In his video manifesto, he proclaimed:

I am going to enter the hottest sorority house at UCSB and I will slaughter every single spoiled, stuck-up, blond slut I see inside there. All those girls I've desired so much. They have all rejected me and looked down on me as an inferior man if I ever made a sexual advance toward them.[41]

When all was said and done, he'd injured thirteen and murdered six. Then he killed himself.

Rodger felt that he was positioned unfairly low in the masculine hierarchy. Of both Chinese and European ancestry, he considered himself superior to Asian men by virtue of being half-White. He was especially infuriated when Black and Asian men, whom he considered lesser, "won" the "prizes" to which he believed he was entitled.

Ultimately, Rodger did not believe that women had the *right* to deny him their bodies. He felt *entitled* to sex with these women. His desire to kill them, in other words, was motivated by the belief that they were not obeying the rules of femininity, which included subordinating themselves to his sexual needs. His mass shooting was an act of gender policing and an example of hostile sexism rooted in aggrieved entitlement.

Other men, many of whom describe themselves as incels, have found inspiration in what Rodger did at UCSB. In 2015, an Oregon community college student entered his Introduction to Composition class and killed the teacher and eight fellow students, injuring eight others. A thumb drive he handed to a survivor revealed that he'd studied what Rodger had done. In 2018, at least three men would praise Rodger shortly before engaging in their mass murders. One of them walked into Marjory Stoneman Douglas High School in Parkland, Florida, carrying a semiautomatic weapon. Promising "Elliot Rodger will not be forgotten," he killed three adults and fourteen teenagers.[42]

Sometimes these violent men deliberately target specific kinds of women. In 2021, for example, a man visited three massage parlors in Atlanta, Georgia, seeking out and targeting Asian women. The perpetrator explained that he had a "sex addiction" and that Asian women were "a temptation . . . that he wanted to eliminate."[43] He killed eight people. As in Rodgers's case, gender and race formed a hierarchy of entitlement. The sexualization of women, and the fetishization of Asian women in particular, can quickly turn deadly.

One in four known mass killers have a history of intimate partner violence.[44] Across both public and private settings, at least 53 percent of mass shootings between 2009 and 2020 involved a perpetrator shooting a (former) partner or family member. In fact, most mass killings occur in the home, even if the ones that occur in public involve more victims on average and draw more media attention. A quarter of all the victims of mass shootings are children.[45]

About a quarter of women experience intimate partner violence, compared to 11 percent of men.[46] This includes about 4.5 million women who've had an intimate partner threaten them with a gun.[47] Violence of this kind may have been exacerbated by the Covid-19 pandemic, with early research showing increases in some types of violence or in its severity.[48]

Intimate partner violence is often deadly. Fully 39 percent of women murder victims were killed by their boyfriends or husbands; in contrast, men murder victims are killed by their girlfriends or wives only 3 percent of the time.[49]

Gender and sexual minorities or people who are gender nonconforming are also frequently targeted by violent men. The Human Rights Campaign—an organization that has been tracking the murder of people who are trans and gender nonconforming since 2013—reported that 2021 was the deadliest year on record.[50] By one estimate, trans women in the United States are more than four times more likely than other women to be killed.[51] Trans women of color are at the highest risk. In 2021, fully thirty-six of the forty trans women who were killed were non-White.

Such murders, and other forms of hostile sexism, are a result of men's homophobia and **misogyny**, or men's fear and hatred of women with power.[52] Though individual men commit these crimes, their violence is a *social* problem. It's the stubborn persistence of patriarchal ideas—the idea that women, feminine people, and others who violate gender rules should subordinate themselves to the gender binary and to the men on one side of it—that fuels aggrieved entitlement and the violence that comes with it.

(MIS)MANAGING HARM Some people believe that women can behave in ways that reduce their vulnerability to men's anger, but this is a form of **victim blaming**: identifying something done by victims as a cause of their victimization. In one study, even the volunteers at a domestic violence shelter often offered women's own behavior to explain what "set him off."[53] When we are the victim, we also often blame ourselves.

On college campuses, students sometimes accuse sexual assault victims of being "naive" or "stupid." "She somehow got, like, sexually assaulted," said one woman about an acquaintance who'd been victimized. "All I know is that kid [that raped her] was like bad news to start off with. So, I feel sorry for her but it wasn't much of a surprise for us. He's a shady character."[54] By suggesting that she and her friends knew better than to hang out with the perpetrator, she implies that information and social savvy can keep women safe.

For many of us, imagining that victims "must have done something" wrong or stupid gives us a false sense of security. And this comes at the expense of women's freedoms. As the journalist Laurie Penny put it:

> *What makes victim-blaming so insidious is that it isn't just about shifting the blame—it's about sending a message to anyone else who might be dumb enough to think they can do whatever that victim was doing and get away with it.*[55]

Being a "smart" woman means not being out after dark, making sure not to get too drunk, always keeping an eye on friends at parties, and never taking drinks from anyone. It also often means keeping her opinions to herself, lest they provoke men.

Exculpatory chauvinism also comes into play when we offer excuses for violent men that explain away or trivialize their behavior. We say the harm was not so bad or that he didn't mean it, that it was certainly a onetime thing or that he has already suffered enough. The philosopher Kate Manne coined the word "himpathy" to describe the outsize sympathy often granted to violent men—a phenomenon observed especially when the man in question is well known or otherwise powerful.[56]

Himpathy was on full display when Christine Blasey Ford and Brett Kavanaugh both testified in front of the US Congress in 2018.[57] Kavanaugh had been nominated to serve a lifetime term as a Supreme Court justice, prompting Blasey Ford to go public with an allegation of sexual assault against Kavanaugh. In the hearing, she testified to an incident in which Kavanaugh and his friend laughed while they trapped her in a bedroom at a party, turned up the music, pinned her down, groped her, and ground against her. They tried to pull off her clothes and covered her mouth when she tried to scream. Blasey Ford was fifteen years old; Kavanaugh was seventeen.

Reflecting himpathy, much of the media coverage of the hearings centered on Kavanaugh's feelings rather than Blasey Ford's, framing the hearing itself as the traumatic event, not the assault. Himpathy was detected, too, in commentary that tried to explain Kavanaugh's behavior as something typical of teenage boys. "Tell me," said one man who was interviewed about the hearing, "What boy *hasn't* done this in high school?"[58] Journalist Bari Weiss expressed himpathy when she suggested that having his behavior "paraded out in front of the country" was "a horrible reality" for him.[59] For sure. But what about Christine Blasey Ford's horrible reality? It's good to have sympathy for others; himpathy is excess sympathy for Kavanaugh at Blasey Ford's expense.

Like exculpatory chauvinism, himpathy deflects our attention from the fact that men's violence is a social problem. So does the social construction of women's bodies as weaker and more fragile than men's.[60] Women are often presumed to be inherently vulnerable to and helpless in the face of men's violence. This idea is often internalized by women and reinforced in those interactions with men, where subjecting women to sexually objectifying gazes and touching them without permission brings no negative consequences. Consequently, women often feel like they're incapable of fighting off men's violence.

Even women who were assigned male at birth often come to believe this. Interviews with trans women show that most learn to embody a sense of physical vulnerability as they transition.[61] Trans women, like cis women, are more likely than cis men to be subject to sexually objectifying gazes and touched without permission. Meanwhile, adopting feminine fashions—heels that shorten and unbalance their stride and skirts that restrict how they bend and sit—reduces how powerful a person can feel in their own body. A trans woman named Rebecca, for example, said the following when asked if she walks alone at night:

> *I just don't do it. I used to when I was a man. Yeah, I'd be anywhere I wanted to. I didn't fear anything but as a woman, yeah, I'm very cautious. . . . Because we are victims. We're the type of person that other people prey upon because we're the weaker sex, so to speak.*[62]

Despite being socialized as men and being, on average, taller than cis women, trans women often come to feel similarly vulnerable.

But neither trans nor cis women are powerless in the face of men's violence. Maneuvers that take little strength can often bring an attempted assault to an end: a thumb to the eye socket, a punch to the throat, an elbow to the nose, a quick kick to the knee cap, or a twist of the testicles.[63] Research has shown that hollering, fighting back, or fleeing reduces the likelihood of a completed rape by 81 percent, without increasing the severity of injuries sustained by victims.[64] Women don't always recognize this power because forces in our culture go to great lengths to keep it from them.

Part of the struggle is helping women embrace the idea that they can be loud, strong, angry, or dangerous. This is a challenge even in one of the most gender-egalitarian countries in the world: Sweden. Kindergarten teachers there are now actively and effectively teaching girls how to yell. The goal is to counter the gender-stereotypical socialization the kids are getting elsewhere. Boys, then, are being taught to give massages, and girls are being told to "throw open the window and scream."[65]

How we as individuals manage men's violence will vary. The collective challenge is to change societies that normalize and elicit it. Until then, conventional femininity offers only a choice between victim (helpless but protected by benevolent sexists) or pariah (powerful but punished by hostile ones), while victim blaming and himpathy undermine efforts to place the blame where it belongs.

Bargaining with Patriarchy

Though women have choices about how to do femininity, and options for mixing in masculinity, they're still subject to rules and restrictions when it comes to their gender performances. Women make patriarchal bargains, as men do, in an effort to maximize their autonomy, safety, and well-being in the face of sexism, androcentrism, and subordination. Men are presented with essentially one kind of bargain: adopt hegemonic masculinity as much as they can, or accept low status in the masculine hierarchy. Women, though, can choose among three types of bargains.

One bargain involves trading one's own attainment of power for the protection and support of a man. This bargain involves performing **emphasized femininity**, an exaggerated form of conventional femininity "oriented to accommodating the interests and desires of men."[66] Women who adopt this strategy do so in exchange for the support of a man who will share his privilege with her. Stay-at-home moms, for example, have struck this patriarchal bargain. They stay family focused as part of a gendered economic deal. They provide unpaid work in the home for their husbands and children. In turn, they expect their husbands to share their income and its benefits.

Aspiring models who work the high-end party circuit in the United States are making a slightly different patriarchal bargain. Adopting emphasized femininity, they work as nonsexual companions to very wealthy men.[67] The women get designer clothes, gourmet meals, and luxury trips in exchange for performing a femininity that makes men feel attractive and important. Likewise, in high-end clubs in Vietnam, corporate men hire beautiful women to smooth their negotiations with clients.[68] In some cases, a woman doing emphasized femininity may become a rich man's wife. In exchange for financial support, these women promise to keep their bodies taut, their clothes flattering, and their hair and faces attractive. The man has a lovely companion, then, to appreciate and display.

To this day, Marilyn Monroe remains an icon of emphasized femininity.

The family-focused wife and the lovely companion are making similar patriarchal bargains. In both cases, women's performances of emphasized femininity contribute to men's relative status, help men succeed economically, and enhance men's quality of life. Notably, neither raising kids nor being beautiful pays the rent, ensures a comfortable retirement, or makes women's voices heard. Instead, such women have traded the direct attainment of their *own* power for the indirect attainment of *his*. These are risky bargains, even for privileged women. What upper-class men have to offer (money and status) are universally desirable goods and likely build over their lifetimes, whereas the bargaining position of women who adopt emphasized femininity inevitably weakens as beauty fades and kids grow up.

Many women decide it's safer to make a different bargain. Women with ambitions to enter professions occupied primarily by men may be able to position themselves as "one of the guys" and thus directly receive some of the benefits that come with being a man. This strategy is **emphatic sameness**.

Najiah Knight is an example of a young woman doing emphatic sameness. At ten years old, this Native American of Paiute ancestry became the first girl to join the Mini Bull Riders circuit (in which young children ride eight-hundred-pound "mini" bulls). At fourteen, she became the first to ride a bull in Madison Square Garden and the first Mini Bull Rider of any gender to earn a corporate sponsorship. Asked if it felt strange to be the only girl on the circuit, she replied: "Yeah, but I kind of earned the boys' respect the first year I competed, because I ended up on some of the rankest bulls."[69] In her spare time, Knight works out and plays sports. "I'm not really into makeup and that kind of stuff," she revealed.[70] And her fashion sense is 100 percent cowboy.

So far, Knight's strategy of emphatic sameness is mostly working out for her. "Sometimes you feel like you're just part of the boys. Like, you don't feel any different and they just accept you," she told a reporter. "But sometimes they'll be like, 'So I can't get beat by a girl.' But, you know, you just gotta show him who's boss."[71]

Many women do emphatic sameness, downplaying the feminine in themselves in exchange for the right to do quite a bit of masculinity. These women may declare majors associated with men, make sports a central part of their

Adopting a gender strategy known as emphatic sameness, bull rider Najiah Knight greets the crowd in jeans, chaps, and a cowboy hat.

lives, and dress in baggy clothes and baseball hats. They may identify as tomboys and distance themselves from other women. This is one way some women gain power in a society that values masculinity.

This bargain has limits, though. First, this strategy is possible only in masculine arenas in which men have agreed to tolerate the presence of women who are very successful in the performance of masculinity. Everyone in military school, for instance, is doing a specific kind of masculinity. That's how all cadets are taught to fit in and succeed. In such a context, the requirement that women balance masculinity with femininity may be relaxed, at least some of the time.

Second, emphatic sameness ultimately harms women—even those who perform it—because it depends on the denigration of femininity in general. The majority of women who do emphatic sameness reject femininity but are still understood to be women. Accordingly, the expectation remains that they'll reveal their intrinsic femininity at some point—when they start dating, for example, if they plan to date men; or, in certain circumstances, like when they attend dressy events; or when they become mothers, unless they are lucky enough to have a family-focused partner.

Moreover, this bargain reinforces the idea that women and girly stuff are trivial and worthless. So emphatic sameness undermines attempts to empower women *collectively*, even if it allows some individual women to have more power than they would otherwise. Notice that the most successful women (surgeons, judges, politicians) usually rely on a team of less advantaged women (housekeepers, nannies, nurses, secretaries). The woman who becomes a neurosurgeon, tech entrepreneur, or engineer may have achieved a level of prestige usually reserved for a man, but she does so like a man, on the backs of women who do devalued, still-feminized work on her behalf.

Most women don't do either emphasized femininity or emphatic sameness consistently. In different contexts or times of their lives, they may strike different bargains. They alternate between masculinity and femininity in accordance with the third patriarchal bargain, **gender equivocation**, using masculinity and femininity strategically when either is useful and culturally expected.

This was the case, for example, for a group of young women studied by sociologist Nikki Jones.[72] These women were all enrolled in a violence-intervention project located in a low-income, mostly Black neighborhood of Philadelphia. Living in violent neighborhoods, the women had developed strategies for both doing gender and staying safe. Like their men peers, they were willing to fight to protect their reputation but also understood that sometimes there was advantage in performing femininity.

Jones documents a young woman, Kiara, collecting signatures for a neighborhood petition. She approached strangers assertively to discuss the petition, strategically drawing on both feminine flirtation and masculine argumentation to get signatures. She would flirt with acquaintances walking by but then defiantly criticize the police as they passed the station. She was, she said, "aggressive for the streets" but "pretty for the pictures."[73] When it came to her gender performance, Kiara equivocated, using whichever strategy provided the best bargain at the moment.

These patriarchal bargains—emphasized femininity, emphatic sameness, and gender equivocation—are not equally available to every woman. The women studied by Jones largely didn't have the option to choose emphasized femininity; their Tough Gal strategy was an acknowledgment that fighting "like a man" was sometimes necessary. Likewise, the ability for any woman to perform emphasized femininity to land a rich husband depends in part on their particular body and face. Not everyone is born with a conventionally attractive, physically able body that they can train to be slim and graceful. It helps to have some money to start with too. Conversely, some women may not have the temperament to be a family-focused parent or the ambition or opportunity to pursue a demanding career. Most women aim to find a bargain that seems practical and potentially rewarding, even if not ideal.

No matter what bargain women make, however, there is always a cost. This state of affairs is called a **double bind**, a situation in which cultural expectations are contradictory, making success unattainable. Satisfying only one or the other expectation inevitably means failure, and it's impossible to do both. In the case of women in contemporary societies, the double bind refers to the idea that to be powerful is to fail as a woman, and to succeed as a woman is to give up power.

Women can and do fall from grace in either direction. We see this phenomenon, for example, in sports. South African Olympic sprinter Caster Semenya is an example of a woman who was attacked for doing too little femininity, whereas tennis player Anna Kournikova is an example of an athlete who did too much. Semenya's body, fast races, and refusal to do femininity both on and off the track led to an investigation of her biological sex that upended her career. Under this pressure, she submitted to a public makeover—a last-ditch attempt at a feminine apologetic—but the dresses and hairstyles ultimately failed to protect her.[74]

In contrast, Kournikova's successful embodiment of femininity pushed her out of her tennis career and into modeling. Today, she is frequently mocked as one of the worst professional athletes of all time; the fact that she was once ranked eighth in the world is eclipsed by her sex appeal. She still frequently graces the covers of men's magazines.

Backlash against women politicians also often reflects the double bind. Women candidates have some ability to gender equivocate on the campaign trail, but this bargain doesn't necessarily help them.[75] On the one hand, women are criticized for being insufficiently feminine. In 2012, Park Geun-hye, a candidate for president of South Korea, was accused of having "no femininity" because she hadn't had children and therefore hadn't been "agonizing over childbirth, child-

Caster Semenya's astonishingly fast times on the track and disinterest in performing gender while she raced prompted World Athletics to investigate her biological sex. Her makeover for *You* magazine (*right*) was an effort to assure others of her femininity.

care, education, and grocery prices."[76] Similar charges were made of Julia Gillard, former prime minister of Australia, and Angela Merkel, the former chancellor of Germany.[77]

On the other hand, if women candidates do emphasized femininity, this tends to hurt them too.[78] Consider the treatment of Sarah Palin, the Republican nominee for vice president in 2008.[79] On the campaign, she kept her hair long, wore stylish clothes that hugged her body, and maintained a cheerful demeanor. Commentators gushed over her attractiveness, saying that she was "by far the best-looking woman ever to rise to such heights" and "the first indisputably fertile female to dare to dance with the big dogs."

But they also pejoratively called her "girlish," compared her to a "naughty librarian," and dubbed her "Caribou Barbie." A pundit for CNBC claimed that she was politically successful only because "men want to mate with her." It wasn't long before she became a joke to much of America, inspiring look-alike stripper contests in Las Vegas. While Palin certainly had her faults, her downfall was also distinctly gendered.

On a national stage, how could an ambitious woman politician possibly strike a balance between masculinity and femininity that pleases everyone? Voters tolerate some kinds of balances but not others, and the balances they tolerate differ across regions: among the cities, suburbs, and countryside; up and down the class ladder; and along the political spectrum, among other divides. Under these circumstances, women politicians can never escape the double bind.

Women, like men, make patriarchal bargains to maximize their autonomy and well-being. Men face substantially tighter restrictions than women, but the bargains available to them—while fewer than those available to women—offer greater rewards. Women enjoy more flexibility because there are more socially endorsed strategies for them to use, but no matter what bargains women make, the outcomes are not in their favor.

CAN FEMININITY BE HEGEMONIC?

Scholars disagree.

Some argue that it cannot.[80] Recall that the hegemonic man embodies all the traits valued in an ideal *person*, such that both men and women are encouraged to emulate him. Scholars who are a "no" on the idea of a hegemonic femininity conclude that feminine traits and activities are seen as desirable *only* for women. If this is so, women will always be seen as women first and people second.

Opponents of the idea also observe, and rightly, that there's no straight-forwardly advantageous patriarchal bargain for women. Women politicians, for example, won't ever be able to strike just the "right" balance because there's no version of femininity that has almost universal endorsement. There's always a double bind. Hence, no single type of femininity can sit neatly atop a hierarchy of women in the same way that hegemonic masculinity sits atop a hierarchy of men.

Other scholars argue that an intersectional lens allows a hegemonic feminin-ity to come into view. They see hegemonic femininity as a type of feminine per-formance, idealized by people of all kinds, that encourages consent to multiple forms of inequality.[81] By definition, the women who best approximate hegemonic femininity are advantaged on all other axes of oppression. So, like the hegemonic man, the hegemonic woman is White, wealthy, fit, conventionally attractive, het-erosexual, cisgender, and so on. She is also a similarly impossible fiction. She's fashionable, alarmingly thin, and sexually alluring to men. She's sexually free but not a slut. She's unattainable but also the "girl next door." She gets a good educa-tion and builds a thriving career. She marries a successful and attractive man and becomes a conscientious mother to his children and a volunteer in her community.

Proponents of the idea of a hegemonic femininity argue that women who attempt to approximate it inevitably uphold rather than challenge other forms of inequality. This is because the process of accessing the advantages that come with having privileged identities is itself gendered. That is, for women, the only way to access the advantages of Whiteness is to do White femininity. Likewise, the only way to access the advantages of heterosexuality is to do heterofemininity. The same is true for all axes of oppression. Most women lean into at least some of the advantages they carry. In doing so, their femininities are affirmations of racism, heterosexism, and more.

Disagreement as to whether there's a hegemonic femininity reveals that gender studies scholars are still working hard to understand why and how gender inequality persists, especially in relation to other forms of inequality. Below, the final section summarizes the fundamentals, starting with a definition of the f-word.

THE BIG PICTURE

From the earliest democratic revolutions, when the idea of equal rights inspired resistance to tyranny, people have been actively challenging the basis, logic, and fairness of patriarchal ideas and practices. Today, those people are called feminists. **Feminism**, most simply, is the belief that all men and women should have equal rights and opportunities. The word was borrowed from the French in the late 1800s, when many women around the world were still the property of men by law. It has been used ever since to describe the variety of efforts to reduce women's disadvantage relative to men and free both men and women from oppressive gender practices and harmful stereotypes.

Today's feminism is increasingly intersectional. Intersectional feminists argue that a feminism that aspires only for women's equality with men is not really feminist because it leaves all other axes of oppression untouched, and that harms women.[82] To such feminists (including the two writing this text), feminism is a project that aims to tear down the entire **matrix of domination**, or the structure in which multiple hierarchies intersect to create a pyramid of privilege, leaving on top those people who are advantaged in every hierarchy.[83]

Do Americans still need feminism? Emphatically, yes.

The gap between women and men's pay and workplace participation narrowed substantially beginning in the 1960s, but it's barely budged since the mid-1990s (Figure 6.1).[84] Likewise, women's integration of well-paying white-collar occupations stalled out in the mid-1980s. Meanwhile, men have largely resisted entering previously women-dominated occupations, and it's rare for them to play supporting roles to wives' careers.

This state of affairs inspired scholars to argue that many countries, including the United States, are in the middle of a **stalled revolution**, a sweeping change in gender relations stuck halfway through.[85] Women have increasingly

FIGURE 6.1 | WORKPLACE PARTICIPATION RATE BY GENDER, 1972–2020

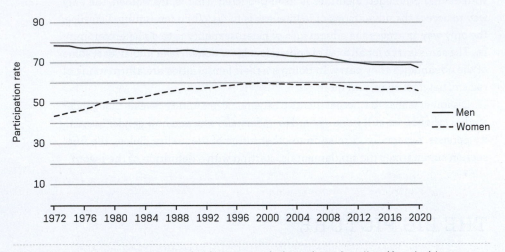

Source: US Bureau of Labor Statistics, "Women in the Labor Force: A Databook," March 2022, https://www.bls.gov/opub/reports
/womens-databook/2021/home.htm.

embraced opportunities to enter masculine arenas, but few men have moved toward feminine ones. This new gender order hurts both men and women but differently: Men suffer more *as individuals*; women are harmed more *categorically*.

Men are harmed as individuals because hegemonic masculinity pushes them to obey its imperatives. Even as sexism has declined, androcentric attitudes have gotten stronger.[86] This has increased the pressure many men feel to conform to a narrow range of acceptable masculinities. This restricts men's lives, asking them to destroy or hide parts of themselves that don't fit the hegemonic model. As a result, they have fewer life options than women do.

Some men find this oppressive; others don't, but not because it isn't a form of repression. It's just that, for many men, there are worse things than being boxed into valued and rewarded roles in society. A lot of men aren't that upset, it turns out, by being told they shouldn't do something they learned to not want to do, concluding that it's okay to leave high heels, dirty diapers, and salads to women. In other words, *masculinity is oppression dressed up as superiority*.

Whether gender rules for men feel oppressive will depend on how well men's intersectional identities position them to reap patriarchy's rewards.[87] Many men— perhaps even most men—are unable to reap these rewards to the extent they feel they should. They may take this failure personally. Some of these men die "deaths of despair," ones caused by addiction, overdose, or suicide.[88] Other men may respond with aggrieved entitlement, angry at the possibility that men's power is slipping away. And entitlement breeds violence.

Our gender regime is terrible, then, for the mental and physical health of many men. But it's not because men aren't advantaged over women. The playing field remains tilted by sexism, androcentrism, and subordination. Whatever suffering ensues, men as a whole still benefit. Men face less pressure to defer to others, sacrifice their own needs, or bother with things we've learned to belittle. They are free to grab brazenly for power, act on self-interest, and mobilize support from other men for their success. Theirs is the face of power, even if some individual men feel quite powerless.

In contrast, women benefit from the greater flexibility that modified patriarchy affords them as individuals. But collectively, women are harmed by the costs that sexism, androcentrism, and subordination still impose on women. Women who face disadvantages other than gender will find that their oppression is multifaceted. They may also find that they have fewer opportunities to make patriarchal bargains or that the deals they can make with patriarchy are substantially less advantageous.

But all women, regardless of whether they enjoy other privileges, still must contend with the risk of assault and the possibility of becoming a pariah. All their diverse strategies are fitted within the boundaries of gender inequality. Collective costs include facing benevolent and hostile sexism, being hamstrung by the double bind, relying on men for safety and support, and being channeled toward devalued, subordinating, and sexualized gender performances.

Revisiting the Question

Q+A **If both men and women are constrained by a binary gender system, why is it that more women than men find this system unfair?**

The gender binary isn't just about difference; it's about hierarchy. The masculine side of the binary is presumed to be not just different but *better than* the feminine side. And most of us have internalized this idea, at least a little, learning to see men and masculine people as more valuable and impressive than women and feminine people.

As a result, girls and women are generally encouraged to mix a little masculinity into their personality and enter leisure activities and occupations previously reserved for men. In fact, women's eagerness to incorporate masculinity is proof of femininity's low value. In hindsight, one of the reasons women have been so keen to embrace masculinity is because it feels good to be seen as better than the women who do not.

Yet all women must do at least some femininity, and when they do, they'll be performing a devalued identity. As individuals, women can resist these

mechanisms of oppression by deftly doing masculinity and strategically appro-
priating masculine roles. Some women will do so spectacularly, rising to the corner offices of the biggest companies and powerful positions in our government.
But women collectively will not be on an equal footing with men because men
aren't required by virtue of their gender to perform powerlessness and deference.

This is why women, more so than men, have fought to dismantle patriarchy.
It's also why the word *feminism*, and not *humanism*, has come to represent the
movement, though today feminism aims to draw more attention to the diverse
ways that gender affects everyone. Today, the goals of feminism include freeing
individual men from repressive gender rules, giving women the choices patriarchy denies them, reconsidering the ways masculinity expresses value and
power, and challenging the gender binary itself.

Likewise, feminism today involves challenging every axis of all our societies'
intersecting oppressions: racism, colorism, ableism, heterosexism, class inequality, and prejudices based on religion, immigration status, cognitive difference,
physical size, mental health, and more. The real story about gender and power
isn't a simple one about women's disadvantage, then, but a complicated one that
reveals the costs that a hierarchical gender binary imposes on the vast majority
of us. Gender inequality is one significant part of the wider matrix of domination. Feminism refers to all the gender-aware efforts to dismantle this system.

Next . . .

Thus far this book has discussed the social construction of gender in our ideas,
the policing of gendered performances in interaction, and intersectional patriarchal power relations. These are all very powerful forces. But what about free
will, self-determination, and personal initiative? We're a free country, after all—
isn't it still possible to reject the gender binary; ignore what other people say;
refuse to accept or enact sexism, androcentrism, and subordination; and live a
life free of all this gender stuff, even if that means paying some social costs?
Why can't we just give up male privilege or live as a pariah? That line of inquiry
leads to the next chapter:

 **When it comes down to it, regardless of social
construction and social pressure, don't we live in a
society in which it's possible to just be an individual?**

It turns out, no.

FOR FURTHER READING

Britton, Dana M., Shannon K. Jacobsen, and Grace E. Howard. *The Gender of Crime.* New York: Rowman & Littlefield, 2017.

Brownmiller, Susan. *Femininity.* New York: Open Road, 2013.

Glick, Peter, and Susan Fiske. "An Ambivalent Alliance: Hostile and Benevolent Sexism as Complementary Justifications for Gender Inequality." *American Psychologist* 56, no. 2 (2001): 109–18.

Halberstam, Jack. *Female Masculinity.* Durham, NC: Duke University Press, 2018.

Hamilton, Laura, Elizabeth A. Armstrong, Lotus Seeley, and Elizabeth M. Armstrong. "Hegemonic Femininities and Intersectional Domination." *Sociological Theory* 37, no. 4 (2019): 315–41.

Jenness, Valerie, and Sarah Fenstermaker. "Forty Years after Brownmiller: Prisons for Men, Transgender Inmates, and the Rape of the Feminine." *Gender & Society* 30, no. 1 (2015): 14–29.

Mears, Ashley. *Very Important People: Beauty and Status in the Global Party Circuit.* Princeton, NJ: Princeton University Press, 2020.

Schippers, Mimi. "Recovering the Feminine Other: Femininity, Masculinity, and Gender Hegemony." *Theory & Society* 36, no. 1 (2007): 85–102.

NOTHING IS POSSIBLE WITHOUT
MEN, BUT NOTHING LASTS
WITHOUT INSTITUTIONS.

—JEAN MONNET[1]

Institutions

Thus far we've talked about looking through gender binary glasses, learning gender rules, and performing gender. We've also talked about how we're held accountable to gender rules and how this produces gendered inequality as well as gender difference. Finally, we've considered how people get away with breaking gender rules and form communities that support the gender rules they prefer. All this makes it seem like no matter how pervasive the gender binary lens and how strong the pressure to do gender, an individual *can* make the difficult decision to do gender however they want or not at all. In other words:

Q+A **When it comes down to it, regardless of social construction and social pressure, don't we live in a society in which it's possible to just be an individual?**

The answer to this question is, in fact, no. Gender is a set of ideas and something one does when interacting with other people, but it's also an organizing principle that permeates our social institutions. Because ideas about gender shape the environments in which we live, these ideas exert an influence on our lives independent of our own beliefs, personalities, and interactions. It's simply not true that if we reject the gender binary as individuals, and refuse to be held accountable to gender rules, we'll be free of gender. Gender—and gender inequality too—is part of the fabric of our lives.

This chapter starts by introducing the idea of the institution, then discusses how institutions are gendered in ways that reproduce both difference and inequality.

THE ORGANIZATION OF DAILY LIFE

Most schools in the United States—from kindergarten to college—take a three-month break during the summer. Most kids enjoy the break without asking why, but there's a reason we do it this way. Not a natural reason, but a social one.

Before the late 1800s, urban schools met year-round, but rural schools met for only six months.[2] They let students off to help on their families' farms. Later, urban schools introduced a summer break; that was when the wealthy liked to travel, and also, before the invention of air conditioning, schools were oppressively hot and stuffy during those months. As education became more important and fewer kids were growing up on farms, rural schools increased the length of their abbreviated school year to match that of urban schools. Our precious summer vacation was born.

Summer vacation has a history, but today we mostly just accept that this is how things are done. It's now part of how Americans "do" school, one of countless policies, rules, traditions, and habits that guide kindergarten through twelfth grade education. Altogether, those practices make American education an **institution**, a persistent pattern of social interaction aimed at meeting a need of a society that can't easily be met by individuals alone. The institution of education strives to give children the information and skills they'll need to be productive workers and responsible citizens. This would be difficult or impossible for today's parents, who generally don't have the knowledge, the know-how, or the time to teach their kids themselves. In response, we take on education collectively, creating a systematic way to achieve the goal of an educated citizenry.

Carefully organized and controlled by individual states, the institution of education in the United States dictates the when, where, and how of teaching: the standards, curricula, and credentials students and teachers are held to; occasions for enacting them (like the first day of school, graduation, field trips, and snow days); and teachers' unions that negotiate with districts and states to determine pay. The institution of education involves organizations: primary and secondary schools, colleges, and universities as well as federal and state departments of education, private and charter schools, and companies (like those offering the

American high school students toss their caps to celebrate completing one stage of education as institutionalized in the United States.

SAT, ACT, and other tests, as well as test-prep courses). There are also commonly accepted routines (like parents helping with homework, organizing carpools, and holding fundraising events) and spectacles (like swim meets, senior prom, and graduation).

For the most part, these organizations and routines (like summer vacation) are taken for granted as just what school is like. In this sense, much of how we achieve institutionalized tasks is simply normative. **Norms** are beliefs and practices that are well known, widely followed, and culturally approved (like back-to-school shopping trips). Conformity with institutionalized ways of doing things is also secured with formal **policies**, which are explicit and codified expectations, often with stated consequences for deviance (like rules related to attendance). Many policies elaborate on and reinforce norms, transforming common sense into regulations (like no cheating on tests); some policies explicitly are intended to override and change beliefs and practices (like the rule against texting in class). Some policies are contentious: school dress codes or sex education curricula, for example. Some norms and policies are strongly enforced, while others are enforced only weakly.

Because institutions are about *collectively* meeting the needs of individuals, they're very different from the social forces we've discussed so far. We can try to get cultural ideas we don't like out of our brains, surround ourselves with people who support our personal choices, and accept whatever consequences come with breaking social rules, but it's essentially impossible to avoid institutions. They impose themselves on our lives.

If we didn't have a stay-at-home parent or guardian, or one who was a teacher, for example, our summer vacation was likely inconvenient or expensive. Child-care during those months may have strained our family's budget, and, depending on our age, leaving us at home to fend for ourselves might have been criminal neglect. Yet the trouble it may have caused our parents didn't make the institution magically transform. In this way, institutions affect our lives whether we like it or not. Our institutions are social inventions, but they are also nonnegotiable facts of life.

We can't just be an individual, then, because we're part of a society that's replete with institutions. Education is but one example. We also have institutions designed to promote global peace and prosperity (including, but not limited to, the United Nations, the World Health Organization, and Doctors Without Borders); defend the country (the military, the Central Intelligence Agency, the US Department of Homeland Security); keep citizens safe from violent crime (neighborhood watch programs, prisons, law enforcement, the judiciary); enable transportation (airlines, public buses and trains, road construction, highway patrol, waterways); promote social welfare (food-stamp programs and Social Security, psychiatric institutions, child social services); raise the next generation (schools, camps, youth groups, and families); deliver and monitor health care (the US Centers for Disease Control and Prevention and state health departments, hospitals, insurance companies, the American Medical Association); promote the national economy (regulations on printing money, incorporating businesses, borrowing and lending, insuring property); entertain, inform, and make life meaningful (newspapers, organized religion, professional sports, art, the film industry); and shape the overall conditions of life and the future of our societies (advocacy organizations, labor unions, nonprofit groups, political parties, and legislative bodies).

These are all institutions. Together, they form the **social structure**: the entire set of interlocked institutions within which we live our lives. We call it a "structure" because institutions, in concert, create a relatively stable *scaffolding*. If we want to be a doctor, for instance, we know we have to go to college and then medical school. The path, or structure, already exists. We know we're expected to follow it, and we trust that a medical degree will still be a requirement to begin a career in medicine when we finish our schooling eight or more years later. In this way, the stability of institutions, and the relationships among them, provide a framework that enables us to make rational decisions about our future. Structures are essential because they help us know what we wish to accomplish and provide guidelines for doing so.

And yet the social structure is also a source of constraint. Social structures often make differences into consequential distinctions, providing a scaffold that offers an unequal mix of access and barriers to people who are differently equipped. Sometimes climbing the scaffolding requires resources we don't have. If we can't afford the combination of tuition, time, and dedicated attention to go to college, for example, we won't get into medical school. It won't matter how much medical knowledge and experience we amass on our own; we'll still be criminals if we practice without a license.

Institutions aren't always convenient or fair, but there's no opting out. We can condemn state and federal governments as incompetent and corrupt, become an anarchist, and stay home on Election Day, but Congress is still going to pass laws to which we'll be held accountable. And if we break the law and get caught, we'll face legal penalties even if we personally object to the law. We live in, through, and with institutions. By shaping our opportunities, they shape our lives. And they do this in gendered ways.

GENDERED INSTITUTIONS

A **gendered institution** is one in which gender is used as an organizing principle. In a gendered institution, men and women are channeled into different, and often differently valued, social spaces or activities, and their choices have different and often unequal consequences.

Education, for example, isn't just an institution; it's a gendered institution. Education is gendered with both policies and norms. Policies like gendered honorifics for teachers ("Mr." and "Ms."), gender-specific dress codes (like skirts for girls but not boys), and gender-segregated classes (such as separate sex education units), make gender an organizing principle of schooling. Meanwhile, informal norms make gender part of the routine practice of school. There is no policy requiring that girls populate the monkey bars and boys populate the sports fields at recess, for instance, but that's often how kids distribute themselves.[3]

While many American elementary school playgrounds feature this kind of "geography of gender," gender is less important in other parts of the school or at other times of day.[4] In elementary-school classrooms, for example, students are usually seated alphabetically or in other ways conducive to an orderly classroom, not according to gender. Kindergarten play kitchens may be more gendered than nap time. In high school, AP Calculus may be more gendered than Algebra I. In other words, **gender salience**—the relevance of gender across contexts, activities, and spaces—rises and falls across the different parts of the institutional landscape.

Gender is a persistent, if uneven, feature of education, making education a gendered institution. When new students arrive, they're inserted into this already-existing system. The system is reproduced and enforced by a collection of others who assign esteem and stigma, or success and failure, according to how well new students follow or otherwise contend with existing gendered norms and policies.

If you, an intrepid first grader, were to arrive at one of these schools, you would quickly learn when and how gender was important. You could then choose whether to conform or deviate, but you *would* contend with it one way or another. You would also contend with how your other identities—your class, ability, sexual orientation, gender presentation, and more—intersected with your gender. Together, these features would determine how policies and norms applied to you.

Gendered institutions are interesting sociologically because they affirm and enforce both gender difference and inequality. And they do so intersectionally. In this way, inequalities are *institutionalized*, meaning that they are produced and reproduced by the routine functioning of our institutions. When people talk about "structural racism," "structural sexism," or any other structured inequality, this is the phenomenon to which they're referring.

THE INSTITUTIONALIZATION OF GENDER DIFFERENCE

This section elaborates on how institutions institutionalize gender difference. It does so with an intimate example: our plumbing.

A Room of Her Own

In most parts of the world today, public sanitation is an institution, and thank goodness. It would be impossible for every individual in a complex society to build and maintain a personal toilet in every location where they might find themselves, so providing a safe and sanitary way to eliminate personal waste is a social task. Without sanitary institutions, our daily lives would include routine exposure to both the act and product of urination and defecation, including the diseases that humans harbor in bodily fluids. In fact, around 10 percent of the world's population lives without public sanitation.[5]

Where you live, however, you likely benefit from a sewer system that quietly and invisibly whisks human waste to treatment plants where it's variably burned, hauled off to landfills, given to farmers, or released back into the water supply. Aboveground, sanitation policies ensure the provision of bathroom facilities in workplaces, schools, restaurants, department stores, government build-

When middle-class White women first entered the workforce, workplaces provided "rest rooms." The idea that such women couldn't work without taking frequent breaks protected the gender binary notion that women were more fragile than men.

ings, airports, and elsewhere. We typically find men's and women's rooms in these locations, requiring us to pick one or the other. This makes public sanitation a gendered institution.

The idea that men and women should have separate bathroom facilities emerged during the late 1800s. During that era, women and men were first brought together as workers in factories. The idea of men and women working side by side on the factory floor threatened to upset cherished Victorian beliefs about the differences between them. One such belief was that women were more fragile than men and therefore less suited to working for pay. Reflecting this belief, the US Department of Labor reported in 1913 that a "woman's body is unable to withstand strains, fatigues, and deprivations as well as a man's."[6]

As a solution, a study recommended the provision of "rest or emergency rooms" on the assumption that women were "likely to have sudden attacks of dizziness, fainting or other symptoms of illness."[7] The word *restroom* emerged from this recommendation. These were small private rooms with a bed or chair available to women workers struck by some sudden feminine malady. Their presence reasserted women's fragility, easing the threat that women's presence in the workplace posed to the Victorian gender ideology.

Women's restrooms served a second purpose too. Employers placed them between the factory floor and the women's toilets so that women had to pass through them on their way to the bathroom. Whenever a woman went into the restroom, then, men could pretend she was just going to *rest*; they could be in happy denial that women ever went in to *poop*. In other words, gender-segregated bathrooms, with the restroom as a buffer, allowed Victorian women to carefully conceal any sign of bodily functions and allowed men to pretend that women never used the bathroom at all.

The idea caught on. In 1887, Massachusetts enacted the first law mandating gender-segregated toilets.[8] By 1920, forty-three states had followed suit. Today, every state in the United States requires the provision of separate bathrooms for men and women in every public building and private business with a minimum amount of foot traffic.[9] And the occasional women's bathroom still provides a couch or chairs upon which women can rest.

Gender and Bathrooms Today

Gender segregation of toilet facilities has become a powerful norm, if an increasingly contested one. Even if we think it's silly, most of us use the "correct" bathroom in public if at all possible. This is often true even when the bathrooms in question are standalone rooms with a single toilet and a door that locks. Accordingly, most women have likely found themselves waiting patiently in line to use the proper toilet while the one designated for men sits empty.

Notably, if there *isn't* a single stick figure on the door, we use the same bathroom as someone of the other gender without hesitation. This is true in many smaller businesses and workplaces with only one bathroom. It's also true on airplanes. The bathrooms at the back of the plane *could* be designated for men or women, but out of a concern that passengers get back to their seats as soon as possible, they aren't. Men and women also use the same bathrooms at home. Having men's and women's bathrooms in your house would be a novelty, a gag. Everyone knows it's completely unnecessary.

Just as in the Victorian era, then, today's gender-segregated bathrooms serve *social*, not biological, functions. Most people don't think that women need a fainting couch within arm's reach, but different bathrooms continue to allow women to keep "unladylike" bodily functions away from men. Likewise, gendered bathrooms allow women to do body work that's supposed to remain invisible; when done in public, fixing one's hair, smoothing one's clothes, checking for blemishes, and reapplying lipstick all reveal to the viewer that appearing effortlessly feminine requires a lot of effort. To a lesser extent, the same is true for men.

Gendering public bathrooms also reinforces heteronormativity. This separation assumes, for example, that there's a need to protect our private parts from people of the other gender but not of the same gender. That our bathrooms are not planned with same-gender desire in mind is obvious when we consider that men's rooms are often designed with the expectation that men will expose their penises to one another when urinating.

And, of course, gender-segregated bathrooms uphold the gender binary. This creates challenges for people who are nonbinary or in transition, as well as people whose gender doesn't come across clearly to others. "Encounters in public rest rooms are an adventure," writes Betsy Lucal, the sociologist we discussed earlier who is often misgendered.[10] Lucal has a set of strategies she uses to avoid stares, uncomfortable questions, and confrontations:

> If I must use a public rest room, I try to make myself look as nonthreatening as possible. I do not wear a hat, and I try to rearrange my clothing to make my breasts more obvious. . . . While in the rest room, I never make eye contact, and I get in and out as quickly as possible. Going in with a woman friend also is helpful; her presence legitimizes my own.[11]

While trans, gender-fluid, and ambiguous-appearing individuals like Lucal can be significantly inconvenienced by gender-segregated bathrooms, the binary approach to sanitation can cause everyone problems from time to time, like when we really have to go and there's a long line for one bathroom but not the other. Or when we're trying to help a child or elderly person of the other gender use a public toilet. Or even when we're just stuck waiting because a friend of the other gender faces a line and we don't. Providing gender-neutral bathrooms is often described as an institutional policy that would help nonbinary people, but it would actually help all kinds of people.

Nonetheless, in the past decade, the politics of bathrooms have increasingly become a topic of public debate. Americans are divided about equally as to whether they support laws protecting trans people's rights in the bathroom.[12] Currently, US federal law does not protect people's rights to use the bathroom of their choice.[13] In 2021, President Joe Biden issued an executive order aimed at preventing discrimination based on gender identity and sexual orientation. Likewise, the US Department of Labor recommends that trans employees be granted access to bathrooms consistent with their gender. These, however, are guidelines, not law.

Forty-four states, plus Washington, DC, have laws against discrimination based on sex. Some interpret these laws as prohibiting not just discrimination against men or women but also discrimination against people who identify as trans, nonbinary, or gender fluid. Seventeen states and more than two hundred cities and counties have institutionalized this interpretation, making it illegal to force people to use the bathroom consistent with the sex they were assigned at birth.[14] Many airports, sports arenas, and other large facilities have added "family bathrooms" or gender-neutral "disabled" ones, which offer a way around the gender binary.

Other states, mostly in the South, have passed or considered bills restricting bathroom rights. These are often justified with the argument that trans people are dangerous to women and children (but, notably, not to men). Tennessee, for example, passed a law in 2021 requiring businesses to post signs if they let trans people use the bathroom of their choice.

These kinds of laws are nothing new: There is a long history in the United States of justifying rules around bathroom use by appealing to the vulnerability of (White) women and girls. In fact, this was the argument made against desegregating bathrooms by race. In the 1940s, the specter of race-integrated bathrooms was used to argue against racial integration and the rights of Black Americans more generally.[15] Opponents of integration pointed out that it would mean the end of White-only bathrooms. This, they falsely claimed, would put White women at risk of dangerous diseases carried by Black women. A few decades later, in the 1970s, fearmongering about bathrooms helped sink the Equal Rights Amendment to the US Constitution.[16] Today, it's supposedly trans women who are the threat. The details have changed, but the strategy is the same.

Sanitation is an example of a gendered institution, one that enforces gender difference. Institutions, though, do more than reflect the gender binary, as harmful as that can be. They also contribute to gender inequality. To illustrate how, the next section turns to an institution many of us first encounter on the playground: sports.

THE INSTITUTIONALIZATION OF GENDER INEQUALITY

How individuals experience sports varies tremendously. Some find it intimidating; some, exhilarating. Some shrink from the competition, while others come alive under pressure. Some of us are blessed with strong and graceful bodies that bound, bend, and twist, but others of us struggle to gain quickness, coordination, and endurance. We all have to work harder at this as we get older and our bodies become less spry.

Regardless of whether we like sports, they're part of an institution that shapes our experiences. Little Leagues and after-school programs are complex organizations that engage children in sports in prescribed ways. Once American children start school, they may be required to take physical education classes that teach certain sports but not others. Schools are also sites where team play and competition are taught and encouraged. Our teams need opponents with whom to have matches, bouts, or games, so other schools nearby also need to

The aerial view of a high school in Idaho is a testament to the infrastructure required to support the institutionalization of popular American sports.

field teams for the same sports. The space and equipment requirements for various sports—tracks, courts, fields, balls, bats, mitts, and sticks—are provided by schools and city and state parks departments and are manufactured and sold by companies for profit.

In the United States, colleges and universities also allocate money, space, and time to athletics. Colleges have relationships with middle and high schools that funnel talented students to their campuses. They do so not just because sports are entertaining but because they bring attention and revenue. Successful or otherwise beloved teams bring public exposure and potential alumni dollars. The mass media follow certain college sports, making games lucrative for some colleges. Companies, in turn, can count on televised or streaming sporting events to find audiences to whom they can advertise their goods and services. Regulatory bodies, such as the National Collegiate Athletic Association (NCAA), define the rewards that sports can offer to athletes and the standards of the competition.

In fact, the entire economy benefits from the institution of sport. In the United States in 2020, sales of sporting goods exceeded $96 billion.[17] The year before the Covid-19 pandemic temporarily tanked revenues, Major League Baseball and the National Football League (the two most lucrative sports in the United States) earned $11 billion and $16 billion, respectively.[18] The US sports industry, put together, is worth $420 billion.[19] Individuals who profit—a list too vast to compile here but one that includes not just owners, athletes, merchandisers, and marketing executives but also cashiers, janitors, vendors, ticket takers, sports journalists, and owners and employees of nearby souvenir shops, hotels, bars, and restaurants—are all invested in the industry. Meanwhile, there are a vast infrastructure (stadiums, arenas, tracks) and media empire (an ever-multiplying number of ESPN channels and other sports networks).

Sport is an impressive behemoth of an institution. It's also strongly gendered, making it an institution that despite having changed dramatically in the past several decades continues to establish a hierarchy among men and demonstrate women's supposed inferiority.

Separating the Men from the Boys

One of the first recreational physical activities taken up by women was bicycling. It was the 1890s, and it changed women's lives.[20] Bicycles made women mobile, enabling them to travel miles from their homes. Bicycles required lighter garments with fewer restrictions of movement, inspiring changes in the norms of women's dress. "Let me tell you what I think of bicycling," said the women's rights activist Susan B. Anthony. "I think it has done more to emancipate women than anything else in the world. I stand and rejoice every time I see a woman ride by on a wheel."[21] Bicycles gave women *freedom*.

People didn't like it.

Doctors warned that women were unfit for exertion, claiming that riding bikes would cause headaches, heart trouble, depression, insomnia, and exhaustion.[22] They said women who rode bikes might get "bicycle face," a possibly permanent clenching of the jaw and bulging of the eyes caused by strain. Bicycling caused women to be flushed or pale, and grimacing but weary. The activity should be reserved, the doctors insisted, for men.

Women didn't listen. They rode bikes and, in the next one hundred years, would progressively risk their faces and put their bodies to the test, integrating sport after sport. Today, millions of women around the world play sports, though they often still face resistance. "Convincing my dad [to let me skate]," said the six-time X Games gold medalist skateboarder Letícia Bufoni, "was harder than getting to the Olympics."[23]

Her father's reservations reveal that many sports are still considered masculine, even when women are allowed to participate.[24] Sports are part of a boy's basic "manhood training."[25] They epitomize masculinity, such that thinking, watching, and talking about sports is a central way in which men perform their gender.[26] A boy's first plush toy may be a soccer ball; their first T-shirt may feature a baseball and bat. A boy's first memories of bonding with his father may involve watching football on TV or playing T-ball in the backyard. Informal

Even though women like X Games gold medalist Letícia Bufoni have taken the sport to great heights, skateboarding is still considered a masculine pursuit.

games in the neighborhood may transition into Little League and then participation on school-based teams. Not surprisingly, most boys get involved with sports at some level.

Because sports are so strongly associated with masculinity, excelling in them is one way for young boys to show they're "big boys" and, later, "real men." Sports, though, don't simply offer boys and men an avenue through which to claim esteem; they slot individual boys and men into the hierarchy of masculinity. Recall that sociologist Michael Messner described his decision to embrace sports as his first "engagement with hegemonic masculinity," a moment in which he accepted that he would have to belittle other men if he was to ascend the hierarchy.[27] Importantly, he notes that sports aren't just about individual accomplishment; they're also about competition: "It is being better than the other guys— *beating them*—that is the key to acceptance."[28] As Messner argues, sport "serves partly to socialize boys and young men to hierarchical, competitive, and aggressive values."[29] While some men excel, others fail.

Most men eventually focus their energies elsewhere. As men recognize that it's unlikely they'll become professional athletes, many turn their attention to education, careers outside of athletics, or the daily rhythms of raising a family. But the institution of sport will likely continue to play a symbolic role in their lives. Some men trade the physical competition for a more passive consumption of televised sports and sports news. Men cheer for their respective teams on flat-screen

TVs, engaging in friendly trash-talking. They jostle for relative position by owning better paraphernalia, holding season tickets with better seats, knowing sports history and statistics more thoroughly, and, of course, bragging when their team wins. It's a culture-wide, feel-good, male-bonding extravaganza, one that retains a competitive aspect. And men who aren't interested in sports suffer many of the same disadvantages as men who don't play well.

No matter that most men aren't especially impressive athletes themselves. Because they're men, even couch potatoes can point to the game and claim they share something important and meaningful with Kevin Durant, Patrick Mahomes, or Cristiano Ronaldo.[30] As one man said: "A woman can do the same job I can do—maybe even be my boss. But I'll be damned if she can go on the football field and take a hit!"[31] Of course, the vast majority of men couldn't "take a hit" either, but that's beside the point. Instead, sports like football serve as a *cultural* testament to the idea that no matter what happens, men are something women are not.

A Team of Her Own

Most Americans will agree that men are naturally better athletes by virtue of their size and strength. But the truth is that our culture specifically prizes sports that emphasize the few physical advantages men have over women. We even go so far as to define physical activities in which women outperform men as not sports at all.

In an alternative reality, we could imagine a world of sports that worships the physical skills the average woman performs better than the average man. The philosopher Jane English tried such a thought experiment, pondering:

> Speed, size, and strength seem to be the essence of sports. Women are naturally inferior at "sports" so conceived. But if women had been the historically dominant sex, our concept of sport would no doubt have evolved differently. Competitions emphasizing flexibility, balance, strength, timing, and small size might dominate Sunday afternoon television.[32]

In English's thought experiment, basketball and football are replaced by gymnastics and horseback riding, with nonstop coverage of long-distance marksmanship and billions of dollars spent on dance competitions.

This is not our world. Instead, media coverage of sports keeps a raw, grimacing, bulging, powerful man's body front and center.[33] It's no accident, argues Messner, that the most popular sports in America are also ones based on what he terms "the most extreme possibilities of the male body."[34] Using American football as an example, he explains:

Gymnastics is exceptionally athletic and offers feats of strength and skill, but it is not a prized and well-rewarded part of US sports culture.

Football . . . is clearly a world apart from women. . . . In contrast to the bare and vulnerable bodies of the cheerleaders, the armored male bodies of the football players are elevated to mythical status, and as such, give testimony to the undeniable "fact" that there is at least one place where men are clearly superior to women.[35]

The bodies of these professional athletes serve as icons of masculine physical achievement. In this way, the symbolic link between the male spectator and the male athlete establishes men's supposed superiority over women.

On the assumption that women are lesser athletes than men, the institution of sport segregates women and men in almost all cases. This is true even when there is little reason to expect that men's and women's bodies give them differing advantages, as in the case of skateboarding.[36] Almost all team sports ensure that men and women never compete with or against one another. Likewise, individual sports like long-distance running, swimming, and ski jumping usually do not put men and women in direct competition. They even rank records separately. (There are some exceptions: Equestrianism, NASCAR, and synchronized swimming are gender integrated, and the 2020 Tokyo Olympics introduced nine new mixed-gender events in which men and women compete together on the same team.)

Both those on the political left and political right tend to think sports should be segregated by gender, given the assumption that men are stronger, faster, and bigger than women. If women played with or against men, it is argued, they'd get hurt; if they competed against men, they'd lose; and if they tried out for the same team, they'd get cut. Accordingly, gender-segregated teams are supported by both conservatives who think women are more fragile than men and liberals who want women to have the same opportunities.

Sorting by gender, however, also organizes sports in ways that affirm cultural beliefs in gender difference and inequality. The next section explores two ways gender segregation is used to affirm a hierarchical gender binary.

Different but Equal?

First, sorting allows us to require—with both policies and norms—that men and women play the same sports in different ways. Both women and men play hockey, for instance, but whereas men are allowed to "check" (body slam) one another, it's against the rules for women to do so and is punishable with penalties. Likewise, tackle football is the province of "real men"; women (and "lesser men") are allowed to play "flag" (also sometimes called "powder puff") football. At the Olympics, women competitors in BMX, or bicycle motocross, ride a shorter course with less difficult obstacles than their men counterparts do; the same is true for women who compete in slalom, downhill, and cross-country skiing.[37] In the case of baseball, women are sorted into softball, a related but different game with its own equipment and rules.

These differing policies—especially those that forbid women to be as physically aggressive or take on the same challenges—mean that women and men are required to do sports both differently and unequally, with women doing a lesser version. This way, whether women and girls *could* play or ride the way men and boys do remains an open question. The rules ensure that we'll never know.

Different artistic expectations for men and women athletes, sometimes encoded in judging guidelines, also create sports that reinforce beliefs about men's and women's talents and abilities. Writing about the feminine apologetic in figure skating, sociologist Abigail Feder keenly observed that one of a woman skater's most useful talents is the ability to disguise the incredible athleticism required and instead make it look effortless.[38] Whereas men who figure skate are valued for appearing powerful and aggressive on the ice, the judging norms for women frown upon this. Instead of athleticism, an ability to look beautiful and graceful is valued in women. The woman skater is supposed to look serene and at rest, no matter that she is launching herself into the air at twenty miles an hour or rotating so quickly through a flying sit-spin that she might give herself a nosebleed.

Bodybuilding is on the flip side of the gender binary but has the same gendered expectations. Judges are instructed to evaluate men only on how muscular they are but to judge women on both their muscle development and their femininity.[39] The International Federation of Bodybuilding and Fitness, the organization that sets the rules for judging competitions and serves as the gateway to the Mr. and Ms. Olympia competitions, slots women into divisions that limit accumulation of muscle mass: "bikini fitness," "fit model," and "wellness fitness" (some of which have parallel men's divisions and some of which do not).[40]

In these competitions, women can be penalized for being "too big." One judge confessed to a bodybuilder who had taken a disappointing eighth place: "As a bodybuilder you were the best, but in a *women's* bodybuilding competition I just felt that I couldn't vote for you."[41] In 2005, the federation officially requested that women bodybuilders reduce their muscle mass by 20 percent. In 2015, the federation ended the Ms. Olympia competition altogether.

The examples of figure skating and bodybuilding show that separating women and men allows us to require that even the most elite of athletic performances conform to gendered expectations. It's circular logic: The idea that men and women have fundamentally different physical abilities is used to institutionalize policies that ensure women and men don't participate in the same sports in the same way. And because they don't, we can easily go on believing that men and women have fundamentally different physical abilities.

Who Loses if Women Compete with Men?

A second way gender segregation in sports protects a belief in the hierarchical gender binary is by ensuring that men and women never compete against one another. But whom does this protect? On the assumption that women would always come in second to men, it might seem like gender segregation protects women, giving them a "chance." And maybe that's true for some individual women. But if we zoom out, it becomes clear that it's men, not women, who benefit from gender-segregated sports.

Segregation allows the assumption that men outperform women to go untested. If we integrated sports, this assumption would be put to the test repeatedly. In those tests, if women always lost, it would only maintain the status quo; we already think they're inferior athletes. But if men lost, the status quo would be upended. They wouldn't lose only the competition; they'd also lose the presumption of male superiority.

This is Messner's argument. Reflecting on his own experience in elementary school, he writes:

> *The best athlete in my classes never got to play with us. She was a girl. Somehow we*
> *boys all knew that she was the fastest runner, could hit a baseball further than any*
> *of us, yet we never had to confront that reality directly. Our teachers, by enforcing*
> *strict sex segregation on the playground, protected our fragile male egos from the*
> *humiliation that presumably would result from losing to a girl.*[42]

Many young boys and their parents intuit this. In 2011, a high school threatened to forfeit a junior varsity football game unless a girl on the opposing team sat out.[43] Mina Johnson, a five-foot-two-inch 172-pound linebacker, had "gain[ed] a reputation in the league as a standout junior varsity player"; she sacked a six-foot quarterback in her very first game. Nevertheless, not wanting to be the cause of a lost opportunity for her team, she agreed not to play. The opposing team still lost—60 to 0, in fact—but apparently that was less humiliating than losing to a girl.

In 2017, high school golfer Emily Nash competed alongside boys in the Central Massachusetts Division III Boys Tournament.[44] She was allowed to play as a member of the team because her school didn't have a girls' golf team. But because it was otherwise a boys-only tournament, her individual scores didn't count. So even though she had the best tournament-wide score, beating every other boy on every team, the first-place trophy went to the boy runner-up. Still, by virtue of just being able to play, the message came through loud and clear: *Sometimes girls beat boys.*

What does gender segregation in sports do? It protects boys and men. As one mother of a boy wrestler put it: It's "unfair for girls to compete against boys. . . . [It puts boys] in a no-win situation. . . . If he wins, it's just a girl, and if he loses, his life is over."[45] It's important to be empathetic to the experiences of boys in a world characterized by sexism and androcentrism, but unfair? Hardly. It's extra humiliating to lose to a girl only because we've already decided that girls *should* lose.

Still, we might object, doesn't segregating sports by gender give girls and women an opportunity to play that they might otherwise not have? Not really. Gender is neither a necessary nor logical way to organize sports and make competitions fair.[46] Any justification for this criterion is based on using gender as an imprecise substitute for better variables: height, weight, or athletic ability.

Consider wrestling, the sport causing such angst for mothers of sons. Traditionally, wrestling matches have been organized by weight class. People in the same weight class, considered equally paired, wrestle each other. The relevant characteristic here isn't gender at all—it's weight. So men and women of the same weight class should be considered good competitors.

Using this logic, girls and women have been pressing coaches to allow them to wrestle and have been joining previously all-boy high school wrestling teams since the 1990s. In 2006, Michaela Hutchison from Alaska became the first girl

Two high school students compete in a 131-pound match. Girls' wrestling is one of the fastest-growing sports in the United States, spurred in part by the introduction of women to Olympic wrestling in 2004.

to win a state high school mixed-gender wrestling championship.[47] She wasn't the last. Today, there are thousands of girl wrestlers on teams.

Basketball could also be organized according to size and skill instead of gender. Instead of gender-segregated teams, you could separate teams into taller and shorter players. Tall women could play with tall men and shorter men and women could play together. Or, alternatively, we could set up mixed-gender teams and then sort them into "fair play" leagues by average height and relative successes. Then agility, speed, and shooting skill could be more directly compared, with all teams competing for the players who have what they need.

The same logic applies to American football, where being big and heavy is an advantage in several positions. Women are almost entirely excluded from football on the logic that they're too small to play. But most men are also too small to play football. Having two or more teams organized by size would give everyone a chance to play: men, women, and other folks too. People of all sizes could opt into flag teams, too, giving anyone who wanted to avoid the known risks of concussions the opportunity to join.

Or, if the issue is ability, why not divide up competition that way? Footraces are already organized according to qualifying times, so why is it necessary to further break them down by gender? If we desegregated these gendered sports, the top ranks of many might be disproportionately populated by cis men, but they would also likely be disproportionately populated by the young, people with opportunities to train, and other variables that predict talent and the ability to develop skills. We let the chips fall where they may.

We could do the same with gender. Beginning in 2012, Lindsey Vonn, one of the most decorated skiers of all time, started asking international ski racing officials for permission to enter men's races. She trained alongside men and often had better times than them. Maybe she wouldn't win as often if she competed against men. "But," she said, "I would like to at least have the opportunity to try."[48] She never did get that opportunity. The officials denied her request all the way to her retirement in 2019.

Vonn might be right. If we organized sports by weight, height, skill, or qualifying times, women like her might be less likely than men to rise to the top of some sports. Still, it'd be much more difficult to claim that women are too small, weak, slow, or fragile to compete with men *at all*. Some women would outperform even some of the best men, as is already the case. If we allowed this fact to become clear, the belief that women are lesser athletes than men would be much more difficult to justify. Meanwhile, we'd open sports to everyone: men and women of all shapes and sizes, along with people who have historically been excluded from gender-binary sports almost entirely: trans men, trans women, nonbinary folks, and people known to be intersex.

We might even come to question whether the "top" leagues with competitors with the most extreme body types are the most interesting ones to watch. Football played without a premium on huge bodies or basketball played by teams of people with average heights might look more exciting than the leagues that are valued merely because they are "men's" and thus presumed to be "the best." Hockey fans often speak admiringly of the excellent stick work of the women's teams and, with more assists and fewer dunks, women's basketball showcases an impressive cooperation that better reflects the sport's roots. Some men might fit in better in these leagues, and more fans might turn to them, if only they weren't disparaged by being marked as "women's."

Gender-integrated sports would also help ensure that women get paid what they're worth. Segregated sports make it possible to justify paying women less than men. Given the sexist assumption that women are inferior athletes, media companies don't feature women athletes as often or as prominently as men. As a result, prize monies and salaries for men far exceed those for women. In 2021, for example, the *average* salary for players in the Women's National Basketball Association (WNBA) was about $121,000. Meanwhile, the *minimum* salary for National Basketball Association (NBA) athletes was $582,000. The *average* salary for players in the NBA was $7.7 million. We see this huge discrepancy even after the women of the WNBA won a historic salary increase in a collective bargaining agreement in 2020. All told, only two women made the 2021 *Forbes* list of the one hundred highest-paid athletes: Serena Williams and Naomi Osaka.[49] The other ninety-eight were men.

Sports salaries don't simply reflect economic reality, nor are they tied merely to levels of athleticism. Consider a study of salaries in professional golfing by sport management professor Todd Crosset. He found that men golfers outperform women golfers on average, but these differences are, all things considered, very small.[50] Both sets of golfers are remarkably dedicated, skilled, and talented. To Crosset, the vast differences in prize money—nearly $400 million for the men's Professional Golf Association Tour, compared to just over $73 million for the Ladies Professional Golf Association Tour—largely reflect the "social significance" of men and women in athletics, not their respective athleticism.[51]

Sports fans, he explains, often argue that men's sports get more support and attention because men are better athletes. But, he counters:

> If it was truly skill that fans were going to see, how can we explain the lack of fan support for women's college teams that could easily handle boys' high school teams, which draw more fans. Quite simply, sports have more significance for men regardless of skill level.[52]

It's sexism that drives the unequal attention and rewards that accrue to men and women in sports, and institutionalized gender segregation is the foundation on which unequal attention and rewards rest.

The policies and norms of gender segregation make sports an institutional arena in which beliefs in difference and inequality are routinely and ritualistically rehearsed. This is part of the institution of sport, one we can opt into or out of but can't ignore. If we want to be athletes, we have to play by these rules. If we're a girl and we want to play baseball, we're up against more than the discomfort that sometimes comes with breaking gender rules and the policing that follows. We're also confronted by the fact that there isn't a girls' baseball team at our school. And if there *were*, who would we play? Girls' baseball teams haven't been institutionalized and it takes a community to field an entire league.

INSTITUTIONAL INERTIA AND CHANGE

As individuals, we may wish to change or ignore the institutions we confront, but this is far more difficult with institutions than it is with ideas or social interactions. Institutions are more resistant to change and more difficult to ignore because institutional patterns reflect widespread norms that are often encoded in formal policy. A return trip to the restroom offers a case study.

Sociologist Harvey Molotch was part of a failed effort to install a gender-neutral bathroom during the renovation of a space designed for the New York University Department of Social and Cultural Analysis.[53] While the department included trans faculty members who might benefit from a gender-neutral bathroom and other faculty members intrigued by the opportunity to push gender boundaries, they nevertheless ended up with conventionally segregated toilets. Why?

The first reason was related to inconvenience and expense. Contractors and designers are intimately familiar with the design requirements of gender-segregated bathrooms, making the installation of integrated ones a new challenge. Sitting down to design a new kind of bathroom takes time, and this is expensive. The administration was reluctant to draw out the process and spend extra money on a brand-new restroom design. It was cheaper and faster to rely on the tried-and-true approach. Molotch writes:

> Everyone "knows" what a building restroom should be like. . . . To innovate means going back to the drawing boards, rethinking architectural opportunities and constraints, and checking continuously to make sure everyone is aware of the plan now being implemented. This is a hassle, one with financial implications and new potentials for error. . . . Working through details of restroom innovation was an extra, one that burdened an already crowded agenda.[54]

The second reason the initiative failed had to do with the discomfort institutionalized in city policy. The New York City Department of Buildings requires all large new buildings to install gender-segregated facilities, so the university had to submit a petition for an exemption. The city turned them down. The university appealed but lost. The building commissioner expressed "concerns about security and liability."[55]

Molotch's hopes for change were crushed.

As this example shows, doing things differently can be challenging on multiple fronts. This isn't to say that institutions can't be changed, but changing them requires a *collective* shift in norms and routines. Sometimes this simply means a slow but steady disinvestment in the old ways, as when school and workplace dress codes began to allow girls and women to wear pants. Other times, institutions change in response to shifts in the broader social structure, as when women entered the workforce during World War II.

Sometimes change is a result of the work of activists and politicians. It was this kind of work that resulted in the passage of Title IX, an amendment to the Civil Rights Act of 1964, which states, "No person in the United States shall, on the basis of sex, be excluded from participation in, be denied the benefits of, or be subjected to discrimination under any education program or activity receiving Federal financial assistance."[56] Passed in 1972, Title IX meant that schools and colleges receiving federal funding could not legally give preference to men. Instead, they had to allocate their resources to men and women in proportion to their interest and enrollment.

Here is where sports come back in. The intention of Title IX was to change the norms that gave preference to men across the board, from medical school enrollment to Greek life. Because most schools and colleges have extensive athletics departments, sports were included among the resources that schools were required to dole out fairly. Eventually, even grudging and partial compliance with the requirements of Title IX dramatically increased the opportunity for women to play sports (Figure 7.1). In the fifty-plus years since the passage of Title IX, the number of athletes climbed more than tenfold among high school girls and more than threefold among college women. Today, 43 percent of high school athletes and 44 percent of college athletes are women.[57]

The changes in the institution of sport are visible in baseball. When Kay Johnston wanted to play Little League in 1950, she cut off her braids, put on her brother's clothes, and signed up under the name "Tubby." She made the team, but when she was found out, the national organization instituted a formal policy forbidding girls from playing.[58]

FIGURE 7.1 | PARTICIPATION IN NCAA CHAMPIONSHIP SPORTS

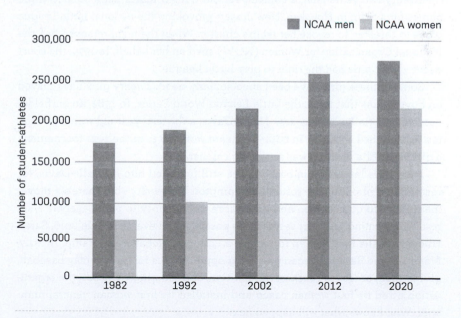

Source: NCAA Sports Sponsorship and Participation Rates Database, accessed January 10, 2022, https://www.ncaa.org/about/resources/research/ncaa-sports-sponsorship-and-participation-rates-database

Mo'ne Davis made the cover of *Sports Illustrated* for her Little League World Series shutout. Seen in the middle of what might be a 70 mph pitch, Davis is an example of what girls and women can do when given the opportunity.

Twenty-two years later, a twelve-year-old named Maria Pepe pitched three games for a team in Hoboken, New Jersey, provoking the national Little League office to threaten to revoke her team's charter. When the team removed her, the National Organization for Women (NOW) sued on her behalf. In 1974, the court decided that girls had the right to play Little League.

Some of these girls have been spectacularly good. Twenty girls have played on boys' teams that made the Little League World Series. In 1982, an outfielder named Victoria Roche was first. Mo'ne Davis, a thirteen-year-old with a 70 mph fastball, pitched a shutout in 2014—her team won 4 to 0. In the 2021 tournament, a girl name Ella Bruning was a starting catcher.

Most girls interested in baseball are still funneled into softball—Davis, for instance, went on to play softball at Hampton University—but there's a movement afoot to give women and girls more opportunity to play baseball. As a result, integrating the sport seems more possible than ever before. In 2016, Sarah Hudek was the first woman to receive a college baseball scholarship. In 2017, Major League Baseball began providing opportunities for girls to play baseball, giving them access to coaches, competition, and scouting.[59] In 2021, the organization hired its first woman coach and installed its first woman general manager. Who knows what will happen next.

The remarkable increase in the number of women playing sports—from Little League to Major League—reveals the power of institutions to shape the experiences of individuals and change social ideas. New policies allowing women to play will shift norms, making the idea that women are biologically fated to lose to men seem increasingly unreasonable. Though we've got a long way to go, we've also come a long way from the idea that women are so weak they need a room to rest.

Institutions often resist change, but they are not unchangeable. When even a minority of people recognize that institutionalized practices are cultural, not natural and inevitable, they create opportunities for themselves and others who want to do things differently. This isn't always easy, but it's always possible. And institutions never change unless people—like you—begin to question them. Taking chances and bucking expectations may not lead anywhere in your lifetime—both Kay "Tubby" Johnston and Maria Pepe were booted out of Little League—but over time a few rocks can become a landslide. In any moment, one never knows what small acts of defiance are making history, but one thing is for sure: History will be made.

Alyssa Nakken made history in 2020 when she became the first full-time woman coach in Major League Baseball.

Revisiting the Question

Q+A **When it comes down to it, regardless of social construction and social pressure, don't we live in a society in which it's possible to just be an individual?**

When someone is so focused on the details that they miss the big picture, they're sometimes told they can't see the forest for the trees. Each tree is a unique individual well worth understanding, but together they form a landscape and an ecosystem that's equally important to understand. Thinking in terms of institutions requires us to zoom out and look at the forest in which we live.

To understand gender, we need to examine the institutional structures and persistent patterns of interaction that are *our* landscape and ecosystem. Because these structures and patterns sometimes present men and women with different opportunities and obstacles, they produce gender difference and inequality regardless of the inclinations or attitudes of the people who move through them. It's not possible, then, to just be an individual. Some things simply resist our personal beliefs and desires.

Once we recognize that some of the institutions we live with are strongly gendered, it becomes clear that, as sociologist Raewyn Connell once argued, there are "gender phenomena of major importance which simply cannot be grasped as properties of individuals."[60] Societies are bigger than the sum of their parts. Gender isn't just an individual phenomenon; it's an institutional one. These institutions present *real* opportunities and obstacles. Because institutions are designed to last, they prove hard to change. Policies will be stubbornly defended by those who benefit from them, and norms create habits and taken-for-granted expectations that are inherently sticky. Still, individuals working together absolutely can change societies—and they have.

Next . . .

By now you have a strong understanding of how sociologists theorize gender as a set of ideas, a relationship between our bodies and our societies, a series of ongoing actions and interactions, and multiple interconnected institutions. Together they form the **gender order**, the social organization of gender relations in a society. The gender order is pervasive, expanding horizontally to affect all dimensions of a society and vertically to shape everything from the individual to the whole society. It intersects with other social hierarchies, establishing a matrix of domination that includes and inflects other inequalities beyond gendered ones.

You've gained a set of theoretical tools to help you better understand what's going on around you and how your participation both affirms and disrupts gendered ideas, interactions, and institutions. The next part of this book takes a different approach. Using the theory you now know, it takes a closer look at some important parts of life: sexuality, family, the workplace, and politics. Before talking about where we are, however, it's helpful to talk about how we got here. The next chapter picks up where this one left off, with the process and politics of social change.

FOR FURTHER READING

Berger, Peter, and Thomas Luckmann. "Society as Objective Reality." Sec. II in *The Social Construction of Reality: A Treatise on the Sociology of Knowledge*. Garden City, NY: Doubleday, 1966.

Britton, Dana. "Gendered Organizational Logic: Policy and Practice in Men's and Women's Prisons." *Gender & Society* 11, no. 6 (1997): 796–818.

Cooky, Cheryl, and Michael Messner. *No Slam Dunk: Gender, Sport, and the Unevenness of Social Change*. New Brunswick, NJ: Rutgers University Press, 2018.

Davis, Alexander. *Bathroom Battlegrounds: How Public Restrooms Shape the Gender Order*. Oakland, CA: University of California Press, 2020.

Johnson, Allan. "Patriarchy, the System: An It, Not a He, a Them, or an Us." Chap. 2 in *The Gender Knot: Unraveling Our Patriarchal Legacy*, 3rd ed. Philadelphia: Temple University Press, 2014.

Jones, Charlotte, and Jen Slater. "The Toilet Debate: Stalling Trans Possibilities and Defending 'Women's Protected Spaces.'" *Sociological Review* 68, no. 4 (2020): 834–51.

THE ONLY LASTING TRUTH
IS CHANGE.

—OCTAVIA BUTLER[1]

Change

We all know the scene. He gets down on one knee in a restaurant a tad above his price range. The ladies at the next table spy him kneeling. They clasp their hands to their chests and inhale. The room is suddenly hushed. All eyes turn toward the couple. Out pops the box. Her eyes widen and her bottom lashes moisten with the first sign of tears. He pushes out his arms, meaningfully pressing the box upward in her direction, imploring as he pulls back the velvety lid to reveal a glimmering dia ... The ladies lean in. A thimble!

The thimble is a small metal cap worn over the tip of one's finger to protect it from needle points. It was the engagement item of choice for early Americans and just one of many items that have served as a symbol of a commitment to marry.[2] Rings didn't become the standard sign of betrothal until the late 1800s. Diamond rings only became standard later still, in the 1930s. Despite the hype about how "diamonds are forever," the diamond engagement ring is less than one hundred years old, with no guarantee of lasting into the next millennia.

Marriage is an institution, and a socially constructed one. Today we think about marriage as a source of love, care, and commitment, but it was and continues to also be governed by informal norms and formal laws that determine the rights and responsibilities of spouses. Marriage is also a gendered institution. It used to be much more unequal, with substantially fewer rights for women. Diamonds, it turns out, haven't always been a girl's best friend.

Marriage has changed and is changing still. The same can be said for the other institutions addressed in this chapter: sexuality, family, and work. Like diamond rings, things that seem timeless are often recent and fragile inventions, including many of the things we take for granted as natural, normal, or inevitable today. This chapter offers a dynamic historical view of what often feel like static traditions. To begin, let's start with one undeniably transformative moment: the arrival of the Puritans on the rocky East Coast of the North American continent.

THE EVOLUTION OF SEX

The word *puritanical* refers to zealous adherence to extraordinarily strict religious or moral rules. It was named after the Puritans, and rightly so. They believed that sex should be restricted to intercourse in heterosexual marriage with the aim of reproduction. All nonmarital and nonreproductive sexual activities were forbidden, including pre- and extramarital sex, homosexual sex, masturbation, and oral or anal sex, even if married. Violations of the rules were punished by fines, whipping, public shaming, ostracism, or even death.

The Puritans believed women were more sexual than men, and thus especially vulnerable to sexual sin. Men were socially constructed as stalwart, strong, stoic, and self-disciplined. Certainly, they were concerned with more important things than sex! Described as a "weaker vessel," women were considered unstable, indulgent, and emotional, with "less mastery over [their] passions."[3] In their reading of the Bible, Eve succumbed to the forbidden fruit not because she was curious, but because she couldn't restrain her desire.

The Puritans were downright scandalized by the sexual lives of the Indigenous peoples of North America.[4] These Native peoples were organized into several hundred ethnolinguistic groups, so their practices and norms varied, but they were consistently more permissive than Europeans, including the zealous Puritans. As discussed in the last chapter, many Native communities accepted intercourse outside of committed relationships, practiced polygamy (the custom of having more than one marital partner), formed and dissolved unions at will, and accepted same-gender sex and gender identities outside the binary.

Indigenous Americans were also less anxious about paternity. After the arrival of the French in the early 1600s, one Naskapi man was warned by a missionary that his failure to police his wife's sexual activity might result in her being impregnated by another man. He responded: "You French people love only your own children, but we all love all the children of our tribe."[5]

Indigenous Americans could be rather nonchalant about paternity in part because they didn't subscribe to the idea of private property. This is typical of societies that migrate seasonally, foraging edible plants and hunting game across the landscape. Anthropologists and archaeologists have shown that both private property and patriarchy emerged together as societies transitioned from foraging to settled **agrarian** societies, ones that cultivate domesticated crops. Once communities put down roots, there can be ownership of land. Once there is ownership of land, there can be the consolidation of wealth. Once wealth is consolidated, people become concerned with passing it down to heirs. And when people are concerned with passing down wealth, it becomes important to make sure wives don't become pregnant with other men's babies. For these reasons, women's sexual freedom is often curtailed when societies transition from foraging to agrarian economies.

The White settlers who came from Europe in the 1600s were property-minded agrarians with very specific ideas about the function of sex. And when they arrived in North America, sex for reproduction was necessary for both survival and conquest.

Adherence to the Puritan moral code was often enforced by stringent punishments, such as being locked in stocks for the purpose of public humiliation.

Sex for Babies

Why *were* the Puritans so darn puritanical? It wasn't merely for cultural or religious reasons. As would-be settlers, they were attempting to replace the Native peoples and take their land.[6] Making baby colonists was essential to group survival, especially because so many of them were dying from exposure, starvation, illness, and war. So, the Puritans channeled their sex drive toward the one sexual activity that made babies: penile-vaginal intercourse. Having intercourse with your spouse was required and all other sexual activities were forbidden. Women who weren't getting pregnant were encouraged to divorce their husbands and marry new ones.[7]

The Puritans' population concerns also led them to be surprisingly forgiving when people broke the rules. Both ostracism and punishment by death harmed their efforts to grow the population, so the harsher penalties were rarely imposed. Fines and public shaming were more common. In other regions, settlers bent the rules for reasons related to the sex ratio. In the Chesapeake-area colonies, for example, men outnumbered women four to one.[8] Women were rare, so even a "disgraced" woman could count on a man being happy to have her. In fur-trading regions far from the agrarian colonies, groups of European men violently seized Native women for sex, and this, too, was accepted by the colonizers.[9]

In fact, when it worked in their favor, the colonizers forgave themselves their own sins, including killing and raping Native peoples. Moreover, they made it impossible for the Africans they enslaved to follow their rules, and then judged them for failing to do so. Enslaved people were legally denied the right to marry, making nonmarital sex and childbearing inevitable.[10] In a cruel twist, White elites would claim that "immorality" was "a natural inclination of the African race."[11] They used this lie as an excuse to rape the people they enslaved and force them to reproduce with one another. The colonists extolled godliness, but their practices were guided by the desire to dominate Africans and Indigenous peoples.

The colonists' sexual values and behaviors were shaped by an economy based on the exploitation and dehumanization of Africans and Native peoples. The Puritan belief in restricting sex to intercourse facilitated their need to reproduce themselves. When population numbers or wealth was at stake, though, they were happy to look the other way, forgive misdeeds, or even make following the rules impossible. Puritans surely earned their reputation for sexual repression, but beneath the strict rules were human beings who were fallible, rebellious, and brutally strategic.

Eventually the early colonizers' approaches to sexuality would fall victim to new and different institutional demands and opportunities: economic change, technological innovations, medical advances, and political upsets. One of those was the Industrial Revolution, and it transformed both Europe and the American continent.[12]

Sex for Love

Beginning in the 1700s and advancing through 1900, the Industrial Revolution first brought metal tools and steam-powered manufacturing, then factories, mechanization, and assembly lines. The need for labor drew many people out of small communities and into cities, where people were more densely packed and more anonymous. This was the beginning of an **industrial economy**, one dependent on the production of material goods intended for the market.

This was a dramatic change. In the pre-industrial agrarian societies of Europe and North America, the majority of people both lived and worked at home, whether on their own farms or those of feudal lords. Together, moms, dads, daughters, and sons grew crops and tended orchards, fed and slaughtered pigs and chickens, milked cows and churned butter, pickled vegetables and salted meat, and made things like soap, candles, and clothes from scratch. Everyone worked together to make what they needed to survive. Children were a necessity. Babies quickly grew up to be helpers and then farmhands.

Industrialization undid all of this. First, it separated work from home. No longer sitting on fertile land, people increasingly had to leave the house to "go to work" in factories, mines, and shops that belonged to others. In return, they received money, their **wage**, with which they would go out and buy the things they once made. The process by which goods transition from something a family provided for itself into something bought with a wage is called **commodification**: the making of something into a **commodity**, a thing that can be bought and sold.

In the era of tenement housing, large families in cramped quarters necessitated the storage of toddlers in wire cages attached to the windows.

Though useful on farms, kids were a burden in cities, where lodging was expensive and overcrowded. This gave couples an incentive to have fewer children. And because industrial production had made condoms increasingly cheap and effective, couples had the tools to limit family size.[13] Marital fertility rates dropped dramatically between 1800 and 1900: from 6 or more children per woman to 3.5 in the United States, England, and Wales.[14]

In this context, a sexual ethic that restricted sex to efforts to make babies didn't make sense. People needed a new logic to guide sexual activity.[15] In response, over the course of the 1800s, Victorians slowly abandoned the idea that sex was only for reproduction, embracing the now familiar idea that sex could be an expression of love.[16] The Romantic Era had arrived.

The Victorians also introduced the **gendered love/sex binary**, a projection of the gender binary onto the ideas of love and sex, such that women are believed to be motivated by love and men by sex.[17] Dualistic thinking about the opposition of body and soul meant that if women were more romantic than men, they were also less carnal.[18] Reversing earlier beliefs about women's voracious sexuality, the Victorians feminized love and masculinized sex.

Early feminists embraced these ideas. They advocated the notion that women took more naturally to both sexual moderation and romantic love. They thought it might elevate women's value in the eyes of their contemporaries. To attract and support women members, Protestant churches repeated these new stereotypes.

As this idea spread throughout Victorian society, women were re-imagined as *naturally* chaste, innocent of the vulgar sexual desires felt by men, and motivated by love instead of lust.[19] Men, in contrast, were believed to be more deeply tied to their bodies. This is when the idea of "opposite sexes" really took hold, as did the **sexual double standard**, different rules for the sexual behavior of men and women.

In fact, during the Victorian era, the idea that women were uninterested in sexual pleasure made it inconceivable that women felt for women what men felt for them. No matter how close women were, or what they did together, no one imagined it to be *sexual*. Out from under any suspicion of lesbianism, women formed intimate and romantic relationships with each other. Correspondence between women in the nineteenth century was full of language like the one found in this letter that Jeannie wrote to Sarah in 1864:

> *Dear darling Sarah! How I love you & how happy I have been! You are the joy of my life. . . . I cannot tell you how much happiness you gave me, nor how constantly it is all in my thoughts. . . . My darling how I long for the time when I shall see you. . . . Goodbye my dearest, dearest lover . . . A thousand kisses . . . I love you with my whole soul.*[20]

It sounded like friendship at the time. Maybe it was, but maybe not.

The Victorians sustained the illusion that women were free of sexual thoughts and men were dens of sexual depravity by giving men an outlet for their more perverse inclinations: prostitution. Early capitalism had worsened life for those at the bottom.[21] Prostitution was a way for poor women to support themselves and their families. At the same time, it functioned to protect "the virgin of the wealthier classes and shield their married women from the grosser passions of their husbands."[22] By one estimate, London alone was home to 8,600 prostitutes in the mid-1800s. Manhattan had one prostitute for every sixty-four men, and there was one for every thirty-nine and twenty-six men in Savannah, Georgia, and Norfolk, Virginia, respectively.[23]

Just as early colonists had used the (impossible to avoid) sexual transgressions of enslaved Africans as proof of their inferiority, Victorian intellectuals would champion the purity of middle- and upper-class women and scorn the "uncivilized" sexual behavior of poor women.[24] Today we know this as the **good girl/bad girl dichotomy**, the idea that women who behave themselves sexually are worthy of respect and women who don't are not. At the time, all these ideas were radically new (though the degradation of poor women and women of color was not). All this would continue to evolve as American society entered the 1920s.

Sex for Pleasure

The 1920s was a period of economic prosperity, technological innovation, and artistic experimentation. Americans call this decade the Roaring Twenties; in France it is called the *Années Folles*, or the "Crazy Years."[25] This era saw the invention of "sexy," literally; the word was first recorded to mean "sexually attractive" in 1923.[26] The '20s were sexy because, unlike the countryside, the city offered unsupervised mixed-gender mingling, flirtation, and romance.

With people concentrated in cities, commercial entertainment developed. Amusement parks catered to flirtatious young people, "nickelodeons" showed newly invented moving pictures with larger-than-life seductions, and burlesque clubs kept the morality police at bay with pasties and G-strings. In Harlem and other centers of African American life, high-end clubs featuring Black musicians attracted White patrons, encouraging racial integration and introducing them to a new form of music: jazz.[27]

Revelers danced the "hug me close" and the "hump-back rag" in dimly lit ballrooms where singers mastered the art of innuendo, singing "keep on churnin' till the butter come" and "it ain't the meat, it's the motion." *Not* songs about food. As historians John D'Emilio and Estelle Freedman wrote, "More and more of

During the 1920s, young people in Harlem and elsewhere began dancing the Charleston. It was the first time in American history that women in ballrooms danced independently from men.

A lipstick advertisement from the 1930s emphasizes women's efforts to "fascinate" men while also stressing how "natural" rather than "theatrical" or "painted" she would appear.

life, it seemed, was intent on keeping Americans in a state of constant sexual excitement."[28]

People in small communities, as well as in the upper classes, continued the Victorian tradition of "calling" in which young men were invited to the homes of young women for chaperoned visits. In cities, though, young working people invented "dating."[29] This wasn't dating as we know it today (an effort to find a romantic partner); it was a social strategy. In the interest of being seen and having fun, a successful dater would "go out" with a different person, preferably an attractive and well-regarded one, every night of the week.

Dating shifted the balance of power. Because calling took place in the home, women had substantial control over the activity. Women decided who came over and when, determined how young people socialized, and provided the snacks or entertainment of their choice. As historian Beth Bailey writes, dating "moved courtship out of the home and into the man's sphere."[30] Whereas advice books during the Victorian era strongly discouraged men from calling without being invited, advice books on dating scolded women who would dare "usurp the right of boys to choose their own dates."[31]

Part of the reason men were accorded such an exclusive right involved the expense. Unlike calling, dating required that someone pay for transportation, food, drink, and entertainment. With no equal-pay laws protecting women's wages, working women could barely afford rent; entertainment was an impossible luxury.[32] This was the basis for **treating**, a practice through which a man funds a woman's night on the town. One government vice investigator, horrified by this new development, reported, "Most of the girls quite frankly admit making 'dates' with strange men. . . . These 'dates' are made with no thought on the part of the girl beyond getting the good time which she cannot afford herself."[33] The owners of establishments, hoping to keep the customers coming, worked hard to convince the public that "treating" was not tantamount to prostitution.

The inequitable responsibility for the cost of dating was not lost on men. Some were resentful that women now expected men to pay for dates. Men were nostalgic for the good old days of calling, which cost them nothing. For their part, women tried to make themselves, literally, worth it. This meant being an attractive and pleasing companion.

Likewise, women began wearing makeup and nail polish, previously used only by sex workers. During the '20s an attractive face and body, as well as a certain degree of sexual accessibility, became more central to a woman's value. Claimed one ad:

The first duty of woman is to attract. It does not matter how clever or independent you may be, if you fail to influence the men you meet, consciously or unconsciously, you are not fulfilling your fundamental duty as a woman.[34]

Cosmetics industry profits increased more than eightfold in just ten years, from $17 million in sales to $141 million.[35]

There were ways in which the '20s created new potential for gender equality too. Women's growing freedom meant that men and women could mix socially and hold intimate conversations. Half of all women coming of age during the Roaring Twenties had premarital intercourse; being a virgin at marriage was beginning to seem quaint. For middle-class men, this freedom meant that they could have sex with women peers instead of with poor women, women they enslaved, sex workers, and each other. These changes brought both men and women pleasure and paved the way for more gender-egalitarian relationships. Many young people were excited by this development and liked the idea of finding a partner who would be a "soul mate," someone who brought them joy and happiness.

Still, sex remained dangerous for women. With birth control information limited by law and still condemned by most churches, 28 percent of women became pregnant before marriage, up from 10 percent in 1850, a rise seen disproportionately among the urban working class.[36] Without a community in place to force men to "do the right thing," and with abortion newly illegal (in all states but one by 1910), women in the '20s were more likely than those of earlier eras to have a child outside of marriage.[37] Since women were still paid wages much below men's, raising a child alone could lead to a lifetime of poverty, assuming the mother was not forced to hand over the child to an orphanage. In other words, while the era was a time of rising heterosexual opportunities, these opportunities came with huge costs to women.

Cities also made it possible for queer communities to emerge.[38] As early as 1908 it was reported that "certain smart clubs [we]re well known for their homosexual atmosphere."[39] No longer tied as tightly to family farms (where having large numbers of children was essential for survival), young people could consider putting their personal passions ahead of family responsibilities.[40] Cities offered anonymity that made same-gender relationships less risky and more rewarding.

In the 1920s, college girls breathlessly talked about girls on whom they were **smashing**, a term they used to describe a same-gender crush.[41] These crushes weren't all platonic. In a survey of 1,200 college graduates from the 1920s, 28 percent of women enrolled in single-gender schools reported that they had been in a sexual relationship with another woman, along with 20 percent of women at mixed-gender schools.[42] They would write letters to their mothers about it. No one thought it odd. So long as young women eventually married men, sexual and romantic relationships with other girls were considered harmless.

Queer culture gained mainstream appreciation too. In the 1920s and '30s, American cities hosted a "pansy craze." Songs with titles like "Let's All Be Fairies" (*not* a song about fairies) hit the mainstream charts. Patrons of all genders and sexualities flocked to widely publicized drag shows in both White and Black neighborhoods, taking delight in the bawdy humor and breaking of gender rules. "While dominant American society disapproved of LGBTQ people," wrote one commentator, "they were very fond of their parties."[43]

In sum, unmarried people could congregate without supervision in cities. This freedom altered the environment in which sexuality was experienced, as well as the norms for sexual behavior. Eventually the lifestyle first enjoyed by working-class youth in cities would become mainstream and the expression of same-gender desire would become increasingly normalized. With the exception of a short-lived detour in the 1950s, the sexual attitudes and behaviors of young people have become increasingly permissive ever since.[44] Marital practices have changed just as dramatically.

THE EVOLUTION OF MARRIAGE

For thousands of years, marriage served economic and political functions unrelated to love, happiness, or personal fulfillment.[45] Prior to the Victorian era, love was considered a trivial basis for marriage and a bad reason to marry. There were much bigger concerns afoot: gaining money and resources, building alliances between families, organizing the division of labor, and producing legitimate male heirs.

For the wealthy and, to some extent, the middle classes, marriage was important for maintaining and increasing the power of families. The concerns of the working classes were similar, if less grand: "Do I marry someone with fields near my fields?" "Will my prospective mate be approved by the neighbors and relatives on whom I depend?" "Would these in-laws be a help to our family or a hindrance?"[46] Marriages were typically arranged by older family members. They thought it foolish to leave something so important to the whims of young people.

These marriages were patriarchal in the original sense of the term. White men were heads of households and White women were human property, equivalent to children, enslaved peoples, and servants. A woman was entered into a marriage by her father, who owned her until he "gave her away" at the wedding. There are many stories in the Bible that reflect this culture of marriage. We call it **patriarch/property marriage**. The husband was the patriarch and his wife was his property.

This logic—that marriage is a form of property ownership—led to many laws that seem outrageous today. If an unmarried woman was raped, for instance, the main concern was the harm to her father's property. She became less valuable when she lost her virginity, so the rapist could make amends for the bad deed by marrying her. It was a "you break it, you buy it" rule.

A wife who was believed to be infertile could be discarded, like a broken TV, as she was useless if she couldn't produce sons to pass on her husband's wealth, power, and legacy. If her husband died, she could be inherited like livestock. In many cultures, she was passed on to her husband's brother; the important thing was that her future children still carried her husband's last name.

Feminist activists of the 1800s and early 1900s fought to end patriarch/property marriages. One of the earliest feminist demands was for women to have the legal right to *own* property rather than *be* property. This right would eventually make many other rights possible: the right to vote and serve on juries; the right to work, keep one's own wages, and build financial credit; the right to have a voice in family decisions; and, if divorced, the right to ask for custody of one's children. All these issues were part of early feminist struggles.

In response to feminist activism, and in the face of opposition from clergy and others, marriage would change. By the 1950s, on the heels of industrialization, a new kind of marriage would be institutionalized, the one that we typically and misleadingly call "traditional" today.

The Breadwinner/Housewife Marriage

Industrialization broke up the then-traditional family. As Americans were increasingly pulled into the workplace, control over money and time shifted from husbands and fathers to employers. Capitalism valued cheap labor regardless of the costs to the family. Since the subordinate status of women and children made their labor especially low-priced, capitalists were happy to employ them. Men's wages were typically insufficient to support dependents, so the survival of a family relied on women's and children's wages too. Now that even men had bosses, a patriarch's role as head of household could be called into question.

Intellectuals of the time worried that capitalism would destroy the family completely, but instead of abandoning patriarchal marriage altogether—an option advocated by some at the time—men organized to modify and modernize patriarchy. They did so, in part, through unionization. Pushing back against capitalism, labor unions argued that working men had the right to support a "home and family" on their wages alone.[47] Through protests, strikes, and boycotts, unions carved out a new way of life for adult White men. They supported state laws meant to reduce competition among workers (like restrictions on child labor and legislation that barred women and men of color from well-paying jobs) and enable mothers to stay home (such as child-rearing allowances and maternity leave).

Unions eventually succeeded in institutionalizing a **family wage**: an income paid to one man that was large enough to support a home, a wife, and children. Built upon the family wage, a new kind of marriage emerged, the **breadwinner/housewife marriage**: a separate but equal model of marriage that defined men's and women's contributions as different but complementary. Unlike patriarch/property marriage, breadwinner/housewife marriage did not legally subordinate wives to husbands (that is, she was no longer his property), but it did rigidly define roles: Women owed men domestic services (cleaning, cooking, child care, and sex); in return, men were legally required to support their wives financially. If either failed to play their part, they could divorce and receive reparations for breach of contract.[48]

Other societies had stronger labor unions and, therefore, stronger breadwinner/housewife policies than the United States. West Germany and the Netherlands, for example, offered cash bonuses for each child. These countries also paid women a wage for raising their children during the early months (and sometimes years) and gave big tax breaks to married couples with only one earner. When breadwinners wouldn't or couldn't support their wives and children, states often stepped in. Weaker breadwinner policies, like those in the United States, made it more difficult for men to support a housewife, which pushed many women into the workforce.

Policies put in place in the aftermath of World War II further changed how Americans organized families. Most notably, during the '40s and '50s the US government collaborated with private investors to build suburbs and facilitate homeownership. This was the birth of the "American dream." The G.I. Bill—designed to reward soldiers and help them reintegrate into society—offered college scholarships and cheap mortgages to veterans who were men (but not women, whose service to the military was deemed "auxiliary"). Meanwhile, the government funded the building of an interstate highway system that connected the cities to the countryside much more efficiently. This led to a boom in housing developments, to which cities strung power lines and dug sewer tunnels. These government investments transformed America into a land of homeowners for the first time in history.

Home was farther from work than ever and the growing distance between the two cemented the idea of **separate spheres**, a masculinized work world and a feminized home life, especially for White people. At work, employees engaged in **production**, the making of goods for sale. Since capitalism is a competitive system, factory owners pushed workers to be as efficient as possible. Men, then, were pressed to become the kind of people capitalism found most useful: those who were more interested in work than family and concerned with maximizing economic success. Living in such a world required that men master the qualities of competitiveness, aggression, and ruthlessness. "'It's a jungle out there,' says the stereotypical male provider when his wife and kids meet him at the door."[49]

Inside that door, he was supposed to find not just a house, but a *home*: a warm, comfortable space filled with people who cared for him: his loving children, doting wife, and devoted dog. Under the glow of their admiration, he could recharge to fight another day. At home there was supposedly no production, only **reproduction**, the making and nurturing of human beings.

After World War II, the US government subsidized the building of the first suburbs, where normative ideas of the family came to be signified by a married man and woman with two to three fresh-faced, smiling children. The families that received loans to move into these neighborhoods were almost entirely White.

Women, then, were expected to specialize in a particular kind of supportive and loving emotion work. The notion that women could and should wholeheartedly embrace this work is called the **cult of domesticity**.[50] It emerged as an idea during the Victorian era—at the same time that we feminized the idea of love—and spread downward through the social classes along with homeownership and the family wage. Together with the ideology of separate spheres, the cult of domesticity protected at least one part of life from the harsh capitalist values of rationality and cost-benefit analysis.

This was an entirely different kind of family. In the mixed-gender environments innovated in the 1920s and mainstreamed over the next several decades, men and women met and got to like one another. They married by choice and were expected to find comfort in their relationship. But becoming whole in the process of marriage meant joining the feminine and the masculine together into one household. Doing this required strict enforcement of gendered family roles and heterosexuality, leading to a short-lived and uneasy experiment: 1950s America.

THE FUNNY '50s

The icon of Rosie the Riveter signifies the work opportunities offered to women during World War II. In fact, in wartime, women entered many occupations previously dominated by men. After the war ended in 1945, however, they were subject to a counter-campaign designed to push them back into the home. Marketers, columnists, scientists, public intellectuals, and the US government all decried the undoing of the breadwinner/housewife family, defending its gender-specific family roles as natural. This resulted in an entrenchment of the nuclear family. As the historian Stephanie Coontz explains:

> At the end of the 1940s, all the trends characterizing the rest of the twentieth century suddenly reversed themselves. For the first time in more than one hundred years, the [average] age for marriage and motherhood fell, fertility increased, divorce rates declined, and women's degree of educational parity with men dropped sharply. In a period of less than ten years, the proportion of never-married persons declined by as much as it had during the entire previous half century.[51]

All these trends would reverse again within a few decades. Historically speaking, then, middle-class marriages in the 1950s were *unusually* family-oriented.

The era was unusually conservative in other ways too. If city life in the 1920s was high energy, sexy, and fun, the 1950s was relatively prudish. The government passed decency standards for Hollywood movies, ensuring that sex was kept off the screen and bad things always happened to "bad" girls. In 1952, books and magazines with sexual content were banned. Comic books were considered especially corrupting. In an official report, Congress argued that comic books gave "short courses in . . . rape, cannibalism, carnage, necrophilia, sex, sadism, masochism, and virtually every other form of crime, degeneracy, bestiality, and horror."[52]

Homosexuality was also ruthlessly repressed.[53] In the United States, the idea of a queer *person*, as opposed to a person who engages in same-gender sexual activity, was new. The Victorians knew, of course, that people of the same gender sometimes had sex, but it had never occurred to them that particular people distinctively desired such behaviors. In a Puritan-inspired view, they believed all humans were brimming with the potential for sin. Variation in how likely a person was to have sex with someone of the same gender was considered a measure of how godly they were, not an innate preference for one gender or the other.[54] So, while Puritan and Victorian men who felt same-gender desire may have experienced guilt and shame, they would not have paused to wonder if they were different kinds of people than anyone else.

The idea of a queer *person* didn't become a part of the collective consciousness until World War II. Almost every young, fit man between eighteen and

A housewife stops to feed her son while ironing as the Army-McCarthy hearings of 1954 play on television. The politics of the 1950s were aimed at rooting out "communist" ideas like child care and gender equality.

twenty-six years old served in the war.[55] As a result, unmarried people on both the front lines and the home front found themselves largely in the company of the same gender. Indulging in homoerotic encounters became easier and more tempting. Wrote one young man: "The war is a tragedy to my mind and soul . . . but to my physical being, it is a memorable experience."[56] World War II was so conducive to exploring same-gender attraction that it's been called "a nation-wide 'coming out' experience."[57]

After the war, some soldiers pursued a gay "lifestyle."[58] The first gay bars in the United States opened in the 1940s and the first gay advocacy organization would be founded in 1951.[59] Notably, these new communities were mostly for men. Gay women would remain less visible to the public and each other, at least for a while. Women in same-gender relationships were still often read by others as "celibate" spinsters.[60]

Growing awareness of and more community among men who identified as gay invoked a backlash. Cities passed laws saying alcohol couldn't be sold to gays and lesbians and outlawed same-gender dancing and cross-dressing.[61] In response to the so-called homosexual menace, the US government sought to purge men who had sex with men from public jobs on the assumption that they were "by definition morally bankrupt and, as such, politically suspect."[62] Much of the private sector followed suit.

Meanwhile, the Cold War's "red scare" spread a moral panic about socialism while a "lavender scare" framed homosexuality as a threat to the heterosexual family.[63] Senator Joe McCarthy, famous for these efforts, said that anyone who opposed him was "either a Communist or a cocksucker."[64] While lesbians were not especially visible, those who appeared in fiction invariably met a bad end. Unmarried women who refused to perform a feminine apologetic at work were often fired or forced to quit.

The politics of the 1950s were unique. They were unusually family focused, homophobic, and sexually repressive. But people don't always live up to their own expectations. What was happening behind the closed doors of so-called traditional marriage in the 1950s? And what has happened since?

Sex and Marriage in the '50s

A young woman in the 1950s might have been seriously worried about her marriage prospects. Hundreds of thousands of men had been killed in the war and tens of thousands of soldiers married foreign women while abroad.[65] *The New York Times* reported that 750,000 young women would likely never marry. The process of securing a husband, then, became serious business. So, while it may have made sense to go out with a different guy each night in the 1920s, flitting from guy to guy didn't seem so smart when there weren't enough guys to go around.

Accordingly, during the 1950s dating was edged out by a new practice: **going steady**, an often short-lived, but still exclusive, public pairing off. Going steady was "social security."[66] It ensured that a girl would always have a date on important nights and lessened the chances that she would end up an "old maid."

Ironically, going steady accelerated premarital sexual experimentation in exactly the decade known most for its conservatism.[67] Compared to couples who might enjoy just one night together, couples that went steady were more likely to "neck" (kissing on the neck and mouth), "pet" (touching below the neck), or "go all the way" (having penile-vaginal intercourse). Adults objected to these new trends but couldn't stop them. Sexual activity became an expected part of any youthful romantic relationship. According to one 1952 advice manual, if a girl "wishes to be a member of the dating group," then "mild sexual contact" is "one of the requirements."[68]

Despite the conservative overtones, the undercurrent of the 1950s—represented by the swinging hips of Elvis and the flamboyance of Little Richard—was a sexy one. Meanwhile, the new ubiquity of the automobile did for suburban youth of the '50s what living in cities had done for the working-class youth of

In the 1950s, the custom of going steady among teenagers guaranteed that girls would have companions to institutionally organized events, such as the senior prom, and facilitated both romantic and sexual experimentation.

the '20s: It provided the opportunity to socialize without parental supervision. Hence the invention of "parking," driving off to a remote location, pulling off the road, and necking, petting, or more in the backseat.

Emotionally intense relationships led to sex and the highest rate of teen pregnancy in American history. At its peak in 1957, one out of every ten women aged fifteen to nineteen gave birth.[69] But there was no teen pregnancy crisis. Instead of a rash of single teen mothers, the age of marriage dropped to a one-hundred-year low and babies born "premature" (healthy-weight babies that arrived less than nine months after the wedding) reached a one-hundred-year high. At the end of the Victorian era, the median age at first marriage was twenty-six for men, twenty-two for women, and rising. By 1950, it had dropped to twenty-three for men and twenty for women, and it would remain this way throughout this decade (Figure 8.1).[70]

Eventually it would be impossible to pretend that either the youth or the adults in the 1950s were sexual goody-goodies. The fable was dealt a heavy blow with the publication of sexologist Alfred Kinsey's extensive reports on the sexual behavior of 18,000 men and women.[71] Published in 1948 and 1953, his books sold a quarter of a million copies. They roundly discredited the idea that it was only teenagers who were breaking the sexual rules, revealing that premarital "petting" was nearly universal, 90 percent of men and 50 percent of women had premarital sex, 90 percent of men and 60 percent of women masturbated, and 50 percent of men and 25 percent of women had extramarital sex. A third of men and 13 percent of women reported having sex with someone of the same gender, while fully 50 percent of men and 37 percent of women reported same-gender attraction. The cat was out of the bag.

If sex was hiding behind the happy innocence of poodle skirts and saddle shoes, unhappy marriages were disguised by the flower beds and fresh lawns of suburban homes. By 1963, the gig was up. A book called *The Feminine Mystique* forever changed the way America thought of housewives. The title referred to a mythology—the idea that women were gleefully happy as wives and mothers—that strongly contrasted with reality. Written by feminist Betty Friedan, it documented

FIGURE 8.1 | MEDIAN AGE AT FIRST MARRIAGE, 1900–2021

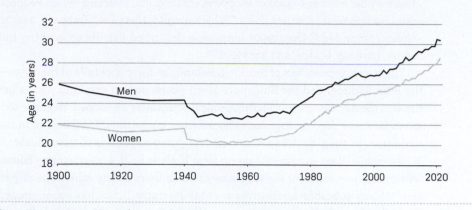

Source: US Census Bureau, Historical Marriage Status Tables, Nov. 22, 2021, https://www.census.gov/data/tables/time-series/demo
/families/marital.html.

widespread unhappiness among middle-class White married women in the 1950s
and 1960s. Writes Friedan:

> *Each suburban wife struggled with it alone. As she made the beds, shopped for
> groceries, matched slipcover material, ate peanut butter sandwiches with her chil-
> dren, chauffeured Cub Scouts and Brownies, lay beside her husband at night—she
> was afraid to ask even of herself the silent question—"Is this all?"*[72]

The book spent six weeks on *The New York Times* best seller list; its first printing sold 1.4 million copies.[73] Women wept with recognition, claiming that it was
a "bolt of lightning," a "revelation," a "bombshell."[74] Friedan's book revealed the
cracks in the breadwinner/housewife model, fault lines that would contribute
to its demise.

STRAINED BY SEPARATE SPHERES While people were now marrying for
love, the separate roles of breadwinner and housewife drained the life out of the
friendships that couples had built before marrying. The differences in their daily
lives left them strangers to one another. Less than a third of spouses described
their marriages as "happy" or "very happy."[75]

Stranded in the suburbs and with few other adults to talk to, privileged wives
living the American dream often felt isolated, lonely, and bored. Many had earned
college degrees and resented being pushed out of the workforce at the end of
World War II.[76] Instead of finding housework and child care endlessly stimu-
lating and enjoyable, many chafed under the expectation that they would find
fulfillment this way.[77] Gleaming linoleum could only bring so much joy. Child

care was tedious and tiring. They worried that their brains were wasting away while they did endless rounds of shopping, cooking, and cleaning. When *Redbook* asked readers to send letters about "Why Young Mothers Feel Trapped," 24,000 women responded.[78] One 1950s housewife described her life as nothing but "booze, bowling, bridge, and boredom."[79]

There was, indeed, lots of drinking. Behind the flirty cocktails of the 1950s—the Pink Squirrel and the Singapore Sling—were women drinking just to get through the day. Drugs, too. Pharmaceutical companies developed "daytime sedatives for every day" in response to housewives' complaints.[80] Unheard of in the mid-fifties, in 1959, doctors prescribed over 900,000 pounds of tranquilizers.[81] White middle-class women—the group most likely to be in a breadwinner/housewife marriage—were four times as likely to take them as any other type of person.[82] "Many suburban housewives were taking tranquilizers like cough drops," wrote Friedan.[83] The pills were known, colloquially, as "mother's little helpers."

Wives weren't the only ones unhappy, though. Marriage was essentially compulsory for men. Often, jobs and promotions depended on their ability to show that they were good family men. Bachelors were considered immature ("Why can't he settle down?") or deviant ("Is he gay?"). Meanwhile, men were wary of women who saw them only as a "meal ticket," or felt overwhelmed by being the only person on whom their wives could rely for emotional support, not to mention adult conversation. A whole genre of humor emerged, designed to resonate with men's sense of being trapped (hence the idea of the wife as a "ball and chain").

Tapping into this sentiment, Hugh Hefner launched *Playboy* magazine in 1953, forever changing ideas about masculinity.[84] Encouraging men to stay single and avoid commitment, he mainstreamed the notion of a man who didn't marry but was anything but gay. As the writer Barbara Ehrenreich explained, "The playboy didn't avoid marriage because he was a little bit 'queer,' but, on the contrary, because he was so ebulliently, even compulsively heterosexual."[85] Hefner introduced a new set of gender rules that rewarded men's resistance to marriage, leading to the still-present myth that men must be dragged, kicking and screaming, to the altar.[86]

Both men and women, then, enjoyed fantasizing about a life without a spouse, kids, and a mortgage, but it was women who were truly vulnerable in marriage.

SEPARATE AND UNEQUAL While both men and women had their dissatisfactions, women carried virtually all the risks of a breadwinner/housewife marriage. These marriages weren't overtly patriarchal—just as Victorian feminists had hoped, women were now seen as men's equals: different and complementary instead of better and worse—but women were still financially dependent on men. In classic androcentric fashion, the masculine sphere of work was evaluated as important and admirable, while the feminine sphere of the home was seen as decidedly less so.

Hugh Hefner, the founder of *Playboy*, made a fortune by offering an alternative image of masculinity to White men who chafed under the repressive rules of breadwinner/housewife marriage.

The imbalance in the value attributed to work and home was literal. Men's work was *worth* something; they received a wage in exchange for it. In contrast, women were working in and around the home just as they'd been doing since agrarian times but getting less credit for it than ever. Capitalist rationality replaced explicit patriarchy. It wasn't his penis anymore that made him the "head of the household"; it was his paycheck.

Prior to industrialization, women's labor—both the work of maintaining a household and the birthing and rearing of children—was understood to be *work*. After industrialization, however, with the separation of work from home, women's labor seemed to disappear; it was men who "went to work," while women just "stayed home." Because women's work was newly invisible, housewives seemed dependent on men, but not vice versa. Her dependence on his wage was obvious to everyone, but his dependence on her cooking, cleaning, shopping, and child care often was not.

To be fair, a housewife would be in big trouble if she lost her breadwinner, but a breadwinner needed his housewife too. Without her, he had hungry, dirty, misbehaving children he couldn't leave alone, plus no clean clothes to wear, an empty belly, nothing in the fridge, and a filthy house. He either had to stay home himself or hire someone to replace his wife. Even a family wage wasn't designed to support a house, children, *and* a full-time, paid babysitter and housekeeper; it relied on him getting the domestic work for free. The degree to which wives supported husbands' breadwinning activities was swept under the rug, so to speak.

Middle- and upper-class women didn't just become unpaid and unrecognized housewives; they also gave up incomes of their own. This was okay *if* the marriage lasted, her husband valued her contribution, and he consistently earned a good income. If the marriage fell apart, wives could end up divorced and destitute, often with children. This was not an unlikely scenario; between a quarter and a third of marriages in the 1950s ended in divorce.

The government tried to protect "displaced homemakers," as they were called, by requiring alimony (monthly cash payments to ex-wives from their former husbands) and making divorce legally difficult (by requiring proof that a spouse had broken the marriage contract, for example), but marriage remained an intrinsically risky bet for women. Pretty soon the idea that they needed to secure their own future "just in case" carried quite a bit of weight.

Women looked to the workplace for answers.

GOING TO WORK

Even at its height, the 1950s version of the traditional marriage was more myth than reality. Due to legal discrimination, the family wage was elusive for most men of color and immigrant men. Black and American Indian soldiers were also systematically excluded from the G.I. Bill that made the American dream a reality for so many soldiers.[87]

The bill's mortgage program didn't apply on reservations where many American Indians lived because the US federal government holds that land in trust. Though Native veterans technically qualified for low-interest loans under the G.I. Bill, the government refused to waive title to the land to allow for homeownership. So, many veterans couldn't access that benefit.

Black veterans were also denied the college loans and mortgages that launched many White and some Asian and Hispanic families into the middle class. Even if they could afford to move into the suburbs without government help, most of these communities explicitly barred Black people. As a result, many Black families were left behind in cities that governments neglected.

The breadwinner/housewife marriage was also elusive for many White families. Only a third of these families could survive on a single wage. Poor White women and most women of color were in the wage economy from the beginning and stayed there.

Soon middle-class White women were joining them. Before 1940, more than 80 percent of women who married left the labor force on their wedding day and never came back.[88] In the next twenty years, the proportion of married women

who worked doubled.[89] Most of these were "returning workers," mothers of older children who gave
up sewing their children's clothes and baking
cookies in exchange for the money to buy these
products.

These women filled the offices of the growing
corporate class, often serving as secretaries to
white-collar men who held a growing number of
managerial jobs.[90] Mirroring the breadwinner/
housewife at home, "office wives" filled an important role in the expanding economy. By the 1960s,
when Betty Friedan condemned the "feminine mystique," many married women had already decided
they wanted to work.

The economy also needed more workers.[91]
America had lost a quarter million men in World
War II and the birthrate was low during the Great
Depression.[92] Industry needed bodies, even if that
meant hiring middle-class married women.[93] To do
so, rules that limited women's working were often
discarded.

Beginning in the late 1800s, for example,
marriage bans—policies against employing married women—were common in banking, teaching,
office work, and government jobs. A majority of US
school districts had bans against hiring married
women, as did over half of all firms employing
office workers.[94] Bans were expanded to manufac-

The US economy needed workers after
World War II, giving more women the
opportunity to earn their own living. Some
went to work in factories, like the woman
at a television tube plant pictured here.
Other women entered white-collar workplaces as secretaries or teachers.

turing work during the 1930s in an effort to save jobs for men during the Great
Depression. After the war, some employers rejected these bans; they wanted all
their options. By 1951, the percent of school districts that had a marriage ban had
dropped from 87 to 18 percent (though pregnancy bans were often put in their place).

Other policies were more resistant to change. These included **protective
legislation**, policies designed to protect women and children from exploitation
by restricting their workplace participation.[95] Women were banned, for example,
from working long hours, doing night work, lifting even moderate weights, or
taking dangerous jobs (though exceptions were made for jobs like waitressing,
housekeeping, and nursing that were "for women" regardless of these demands).
Beginning in the mid-1800s, almost every American state passed some protec-
tionist laws.[96] Many feminists at the time recognized that protective legislation
was benevolent sexism (young women being slotted into largely dead-end jobs
for their own good).

FIGURE 8.2 | HISTORICAL COMPOSITION OF FEMALE LABOR
FORCE BY MARITAL STATUS, 1890–1980

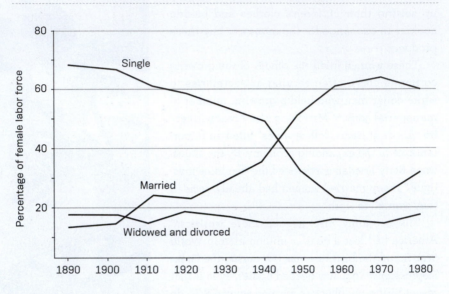

Source: Lynn Weiner, *From Working Girl to Working Mother: The Female Labor Force in the United States, 1820–1980*
(Chapel Hill: University of North Carolina Press, 1986).

As long as employers assumed that women would quit working when they
got married or pregnant (and planned to fire them if they did not), "working girl"
was merely a life stage. Accordingly, employers had little reason to give women
on-the-job training or consider them for promotions. Women who sought higher
education were assumed to be there to meet and marry a man with a promising
career (or get an "MRS degree," as it was jokingly called).

As Figure 8.2 shows, after World War II, this began to change. In 1964 discrimination against working women became illegal in the United States. In a
last-ditch effort to ensure that a bill mandating equal treatment of Black Americans would fail, a Virginia Democrat added "sex" to the Civil Rights Act, including it in the list of characteristics against which workplace discrimination would
be illegal: race, color, religion, and national origin.[98] He thought the idea of equal
treatment for men and women was so preposterous that it would surely kill the
bill. Much to his chagrin and surprise, it passed anyway.[99]

Two years later the National Organization for Women (NOW) was formed
to enforce the new law. First up was challenging the then-prevalent practice of
segregating all job advertisements by gender category ("help wanted: female"
or "help wanted: male"). The Supreme Court ultimately sided with the feminists.
Then, in 1973, the Court affirmed women's right to an abortion. After these developments, women could at least *try* to design their work and lives as they chose.

Throughout these decades, married women and mothers of older children increasingly entered a changing workplace. The United States transitioned from an industrial economy (founded on producing material goods) to a **service and information economy**, one dependent on jobs focused on providing services for others (such as waiting tables, working in nail salons, or providing administrative assistance) or working with ideas (like engineers, computer programmers, and college professors). By 1980, 51 percent of all women were employed. Even 40 percent of mothers with children under eighteen had at least a part-time job.[100] Women were even entering white-collar professions at rising rates.

Despite optimism and economic need, however, many women found that their opportunities were *still* blocked. Discontent grew.[101] As the 1990s came to a close—with 78 percent of mothers in the labor force—a wave of family change was cresting.[102]

MARRIAGE IN THE 2000s

In 2003, James Dobson Jr., founder of Focus on the Family, wrote: "Unless we act quickly, the family as it has been known for 5,000 years will be gone."[103] The truth is, by the turn of the millennium the patriarch/property marriage was already gone, and the breadwinner/housewife marriage was fading fast. Most Americans now agree that good fathers do more than drop a paycheck on the kitchen table. Likewise, the expectation that women will leave the labor force permanently when they marry or have children has vanished.

Divorce laws have changed, too, allowing people to initiate proceedings without proving infidelity, physical abuse, or failure to provide economic support.[104] The stigma of divorce has faded, and many women have decided that an uncooperative husband—one who refuses to let them go to school or work or fails to do his share of the housework—is something they can do without. Today, 69 percent of divorces between men and women are initiated by wives, even though women's living standards fall much more than men's do.[105] Paradoxically, today divorce rates are highest in the parts of the country where conservative Protestantism is most common and politicians are most vocal in denouncing changes in marriage norms.[106]

After over a century of feminist activism and demands, the marriage contract was rewritten to be gender-neutral. Married men are no longer owed domestic labor, nor are married women owed economic support. Obligations now fall on "spouses" rather than "husbands" and "wives." Both men and women are responsible for paying alimony to a spouse who spent time out of the workforce to take care of the family. A widower can now collect his wife's Social Security check instead of his own (until the 1970s, only bereaved wives could do this).

Nearly all states today confer equal standing to both spouses in issues of child custody.

This gender-neutral legal contract also opened the door to same-sex marriage. If marriage no longer has different rules for men and women, then it doesn't need a man and a woman at all. In 2015, the US Supreme Court acknowledged that marriage was a fundamental right that could not be restricted to heterosexual couples. Sixty (and now 70) percent of Americans agreed.[107]

If they need to, people in the United States can do without marriage. If a man with means prefers to stay single, it's now easy to buy a homemaker's services in the market. Dinner can be eaten at restaurants; housekeepers can clean your house and wash your laundry; and companionship (both free and paid) is an app away. Given how risky marriage can be for women, and its questionable benefits, women who can support themselves sometimes hold out until they can find spouses with whom to innovate a new model of marriage or don't marry at all.

While marriage is still normative, it's not so surprising anymore when people reach their thirties, forties, or fifties without marrying.[108] Just half of US adults today are married and about one in seven lives alone.[109] It's totally normal to be single, even as a "grown-up." While it may be preferable to some, marriage is no longer necessary for entrance to adulthood, nor is it a prerequisite for having a child. In fact, 40 percent of children are born to unmarried parents.[110] Marriage is certainly no longer a job requirement. And it's rarely used, at least explicitly, to cement political alliances or hoard wealth.

If people do marry, they can organize their marriages however they wish. And they do. Today we see couples in which two parents work part-time and share child-rearing responsibilities and couples in which both work overtime and hire gardeners, housekeepers, and nannies for their kids. We see breadwinners married to housewives and, in small but growing numbers, breadwinners married to househusbands too. Both same- and mixed-gender couples adopt all these family forms. Grandparents are stepping back in to offer child care and income support in a way that had become rare in the 1950s.[111]

US laws restrict marriage to two and only two people, reflecting the presumption of **monogamy**: long-term intimate relationships with only one person. But Americans are increasingly exploring forms of consensual nonmonogamy like **polyamory** (long-term intimate relationships with more than one partner at a time) and **open relationships** (long-term intimate relationships that allow sexual but not romantic encounters with others). Twenty percent of Americans now say polyamory is morally acceptable and 11 percent have tried it.[112] These relationship forms have existed in many parts of American culture since the founding—among Indigenous peoples, in early Mormon communities, and among early feminists—but today they are more "mainstream" than ever.[113]

Since the primary reason to marry in Western cultures today is still love, marriages are both more voluntary and less stable. As the historian Stephanie

Coontz explains, the "same things that made marriage become such a unique and treasured personal relationship during the last two hundred years, paved the way for it to become an optional and fragile one."[114] People divorce. When they do, they often take children with them, sometimes into new marriages, creating **blended families**, ones consisting of partnered adults with at least one child from a previous relationship. Today, about one in six children are living in blended families.[115]

The high rate of divorce does not signal a decline in the value of marriage. Instead, Americans engage in what sociologist Andrew Cherlin calls the "marriage-go-round." They both marry *and* divorce more frequently than people in other countries.

Putting this all together, Coontz writes:

> Almost any separate way of organizing caregiving, childrearing, residential arrange-
> ments, sexual interactions, or interpersonal redistribution of resources has been
> tried by some society at some point in time. But the coexistence in one society of
> so many alternative ways of doing all of these different things—and the compara-
> tive legitimacy accorded to many of them—has never been seen before.[116]

Amid all this variety, one thing is clear: Since the 1980s, the breadwinner/housewife marriage has been slowly replaced by **partnership marriage**, a model of marriage based on love and companionship between two equals who negotiate a division of labor unique to each couple.

This continues to be alarming to people who believe the breadwinner/housewife marriage model is ancient, natural, and universal. Since the 1960s, people opposed to partnership marriage have mobilized in defense of what they call "family values." Phyllis Schlafly, for example, was a vocal anti-feminist campaigner of the 1970s. She denounced women who left abusive husbands as "runaway wives" and fought the emergence of new feminist social services like hotlines supporting rape victims and shelters for women fleeing intimate partner violence.[117]

The long-running "mommy wars"—fueled by the media—have pitted women against one another. The wars portray working mothers as disdainful of women who choose to be homemakers, encouraging the latter to see working women as adversaries, not allies.[118] Like the middle-class White Victorian women who advocated for the ideology of intensive mothering, homemakers have mobilized to defend the value of their work.

In the 1970s, the singer Anita Bryant joined with James Dobson Jr. to rally against homosexuality. Bryant campaigned under a "Save the Children" slogan, arguing that sexual minorities were sinful and dangerous to children. When the HIV/AIDS pandemic arrived in the United States, they and other anti-gay activists exploited the tragedy to stoke fear, anger, and disgust. Pat Buchanan, then-communications director for US President Ronald Reagan, called it "nature's revenge."[119]

Men's rights groups have also arisen, objecting to some of the changes of the past decades. These include the ease with which women can file for divorce, efforts to make it easier for sexual violence survivors to get justice, and women's right to abort fetuses to whom men are biologically related.[120] They also draw attention to many of the harms disproportionately suffered by men, including incarceration, poor health, and circumcision.

The backlash to changes in family life, however, has been no match for economic demands. Politicians in both parties began rolling back the social safety net in the 1980s, and the gap between the richest and poorest Americans has grown wider and wider.[121] Most families *need* two earners, whether they like it or not. Under these conditions, the goal is "work-life balance."

Women especially want to strike this balance.[122] Women more than men aspire to find a way to combine the historically valued role of breadwinning with the equally essential role of caregiving.[123] To do this, women need more than non-discrimination laws. They need proactive governmental policies that support working parents, like flexible working hours and benefits for part-time workers. Policies like these, however, have been slow to come.

Despite the ascendance of the partnership model, then, as well as the degendering of marriage law and legalization of same-sex marriage, the breadwinner/housewife model still echoes through our personal lives and political debates. It competes with and sometimes lives quietly alongside the partnership model, producing the types of trouble that contradictions cause. Still, despite the trouble, and despite the clamor to return to the breadwinner/housewife model of marriage, partnership marriage is here . . . maybe not to stay, but for now.

CONCLUSION

When people defend the idea of "traditional marriage," we would be smart to ask which one they mean. The patriarch/property model of marriage reigned supreme for thousands of years, while the breadwinner/housewife model emerged quite recently, only to be rather quickly replaced. Today's marriage contract reflects a partnership model, ideally flexible enough to accommodate a wide range of family forms. But it also strains under the continued influence of the breadwinner/housewife ideal.

The institution of marriage has changed because feminists and others insisted that prior models were unfair. It changed, too, because sexual and gender minorities worked to discover alternatives that were better for them. All found opportunities as well as obstacles in historical events—industrialization, the rise of cities and then suburbs, the demands of capitalism, global competition, technological innovation, and more—as well as backlash from people who defend the breadwinner/housewife model.

All the other institutions discussed in this chapter are also changing. Our sexual practices reflect shifts in opportunity provided by social activists and social change. Likewise, the workplace has evolved, pushing and pulling us into different kinds of work and changing and being changed by its relationship to the home. When we take the long view, we see continual upheavals of social norms and institutions, making any natural and universal idea of gender relations—based on biology or religion or anything else—seem increasingly implausible.

Next . . .

In the four chapters to come, we explore the on-the-ground realities that people face today, starting with sexuality. It's difficult to imagine, perhaps, that social forces shape this most intimate part of our personal selves. Desire for sexual and romantic connection is felt so deeply that it seems impervious to outside influences. You might ask, in a hopeful tone:

Gendered ideas, interactions, and institutions may affect almost every part of my life, but some things are personal, and my sexuality is mine and mine alone. Isn't it?

Alas, dear reader.

FOR FURTHER READING

Coontz, Stephanie. "The World Historical Transformation of Marriage." *Journal of Marriage and Family* 66, no. 4 (2004): 974–79.

Edin, Kathryn, and Maria Kefalas. *Promises I Can Keep: Why Poor Women Put Motherhood before Marriage.* Berkeley: University of California Press, 2011.

Ehrenreich, Barbara. *The Hearts of Men: American Dreams and the Flight from Commitment.* New York: Anchor Books, 1987.

Goldin, Claudia. "The Quiet Revolution that Transformed Women's Employment, Education, and Family." *The American Economic Review,* 96, no. 2 (2006): 1–21.

Katz, Jonathan. *The Invention of Heterosexuality.* Chicago: University of Chicago Press, 2007.

Macht, Alexandra. *Fatherhood and Love: The Social Construction of Masculine Emotions.* London: Palgrave Macmillan, 2020.

Strasser, Susan. *Never Done: A History of American Housework.* New York: Macmillan, 2000.

SEX IS NOT A NATURAL ACT.

—LEONORE TIEFER[1]

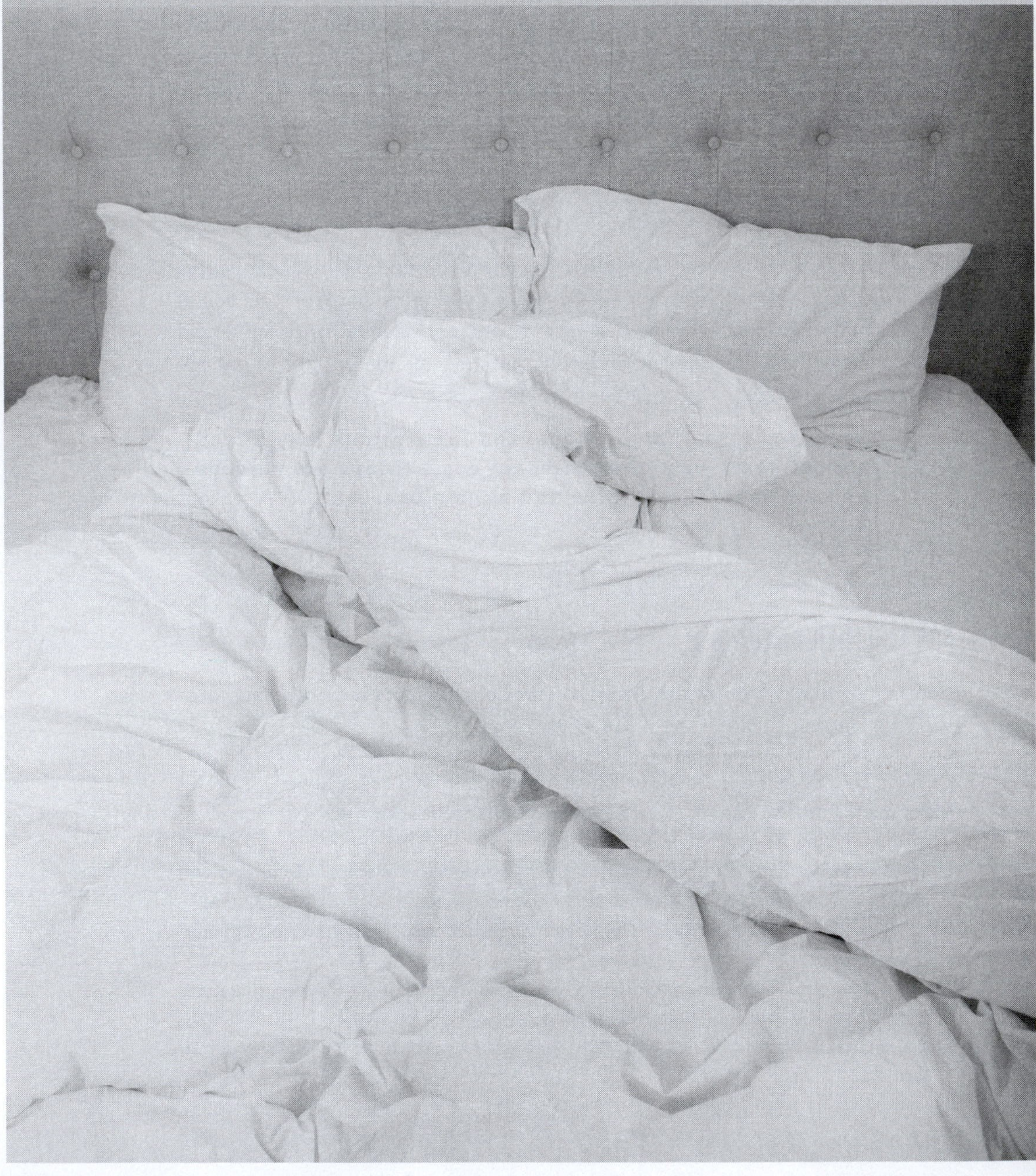

9

Sexualities

"There's this system," said a student about hooking up in college. "You're gonna get drunk, randomly meet randoms, and just, like, whatever happens."[2] Social scientists call the "system" she's referring to **hookup culture**, an environment in which casual sexual contact is held up as ideal, encouraged with rules for interaction, and institutionalized. Hookup cultures are found on most residential college campuses. All told, 70 percent of students will hook up at least once before graduation.[3]

By now, scholars understand hookup culture well. In fact, the first author of this textbook wrote a book about it. *American Hookup: The New Culture of Sex on Campus* follows 101 college students as they navigate a semester of their first year. You'll hear from some of these students throughout this chapter.

Most students report being eager to experiment with their sexuality, at least a little. They also report feeling pressure to do college "right," which seems to require a casual attitude toward sex. Many students believe, or think their peers believe, that college is a time to go wild and have fun. Some even believe that separating sex from love is what liberation looks like.

This works out well for the 25 percent of students who are truly enthusiastic about casual sex.[4] Hooking up raises their self-esteem and lowers rates of anxiety and depression. The students who don't like hookup culture, though, often struggle. About a third abstain altogether. The remainder, just under half, participate with mixed feelings and mixed experiences.

This chapter will explain how casual sex has so captured college life. It will demonstrate that sexualities, though deeply personal, are also thoroughly social. Gendered ideas, interactions, and institutions shape our sexual experiences, producing asymmetries in the distribution of pleasure, violence, and power.

 Q+A   **Gendered ideas, interactions, and institutions may affect almost every part of my life, but some things are personal, and my sexuality is mine and mine alone, isn't it?**

Unfortunately, no. Just like in the past, today's sexual attitudes and behaviors are strongly influenced by the cities, circumstances, and societies in which we live. To understand how, we'll start with three examples of historical change, take a look at sexuality today, and end somewhere that might be familiar.

SEX AND SOCIAL FORCES

The last chapter discussed the contrasting sexual regimes of Indigenous Americans and European colonizers, which emerged in response to different ideas about and relationships to the land. It discussed how the emergence of cities led working-class youth in the Roaring Twenties to invent "dating." And it showed how "going steady" was a response to the massive loss of life in World War II. All these examples reveal that our sexualities are influenced by often large-scale social change. In the past several decades, the sexual terrain has continued to shift in response to activism, innovation, and disease.

The young people born after World War II are collectively described as the "baby boomers." Youth often push boundaries, and this generation went down in history for doing so.[5] Engaging in widespread activism, the boomers protested the Vietnam War, fought for Black Americans' civil rights, and led the women's movement, the gay liberation movement, and the sexual revolution. These movements reinforced permissive rather than punitive attitudes about sex, including rising approval of nonmarital sex.[6] Since women had historically shouldered the brunt of sexual repression, the sexual revolution and women's movement especially freed women from constraints.

Serendipitously, all this occurred alongside a world-changing medical breakthrough: the birth control pill. "The Pill" went on the market in 1960. Five years later, the US Supreme Court deemed state laws against the use of birth control in marriage unconstitutional. It affirmed this for single people in 1972. In 1973, the Court legalized abortion; a decision that would stand until 2022. For a time, everyone was free to have sex with less fear of an unintended pregnancy.

Life was changing for sexual and gender minorities too. In 1969, a group of trans and queer people revolted during a police roundup of patrons of the Stonewall Inn, a bar in New York's Greenwich Village. They resisted arrest and threw pocket change, beer cans, and bottles at the police officers, forcing them to barricade themselves inside the bar. Their actions kicked off several nights of protest against police harassment of queer people.

On the anniversary of the riots, the first gay pride parades were held in New York, Los Angeles, Chicago, and San Francisco. Americans began coming out in record numbers. Sexual minorities weren't just out of the closet; they were out and proud.

Then horror struck. Beginning in 1981, gay men's communities would be devastated by the AIDS pandemic. In the United States, men who had sex with men were especially likely to contract the human immunodeficiency virus (HIV), the virus that causes AIDS. In the early years, more than 90 percent of people who contracted HIV died.

It took six years for the first treatment to be developed. Queer people protested government inaction and exploitation by pharmaceutical companies, arguing "Silence = Death."[7] They also organized the most effective safer sex campaign the world has ever seen. Way ahead of the medical community, and light-years ahead of heterosexual people, gay and bisexual men normalized condom use.

Because of HIV, many teenagers in the 1980s and 1990s received at least some comprehensive sex education in school, but there was swift backlash.[8] The federal government soon refused to offer funding for anything other than abstinence-only sex education, the kind that instructs students to refrain from sex until marriage. Since the mid-1990s, tens of millions of federal dollars have been spent on these programs each year, including $110 million in 2021.[9]

If you *really* love him...

Rubbers – Every Time!

Facing a hostile federal government, gay men in the early HIV era organized their own safer-sex campaigns. Love for each other, and for their community, was one basis on which they mainstreamed the use of "rubbers," or condoms.

Just as comprehensive sex education was becoming rarer, the internet arrived. By 2000, there were over 17 million websites on the internet, 1 website for every 360 people on the planet. With so much competition for attention, producers of media both on and off the internet learned that more was more.[10] More fighting, more explosions, faster cars, cruder humor, and bigger disasters. And more sex too. Most people still aren't receiving much sex education at school, but they are getting quite an education online.

In 2017, the internet enabled the #MeToo movement. Coined in 2006 by the activist Tarana Burke, the hashtag is meant to draw attention to the frequency with which women experience sexual violence and abuse. It catapulted into awareness in 2017 after movie producer Harvey Weinstein's decades of abuse of women became public. When actress Alyssa Milano invited people on Twitter to say #metoo, half a million people responded within twenty-four hours.[11]

Soon it became a chorus of #allwomen, including those in middle- and low-status and underpaid occupations.[12] It was also used by sexual minorities, trans women, and cisgender men to draw attention to their abuse.[13] The hashtag resonated with already-organized feminist efforts, spurring mobilization around gendered violence globally.[14] A study of thirty-one countries found a 10 percent increase in the reporting of sex crimes in the following year.[15]

In the United States, news coverage of sexual assault became more expansive in the aftermath of #MeToo, helping dispel rape myths.[16] Over half of Americans report having a favorable view of the #MeToo movement.[17] Nearly three-quarters say they're inclined to believe women when they report being assaulted.[18] There's evidence, too, that sexual coercion and unwanted sexual attention in the workplace has declined.[19]

Then, in early 2020, the Covid-19 pandemic sent much of the world into "lockdown." Soon after, Tinder reported its strongest engagement in its entire history. A marketing officer for OkCupid reported that the company saw a 700 percent increase in virtual dating. Match, too, reported that use of video platforms skyrocketed.[20] Early data suggest that some college students using apps were Covid-conscious, asking potential partners about their levels of exposure, but it's unclear whether that translated into being more conscious and communicative about the risk of sexually transmitted infections.[21]

Among people without established partners, Covid-19 may have spurred some to broaden their sexual repertoire to include activities consistent with social distancing, like sexting and sharing fantasies. Some reported hooking up with their roommates as a way to have sex safely during the pandemic. Many said that long-term isolation left them longing for the kind of meaningful connection that hookups don't usually provide.[22] Married and cohabiting people initially had more sex, but the stress and anxiety brought by the pandemic suppressed their sexual activity over time.[23]

In sum, as the pandemic revealed rather abruptly, the context in which sex plays out changes, often in surprising ways. This has always been the case. Sex is subject to not only interpersonal dynamics but also institutional forces. These include disasters like pandemics and technologies like the birth control pill and the internet. Social change is also the result of activism: the revolutions of the 1960s and '70s and the #MeToo movement today. Everyday people have fought back against sexual oppression, and they still do.

Today, one core tenet of the sexual revolution—the idea that we should be free to consensually explore our sexualities—has become widely accepted in the United States. Has sexual liberation arrived?

ON "SEXUAL LIBERATION"

Many young Americans feel that sexual liberation involves saying yes.[24] Yes to learning about sexuality; to talking about it, brashly; to feeling comfortable seeing it, explicitly; and to displaying one's body in a sexual way. Yes to kink and sexual experimentation, however adventurous. And yes to doing it casually, just for fun. To say no to any of these things, the logic goes—to be conservative about sex, take sex seriously, or simply be uninterested in sex—is to deprive oneself of sexual freedom.

This definition of liberation, however, is a gendered social construct. The cavalier approach to sex described as "free" is consistent with a stereotypically masculine approach to sex, while the more careful and stereotypically feminine approach to sex is seen as prudish, even repressed.[25] This amounts to defining women's liberation as doing what men supposedly do. While this approach to sex is less sexist, it's still strongly androcentric.[26]

Still, many women—especially White, heterosexual, class-privileged women—believe that adopting a masculine approach to sex is what sexual freedom looks like. One such woman quoted in *American Hookup* put it this way:

> *I figured the best way for a girl to reject oppressive sexism would be to act in exact opposition of what our sexist society expects of a decent woman; to get exactly what she wants from men, whenever she wants it. In essence, objectify them back.*[27]

Granted, there are many good things about women feeling free to say yes to sex. It's meant greater tolerance for other peoples' choices, identities, and practices.[28] But it isn't freedom; it's just a new set of rules. And one of those rules is: *Say yes!* This led a student in *American Hookup* to worry she was being a prude when she turned down an opportunity to hook up:

I'm so embarrassed by that. . . . I "know" that I should want to have sex all the time,
and should take advantage of it when I get the chance; especially when it's a girl
who's showing interest in me. But I didn't. . . . Pressure to be sexual was and has been
SO CONSTANT for so long. . . . I feel as if by not voluntarily taking part in it, I am
weird, abnormal, and a prude.[29]

For people who don't want to say yes, don't want to say yes right now, or don't
want to say yes to just anyone or any activity, the imperative to say yes can feel
quite oppressive. There is also the matter of what it is that we're saying yes to.
Moreover, this new sexual playground isn't equally fun for everyone. This is
because sex is still saturated with gendered power and other kinds of power
imbalances too.

SEX, POWER, AND PLEASURE

In the 1980s, a debate among feminists spilled into mainstream culture. Dubbed
the "sex wars," it was an argument about what kind of liberation feminists
wanted.[30] On one side were "anti-porn" feminists who argued that pornography,
prostitution, and BDSM promoted men's violence against women. Some claimed
that even conventional penile-vaginal sex between women and men was exploitative, given that it carried patriarchal meanings that empowered men and disempowered women.

On the other side were feminists who cast themselves as "pro-sex." They saw
any attempt to stigmatize or control sexuality as a form of sexual oppression.
They accused the other side of seeing women as victims and denying their sexual agency. Feminists who would later be called "sex positive" were on this side
of the sex wars, as were many queer women who knew firsthand what it meant
to demonize a form of sexuality.

Ever since, feminists have struggled to reconcile the pleasure and danger in
sex.[31] Look no further than the controversy over the erotic novel *Fifty Shades
of Grey.* The story follows a sexually naive college woman's relationship with a
wealthy businessman who introduces her to BDSM. The book was a smash hit.

Feminists disagreed whether *Fifty Shades* was good for women. "*Fifty Shades*
has given tons of people—mostly women—permission to tap into desires that they
maybe did not have the okay to tap into before," said one feminist.[32] Another
described the protagonist as a "sexual sociopath," arguing that the film "glam-
ourised and eroticised violence against women and rebranded it as romance."[33]

For decades, women have wanted to say "yes to sex and no to sexism," but
sex and sexism have historically gone hand in hand.[34] Consider that we refer to

In the late 1970s and 1980s, the "sex wars" pitted feminists against one another. While some saw great potential for liberation in sex, others—like the feminists pictured here—focused more on the potential for harm.

sex with an f-word that also means "I hate you." In sex, someone gets f***ed—and it's not usually a man. Unless, of course, that man plays a receptive role in sex like women supposedly do.

This use of sex to enact power is ubiquitous in porn. Pornographers make billions each year producing material that is more exploitative and violent than in earlier eras.[35] One study found that 45 percent of scenes included physical aggression, most commonly, spanking, gagging, slapping, hair pulling, and strangulation.[36] Men were the aggressors 76 percent of the time and women were the targets of the aggression 97 percent of the time.[37] Sex can be many things, but unfortunately, one of those things is the enactment of masculine dominance and feminine submission.

The pro-sex feminists of the 1980s were probably too optimistic. If it's possible to drain sex of its nonconsensual power dynamics, we haven't done it yet. But the pro-sex feminists definitely won the sex wars. Today, 43 percent of Americans—a record-setting number—find pornography morally acceptable.[38] The percentage of people who want sex work legalized has doubled since 1978, to 52 percent of Americans.[39] And college students have largely embraced having sex just for fun.

In so many ways, this is great. There has been far too much sexual shame, stigma, and secrecy. But the anti-porn feminists weren't entirely wrong. Sex is socially constructed, and routinely enacted, to reflect gendered power dynamics. Accordingly, the remainder of this chapter focuses on exploring how this shapes how we think about and engage in sexual activity. It looks at how we define sex, divide up desire, eroticize inequality, and racialize sexuality. It also discusses how we "do" sex and the relationship between our sexual scripts and sexual violence.

DEFINING SEX

Most Americans continue to assume that new people they meet are heterosexual and monogamous, absent any signs otherwise. Likewise, our institutions are still organized around the idea that couples include one man and one woman. This is especially obvious around Valentine's Day, when companies offer hotel rooms fit for a "king and queen," spa packages for "beauty and her beast," and romantic dinners for "Romeo and his Juliet." Gifts like these are both heteronormative (designed on the assumption that everyone is heterosexual) and **mononormative** (designed on the assumption that everyone is monogamous).

Our definition of "sex" is also hetero- and mononormative. Generally, it's used to refer to one sexual activity in particular: penile-vaginal intercourse involving exactly one penis and one vagina. Essentially 100 percent of young people agree that penile-vaginal intercourse is sex.[40] About 90 percent agree that penile-anal intercourse is sex. But there's substantial disagreement about everything else.

People are especially thrown by sexual activities that don't involve a penis at all. When asked to define sex for lesbians, for example, a sample of college students struggled.[41] A heterosexual cisgender man named Brent, for example, floundered as he talked about what counts as sex between two women:

"Mr." and "Mrs." decorative pillows and other his-and-hers sets highlight how our institutions still assume that all sexual couples include one man and one woman.

It's so easy to define [sex] when there's a penis involved. . . . I'm gonna go on a limb and say there isn't lesbian sex. . . . There's no lesbian sex with only the human body being involved. . . . You could define lesbian sex with uses of dildos or strap-ons or what-not. It's almost like I want it to be more of like penis in a hole to be sex.[42]

Brent can't imagine sex that doesn't involve a penis or penis-shaped object. It's tempting to blame this on his gender and orientation, but people of all sexualities struggle to answer this question. Grace, a woman who's had sexual relationships with both men and women, was also unable to provide a clear answer:

> No one really knows what lesbians do, ever. . . . I feel like it's a lot less definable simply because society defines sex as penetration. So, because there's no penis usually, I mean no natural penis, in a same-sex female relationship, it's a lot less easy to define.[43]

The problem is not with either Brent or Grace but with a society that continues to define sex as whatever penises do.

Defining sex as penile-vaginal intercourse also positions it as the ultimate goal of all sexual activity between men and women. Euphemisms like *home base* and *all the way* are widely understood to refer to that specific activity. This is the **coital imperative**, the idea that any sexually active couple must be having penile-vaginal intercourse (also known as "coitus") and any fully completed sexual activity will include it.[44]

The coital imperative is heteronormative—making lesbian sex inscrutable, for instance—but it also creates problems for men and women who have sex together. When coitus is "real sex" and everything else is just "foreplay," having penile-vaginal intercourse can feel compulsory. If intercourse is undesired, difficult, or impossible—if women experience pain when penetrated or men struggle to maintain erections—the coital imperative defines their sex as dysfunctional.[45]

Since most heterosexual men reliably have orgasms during intercourse, but many women do not, the coital imperative also prioritizes an activity that privileges his orgasm at the expense of hers.[46] This contributes to an **orgasm gap**, a phenomenon in which women who have sex with men report fewer orgasms than men who have sex with women. Women having sex with men enjoy, on average, between one and two orgasms for every three of their partners'.[47]

Gendered myths about bodies suggest that this gap is inevitable, but it isn't.[48] Some countries have larger orgasm gaps than others. The gap in the United States, for example, is twice as large as the ones in Brazil and Japan.[49] Women who have sex with women have two to three times as many orgasms as women who have sex with men.[50] When women are alone, their rate of orgasm is as high as 96 percent.[51] Women have just as many orgasms as men when their orgasms are prioritized.

We naturalize the orgasm gap, though, treating it as inevitable, because we tend to believe that women are genuinely less sexual than men. But that isn't true either. Instead, we've divided up desire, taking from women the pleasure of lust and taking from men the pleasure of being lusted after.

DIVIDED DESIRE

Recall that the idea that home and work were distinct places emerged during the Industrial Revolution. That was when work was masculinized and the home feminized. With this move, women were charged with saving one part of life from the vagaries of capitalism. They did so by embodying love. The result was a gendered love/sex binary that framed men as sexual and women as romantic. This still pervades our understandings. In American culture, the two halves of desire—desiring and being desired—have been cleaved by the gender binary.

Women are sexy. Men are sexual. To be *sexy* is to be an object of desire for others; to be *sexual* is to have the capacity to experience sexual desire.[52] Most of us want to both feel sexual and be sexy, but the stereotypes tell us otherwise.[53] Men desire, they say, and women are desirable. Men want women. And what do women want? Women want to be wanted.

Reflecting these ideas, media assumes a **heterosexual male gaze**, meaning that content is designed to appeal to a hypothetical heterosexual man.[54] Over repeated exposure to the sexualization of a specific kind of woman (usually White, feminine, blond, and thin but curvy), men undergo a process of **sexual subjectification**: They are told what their internal thoughts and feelings should be. This may limit a man's ability to recognize when he's attracted to women outside the very narrow ideal, as well as when he's attracted to other men or nonbinary people.

For women, the heterosexual male gaze means being regularly exposed to idealized images of women's bodies. **Sexual objectification** is the reduction of a person to their sex appeal. To be clear, it's not the same thing as finding someone's body desirable; it's reducing

Real women and girls are seen through lenses formed by omnipresent sexually explicit images of women's bodies presented as desirable objects for the gaze of the presumptively heterosexual male consumer.

a person to nothing *but* a desirable body. Both men and women are objectified in popular culture, but women overall are objectified much more.[55] As a result, many heterosexual women internalize the idea that their value is heavily dependent on their ability to conform to a narrow and largely unattainable definition of attractiveness, whereas heterosexual men's value is somewhat less so.[56]

Men who have sex with men can be positioned as the objectifier, the objectified, or both. Standards of attractiveness in media content aimed at queer men can be as unrealistic as the content aimed at women. Research on lesbians is mixed. Media often portrays them as "hot" and "heteroflexible," therefore theoretically available to a sufficiently seductive man.[57] Some studies suggest that their lack of interest in men's sexual attention protects them, but other research suggests that the idealized images still take a toll.[58]

Consequently, many people—especially women and gay men—**self-objectify**, internalizing the idea that their physical attractiveness determines their worth. During sex, self-objectification may translate into a process called **spectating**, watching one's sexual performance from the outside.[59] Women might try to stay in sexual positions they think are flattering, arrange their body to make themselves look thinner or curvier, try to keep their face looking pretty, and ensure they don't make embarrassing noises.

Because of spectating, some people have "out-of-body sexual experiences" in which they don't focus much on how sex *feels*. Women may even avoid orgasm because doing so means losing control of these things. And, sure enough, research has shown that the more a woman worries about how she looks, the less likely she'll experience sexual desire, pleasure, and orgasm.[60]

EROTICIZED INEQUALITY

Not everyone is considered worthy of an objectifying gaze. The phrase **erotic marketplace** refers to an intersectional ranking of people according to their perceived sexual desirability.[61] It's impossible to live in the United States and not know what kind of person Americans place at the tippy top of the erotic marketplace. We see the young, tall, taut, able-bodied, light-skinned physiques in essentially all advertising and entertainment. These individuals are also usually presumed heterosexual, in part because they perform gender in conventional ways. Gender conformity is hot, at least among heterosexual people.

Perhaps for queer people too. The limited research on the preferences of women seeking women indicates a slight preference for gender-conforming partners.[62] The research on men seeking men suggests a strong preference for men who approximate hegemonic masculinity.[63] Recognizing a preference for "straight acting" men, some men try to enhance their erotic capital on Grindr and other apps by advertising their masculine qualities, a practice described as **mascing** (a portmanteau of *masculine* and *masking*).[64] Mascing may include expressing an interest in sports, emphasizing one's interest in the outdoors, or growing a hearty beard. It may even include identifying as heterosexual.

Sex, though, takes two. That makes attractiveness *relative*. In other words, we're often not looking for the hottest possible partner but one that "fits" with us, given our personal characteristics. Cultural norms, for instance, dictate that men pairing with women be a little taller, stronger, bigger, older, and more educated than their partners and have a higher-status, better-paying job. We have learned to feel attracted to a gentle asymmetry, one that gives men in such couples a tad more power than women.

The data on age put this in stark relief. Age is an imperfect measure of attractiveness, career success, and financial security. Online, men seeking women report that they'll date women who are quite a lot younger but only a bit older.[65] As they age, men become increasingly comfortable with larger and larger age gaps. In practice, men mostly seek contact with the youngest women in their reported age bracket and women whose ages fall below it.[66]

Men's willingness to date "down" suggests they prefer or will accept a mate whose career is "behind" their own. The average woman, conversely, prefers to date a man who is her age or older. As women age, they generally accept about five years on either side. In actual messaging, they tend to focus on men their own age.

For men seeking women, having advanced degrees and a well-paying job is always advantageous. For women seeking men, these things carry both advantages and disadvantages. A good education and high income may help a middle-class woman catch an accomplished man, but too much school or money could make her seem less appealing. Meanwhile, she's dinged on attractiveness as she ages, while same-age men become relatively *more* attractive by virtue of their mounting accomplishments.

Many women understand this. In a study of newly admitted MBA students, respondents were asked to share their salary goals. Half were told that their peers would see their answers and half were told they'd be confidential. Single women who thought their goals would be public reported salaries $18,000 lower than single women who were promised confidentiality.[67] They also reported lower ambitions, less interest in leadership, and less willingness to travel. Single men's answers didn't differ by condition. Concerned that seeming too ambitious or being too successful might make them unattractive to men, heterosexual women sometimes moderate their career goals.

The determinants of erotic attractiveness are not merely gendered, though; they're also intersectional. Next, we focus on the intersection of race, gender, and sexuality.

SEXUAL RACISM

Chapter 4, on intersectionality, reviewed the origins of racist sexual stereotypes about Black and Asian people, with Black people portrayed as hypermasculine and Asian people as hyperfeminine. These gender ideas often play out in stereotypes about sexuality. Racist sexual stereotypes about Black men and Latino men, for example—epitomized in the Black Buck and Latin Lover archetypes—portray them as especially sexual and sexually skilled compared to White men.[68] But this is a double-edged sword, and a sharp one.

On the one hand, by virtue of these stereotypes, Black and Latino men may be desired as sexual partners. But this doesn't necessarily feel good.[69] Desiring a partner because of his race is just another type of sexual objectification. On the other hand, Black and Latino men are often framed as *too* masculine and, therefore, sexually dangerous. Likewise, Muslim men are often stereotyped as violent, sexist, and untrustworthy.[70]

For Asian men, sexual stereotypes based on race are straightforwardly negative. Asian men are seen by some as unmasculine and, therefore, sexually deficient.[71] As Michael, a Chinese American, put it: "Asian men are smooth. Expected to be submissive. Expected to be quiet and not speak up and express their feelings. And they're supposed to be small-dicked."[72] Research shows that even some Asian women may hold these views.[73] Among men seeking men, there's some evidence that Asian men are expected to play a feminized sexual role.[74]

In a society that centers and elevates Whiteness, we would expect that White men would have an advantage in the erotic marketplace, and they do.[75] On dating apps, Black, Latino, and Asian men are substantially less likely than White men to get a response from either women or men. In one study of online dating behavior, college-educated White women were actually more likely to respond to a White man without a college degree than an Asian man with one.[76]

Racism and colorism also affect the desirability of women. Asian women are seen as hyperfeminine and therefore more sexually malleable than White women. This makes them appealing to men who are looking for subservient partners. One White American man who prefers Asian women explained: "I'm kind of a soft guy. I really find [White] American women overly aggressive."[77]

Asian, Pacific Islander, South Asian, and Middle Eastern women do well in the US erotic market. In contrast, Black women face a situation similar to that of Asian men: Racial stereotypes that masculinize Black Americans relative to Whites undermine a Black woman's erotic value. Black women are least likely to receive a response on dating apps. Latinas fall somewhere in between.

Actual dating and marriage patterns reflect what we see on apps.[78] White men are more likely to marry Asian women than Black women, and White women are more likely to marry Black men than Asian men.[79] Reflecting colorism, lighter-skinned racial minorities are more likely to intermarry with Whites than with darker-skinned minorities. A preference for a submissive wife sometimes sends White American men abroad looking for partners in Thailand or other Asian countries.[80] Asian women may choose to marry internationally in exchange for economic security; being a wife and mother in a foreign country may be preferable to being a nanny or maid at home. Of course, many of their husbands may well discover that their Asian wives aren't as deferent as they expected them to be.

Notably, most of these data were collected before George Floyd's murder in 2020 and the summer of protest in defense of Black lives. In a 2021 study of single people, 70 percent of respondents said they were open to dating someone of a different race or ethnicity, a 22 percent increase over prepandemic levels.[81] More than two-thirds of young people now prefer to date someone who supports Black Lives Matter and Stop Asian Hate, which may translate into being more open to dating someone of a different race. Sexual preferences may now be shaped at least as much by political identities as by racial ones. Cultures change—sometimes fast.

GENDERED SCRIPTS

By the time we have our first intimate experiences, we've watched hundreds, possibly thousands, of sexual and romantic interactions play out. Maybe we've watched pornography, where scenes are explicit, but we see "tasteful" representations of sex in all media. Notably, these sex scenes are written, edited, directed, and produced primarily by White men. An analysis of the top-grossing two hundred films of 2018 and 2019 found that 85 percent of directors and 83 percent of screenwriters were men; even higher percentages were White.[82] These men have valid points of view, but their perspectives, like everyone's, are shaped by their structural positions.

Of course, we also learn from our friends. But whoever they are, they're also trying to put the pieces together from media they consume. Eventually we start having our own sexual experiences, probably with people who learned similarly biased cultural lessons about what sex is supposed to be like, and those inform us too.

All these sources teach us what sex is, how it works, who does what, and what it means. So, when sexual interactions unfold in real time, they're guided not just by our own desires and the desires of our partners but also by the information we've gathered. The resulting knowledge is called a **sexual script**, a phrase that refers to the social rules that guide sexual interaction.[83] Sexual scripts are culturally derived and often shared sets of instructions for how to have sex.

Generally, US sexual scripts assume sex occurs between two and only two people. These two people kiss first (closed mouth), then have close body contact with more kissing (open mouth), and only then move to grabbing and squeezing. Once this has occurred, there's more kissing and groping, including the touching of genitals through clothes. Clothes start coming off, usually tops before bottoms. If it's a man and a woman, her clothes usually come off first (her shirt, his shirt, her pants, his pants, and so forth); it's a toss-up if it's a same-gender couple. Scripts have a somewhat rigid ascending order of intimacy: fellatio before cunnilingus, oral before penile-vaginal, penile-vaginal before anal, and oral before anal, depending on what body parts are involved.

We tend to be especially careful to follow sexual scripts when we're first becoming sexually active or when we're first becoming active with a new partner. Scripts are particularly helpful when we're concerned about doing sex "right." They create predictability and ease social interaction: *Did they kiss me back? Aha, now I have clearance to try for second base.*

The sexual script is also gendered.[84] Because masculinity is conflated with power, the masculine role in sex is an assertive one. The more masculine person makes the first move, touches first, pushes the interaction along, and removes their partner's clothes. The feminine role in sex is responsive. A feminine sexuality is one which waits, never acts or initiates. The feminine partner is put into sexual positions by the masculine partner. The masculine partner penetrates; the feminine partner is penetrated.

Conflating sexual power and desire with masculinity is behind the **push-and-resist dynamic**, a situation in which it's normal for men to press sexual activity forward and for women to stop or slow things down when he goes "too far."[85] This interferes with people's ability to enjoy sexual activity. Men may be thinking about what they *aren't yet doing*. Women, in turn, may be thinking about what her partner *might do*.

In practice, of course, people rarely behave in purely feminine and masculine ways, but men who have sex with women and women who have sex with men will probably recognize these dynamics. People who have sex with people of the same gender may recognize them, too, as masculinity and femininity can be "done" by anyone. Women are quite obviously capable of playing an assertive role—otherwise, they would never have sex with each other.

People who have sex with people of the same gender also follow sexual scripts. Gay culture in the United States differentiates among three distinct roles: tops, bottoms, and versatiles (each referring to whether a person is keen to adopt an active and sometimes penetrative role, a passive and sometimes receptive role, or both).[86] Consistent with heteronormative stereotypes, these roles are gendered: Topping is framed as masculine and bottoming as feminine.[87] Men who identify as tops are often ascribed masculine characteristics, while men who identify as bottoms are often assumed to be more feminine.

Because sex and power are linked in US society, gay and bisexual men, no less that heterosexual men and women, often think about topping as not just masculine but also dominating, and bottoming as not just feminine but subordinating too. Some gay men look down on bottoms and try to avoid being perceived as feminine themselves. Andy, a versatile, said he felt the "most manly" when topping, adding: "I don't want to be seen as just—as just a bottom.... That's seen as a more effeminate thing, I guess.... It's quite important for me to come across as masculine."[88]

Craig said that topping gives him a "surge of dominance," even though he identified as a bottom. To resist the stigma of taking on a feminine role, he described himself as an "active bottom." "Cause I'm quite keen on portraying myself as not just being a lying-on-your-back kind of bottom," he explained. "It doesn't affect my masculinity, because I'm not the kind of person to just lie there."[89]

Race and gender intersect here too. Asian men are stereotyped as feminine and therefore rightful bottoms, subordinated. Conversely, Black men are fetishized as hypermasculine and therefore rightful tops, dominant.[90] Among men who have sex with men, sex is sometimes used to establish one man's power over another.

Some White men, then, might seek out Black men as tops because they want to be dominated. But race can also twist the dynamics of topping and bottoming, serving to reproduce racial hierarchies.[91] Black men who have sex with White men report being expected to top on the assumption that they're sexually aggressive. When they do, White men may recast bottoming as being "served." When Black men are topped, their White partners may racialize their experience of power. A Black gay man named Paul, for example, reported that he doesn't bottom for White men anymore.[92] When the researcher asked why, he recounted several experiences with White men who sprung the n-word on him during sex.

Not all gay men adopt a top or bottom identity, and in fact some identify as versatiles specifically to avoid replicating heterosexual sexual scripts. Others reject the labels altogether. But the continued salience of these terms reveals how gendered power shapes sex, even when it's between people of the same gender.

Women who have sex with women appear to have the least scripted sexual encounters. The limited research on lesbian sexual scripts, most of which focuses on White women, suggests that they're more likely to talk about and ad-lib their sexual encounters.[93] They may not have a single "gold standard" that defines encounters as sex (like penile-vaginal intercourse for women with men).[94] "There's an awful lot of sex acts," said one bisexual woman in a long-term relationship with a woman, ". . . and we don't seem to run out."[95] Having fewer guardrails on what sex is might allow lesbians to have more creative sex lives, with more communication, than people who have sex with men.

Perhaps the people with the most imaginative sexual experiences are people of all genders and sexual orientations who have physical disabilities.[96] Research on this population reveals the flexibility of erotic sensation. People who acquire spinal cord injuries, for example, sometimes become sexually responsive outside of the conventional erotic zones. The experience of orgasm can change, too, becoming more abstract or full body. People with disabilities may also be more in touch with their bodies than people without, making them more comfortable with sex, less self-conscious about their attractiveness, and more sensitive to their bodies' capacity for pleasure.

Those of us with disabilities may not be able to follow our culture's sexual scripts, meaning we have to rewrite them. We might change our minds about or expand what counts as sex. And we might write scripts that are less rigid, more egalitarian, and degendered. As one woman with a disability said, "If you are a sexually active disabled person, and comfortable with the sexual side of your life, it is remarkable how dull and unimaginative non-disabled people's sex lives can appear."[97] Since all of us who are lucky enough to age will inevitably acquire disabilities, this is a freedom that can come with time. By freeing us from the ability to follow old scripts, aging and disability can be liberating.

SEXUAL VIOLENCE

That we even identify sexual assault as a crime is rather new. The Europeans who colonized the United States considered women property. Men could do whatever they wanted with their property, including rape it. If you raped someone else's property, though, you damaged the goods. So rape was more like theft than assault. Because enslaved people were also defined as property, the men given legal right to own them could abuse them with impunity.[98] The colonists denied Native men property rights, so unless Native women were owned by or married to White men, raping them wasn't a crime at all.[99] Much of this was true until about 150 years ago.

Even as patriarch/property marriage was replaced by a breadwinner/housewife model, men's right to sex didn't change right away.[100] Well into the 1970s, domestic violence, sexual harassment, and sexual assault went largely unregulated by the government. Violence between intimate partners was seen as part of men's legitimate right to "govern" their own homes. Sexual harassment was so routine there was no name for it.[101] And rape was normalized, especially when perpetrated by friends or acquaintances. Rape of men didn't legally exist until 2014 when the US government redefined rape as a crime against people rather than women.[102]

These things changed because activists raised money, recruited volunteers, opened domestic violence shelters, and staffed rape crisis lines.[103] They redefined sexual violence as a crime, collected data to demonstrate its prevalence, and argued that governments needed to protect survivors.[104] Rates of rape began to decline.[105] In 1986, the Supreme Court criminalized sexual harassment. In 1993, marital rape became illegal in all fifty states. In 1994, Congress increased criminal penalties for sexual violence and began funding special sexual assault units in police departments. In 2013, this was extended to expand protections for immigrant and Native women.

These are impressive accomplishments, but there's a lot of work left to be done. It's still hard for survivors to get justice. Often they're unsure whether what happened to them was a crime and worry they won't be believed.[106] Victim blaming is common, and many survivors (sometimes rightly) fear that they'll face more trouble than the person who assaulted them.[107] Only one out of every four sexual assaults is reported to the police.[108] Of those that are reported, only 2 percent lead to a conviction.

Justice is even more elusive for men, women of color, and anyone who carries socially stigmatized characteristics. Police officers sometimes decide whether to investigate reports of sexual assault based on the survivor's race, age, sexual orientation, or income level.[109]

Even in best-case scenarios, convictions can be cold comfort. In 2015, a Stanford student named Brock Turner was discovered behind a dumpster with his hands inside a woman named Chanel Miller. She was unconscious. Her underwear had been removed, and her skirt was pulled up over her body. She had pine needles tangled up in her hair and inside her body. Thanks to two eyewitnesses, Turner was convicted of assault with intent to rape and sexual penetration with a foreign object.

Turner's father pleaded for leniency, saying that prison time was a "steep price to pay for 20 minutes of action." The judge also minimized Turner's criminal behavior. He expressed concern for Turner's future and stated that he didn't believe that the newly convicted sex offender would be "a danger to others." Chanel Miller was there, listening. "I had to fight for an entire year," she would later write, "to make it clear that there was something wrong with this situation."[110] The judge worried that prison time "would have a severe impact" on Turner. He was sentenced to six months in prison. He would serve only half that. Three months—a summer vacation's worth of punishment.

Rape myths frequently underlie the decisions and judgments of police officers, medical examiners, lawyers, judges, jurors, and the survivors themselves, including the persistent belief that sexual crimes are falsely reported more often than other crimes.[111] They're not.[112] In fact, men are far more likely to survive a sexual assault themselves than to be falsely accused of one.

Sexual violence is not inevitable. In fact, it's extraordinarily rare in some societies.[113] Some environments, though, facilitate sexual assault. These are **rape cultures**, environments that justify, naturalize, and even glorify sexual pressure, coercion, and violence. The idea that men are naturally sexually aggressive is part of US rape culture, as is the idea that women are inherently vulnerable to

DON'T LET A NIGHT FULL OF PROMISE...

TURN INTO A MORNING FULL OF REGRET...

DON'T LEAVE YOURSELF MORE VULNERABLE TO REGRETFUL SEX OR EVEN RAPE. DRINK SENSIBLY AND GET HOME SAFELY.

For advice and information, visit www.herts.police.uk and www.hertssunflower.org
Always dial 999 in an emergency.

This campaign is funded by the County Community Safety Unit, a joint unit between Hertfordshire Constabulary, Hertfordshire County Council and Hertfordshire Fire and Rescue Service.

Images courtesy of Safer Watford

This British police campaign that intends to reduce the incidence of rape does so by putting the onus of preventing sexual assault on the woman, as do campaigns on many US college campuses.

men.[114] Vulvas and vaginas are socially constructed as passive and physically delicate (flower-like, easily crushed or bruised) or simply thought of as a vulnerable space (a "hole").[115] Penises, in contrast, are symbolically active and strong; they become "rock hard" and are used to "hammer" and "pound."[116] This contributes to a belief that men can use their penises as weapons.

In cultures where rape is rare, the vulnerability of the penis and testicles are more likely to be stressed. These cultures may also socially construct women's genitals as less delicate, emphasizing the power of the muscles surrounding the entrance to the vagina and the mysterious depths into which penises must blindly go.[117]

In the United States, media often promotes rape culture too. Routine in regular programming are images that glamorize scenes of sexual force, sex scenes in which women say no and then change their minds, and jokes that trivialize sexual assault, especially of men.[118] Rape scenes in movies and on television are common plot twists or character devices, purposefully designed to be sexually titillating. The hit series *Game of Thrones*, for example, used rape as a plot device at every turn. By one count, at least fifty times.[119] Fictional perpetrators are disproportionately men of color.

When news media cover sex crimes, they still often focus on the survivor's behavior, reporting on whether she was drinking, flirting, dressed provocatively, or making risky choices.[120] White women get more sympathetic coverage. Perpetrators who seem "respectable"—wealthy White men, for instance—are most often given the benefit of the doubt. Not uncommonly, stories about affluent men accused of rape are described as "sex scandals" instead of "sex crimes."

Rape culture also encourages and excuses the push-and-resist dynamic. Because they're expected to push for sex, men are at the highest risk of behaving in this way. Because women are expected to act polite and be nice, pushing is often effective.[121] People sometimes consent to sex they don't want or offer oral sex in place of intercourse to avoid making things "weird" or because they've been taught to expect violence from men if they don't give them what they want.[122]

Because of the push-and-resist dynamic, many sexualized interactions end up being coercive and manipulative. Much of this isn't criminal, just cruel and dehumanizing. So most women and femme-presenting people will experience a range of sexual pressure, manipulation, coercion, and force throughout their lives. Altogether, it is what feminist writer Robert Jensen calls a "continuum of sexual intrusion."[123] This is part of why the revelation of Weinstein's decades of abuse, alongside dozens of other men outed for similar behavior around the same time, snowballed into a hashtag. By saying #metoo, millions of people confirmed the sheer ubiquity of coercive behavior, from the merely selfish to the truly egregious.[124]

This doesn't just make for confusing and uncomfortable sexual interactions; it also gives camouflage to people who are intent on exploitation. The push-and-resist dynamic normalizes aggressive sexual behavior. When men behave this way, it is often brushed aside as "boys will be boys." This is exculpatory chauvinism: giving men a pass for exploitative, cruel, and otherwise thoughtless and dehumanizing behavior. The dynamic is also a catalyst for sexual assault. We teach men, and even women, that being sexually assertive is good, then expect them to parse the difference between pushy and criminal. It can be a thin line, and sometimes people cross it.

Fully 44 percent of women and 25 percent of men have experienced sexual violence, ranging from rape and forced penetration to sexual coercion and other forms of nonconsensual sexual contact.[125] Those of us at highest risk include low-income people, people of color, people with disabilities, people who are imprisoned, sexual minorities, and gender-nonconforming people. Sexual violence is most commonly experienced when people are young.

Almost all perpetrators of sexual violence are known to the victim. Men are the vast majority of perpetrators, representing 97 percent of people arrested for sexual assault.[126] Many perpetrators are also survivors of sexual abuse or violence, complicating a simple perpetrator/victim binary.

Sexual violence is a problem on many US college campuses. In fact, hookup culture is characterized by all the dynamics discussed thus far. The final section takes a closer look at the sexual culture found on many residential campuses.

COLLEGE HOOKUP CULTURE

The American college party today is a drunken mix of elation and recklessness. "Things get out of hand," sociologist Thomas Vander Ven observes, "but in an entertaining sort of way."[127] The party is euphoric in part because it's just a little dangerous. At its climax, it's a world apart, a place where it's normal for people to "fall down, slur their words, break things, laugh uncontrollably, act crazy, flirt, hook up, get sick, pass out, fight, dance, sing, and get overly emotional."[128] Casual sex, by virtue of being slightly reckless but oh so exhilarating, fits right in.

Well into the 1970s, colleges acted like substitute parents, treating students like children by imposing curfews and punishing them for drinking and sexual activity.[129] The boomer generation successfully pushed back against these practices, and that's when things got wild. The drinking age was eighteen, so students partied pretty much as hard as they wanted.[130] By 1978, when the movie *Animal House* cemented the relationship among college, alcohol, and sex, students were having all-out parties in residence halls. The alcohol industry took notice, spending millions of dollars in the 1980s to convince college students to drink.[131]

Then, in 1987, the balance of power on campus shifted. The federal government convinced all fifty states to raise their drinking age to twenty-one. Now students who wanted to party faced problems: Campus authorities were policing residence halls, bars required an ID, and most sororities weren't allowed to throw

Because fraternity houses are given implicit permission to serve alcohol to minors, fraternity men often control the one place where college students under twenty-one can drink and party. This gives these men an outsize influence over the social and sexual lives of their peers.

parties with alcohol. First-year students, especially, were unlikely to have friends living in private apartments and houses. Where could college students go to party?

The men who belonged to wealthy fraternities with private houses happily stepped up.[132] And, in a striking example of the privilege carried by wealthy White men in America, an unspoken agreement emerged: They were going to be allowed to serve alcohol to minors. Today, everyone knows that fraternity parties involve underage drinking. The students know. Their parents know. The professors know. The university administrators know. The police know. The mayor knows. *Everyone knows.* But no one meaningfully tries to stop them.

This gives a small group of students—men in wealthy, historically White social fraternities or, on some campuses, men in fraternity-like brotherhoods—a lot of power to shape their peers' social and sexual lives. Their parties are now iconic, standing in for *the* college party.[133] These sexy, rowdy environments also resonate with the current definition of sexual liberation: saying yes instead of no and, for women, grasping one's "liberation" by acting like a stereotypical guy.

Thus, the outsize influence and privilege of a small slice of men has become institutionalized on many college campuses. We see hookup cultures in higher education because the students who *do* like it have a great deal of power. It's *not* because everyone likes it. Up to three-quarters of students want more opportunities to find a romantic partner.[134] A third say their intimate relationships have been "traumatic" or "very difficult to handle."[135] Lots of students would like more options, even if they'd also like to hook up.

Who Hooks Up?

Most students overestimate how often their peers hook up, as well as how "far" they go and how much they enjoy it.[136] According to a survey of more than twenty-four thousand students at twenty-one colleges and universities, a third of students don't hook up at all. Fraternity and sorority members hook up almost twice as much as everyone else. Students of color, low-income students, immigrants and international students, and lesbian and bisexual women hook up with their peers less often than their counterparts.[137]

For students who experience same-gender desire, college parties aren't always safe or friendly. This is partly why Grindr arrived on college campuses years before Tinder. Facing hostility from the predominant heterocentric hookup culture, gay and bisexual men turned to apps to find potential partners off campus.[138]

Women interested in exploring same-gender desire are more likely to meet each other in small social gatherings friendly to queer people.[139] College parties may also be less exclusionary. Girl-on-girl kissing is often allowed as long as it's assumed to be for men's attention.[140] This allows some women with same-gender desire to hide in plain sight. They're able to experiment sexually under the guise of heterosexuality. Ironically, then, the hyperhetero college party is one place women can learn they're queer.

While Black men hook up somewhat more than average, Black women and Hispanic and Asian students are less likely than White students to hook up.[141] These students both pull themselves out and are pushed out of hookup culture. Students of color are, on average, more religious than White students, more serious about studying, and less interested in partying.[142] They also often face disinterest or even hostility from their peers, many of whom have internalized racist standards of attractiveness and racialized sexual stereotypes. Some students of color even see hooking up as a White thing.[143] "We don't sleep around like white girls do," said a Filipina American expressing this view.[144] "If I started hooking up," said a Black man, "my friends would be saying I'm, like, 'acting white.'"[145]

In general, college students who've immigrated to the United States are less likely to hook up than students who share their race and gender but not their immigration status.[146] These data best apply to Black men and Black, East Asian, and Latina women. Among East Asian and Latino men, both immigrants and nonimmigrants have relatively low rates of hooking up. And White men and women hook up frequently regardless of their immigration status, perhaps in part because White immigrants are more likely than non-White immigrants to be class privileged and come from countries that are culturally similar to the United States.

Research also suggests that class-privileged students hook up more often than other students.[147] Students are much quicker to ascribe the "slut" label to low-income women, even when they're less sexually active than their richer peers.[148]

Low-income women, then, hook up at the risk of being criticized for being too sexual. They are also often the first in their family to go to college, and so they may be more focused on their studies.[149] They may try to emulate the "rich girls" who take light course loads and party hard. If they do, low-income students may get caught in a lose-lose situation: The quality of their schoolwork declines. Meanwhile, they don't have parents who know people who can hand them fancy internships or great jobs upon graduation.[150]

Students from families with tight budgets (disproportionately students of color) are also likely to have a job outside of school and may live at home to save money. Sharing a small house with one's parents—often a car or bus ride from the party—isn't conducive to casual sex or heavy drinking. Students who live at home are also surveilled by parents who may have rules against partying, hooking up, and staying out late.

Men and women hook up at similar rates, but women report higher rates of regret, distress, and lowered self-esteem.[151] The gendered love/sex binary introduced by the Victorians would suggest that this is because women are more interested in love than sex. But college men are more romantic and more likely than women to say they're interested in a committed relationship.[152] So it's not true that women are sappy and men stoic about love. That women are specifically dissatisfied by hookup culture is better explained by their greater exposure to sexist and subordinating experiences.

Power

The myth of a gendered love/sex binary leads many of us to assume that men want casual sex and women don't. Many people presume that women are hooking up in search of a relationship while men aren't. Women may enthusiastically participate in hookup culture, then, only to discover that many men don't see them as equals.

Deanna reflected on just such an experience for *American Hookup*. She'd been hooking up with a guy named Reid. One day he pulled her aside to glumly tell her that he wasn't interested in a relationship. She told him she was fine with that (and she was), but he pressed on. "He more and more drastically emphasized asking if I was OK," she recounted, "seeming to expect a flood of tears."[153] His behavior was revealing. She thought they were both having fun, but he hadn't seen it that way. Reflecting on their encounters, she wrote:

> *The stigma attached to women being the emotional creatures in the relationship and the men being the physical ones had never been so apparent to me. . . . He clearly thought that he was the one with the power to hurt and I was the one that was expected to cry with anguish.*[154]

This experience made Deanna realize that the men she was hooking up with may in fact be looking down on her. "The hardest part of the whole affair," she wrote, was "seeing in an equal's eyes their opinion that I was inferior."[155] This is a benevolent form of sexism, an assumption that women are too in touch with their emotions to be able to hook up without catching feelings.

The sexist assumption that women have an insatiable desire for a boyfriend leads some men to stiff-arm women after hooking up with them. They may act aloof to ensure their partners don't get the "wrong idea." Women may act aloof too. They understand that some people don't believe women are capable of being casual about sexual activity, so they go to extra lengths to prove they can be.

Recall that men are also aligned in a hierarchy all their own, policing one another for their approximation of hegemonic masculinity. For college men who buy into hookup culture, climbing that hierarchy means hooking up a lot with women who "count"—that is, women who are hard to get. When they hooked up with women their friends thought were easy or desperate, they'd get teased.

Hooking up with all the hottest women, though, is possible only for the most sought-after men. For most, it's a recipe for failure. Corey—a White, heterosexual student in *American Hookup*—went so far as to call it a "hostile environment." It left him with an uneasiness that he talked about with his closest friend: "I don't want our reputations to be hurt or judged" after a hookup with the "wrong girl."

Fraternity men are especially likely to find themselves in the hostile environment that Corey observed, and research with men in fraternities finds that some respond with hostile sexism. Sociologist Brian Sweeney interviewed men in fraternities, finding that some preserved their rank by turning their hookups with low-status women into fodder for male bonding. They reported that when having sex with the "wrong" women, they'd be "rough, lewd and overly self-gratifying." They would try to "get something . . . without giving in return."[156] If they treated the low-status women they hooked up with badly, they could at least go back to their buddies and talk contemptuously about her. It's a way of saying, "I know she didn't count, and I made sure she knew it too."

Women who participate in hookup culture may encounter both benevolent and hostile sexism, leaving them feeling acutely disempowered.

Pleasure

American Hookup features a story in which two heterosexual White women—Ashlynn and Izzy—both laugh hysterically while recapping a hookup. Izzy had performed oral sex on her partner and was surprised when he appeared to be ready to return the favor. But then he went down and came right back up. He licked me, Izzy said to Ashlynn, just "once."

Ashlynn was astounded. "A single lick?" she asked. "We laughed until our stomachs were sore." They couldn't imagine a woman licking a man's penis just one time. It was funny but also irritating. "His short attention span indicates something more than laziness," Ashlynn wrote. It reflected a more pervasive phenomenon on campus: a "fellatio-cunnilingus double standard."[157]

Ashlynn is right about that double standard. Young people in America tend to think that performing oral sex on women is "a bigger deal" than performing oral sex on men.[158] Accordingly, men are less likely to perform cunnilingus (oral stimulation of a vulva) than women are to perform fellatio (oral stimulation of a penis).[159] When they do, men may also be less inclined to persist until their partner has an orgasm. When college students receive oral sex in hookups, men have orgasms nearly twice as often as women.[160]

The double standard contributes to an uneven distribution of sexual pleasure on campus.[161] In first-time hookups, women hooking up with men report 35 percent as many orgasms as their partners.[162] This is similar to the orgasm gap we see off campus.

FIGURE 9.1 | PERCENTAGE OF WOMEN HAVING AN ORGASM IN FOUR SEXUAL CONTEXTS, BY OCCURRENCE OF SELECTED SEXUAL BEHAVIORS

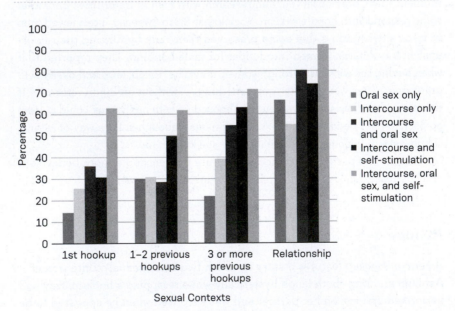

Note: Oral sex refers to receiving oral sex.
Source: Elizabeth A. Armstrong, Paula England, and Alison C. K. Fogarty, " Orgasm in College Hookups and Relationships," in *Families as They Really Are*, Second Edition, ed. Barbara Risman (New York: W. W. Norton, 2015), 291.

Interestingly, we know that at least some college men are excellent at giving women orgasms. As Figure 9.1 shows, when a man and a woman hook up together repeatedly, the orgasm gap shrinks. It shrinks further if they decide to become a couple. The far-right column shows that when couples use a variety of forms of stimulation, women have orgasms 92 percent of the time.[163]

Research suggests that some college men care about their girlfriends' pleasure but not their hookup partners'. One put it this way:

> If it's just a random hookup, I don't think [her orgasm] matters as much to the guy.... But if you're with somebody for more than just that one night ... I know I feel personally responsible. I think it's essential that she has an orgasm during sexual activity.[164]

To be fair, women hooking up with men often don't put their own pleasure first either: "I will do everything in my power to, like whoever I'm with, to get [him] off," said one woman about her priorities during a hookup.[165] Both men and women tend to believe that men are more entitled to orgasms. This is illustrated most strikingly by a bisexual student who realized, upon putting some thought into it, that he concentrated on giving his partner an orgasm when he hooked up with men but on getting one when he hooked up with women.[166]

Danger

If college women have less power and experience less pleasure in hookup culture than men, they also face more danger. Fully 26 percent of cisgender women and 7 percent of cisgender men report being sexually assaulted in college. Sexual minorities of all kinds, but particularly people who are bisexual, experience especially high rates of sexual violence. And 23 percent of trans, nonbinary, gender-fluid, and gender-questioning students are victimized in college. Almost all undergraduates believe that sexual assault is a problem at their school, including 92 percent of women, 87 percent of men, and 95 percent of gender minorities.[167]

As with the national statistics, the vast majority of perpetrators are men, regardless of the gender or sexual orientation of the survivor. Eight percent of college men report behavior matching the definition of sexual assault.[168] About half of these incidents involved physical force, and about half involved incapacitation with drugs or alcohol.

Rates of sexual violence are high on campus in part because hookup culture is a rape culture.[169] Its sexual scripts make coercive behaviors look and feel normal (plying people with alcohol or pulling them into secluded parts of a party) while making a feminized interest in and concern for one's partner off-script (including caring about their pleasure and consent). This camouflages the behavior of students who are intent on raping their peers, but it also puts students at

Emma Sulkowicz, a visual arts student at Columbia, made national headlines when she began carrying her mattress around campus to dramatize the inaction of university officials after she reported being sexually assaulted by a fellow student.

risk of perpetrating rape. And if men are put in the "push" role in the push-and-resist dynamic, we might expect men in particular to be perpetrators.

Serial perpetrators are a problem on college campuses, but a longitudinal study of rape perpetration found that four out of five college men who commit rape before graduation are not serial perpetrators.[170] They rape only once. It may not be the content of one's character but the context of hookup culture—the risk-loving parties, the pressure to "get" sex, and the normalization of aggressive sexual behavior—that leads some students to commit sexual crimes.

The role of context in creating a dangerous sexual environment cannot be overstated. As an example, consider the death of Timothy Piazza. In 2017, Piazza was a nineteen-year-old sophomore at Pennsylvania State University. While pledging Beta Theta Pi, he was exhorted to drink what a forensic pathologist called a "life-threatening" amount of alcohol.[171] Soon after, he tried to leave the house, but he was too drunk to work the lock on the front door. Looking for another exit, he found the door to the basement. He opened it and fell headfirst—and hard—down the basement stairs.

He was found unconscious, and some fraternity brothers carried him to a couch. Surveillance footage showed the Beta Theta Pi brothers poking his face; slapping, punching, and throwing shoes at him; sitting on him; and pouring beer on his face.[172] A large bruise is visible on his side; his ruptured spleen was pouring blood into his abdomen. His would-be brothers watched as his limbs twitched. At one point, he appears to have a seizure. A man Snapchatted a picture of him.

At various times over the course of the night, Piazza wakes up, gets up, and falls again. He falls onto the stone floor of the basement. He falls into a metal railing. He falls behind the bar . . . again, and again, and again. His face becomes bloodied, distorted.

The fraternity brothers didn't call 911 until nearly 11:00 a.m. the next morning, twelve hours after his first fall.

Those men let Piazza die. But here's the thing. If any of those men had found Piazza in that condition on a sunny sidewalk on a Sunday afternoon, they almost certainly would have gotten help immediately. Yes, their behavior reflects their characters, but it was also strongly conditioned by the fact that fraternity parties are places where people are *supposed* to get incredibly drunk, even dangerously drunk. And when they do, it's not a cause for concern. It's *hilarious*. That's why someone Snapchatted it.

Our environments powerfully shape our behavior, often bending it to fit the culture we're in. The sexual cultures on college campuses are environments like these. They're present, perhaps most strongly, in places like fraternity houses. When these cultures are rape cultures, they don't just camouflage rape; they generate it.

Rape culture also makes it difficult for campus activists fighting sexual violence to hold colleges accountable for effective prevention and fair resolution, though much progress has been made on this front. In 2011, the Office for Civil Rights released a statement explaining that Title IX, a law that prohibits sex-based discrimination in education, requires colleges to be proactive in reducing rates of sexual violence.[173] In the following years, students at hundreds of colleges submitted complaints to the federal government, arguing that their institutions were ignoring or mishandling sexual assault.

The Trump administration rescinded the 2011 statement, ultimately delivering new guidelines. These raised the burden of proof, narrowed the range of behavior that could prompt intervention, allowed for hostile interrogations of survivors, and excused colleges from responding to incidences of sexual violence that occurred off campus (including at fraternity and sorority houses and off-campus apartments).

The year 2021, however, ushered in a new wave of survivor-activism. Protests erupted across the country. Student activists held walkouts, vigils, and demonstrations at more than one hundred colleges.[174] They're protesting Greek life's promotion of rape culture and how colleges handle both sexual violence prevention and response.

Student-activists have changed their campuses in the past and they will continue to do so.[175] A next step may be thinking bigger, not only about the acute problem of sexual assault but about the many problems in the wider sexual culture

Students at Virginia Tech participate in a rally against sexual assault. In 2021, students at more than one hundred schools engaged in activism aimed at addressing sexual violence on campus.

as well. Promoting a culture that values care and consent, gives equal importance to women's pleasure, embraces sexual minorities and gender-nonconforming students, and addresses intersectional inequalities would make colleges, and the country, safer spaces for all.

Revisiting the Question

Q+A Gendered ideas, interactions, and institutions may affect almost every part of my life, but some things are personal, and my sexuality is mine and mine alone, isn't it?

Sex, no less than anything else, is shaped by interactional norms, institutional forces, and social activism. The women's movement, gay liberation, and sexual revolution changed the sexual landscape for today's young Americans, but there is much left to do. The new imperative to say yes to sex is not the same thing as sexual freedom. Sex, like so much of our culture, is still plagued by gendered power dynamics and intersectional inequalities.

These problems are a big part of why so many college students find hooking up unpleasant or even awful. And these problems are spurring activism that may usher in new sexual cultures still.

Before long, though, students will be graduates. In the next decade, most will find themselves juggling engagements and weddings and extended families.[176] Their marriages will be unlike any in history. For the first time in thousands of years, marriage law prescribes to men and women the same rights and responsibilities, meaning married couples today have the capacity to build truly egalitarian partnerships. One source of oppression for women appears to have crumbled.

And yet, despite changes aimed at giving women equal footing, women who marry men have become increasingly unhappy with their marriages over the last thirty years. Why?

Next . . .

Women today experience significantly less wedded bliss than men married to women, women married to women, and single women.[177] In fact, despite the cultural messages that insist that women crave marriage and children more than men do, research shows us that the happiest women are single and child-free. This prompts us to ask:

If marriage is better for women than ever, why do women married to men report lower levels of happiness than men married to women, women married to women, and single women?

An answer awaits.

FOR FURTHER READING

Armstrong, Elizabeth. "Accounting for Women's Orgasm and Sexual Enjoyment in College Hookups and Relationships." *American Sociological Review* 77, no. 3 (2012): 435–62.

Armstrong, Elizabeth, Laura Hamilton, and Beth Sweeney. "Sexual Assault on Campus: A Multilevel, Integrative Approach to Party Rape." *Social Problems* 53 (2006): 483–99.

D'Emilio, John, and Estelle Freedman. *Intimate Matters: A History of Sexuality in America*. Chicago: University of Chicago Press, 1997.

Ghaziani, Amin. *Sex Cultures*. Cambridge: Polity Press, 2017.

Harding, Kate. *Asking for It: The Alarming Rise of Rape Culture and What We Can Do about It*. Boston: De Capo Lifelong Books, 2015.

Wade, Lisa. *American Hookup: The New Culture of Sex on Campus*. New York: W. W. Norton, 2017.

Ward, Jane. *The Tragedy of Heterosexuality*. New York: New York University Press, 2020.

OTHER COUNTRIES
HAVE SOCIAL SAFETY NETS.
THE US HAS WOMEN.

—DR. JESSICA CALARCO[1]

10

Families

Thanks to hundreds of years of legal reform and social change, individuals have substantially more freedom to arrange their relationships as they wish. This is what feminists have been fighting for. Yet for women married to men, this has not translated into happiness.[2] On average, American women married to men are the least happy. They're less happy than single women, the men they're married to, women married to women, and men married to men.[3] Less than a quarter of women, but more than a third of men, think happiness comes more easily to married people than single people.

Partly for these reasons, women married to men are as likely as their husbands to have an affair that precedes divorce.[4] They're also more likely to initiate a separation. After divorce, women are happier than they were when married; for men, the opposite is true. Accordingly, divorced women are more likely than divorced men to say they'd prefer to never marry again.

All this prompts the question:

> **Q+A** If marriage is better for women than ever, why do women married to men report lower levels of happiness than married men, women married to women, and single women?

The reasons have to do with the gendered nature of childcare and housework and the surprising contrast between what people say they want and what they actually do. This chapter reviews the many different ways that families attempt to balance paid and unpaid work, with an emphasis on how gender intersects with other features of families. Throughout, it will show how women's disproportionate responsibility for devalued and unpaid categories of labor creates disadvantages for all women, exacerbates inequality among women, and places women married to men at odds with their husbands. Unfortunately, while love and care are central to families, both gender difference and inequality are reproduced in families too.

THE SECOND SHIFT

Sociologists use an expansive definition of family, inclusive of all kinds of emotionally meaningful connections. Among families, we often see shared genetics, cohabitation in the same household, and relationships formalized by marriage or adoption. But many families have other features.

In the United States, the "traditional family" is imagined to include a husband, a housewife, and a child or children. Today, however, only 3 percent of households fit this description. Nearly 28 percent of households are made up of adults living alone and 2.4 percent comprise roommates. Another 7 percent of households include a cohabiting couple and 47 percent of households a married one. Single parents represent 11 percent of households.[5]

Even when we consider parents, only 22 percent of married couples with kids under fifteen years old include a breadwinner and a full-time homemaker. In fact, prior to the Covid-19 pandemic's interruption of employment, nearly three-quarters of all mothers, including almost two-thirds of mothers with preschoolers, were in the workforce. Accordingly, breadwinner/homemaker households were outnumbered by both single-parent families and dual-earner two-parent families (in which both partners engage in paid work).

People without a homemaker—including people with roommates, people who live alone, single parents, and dual-earner families—face a specific challenge: finding time to do the cleaning, cooking, errand running, bill paying, and parenting (if there are children) that housewives have historically done for breadwinner husbands. That work is described as the **second shift**—the work that greets us when we come home from paid work.[6] Groceries must be bought, dinner must be cooked, messes must be cleaned, budgets must be balanced, and plants and pets must be tended to. If there are children, there are chores to supervise, homework to review, and games to play. At the end of the day, kids must be bathed, soothed, and put to bed. In short, the second shift is a lot of work, *especially* when it involves taking care of young children.

In addition to all the physical activities, the second shift requires cognitive attention. The phrase **mental load** refers to the intellectual and emotional work of parenting and household maintenance.[7] This includes learning and information processing (like researching pediatricians), worrying (like wondering if your child is hitting developmental milestones), and organizing and delegating (like deciding what to cook for dinner).

Carrying the mental load is an invisible kind of work. Thinking and worrying can't be seen. It's also never done. It weighs on us in the shower, when we're trying to sleep, and when we're out with friends. As you can imagine, those of us who carry the mental load for a household often wear ourselves out.

Compared to previous eras, caring for children is also especially time intensive today. American parents have become more anxious about their children's financial futures, and rightly so; middle-class livelihoods are increasingly precarious. In response, parents in the United States—especially middle- and upper-class parents—engage in **concerted cultivation**, an organized effort to develop a child with a wide range of skills and talents, with the goal of making sure they get ahead in a fiercely competitive society.[8] This means preparing a child from birth for the attainment of an undergraduate or graduate degree from the best

In the hopes of giving their children every possible advantage, parents today engage in concerted cultivation. By signing their children up for track and field, for example, these parents may be trying to stoke a competitive spirit.

possible college, an achievement that's believed to be the key to decent wages and a stable job.

Upper middle-class families in China today are also adopting this strategy. Their version of concerted cultivation includes developing fluency in English as well as researching and investing in tutoring that prepares children for university exams.[9] The Chinese are explicit about the goal of producing a "high quality" (*suzhi*) child who will reflect well on the Chinese nation.

Called the "rug rat race," concerted cultivation puts no boundaries on the time parents should be devoting to their child's development.[10] When children are little, this may mean providing constant interaction and brain-stimulating activities. It may also include teaching children how to navigate adults' expectations and institutional structures. When getting dressed or having dinner, upwardly striving parents often negotiate with young children rather than simply telling them what to do, offering them important lessons about how to interact with authority figures. Black middle-class parents rely on concerted cultivation not only to pass on class privilege but also to give their children lessons about systemic inequalities and coping skills for weathering racial discrimination.[11]

For older children, concerted cultivation includes maximizing their educational achievement by volunteering at school, meeting with teachers, and helping with homework. Such parents may keep a close eye on their kids' grades, enrolling children in after-school and weekend activities like piano lessons, Little League, and dance classes. Since many of these activities are costly, concerted cultivation may require mom's employment or dad adding a second paid job to cover the costs. Indeed, in less affluent families, both parents put most of their effort into providing economically for children.

The second shift demands that we perform a range of household activities, carry a heavy mental load, and prepare our children for an uncertain future. This is a lot for anyone to handle, and in the United States women do the lion's share of this work. A quick exploration of the feminization of housework and childcare is next.

THE FEMINIZATION OF HOUSEWORK AND CHILDCARE

In America today, the proportion of time men and women spend in paid and unpaid work differs in gender-stereotypical ways, especially after children arrive. To put it more simply, parents of all sorts are working hard, but fathers partnered with women do about two-thirds of the paid work and one-third of the unpaid work, and mothers partnered with men do the inverse.[12] Specifically, the average mother married to a man spends twenty-five hours per week working for pay, while her husband spends nearly forty-three hours, an eighteen-hour difference. Meanwhile, he spends about eighteen hours per week on the house and kids and she spends thirty-two, or fourteen more.

Why are women doing so much more housework and childcare and men doing so much more work for pay?

Idealizing Motherhood

Throughout most of American history, children were seen as "sturdy innocents" who were capable of "self-correction."[13] Experts assumed children would "grow up well unless corrupted by adult example." In other words, as long as they didn't encounter a person who set out to harm them, children could be expected to look after themselves, learn about life, and become well-adjusted adults.

Well into the 1900s, some experts even argued that catering to children was harmful. In 1907, the doctor who pioneered the science of pediatrics wrote a child-rearing advice book in which he argued that infants "should be left much alone" and "never be played with."[14] In fact, mothers were given strict warnings not to over-love. In 1928, the author of one of the best-selling child advice books of all time cautioned that "mother love is a dangerous instrument":

> An instrument which may inflict a never-healing wound, a wound which may make infancy unhappy, adolescence a nightmare, an instrument which may wreck your adult son or daughter's vocational future and their chances for marital happiness.[15]

As for affection, he advised: "Kiss them once on the forehead when they say goodnight. Shake hands with them in the morning." But only, he said, "if you must."[16]

It was in this context that the psychologist Harry Harlow set about proving that babies needed more than just food, water, and shelter. In the 1960s, he did experiments in which he deprived baby Rhesus monkeys of a warm mother figure, showing that such deprivation led to psychological harm.[17] He concluded that monkey babies, and human ones, too, needed comfort and even love.

This conclusion resonated with the argument that middle-class White Victorian wives had been making for decades. Recall that the gendered work/home distinction was new at the time that child-rearing experts were warning about the dangers of mother love. Wives knew that their freshly separated sphere was devalued, and the idea that children didn't need much from their mothers contributed to the falsehood that housewives weren't working. To preserve their social standing, these women claimed that mothering was an essential, skilled, and time-consuming enterprise.[18]

This was the birth of the ideology of **intensive mothering**, the idea that child-rearing (1) requires "copious amounts of time, energy, and material resources"; (2) should take priority over all other interests, desires, and demands;

and (3) is the responsibility of mothers specifically.[19] Epitomizing the ideology, a mother named Debbie proclaimed:

> For me, I feel it is vital to be there for my children every day, to consistently tend to their needs, to grow their self-esteem, and to praise them when they're right, to guide them when they're not, and to be a loving, caring mom every minute of the day.[20]

Today, intensive mothering is the predominant ideology of care in the United States. That's certainly the case among middle- and high-income people, and it increasingly influences all socioeconomic classes.[21] In fact, its demands have grown even more intensive: Today mothers who work full-time spend about as much time with their children as stay-at-home moms did in the 1970s.[22]

Parenting in Pop Culture

The ideology of intensive mothering is seen plainly in pop culture. A recent analysis of Mother's and Father's Day cards, for example, revealed that dads were often thanked for earning money and passing down useful skills.[23] "A good dad teaches you how to properly swing a hammer," said one card. "A great dad teaches you what to yell when you smash your thumb. Thanks, Dad, for all the lessons." In contrast, cards for moms emphasized emotional support and self-sacrifice. One expressed gratitude "for all the little things you've done . . . and still do . . . to make me feel loved in a big way."

In sitcoms, mothers are presented as nurturing and involved parents, while fathers are often portrayed as inept. An analysis of top-rated family sitcoms from 2000 to 2020 found that fathers were depicted as "humorously foolish" in more than half of a random sample of scenes.[24] Low-income fathers and married fathers are especially likely to be portrayed this way.[25] The classic example is Homer Simpson of *The Simpsons*. Wikipedia describes the character as stupid, lazy, and impulsive.

This theme is reproduced in apps for expectant parents.[26] Many apps assume that fathers are only moderately interested in learning about pregnancy, birth, and newborns. One app offers "short, punchy tips" that men can absorb while "sitting on the train, in front of the TV, or on the toilet." Learning about pregnancy is gamified for men, whereas women are assumed to be intrinsically motivated.

Americans receive daily messages affirming the idea that it is women's specific responsibility to go above and beyond in caring for children, even when they share them with men.[27] There's even a sneaky linguistic switcheroo that reveals that mothers are considered the primary parent and fathers the secondary one. The masculine version of a term usually comes before the feminine:

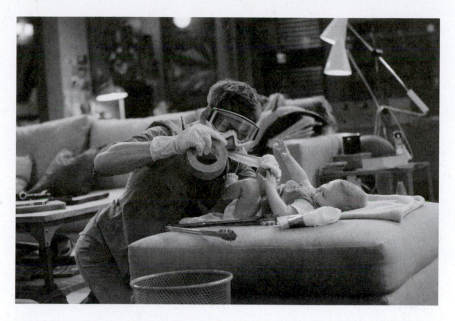

In pop culture, fathers are often portrayed as incompetent caregivers to comedic effect, reinforcing the idea that childcare is best left to women.

"men and women," for example, "Mr. and Mrs.," "his and hers," and "boys and
girls." But writing about parenting usually addresses "mom and dad."

But what happens when households don't consist of a cisgender man paired
with a cisgender woman?

Housework and Childcare across Households

Even in households without any women, housework and childcare are still
considered "women's work." Men who live with other men as roommates, for
example, still often think of cleaning as "girly." This makes for difficult negotiations over chores. In one study, men roommates did masculinity specifically by
being blasé about cleanliness.[28] When asked about how he and his roommates
kept the house clean, Rick insisted that he didn't even think about it. "It doesn't
really matter. I mean, it's not like something I consider. It's not like I'm caring
about it if it happens or not."

Since caring about cleanliness is feminized and our society is androcentric,
these men avoided doing household tasks whenever possible. Jeremy explained
that they'd eat out or order in when all the dishes were dirty rather than wash
them. Likewise, they'd put off doing laundry until they had nothing left to wear
or wait to clean the toilet until their moms were coming to visit. Smelly clothes

and visiting moms were accounts: a motivation for cleaning *other* than a femi-nized desire for cleanliness.

Interviews with cis women partnered with trans men also illustrate the femi-nization of domestic work.[29] In a study of these partnerships, cis women usually did most of the housework, and this arrangement justified the trans men's mas-culinity. "He's very forgetful and he doesn't take care of himself and he's messy and all this other stuff," said one interviewee named Lilia. "I feel like he's very specifically like a boy in this way."[30]

Studies of gay fathers reveal that childcare, too, is feminized. In one study, gay dads used language associated with women to describe their caregiving. They talked about their "biological clocks" and "maternal instincts" and described themselves as "housewives" and "soccer moms."[31] Nico and Drew, a couple with twin toddlers, used this kind of language when describing how they shared their childcare responsibilities:

> Nico: Since I don't work as often, I am more of the mom role. I am home more with them. I'm the one who takes them to the park during the week and I usually feed them and . . .
>
> Drew: Wait, I am just as much a mommy as you! Just because my job is more lucra-tive does not automatically make me the dad, and besides, we both feed them din-ner, read to them, get them to bed and I always do the dishes so that you can relax.[32]

Even when you're a gay man, parenting makes you a "mommy."

When men actively parent, the feminization of childcare causes others to see them as the exception rather than the rule.[33] In a study of stay-at-home fathers, a dad named Lew explained that strangers are regularly inspired to comment on what they view as an odd sight—a man alone with kids:

> People always say, "Oh, so you're babysitting the kids today?" Or, "Oh, it's daddy's day," or "You must have the day off from work," or something like that. They assume that I work somewhere and this is just this random day that I happen to be with the kids, which really irritates me.[34]

Other stay-at-home dads report similar experiences.

Studies of all-men roommates, gay couples, cis women partnered with trans men, and single dads all reveal the feminization of both housework and child-care. This brings some level of stress to nearly every family in America. In fact, conflict over household chores and parenting is among the top reasons for divorce.[35] Accordingly, finding ways to balance paid and unpaid work is one of the most important things couples can do, especially if they decide to have children.

BALANCING PAID AND UNPAID WORK

Sexism has declined since the 1960s, and professional opportunities for all women have expanded. White and Black women are now, on average, more educated than their men counterparts. Economically, most families need two incomes to make ends meet. This combination of structural and ideological changes has shifted expectations for mixed-gender marriages.[36]

Compared to previous generations, few people today are **traditionalists** (advocates of breadwinner/housewife marriages in which men are responsible for earning income and women are responsible for housework and childcare) or even *neo-**traditionalists*** (advocates of breadwinner/superspouse marriages in which men remain responsible only for earning income and women *both* work outside the home and retain responsibility for housework and childcare). Instead, most young adults are **egalitarians**, preferring relationships in which all partners share breadwinning, housekeeping, and child-rearing.

Women, younger people, people with college educations, and Black Americans are especially likely to be egalitarians.[37] Black and Hispanic fathers do somewhat more housework and childcare than White fathers.[38] This is partly because Black and Hispanic families have rarely been able to afford stay-at-home wives. Regardless of race or ethnicity, same-gender partnerships are somewhat more balanced than mixed-gender ones.[39] Whether partnerships involving trans or nonbinary people are more egalitarian is still unclear.[40]

Because Black men and immigrant men of all races and ethnicities have largely been shut out of the "family wage" that allowed some American men to support a housewife, Black and immigrant families have a stronger tradition of sharing. In such cases, both partners are well aware that women's earnings are critical to a family's well-being. This is part of why Black Americans are more likely than others to be egalitarians and why Black and Hispanic men are more likely than White men to do household chores and childcare.

By contrast, social norms in East Asia have put primary emphasis on men as earners and family authorities, but these traditions are challenged at home by women's aspirations and in the United States by the challenges of immigration. In South Korea, grandmothers may provide childcare if their daughter's educational and occupational trajectory is upward. In the United States, young Asian American men are ambivalent about their fathers' single-minded focus on jobs and achievement; they want to be more involved parents, but like most men, they struggle to let go of the role of breadwinner.[41]

In the 1980s and 1990s, White non–college educated men were increasingly shut out of a family wage, thanks in large part to the decline of union jobs in the United States. Married women's employment was becoming essential for nearly all families. As a result, more White families moved toward an egalitarian model. By the 2000s, it was normal for both men and women to want to share bread-winning, housework, and childcare.

In fact, when the sociologist Kathleen Gerson asked eighteen- to thirty-four-year-olds how they would ideally divide homemaking and breadwinning, the majority said they wanted to **share**, or have each member of the couple do more or less symmetrical amounts of paid and unpaid work.[42] Sharing was preferred by about 80 percent of women and 70 percent of men, and the desire to share spanned race, class, and family background. And yet in practice, most couples don't share. They **specialize**; they split unpaid and paid work so that each partner does more of one than the other.

This raises a question: If most people want relationships in which they share paid and unpaid work about equally, why do studies find that couples specialize in practice? As you might have learned in your own families, sharing is hard.

The Struggle to Share

Both work and family are **greedy institutions**, ones that take up incredible amounts of time and energy.[43] In these greedy institutions, high expectations for workers conflict with high expectations for parents. This makes it difficult for people to excel at work, thrive at home, *and* engage in sufficient self-care.[44]

Sometimes both members of a couple have the resources and inclination to lean out of work and into the family. These families are comprised of **dual nurturers**, couples who turn away from work and toward the home to focus together on the housework and childcare.[45] In some cases, the opportunity arises because of the nature of a couple's work. They may share farm labor, run a small business together out of their home, or hold jobs with odd but complementary schedules, like teachers and emergency medical technicians.[46] It helps to have jobs with hourly rates that are high enough that they can pay their bills even while working part-time. A therapist and an accountant, for example, might make enough money to make ends meet while taking turns being home during the day with their children.

Dual nurturing challenges the sexist idea that women should be held uniquely responsible for the undervalued work of housework and childcare. And, on average, dual nurturing is great for families. Because their relationships are more egalitarian, dual nurturers are among the happiest of mixed-gender couples.[47] In fact, a greater likelihood of sharing is one theory for why same-gender couples are happier on average than marriages between a man and a woman.[48]

Even in dual-nurturer mixed-gender couples, though, ideological commitment to the breadwinner and housewife lingers. Sociologists generally consider duties shared if the division of labor is between 40/60 percent and 60/40 percent. Fifty-

fifty arrangements—where a man and a woman split paid and unpaid work exactly—are the second happiest of sharing arrangements.[49] The happiest are ones in which there's a slightly asymmetrical division of labor tilted in the stereo-typical direction: a woman who does 60 percent of the domestic work and a man who does 60 percent of the breadwinning. Gender-swapped relationships—in which the man does 60 percent of the homemaking and the woman does 60 per-cent of the breadwinning—are the least happy of the three (though they're still happier than spouses who specialize). This suggests that men and women are more comfortable with *almost* sharing than with sharing and that flipping the script can strain relationships.

Though dual nurturing undermines sexism and subordination, it doesn't mit-igate the androcentric devaluation of childcare and housework. Instead, both partners simply have to live with it. The low status and economic risks of being family focused accrue to *both* members of a dual-nurturer couple. It takes a real ideological commitment to make it work.

It also requires the ability to afford *two* compromised incomes and the eco-nomic penalties that come with this strategy. Many families access health insur-ance through a parent's employer, but this benefit typically accrues only to employees who work a forty-hour workweek. Many dual nurturers, especially if both are self-employed or neither has a full-time schedule, have to be able to buy health care out of pocket. (Citizens of countries with nationalized health care don't face this problem, giving them more options for how to organize their families.)

Moreover, dual nurturers face higher taxes. Among high-income earners, the Social Security tax rewards breadwinner/homemaker families over those who share these duties; the income of a couple in which one earns $150,000 a year and the other earns nothing is taxed less than a couple in which both partners earn $75,000.[50] This is a tax incentive for specializing couples and a tax burden for sharing ones.

The placement of homes, childcare centers, workplaces, and doctors' offices in different parts of town poses another institutional barrier to sharing. Long commutes add to the workday, making it difficult for two earners to participate fully in home life. Commutes are a consequence of zoning laws that separate residential and commercial districts. If we zoned differently, it might be easier for families to share.

When couples realize that specialization is necessary, the smartest option may be to invest in the career of the partner who has a higher salary and greater oppor-tunity for advancement. But the workplace, as the next chapter will make clear, is no more gender neutral than the family. Men married to women typically earn more than their wives, making it sensible for many families to prioritize the man's career for purely economic reasons.

If a child arrives, it may be financially smart for the new mother to take time off from work instead of the new father. As new mothers focus on the child, new fathers ramp up at work.[51] They then do even less housework than before.[52] In response, wives often work even less, citing their husbands' hours and the new housework demands as a reason why.[53]

Many moms relish the opportunity to focus on the family (and many dads are jealous). Still, there's a price to pay: Each month a woman stays out of the workforce is a month during which her partner is building a career. With her taking care of their domestic life, he can lean into breadwinning and aim for raises and promotions. By the time she's ready to work full-time again, he'll likely be "ahead" of her. When the next baby comes along, it makes even *more* economic sense for the couple to prioritize his career instead of hers. Once a couple specializes, the disparity only grows.

Consider Daniela and Matthew, a couple profiled in the *New York Times*.[54] They met in college and both earned law degrees. Before they had children, they both worked at big law firms. Ten years and two kids later, Daniela works half-time and Matthew is making six times her salary. Like 20 percent of fathers and just 6 percent of mothers, Matthew works at least fifty hours a week.[55] Sometimes more.

Importantly, Matthew could not have been as successful at work without Daniela's help. "If he has to work late or on weekends," she explained, "he's not like, 'Oh my gosh, who's going to watch the children?' The thought never crosses his mind." She adds:

> *I'm here if he needs to work late or go out with clients. Snow days are not an issue. I do all the doctor appointments on my days off. Really, the benefit is he doesn't have to think about it.*[56]

Like many couples, Daniela and Matthew were egalitarians, but it wasn't feasible for both to pursue work with equal fervor. Corporate law requires lawyers to respond to their clients quickly and at all times of the day or night.

It also didn't make financial sense for both Daniela and Matthew to switch to a less demanding specialty. Since about 2000, working very long hours has become increasingly lucrative for white-collar professionals.[57] In corporate law, Daniela estimated, "being willing to work 50 percent more doesn't mean you make 50 percent more, you make like 100 percent more." Accordingly, investing in just one career made financial sense.

Same-gender couples also face the pressures of time and money. Three-quarters of same-gender couples specialize, and they're especially likely to do so if they have children.[58] Their divisions of labor are generally more equal than those of mixed-gender couples, come in more diverse forms, and follow logics other than gender, but the same social forces push them toward specialization. "The truth is," said psychologist Abbie Goldberg, "same-sex couples wrestle with the same dynamics as heterosexuals. Things are humming along and then you have a baby or adopt a child, and all of a sudden there's an uncountable amount of work."[59]

Institutional forces like tax and zoning laws make sharing difficult, pushing couples of all kinds toward specialization. Further ideological pressures make that specialization gendered. When push comes to shove—when the "uncountable amount of work" descends upon their families—many women are still drawn to the idea of being the center of family life and many men have a hard time abandoning the breadwinner role. Asked about their "fallback plan"—what they would like to do if they discover that sharing isn't possible—70 percent of otherwise egalitarian men choose a neo-traditional arrangement (Figure 10.1). It turns out, if equal sharing proves too difficult, men overwhelmingly hope to convince their partners to deprioritize their careers and focus on homemaking and raising children. Matthew exemplifies this plan:

> If I could have the ideal world, I'd like to have a partner who's making as much as I am—someone who's ambitious and likes to achieve. [But] if it can't be equal, I would be the breadwinner and be there for helping with homework at night.[60]

Most men value their role as workers too much—and perhaps homemaking too little—to imagine deprioritizing their own career. "If somebody's gonna be

FIGURE 10.1 | MEN'S AND WOMEN'S FALLBACK PLANS

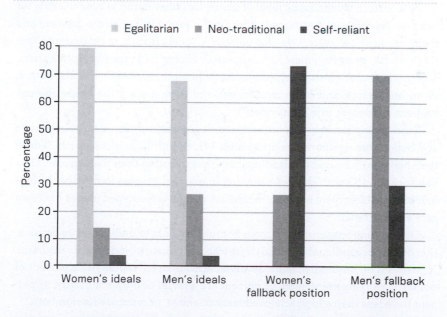

Source: Kathleen Gerson, *The Unfinished Revolution: Coming of Age in a New Era of Gender, Work, and Family* (New York: Oxford University Press, 2010), 129.

the breadwinner," Jim said, "it's going to be me."[61] Even when it comes to the new ideal of engaged fathering, men pull back when the demands are at odds with what they see as their primary role: financial support.[62]

Only a quarter of egalitarian women prefer neo-traditionalism as a fallback plan, but they may find themselves negotiating with a husband who does. Studies suggest that wives are rarely able to convince a neo-traditional husband to adopt an egalitarian division of labor.[63] For class-advantaged families, one solution to this stalemate is to hire outside help. While this approach allows both partners to pursue time-intensive careers and preserve their identities as egalitarians, it comes with costs.

Paying for the Privilege

One sharing strategy involves both members of a couple prioritizing their careers. These are dual breadwinners, couples in which both partners lean in to demanding, high-paying occupations. Such arrangements are especially common among highly educated, professional-class couples. Especially if they have children, dual-breadwinning families almost certainly engage in extensive **domestic outsourcing**: paying nonfamily members to do family-related tasks. If both parents want to remain on accelerated career tracks, most of these families will need to hire a substantial amount of outside help.

To a certain extent, some level of domestic outsourcing is now the rule for families. Nannies are outsourced childcare, for example, but so are day care and the occasional babysitter. We also outsource meals (eating in restaurants, getting takeout, or having meal kits delivered), chores and errands (dry cleaners, dog groomers, or mechanics), education (schooling, of course, but also tutors, swim instructors, and camp counselors), and work around the house (housekeepers, gardeners, and "handymen").

Outsourcing can help economically privileged couples offload the second shift and build more egalitarian relationships. Wives with high incomes can reduce their housework hours by offloading it onto people other than their spouse. Husbands can too. One study of outsourcing in married couples found that the first investments often went to reduce husbands' gender-stereotyped chores like lawn care and car repair.[64]

Outsourcing feminized work does nothing, though, to undermine its devaluation or give professional status to those who do it. Instead, it displaces the harm. It pushes it off onto other, more disadvantaged people.[65] Ninety-two percent of domestic workers are women, 52 percent are a racial or ethnic minority, 32 percent have less than a high school education, and 35 percent are foreign born.[66]

Domestic jobs are generally considered "bad jobs," ones with long hours, low pay, little flexibility, no security or chance for advancement, and few benefits.

The average wage for a live-in nanny, for example, is $11.60 an hour.[67] Only as of 2013 were domestic workers legally entitled to pay at or above the minimum wage and to days off, overtime, and contributions to their Social Security accounts. The Supreme Court has still denied them the right to unionize, and enforcement of their legal rights is thus difficult and rare.

Importantly, many women who perform housework and childcare for other people also have children of their own, and they're usually not allowed to bring them to work. Because their wages are low, they purchase the even lower-wage services of even poorer women. These women, in turn, leave their own children with family members or friends. Sociologist Rhacel Parreñas calls this a **care chain**, a series of nurturing relationships in which the care of children, older adults, or people with disabilities is displaced onto increasingly disadvantaged paid or unpaid carers.[68]

Caring brings decreasing financial returns as you go down the chain. A nanny working for a wealthy family in the United States might earn $450 a week. She, in turn, may pay a live-in domestic worker in her country of origin $45 a week. That worker may leave her children to be taken care of by their older sister or grandmother for free.

At the top of the care chain, the caregiving of middle- or upper-class children becomes the responsibility of poorer women, often women of color, whose own children receive less care as a result.

These care chains are not only economic; they displace love and its benefits by pushing them up the chain.[69] Nannies spend weekdays doting on their employers' children.[70] On weekends and evenings, they fit time with their own children around their own errands, housecleaning, and other routine activities. Their own second shifts leave little opportunity for quality family time.

This displacement is especially extreme for migrants. Vicky is a thirty-four-year-old mother of five. She left the Philippines to work for a family in Beverly Hills. "[It's] very depressing," she said, sighing, referencing how much she misses her children. She finds solace in loving the child for whom she nannies: "The most I could do with my situation is give all my love to that child."[71]

The child in Beverly Hills benefits from Vicky's love as well as the love of their own parents. Vicky's time and attention are diverted from her children, whom she can love only from afar. That absence is partially filled by attention from their lower-paid nanny in the Philippines, who likely has her own child or children in an even less secure arrangement, where they're deprived of a certain amount of love and attention from their own mother. In other words, the excess love that the child in Beverly Hills receives comes at the expense of other, less fortunate children.

Because of androcentrism, we devalue the feminized domestic sphere relative to the masculinized work sphere. Because of sexism, we expect women to bear the brunt of this trivialized, unpaid, and sometimes disparaged activity. In this way, the relationship between husband and wife is a systematic form of gender subordination not unlike the relationship between doctor and nurse or boss and secretary: In each case, the relationships reproduce both difference and inequality.

Class-privileged families can replace some of women's conventional efforts with outsourcing. In making this patriarchal bargain, wealthier women may excel at work, but this isn't "women's liberation." An intersectional lens reveals that the harm is merely displaced and mostly onto women of color, poor women, and migrant women.

Blending and Extending Families

Few Black families in history would have had the financial means to outsource feminized household duties or leave a wife at home to perform them. As a result, Black Americans are less likely to endorse the ideology of intensive mothering.[72] Instead, many Black people—including the contemporary middle- and upper-class Black mothers studied by sociologist Dawn Marie Dow—ascribe to **integrated mothering**, an ideology that promotes women's work outside the home, financial self-sufficiency, and a network of support.[73]

As an alternative to intensive mothering, integrated mothering helps protect many Black mothers from the guilt felt by some White mothers, since it doesn't position working and mothering as inherently contradictory. It also proposes a diffusion of responsibility: Black mothers may be less likely than White mothers to think they're supposed to do it all by themselves.

Believing in integrated mothering, many Black mothers reach out to extended family and friends for help raising their children. They've traditionally relied on **othermothers**, women who provide care for the children of friends, family members, and neighbors.[74] Faith, a Black mother interviewed by Dow, said:

> I think of my network as my village.... My mother is a member, my sister is a member, and my girlfriends are members. I also am beginning to become friends with stay-at-home moms who are willing to lend their support.[75]

Fatherhood is also less closely connected to biology in Black American culture. Brothers, cousins, uncles, and grandfathers, as well as neighbors and friends, often act as **otherfathers**, men who provide care for the children of friends, family members, and neighbors.[76] In these communities, both maternal and paternal attention come from many different sources. This may be why Black children who grow up with single parents don't struggle as much as White children do.[77]

This network of support typical in Black communities is a form of **extended family**, a more expansive family form that includes grandparents, aunts, uncles, and friends. Reliance on extended families is common across most of the world, including the Middle East, Central and South America, southern Europe, sub-Saharan Africa, and Asia.[78] In many places around the world, grandmothers watch their daughters' children during the workday, making women's wage earning possible.[79] In the United States, this is typical in White working-class families, immigrant families, and Black families. Help from grandparents, whether they live in the same household or nearby, is often critical for families lacking the high wages that college-educated White women expect to earn by the time they feel ready to have children.

Extended families most resemble the oldest human family form and have persisted across the world in different ways. The Mosuo in China, for example, have long separated the raising of children from sex and romance.[80] Women live with their sisters, mothers, and grandmothers, with the eldest woman as head of household; they all raise their children together. Mothers may also maintain romantic relationships with the father(s) of their children, but fathers live with their own mothers. From the Mosuo point of view, separating romantic and sexual

Among the Mosou people in China, children are raised in multigenerational households headed by women.

relationships from the bearing and raising of children is smart. It ensures that romantic whims and sexual urges don't disrupt children's home lives.

In the United States, sexual minorities have been forced to be creative about family. Especially before adoption and reproductive technologies were legally available to them, same-gender couples formed "families by choice."[81] Two men in a relationship may have recruited a close woman friend to be the mother of their child, or a lesbian couple may have asked a best friend to donate sperm. These adults then sometimes collaborated as co-parents, with three or four adults collectively committed to building a family together.

Polyamory is another way to build an extended family. Children with poly-amorous parents may have three or more adults on whom they can depend.[82] Many hands make light work, so polyamorous families can share the burden of the second shift with more than one or two adults. It's easier to pick up the kids from school, help with homework, and make dinner when there are three or four people to do it. Moreover, income from several adults may give the family more economic stability and each individual greater flexibility, perhaps enabling many adults to work less (not a dual- but a triple-nurturer arrangement).

Because divorce and remarriage are so common, many Americans live in blended families, a type of extended family consisting of partnered adults with at least one child from a previous relationship. Forty percent of married couples with children have blended families.[83] In some cases, children in blended families split their time among multiple households. In these cases, many adults may share responsibility for children, and each child will have more grandparents who can help care for them.[84]

In all extended family arrangements, women are still probably the ones taking primary responsibility for housework and childcare. And there's no guarantee that they won't suffer reduced status, interpersonal power, and economic security as a result. Moreover, as much as such arrangements have the potential to ease the burden of the second shift by distributing it among many adults, there's also the potential of burdening just one family-focused adult with supporting multiple breadwinners. Bigger families do not necessarily translate into an absence of gender ideology, but they do present an opportunity to challenge gendered divisions of labor.

Blending and extending family are ways that people cope with the barriers to sharing. Faced with insufficient time or money to make their families hum, others turn to specialization.

Deciding to Specialize

In practice, most families can't afford either the extensive outsourcing needed for dual breadwinning or the two compromised careers required for dual nurturing. Staring down the institutional barriers to sharing, and familiar with the ideological lessons about men's and women's "roles," most families adopt some version of specialization.

"TRADITIONAL" FAMILIES Some people idealize the 1950s-style breadwinner/homemaker marriage. Advocates of this specialized family model are traditionalists. Frank, for instance, explains: "I look at myself as pretty much a traditionalist. It's the way I am inside. I feel that the man should be the head of the house. He should have the final say."[85] Carmen, Frank's wife, agrees. She just wants to be "taken care of," she says.[86]

We see traditionalist breadwinner/homemaker families mostly in religiously conservative families and at the highest and lowest family income levels. Highly paid men who make the elusive "family wage" can afford for one parent to stay home. Fully 46 percent of mothers whose husbands bring in $250,000 or more in annual income, for example, stay at home. These families may rely on one earner voluntarily.[87]

Over a third of mothers whose husbands have annual incomes under $25,000 also stay home full-time.[88] Instead of being voluntary, this is often the only choice for poorer families. While many countries heavily subsidize childcare, the United States does little to ensure that access is universal and affordable.[89] As a result, the average cost of infant care is $15,888 a year.[90] In many states, this is more than average in-state college tuition and exceeds the entire pretax income of a full-time minimum-wage worker. If both parents are low income, they may *save* money by leaving a partner at home.

In one-earner two-parent families, whether high or low income, the full-time homemaker is usually a woman. Only about one in five stay-at-home parents is a father, though that's twice as many stay-at-home dads as there were twenty years ago.[91] Fathers of color and fathers without college degrees are more likely to stay home than their counterparts.[92] Most stay-at-home dads, however, are not home because they *want* to be a primary caregiver for their children. Instead, they're home because they're unemployed, ill or disabled, in school, or retired.[93]

The highest- and lowest-earning households are most likely to leave a spouse at home, but middle-income families are up against somewhat different pressures: Their incomes are high enough to allow them to afford childcare but not so high that they can live on one income alone. They typically respond to the time crisis produced by the second shift and ideology of intensive mothering by adopting a more gentle form of specialization.

BALANCING TRADITION AND CHANGE In breadwinner/superspouse marriages, one partner focuses on breadwinning, and the other *both* works and takes care of the home. Advocates of this model are *neo*-traditionalists: They believe that a woman can work if she needs or wants to but only if it doesn't interfere with her "real" duty to take care of her husband and children. A neo-traditionalist named Sam, for example, explains that he would accept a working wife, but "if she wanted to work, I would assume it's her responsibility to drop the kids off at grandma's house or something. She's in charge of the kids. If she's gonna work, fine, but you still have responsibilities."[94]

By definition, superspouses work full- or part-time and still take on most of the second shift: juggling a paid job, the logistics of day care, and the needs of a spouse and children. These folks are busy. In fact, the average employed mother spends over sixty-three hours a week on paid and unpaid work.[95] She has four and a half fewer hours of leisure time than your average employed father and spends more time multitasking.[96]

Especially if they're women, superspouses also shoulder most of the mental load. They do more of the planning, worrying, and information collecting. This is often justified with the benevolently sexist idea that women are simply better at this than men. "I know the basics," said a dad named Matteo about his one-year-old daughter's dietary requirements:

> Each month [our daughter] kind of changes in terms of what she can eat and can't eat and how you prepare it—I think [my wife] Leah has all the knowledge. I'm always surprised with what she came up with . . . because I would have never thought about it.[97]

Matteo attributed Leah's capacity to keep track of their daughter's needs to Leah's personality, stating that she would "always be better at sensing what our daughter needs as a next developmental step."

When dads step in to do the second shift, it's often described as "pitching in."[98] Traditionalist and neo-traditionalist husbands can be good "helpers" but usually only if their partners actively give them tasks to do. Nina, for example, who is partnered with a trans man, describes her management of their household this way: "I remind him to do a lot, and am the planner and really sort of controlling about a lot of things. He is the one who is super flaky and forgetful. . . . So the dynamic is me trying to keep on the ball about things and him assuming that I'm going to take care of it."[99]

Because superspouses are constantly organizing and delegating, it may seem like they're in charge at home. In a sense, they are. They decide what gets done, when, and how. But they don't have the freedom to walk away from these responsibilities. In this sense, breadwinners hold plenty of power because superspouses can get a break only with the breadwinners' cooperation.

Meanwhile, getting breadwinners to help can be a job all its own, and one that contributes to ugly interpersonal dynamics: "nagging" superspouses and "henpecked" breadwinners.[100] Ruth, in a relationship with Cindy for nearly a decade, comments:

I have learned how to read Cindy for moods. . . . I don't know if she realizes that I am scanning the moments waiting to ask her to clean out the fireplace or hose out the garage, but that's what I do. I sort of get in tune with the rhythm of her life now and it seems to work.[101]

Don had something similar to say about his partner, Gill:

I have to prod him; "bitch at him" is what he would say. I have found it difficult to figure out ways to bring up the condition of the house without creating too much of a fight. I sort of have learned that there are certain times to bring it up. . . . Of course, he doesn't see any of this—it's annoying—nor does he recognize what an effort it is to get him to help.[102]

The fact that we see this same dynamic in both same-gender and mixed-gender partnerships reminds us that the demands of housework and childcare force even gender-unconventional thinkers to do gender in conventional ways. This gendered dynamic also puts all people who do household work into a subordinate role, one that harms not only their egos but also the quality of their relationships and the size of their bank accounts.

The Price of Specialization

Victorian women introduced the ideology of intensive mothering to resist the androcentric devaluation of the domestic sphere, but these efforts were not wholly successful. Housework and childcare remain low-status activities. When we've asked our students what their parents would think if they decided to have a child and become a stay-at-home caregiver after graduation, people of all genders often suggest that their parents would be disappointed, even aghast. Students imagine their parents would exclaim, "What did we spend all that money on college for!?" or "That would be a waste of your intelligence!" It's as if people think parenting requires no skills, zero knowledge, and even less brain power.

People sometimes say that a woman who stays at home "doesn't *do* anything." Even homemakers sometimes refer to their work as "*just* staying home"—doing nothing important, in other words. "Oh, so you don't work?" a homemaker might be asked as she quickly mops the kitchen floor so she can run by the dry cleaner before picking up her child from preschool, feeding him a snack, and finding something for him to do so she can begin preparing dinner.

This androcentrism can motivate women to take on the superspouse role, since staying in a paid job after having a child, no matter how draining, becomes a way to continue to assert one's value. Even women who are in physically demanding and underpaid jobs may see staying home full-time as a worse option. One

White woman with a factory job said she'd advise the wife of a traditionalist husband this way: "Do what I did; tell him you will either get a job or have an affair,
just to have some time away—but he's the boss, so it's his choice!"[103]

It's no wonder so few men choose to be stay-at-home fathers. Though the typical man wants their wife to specialize in domestic labor if they can't manage to
share, most would be loath to take on that role themselves. "I would never stay
home," said a young man named Josh. "I have a friend who's like that, and I
strongly disapprove. . . . I think it's wrong because his wife's out there working
seven days a week, and he's doing *nothing* except staying home."[104]

Gay men often view the role similarly. Rich, for example, asked, "What about
one's self-respect?" when he contemplated being a full-time homemaker. "I don't
see how one could live with oneself by not doing *something* for a living."[105] Note
how Josh and Rich's language—"doing nothing" vs. "doing something"—betrays
their belief that feminized household labor isn't really anything at all.

In interpersonal relationships, those who specialize in domestic work sometimes feel as though their partners don't value their contribution to the household, and they might be right. They may also have lost bargaining power in their
relationships. One wife who quit her job to stay home with her children gave an
example:

> It's funny now because he is the breadwinner so there have been . . . opportunities
> to relocate and get a better position and the money was better. You're just put in a
> position where you have to just follow. Before when we were both working we would
> talk it out.[106]

Stay-at-home fathers can feel similarly. About his wife, one explained,

> She's the one bringing home the money right now so I feel, in financial decisions, I
> feel a little . . . bit more uncomfortable about, saying oh, we should spend, we should
> buy this or do this or that sort of thing.[107]

We see these status and power differences in all kinds of couples where one
person specializes in domestic work: among neo-traditionalists, mixed-gender
couples in which men are primary caretakers, same-gender relationships, and
even polyamorous relationships involving three or more people.[108] In losing status,
homemakers often feel at least somewhat subordinated to their breadwinners.

Caregivers' vulnerability isn't limited to status and interpersonal power. It's
also economic. In the United States, taking time out of the workforce to raise small
children means lost wages, benefits, and Social Security contributions, which
means less money in retirement. Wryly, this is called the "mommy tax."[109]

When a person reenters the workforce, they'll be on a less lucrative trajectory
for the rest of their lives. The typical college-educated American will sacrifice

nearly $2.1 million over the course of their lifetime for the pleasure of staying home with their children.[110] Mothers who take less than a year off see a drop of 11 percent; mothers who take three years or more off incur, on average, a 37 percent decrease in income.[111]

In sum, most Americans want to build families in which both spouses balance paid and unpaid work in an egalitarian way. In practice, both ideological and institutional forces make this difficult or impossible for most. Dual-nurturer spouses are up against health care and tax laws, for example, that penalize them for choosing family over work. Dual-breadwinner families must be able to afford to pay for the work that wives have historically done for free; even if they can, it will require outsourcing low-status domestic work to (mostly) less privileged women.

Some spouses respond by specializing, adopting either traditionalist or neo-traditionalist models. People in these families are less happy than those in dual-nurturer families, and women married to men are the least happy of all. Faced with a husband who insists they should be a homemaker or work for pay and still take care of the house and children, almost three-quarters of women would rather divorce and raise their kids alone (Figure 10.1).

GOING IT ALONE

What appears to be a happy convergence between young men's and young women's ideals—almost all egalitarians—can turn into an intractable situation. When their ideals bump up against an institutional context that makes sharing difficult, and their fallback plans come to the fore, the man is likely to want his wife to focus on the home. In that case, she might prefer to end the marriage altogether. When couples separate, custody is granted to the mother most of the time. A quarter of American children live in single-parent households and 80 percent of custodial parents are mothers.[112]

Other people go it alone from the get-go. Today, about a third of adults—including both people who are heterosexual and sexual minorities—will spend their prime childbearing and child-rearing years without a spouse.[113] Many of these individuals will choose to have and raise children anyway.

Sociologists Kathryn Edin and Maria Kefalas, for example, spent five years getting to know 162 racially diverse low-income single mothers in Philadelphia.[114] Many of them had children while they were young and unmarried, something middle-class Americans believe to be self-defeating. Why did these women make this choice?

The answer to this question is counterintuitive. Low-income women sometimes have children while they're young and unmarried out of a deep respect

Women attend a Single Mothers by Choice support group. Women on both ends of the class spectrum sometimes opt to have children without the help or support of a spouse.

for the fragility of marriage. They value the idea of marriage but also watch as relationships around them are so often torn apart by poverty and imprisonment. While they remain hopeful about the possibility of building a stable relationship, they're also skeptical. Accordingly, young women like these often vet potential husbands very carefully, dating for five or ten years before marrying.

Moreover, when young low-income women do get pregnant, they may have more reason to have the child than not. Young class-privileged women see a child interfering with their plans for college and a career. In contrast, low-income youth don't often imagine that these things are on the horizon for them. So why should they wait? They consider an early pregnancy less than ideal but something they can embrace.[115]

On the other end of the class spectrum, some class-privileged women make the same choice at an older age.[116] As having a child "out of wedlock" has become less stigmatized, voluntary unmarried motherhood has increased. Between 1994 and 2014, the number of women who reached their midforties as never-married mothers tripled.[117] Today, 40 percent of babies are born to unmarried people.[118] A rising proportion of these parents have postgraduate degrees like JDs, MDs, and PhDs. Some high-paying tech jobs offer egg-freezing as an employment benefit, encouraging their employees to delay parenthood and keep their focus on work.

Anna, a forty-year-old "single mother by choice," explains how she came to her decision:

> I really believe that children are made from two people that love each other and want to create a family. But if that is not an option, you just have to draw a way around really. Because if you are running out of time, you just have to see what option you have to have a child. And then have a father [later].[119]

When women today have the economic resources, access to technology, and enough social support, increasingly they are choosing to have children without a partner.

Compared to the United States, other countries do quite a bit to support single parents. Many offer over a year of fully paid childcare leave; some, like Sweden and Germany, offer months of extra leave only accessible to fathers. Germany adds years of credit to mothers' pensions too.

Particularly in America, then, solo parenting exposes the economic vulnerability that comes with responsibility for housework and childcare. Forty-four percent of children in single-mother households live below the poverty line, compared to 26 percent of those living with single fathers.[120] Nearly a third of families led by single mothers are food insecure, with 62 percent using food stamps; these families often spend more than half their income on housing.[121]

Some of these single parents are poor because day care costs exceed the earnings of a person working full-time. Or childcare leaves so little money left over that it's impossible to afford even an austere lifestyle. Government subsidies for low-income single parents help some out of this bind, but these programs are woefully underfunded in the United States. In 2020, thirteen American states had children on waiting lists for subsidized childcare. In Texas, the state with the longest waiting list, more than thirty-four thousand children are eligible, but the state has no money for them and nowhere to place them.[122] Even parents who can access federal income support programs are allowed to use them only for two years, after which they're ineligible.

Seventy percent of single moms work for wages, but this doesn't guarantee financial security.[123] The US federal minimum wage is still only $7.25 an hour. A full-time employee earning minimum wage who doesn't miss a single day of work for a year earns $290 a week before taxes; that's $15,080 a year. According to how the government measures poverty, that's not enough to support a single adult with a child.[124] Consequently, 20 percent of single mothers and 9 percent of single fathers are **working poor**, individuals who work but still live in poverty.[125]

The economic costs and structural contradictions of single parenting apply to everyone, but women bear the brunt of the disadvantage. This is because women are more likely to specialize in domestic work, more likely to end up as custodial single parents, and more likely to work in underpaid industries. Shockingly, motherhood is the single strongest predictor of bankruptcy in middle age and poverty in old age.[126] As a result, we're seeing a **feminization of poverty**, a trend in which the poor are increasingly women and, of course, their children too.

Perhaps it's not surprising, then, that more and more Americans are deciding to build families that don't involve children at all.

CHOOSING NOT TO HAVE CHILDREN

Faced with the challenge of balancing work and family life, some adults choose not to have children. In fact, a growing number of people are making this choice. The year 2019 broke a record for the lowest birth rate in modern US history.[127] The birth rate dropped *another* 4 percent in 2020, partly in response to the Covid-19 pandemic.[128] Today, one in six Americans over fifty is child-free.[129] Among adults under fifty, nearly half say they won't or aren't likely to have kids.[130] In the past, women with higher levels of education were most likely to go child-free. Now women with less education are following suit.

Notably, the happiest Americans are child-free. Compared to nonparents, parents feel that their life has more purpose, but they report worse financial problems, lower-quality relationships, and higher levels of depression, distress, and anxiety.[131] This is true even long after the kids have left the house.[132]

We see a happiness gap between parents and nonparents in almost all kinds of countries (social democratic, conservative, and liberal), but the gap in the United States is the largest in the industrialized world.[133] In most cases, the more children people have, the less happy they are. There are two clear exceptions: Parents are happier than nonparents in countries with no safety net for the elderly. If kids literally keep you out of poverty when you're old, you're on average happier if you have them, but only after they're grown. Parents are also happier than nonparents in countries that offer highly generous family-friendly policies. Raising kids brings more joy when there's paid time off, free or affordable day care, flexible work hours, and ample vacation time and sick leave.[134]

Some people intuit this and choose not to have children. For women, this is especially fraught. The cult of domesticity impels women to become mothers, suggesting that it's women's nature and destiny to make homes for husbands and children. Women who don't are turning away from this social construction of womanhood. This places them at risk of being cast as a feminine pariah.[135] Childless women—especially the ones who never marry—are the shrews, spinsters, and old maids of fairy tales. In real life, they're often objects of pity, criticism, and blame. Pariah status ensures that they serve as cautionary tales, warning young women of what will happen to them if they don't fulfill their reproductive duty.

All the contradictions and crises discussed in this chapter became even more acute when Covid-19 swept across the globe. Families with children found their fragile balances upended, and mothers bore the brunt of the fallout.

CARE DURING COVID-19

The Covid-19 pandemic introduced new demands on households. We all had to track the spread of the virus, learn about disease transmission, and make decisions about personal protective equipment. We had to plan for lockdowns and figure out how to shop, work, and socialize differently. This heightened the mental load for everyone but especially for those of us who were making decisions for children or negotiating with teenagers, partners, or parents.

Parents of younger children found their routines upended by school and daycare closures.[136] Other families were cut off from neighbors or family members they previously relied on for childcare. This meant more of the burden of childminding fell on parents than ever before. And now it included homeschooling: figuring out and setting up technology, designing engaging activities and lesson plans, and supervising children's learning. By one estimate, parents doubled the time they spent in direct care of children, from thirty to fifty-nine hours per week.[137]

Meanwhile, the chores piled up. Prior to the pandemic, for example, at least some meals were eaten outside the home (at restaurants, school, or work). Now parents were responsible for planning, cooking, and cleaning up after *every* meal. Adding a classroom to the household meant more mess. With kids home for school and some parents working from home, bathrooms got dirty more quickly. Fear of the virus also prompted many families to limit their outsourcing. Now even class-privileged families were doing more.

About three-quarters of domestic workers were let go or had their hours reduced.[138] Nannies and housekeepers were especially vulnerable.[139] While some lost employment, others were pressured to move in with their employers and lock down with them. This isolated workers from their own friends and family while putting them at risk of being asked to work even longer hours. Many care workers were providing for older adults, which heightened their responsibility to avoid contracting the virus.

Closed borders meant that many migrants couldn't return home. The financial help offered by governments didn't always reach domestic workers, many of whom are undocumented or working without formal employment contracts. In most of the United States, for example, migrant domestic workers don't have access to unemployment insurance, cash payments, or food stamps.[140]

Parents in dual-earner households had to juggle more complex schedules. Even after schools reopened, the inevitability of sudden closings and bouts of quarantine made it challenging for both parents to hold full-time jobs. This was the case for a computer scientist named Erica. When the world went into lockdown, Erica found herself at home with a one-year-old son whom her husband couldn't or wouldn't help watch during the workday. But working while supervising her son was all but impossible:

> Today I was nursing him and trying to read something at the desk, and he swung his leg, and it somehow landed in my tea, and it kicked the teacup over. Tea all over both of us, all over the desk, all over the chair, all over the wall, and then he bit me at the same time.... I had to get us both cleaned up, clean up everything and then keep nursing him.[141]

The situation wasn't sustainable, so Erica slowly pulled back until she was working just two hours a day.

In the early weeks of the pandemic, both men and women increased the time they spent on childcare.[142] But as the pandemic stretched from weeks to months, men reverted to old habits, and the gap between the number of hours men and women spent on housework grew.[143] Soon mothers married to men were putting in fifteen more hours of housework and childcare per week than their husbands.[144] Even women married to men who were furloughed or laid off did disproportionate amounts of household labor.[145]

Partly as a result, mothers were twice as likely as fathers to report feelings of depression and three times as likely to report anxiety.[146] They also reported high levels of frustration with both their partners and their kids.[147] Under pressure from the ideology of intensive mothering, many mothers also felt guilty. "A good parent . . . [is] setting a good example by eating healthy and engaging in meaningful activities with and without the kids," said one mom during the pandemic, but she confessed:

> I don't think I'm meeting this ideal at all. I'm frazzled and stressed and worried all the time. I want to chill and play, but I also want to lock myself in the bathroom and be alone. It makes me feel terrible.[148]

Single parents had it even worse, especially if their job couldn't be done from home. In a voice memo sent to the *New York Times*, a single mom named Elizabeth shared her desperation:

> The pressure is now triple on me.... It's kind of impossible for me to make this work, because I'm not your classic design of a family.... I depend heavily on social things like school to get me by. And then without it, I don't know what I'm supposed to do.[149]

Single parents reported even higher levels of emotional distress than women married to men.[150]

The Covid-19 pandemic was uniquely challenging for working mothers, particularly single mothers, who were more likely to report emotional distress than fathers. To vent their frustrations, some mothers engaged in scream therapy.

The extra demands on the family intensified the pressure to specialize. With family stretched to the limit, mothers were four or five times more likely than fathers to reduce their work hours or quit their job entirely.[151] Latinas left the workforce at three times the rate of White women and four times that of Black women.[152]

Altogether, scholars estimate that the pandemic will almost certainly worsen gender inequality, rolling back even the limited economic gains women have made in the past few decades. Since spring 2020, more women have left the workforce than men, prompting one economist to dub the pandemic a "she-cession." Women's earnings have also declined more than men's. As a result, they're not only losing income in the short term; they're also losing the momentum they've built and the raises and promotions they might have gotten. They're now on a trajectory to earn significantly less for the rest of their lives.

It's possible the pandemic will usher in some positive changes, including a rise in the minimum wage, more flexible working hours or arrangements, or a better appreciation for the challenges of walking a tightrope between two greedy institutions. Still, to take advantage of these changes, parents will have to be able to find affordable, quality childcare. That may be easier said than done.

By one estimate, it may take twenty or thirty years for the childcare industry to recover.[153] Many childcare centers permanently closed during the pandemic, and many migrants who worked as nannies returned home.[154] Some who left are not legally allowed to come back. So when parents *are* able to return to work, they may not be able to find childcare. This will hit families of color hardest, since childcare centers have closed at higher rates in their neighborhoods, which had fewer centers than White-majority neighborhoods even before the pandemic.

Low-wage workers are going to face greater challenges too. The cost of day care increased by nearly half during the pandemic due to new health regulations and the need for additional staff.[155] With fewer spots for children for the foreseeable future, supply and demand may keep prices high. If childcare costs remain elevated, more low-income earners than before may be forced to stay home, even if they'd rather work.

Reflecting on the harm done to women, the writer EJ Dickson described Covid-19 as "a scenario so perfect it's almost as if some misogynistic sorcerer conjured it in a dungeon."[156] But it wasn't just the virus. If Americans hadn't been pushed by ideological and institutional factors to specialize instead of share, the pandemic would still have been devastating to families but not disproportionately devastating to women. State governments could have prioritized schools over bars and restaurants. None did. The federal government bailed out many industries, including the childcare industry, but the money wasn't sufficient. "We gave less money to the entire childcare sector than we gave to one single airline," said economist Betsey Stevenson.[157]

It was facts like these that prompted the sociologist Jessica Calarco to quip: "Other countries have social safety nets. The US has women."[158] Already held disproportionately responsible for the second shift, women also absorbed the majority of the burden placed on families by the pandemic. They did most of the homeschooling, the extra chores, and the worrying. Some may never return to the workforce. And that in itself is bad for families because traditional and neo-traditional households are often embattled and unstable; they are the marriages most likely to end in divorce.[159]

Revisiting the Question

Q+A **If marriage is better for women than ever, why do women married to men report lower levels of happiness than married men, women married to women, and single women?**

Women are less happy than men in marriage because it's an institution that systematically presses them into doing unpaid, low-status work. When families specialize, (usually) women are positioned to have less interpersonal power and financial security than the people (mostly men) on whom they have to depend. Couples in same-gender partnerships may not use gender as a basis for their division of labor, but they specialize too. And when domestic work is undervalued, the person who does it loses status and becomes dependent on their partner for economic support.

Most people would prefer to share, but even sharing comes with its own mix of challenges and consequences. Ideological and institutional forces combine to keep sharing arrangements in the minority in the United States. Consequently, even gender innovators struggle to develop truly egalitarian relationships.

All this is further complicated by that other greedy institution: work.

Next . . .

Since 1964, the federal government has strengthened mandates for gender equality in the workplace. Women now represent 47 percent of the workforce.[160] Still, men reap more rewards at work. Women are less likely than men to be in well-paid, high-prestige jobs. Our question for the next chapter is:

If women now have equal rights in the workplace, why aren't they as successful as men at work?

Let's find out.

FOR FURTHER READING

Blackstone, Amy. *Childfree by Choice: The Movement Redefining Family and Creating a New Age of Independence*. New York: Dutton, 2019.

Hondagneu-Sotelo, Pierrette, and Ernestine Avila. "'I'm Here, but I'm There': The Meanings of Latina Transnational Motherhood." *Gender & Society* 11, no. 5 (1997): 548–71.

MacDonald, Cameron. *Shadow Mothers: Nannies, Au Pairs, and the Micropolitics of Mothering*. Berkeley: University of California Press, 2010.

Moore, Mignon. *Invisible Families: Gay Identities, Relationships, and Motherhood among Black Women*. Berkeley: University of California Press, 2011.

Petts, Richard J., Kevin M. Shafer, and Lee Essig. "Does Adherence to Masculine Norms Shape Fathering Behavior?" *Journal of Marriage and Family* 80, no. 3 (2018): 704–20.

"
WE'RE HERE TO SAVE YOUR
ASS, NOT KISS IT!
—YOUR FRIENDLY FLIGHT ATTENDANT[1]
"

11

Work

Women today are giving men a run for their money. Teen girls aspire to more education and more prestigious careers than teen boys.[2] Among young women, two-thirds say a high-paying job is important to them, compared to 56 percent of young men.[3]

Yet wages don't reflect women's ambitions. A study of the graduating class of 2020 found that women's first jobs were paying about $52,000 on average, while men's were paying about $64,000.[4] Nonbinary college graduates were earning even less, bringing in barely over $45,000. Even among the most high-achieving young people, men's pay outpaces women's. A study of Harvard grads, for example, found that men in finance were four times more likely than women to report a starting salary of at least $110,000.[5] Likewise, among Harvard technology and engineering grads, 79 percent of men reported a salary of more than $90,000, compared with 44 percent of women.

And this is just the beginning for this generation of workers. The gender gap in pay gets wider over a lifetime: Full-time working women in their early twenties earn $0.94 for every dollar earned by men, but by the time they're in their fifties, they're earning just $0.78.[6] These differences in men's and women's earnings persist despite federal laws designed to guarantee equality, which leads to the question:

Q+A   **If women now have equal rights in the workplace, why aren't they as successful as men at work?**

This chapter gets up close and personal with occupations and earnings. Drawing on data from the US Bureau of Labor Statistics, it explains how paid work is gendered in ways that affirm difference and entrench inequality. Some of women's disadvantage is due to simple discrimination, but it also reflects the tendency for jobs to be filled primarily by either men or women, the different value attributed to men's and women's work, the challenge of being both a good parent and a good worker, and employers' beliefs about mothers and fathers.

So buckle up, put your seatbacks and tray tables in their full upright and locked position, and direct your attention to the flight attendant.

THE CHANGING WORKPLACE

"Next to being a Hollywood movie star, nothing was more glamorous," said a starry-eyed stewardess in 1945.[7] Only about 10 percent of Americans had ever flown, and most were afraid to do so.[8] Stewardesses were certifiably adventurous. They took risks, saw the world, and rubbed elbows with the elite: their passengers. As historian Kathleen Barry contends, "Few women journeyed as regularly or as far from home, or came into contact with the rich and famous as often, as a typical stewardess did."[9]

Airlines hired women whom they believed represented ideal femininity. Chosen for their beauty and poise, and almost exclusively from among the White, educated, and slender, they were as much of an icon as Miss America. As one of America's sweethearts, stewardesses appeared in commercials for products from soft drinks to cigarettes.

By the 1960s, airlines were in the "business of female spectacle," unabashedly selling women's attractiveness to customers.[10] Perhaps most famous was a National Airlines campaign: "Fly me," stewardesses saucily invited would-be passengers.[11] Later, National's advertising featured young women who promised, "We'll fly you like you've never been flown before." Feminists later retorted, "Go fly yourself!"

The strategy of sexual objectification was industrywide.[12] Continental stewardesses pledged, "We Really Move Our Tails for You." Air Jamaica promised, "We Make You Feel Good All Over." Air France replied, "Have You Ever Done It the French Way?" Braniff Airlines asked their men passengers, "Does Your

Wife Know You're Flying with Us?" Uniforms emphasized flight attendants' sexiness: mini-skirts, short shorts, and go-go boots.

Still, it wasn't all fun and hot pants. Standards of appearance were strict.[13] Disqualifications and dismissals were issued for big feet, chubby legs, poor posture, the wrong haircut, glasses, acne, short nails, imperfect teeth, or any supposed flaw the recruiters identified. They claimed their objections to broad noses, coarse hair, and full lips were race-neutral, but they weren't.[14] A ban on "hook noses" was used to exclude Jewish women.

Women were required to wear girdles and submit to routine weigh-ins and measurement of their busts, waists, hips, and thighs. They were fired if they gained weight. "You run a $1.5 billion business," said a United Airlines official, "and it boils down to whether some chicks look good in their uniforms. If you have fat stewardesses, people aren't going to fly with you."[15] Airlines also fired women who got married, became pregnant, or reached their early thirties. A manager once told a group of flight attendants: "If you haven't found a man to keep you by the time you're twenty-eight, then TWA won't want you either."[16]

In the 1960s and '70s, airlines sexualized their stewardesses to attract a mostly male customer base. As part of this effort, Southwest Airlines flight attendants were required to wear hot pants and leather go-go boots.

Stewardesses also faced routine sexual harassment, as airlines implicitly, and sometimes explicitly, marketed them as available sex partners.[17] Pacific Southwest Airlines riffed on their acronym, advertising that the A in PSA stood for stewardesses who were "available."[18] Black flight attendants faced their own unique kind of sexual harassment; some White customers were hostile racists, but others would proposition them for a "Black experience."[19]

Meanwhile, women flight attendants were among the most poorly paid employees in the airline industry. They were paid a third of what pilots earned, two-thirds the wages of the mostly men grounds workers, and significantly less than the few flight attendants who were men. Among Pan Am flight attendants, for example, men were paid 140 percent of what women were paid. Men also enjoyed promotions, more responsibility, nicer accommodations on layovers, larger pensions, greater scheduling flexibility, and more sick leave. Plus, they didn't face weigh-ins, girdles, or forced retirements.

In 1964, the Civil Rights Act made such sex discrimination illegal. On the first day the government began considering violations of the new law, stewardesses filed a case against the airline industry.[20] In the next eighteen months, flight attendants would initiate over one hundred lawsuits. Women across the occupational spectrum would follow suit. Over decades, as companies faced potential lawsuits, overtly discriminatory practices slowly eroded.

Yet men today—especially class-privileged White men—continue to be advantaged in the workplace. Men are more likely than women to work for pay, and they work more hours per week and weeks per year. They get better benefits (like health insurance, vacation days, and retirement plans) and are more likely to get on-the-job training. They're more likely to be managers or work in jobs considered "skilled." And they dominate the highest rungs of corporate ladders: Men comprise 65 percent of senior-level managers and directors, 70 percent of board members, and 92 percent of the CEOs of Fortune 500 companies.[21]

The most succinct measure of men's advantage in the workplace is the **gender pay gap**, the difference between the incomes of the typical man and woman who work full-time. In 2021, the median earnings of American men working full-time were $1,097 per week.[22] Comparably, full-time working women earned $912, or 83 percent of men's wages. To put it another way, among workers employed full-time, women earned $0.83 for every dollar made by men.

As revealed in Table 11.1, the gap has been shrinking for nearly two hundred years. Much of the narrowing is due to women's rising wages, but about a quarter reflects falling wages among men (down 7 percent since 2000).[23] The things that used to protect men's wages, like labor unions and manufacturing jobs, have been on the decline.[24] Meanwhile, women have compensated by increasing their education, shifting into better-paying jobs, and working longer hours.

Women of all races make less money than their men counterparts, but the size of the gap differs.[25] It's smaller among groups that have overall lower wages. The gap varies both among US states and across different countries too. As noted earlier, the wage gap increases across the life cycle. Perhaps surprisingly, the gap is largest among men and women who earn professional degrees.[26] In 2021, for example, the annual wage gap between men and women physicians grew to $122,000.[27]

All told, because of the gender wage gap, the average American woman will earn $407,760 less in her lifetime than the average man.[28] Compared to White non-Hispanic men, Black women will be out almost $950,000, and Latinas and American Indian women more than $1 million. This harms women's economic stability throughout their lives. After retirement, nearly twice as many women as men live in poverty.[29]

This chapter explores the gendered forces behind this inequality: job segregation, gender discrimination, and the practice and ideology of parenting. It also

TABLE 11.1 | VARIATION IN WOMEN'S EARNINGS FOR EVERY DOLLAR OF MEN'S FOR FULL-TIME WORKERS

Comparison	Cents/Dollar	Comparison	Cents/Dollar
By state in the United States		*By education (United States)*	
California	$0.88	Less than high school	$0.78
Florida	$0.84	High school graduate	$0.76
New Jersey	$0.82	Some college or associate's degree	$0.76
Texas	$0.87	Bachelor's degree and higher	$0.75
Washington, DC	$0.80		
Wyoming	$0.75	*By race or ethnicity (United States)*	
Utah	$0.73		
		Black women, men	$0.92
By country		Black women, White men	$0.69
		Asian women, men	$0.79
Germany	$0.80	Asian women, White men	$1.04
Ireland	$0.89	Hispanic women, men	$0.88
Italy	$0.95	Hispanic women, White men	$0.64
Poland	$0.92	White women, men	$0.82
Sweden	$0.88		
By year (United States)		*By age (United States)*	
1820	$0.35	16–24	$0.95
1890	$0.46	25–34	$0.89
1930	$0.56	35–44	$0.81
1960	$0.61	45–54	$0.78
1970	$0.60	55–64	$0.78
1990	$0.72	65+	$0.80
2000	$0.77		
2010	$0.81		

Sources: Denis Leythienne and Marina Pérez-Julián, "Gender Pay Gaps in the European Union—A Statistical Analysis, 2021 Edition," European Commission, September 2021, https://ec.europa.eu/eurostat/documents/3888793/13484385 /KS-TC-21-004-EN-N.pdf/69965821-22ed-7c56-c859-cd7b10e011c5?t=1633341826751; and "Highlights of Women's Earnings in 2020," US Bureau of Labor Statistics, September 2021, https://www.bls.gov/opub/reports/womens-earnings /2020/home.htm.

looks at how work experiences are shaped by class, race, gender, sexuality, and age. It concludes with some observations about the current economy and both men's and women's opportunities within it. Throughout, it will discuss how the pandemic has upset the status quo, sometimes for the better but often for the worse.

JOB SEGREGATION

Women and men attracted to the excitement of air travel have pursued their dreams largely through two very different avenues. Men have become pilots and women have become flight attendants. Today, 65 percent of flight attendants

A woman laborer carries bricks needed for a construction site. Construction is gendered female in India.

are women and 95 percent of pilots are men.[30] This is an example of **gendered job segregation**, the practice of filling occupations with mostly men or mostly women workers. Just as we gender all kinds of things, we gender jobs. Collectively, we understand certain jobs as somehow for women and others as for men.

Because jobs are not naturally gendered, we find great variation across cultures. Medicine is a woman's job in Russia and Finland, as is dentistry in Latvia and Lithuania.[31] In Armenia, half of computer science college professors are women.[32] Women dominate computer science in Malaysia, too, where abstract thinking and office work are seen as feminine compared to more "physical" labor.[33] Likewise, Malaysians see chemical engineering as feminine because it involves working in a lab but civil engineering as masculine because it involves going to worksites and overseeing construction. In contrast, women make up a large share of the construction industry in India—despite the fact that it's hard, physical labor—because Indian society holds women responsible for the home.[34] We make work meaningful in gendered ways and slot men and women into occupations accordingly.

How Much Job Segregation Is There?

Table 11.2 presents data for some of the most gender-segregated occupations in the United States. Overall, about four in ten American women work in occupations in which three-quarters or more of their coworkers are women.[35] Men work in even more gender-segregated environments. Internationally, the amount of gender segregation among occupations varies; the United States is in the middle of the pack.[36]

We see gender segregation not just between occupations but within them. Consider that servers at very expensive restaurants tend to be both men and women, but lower-priced restaurants tend to employ mostly women.[37] Among doctors, gender correlates with specialty: Women make up 64 percent of pediatricians but only 6 percent of orthopedic surgeons.[38]

Gender intersects with other characteristics too. Depending on what part of the United States we're in, the (likely women) housekeepers at our local motel will be White, Latina, or Black.[39] The janitor or maintenance workers will proba-

TABLE 11.2 | SOME OF THE MOST GENDER-SEGREGATED OCCUPATIONS

Women-Dominated Occupations	How Female Is It?
Preschool and kindergarten teachers	97%
Speech-language pathologists	95%
Dental hygienists	95%
Childcare workers	95%
Secretaries and administrative assistants	93%
Hairdressers, hairstylists, and cosmetologists	92%
Medical assistants	91%
Receptionists and information clerks	90%
Dietitians and nutritionists	90%
Maids and housekeeping cleaners	89%

Men-Dominated Occupations	How Male Is It?
Crane and tower operators	99%
Electricians	98%
Plumbers, pipefitters, and steamfitters	98%
Automotive service technicians and mechanics	98%
Roofers	97%
Carpenters	97%
Construction laborers	96%
Firefighters	95%
Aircraft pilots and flight engineers	95%
Mechanical engineers	91%

Source: "Labor Force Statistics from the Current Population Survey," "Employed Persons by Detailed Occupation, Sex, Race, and Hispanic or Latino Ethnicity" (Table 11), US Bureau of Labor Statistics, January 20, 2022, https://www.bls.gov/cps/cpsaat11.htm.

bly be the same race but the other gender. Black women make up only 6 percent of the general population but represent nearly a third of active-duty enlisted women in the military.[40] Fully 99 percent of New York City's yellow taxi drivers are men; 23 percent are from Bangladesh alone.[41]

Jobs are also segregated by sexual orientation. Nonheterosexual men are substantially more likely than heterosexual men to be in occupations that require a college degree. And queer men and women are more likely than their counterparts to enter occupations monopolized by the other gender. Lesbian women are more likely than heterosexual women to be architects, for instance.[42] Bisexual men and women are overrepresented in art and design. And, while not all men flight attendants are gay, gay men are overrepresented compared to the overall population.[43]

What causes this divvying up of men and women into different kinds of jobs?

Causes of Job Segregation

Men and women usually end up in gender-stereotypical jobs through socialization, employer selection, or selective exit. The **socialization hypothesis** suggests that men and women respond to gender stereotypes when planning, training, and applying for jobs.[44] In one study, for example, psychologists invited students into a classroom to fill out a questionnaire about their interest in computer science.[45] One set of people entered a room covered in "computer geeky" things: a *Star Trek* poster, comic books, video game boxes, empty soda cans and junk food, and technical magazines. The other group entered a room without these objects. Men were unfazed by the geekery, but women who encountered the geeked-out room were significantly less likely to consider the major. Whether it's the "macho" image of the construction worker or the "bro" image of the tech guy, the message to women is "no girls allowed."[46] Men are similarly attracted to and adverse to certain occupations, depending on whether they're coded masculine or feminine.

The **employer selection hypothesis** proposes that employers tend to prefer men for masculine jobs and women for feminine jobs, slotting applicants into gender-consistent roles during hiring and promotion. Certain kinds of factory work, for example, are predominantly performed by women because employers prefer to hire them. One manager at a manufacturing company told a researcher: "Just three things I look for in hiring: small, foreign, and female."[47] Hiring in Silicon Valley, by contrast, has been driven by employers' belief that nerdy men make the best computer programmers.[48] According to the employer selection hypothesis, then, once a job is dominated by men or women, employers select new workers accordingly.[49]

The **selective exit hypothesis** highlights workers' abandonment of counter-stereotypical occupations. One study found that 61 percent of women in men-dominated occupations left their job within ten years, compared with fewer than 30 percent of their men colleagues; half of these women switched to a women-dominated occupation.[50] Among people who get degrees in engineering, 35 percent of women, but only 10 percent of men, either never enter the field or leave it sometime after they do.[51] A majority of women who choose to leave blame hypermasculine work cultures.[52]

All three of these mechanisms—socialization, employer selection, and selective exit—are sources of job segregation. And that's interesting, but job segregation alone doesn't produce inequality. Gendered job segregation is only a precondition for the gender wage gap. To understand how that happens, let's return to that gender-segregated job in the sky.

Different and Unequal

A Floridian Cuban named Celio Diaz was the first man to claim gender discrimination under the Civil Rights Act.[53] In the 1960s, only 4 percent of flight attendants were men. Pan Am—the airline sued by Diaz—refused to hire men, arguing that men simply couldn't "convey the charm, the tact, the grace, the liveliness that young girls can."[54] Or if they could, Pan Am claimed, it might "arouse feelings" in a man "that he would rather not have aroused."[55]

Celio won his case, and beginning in 1971, airlines were forced to begin hiring men alongside women. The media had a field day. The *Miami Herald* ran a story with a picture of a stocky, hairy-legged man in a miniskirt and knee-high socks, a purse hanging from his cocked arm. It read: "Here's the worst thing that could happen to commercial airlines."[56]

This response by the American media is funny when you consider that the word *stewardess* is a feminized version of the word *steward*. The job was performed almost exclusively by stewards—that is, men—for some time. Pan Am itself maintained an all-steward workforce for sixteen years.

Early airlines modeled their businesses on ocean liners and train cars, which largely employed Black men. Thinking their overwhelmingly White passengers wouldn't feel comfortable placing their lives in the hands of a Black person, Pan Am and the other airlines hired White men as flight attendants.[57] To inspire gravitas, stewards wore military-inspired uniforms and changed into white sport coats and gloves to serve dinner.

Due to the shortage of men on the home front during World War II, Pan Am started hiring women in 1944. By 1958, Pan Am had entirely reversed its policy. And when the aisle was turned over to women, the role was reimagined. As the occupation was feminized, the seriousness of the job was downplayed, and sexually playful service was emphasized. As one flight attendant described it, the job became "part mother, part servant, and part tart."[58]

You might recall that this is exactly what happened with cheerleading, and that's no coincidence. When an occupation transitions from being mostly performed by men to mostly performed by women, or vice versa, prestige and pay tend to follow. During World War II, for example, women typists were funneled into early computer programming.[59] It was believed that the work required patience, something women supposedly had thanks to "maternal instinct." "It's just like planning a dinner," explained the pioneering programmer Grace Hopper to *Cosmopolitan* in 1967; it "requires patience and the ability to handle detail. Women are 'naturals' at computer programming."[60] In fact, as the film *Hidden Figures* reminded us, Black women such as Katherine Johnson served as human "computers" for NASA.[61]

As late as the mid-1980s, computer science was more gender-integrated than other science, technology, and engineering fields. Today, however, computer science is considered a nerd's playground. Not coincidentally, it's among the least gender-integrated occupations and very high in prestige and pay.

We've seen similar changes in response to the feminization or masculinization of many different occupations, including law, medicine, and veterinary

Celebrated in the film *Hidden Figures*, Mary Jackson was NASA's first Black woman engineer. Today, men represent 86 percent of aerospace engineers.

medicine.[62] Clerical work in the United States was performed almost exclusively by men until the late 1800s. At the time, typing was considered "too strenuous for women."[63] Later, as it became feminized, the necessary qualification would shift from "arduous labor" to "dexterity."[64] Today, most people don't think much of "secretaries," but these were highly respected roles when performed by men. This is why the US government still uses the term to refer to high-level positions like secretary of state.

Generally, the rule is clear: As women enter an occupation, status goes down; as men enter it, status goes up.

We call the result the **androcentric pay scale**, a strong correlation between wages and the gender composition of the job.[65] In fact, according to a study by the US Bureau of Labor Statistics, gender composition is the *single largest contributor* to the gender wage gap among jobs.[66] It's more important than industry, level of unionization, supply and demand, the safety or comfort of the work, and workers' education, marital status, and experience. Even controlling for these things, "women's work" pays, on average, between 5 and 21 percent less than "men's work."[67]

If there's an androcentric pay scale, we should expect jobs held disproportionately by men to be among the highest paying. They are. Consider Table 11.3, which lists all US occupations (with reliable demographic data) that pay more than $130,000 a year.[68] In the rightmost columns, we include the gender and race composition of this high-paying work. Since men make up 53 percent of the workforce, any occupation that's more than 53 percent men is disproportionately so, with more men than we would expect by chance alone. Likewise, 63 percent of the workforce identifies as non-Hispanic White, so any job that is more than 63 percent White is disproportionately so. Twelve of the sixteen highest-paying occupations are majority men and all but two of these occupations are disproportionately White.

The concentration of men in high-earning occupations, and their resulting ability to accumulate savings, investments, and assets, can be described as a **masculinization of wealth**.[69] This accumulation of money starts when men are boys. Sons are 15 percent more likely than daughters to get an allowance in exchange for doing chores; even when daughters get paid, sons get paid more.[70] In other words, boys spend fewer hours on chores than girls, enjoy more leisure time, and *still* end up with more money in their piggybanks.

TABLE 11.3 | GENDER AND RACE COMPOSITION OF THE HIGHEST-PAYING JOBS IN THE UNITED STATES

Occupation	Avg. Annual Wage	% Male	% White
Surgeon	$294,520	72%	83%
Physician	$252,480	60%	62%
Chief executive	$213,020	71%	80%
Dentist	$177,770	61%	68%
Aircraft pilot and flight engineer	$169,540	95%	88%
Computer and information systems manager	$162,930	73%	67%
Architectural and engineering manager	$158,970	89%	74%
Financial manager	$153,460	45%	70%
Marketing manager	$153,440	39%	77%
Lawyer	$148,030	62%	82%
Advertising and promotions manager	$142,860	58%	74%
Sales manager	$142,390	69%	78%
Human resources manager	$136,590	19%	69%
Computer hardware engineer	$136,230	87%	51%
Purchasing manager	$134,590	54%	76%
Public relations and fundraising manager	$132,800	32%	84%

Sources: "Labor Force Statistics from the Current Population Survey," "Employed Persons by Detailed Occupation, Sex, Race, and Hispanic or Latino Ethnicity" (Table 11), US Bureau of Labor Statistics, January 20, 2022, https://www.bls.gov/cps/cpsaat11.htm; "May 2021 National Occupational Employment and Wage Estimates," US Bureau of Labor Statistics, March 31, 2022, https://www.bls.gov/oes/current/oes_nat.htm.

The Value of Gendered Work

In 2013, a flight crash-landed at San Francisco International Airport. All but two of the 307 passengers survived. The media called it a "miracle." But it wasn't a miracle. It was the flight attendants.

When the plane crashed, the flight attendants on board successfully executed a ninety-second evacuation. As passengers were fleeing the wreckage, some flight attendants fought the rising flames while others hacked trapped passengers out of their seatbelts with knives. They carried injured passengers out on their backs. "I wasn't really thinking, but my body started carrying out the steps needed for an evacuation," explained Lee Yoon Hye, one of the flight attendants. "I was only thinking about rescuing the next passenger."[71] Later she learned that she'd sustained a broken tailbone.

The top five news stories at the time used passive language that made the work of the flight attendants invisible: "Slides had deployed" and passengers "managed to get off."[72] Instead of being described as first responders, flight attendants were portrayed as just a special kind of passenger. The crash forced "frightened passengers and crew to scamper," read one article. Only one of the five stories acknowledged that the sixteen flight attendants *worked* through the crash and its aftermath.

Which leads us to ask: Do flight attendants have skills?

They do. Flight attendants learn hundreds of regulations and the safety features of multiple types of airplanes. They know how to evacuate a plane on land or sea; fight fires thirty-five thousand feet in the air; keep a heart attack or stroke victim alive; calm or restrain an anxious or agitated passenger; respond to hijackings and terrorist attacks; communicate effectively with people frozen in fear; and survive in the event of a crash landing in the jungle, sea, desert, or Arctic. As one flight attendant said: "I don't think of myself as a sex symbol or a servant. I think of myself as somebody who knows how to open the door of a 747 in the dark, upside down, and in the water."[73]

Even when survival is unlikely, many flight attendants take their job demands seriously. As one flight attendant said:

> If we were going to make a ditching in water, the chances of our surviving are slim, even though we know exactly what to do. But I think I would probably—and I think I can say this for most of my fellow flight attendants—be able to keep [the passengers] from being too worried about it. I mean my voice might quiver a little during the announcements, but somehow I feel we could get them to believe . . . the best.[74]

Many lives have been saved, and many final moments have been less filled with sheer terror, thanks to well-trained and effective flight attendants committed to doing their job well—if necessary, until the bitter end.

Airlines, though, are loath to reveal the intense and ongoing emergency, security, first-aid, combat, and survival training that flight attendants receive. Talking about the "live fire pit" and "ditching pool" used for training might remind passengers of the potential dangers of air travel.[75] It's much better for airlines if we think flight attendants are just "sky waitresses."

So flight attendants' skills are invisible to most of us most of the time, both by circumstance and design. Meanwhile, we tend to dismiss the work we do see as unskilled, but is that fair? Early airlines hired women for their extraordinary beauty, grace, and charm. They were to have a "modest but friendly smile," be "alert, attentive, not overly aggressive, but not reticent either," "outgoing but not effusive," "enthusiastic with calm and poise," and "vivacious but not effervescent."[76] No problem, right? All women *don't* naturally have these skills; that's why flight attendants were cast as perfect women.

This part of the job is referred to as **emotional labor**, the act of controlling one's own emotions and managing the emotions of others. Flight attendants are tasked with seamlessly performing the proper emotions in interaction with an impossibly wide range of people who bring their own (often negative) emotions to the moment. And they have to be nice, no matter what. One flight attendant interviewed in 2001, for example, explained how she managed the problem of sexual harassment without offending her customers: "If someone puts their hand on your bottom," she said, "you should say, 'Excuse me, sir, but my bottom accidentally fell into your hand.'"[77]

During the Covid-19 pandemic, abuse of flight attendants skyrocketed. In 2021, the US Federal Aviation Administration received more than five thousand reports of disruptive passengers. That was more reports in one year than had been received in the previous thirty-one years combined, when recording began. "I'm a twenty-five-year flight attendant," said Sara Nelson, president of the Association of Flight Attendants, "and throughout my career when there was something going on socially or politically in this country, we see ramifications on airplanes. And this is absolutely supercharged this year."[78]

A survey of flight attendants found that 84 percent confronted unruly passengers in 2021.[79] Most involved passengers refusing to follow the federal rule requiring face masks. "They're just looking for a fight," was how one flight attendant saw it. "It becomes a power play—who's going to win?" Sometimes these confrontations escalated to name-calling or physical violence. "I got called a 'bitch' last month," a flight attendant named Jules recalled, "because someone was taking their mask off to cough, and I told them to keep it on."[80]

Nearly two-thirds of flight attendants also reported being called racist, sexist, or homophobic names by passengers during the pandemic, and 20 percent were physically assaulted.[81] Jules took a leave from the job after she was shoved by a man who refused to wear his mask when walking to the bathroom. She was pregnant and worried an angry passenger might hurt her baby. This felt unprecedented: "I'd been verbally abused by passengers before, but nobody had ever put their hands on me."

Airline passengers all too often see flight attendants as "a very accessible punching bag."[82] That means that in addition to managing their own anxieties about contracting Covid-19 at work, flight attendants were forced to manage the emotions of their passengers more often and with even more delicacy. "My goal is always to diffuse," said a flight attendant named Mitra. So she responds kindly and calmly to even the most unruly of passengers. "I would sympathize and say, 'Hey, you know, I get it, it's hot, I'm hot. I'm wearing [a mask] too—I need you to wear it too. Can we please work together?'"[83]

Undeniably, these impressive emotional and interpersonal skills are also *valuable* resources for airlines. And yet airlines have historically framed flight attendants' performances as "natural." As historian Kathleen Barry explains:

> [A]irlines' favorite metaphor for stewardesses' work was that they were playing gracious hostess to guests in one's own home, which suggested their efforts were a natural, voluntary expression of female domesticity and of social rather than economic value.[84]

The work of flight attendants, in other words, was defined as *outside the realm of work*. If being nice just comes naturally, then flight attendants are just being themselves. Being oneself is not a *skill*, and therefore it shouldn't be compensated as one. The benevolently sexist idea that women are naturally gracious, in other words, leads us to dismiss the work of women flight attendants as nothing special.

Lots of the work women do is similarly believed to come naturally. In contrast, "men's work" is usually considered skilled almost by definition. Stereotypes of men include being good with their hands, talented at understanding how things work, and steadfast behind the wheel. If we were inclined to devalue these skills, we could argue that it was only natural that men would become surgeons, engineers, and truck drivers. Since this is just how they *are*, they deserve to be paid only for their time. That is, in fact, exactly how "women's work" is frequently understood.

Traditional women's work—like soothing an autistic child, organizing twenty kindergarteners, making middle school kids care about literature, ensuring a boss's day runs smoothly, or carefully monitoring the health of an elderly patient—all require knowledge, concentration, effort, creativity, problem-solving, practice, and emotional labor. So does responding to sexual harassment in ways that are effective but not explosive.[85] In an article about sexism in the tech industry, entrepreneur Susan Wu discusses

> the countless times I've had to move a man's hand from my thigh . . . without seeming confrontational (or bitchy or rejecting or demanding or aggressive). . . . [It's] a pretty important skill that I would bet most successful women in our industry have.[86]

It seems women are still apologizing for their bottoms falling into men's hands.

If jobs filled by women are devalued, then we should expect these jobs to pay less than jobs filled by men. They do. Consider Table 11.4, which lists all American occupations (with reliable data) that pay less than $30,000 a year.[87] In the rightmost columns, we include the gender and race composition of these low-paying jobs. Since women make up 47 percent of the workforce, any job that is more than 47 percent women is disproportionately so. Likewise, since 63 percent of the workforce identifies as non-Hispanic White, any job that is more than 37 percent minority is more so than we would expect by chance alone.

Two-thirds of the lowest-paying occupations (thirteen of eighteen) are disproportionately women; five are more than three-fourths women. Most of the remaining jobs are filled by men of color. Black men are twice as likely as White men to work in feminized industries, and Latino and Asian men are one and a half times as likely.[88] This is partly because racial discrimination gives men of color fewer options than White men, but also possibly because men of color may need to adopt feminized qualities like care and kindness.[89] With few exceptions, the lowest-paying occupations in the United States are disproportionately

TABLE 11.4 | GENDER AND RACE COMPOSITION OF THE LOWEST-PAYING JOBS IN THE UNITED STATES

Occupation	Avg. Annual Wage	% Female	% Minority
Host and hostess, restaurant, lounge, and coffee shop	$26,000	84%	38%
Fast food and counter worker	$26,060	66%	42%
Cashier	$26,780	73%	47%
Entertainment attendant and related worker	$27,170	46%	28%
Dishwasher	$27,350	24%	55%
Childcare worker	$27,680	95%	43%
Dining room and cafeteria attendant and bartender helper	$27,690	47%	51%
Laundry and dry-cleaning worker	$27,830	67%	67%
Hotel, motel, and resort desk clerk	$28,040	70%	47%
Food preparation worker	$28,810	58%	49%
Waiter and waitress	$29,010	68%	40%
Parking attendant	$29,210	13%	71%
Home health and personal care aide	$29,260	87%	67%
Gambling services worker	$29,340	51%	51%
Food server, nonrestaurant	$29,500	74%	44%
Animal caretaker	$29,520	82%	23%
Cook	$29,560	40%	58%
Maid and housekeeping cleaner	$29,580	89%	69%

Note: Minorities include Black/Black, Asian, and Hispanic/Latino. The US Census does not report statistics for American Indians because their population numbers are so low. Arab and Middle Eastern Americans are considered White by the US government.
Sources: "Labor Force Statistics from the Current Population Survey," "Employed Persons by Detailed Occupation, Sex, Race, and Hispanic or Latino Ethnicity" (Table 11), US Bureau of Labor Statistics, January 20, 2022, https://www.bls.gov/cps/cpsaat11.htm; "May 2021 National Occupational Employment and Wage Estimates," US Bureau of Labor Statistics, March 31, 2022, https://www.bls.gov/oes/current/oes_nat.htm.

staffed by racial minority women (in twelve occupations) or, barring that, mostly women or racial minorities (in one and four occupations, respectively).

The devaluation of feminized occupations is especially acute for **care work**, work that involves face-to-face caregiving of the physical, emotional, and educational needs of others: children, older adults, people who are sick, and people who are disabled. These jobs pay *even less* than other feminized jobs.[90] Consider the job of childcare worker. In 2021, the average yearly income for childcare workers was $27,680.[91] You know who's paid more than the people who are taking care of children? People who take care of coats in the coat check, parked cars, broken bicycles, dry cleaning, motel reservations, and roadkill.

Androcentrism is thus a key mechanism by which job segregation contributes to the gender pay gap. Because we attribute more value to "men's work" than "women's work," an occupation disproportionately filled by women is seen as *legitimately* lower paid than an occupation dominated by men. Because of this, job segregation doesn't just create a differentiated workforce; it creates an unequal one.

Both men and women can lose prestige and income when they enter a feminized occupation. Women working in feminized occupations earn substantially less than women working in masculinized ones; men pay a similar price, though they're more likely than women to abandon feminized careers in response.[92] Because openly gay and bisexual men and women are more likely than heterosexual men and women to work in feminized or masculinized occupations, respectively, androcentrism also explains a bit of the pay gap at the intersection of gender and sexual orientation.[93]

Job Segregation and the Impact of Covid-19

Men tend to work in industries especially vulnerable to downturns in the economy, like manufacturing and construction. Sectors like education, which disproportionately employ women, are more resilient. Because of gendered job segregation, then, economic crises usually hit men harder. Most recessions are "he-cessions."

Covid-19, however, caused a "she-cession."[94] In the first year of the pandemic, 1.8 million men and 2.4 million women left the labor force. Parenting responsibilities were one reason why, but job segregation was another. The hardest-hit occupations were ones dominated by women, including jobs in the service industry and leisure and hospitality. As a result, the total number of women with jobs hit a thirty-three-year low.[95]

As usual, some women suffered more than others. Many of the most severely affected industries were already paying low wages, so non-college-educated and low-income women were especially likely to lose their jobs or have their hours cut. Black and Hispanic women were more likely than Asian and White women to find themselves unemployed, while young women and women with disabilities had the highest rates of unemployment.[96]

Women also make up 70 percent of the health care workforce, both globally and in the United States, meaning that they've disproportionately held some of the most dangerous and stressful jobs of the Covid-19 era.[97] Women are 87 percent of registered nurses and 89 percent of nursing assistants.[98] Women are also nearly 71 percent of respiratory therapists, the experts who help patients breathe and, when necessary, care for those placed on a ventilator.

Being on the front lines of the pandemic was devastating to health care workers' morale and mental health.[99] In addition to witnessing mass death, their jobs directly exposed them to SARS-CoV-2.[100] Health care workers were especially likely to contract Covid-19 and seven times more likely to develop severe Covid-19, the kind that requires hospitalization.[101] This was especially true in the first year of the pandemic—before vaccines, when personal protective equipment was rationed and often improvised.

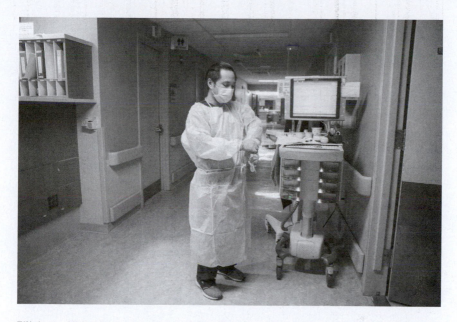

Filipino and Filipino American nurses and other nurses of color died of Covid-19 at a much higher rate than their White colleagues, especially in the early days of the pandemic when personal protective equipment was in short supply.

Among registered nurses, workers of color died at more than twice their rate in the workforce and fully half of the nurses of color who died were Filipino or Filipino American.[102] Though they account for only 4 percent of registered nurses in the United States, 24 percent of all nurses lost to Covid-19 in the United States were Filipino. Shockingly, three times as many Filipino health care workers died in the United States as died in the Philippines.[103]

This is because the United States has historically depended on foreign nurses to serve as emergency health care workers, the majority of whom have been from the Philippines.[104] This practice began when the United States bought the country from Spain in 1898 and installed American-style hospitals to treat US soldiers.[105] When the Philippines achieved independence from the United States in 1946, it continued to train health care workers to work in the American health care system. Ever since, whenever US health care workers are unwilling or unable to provide care, Filipino nurses are there. During the 1980s HIV pandemic, for example, nurses from the Philippines filled in for American workers who were given permission by the American Medical Association to deny care to people with HIV.[106]

During Covid-19, Filipino nurses stepped in again. When they did, they were more likely than US-trained White nurses to be placed at the very front of the front lines: in intensive care units and emergency rooms, for example.[107] The resulting death toll on this community is a tragic example of how job segregation (in this case, at the intersection of race, class, and nation) can protect some communities and place others in harm's way.

Early in the crisis, people around the world sang and clanged pots every day to thank health care workers. Perhaps this will translate into higher wages. Indeed, after being stagnant for nearly twenty years, nursing salaries rose during the pandemic.[108] Will we continue to value the feminized work of providing care? The evidence is mixed but suggests that the future will depend on whether nurses and other medical care workers use the bargaining power that labor scarcity has offered.

Thus far this chapter has discussed how androcentrism interacts with job segregation to explain a large part of the pay gap. But it doesn't explain all of it. Women are not just paid less than men overall; they are also paid less than men *in the same occupations*. What else is going on?

DISCRIMINATION AND PREFERENTIAL TREATMENT

Thanks to the Civil Rights Act of 1964, it's no longer legal to discriminate based on gender, but discrimination didn't simply vanish. Enforcing the new law meant going to court, proving discrimination and intent, and creating consequences. It took decades for the hundreds of cases filed by flight attendants, for example, to make their way through the courts.[109] Despite much progress, there is a pay gap in this profession still: Women flight attendants make $0.82 for every dollar made by their men counterparts.[110] In fact, we see a gendered pay gap in almost every US occupation. Table 11.5 shows the wage gap in the most common occupations for men and women, ranked from smallest difference in pay to the largest.

Gender discrimination accounts for some of the wage gap within occupations: Sometimes men are simply seen as better employees, no matter what qualities are considered ideal for the job. In one study, for instance, participants rated two hypothetical candidates for police chief: one named Michael and the other Michelle.[111] When Michael was described as "streetwise" and Michelle as "formally educated," participants recommended hiring Michael on the basis that he was tough, a risk-taker, and physically fit. When Michelle was the one described as streetwise, however, they *still* recommended Michael, this time on the basis that he was formally educated. In other words, participants moved the goalposts to ensure that, whatever the qualifications, Michael was seen as more qualified than Michelle. Both men and women exhibited this bias, but men more than women.

TABLE 11.5 | WOMEN'S EARNINGS FOR EVERY DOLLAR OF MEN'S IN THE 20 MOST COMMON OCCUPATIONS FOR WOMEN AND MEN

Occupation	Cents/Men's Dollar
Cashier	$0.96
Office clerk, general	$0.92
Customer service representative	$0.91
Laborer and freight, stock, and material mover	$0.89
Elementary and middle school teacher	$0.86
Software developer	$0.86
Registered nurse	$0.85
Nursing assistant	$0.85
Secretary and administrative assistant	$0.84
Manager, all other	$0.79
Janitor and building cleaner	$0.79
Accountant and auditor	$0.78
Retail salesperson	$0.77
Sales representative, wholesale and manufacturing	$0.77
Chief executive	$0.76
First-line supervisor of retail sales workers	$0.75
Driver/sales worker and truck driver	$0.73

Note: Some of the most common occupations for men are also the most common for women, so the total number of occupations is fewer than twenty.
Source: "The Gender Wage Gap by Occupation, Race, and Ethnicity 2020," Institute for Women's Policy Research, March 2021, https://iwpr.org/iwpr-issues/esme/the-gender-wage-gap-by-occupation-race-and-ethnicity-2020/.

If this sounds implausible, consider the stories of people who've been both a man and a woman in the workplace. In a study of twenty-nine trans men, two-thirds reported receiving a post-transition advantage. This was especially true if they were White and tall. Crispin, for example, worked at Home Depot; he said customers had often dismissed his expertise when they perceived him as a woman, but now they heartily welcomed his advice. Henry said he was suddenly "right a lot more" than he'd been before.[112] Keith said that behavior perceived as "assertive" when he was seen as a woman was now "take charge."[113] Thomas, who previously went by Susan, told a story that sums it up: After his transition, a client commended his boss for firing "Susan" and hiring the "new guy" who was "just delightful!"[114]

Conversely, trans women face forms of discrimination they didn't encounter when presenting as men. When a computer programmer named Agape transitioned on the job, her boss worried aloud that it would affect her programming abilities. "I don't really understand why," Agape said, continuing:

He just doesn't really have that high of an opinion of women. . . . He thinks fire and aggression is what gets things done, like, "Grr, I'm gonna beat this thing!" And he sees women as being more passive and was worried my productivity would decrease.[115]

Carolina and Lana had similar experiences after transitioning. "I get walked on all over now," reported Lana. "It's like, before, I could assert myself and people would stop and listen. Now I try to assert myself and practically have to take my shoe off and pound on the table, 'Please, listen to me!'"[116] Carolina described the sudden encounters with sexism as "a huge shift." "As a man in this world, everything you say is taken at face value," she observed. "Everything you say as a woman in this country is automatically questioned."[117]

Because of discrimination of this sort, women and men continue to turn to the courts for justice. Many American companies and public service sectors have lost or settled gender-based class action lawsuits in the last twenty years, including Abercrombie & Fitch, Amazon, Bank of America, Best Buy, Coca-Cola, Costco, the FBI, Goodyear, Hewlett-Packard, Outback Steakhouse, Riot Games, Uber, United Airlines, the US Mint, Walmart, Wells Fargo, and many more.

Sexism is still prevalent in the workplace. The next two sections show how hostile and benevolent sexism produce invisible obstructions for women and opportunities for men.

Hostile and Benevolent Sexism

Most people—including most men—do not exhibit sexist behavior at work. Among those who do, some are more aggressive or persistent than others. It takes only one or two sexist people in a workplace, though, to create a hostile environment. Recent high-profile cases—like those against the mega movie producer Harvey Weinstein, the sports physician Larry Nassar, New York governor Andrew Cuomo, and the television hosts Bill O'Reilly and Matt Lauer (all credibly accused of patterns of sexual abuse or harassment of multiple women)—reveal that just one person can do a lot of damage. Even in less lofty and visible workplaces, a few particularly sexist superiors can do significant harm, even if the employees targeted are generally surrounded by supportive colleagues of all genders. Traditionalist men with homemaker wives are the most likely to be discriminatory.[118]

When asked, 22 percent of men and 42 percent of women report being the victim of gender discrimination at work.[119] Women in workplaces dominated by men are most likely to have this experience. The discrimination includes being treated as incompetent; being passed over for good assignments or promotions; being silenced, slighted, or isolated; and receiving less support from superiors.

Some of this discrimination takes the form of benevolent sexism, or discrimination in the form of chivalry. In this case, men attempt to protect women from unpleasant, dirty, or dangerous parts of the job and, in doing so, end up undermining women's careers. Cynthia, a construction worker, described how her coworker behaved toward her at work and what she did about it:

One journeyman treated me more like his wife because he pampers his wife. [He would say:] "Don't carry this and don't carry that." I started getting in this rut of standing at the bottom of the ladder handing him tools. So one day, I said this is such crap, I've got to do something. I just started doing everything before he had a chance. I'd grab the ladder and make him do the light work. I said, "Let me do some work, I'm an electrician."[120]

In the tech industry, managers give women less concrete negative feedback than men because they don't want to hurt their feelings.[121] As a result, men get the information they need to improve their performance, but women don't. Benevolent sexists may be trying to be "nice," but they harm women employees when "protection" prevents them from learning their job, demonstrating their skills, or becoming better employees.

Discrimination against women also comes in the form of hostile sexism. Especially in some occupations, some men are resentful that they're expected to work alongside women, so they isolate their women coworkers, treat them cruelly, sexually harass them, or put them in dangerous situations. Women construction workers report being forced to do "two-man" jobs all by themselves, for example, by men hoping they'll fail.[122] Such women are in lose-lose situations: If they try to prove they can "work like a man," they end up doing the dirtiest work or getting hurt. If they refuse to do that kind of work, they get accused of demanding "special treatment."

To discriminatory men, women present a **symbolic threat**; their presence potentially degrades the identity of the dominant group. Women in masculinized occupations present a symbolic threat to men coworkers when those men's self-esteem comes, in part, from being a man doing men's work. As long as men's esteem rests on being different from and better than women, men will likely resist women's entry into jobs that men dominate.

Ironically, interrupting the idea that some kinds of work are for "manly men" can be good for both men and women. In 1997, Rick Fox, a man in charge of the then deepest offshore oil well, embarked on an unusual experiment.[123] Oil rig work is a very dangerous job, and Fox figured that men's concern with showing weakness, fear, or ignorance—violations of core tenants of masculinity—was part of why. Accidents were going to happen if men were averse to asking questions, admitting nervousness when something seemed dangerous, or showing weakness if they couldn't handle a task.

So Fox brought in a facilitator to encourage his employees to share their fears and insecurities. In front of their coworkers, men confessed to losing loved ones, drowning their sorrows in alcohol, worrying about being a good father, and more. In the end, they felt more comfortable asking for help, listening, and cooperating—core tenets of femininity—and this transformed the workplace. The accident rate declined by 84 percent.[124]

Men's workplace discrimination against women and other men isn't inevitable. It can be interrupted, especially when employment opportunities are expanding and men aren't worried about losing their jobs.[125] When women are successfully integrated into workplaces, their mere presence reduces sexist and androcentric beliefs and behavior.[126] The presence of high-status women managers also makes a difference, decreasing the pay gap between men and women in their companies.[127]

Hostile and benevolent sexism limit career choices, create toxic and dangerous workplaces, and harm career trajectories. Women pay most of these costs. In many occupations, women also have to contend with invisible obstructions, while men—especially White men—are granted invisible opportunities.

Invisible Obstructions and Opportunities

The costs of hostile and benevolent sexism amount to a **glass ceiling**. Metaphorically, this is an invisible barrier between women and top positions in masculine occupations. Men, on average, enter the workforce at a higher rank with a better salary. They get more training, mentorship, and promotions.[128] And they advance and see their pay rise more quickly than women. This is true even when researchers account for the industry, geographical location, parenthood status, level of ambition, number of years in the workforce, and strategies used for advancement.

Even very successful women feel the strain. In a survey of corporate America, women in leadership positions were more than twice as likely as men to report being routinely interrupted.[129] They were nearly twice as likely to have their emotional state commented upon. And they were 50 percent more likely to have their judgment questioned, even when they were the ones with the relevant expertise. When there's only one woman on a team, the incidence of such discrimination goes up.

The same survey found that Black women, sexual minority women, and women with disabilities were the targets of discriminatory comments most often. Women with disabilities faced the greatest incidence. All these groups—and Asian and Latina women too—also disproportionately encountered people who expressed surprise at their skills or abilities. In addition, some sexual minorities report being forced to stay in a **glass closet**, an invisible place in which sexual minorities hide their identities in order to avoid stigma, suspicion, or censure at work.[130] Rates of discrimination rise when people carry multiple disadvantaging identities.

Consider what happened in early 2022: President Biden was delivering on his campaign promise to choose a Black woman for a vacancy on the US Supreme Court. As he weighed his options, much of the criticism he received was built on

a racist and sexist assumption that he was prioritizing identity over qualifications. Instead of acknowledging that there were many qualified Black women to
choose from, his critics assumed that candidates were *either* qualified *or* Black
women. Senator John Kennedy of Louisiana, for example, criticized Biden's process by saying he wanted "a nominee who knows a law book from a J. Crew
catalog," implying that Black women across the board were unqualified.[131]

For Black women—and Latinas too—the proper metaphor may not be glass,
but concrete. These women are even less likely than White and Asian women to
hold jobs in the top ranks of professions.[132] Stereotypes such as the Angry Black
Woman and the Hot-Blooded Latina doubly penalize women of color for not living up to expectations of White femininity. This requires them to put even more
energy into their feminine apologetic. As one Black woman lawyer explained:

> *Black women in law must perform work—actual mental and emotional work—that is*
> *not expected of our colleagues. This extra labor takes aim at our very dignity, but*
> *we must do it well and with a smile. The smallest mistake could not only harm our*
> *careers but also serve as justification for those who see us as mere affirmative action*
> *beneficiaries. We must do our jobs and continuously prove we deserve them.*[133]

When women of all races do break through glass ceilings, they often encounter
a **glass cliff**, a heightened risk of failing, compared with similar men.[134] In 2018,
for example, the retailer JCPenney appointed its first woman CEO, Jill Soltau, in
the midst of a collapse. Verging on bankruptcy, citing precipitously declining
revenues, and after closing dozens of stores, the board finally decided to install
a woman at the top of the company. Two years later, they fired her for failing
to turn the company around. Soltau's experience is routine.[135] Women tend to
be promoted during times of crisis and given jobs with a higher risk of failure.
This phenomenon is found in contexts as wide ranging as funeral homes, music
festivals, political elections, and law.

If women are seen as less capable than men, why would companies promote
them in times of crisis? The answer has less to do with how managers feel about
women than it does with how they feel about men. When decision makers are
predominantly men, they may make efforts to ensure that men with whom they
feel chummy get the better positions. The bad jobs are then given to whomever
is left over: typically women and racial minorities of all genders.[136] This was the
experience of one woman Marine Corps officer. "The good old boys network,"
she explained, "put the guys they want to get promoted in certain jobs to make
them stand out, look good."[137]

When women succeed in precarious positions, and they often do, their reward
is often to be put in charge of yet another fragile project. Many women, faced with
this revolving door, eventually do fail. Or they burn out from stress. In fact, while

we often hear that women "opt out" of high-pressure jobs to spend more time with their families, in real life women cite this reason for leaving their jobs only about 3 percent of the time (that is, no more often than men). Dissatisfaction, feelings of underappreciation, blocked opportunities, discrimination, and harassment are much more significant factors.[138] If women *seem* less ambitious than men, then, this is partly explained by the barriers they face at work, ones that men, all things being equal, do not.

This resonates with research on work more generally: People in jobs with a **sticky floor**, ones with no or low opportunity for promotion, tend to limit their aspirations.[139] Women, more often than men, once found themselves in positions where it didn't make sense to be ambitious. This is still true for women of color, immigrant women, and non-college-educated women.[140]

Young men without college degrees also increasingly find themselves stuck in jobs with sticky floors. Unlike their fathers and grandfathers, they are often closed out of occupations that offer stable employment, a family-supporting wage, and chances for promotion. Many of these men resist switching to women-dominated occupations, but some do.[141]

Do men who enter women-dominated professions face the same struggles as women in men-dominated ones? Most don't. Men in women-dominated occupations are disadvantaged relative to men in men-dominated occupations, but they aren't disadvantaged relative to their women coworkers. Instead of facing glass ceilings or cliffs, they're often presented with a **glass escalator**: an invisible ride to the top offered to certain men in women-dominated professions.[142]

A glass escalator was documented, for instance, in a study of thousands of secondary- and elementary-school teachers. In the space of two years, men were three times more likely than women to be promoted to administrative positions.[143] Likewise, though women are overrepresented in fashion design, men are more likely to win accolades and awards.[144] This is true especially if they're White and heterosexual. For example, research shows that Black men who are nurses are not especially likely to be promoted or advanced.[145]

Not all men view the glass escalator as a blessing. Sociologist Christine Williams, who coined the phrase, described how a librarian, six months after starting his first job, was criticized by his supervisors for "not shooting high enough."[146] "Seriously," he said, "they assumed that because I was a male—and they told me this . . . that somehow I wasn't doing the kind of management-oriented work that they thought I should be doing." He worked in the children's collection for ten years and had to fight the whole time to avoid being promoted; he enjoyed the job he had. Men nurses, likewise, are often steered to emergency medicine, where salaries are higher.[147] Gender stereotypes are at work here—not just positive ones but also negative ones like the idea that men aren't good with children.

Glass and concrete ceilings, alongside glass cliffs, closets, and escalators, conspire with sticky floors to keep White, heterosexual, college-educated men at the top of many workplaces. Gendered expectations surrounding parenthood contribute as well, especially for parents in white-collar professions.

PARENTHOOD: THE FACTS AND THE FICTION

Two incompatible ideologies shape women's work experiences, particularly for those of us lucky enough to work in middle- and high-income jobs: intensive mothering (discussed in the last chapter) and the **ideal worker norm**. The latter refers to the idea that employees should commit their energies to their careers without the distraction of family responsibilities.[148] Echoing these norms, a senior manager named Bill, interviewed about workplace culture, explained:

> The members of the Management Committee of this company aren't the smartest. . . . We're the hardest working. We work like dogs. We out-work the others. We out-practice them. We out-train them. . . . What counts is work and commitment. . . . I don't think we can get commitment with less than fifty or sixty hours a week.[149]

What Bill is describing is what social scientists call **overwork**, defined as working fifty or more hours a week. In Japan, overwork is recognized as a substantial source of stress. So much so that the language includes a word, *karoshi*, that means death by overwork.

The ideal worker norm behind overwork is strong in the United States. Employees may be cast as insufficiently dedicated if they sometimes take time off to do family-related tasks or can't always exceed stated job responsibilities, like work overtime, on weekends, and on short notice. In Northern California's Silicon Valley, ideal workers are described as ones with "zero drag," meaning that absolutely nothing about their lives interferes with their ability to work.[150] In these high-stakes, high-reward professions, employees who do "just" a good job are penalized; great workers go "above and beyond," creating a cycle in which workers have to outwork each other just to stay in the game.

The ideal worker norm places impossible demands on all individuals with family responsibilities and on many without. But because men, on average, have fewer domestic responsibilities than women, they're more able to fulfill these extreme demands. Mothers, especially, are unable to consistently overwork. And those with high-income, overworking husbands are especially likely to leave the workforce for a decade or more.[151] Scholars estimate that rising rates of overwork have contributed to the persistence of the gender pay gap.[152]

Notably, institutional limits on overwork can open more jobs to mothers and to women who anticipate becoming mothers. For example, when medical residencies for doctors were capped at eighty hours a week, women became more likely to enter the specialties like surgery that formerly had the most punishing schedules. Maximum hours, as well as minimum wages, can contribute to more gender-equal workplaces.[153]

Unrestrained, the ideal worker norm intersects with stereotypes about women, and especially mothers, to make it *seem* as if they'll inevitably be substandard employees.[154] This belief often inspires employers to push women off their career tracks.

Working on the Mommy Track

Overwhelmingly, if a parent in a mixed-gender relationship takes time off work after a child is born, that parent is the mother.[155] If that woman has two children three years apart and takes a break from work that lasts until the second child enters preschool, she'll have been out of the workforce for seven years. Those are unpaid years, and when she returns to work, she'll have less work experience than a person who didn't take time off. Mothers know they'll be penalized, and if they have the kinds of jobs where competing matters, they often keep their leave times to a minimum. Some women even choose to keep their children a secret from their employers.[156]

When women do go back to work, what happens at home matters too. Recall that married mothers and fathers have a tendency to specialize: Men do about two-thirds of the paid work and women do about two-thirds of the housework and childcare. Struggling with work-life balance, mothers may be put on a **mommy track**, a workplace euphemism that refers to expecting less intense commitment from mothers, with the understanding that they're sacrificing the right to expect equal pay, regular raises, or promotions. Women on the mommy track might be sent home when others are asked to stay late, excused from important work-related travel, and kept off projects that require long hours.

In contrast, men may increase their effort at work when they have a child, especially if their partners are spending more time at home. In a striking example from one study, for instance, a new mom started getting sent home at 5:30 p.m. sharp while her husband, who worked for the same person, was given extra work designed to boost his career.[157] Employers sometimes accept that a woman needs to respond to her children's schedule and take care of emergencies, even if they begrudge her this flexibility. Those same employers often do not accept that men need to do the same. Since there is rarely a daddy track, new fathers likely face fewer options than new mothers.

Leave times contribute to mothers' economic disadvantage. They suffer further disadvantage due to employers' *beliefs* about mothers who are also workers.[158] Despite some studies suggesting that mothers are actually *more* productive than nonmothers, employers' assumptions may make it difficult for them to properly evaluate and reward their whole range of employees.[159]

Discrimination against Mothers

Research shows that many employers see mothers as less-than-ideal employees and fathers as especially ideal ones, regardless of how much talent and effort men and women display at work.[160]

Mothers may find themselves put on the mommy track based purely on stereotypes. As law professor Joan C. Williams describes it, "Managers and coworkers may mentally cloak pregnant women and new mothers in a haze of femininity, assuming they will be empathetic, emotional, gentle, nonaggressive—that is, not very good at business."[161] In fact, mothers' value at work is ranked as about equivalent to other stigmatized workers: elderly persons and people receiving welfare. Single mothers and Black mothers are often judged even more harshly.[162] And the more maternal they appear, the less we value them. One study, for instance, found that people think breastfeeding mothers are less competent workers than mothers who bottle-feed.[163]

But, Williams continues, "if these women shine through the haze and remain tough, cool, and committed to their jobs, colleagues may indict them for being insufficiently maternal."[164] What would we think, after all, of a new mother who *didn't* want to go home early? Mothers face an extreme double bind in that they're damned if they do and damned if they don't. If they shine as mothers, their supervisors and coworkers might not take them seriously as employees; if they shine as employees, their coworkers might conclude they're neglectful parents.

The belief that mothers are bad workers sits alongside the belief that fathers are the best workers. Sociologist Shelley Correll and her colleagues did an experiment in which individuals reviewed fictional applications for a marketing job. The résumés were similar but appeared to come from mothers, nonmothers, fathers, and nonfathers. Overall, respondents rated mothers as the least competent, committed, promotable, and suited for management training. Only 47 percent of the mothers were recommended for hire, compared to 84 percent of the nonmothers. If hired, mothers were offered starting salaries nearly $15,000 less per year than those of nonmothers. In contrast, fathers were rated *more* favorably than nonfathers: 73 percent of fathers were recommended for hire, compared to 62 percent of nonfathers. Fathers were seen as more committed and were more likely to be promoted. They recommended an $8,000 bump over the salaries recommended to nonfathers and recommended paying fathers about $17,500 more than mothers.[165]

To test this finding in the real world, Correll and her colleagues sent 1,276 fake résumés, carefully constructed to give hints as to parental status, to 638 actual employers. Mothers received fewer than half as many callbacks as nonmothers. Fathers were called back at a slightly higher rate than nonfathers. Nonmothers received the most callbacks. Employers generally seem to like hiring women in professional jobs; they just don't like hiring moms.

In sum, women's careers are harmed by beliefs about mothers, discrimination against them, and the unfair but very real expectation that they lean into parenting at the expense of work. All this adds up to what social scientists describe as a **motherhood penalty**, a decrease in wages that accrues to people who become mothers. It's found in more than a dozen North American and European countries.[166]

For American mothers, the penalty amounts to a 7 percent decline in their wages, controlling for changes in actual hours worked.[167] That is, mothers make less than nonmothers even when they work the same number of hours. The highest-earning women experience the biggest penalty. Consequently, these women tend to take the least time off and incur the least total cost. The costs are smaller when mothers are not White or not married to men.[168]

Dads, for their part, may receive a **fatherhood premium**, an increase in wages that accrues to some people who become fathers.[169] The evidence is mixed, but certain kinds of married fathers have been shown to earn up to 7 percent more than married men without children. Unlike the motherhood penalty (half of which is the result of bias), the evidence suggests that the fatherhood premium may be mostly about men leaning into work before or after a child is born (with domestic help from the mothers of their children) rather than employers' preference for fathers.[170] It's mostly White men already positioned to earn high incomes who see a fatherhood premium, assuming they are partnered with women.

Motherhood penalties and fatherhood premiums combine to produce real disadvantage and advantage. In the first year after the birth of a mixed-gender couple's first child, the gap between his and her earnings doubles, and it continues to grow for the next five years.[171] American women make 83 percent of what men do, but among parents, women's relative earnings drop to 74 percent.[172]

One study of white-collar workers during the Covid-19 pandemic found that work-from-home fathers were twice as likely as work-from-home mothers to get a pay raise and nearly four times as likely to be promoted.[173] Another found that fathers were not only less likely to get laid off than mothers but also less likely than men without children.[174] In contrast, for those mothers who had previously managed to stay off the mommy track, the pandemic may have finally pushed them onto it. As the last chapter discussed, after schools and daycares closed, women were more likely than similar men to take a less demanding job, switch to a part-time job, take a leave of absence, or work fewer hours.[175]

THE CHANGING WORKPLACE, REVISITED

If being a flight attendant in 1945 was almost as glamorous as being a movie star, it certainly isn't anymore. Commercial air travel today is an unpleasant form of mass transportation—more like riding a city bus than being escorted through the sky by a white-jacketed steward.[176] While airlines once offered plenty of space, free full-course meals, and blankets and pillows, today they do little more than shuttle us from one place to another, with a beverage and snack service sufficient to ensure that passengers don't literally pass out from thirst or hunger.

In the United States, this shift from elite to "economy class" was spurred by the federal government's decision to set fewer standards on air travel.[177] Deregulation of the industry, complete by 1985, left airlines to set their own fares and routes. Capitalist competition sent airlines into a downward spiral as they slashed costs to offer the cheapest fares.

The need to reduce cost is why most airlines today offer only the most basic of amenities for non–first class passengers. It's also meant squeezing as much work out of the fewest employees for as little pay and as few benefits as possible.[178] Flight attendants have a strong history of labor unionization and were organized to protect their rights and interests as coworkers, but legal and illegal efforts by airlines to "bust" unions hindered their ability to collectively bargain. Consequently, flight attendants suffered huge layoffs, heightened work demands, and more unpredictable and erratic schedules. By the end of the 1980s, their income had fallen by a third.[179]

Figure 11.1 shows that US employers stopped sharing growing profits with their employees in the 1970s. Workplace unions—organizations that enabled workers to join together to bargain for good pay, benefits, and safe working conditions—have been on a long, slow decline. Despite recent unionization efforts at places like Starbucks, Amazon, and Walmart, today only 34 percent of public sector workers and 6 percent of private sector workers belong to a union.[180]

Furthermore, jobs today are often part-time, offering few or no benefits (like sick pay) and irregular work hours that make predicting income and arranging childcare difficult.[181] Many people work these part-time jobs involuntarily, meaning they'd rather have a full-time job. In fact, between 2007 and 2018, involuntary part-time work increased five times faster than voluntary part-time work and eighteen times faster than all work.[182] Against their will, many American

FIGURE 11.1 | THE GROWING GAP BETWEEN PRODUCTIVITY AND WORKERS' COMPENSATION

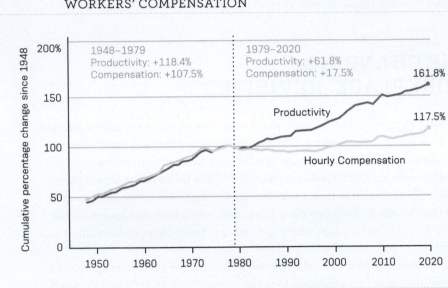

Source: Economic Policy Institute, "The Productivity–Pay Gap," August 2021, https://www.epi.org/productivity-pay-gap/.

workers find themselves cobbling multiple jobs together, juggling unpredictable hours, and still making less than they would had they been able to secure a full-time job.[183]

The absence of good jobs has also pushed up to 40 percent of US workers into the "gig economy," a romanticized form of self-employment that offers neither benefits nor job security.[184] When the pandemic arrived, gig work plummeted, then quickly returned, rising to new heights.[185] Before the pandemic and now, gig workers are disproportionately women, people of color, immigrants, and under thirty-five years old.

All this to say, a middle-class lifestyle has become increasingly elusive in the United States.[186] In 2019, 28 percent of American workers made less than $15 an hour.[187] Men as well as women have been harmed by these changes in the econ-omy (recall that a quarter of the decline in the gender wage gap is due to men's declining wages). The absence of a breadwinner wage—one sufficient to support a family—has contributed to demoralization and family fragility in Black com-munities for decades. Now White men's families are also being affected.[188]

Women breadwinners, though, and especially women of color, are more likely than men to find themselves in a particularly precarious financial situation. This is because they're clustered in industries that pay at or near the minimum wage (or, in the case of tipped workers and home health aides, even less). Families headed by women are increasingly experiencing poverty and homelessness, even as more and more families are depending on women's wages alone.[189]

Scholars estimate that the pandemic will almost certainly worsen gender inequality, but as with any economic change, the long-term consequences will depend on how workers and employers respond to these challenges.

Revisiting the Question

Q+A   **If women now have equal rights in the workplace, why aren't they as successful as men at work?**

Many supervisors, both men and women, go out of their way to ensure women can compete on equal footing with men. Many women are talented and dedicated enough to overcome at least some of the gendered disadvantages. Still, despite many examples to the contrary, women still face collective barriers to success at work that men do not.

The gender pay gap is one measure of this disadvantage. Some of the gap is explained by differences in job experience due to time spent in and out of the workforce; women are more likely to work part-time and to take time out of the workforce to care for children.[190] About half of the gap is explained by current job segregation, the devaluation of women's work, and biases against mothers. The remainder is likely due to discrimination against women and gender-nonconforming people. As a result of these phenomena, women who worked full-time in 2021 earned $0.83 for every dollar earned by comparable men. For the typical woman working fifty weeks a year, that means earning $9,250 less each year.[191]

This isn't just problematic *in principle*. For low-income women's families, economic disadvantage translates into *real* deprivation: an inability to pay rent, keep food on the table, or buy their children back-to-school clothes. For more financially secure women, it translates into fewer opportunities and pleasures. With an extra $9,250 a year, a woman could pay the majority of the tuition and fees at her local state college, get a massage every two and a half days for a year, or learn how to fly an airplane. If she invested it, experts predict it would be worth $100,221 twenty-five years later. Even without interest, ten years of savings would be enough to start a business or put a hefty down payment on a house. Or she could use that money to take an entire year off work, maybe three. It's easy to think about the wage gap in purely theoretical terms, but money buys everything but happiness. It matters.

As women of color have noted in the past, closing the gender pay gap will be a bittersweet victory if the US economy fails to provide well-paying jobs for everyone. Indeed, even if all forms of discrimination were eliminated tomorrow, life-threatening inequalities in income would persist. This is something that many Americans, including ones who identify as feminist, have been working on.

Next . . .

Gender inequality is not just a theoretical exercise. It's a lived experience. Sexism, androcentrism, and subordination play a role in how we understand and express our sexualities, organize and experience our home lives, and earn a living. Gendered ideas, interactions, and institutions structure our lives at every turn, creating both difference and inequality. This is not good for women, but it's not ideal for most men either. This is what motivates many people to get involved in politics. The next chapter asks:

Q+A   **How do we change societies?**

FOR FURTHER READING

Chang, Emily. *Brotopia: Breaking Up the Boys' Club of Silicon Valley.* New York: Penguin Random House, 2018.

Clawson, Daniel, and Naomi Gerstel. *Unequal Time: Gender, Class, and Family in Employment Schedules.* New York: Russell Sage Foundation, 2014.

Collins, Caitlyn. *Making Motherhood Work: How Women Manage Careers and Caregiving.* Princeton, NJ: Princeton University Press, 2019.

Connell, Catherine. *School's Out: Gay and Lesbian Teachers in the Classroom.* Berkeley: University of California Press, 2015.

Fraser, Nancy. "Contradictions of Capital and Care." *New Left Review* 100 (2016): 99–117.

Goldin, Claudia. *Career and Family: Women's Century-Long Journey toward Equity.* Princeton, NJ: Princeton University Press, 2021.

Kessler-Harris, Alice. *A Woman's Wage: Historical Meanings and Social Consequences.* Lexington: University of Kentucky Press, 1990.

Lovejoy, Meg, and Pamela Stone. *Opting Back In: What Really Happens When Mothers Return to Work.* Oakland, CA: University of California Press, 2019.

NOBODY'S FREE UNTIL
EVERYBODY'S FREE.
—FANNIE LOU HAMER[1]

12

Politics

The first democracies excluded women by design. Women did not have the right to vote, serve on juries, give legal testimony, or hold public office. They couldn't weigh in on laws and policies, vote to elect their representatives, or testify at a trial, even in their own defense.

In the United States, the first recorded decision to oppose this situation was in 1848. At the first-ever US women's rights convention, participants resolved that women should act to "secure to themselves their sacred right to the elective franchise."[2] And with that they began a movement for women's **suffrage**, the right to vote. Throughout the nineteenth century, proponents of women's suffrage around the world, called "suffragists," began similar movements.

Opponents of women's suffrage argued that the idea was dangerous. They believed that men were the head of the family and therefore knew what was in their wives' best interests. If wives had their own political opinions, opponents worried, it would threaten family unity. It was much better, they surmised, if women didn't have political opinions at all.

They also thought it absurd for women to bother with politics. Women belonged in the home, they argued, apart from public life. They compared wives to another domestic animal: the housecat. Anti-suffrage propaganda portrayed suffragists exactly this way:

An Advocate for Woman's Rights.

The pro-suffrage cat was introduced by activists who wanted to portray women voters as absurd. Instead, suffragists embraced the comparison, as in this pro-suffrage postcard from 1905.

"I want my vote!" meowed a black-and-white kitten on one such poster.[3] The message was clear: Women's opinions about politics were no more relevant to men than those of a household pet.

Suffragists embraced the insult. Cats are fierce, after all. Hitting back, a pro-suffrage Christmas card issued in 1908 featured a tabby standing on its hind legs holding a "Votes for Women" sign. The accompanying poem was their pledge:

I'm a catty suffragette.
I scratch and fight the P'lice.
So long as they withhold the vote
my warfare will not cease.[4]

It was a long and sometimes violent war. In addition to criticism and ridicule, suffragists faced government repression and violence. More than one thousand would be imprisoned in the United Kingdom and United States. There they endured brutal force-feeding after initiating hunger strikes.[5] Most suffragists were peaceful, but some weren't above aggression themselves. One group in the United Kingdom set buildings on fire and learned jujitsu to defend themselves from attacks by police officers; they made that catty pledge a reality.[6] Still, many suffragists died of old age before their efforts were realized.

Sometimes Black and White women worked side by side to make women's suffrage a reality. Many suffragists were **abolitionists** first, activists in the fight against human slavery. After slavery was abolished in 1865 and Black men were granted suffrage in 1869, Black women continued to fight valiantly for their own vote. As the abolitionist Sojourner Truth observed: "If colored men get their rights, and colored women not theirs, you see the colored men will be masters over the women, and it will be just as bad as it was before."[7]

Anti-suffrage activists tapped into widespread animosity toward Black people, reminding a racist public that women's suffrage would double the Black vote. This led some White suffragists to advocate only on behalf of their own vote.[8] Other White suffragists were proactively racist, choosing to exclude Black women from their organizations. Consequently, some Black women leaders, like Ida B. Wells-Barnett, started suffrage organizations of their own.

Globally, suffragists started working together in the 1880s, and by the early 1900s, public opinion around the world began to shift. New Zealand was the first to grant women the right to vote, in 1893. In 1906, Finland was first to give women both the right to vote and the right to hold public office. After World War I, at least twenty-four different countries, including the United States, gave women the right to vote. Officially, both Black and White women won it in 1920, but the emergence of a Jim Crow regime in southern states meant that all Black people were denied the right to vote in practice. Voting as a formal right did not reach Native American women and men until 1924, and the law barring Asian immigrants from becoming citizens effectively disenfranchised them as well.

Just one hundred years ago, women's suffrage was a **radical claim**: an idea that doesn't (yet) resonate with most members of a population.[9] Over time, however, women's right to vote became noncontroversial, even matter of fact. Eventually all countries in the world extended the right to vote to women. In 2015, Saudi Arabia was the last country to do so.[10] Today, **universal suffrage**, the right of all citizens to vote, is part of the definition of democracy.

That universal suffrage is now the norm is evidence that change—even radical change—is possible. In fact, as the timeline in Table 12.1 illustrates, feminists and other activists have turned plenty of radical ideas into the status quo. We don't know what will come next. Many things that seem radical today may be taken for granted a hundred years from now, for better or worse.

Our final question, then, is:

Q+A   How do we change societies?

We change them with politics.

Politics is the word used to describe the various activities involved in determining public policies and electing people to guide this process. Politics, in other words, is how people in democracies make decisions. It's always contentious, and the current moment in the United States is especially so.

This chapter is about the **politics of gender**: how people change and resist change to the gender order. Because people of all genders carry a mix of identities, the politics of gender is inherently intersectional. **Intersectional feminist politics** involves fighting all the forces that contribute to women's

TABLE 12.1 | KEY MOMENTS IN US GENDER POLITICS SINCE SUFFRAGE

1920	Most American women win the right to vote.
1922	The Supreme Court decides that US women who marry noncitizen men may retain their own citizenship.
1923	The Equal Rights Amendment is introduced into Congress.
1924	Native American men and women win suffrage.
1928	Puerto Rican women win suffrage.
1933	Frances Perkins becomes the first woman member of a presidential cabinet.
1963	The Equal Pay Act makes it illegal to pay men and women different wages for the same job.
1964	The Civil Rights Act outlaws discrimination on the basis of racial, ethnic, or national origin, religion, and sex.
1965	The Supreme Court decriminalizes the use of birth control by married people.
1968	The Equal Employment Opportunity Commission rules that gender segregation of "Help Wanted" ads is illegal.
1970	The last "marriage ban" barring women from paid employment is struck down.
1972	The Supreme Court extends to single people the right to use contraceptives.
	Title IX bans sex discrimination in schools receiving federal funding.
	Congress passes the Equal Rights Amendment. Thirty-five states ratify the amendment, falling short of the thirty-eight needed.
1973	The Supreme Court grants women the right to abortion in the first and second trimesters.
1974	The Equal Credit Opportunity Act establishes married women's right to have a credit card in their own name and, thus, have a credit history and score.
	The Supreme Court rules that mandatory dismissals of public school teachers who become pregnant are unconstitutional.
1975	The Supreme Court grants women equal rights and responsibilities for jury duty.
1976	Military academies are ordered to admit women.
	Nebraska becomes the first state to make marital rape illegal.
1978	The Pregnancy Discrimination Act requires employers to treat pregnancy like any other temporary disability.
1981	Women are allowed to enlist in all military branches.
1992	The "Year of the Woman" sees an unprecedented number of women elected to Congress.
1993	"Don't Ask, Don't Tell" is introduced, requiring sexual minorities to remain closeted if they want to serve in the military but protecting them if they do.
1996	President Bill Clinton signs the Defense of Marriage Act, defining marriage as an act possible only between a man and a woman.
	The Supreme Court declares that states cannot deny gays and lesbians protection from discrimination.

1999	Tammy Baldwin becomes the first openly gay person to serve in Congress.
2004	Massachusetts becomes the first state to legalize same-sex marriage.
2009	The Lily Ledbetter Fair Pay Restoration Act overturns a Supreme Court decision that prevented women from challenging past pay discrimination.
	Sonia Sotomayor becomes the first woman of color confirmed to the Supreme Court.
2010	The US Navy ban on women serving on submarines is overturned.
	"Don't Ask, Don't Tell" is repealed.
2012	The Affordable Care Act requires health insurance to cover contraception.
2015	The Supreme Court declares same-sex marriage a legal right in all fifty states.
	The military begins allowing women to serve in front-line combat roles and lifts the ban on military service by trans people.
2016	Hillary Rodham Clinton becomes the first woman nominated by a major political party for president of the United States.
2017	After Donald Trump's inauguration, Americans march for women's rights, Black lives, and science in the largest protest in US history.
	Danica Roem becomes the first openly trans state legislator (Virginia).
2018	Tammy Duckworth becomes the first senator to give birth while in office.
2019	Nevada becomes the first state to have a legislature that is majority women.
2020	Kamala Harris, a woman of color, is elected as the first woman vice president of the United States.
2021	Debra Haaland, a tribal citizen of the Laguna Pueblo, is confirmed as secretary of the interior, becoming the first Indigenous American in the presidential cabinet.
2022	Kentanji Brown Jackson becomes the first Black woman confirmed to the Supreme Court.
	In *Dobbs v. Jackson*, the Supreme Court strikes down the constitutional right to abortion.

oppression, including class inequality, racism, heterosexism, and more. Intersectional feminists believe that gender equality requires ending inequalities of all kinds.

Feminist progress has always been incremental, a slow dismantling of many different social hierarchies. As the timeline in Table 12.1 shows, wealthy White women are usually the ones to break glass ceilings because they generally have more opportunity than other kinds of women. The first woman to serve in Congress, for example, was Jeannette Rankin, a White woman from Montana. She was elected in 1916, after Montana granted women the right to vote but before the federal government had. It would be another eighty-three years before the first openly gay woman was elected. Likewise, in 1981 Sandra Day O'Connor, a White woman, became the first woman appointed to the Supreme Court. The first woman of color was appointed in 2009. Each gain opens another door, and many "small wins" can add up to big changes.[11]

Table 12.1 is proof that feminists do win, but it may also give a false impression that feminists never lose, or that rights, once won, cannot disappear. In fact, all feminist politics encounters **anti-feminist politics**, the kind that aims to prevent feminist change. This isn't about going "back" to how things used to be but producing a future gender order that affirms gender difference and hierarchy. Anti-feminist politics is intersectional, too, in that it often resists policies that would help marginalized women, such as policies that would undermine the feminization of poverty or the criminalization of Black girls in school. Feminists and anti-feminists are on opposite sides of a struggle for more inclusive societies.

Feminists don't just wrestle with anti-feminists. They also often disagree with one another. There is debate as to what a **feminist utopia**—or a perfectly gender-egalitarian society—might look like, and there are always trade-offs in choosing strategies to get there. This sometimes leads to tough negotiations, but these struggles often lead to a feminism that's more responsive to people of all genders and intersectional positions.

Nothing about politics is simple. It's a thorny, often heated enterprise with lots of moving parts. It can be both exciting and intimidating, as there are no predetermined endings or guarantees. What comes next is uncertain, but one thing is for sure: Politics will be involved.

THE STATE

States are institutions entrusted with the collective power to regulate everyday life. They are what we, in more ordinary language, refer to as countries or nations. The term can also refer to the component parts of countries or nations, as in the United States. States matter because they wield a greater power than almost any other social entity on earth, second only, perhaps, to global alliances like the United Nations and transnational corporations like Google and Amazon. States have vast resources and the exclusive right to pass laws, collect taxes, and detain and imprison citizens. States can even legally wage war according to a set of international rules.

Today, states are the dominant way of promoting collective welfare. This is called **governance**: the process of making decisions for the state, enforcing the laws of the land, and—to the extent that a state is a democracy—ensuring the state's accountability to its citizens. There are two ways to think about gender and governance.[12] The first involves the **governance of gender**: how gender is used to produce distinctions and regulate residents accordingly. The second is the **gender of governance**: who holds political office and how it matters.

The Governance of Gender

Though the state can seem abstract and distant, its policies affect all aspects of our daily lives, from what we're paid for our work, to the health of our environments, to the content of our education, and more. State policies are also gendered. For example, states decide whether to require gender binary spaces. In the United States, public restrooms, prisons, and military barracks all come in "men's" and "women's." Likewise, if a Transportation Security Administration agent decides to pat down a passenger at the airport, the task must be carried out by a same-gender attendant.

States also decide how many and which gender categories to recognize. In India and Bangladesh, people can formally identify as a man, woman, or hijra. Australia, Canada, and Germany have broad third gender categories. The United States leaves such rules in the hands of its individual states. In 2021, Americans were allowed to identify as neither male nor female on official documents in a dozen states (double the number just five years ago). All but four now allow trans people to acquire birth certificates that reflect their true gender.

Some of the most consequential state decisions involve **pro-natal** and **anti-natal policies**, ones that encourage or discourage childbearing. States pass laws that regulate access to contraception, Plan B, and abortion, and even knowledge about how to get pregnant or prevent pregnancy. They can decide whether health insurance companies are required to cover all these things and, consequently, whether we (and which of us) will be covered when we need these things.

Women exercising a right as citizens to control their own bodies, especially their reproductive power, has always challenged the political power of states to act on the presumption that men in positions of political and religious authority know best. In the now-overturned *Roe v. Wade* decision that legalized abortion in the first and sometimes second trimester, the US Supreme Court framed this right as a matter of individual choice.

Notably, abortion wasn't a partisan issue when *Roe v. Wade* was decided in 1973. Most Evangelicals—one of the religious groups most opposed to abortion today—didn't even have strong opinions about it. By 1980, however, religious conservatives had allied with the Republican Party to politicize abortion and frame resistance to abortion as a fundamental matter of "family values."[13] Evangelical Protestants and Roman Catholic leaders came together to wield political influence, exploiting abortion as a central issue in a battle over "traditional morality."

This right-leaning coalition has now successfully repealed the constitutional right to abortion. In June 2022, the US Supreme Court struck down this right in *Dobbs v. Jackson*. This landmark decision leaves it up to the individual states to decide how to regulate abortion. Eleven states have already banned all or most abortions, and experts predict that many more states will follow. These states are also among the least likely to provide sex education, maternal health care, paid parental leave, and a social safety net. People in these states now have to overcome substantial hurdles to access abortion. The scope of this crisis is vast given that 45 percent of pregnancies in the United States are unintended. This is a coercively pro-natal policy.

Whether women choose to have children is very serious business for states. Fertility rates determine whether a country can feed and educate its citizens, fill its jobs, support older adults, or fight wars. In Japan, for example, the fertility rate has fallen to 1.3 children per woman, far below the number required to maintain the population.[14] In an attempt to prompt more childbearing, the country gives tax credits to caregivers for each of their children. It also allows both new moms and dads to each take a full year of paid parental leave. They can stay home with their new baby and still receive 67 percent of their wages for the first six months and 50 percent for the next six.

Figure 12.1 shows that most countries are like Japan; they offer at least some paid parental leave (paid by the employer or the government). Most European states offer around six months of paid leave. Many other countries offer affirmatively pro-natal benefits. Finland gives new mothers a "baby box" filled with diapers, baby clothes, crib sheets, and other goods worth several hundred dollars. France provides day care at virtually no cost. Each of these policies encourages childbearing by making it more affordable and convenient.

States also pass anti-natal policies. Worried about overpopulation, China, for instance, imposed a one-child policy in 1979, revising it to a two-child policy in 2015 in response to a shrinking workforce and then to a three-child policy in 2021. India distributes educational material encouraging couples to have just one child and offers money in return for undergoing sterilization.

Both pro- and anti-natal policies can have unintended consequences. Because of preferences for boys over girls, and illegal but widespread sex-selective abortion, China and India now have more men than women.[15] This has led to a crisis in which millions of men who wish to have wives are unable to find women to marry. But Chinese daughters who are only children are winning more parental investments in their education and careers, with the expectation they will carry the responsibility for parental support that conventionally fell on sons.[16]

The US federal government guarantees only twelve weeks of leave and only to some employees. And it is wholly unpaid. This is one of the least generous parental leave policies in the world. Nine US states and the District of Columbia guarantee at least some paid leave. Some cities and large private employers offer paid leave to their own employees too.[17] In March 2021, the federal government estimated that 89 percent of civilian employees had access to some unpaid leave, but only 23 percent were entitled to any paid care leave.[18]

FIGURE 12.1 | STATE VARIATION IN PAID LEAVE FOR MOTHERS, 2020

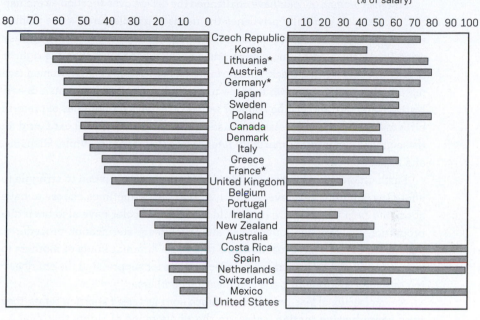

*Payment rates based on net earnings.

Source: "Parental leave systems," Table PF2.1.A. Summary of paid leave entitlements available to mothers, OECD Database, updated October 2021, https://www.oecd.org/els/soc/PF2_1_Parental_leave_systems.pdf.

The type and extent of parental leave has gendered effects. Generous leave given to mothers may help families, but it may also encourage women to stay out of the workforce longer, exacerbating the gender pay gap. Studies show that leave given to fathers often goes untaken.[19] In response, some countries now set aside one or two months specifically for the father, pressing men to get more involved in infant care; the share of fathers taking such leave has grown steadily.[20] Researchers find that fathers who take paternity leave are more likely to have a close relationship to their child even years later.[21] They're also more satisfied with their relationships and less likely to divorce.

Pro- and anti-natal policies may also be targeted differently to different kinds of mothers and fathers, producing intersectionally unequal outcomes.[22] Some US states have "family caps" on their income support for poor parents, for example, hoping to discourage them from having more babies. Other policies push poor mothers into the workforce by requiring them to hold a job to be eligible for benefits like low-income housing, childcare waivers, and "food stamps." This is in stark contrast to tax policies that encourage high-income earners to specialize and leave one spouse at home. Regardless of whether we think mothers of young children should hold paid jobs, it's noteworthy that US states encourage one kind of mothering for poor kids and another for wealthier ones.

Likewise, women of color have challenged the debate over abortion as too narrowly focused. It generally privileges the needs of middle-class White women with the ability to both access abortion and comfortably keep the children they want. Poor women, including many women of color, need more than the right to bear or not bear a child. Black, American Indian, and Alaska Native women face maternal mortality rates two to three times higher than White women. Black, Native Hawaiian, and Pacific Islander women also have higher rates of preterm birth and low birth rates, related to inadequate access to prenatal care. And all these groups suffer infant mortality rates at least twice that of White, Hispanic, and Asian women.[23]

Furthermore, poor women are more likely than other women to struggle to afford the children they have, so much so that they sometimes choose to have abortions even when they want a child.[24] Women of color have also been disproportionately targeted for coercive and involuntary sterilization procedures. Just as states often have mechanisms that press different kinds of mothers to parent in different ways, states have mechanisms for suppressing the childbearing of some and promoting the childbearing of others.

An intersectional lens reveals that women don't just need abortion rights; they need **reproductive justice**, access to the whole range of rights that enables people to choose whether and how to have and raise children. Reproductive justice includes not only the right to have children or not but also the right to safely bear the children they conceive, the right to safe neighborhoods and functioning schools, and the right to medical care and social supports that provide economically.

Policy makers aren't usually trained to think about gender when making policy, let alone how gender intersects with other identities. Accordingly, some feminists want politicians to commit to **gender-aware policy making**, a practice of carefully considering the likely effects of a policy on people of all genders, as well as the intersectional differences among them. This kind of policy making influenced a recent reorganization of the public transit system of Vienna, Austria. A gender-aware approach revealed to city planners that the city's transit system was designed around the needs of men commuting to work.[25] The typical woman had more diverse transit needs than men, including running errands, taking children to school and doctor appointments, and getting to work and back again at more irregular times. To make the transit system friendlier to the typical woman, the city instituted zoning rules to minimize distances among housing, stores, and medical clinics and scheduled more trains and buses during the day.

Changes like these not only reduce the isolation and stress of mothers but also address the needs of "atypical" men: single, stay-at-home, or primary-caregiver dads, or men who are retired, disabled, or unemployed. They help these men because systems are rarely organized around men to begin with; they're organized around the *stereotype* of a man. In fact, decisions made to help women often also make life a little easier for all people who don't meet hegemonic expectations.

Gender-aware policy making is a good start, but politicians and feminists alike must also be thoughtful about what kind of equality they're aiming for.

THEORIZING GENDER EQUALITY There are roughly three models of gender equality, each corresponding to the three types of gender inequality: sexism, androcentrism, and subordination. Most countries incorporate at least some policies that reflect each, and many policies combine these models.

The United States is a good example of a society that emphasizes **equal access**, an approach to ending sexism focused on dismantling legal barriers and reducing gender discrimination. Equal access emphasizes enabling individuals to make free choices. Examples of such policies include the guarantee of equal access to education, allowing women to enlist in the military, and laws that make it illegal to discriminate in the workplace.

Policies that enhance individual choice can significantly reduce the degree to which women are excluded from opportunities to earn money, gain experiences, and enhance their status. And that's good. In other ways, though, equal access falls short. First, such policies exist quite comfortably alongside other forms of intersectional disadvantage. This is because it's primarily privileged women who are able to take advantage of equal access policies.

Second, these policies sidestep the costs of androcentrism and subordination. That is, they don't do anything to encourage people to value femininity, nor do they ensure that women won't be hobbled by unpaid care responsibilities and other forms of service to others.

Third, they do nothing to expand men's opportunities. They merely require men to compete alongside women. This, as we know, sometimes prompts backlash.

Fourth, equal access policies may not appeal to people who prefer the feminized spheres of life. Equal access strategies work pretty well, in other words, for women and nonbinary people who aim to be where men already are, whether in a coal mine or a boardroom. But they do little to enhance the lives of people who prefer the work women have traditionally done; that work can remain low pay and low status.

Finally, if women's efforts to grasp for equality with men don't pan out, equal access policies point the finger at individuals. If access is equal, after all, there's no one to blame but oneself.

An alternative model of gender equality is **equal value**. Instead of addressing sexism, this model targets androcentrism by raising the value of the feminine to match the value of the masculine. This strategy allows for a gendered

division of labor but resists the idea that different is unequal. A society characterized by equal value, for example, would reward reproductive labor (pregnancy,
breastfeeding, and childcare responsibilities) so that this didn't result in economic insecurity. It would also raise the prestige and pay of all people who work
in feminized jobs. It might even challenge the aspects of masculinity that value
physical violence, militarism, and ruthless economic competition.

For people who embrace femininity, equal value is a more promising model
than equal access. It destigmatizes the feminine side of the binary, giving men
more opportunity to balance femininity and masculinity, much as women already
do. Further, if gender were no longer a metaphor for power, men wouldn't feel the
need to exhibit masculinity to feel powerful. This strategy, then, has the most
potential to free men from the constraints they face under gender inequality.

Equal value also pleases feminists who see gender difference as a significant
source of pleasure.[26] Difference might thrive in the absence of devaluation. If
the binary was no longer an infrastructure for inequality, its importance might
fade, making more room for people who don't identify as men or women. New
femininities and masculinities might emerge. Or gender might wane in significance, becoming only as important as whether one is right or left handed.

Challenging androcentrism, though, without also tackling sexism and subordination is a risky strategy. Equal value can provide a justification for coercively
enforcing gendered roles. Today, the Vatican, the Arab states of the Middle East,
and some evangelical Protestant churches in the United States invoke the idea
of equal value to resist equal access. That is, they argue that it's OK to require
men and women to form gender-complementary marriages because they value
the feminine and masculine roles alike. Similarly, they argue that it's OK to
require children to obey gender rules because each set of rules offers positive
contributions. Feminist progress is vulnerable to co-optation by people who claim
that rigid gender expectations are not oppression when masculinity and femininity are valued equally.

If equal access most directly tackles sexism and equal value targets androcentrism, then the **equal sharing** approach takes aim at subordination. As a
strategy, equal sharing attempts to ensure that all people participate equally
in positions conventionally understood as masculine and feminine. Unlike the
equal access approach, this model presses for changes in the rules of the game,
promoting structural change. It would put policies in place that press men to do
half the housework and childcare while aiming to have men and women spend
equal amounts of time in paid work. It would also aim to integrate all occupations. Equal sharing of governance, for example, requires that the composition
of legislatures and corporate boards roughly reflect the gender distribution in
the population (60/40 shares).

Equal sharing wouldn't necessarily end sexism; discrimination against women
or mothers at work is compatible with workplaces that are 60/40 or 40/60. Like-

wise, it wouldn't bring an automatic end to androcentrism. It merely expects men to do half the devalued work. Still, it would go a long way toward closing the gender pay gap and equalizing divisions of labor at home—if, that is, proponents were comfortable with states using their power to strongly influence how people of all genders spend their time.

State policies around the world reflect all three of these models. Reducing the barriers to women's participation in the workforce is an equal access strategy. Paying new parents to stay home with their children reflects equal value; the money indicates that childcare deserves compensation. And policies that reward families when fathers take paternal leave are encouraging equal sharing. Feminists disagree about which approach, or combination of approaches, is best.

In sum, people who call themselves "feminist" often have very different ideas about how to solve the problem of gender inequality. This can cause disagreement, but it can also spark productive conversations about what feminist activism should look like. This is part of why it's helpful to think of feminism as an evolving *conversation* instead of a set of *positions*. This next section is about who has a seat at the table where these conversations are happening.

The Gender of Governance

Historically, the politicians granted the power to govern our countries have been men. Today, however, women running for office in the United States are equally likely to win.[27] The average man is rather indifferent toward a candidate's gender, whereas the average woman tends to prefer women.[28] So what do we know about how women govern?

GENDER IN THE LEGISLATURE Women's presence in government is a form of **symbolic representation**, an acknowledgment of women's standing as citizens. One place to look for such representation is in **legislatures**, or groups of individuals elected to represent constituents in regulating the affairs of the country. Across the world, the percentage of women in legislatures ranges from 0 to 56 percent, with a global average of 26 percent.[29]

The primary way that feminists have increased the presence of women in legislatures is quotas, or rules that state that a certain percentage of legislators be women. While all countries have seen substantial increases in women's representation, those with quotas have been on a faster track.[30] Mexico, for instance, requires that half the seats in its Chamber of Deputies be filled by women. Generally speaking, the countries that come closest to parity are those with highly egalitarian approaches to gender, such as in Scandinavia. Women are also particularly well represented in countries where wars have discredited men's leadership, as in Rwanda.[31] In these countries and in some with effective quotas, like Argentina, women represent 40 percent or more of members of legislatures.[32]

As of 2022, US women hold 31 percent of states' elective executive offices, 31 percent of seats in state legislatures, and 27 percent of seats in Congress.[33] Internationally, this level of representation is only middling.[34] Still, the rapid rise of women in American politics is remarkable. Of all the women who have *ever* been elected to Congress in its more than 230-year history, more than a third are holding seats at the time we are writing this book.[35] Fifty of these, or 9 percent of all seats in Congress, are held by women of color.

Symbolic representation—merely having women in legislatures—suggests, at least in principle, that decision-making in important collective matters should be shared. When women are there, it's harder for men politicians to ignore issues that impact women's lives. In other words, just having women in office may make policy makers more gender-aware, and having more kinds of women in office can make them intersectionally so.

Consider the pathbreaking career of Tammy Duckworth, US senator from Illinois. Duckworth was a Blackhawk helicopter pilot in the Iraq War. In 2004, she was injured when her helicopter was hit by a rocket-propelled grenade. She lost both her legs. In 2017, she became the first disabled woman and the first person born in Thailand to be elected to Congress. And in 2018 she became the first sitting senator to give birth. Ten days after her daughter was born, Duckworth rolled into the Senate chamber to take a vote with her baby in her lap.

It caused quite a kerfuffle.[36] Senator Orrin Hatch worried that allowing Duckworth to bring the baby would invite a congressional baby boom, asking what would happen if there were "ten babies on the floor of the Senate?" Duckworth had to promise not to change the baby's diaper or breastfeed. Eventually they voted in favor. Since no baby had ever been on the Senate floor for proceedings, they had to make exceptions to the dress code. Babies are now officially exempt from donning formal attire, wearing proper footwear, and abiding by rules regarding hats.

Of course, Duckworth isn't the first parent of an infant to serve in the Senate. She is just the first *mother* of an infant to do so. When she came to work that day with a baby in tow, then, she served as a real reminder not just that women

Senator Tammy Duckworth beams as she arrives at the US Capitol Building with her ten-day-old child. "It feels great," she told reporters. "It is about time, huh?"

exist but, more importantly, that mothers exist—*working* mothers even—and that made the struggles faced by working parents of all genders just a little harder to ignore.

Does the presence of women politicians like Duckworth, however, matter in practice? Does symbolic representation, that is, translate into substantive representation? **Substantive representation** refers to the proposing and passing of policies important and helpful to women. The answer is both yes and no.

The answer is no in that gender by itself does not predict how people will legislate. Feminists themselves disagree as to how to promote gender equality, so it shouldn't be surprising that women politicians do too. On some issues, women have been more favorable than men for decades, including gun control and aid to children, for example, but party affiliation is a much more powerful predictor.[37] Men and women politicians in the same party tend to vote largely similarly.

The answer is yes in that women legislators in the United States tend to vote differently than men on issues that obviously affect women constituents, like education and health care.[38] Women politicians are also more likely than men to introduce bills that directly address women's needs.[39] So the presence of women politicians changes what legislators of both genders are voting *on*. Black women politicians, specifically, have done the most work of any group to combat poverty and exclusion.[40] Outside of the United States, women politicians have also been more supportive of measures to reduce climate change, even after controlling for party affiliation.[41]

Despite a long fight for political representation, a slow rise in the percentage of women politicians, and voters' slight preference for women in elected roles, no woman has served as president of the United States. Many other countries have elected women into such positions. Sri Lanka became the first to do so, in 1960. Since then, more than fifty women have served as head of state. Women leaders have been found disproportionately in Europe, but every region on earth has seen at least one. Why has the United States not yet elected a woman president?

GENDER AND THE US PRESIDENCY Scholars argue that the US presidency is possibly the most masculine job in the nation. If our nation is "the homeland," and our internal politics is "domestic," then the president is the metaphorical "head of the household": a leader taking care of a national family, setting the house rules, disciplining the disobedient, and above all, protecting its members from the outside world.[42] Family is the dominant metaphor for the state, and it's a gendered one.[43]

This has long made candidates' masculinity a central feature of political campaigns.[44] To this day, many presidential candidates refer to their masculinity to justify their fitness to lead. They publicly take up masculine hobbies (like ranching or football), emphasize masculine characteristics (like being adventurous or a risk-taker), talk in masculine ways (brashly and combatively), discuss policy in terms of power (by being "tough on crime" and "strong on national security"), and always remind the public of the risk of war.

In his run for the presidency in 2016, Donald J. Trump performed an especially "unapologetic masculinity."[45] At its core, his masculinity was about dominating others: "winning" in business, with women, in politics, and over other men. He had a signature violent handshake, promised to "bomb the shit" out of enemies, and claimed immigrants were rapists.[46] One month before the election, a tape was released in which he boasted of kissing and grabbing women without their permission. When critics questioned his fitness for office, he invoked exculpatory chauvinism—the idea that men are naturally "bad boys" and that being bad is part of what makes men great—calling it "locker room talk." *I'm a bad boy*, Trump seemed to say unapologetically, *but a bad boy is exactly what America needs right now.*

Challenging his 2016 Democratic rival, Hillary Clinton, Trump claimed that Clinton didn't have a "presidential look," implying that because women don't look the part, they can't perform the part. In turn, Clinton criticized Trump's embodiment of masculinity.[47] When Trump repeatedly questioned Clinton's strength, she interrogated what *kind* of man he was. "A man you can bait with a tweet," she warned, "is not a man we can trust with nuclear weapons."[48] In her own way, Clinton was asserting that Trump was not man enough to be president.

Trump did become president, and throughout his presidency, he and his supporters continued to portray him as a dominating man. His approach to Covid-19 is a case in point.[49] Two days after the first case was detected in the United States, and then again a month later, Trump claimed to have the virus "under control." When that was no longer a viable position, he pivoted. After months of minimizing the threat, he started describing himself as a "wartime president" and the virus as an "invisible enemy." He promised an "aggressive strategy" and "victory."[50]

Our best strategy for dealing with pandemics, of course, is nonviolent: handwashing, mask-wearing, quarantining, and vaccinating. Trump's strategy, however, only ambivalently embraced these public health recommendations, partly because they didn't enhance his masculine image. In particular, he resisted wearing and recommending face masks on the claim that they made people look "weak."

When Trump himself contracted the virus, he used his recovery to bolster his masculinity. He flexed his metaphorical muscles, portraying Covid-19 as a vanquished foe. He encouraged Americans to stand up to Covid too. "Don't let it dominate you," he said in a video. "Don't be afraid of it. You're going to beat it."[51]

His political allies—women as well as men—echoed this message, embracing his idea of masculinity. Representative Matt Gaetz of Florida, for example, tweeted: "President Trump won't have to recover from COVID. COVID will have to recover from President Trump."[52] Then senator Kelly Loeffler of Georgia released a video showing Trump winning a wrestling match with the coronavirus. "The president showed he's a true Commander-in-Chief by defeating the coronavirus," said the political commentator Glenn Beck, adding: "He should award himself the Medal of Freedom."[53] Politician Newt Gingrich praised Trump for being "fearless."[54]

An alternative approach to managing the Covid-19 pandemic may have involved embodying a "caring masculinity," wrote the sociologist James Messerschmidt, one "that recognizes the horrors of this virus, sympathizes with those infected, [and] respects all human life."[55] In fact, many world leaders embraced a caring approach, perhaps especially women leaders. Erna Solberg, the prime minister of Norway, for example, held a press conference aimed at her littlest constituents. "Many children are finding this scary," she acknowledged, and she aimed to help them understand what the country was doing and why.[56]

Jacinda Ardern, the prime minister of New Zealand, imposed aggressive lockdowns and border closures, but she also chose to console and comfort the people of her country. At the start of the lockdown, she released a Facebook Live video from her home. Dressed in an old sweatshirt, she apologized for the informality, noting that "it can be a messy business putting toddlers to bed."[57] (She's only the second world leader to give birth in office.) Channeling a maternal role, she urged New Zealanders to be kind and caring to one another.

Interestingly, media outlets responded quite positively to women leaders during the pandemic, especially when they performed femininity.[58] In contrast, the media were quite critical of "strongman" leaders like Trump, China's Xi Jinping, Brazil's Jair Bolsonaro, and the United Kingdom's Boris Johnson. The media frequently described them as "reckless," "incompetent," and "self-interested."[59] Media depictions were no less stereotypical than usual but were more likely than in normal times to portray women as specifically well suited to lead.

Perhaps this is why Joseph Biden's brand of masculinity—and the fact that his vice presidential running mate, Kamala Harris, was a woman—appealed more strongly to American voters than Donald Trump's. Biden played "nice guy" to Trump's "tough guy."[60] Drawing on his many decades in the Senate and his personal experience with loss, he cast himself as a "seasoned protector of the nation in its time of need."[61] He was quick to show empathy and emotional vulnerability, but he also performed a "working-class Joe" masculinity, one that centered on a hardworking, fair-playing, honorable, and ultimately decent family man.

On the campaign trail, Biden balanced his fatherly compassion with traditional symbols of masculinity.[62] He wore his signature aviator sunglasses, jogged alongside parades, and touted his own athleticism. He filmed ad campaigns featuring football and Ford F-150s. At one campaign stop, when questioned about his age, he suggested a push-up contest. Like Clinton, Biden also criticized Trump's version of masculinity, derisively calling Trump's resistance to mask-wearing

On the campaign trial, Biden performed masculinities designed to appeal to voters and signal his ability to lead.

a "macho thing." Yet more than once, he suggested that under different circumstances he'd "take [Trump] behind the gym and beat the hell out of him."[63]

Biden's softer masculinity may have appealed to Americans in part because the Covid-19 pandemic exposed the false binary between the femininized sphere of the home and the masculinized sphere of politics.[64] That is, it had never been more clear that politicians' decisions affect what happens to our families. Yet Democrats weren't so sold on a softer leadership that they chose one of the many women running in the Democratic presidential primary.[65] Despite a record number of women and people of color on the ballot, a White man still prevailed. "Ultimately, masculinity still matters," reflected sociologist Marianne Cooper. "It's how candidates still try to prove they are the best candidate. And so, even in 2020, Democrats decided the safest bet to beat a white man in his 70s is another white man in his 70s."[66]

Still, relative to the Trump/Pence ticket, Biden/Harris was gender balanced and not only because one of the candidates was a woman. The latter's win suggests that many Americans may be less opposed, and perhaps even inclined, to choose candidates, regardless of gender, who balance masculinity and femininity.[67] Further progress on this front faces two significant threats: gendered party polarization and the rise of authoritarianism.

THREATS TO FEMINIST PROGRESS

The 2016 election was uniquely gendered in that a man and a woman faced off for the presidency for the first time in American history, but the 2020 election had masculinity at its core too. Moreover, political parties themselves are increasingly portrayed in gendered ways. This rising polarization is threatening not only feminist progress domestically but also democracy worldwide.

Gendered Party Polarization in America

In the United States, the race and class backgrounds of voters have historically correlated with voting behavior. Today, for example, the typical Black American is likely to vote Democratic and the typical White American is likely to vote

Republican (though at times in history the reverse has been true). Before the 1980s, however, political party affiliation didn't correlate with gender. In other words, women as a group weren't more or less likely to vote Democratic or Republican.

This is no longer true. Today, we see a significant and increasing **partisan gender gap**, a tendency for men and women to align with different political parties. In the 2016 presidential election, for example, women voted for Clinton over Trump by about 12 percentage points, and men voted for Trump over Clinton by about the same margin.[68] This gender gap was bigger than any seen since 1972. It shrank just slightly in 2020, to 11 points (mostly because Trump attracted more women voters in 2016 than he did in 2020).[69]

The partisan gender gap is a new phenomenon in the United States, and it's unique to this country. It's explained by another trend: **gendered party polarization**, a situation in which political parties are divided on gender issues and have asymmetrical levels of women's representation and support.[70] Like the partisan gender gap, gendered party polarization is new. It arose in the 2000s, is still on the rise, and is specific to the United States.[71]

The polarization of the Republican and Democratic parties begins with the gendered social construction of each party. Since the 1980s, Republicans have consistently characterized their party as more masculine than the Democratic Party.[72] Republican presidents Ronald Reagan (elected in 1980) and George W. Bush (elected in 2000), for example, both fashioned themselves as cowboys. An actor before he became a politician, Reagan literally played cowboys on film, while Bush regularly staged photo-ops at his ranch in Texas.

By claiming to be the more masculine party, Republicans cast the Democrats as feminine and, accordingly, politically feckless: "soft" on crime, for instance, and "weak" on foreign policy. They also accuse Democrats of promoting a "nanny state," one that is overprotective of its citizens and overinvolved in ensuring people's well-being. Republicans emphasize **individualism**, a focus on the individual over the group, requiring that people take responsibility for the self and only the self. Democrats, in contrast, are seen to embrace **civic awareness**, a focus on the well-being of groups and societies as wholes, requiring that people consider the welfare of others.[73]

Ordinary people see the parties in these terms too.[74] The political scientist Monika McDermott described it this way: "The Democrats are [seen as] the more feminine party: They're willing to tax more and have bigger government because they're willing to care for people. Republicans are [portrayed as] more about rugged individualism, being independent and fending for yourself."[75]

The Republican and Democratic Parties also differ in the extent of their efforts to recruit women politicians. The latter has devoted substantially more resources toward this end. As a result, at the state and federal level, Democrats have been steadily increasing their share of representatives who are women. Republicans have not. To be fair, the number of Republican women in Congress reached a new high of thirty-nine in 2021, but that number is dwarfed by the 108 Democratic women in Congress.[76]

Contributing to this asymmetrical symbolic representation, the Republican and Democratic Party platforms reflect increasingly polarized approaches to gender and gender equality. Today's Democratic Party platform includes intersectional justice issues: support for social welfare, women's health, family-friendly workplaces, and social equality.[77] It now stands not only for gender equality, in other words, but also equality on the grounds of race, sexuality, disability, and more.

In contrast, Republicans increasingly oppose the newly gained and often fragile rights of historically oppressed groups. At the state level, Republican politicians are involved in curtailing discussions of racism and gender identity in classrooms and denying trans kids gender-congruent bathroom access and the opportunity to play sports with like-gender peers. These strategies appeal to mothers who mobilize against both gender and race reforms in schools. Often, these are White non-college-educated women who see themselves as defending "the family." The Republican Party is also acting to support the right to discrim-

Dubbed "the Squad," Ilhan Omar of Minnesota, Ayanna Pressley of Massachusetts, Alexandria Ocasio-Cortez of New York, and Rashida Tlaib of Michigan were all elected as Democratic representatives in the 2018 midterm elections.

inate against LGBTQIA people, ban gender-affirming health care for trans kids, and eliminate ethnic studies and gender programs at state colleges.

Because of gendered party polarization, support for a wide range of social justice issues—from sexism, to trans rights, to racial equity—are found in one party more than the other. Consequently, all these issues are now tied together into one big intersectional social justice issue: To be a Democrat today is to be for intervening in social inequalities of all kinds, while to be a Republican is to be ambivalent about all these things. White non-college-educated men, especially, tend to oppose policies and practices intended to reduce interpersonal discrimination and institutional inequalities; Black women are the most consistent supporters of such changes.[78]

Basic human rights, in other words, have been politicized. This places people who care about politics—whether voters or politicans—sharply on one side or the other of a **culture war**, a partisan strategy for dividing Americans into those who do and do not support intersectional social justice issues. As a result of this strategy, partisan identities have become increasingly conflated with attitudes about race, gender, sexuality, and immigration, as well as emotionally loaded issues like abortion and gun control.[79] Politicians on both sides of the aisle are happy to exploit the culture war to mobilize their voters, but it's contributing to growing animosity both at dinner tables and in legislatures.

The culture war waged by activists in both parties has also polarized the electorate: Democrats continue to be more favorable on gender matters and Republicans less so.[80] Over three-quarters of Biden voters believe that there "are still significant obstacles that make it harder for women to get ahead than men," compared to only a quarter of Trump voters. That's a gap of a whopping 53 percentage points, up 12 points from just 2016. Likewise, 75 percent of Democratic-leaning women describe themselves as feminists, compared to just 42 percent of Republican-leaning women.[81] Republicans are also much less enthusiastic than Democrats at the prospect of a woman being elected president "in their lifetime."[82] Only a quarter of Republicans hope so, while nearly two-thirds of Democrats do.[83]

Reflecting data like these, attitudes about gender strongly influenced voter behavior in the 2020 presidential election.[84] Among both men and women, endorsement of hegemonic masculinity correlated with the choice to vote for Trump, even controlling for other factors.[85] Likewise, support for Trump has been found to be associated with sexist, racist, homophobic, and xenophobic attitudes.[86]

While we see a partisan gender gap overall, voters also have complex intersectional identities that increasingly align with political parties. Among White voters, both women and men voted for Trump, unless the data are broken down by education. White college-educated women leaned in the direction of Biden, while White college-educated men split rather evenly between Biden and Trump.

Black and Hispanic men and women overwhelmingly voted for Biden (regardless of education level), with women in both groups more likely to do so than comparable men. Evangelical Christians regardless of gender voted overwhelmingly for Trump.

In sum, the Democratic Party increasingly supports intersectional justice, which is presented as a feminized concern. This attracts some women and repels some men. Conversely, by virtue of its claim to masculinity as symbolic and actual power and its growing attacks on racially and sexually marginalized groups, the Republican Party is increasingly attracting some men and repelling some women.

Unfortunately, gendered party polarization is likely to harm the cause of gender equality over the long term. If only one of two parties is meaningfully expanding women's representation, the number of women in positions of political power will grow only by half. And as long as social justice is cast as a partisan issue, the human rights of some Americans will be up for debate instead of taken for granted.

The Global Rise of Authoritarian Nationalism

Before 2016, most people would have found it inconceivable that a candidate like Trump could become president of the United States. On the campaign trail, Trump insulted women's faces, bodies, and temperaments; said working wives were "dangerous"; described pregnancy as an "inconvenience"; and bragged about grabbing and forcibly kissing women. Prior to Trump, neither Republican nor Democratic candidates spoke in these ways or defended such behaviors. Even relatively minor gaffes were often lethal to a campaign.[87]

Trump seemed immune to the consequences of his gaffes, however, even as he faced a climbing number of accusations of sexual harassment and abuse. A substantial minority of Americans stayed strong in their support of him in spite of, or perhaps because of, his style and temperament. Over time, he normalized speech and behavior previously outside the bounds of politics. It turned out Trump wasn't an anomaly. Instead, he mainstreamed a set of values that was alive and well in American society. Trump made clear that the world can change, radically, and not always in ways that feminists want.

One of the things that set Trump apart from previous politicians was his embrace of nationalism and authoritarianism. **Nationalism** is a belief in the superiority of one's own country and its rightful dominance over others and the promotion of exclusionary policies that restrict citizenship by race, ethnicity, or religion. Throughout his presidency, Trump promised to put "America first" and enacted many policies aimed at preserving the United States for White people, including reducing immigration from non-White countries, banning Muslims from entering the country, and aligning with White nationalists (groups that claim that the United States is and should be a White country).

Nationalism goes hand in hand with patriarchy.[88] This is because nationalists know their vision of the future depends on women not only choosing to have children but also choosing to have them with some men and not others. White nationalist projects, for example, require White women to have the children of White men generation after generation. Nationalists, then, often aim to control women's sexual behavior, relationships, and reproduction. Often they do this by aiming pro-natal policies at White women (like restrictions on abortion and laws against contraception) and anti-natal policies at women of color (like forced sterilization and grinding poverty).

While in office, Trump also exhibited qualities described as authoritarian. **Authoritarianism** is a political system without democratic accountability for how it governs. It subverts elections, suppresses free media, uses state power to punish rivals, and accumulates private wealth for an economic elite. Authoritarianism is a style of leadership that appeals primarily to people socialized to value masculinities characterized by the ability to exert power and control. Like nationalism, it celebrates patriarchal dominance over women.

Throughout his presidency, Trump drew from what political scientists describe as the "authoritarian playbook," but it was his actions in regard to the 2020 election that most alarmed scholars of authoritarianism.[89] Trump refused to acknowledge that he lost the election, becoming the first president in US history to reject that linchpin of democracy: a peaceful transfer of power. He also actively attempted to stay in power. He tried to overturn legally cast ballots in several states, asked the Georgia secretary of state to "find" nonexistent votes for him, encouraged state leaders to give him electoral votes rightfully belonging to his opponent, and pushed Vice President Michael Pence to decline to certify the election on January 6, 2021, the day Trump sent his followers to the US Capitol to disrupt the certification of Biden's victory.

Trump's presidency exacerbated a slide away from democracy that was well underway in the United States. The *Economist*, a magazine that has published a regular report on the state of democracy since 2006, now defines the United States as a "flawed" democracy.[90] "Full" democracies get high scores on sixty measures, including ones on voting rights, inclusion and participation, political culture, and civil liberties. Low scores indicate an authoritarian regime, one controlled by an authority with near total power and little accountability. The United States is nowhere near being labeled authoritarian, but Trump's continued popularity suggests that there's plenty of support among Americans for authoritarian leadership.

Importantly, the erosion of democratic norms isn't just happening in the United States.[91] It's a global trend. Between 2016 and 2022, more than half of the 167 countries measured by the *Economist* fell away from democracy and toward authoritarianism.[92] Likewise, nationalist sentiment is on the rise worldwide. Today, only 6.4 percent of the world's citizens live in full democracies. Such developments have led the economist Scott Sumner to write: "Authoritarian nationalism is by far the most important political development of the 21st century—nothing else even comes close."[93]

Among other bad outcomes, authoritarian nationalism usually brings greater prejudice, more aggressive forms of discrimination, and heightened levels of inequality, including sexism, androcentrism, and subordination. It is a type of politics, further, with intersectional implications for minorities. In 2021, for example, the Hungarian Parliament banned teaching about sexual and gender minorities in public schools and also resisted admitting non-European migrants. In China, Xi Jinping has forced birth control, abortion, and sterilization on members of the Uyghur minority. In Poland, more than one hundred regions now describe themselves as "anti-LGBT zones." Turkey withdrew from an EU convention, objecting to the use of the word *gender* in describing opposition to violence against women and children. In Brazil, President Jair Bolsonaro has said that "gender ideology" violates the tenets of Christianity.

The international "anti-gender" movement frames the idea of gender as threatening, even though the content of this idea is left vague. Indeed, as you have learned throughout this book, thinking critically about gender does in fact raise all kinds of questions about the necessity of and reasons for narrowly prescribed gender identities, roles, and relationships. This includes ideas like the gender binary, heteronormativity, mononormativity, the nuclear family, men's entitlement to women's subordination, and the control of reproduction necessary for achieving nationalist aims.[94] Accordingly, nationalists around the world are fighting the very idea.

These anti-gender politics are necessarily authoritarian because they must quash alternative ways of thinking and being. Authoritarians also directly oppress women and nonbinary people by seeking to control sexuality, reproduction, and gender expression.[95] Unsurprisingly, women have not only fought for their own rights but have also played notable roles in popular revolts against authoritarians in many parts of the world. Research suggests that when women lead or participate in such uprisings, they are more likely to be nonviolent and to succeed. And when these uprisings succeed, the resulting democracies are more stable.[96]

Authoritarianism rises and falls alongside the oppression of women: Women's participation in politics enhances democracy; their participation in mass movements are part of why uprisings succeed; and when authoritarianism spreads around the world, women around the world lose their freedoms. The rise of nationalism and authoritarianism, then, is of great concern to feminists.

In 2022, Vladimir Putin, the authoritarian leader of Russia, invaded Ukraine with the nationalist aim of taking over the independent country. Some Russians showed up in the streets to protest Putin's invasion of Ukraine. In doing so, they risked fines, arrests, and jailtime: part of Putin's authoritarian suppression of democracy.

Among the protesters were Russian feminist activists. On International Women's Day, two weeks after Russia initiated the invasion of Ukraine, these activists staged anti-war protests in nearly one hundred cities.[97] "As Russian citizens and feminists," read a statement released by several dozen feminist groups, "we condemn this war." Standing for anti-violence, social justice, and peace, they continued:

> Feminism as a political force cannot be on the side of a war of aggression and military occupation. The feminist movement in Russia struggles for vulnerable groups and the development of a just society with equal opportunities and prospects, in which there can be no place for violence and military conflicts.[98]

In making this bold statement in favor of peace, Russian feminists are doing their part to end the war against Ukraine. They're adding their voices to the call to save Ukrainian democracy. As Russian feminists proclaimed when their country was rising from the ashes of the Soviet empire, "A democracy without women is not democracy."[99]

Today's feminists are fighting a rising tide of authoritarian nationalism, one that deploys harsh tactics designed to roll back feminist progress. These anti-democratic changes have alarmed feminists, but they have mobilized them too. And feminists know how to fight.

SOCIAL MOVEMENTS

In the latter half of the 1900s, the founding documents of many countries around the world were amended to grant equal political rights to women. The US Constitution was not among them. Instead, the Supreme Court first held that women were a "new class of citizens" who could vote but did not automatically have other rights.

To change the US Constitution to ensure women's rights, American feminists introduced an Equal Rights Amendment. They did so first in 1923 and have done so every year since. If adopted, the Constitution would include this statement: "Equality of rights under the law shall not be denied or abridged by the United States or by any state on account of sex." Feminists are still waiting to see it passed and ratified.[100]

Because the US Constitution doesn't guarantee women equal rights, the US Congress *can* pass laws in favor of women's equality, but it doesn't have to. Nor does it have to renew the ones now on the books. Women's right to credit cards, jury duty, and equal education—truly, *all* women's rights—are contingent on the whims of legislators and the will of their constituents. It might sound impossible that such rights could disappear, but there's no rule that radical changes can't involve a return to somewhere we've already been or to a place we think is even worse.

In fact, reproductive rights have been facing just this kind of rollback. In the ten years leading up to the repeal of the constitutional right to abortion, US states adopted 288 laws aimed at restricting women's access to abortion, including mandatory counseling and waiting periods, required parental consent or notification, and new regulations on abortion clinics, many of which were forced to close even before *Dobbs v. Jackson*. By 2018, 90 percent of counties in the United States did not have a single abortion provider.[101]

Now abortion is not only inaccessible but criminalized in some states. How these laws will be enforced remains to be seen. Texas, for example, gives financial rewards to private citizens for bringing charges against anyone who gets an illegal abortion, performs one, or even helps a person obtain one. Exceptions for rape and incest assume that authorities will believe people who report that their pregnancies were a result of nonconsensual sex. Even mortal threat to a person's life may not guarantee that someone can obtain an exception if doctors fear that a prosecutor will challenge their medical opinion. Furthermore, people who experience miscarriage may increasingly face charges of murder. Authorities may accuse people of inducing illegal abortions or merely claim that they didn't behave in ways that prioritized the life of the fetus.[104] The result will be two Americas, one in which states take greater control of people's reproductive rights and another in which people have access to a fuller range of options for controlling their fertility.

President Trump's successful nomination of three religiously conservative, anti-abortion Supreme Court justices showed that the Republican Party was willing to severely curtail existing reproductive rights. In addition to repealing the constitutional right to abortion, the now-strong conservative majority also threatens rights to contraception, same-sex marriage, sexual freedom, and gender expression.[102] This court's recent decisions indicate a particular view of Christian morality is being privileged in the governance of American people.

Because the US Constitution has never been amended to guarantee equal rights to women, feminists have had to fight for each right individually. They have done this work through "regular" politics like voting, supporting legislation, and lobbying, and also "irregular" politics like protest campaigns, public marches, and demonstrations. This latter type of politics is part of what we call **social movements**: collective, nongovernmental efforts to change societies. The remainder of this chapter is about how feminists and their allies have used social movement tactics to secure rights for women and gender-nonconforming people and continue to do so.

Intersectional Feminist Politics across the Generations

Periods of heightened feminist activism are commonly called "waves." Social movements, then, prompt waves of activism that run through society, picking up their strength from like-minded people and leaving new organizations and commitments in their wakes. Like throwing a rock into a pool of water, social movements create ripples in society. These ripples have power, though they are inevitably influenced by the obstacles they encounter and the underlying sediments of the pool. Those ripples can also inspire other people to create their own waves.

As we noted earlier, the first wave of feminist activism began in the mid-1800s. Lacking the right to vote in most states until the 1920s, these early feminists campaigned on many political issues in which they believed women had special interests: They campaigned against drunkenness (which often led to domestic violence and poverty for women) and in favor of birth control, maternal and child welfare, public education, and world peace.[105] Many women-led organizations were founded in this first wave, including parent-teacher organizations, the League of Women Voters, the National Association of Colored Women, and the Women's International League for Peace and Freedom. Many of these organizations were racially segregated.[106] Black and other racial and sexual minority women largely followed separate roads after the 1920s and up into the 1970s.[107]

In the 1960s and '70s, a second wave of feminism rose up alongside the civil rights movement. This second wave aimed to end gender segregation in higher education, challenge job and wage discrimination, make marriage and family law gender neutral, and give women control over their own sexuality. In 1996, the first national women's advocacy organization, the National Organization for Women (NOW), was founded.[108]

Second-wave feminists echoed the first wave in building **women's movements**, social movements organized by women for women. Most women's movements are autonomous in that they can function independently of men's participation and approval.[109] Some women of color led feminist organizations like NOW and Planned Parenthood, some worked primarily in the racial justice movement, and some formed their own autonomous organizations focused on rights for Black, Asian, Hispanic, and Native women.[110]

Anti-feminists also organized.[111] They cast single motherhood, homosexuality, the right to divorce, and "career women" as threats to the family and raised concerns about gender desegregation: gender-neutral bathrooms and women in the military. In 1972, they celebrated a major success when they blocked the passage of the Equal Rights Amendment, which, after nearly fifty years of organizing, was nearly ratified.[112]

Despite this success, anti-feminists—and US Republican Party politics—were becoming increasingly out of touch with global norms. In 1975, the United Nations sponsored an International Women's Year, hosting conferences around the globe. In 1977, when the United States had its own International Women's Year Conference in Houston, it became a battleground for struggles between feminists and anti-feminists and spurred Republican candidate Ronald Reagan to remove the Equal Rights Amendment from his party's platform.

In 1979, the UN released a statement called the Convention on the Elimination of All Forms of Discrimination against Women (CEDAW). The United States did not sign on. Sixteen years later, the United States did join 182 other countries in Beijing and agreed to a global "Platform for Action" to affirm that "women's rights are human rights."[113] Though there is now an international norm in favor of gender equality, the United States has only ambivalently committed itself to it.

The third wave of feminist activism started in the early 1990s, after a Black American law professor's testimony splashed across television screens. Anita Hill had been called before the Senate Judiciary Committee to testify that a Black Republican nominee for the Supreme Court had sexually harassed her. Transfixed, the public watched as an all-White, all-man panel of fourteen senators delivered an "aggressive, gloves-off" attack on Hill's character.[114] The nominee—Clarence Thomas—was confirmed. This event encouraged women to run for office, and in 1992 women won congressional seats in then-record numbers.

The 1990s also saw Black feminist law professor Kimberlé Crenshaw formalize intersectionality as a concept. This facilitated a rethinking of the unique experiences of Black women. Infections of HIV/AIDS peaked during this decade, too, inspiring a high point in gay rights activism. The idea of intersectionality was evolving, coming to incorporate gender nonconformity and sexual diversity, alongside race and gender identity. As scholars and activists increasingly noticed the relationships among sexism, racism, heterosexism, and other forms of inequality, they spread practices of an intersectional feminist activism, the kind that attends to the lived experiences of different kinds of women and men.[115]

Intersectional feminism also prompted introspection about the role of Western feminists in global politics. American and European feminists often exhibited a troublesome tendency to think they were more *advanced* than women in other countries, leading them to try to export their own version of women's liberation around the globe. Critiquing nonintersectional understandings of feminism brought more awareness that there are many feminisms, not one feminism.

This cartoon by Malcolm Evans draws attention to the fact that definitions of women's oppression and liberation can vary tremendously.

Feminist Social Movements Today

In the aftermath of Trump's election, many Americans who had believed that feminist progress was secure and inevitable suddenly realized that it was neither. This energized existing feminist activists and inspired new ones, creating a potential fourth wave. One sign of the gain in momentum was the 2017 Women's March on Washington. Held the day after Trump's inauguration, it was organized by a team with an array of backgrounds.[116] This made the march inclusive and resulted in a platform that emphasized not only traditional feminist concerns like reproductive rights and violence against women but also environmental justice, violent policing, civil rights, equality for sexual and religious minorities, and workers', disability, immigrant, and Indigenous rights.[117]

This broad platform inspired an incredible turnout, the largest in American history.[118] The three to five million marchers included men, women, nonbinary and trans individuals, the young and the old, and people of all colors and religions. A third of attendees reported that this was their very first protest. Clever handmade protest signs revealed a heightened energy. "So outraged," said one sign, "I'm running for office."[119] "Gun violence is a woman's issue" and "Destroy the patriarchy, not the planet," said two more.[120] A white-haired woman held a sign declaring "Ninety, nasty, and not giving up!"[121] And a young woman's sign pledged: "I have only begun to fight."[122]

In 2020, the United States elected its first woman vice president in Kamala Harris. She is also the first Asian American and African American to hold the office.

It remains to be seen whether this era will generate longer-term organizing. Trump's election spurred a second upsurge in women running for political office. The proportion of non-Hispanic White men in Congress shrank to its lowest level ever (61 percent), as record numbers of men and women of color and White women were elected in 2020.[123] The 2020 election also brought Kamala Harris, the first woman vice president of the United States, into office.

The politics of the future will depend not only on who is elected but also the passion and energy of everyday people. It has always been that way. And—at least for now—feminism has broad support in the United States. A substantial majority of Americans today believe men and women are inherently equal and should be treated as such.[124]

Those coming of age in the first decade of the 2000s and later show the strongest support for gender equality.[125] And today's young feminists are also more diverse than those in previous generations: They are more likely to identify as queer, nonbinary, non-White, or multiracial, and they're more politicized around disability, immigration, the climate, and other issues. Women are still more likely than men to be feminists, but the proportion of men is growing too. Thanks to the work of previous generations, today's feminists are well poised to take advantage of international norms of gender equality, prebuilt feminist movement organizations, and the continuing hard work of making feminism more intersectional.[126]

Truly, it's an exciting time to be a feminist.

Revisiting the Question

Q+A   How do we change societies?

We do it with passion, commitment, and cooperation. In every society there's tension. On the one hand, there is the gender order: entrenched and often unquestioned ideas about gender, interactions that reproduce it, and gendered institutions entwined in systems of inequality. And on the other, there's the power of individuals to resist and transform the gender order. Every individual has at least a little bit of power and, when individuals join together, that power accumulates. In other words, the system is bigger than any one of us, but *we're in it together.* If enough of us decide we want to change it, we can.

The best strategies involve getting feminist-friendly politicians and decision makers on the "inside" to work with an intersectional group of feminists and their allies on the "outside."[127] Using that strategy, feminists have changed states dramatically in the last hundred years. They've changed one another as well, adding texture and depth to feminist politics by widening the scope of their attention to many of the inequalities with which women live, setting up a new generation of activists to imagine an even more radical future.

Next . . .

A farewell and some advice!

FOR FURTHER READING

Celis, Karen, and Sarah Childs. *Feminist Democratic Representation.* New York: Oxford University Press, 2020.

Crossley, Alison Dahl. *Finding Feminism: Millennial Activists and the Unfinished Gender Revolution.* New York: New York University Press, 2017.

Dahlerup, Drude. *Has Democracy Failed Women?* Malden, MA: Polity, 2018.

Kimport, Katrina. *No Real Choice: How Culture and Politics Matter for Reproductive Autonomy.* New Brunswick, NJ: Rutgers University Press, 2021.

Luna, Zakiya. *Reproductive Rights as Human Rights: Women of Color and the Fight for Reproductive Justice.* New York: New York University Press, 2020.

Olcutt, Jocelyn. *International Women's Year: The Greatest Consciousness-Raising Event in History.* New York: Oxford University Press, 2017.

Wolbrecht, Christina. *The Politics of Women's Rights: Parties, Positions, and Change.* Princeton, NJ: Princeton University Press, 2010.

NOT EVERYTHING THAT IS FACED
CAN BE CHANGED; BUT NOTHING
CAN BE CHANGED UNTIL IT IS FACED.

—JAMES BALDWIN[1]

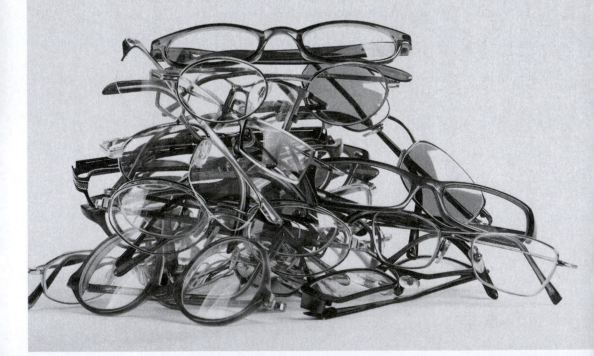

Conclusion

Gender is a powerful idea that shapes our experience of ourselves, one another, and the institutions with which we interact. It's pervasive and unavoidable. And while it's fun sometimes—more for some of us than others—it's also unfair. Our ideas about gender support a hierarchical system, one that intersects with other hierarchies in ways that ensure some men have more power than other men, most women, and people who are neither.

Everyone pays a price.

We all contend with forces that narrow the options for the type of person we're allowed to be. It may not feel like oppression—men are told that masculinity is better than femininity, and many have internalized an aversion to the feminine that has come to feel natural—but masculinity, even for men who take to it easily, is not the same thing as freedom. It's a set of rules that threatens to undermine men's value in their own eyes and those of others. Still, many men embrace the gender order because it offers a psychological wage: the idea that they're superior to women and at least some other men.

Some women, in turn, might feel that in certain ways gender isn't the oppressive force it used to be. Their daily lives may feel freer than those of the men around them, and they may be right. But the cultural permission to perform masculinity isn't liberation; it's an "homage to patriarchy."[2] It affirms the superiority of men and masculinity, just as men's avoidance of femininity is a sign that they think less of it. Women are allowed a taste of the privileges that come with being a man (and if they are otherwise advantaged in society, they may enjoy other privileges as well), but ultimately the requirement to do femininity translates into a social system in which women as a group will be seen as less valuable than men and will do a disproportionate amount of the least rewarded work. If they do defy these expectations—if they demand or enact equality with men in sex, family life, at work, or in politics—they risk being a pariah.

For young people in college, this might sound absurd. The average girl out-performs the average boy throughout school: She gets better grades, runs the clubs, and dominates student government. In higher education, women out-number men. But that's exactly why what happens after college is unfair. Priv-ilege is, by definition, unearned. So men as a group will still be advantaged. This is already acutely noticeable in heterosexual interaction (where women enjoy fewer orgasms and face greater danger) but will also be more obvious in the workplace (where the average man earns more than the average woman from day one), in families (where the responsibility for unpaid housework and childcare falls disproportionately on women), and in the power centers of our societies (where men still are positioned to make most of the big decisions).

Those are the facts. The gender binary isn't real, it isn't fair, and we can't pretend it doesn't affect us. For four thousand years, its purpose has been to differentiate us and place us in a hierarchy. And good and bad things in life are still distributed along that hierarchy in unequal ways. That's the world we live in and there's no guarantee that it will be better, or even as good as it is now, in the future.

This is an unpleasant reality. And it's lessons like this that inspired the sociologist C. Wright Mills to say that the study of society can be "terrible."[3] Truly, this book has given you plenty of good reasons to be angry, sad, scared, or frustrated. But Mills points out that knowledge, even of terrible things, can also be magnificent. This is because understanding the system in which we live is the first step toward changing it. Knowledge helps us make more informed decisions for ourselves, treat others with more empathy, and get to work making a better world. So before we end, here are some suggestions for how to put this book's lessons to work in your daily life.

Consider tossing your gender binary glasses

With your glasses off, you can now see the gender binary for what it really is— a social construction—but you'll still encounter the idea that men and women are "opposite" sexes every day. Try to be skeptical. Don't forget the basics: All differences are average differences with a great deal of overlap; men are not all alike and neither are all women; differences and similarities are caused by the intersection of nature and nurture, not one or the other; and science shows that we are more alike than different, and probably for good evolutionary reasons.

That the gender binary is a social construction applies to *you*, too, of course. If you're a person who sometimes worries about whether you fit into the binary, know that it's perfectly normal to wonder. The binary isn't real, so, to a greater or lesser degree, we're all square pegs being hammered into round holes. Don't blame yourself for how uncomfortable it is. And even if you personally feel quite comfortable, try to be understanding toward people who aren't and give them space for finding their own comfort zone.

Think about how you want to interact with others

You already break gender rules all the time, but now you probably do so more consciously. When you're policed, remember there are three options: Obey and refrain from breaking the rule, break the rule but offer an account that affirms it, or renounce the rule as arbitrary and unnecessary. The last option has the most potential for destabilizing the rules and the gender binary they protect. Think about if and when you might want to do this. It would be exhausting to do it all the time, and in some cases the price you could pay might be too high. Sometimes, though, the rewards outweigh the costs.

You can also choose to police the policers by pointing out other people's efforts to enforce gender rules. Challenging the entitlement of others to demand obedience to gender rules can provoke both mild and severe negative reactions: irritated parents, alienated friends, angry bosses, or retaliation from peers. Pay attention to when other people are likely to get your point and then balance the harm of their policing with the penalties you might face. Sometimes it will feel like the right thing to do.

Another possibility is to personally opt out of gender policing. This will take practice, since most of us police gender out of habit. Don't forget that policing people away from gender stereotypes (like pushing a little sister to be less concerned with her appearance) is not the *opposite* of policing; it's just enforcing a different set of gender rules. Opting out means not reacting to gender performances *at all*, refraining from making comments aimed at endorsing, questioning, or attacking someone's choices. This isn't the final answer to the problem—there will still be people who defend the gender binary, marketers with products to sell, and policy makers who pass gendered laws—but you'll be making a real difference by quietly contributing to a freer and less judgmental space for your friends, family, and coworkers.

Reflect on your relationship with the institutions around you

Gendered institutions push us to make gendered decisions while also making these choices seem natural and inevitable. Now you can see these forces for what they are. Use this knowledge to wrest some autonomy from the institutions that bear down on you.

You may want to do this in order to satisfy your individual preferences; resisting institutional pressures can mean living a life more in tune with who you are. Or you may choose to resist these pressures because of the way institutions place you into unequal relationships with others. Because institutions reflect not only gender inequality but all social inequities, our participation in them typically means being advantaged by virtue of someone else's disadvantage. We hope you keep sight of this fact and make it a practice to ask how institutions are tying you to both visible and invisible others in ways you may not like.

Some institutions are in real flux, making it easier to get around them. At this point in history, for example, the way we institutionalize family life is undergoing rapid and dramatic change. When so many people are making unconventional choices, it becomes easier for others to do so. Neither marriage nor heterosexuality nor parenthood is mandatory anymore. Consider all your options. And think about how your career choices might help or hurt your ability to live the life you want. You might have to make some sacrifices. They might just be worth it.

Do your best and be creative, but be flexible too. One of the most striking findings in the study of gender, work, and marriage is that young people's plans for their future families have almost no relationship to their lives a decade or more later.[4] Our ideals have to compete with other realities, like unexpected fertility or infertility, whether we end up with a well-paying job that we enjoy, surprising reactions to the practice of parenting, and the unpredictable qualities of the person we fall in love with, as well as the not-unlikely possibility that we'll pass through our childbearing years without meeting someone at all. Happiness isn't about getting what we want; it's about finding a way to enjoy what we get.

While the institution of the family is in flux, other institutions are much more deeply entrenched. Even in these cases, there are some things we can do. The institutions that function to produce, transport, and sell the vast majority of goods and services we consume are incredibly hard to avoid, for instance, but there are some choices you can make. Buying clothes secondhand is a way to avoid supporting a garment industry that exploits mostly female labor. Buying gender-neutral products over gendered ones—from deodorant, to exercise equipment, to cell phone covers—can discourage companies from exploiting gender stereotypes to get your money. Paying feminized labor a living wage can help, too, whether in the tips you leave for your server or the wages you pay to a housekeeper. Think about how you can opt out, even in small ways, of institutions you feel have harmful effects on people's lives.

Some of you may have more freedom than others to make choices that oppose institutionalized norms; it depends on your particular mix of advantages and disadvantages. If you *can* make counterinstitutional choices, and you choose to do so, know that you'll slowly be helping to dismantle ideologies and practices that others have less freedom to resist. You'll be using your privilege, in other words, to help others with less of it.

Remember that the mechanisms that produce inequality aren't simple

Compared to the average person, you have a much more sophisticated understanding of how gender inequality is maintained. Most people are familiar with the idea of sexism and object to the idea that one gender should receive preferential treatment, but androcentrism and subordination are less well understood and less obviously problematic. *You*, though, understand. You're tuned into the hierarchy of men and the way that gender inequality places men in competition for the rewards that accrue to masculinity; you are also aware that not all men benefit equally from gender inequality.

You see that intersectionality complicates the notion that anyone is subordinated or elevated by virtue of their gender alone. You're more likely to notice how women, too, enjoy certain privileges and enter into relationships of exploitation. You're aware of how much is going on when people make patriarchal bargains, and you can be both more critical of *and* sympathetic to these choices. Relatedly, you have a more nuanced sense of the attitude, behavior, and policy changes required to challenge gender inequality, as well as a healthy appreciation for just how intensely feminists debate their utopias and weigh their trade-offs.

Use this knowledge to resist the common misperceptions about feminist progress, like the idea that equality is simply a matter of ensuring equal access and that we can proclaim "mission accomplished" once we get a few privileged women into corner offices. Or the notion that men have nothing to gain from reducing gender inequality, as if they aren't in many ways constrained by the gender binary and its masculine hierarchy. Or the idea that being queer or gender nonconforming yourself is sufficient to break the back of rigid gender hierarchies. Question the suggestion that feminists are driven by anger instead of empathy; feminists are in it not because they hate men, but because they care about all people and the struggles they face. Recognize, too, that because most feminists are concerned with racism, poverty, and other -isms and injustices, their goal is not to point fingers; since there is always some dimension on which any given person has some privilege, it would be self-destructive to think about activism as a matter of assigning guilt and claiming innocence. Finally, be suspicious of anyone who tells you liberation can be found in the right purchase, a good slogan, or sheer narcissism.

All this may leave you with more questions than answers, which is a really good place to be. Keep asking those questions, trying out answers, listening to others' perspectives, and forming your own theory of how the world works. No one has the last word on truth. So continue to puzzle over the ideas shared here, add them to the bank of information you've learned from others, see if they explain your own experiences, and let your understanding of the world evolve.

Know that change is always possible

Sometimes problems seem overwhelmingly large and entrenched, but you now know that gender relations change, sometimes dramatically and surprisingly quickly, sometimes painfully slowly, and often in unpredictable ways. Small changes can cascade and help remake institutions. Some changes can also spur powerful resistance. At the core of these contentious efforts to change society are people. Social change is about power and everybody has some. Individuals work—alone or together—to imagine, enact, and share new ways of doing things.

Some of you may be passionate about reducing gender inequality and may decide to make activism a central part of your life. There are lots of ways to do this. You can write and speak about injustice, donate time or money to feminist organizations, or be an activist in your workplace, your house of worship, or a political campaign. Others of you may not be interested in activism, but that doesn't mean your choices aren't political ones. We're all political whether we like it or not: We either accept the status quo or try to change things. Doing nothing *is* doing something. That's OK, but be aware that this is a political choice too.

Even if you're not a passionate activist, there are probably *some* things you'd like to see change. Go ahead and pick a battle or two. That's how most of us do it.[5] Maybe you decide to be the person in your social circle who tries out a gender-neutral pronoun just to see what it's like; you might give relief to a nonbinary friend you didn't know you had. Or maybe you're a woman who decides to quit wearing makeup every day; suddenly you're an inspiration for a friend who isn't as brave or motivated. Or maybe you're the man who commits to calling himself a feminist; now you're pushing back against the idea that feminism has nothing to offer men, as well as the idea that men don't care about women's rights.

If you're a student, you can question the gender order in your immediate environment. Maybe you'll be the one to start an organization on campus dedicated to exploring what it means to be a man, the one who ensures that the college provides all-gender bathrooms for nonbinary students, or the one who does the research to find out whether your school's sexual assault policy complies with federal law.[6] It might be intimidating, and it's impossible to know if you'll succeed, but these are all things you could do *today*. Think about what inspires you.

Once you leave school, you'll have even more opportunities to remake the world. As a police officer, parent, teacher, or religious leader, you will be a part of the institutions that maintain order, raise and educate young people, nurture spirituality, and promote social responsibility. You may be an employee of a corporation with a hand in making key decisions about how its goods are designed, produced, or marketed; its profits allocated; or its impact on the environment managed. You might see ways to improve these institutions from the inside, or you might take your critique outside and try to press for change from there. Make like-minded friends and see what you can do. As the anthropologist Margaret Mead famously said, "Never doubt that a small group of thoughtful, committed citizens can change the world; indeed, it's the only thing that ever has."[7]

Ultimately, no matter how passionate you are, aim for balance. As legal scholar Joan Williams reminds us, "Equality is not everything, even for feminists themselves."[8] Maybe another political issue is more important to you: immigration reform, the climate crisis, or the opioid epidemic. All these issues are important and, as you already likely suspect, gendered. It's also OK to want peace at the holiday dinner table, even if your grandfather still thinks it's strange that men today wear earrings and women get tattoos. It's OK to want to look beautiful in an evening gown or dashing in a tuxedo. That craft beer with the sexist ad campaign is *delicious*; we get it. Even the most dedicated feminists make trade-offs. They balance a desire for social justice with the need for happy, productive, meaningful lives. Feminist principles win out sometimes and not others. And that's life.

Enjoy the vertigo

For better or worse, the gender binary offers many of us a clear path; it helps us make decisions, from the minor to the momentous. Without gender to push some options off to the side and place others in front of us, we're left to make these decisions with fewer guidelines. This can be incredibly disorienting. The sociologist Barbara Risman calls it "vertigo," capturing how dizzying letting go of gendered logic can be.[9] Standing at a precipice, looking at a vast expanse of possibility, you're no longer protected by familiar boundaries. It's both exhilarating and frightening. Enjoy the magnificent lessons you've learned: the way that understanding how gender is a social construction makes life a little more fun, a little more interesting, and a little freer.

It's pretty great, actually.

But know, also, that the terrible part never fully goes away. At times it will be upsetting. Feel free to be annoyed and share your frustrations. This might make people a little annoyed with *you*, but there are worse things. Sometimes the terrible part will be deeply personal, as you struggle with your own challenges. Other times you'll be angry with what you see around you and feel small and powerless to change things. We all do from time to time. And, of course, sometimes you can only laugh.

In the mix of frustration, disorientation, and hope is the magic. It's what frees our minds and gives us the motivation to think up alternative realities. Remember that "radical" ideas are only ideas that haven't been accepted *yet*. So go ahead and imagine the unimaginable. The future is yet unwritten.

GLOSSARY

ableism individual and institutional biases that deny critical resources to differently abled bodies

abolitionists activists in the fight against human slavery

account an explanation for why a person broke a gender rule that works to excuse their behavior

accountability an obligation to explain why we don't follow social rules that other people think we should know and obey

ageism an institutionalized preference for the young and the cultural association of aging with decreased social value

aggrieved entitlement anger over something men feel they rightfully own or deserve that is being unjustly taken or withheld from them

agrarian a type of society in which the invention of agriculture—the cultivation of domesticated crops—allows groups to put down roots

androcentric pay scale a strong correlation between wages and the gender composition of a job

androcentrism the granting of higher status, respect, value, reward, and power to the masculine compared to the feminine

anti-feminist politics activities of those committed to the value of gender difference and hierarchy and who aim to prevent feminist change

anti-natal policies those policies that discourage childbearing, whether intentionally or not

assigned sex an outcome of the interpretation of known sex-related characteristics before and at birth

associative memory a phenomenon in which cells in our brains that process and transmit information make literal connections between concepts, such that some ideas are associated with other ideas

authoritarianism a political system without democratic accountability for how it governs

benevolent sexism the attribution of positive traits to women that, nonetheless, justify women's subordination to men

binary a system with two and only two separate and distinct parts, like binary code (the 1s and 0s used in computing) or a binary star system (in which two stars orbit around each other)

biocultural interaction how our bodies respond to our cultural environment and vice versa

blended families families consisting of partnered adults with at least one child from a previous relationship

brain organization theory the idea that men's and women's brains may have different strengths and weaknesses

breadwinner/housewife marriage a model of marriage that did not legally subordinate wives to husbands but continued to define the rights and responsibilities of husbands and wives differently; women owed men domestic services and men were legally required to support their wives financially

care chain a series of nurturing relationships in which the care of children, older adults, or people with disabilities is displaced onto increasingly disadvantaged paid or unpaid caregivers

care work work that involves face-to-face caretaking of the physical, emotional, and educational needs of others

cisgender a term that describes people who are assigned male at birth who identify as men and people who are assigned female at birth who identify as women

civic awareness a focus on the well-being of groups and societies as wholes

classism a form of prejudice against people of lower socioeconomic status

coital imperative the idea that any fully sexually active couple must be having penile-vaginal intercourse (also known as "coitus") and any fully completed sexual activity will include it

colorism a racist preference for light over dark skin

commodification the process by which goods transition from something a family provided for itself into something bought with a wage

commodity a thing that can be bought and sold

compensatory masculinity acts undertaken to reassert one's manliness in the face of a threat

compulsory heterosexuality a rule that all men be attracted to women and all women to men

concerted cultivation an active and organized effort to develop in children a wide range of skills and talents

cult of domesticity the notion that women could and should wholeheartedly embrace the work of making a loving home

cultural competence a familiarity and facility with how the members of a society typically think and behave

cultural traveling moving from one cultural or subcultural context to another and sometimes back

culturalism the idea that we are "blank slates" that become who we are purely through learning and socialization

culturally unintelligible to be so outside the symbolic meaning system that people will not know how to interact with you

culture a group's shared beliefs and the practices and material things that reflect them

culture war a partisan strategy for dividing Americans into those who do and do not support intersectional social justice issues

deceptive differences those differences that, by being observed, can make it seem as if groups are more different than they really are

democratic brotherhood the distribution of citizenship rights to certain classes of men

distinction efforts to distinguish one's own group from others

doing gender a phrase used to describe the ways in which we actively obey and break gender rules

domestic outsourcing paying non-family members to do family-related tasks

double bind a situation in which cultural expectations are contradictory

drag queens and kings usually cisgender men and women who dress up and behave like members of the other gender

dual nurturers families in which both partners disinvest in work together and turn their energy toward the home

egalitarians people who prefer relationships in which both partners do their fair share of breadwinning, housekeeping, and child-rearing

emasculation a loss of masculinity

emotional labor the act of controlling one's own emotions and managing the emotions of others

emphasized femininity an exaggerated form of femininity "oriented to accommodating the interests and desires of men"

emphatic sameness a strategy by which women try to be "just one of the guys"

employer selection hypothesis a theory that proposes that employers tend to prefer men for masculine jobs and women for feminine jobs, slotting applicants into gender-consistent roles during hiring and promotion

equal access a model of creating egalitarianism by dismantling legal barriers and reducing sex discrimination

equal sharing a model of creating egalitarianism that targets subordination by attempting to ensure that men and women participate equally in masculine and feminine spheres

equal value a model of creating egalitarianism designed to tackle the problem of androcentrism by raising the value of the feminine to match the value of the masculine

erotic marketplace an intersectional ranking of people according to their perceived sexual desirability

exculpatory chauvinism a phenomenon in which negative characteristics ascribed to men are presented as "natural" and offered as acceptable justifications of men's dominance over women

extended family a more expansive family form that includes grandparents, aunts, uncles, and friends

family wage an income paid to a man that is large enough to support a home, a wife, and children

fatherhood premium a wage increase that accrues to married men who become fathers

female a type of sex

feminine things we associate with women

feminine apologetic a requirement that women balance their appropriation of masculine interests, traits, and activities with feminine performance

feminism the belief that all men and women should have equal rights and opportunities

feminist utopia a perfectly gender-egalitarian society

feminization of poverty a trend in which the poor are increasingly female

forager societies societies that migrate seasonally, following crops and game across the landscape

formal gender equality the legal requirement that men and women be treated more or less the same

gender the symbolism of masculinity and femininity that we connect to bodies assigned male and female at birth

gender-affirming care medical procedures and treatments that help people physically embody their gender

gender-aware policy making a type of policy making in which consideration of the effects on both men and women—and different kinds of men and women—is a required part of the policy-making process

gender binary the idea that there are only two types of people—masculine men assigned male at birth and feminine women assigned female at birth

gender binary glasses a pair of lenses that separate everything we see into masculine and feminine categories

gender binary subdivision the practice by which we divide and redivide by gender again and again, adding finer and finer *degrees* of masculinity and femininity to the world

gender equivocation the use of both emphasized femininity and emphatic sameness when they're useful and culturally expected

gender expression a way of expressing one's gender identity through appearance, dress, and behavior

gender fluid without a fixed gender identity

gender identity a subjective sense of one's own gender

gender ideologies widely shared beliefs about how men and women are and should be

gender of governance who holds political office and whether it matters

gender order the social organization of gender relations in a society

gender pay gap the difference between the incomes of the average man and woman who work full time

gender policing a response to the violation of gender rules that is aimed at exacting conformity

gender rules instructions for how to appear and behave as a man or a woman

gender salience the relevance of gender across contexts, activities, and spaces

gender strategy finding a way of doing gender that works for us as unique individuals who are also shaped by other parts of our identity and the material realities of our lives

gendered institution a social institution in which gender is used as an organizing principle

gendered job segregation the practice of filling occupations with mostly men or mostly women workers

gendered love/sex binary a projection of the gender binary onto the ideas of love and sex

gendered party polarization a situation in which political parties are divided on gender issues and have asymmetrical levels of women's representation and support

genes a set of instructions for building and maintaining our bodies

glass ceiling the idea that there is an invisible barrier between women and top positions in masculine occupations

glass cliff a heightened risk of failing faced by women who break through the glass ceiling

glass closet an invisible place in which sexual minorities hide their identities in order to avoid stigma, suspicion, or censure at work

glass escalator an invisible ride to the top offered to certain men in female-dominated occupations

going steady the practice of an often short-lived, but still exclusive, public pairing off

good girl/bad girl dichotomy the idea that women who behave themselves sexually are worthy of respect and women who don't are not

governance the process of making decisions for the nation, ensuring the state's accountability to its citizens, and enforcing the laws of the land

governance of gender how gender is used to produce distinctions and regulate residents accordingly

greedy institutions those institutions, such as work and family, that take up an incredible amount of time and energy

hegemonic masculinity a type of masculine performance, idealized by the majority, that functions to justify and naturalize gender inequality

hegemony a state of collective consent to inequality that is secured by the idea that it is inevitable, natural, or desirable

heteronormative designed on the assumption that everyone is heterosexual, with individuals presuming so unless there are culturally recognizable signs indicating otherwise

heterosexism individual and institutional bias against sexual minorities

heterosexual male gaze a way of looking at society from the perspective of a hypothetical heterosexual man

hierarchy of masculinity a rough ranking of men from most to least masculine, with the assumption that more is always better

homonormativity a practice of obeying every gender rule except the ones that say we must sexually desire and partner with someone of the other sex

hookup culture an environment in which casual sexual contact is held up as ideal, encouraged with rules for interaction, and institutionalized

hormones messengers in a chemical communication system

hostile sexism the use of harassment, threats, and violence to enforce women's subservience to men

hybrid masculinities a collection of gender strategies that selectively incorporate symbols, performances, and identities that society associates with women or low-status men

hypermasculinity extreme conformity to the more aggressive rules of masculinity

ideal worker norm the idea that an employee should have the ability to devote themselves to their job without the distraction of family responsibilities

ideology a set of ideas widely shared by members of a society that guides identities, behaviors, and institutions

individualism an attitude that reflects a focus on the individual over the group

industrial economy an economy dependent on the production of material goods intended for the market

institutions persistent patterns of social interaction aimed at meeting the needs of a society that can't easily be met by individuals alone

integrated mothering an ideology of motherhood that includes work outside the home, financial self-sufficiency, and a network of support

intensive mothering the idea that (1) mothers should be the primary caretaker of their children, (2) child-rearing should include "copious amounts of time, energy, and material resources," and (3) giving children these things takes priority over all other interests, desires, and demands

intersectional feminist politics efforts to fight all the forces that contribute to women's oppression, including class inequality, racism, heterosexism, and more

intersectionality the idea that gender is not an isolated social fact about us but instead intersects with our other social positions and identities

intersex a term used to describe bodies with a reproductive or sexual anatomy that doesn't fit the typical definitions of female or male

kin groups collections of individuals considered family

learned differences those differences that are a result of our familial or sociocultural environment

learning model of socialization a model that suggests that socialization is a lifelong process of learning and relearning gendered expectations and how to negotiate them

legislatures groups of individuals elected to represent their constituents in regulating the affairs of the country

male a type of sex

male flight a phenomenon in which men abandon feminizing arenas of life

marking the act of applying a label to highlight an exception

marriage bans policies against employing married women

mascing advertising one's masculine traits and concealing one's feminine traits in an effort to appease others' preferences for masculine men

masculine things we associate with men

masculinities different ways of doing masculinity, arrayed in a hierarchy, that are more or less available to people with different social positions, intersectional identities, and contexts of interaction

masculinization of wealth the concentration of men in high-earning occupations

matrix of domination a structure in which multiple hierarchies intersect to create a pyramid of privilege, leaving on top only those people who are advantaged in every hierarchy

mental load the intellectual and emotional work of parenting and household maintenance

misogyny fear and hatred of women with power

modified patriarchies societies in which women have been granted formal gender equality but the patriarchal conflation of power with men and masculinity remains a central part of daily life

mommy tax a term for the lost wages, benefits, and Social Security contributions that come with taking time out of the workforce to raise small children and then re-entering it with less momentum

mommy track a workplace euphemism that refers to expecting less from mothers, with the understanding that they are sacrificing the right to expect equal pay, regular raises, or promotions

monogamy the open practice and encouragement of long-term intimate relationships with only one person

mononormative designed on the assumption that everyone is monogamous

motherhood penalty a loss in wages associated with becoming a mother

nationalism a belief in the superiority of one's own country, its rightful dominance over others, and exclusionary policies that restrict citizenship by race, ethnicity, or religion

naturalism the idea that biology affects our behavior independently of our environment

nature/nurture debate argument between people who believe that observed differences between men and women are biological and those who believe that these differences are acquired through socialization

neo-traditionalists people who embrace a modified version of traditionalism: They think that a woman should be able to work if she desires, but only if it doesn't interfere with her "real" duty to take care of her husband and children

nonbinary a gender category that encompasses people who are either both man and woman or neither man nor woman

normative standard the example against which people tend to measure themselves and others

norms beliefs and practices that are well known, widely followed, and culturally approved

nuclear family a monogamous mother and father with children who live together without extended kin

observed differences findings from surveys, experiments, and other types of studies that detect differences between groups

open relationships long-term relationships that allow sexual but not romantic encounters with others

orgasm gap a phenomenon in which women who have sex with men report fewer orgasms than men who have sex with women

otherfathers men who provide care for the children of friends, family members, and neighbors

othermothers women who provide care for the children of friends, family members, and neighbors

overwork working fifty or more hours a week

pariah femininities ways of being a woman that, by virtue of directly challenging men's dominance, are widely and aggressively policed

partisan gender gap a tendency for men and women to align with different political parties

partnership marriage a model of marriage based on love and companionship between two equals who negotiate a division of labor unique to their relationship

patriarch/property marriage a model of marriage in which a woman was entered into a marriage by her father, who owned her until he "gave her away" at the wedding

patriarchal bargain a deal in which an individual or group accepts or even legitimates some of the costs of patriarchy in exchange for receiving some of its rewards

patriarchy literally, "the rule of the father"; it refers to the control of female and younger male family members by select adult men, or patriarchs

policies explicit and codified expectations, often with stated consequences for deviance

politics the activities involved in determining national policies and electing people to guide this process

politics of gender how people change and resist change to the gender order

polyamory long-term intimate relationships with more than one partner at a time

precarious masculinity the idea that manhood is more difficult to earn and easier to lose than femininity

priming a trick in which study subjects are reminded of a stereotype right before a test

privilege unearned social and economic advantage based on our location in a social hierarchy

production the making of goods for sale

pro-natal policies policies that encourage childbearing, whether intentionally or not

protective legislation policies designed to protect women from exploitation by restricting their workplace participation

push-and-resist dynamic a situation in which it is normal for men to press sexual activity consistently in the direction of increasing intimacy (whether he wants to or not) and for women to stop or slow down the accelerating intimacy when he's going "too far" (whether she wants to or not)

race a socially meaningful set of distinctions based on superficial and imagined biological differences

racism social arrangements designed to systematically advantage one race over others

radical claim an idea that doesn't (yet) resonate with most members of a population

rape culture an environment that justifies, naturalizes, and even glorifies sexual pressure, coercion, and violence

reproduction the making and nurturing of human beings

reproductive justice access to the whole range of rights that enable people to choose whether and how to have and raise children

second shift work that greets us when we come home from work

selective exit hypothesis an explanation for job segregation that emphasizes workers' abandonment of counterstereotypical occupations

self-objectify the process by which people internalize the idea that their value is heavily dependent on their physical attractiveness

separate spheres the idea of a masculinized work world and a feminized home life

service and information economy an economy dependent on jobs focused on providing services for others or working with ideas

sex physical differences in primary sexual characteristics (the presence of organs directly involved in reproduction) and secondary sexual characteristic (such as patterns of hair growth, the amount of breast tissue, and distribution of body fat)

sexism the favoring of one sex over the other, both ideologically and in practice

sexual dimorphism degrees of difference in appearance and behavior between males and females of a species

sexual double standard different rules for the sexual behavior of men and women

sexual minorities gays, lesbians, bisexuals, and others who identify as nonheterosexual

sexual objectification the reduction of a person to their sex appeal

sexual orientation whether one prefers men or women as sexual partners, or both or neither

sexual script the rules that guide sexual interaction

sexual subjectification the process by which people are told what their internal thoughts and feelings should be

sharing doing more or less symmetrical amounts of paid and unpaid work

smashing a term used to describe having a same-sex crush

social construct an arbitrary but influential shared interpretation of reality

social construction a process by which we make reality meaningful through shared interpretation

social identity a culturally available and socially constructed category of people in which we place ourselves or are placed by others

social movements collective, nongovernmental efforts to change societies

social structure the entire set of interlocked institutions within which we live our lives

socialization hypothesis a theory that suggests that men and women respond to gender stereotypes when planning, training, and applying for jobs

specialization splitting unpaid and paid work so that each partner does more of one than the other

spectating watching one's sexual performance from the outside

stalled revolution a sweeping change in gender relations that is stuck halfway through

states institutions entrusted with the power to regulate everyday life on behalf of the group

stereotypes fixed, oversimplified, and distorted ideas about what people are like

sticky floor a metaphorical barrier to advancement describing jobs with no or low opportunity for promotion

subordination the placing of women into positions that make them subservient to or dependent on men

substantive representation the proposing and passing of policies important and helpful to women

suffrage the right to vote

symbolic representation women's presence in government

symbolic threat a presence that potentially degrades the identity of the dominant group

toxic masculinity enactments of masculinities that are harmful both to the men who enact them and to the people around them

traditionalists people who ascribe to the values of the breadwinner/housewife marriage that emerged with industrialization and came to be seen as "traditional" and who believe that men should be responsible for earning income and women should be responsible for housework and childcare

trans (or transgender) people whose gender identity is different from the sex they were assigned at birth

treating a practice in which a man funds a woman's night on the town

universal suffrage the right of all citizens to vote

victim blaming identifying something done by a victim as a cause of their victimization

wage money gained from working in places like factories, mines, and shops that belong to others

women's movements social movements organized by women for women

working poor individuals who work but still live in poverty

xenophobia individual and institutional bias against people seen as foreign

NOTES

Introduction

1. Elizabeth Semmelhack, *Heights of Fashion: A History of the Elevated Shoe* (Penzanze, UK: Periscope, 2008).

2. Nancy E. Rexford, *Women's Shoes in America, 1795–1930* (Kent, OH: Kent State University Press, 2000).

3. Shari Benstock and Suzanne Ferriss, eds., "Introduction," in *Footnotes: On Shoes* (New Brunswick, NJ: Rutgers University Press, 1993), 1–13.

Chapter 1: Ideas

1. Carol Lynn Martin and Diane Ruble, "Children's Search for Gender Cues," *Current Directions in Psychological Science* 13, no. 2 (2004): 67.

2. Sarah S. Richardson, *Sex Itself: The Search for Male and Female in the Human Genome* (Chicago: University of Chicago Press, 2013).

3. Georgiann Davis, *Contesting Intersex: The Dubious Diagnosis* (New York: New York University Press, 2015).

4. "Georgiann Davis," Interface Project, accessed Nov. 11, 2021, https://www.interfaceproject.org/georgiann-davis/.

5. Ieuan A. Hughes, John D. Davies, Trevor I. Bunch, Vickie Pasterski, Kiki Mastroyannopoulou, and Jane MacDougall, "Androgen Insensitivity Syndrome," *Lancet* 380, no. 9851 (2012): 1419–28.

6. "Klinefelter Syndrome," National Institutes of Health, last updated February 14, 2018, https://rare diseases.info.nih.gov/diseases/8705/klinefelter -syndrome.

7. "Intersex People," United Nations Human Rights Office of the High Commissioner, accessed June 8, 2022, https://ohchr.org/EN/Issues/LGBTI/Pages /IntersexPeople.aspx.

8. Georgiann Davis, *Contesting Intersex*.

9. Suzanne Kessler and Wendy McKenna, *Gender: An Ethnomethodological Approach* (Chicago: University of Chicago Press, 1985).

10. Esther L. Meerwijk and Jae M. Sevelius, "Transgender Population Size in the United States: A Meta-regression of Population-Based Probability Samples," *American Journal of Public Health* 107, no. 2 (2017): e1–e8, https://doi.org/10.2105/AJPH .2016.303578.

11. Tey Meadow, *Trans Kids: Being Gendered in the Twenty-First Century* (Berkeley: University of California Press, 2018).

12. Carol Lynn Martin and Diane N. Ruble, "Patterns of Gender Development," *Annual Review of Psychology* 61 (2010): 353–81.

13. Georgiann Davis, Jodie Dewey, and Erin Murphy, "Giving Sex: Deconstructing Intersex and Trans Medicalization Practices," *Gender and Society* 30, no. 3 (2016): 490–514.

14. Fran Tirado, "*Queer Eye*'s Jonathan Van Ness: "I'm Nonbinary," *Out*, June 10, 2019, https://www .out.com/lifestyle/2019/6/10/queer-eyes-jonathan -van-ness-im-nonbinary.

15. Wren Sanders, "Gigi Goode Opens Up about 'Fluid' Gender Identity on *RuPaul's Drag Race*," *Them*, April 7, 2020, https://www.them.us/story /gigi-goode-opens-up-fluid-gender-identity-rupauls -drag-race.

16. Jose A. Del Real, "'Latinx' Hasn't Even Caught On among Latinos. It Never Will," *Washington Post*, December 18, 2020, https://www.washington post.com/outlook/latinx-latinos-unpopular-gender -term/2020/12/18/bf177c5c-3b41-11eb-9276-ae0ca 72729be_story.html.

17. "Colleges and Universities That Provide Gender-Inclusive Housing," Campus Pride, accessed October 29, 2021, https://www.campuspride.org/tpc/gen der-inclusive-housing/.

18. "X Gender Markers by State," Lambda Legal, last updated July 28, 2020, https://www.lambda legal.org/map/x-markers.

19. "Gender X Passports," Employers Network for Equality and Inclusion, March 23, 2020, https:// www.enei.org.uk/resources/news/gender-x -passports/.

20. Katrina Karkazis, "The Misuses of Biological Sex in the Art of Medicine," *Lancet* 394 (November 23, 2019): 1898–99, https://doi.org/10.1016/S0 140-6736(19)32764-3.

21. International Olympic Committee, "IOC Releases Framework on Fairness, Inclusion and Non-discrimination on the Basis of Gender Identity and Sex Variations," November 16, 2021, https://olympics .com/ioc/news/ioc-releases-framework-on-fairness -inclusion-and-non-discrimination-on-the-basis-of -gender-identity-and-sex-variations.

22. Margaret McDowell, Cheryl D. Fryar, Cynthia L. Ogden, and Katherine M. Flegal, "Anthropometric Reference Data for Children and Adults: United States, 2003–2006," *National Health Statistics Reports* 10 (October 22, 2008): 1–48.

23. Melissa Whitworth, "Victoria's Secret Show: What Does It Take to Be a Victoria's Secret Angel?" *Telegraph*, November 7, 2011, http://fashion.tele graph.co.uk/news-features/TMG8872623/Victorias -Secret-show-What-does-it-take-to-be-a-Victorias -Secret-Angel.html.

24. "5 Unexpected Gender Differences in Children's Clothing," *ParentCo.* (blog), January 27, 2017, https:// www.parent.com/5-unexpected-gender-differences -in-childrens-clothing/.

25. Thomas Laqueur, *Making Sex: Body and Gender from the Greeks to Freud* (Cambridge, MA: Harvard University Press, 1990).

26. Quoted in ibid., 4n11.

27. Gilbert Herdt, *Same Sex, Different Cultures: Exploring Gay and Lesbian Lives* (Boulder, CO: Westview Press, 1997).

28. Quoted in Jorge Rivas, "Native Americans Talk Gender at 'Two-Spirit' Powwow," *Fusion*, February 9, 2015, https://www.fusion.kinja.com/native -americans-talk-gender-identity-at-a-two-spirit-1793 845144 (website no longer available).

29. Sharyn Graham Davies, *Gender Diversity in Indonesia: Sexuality, Islam, and Queer Selves* (New York: Routledge, 2010).

30. Quoted in "The Beautiful Way Hawaiian Culture Embraces a Particular Kind of Transgender Identity," *Huffington Post*, updated December 6, 2017, www.huffingtonpost.com/2015/04/28/hawaiian -culture-transgender_n_7158130.html.

31. Niko Besnier, "Polynesian Gender Liminality through Time and Space," in *Third Sex, Third Gender: Beyond Sexual Dimorphism in Culture and History*, ed. Gilbert Herdt (New York: Zone Books, 1994), 285–328; and Serena Nanda, *Gender Diversity: Cross-Cultural Variations* (Long Grove, IL: Waveland Press, 2000).

32. Marc Lacey, "A Lifestyle Distinct: The Muxe of Mexico," *New York Times*, December 6, 2008, https://www.nytimes.com/2008/12/07/weekin review/07lacey.html.

33. Shanoor Seervai, "Laxmi Narayan Tripathi: India's Third Gender," *Guernica*, March 16, 2015.

34. Ivan Olita, *Muxes* (documentary short), 2016, www.shortoftheweek.com/2017/01/03/muxes/.

35. Ibid.

36. Ibid.

37. "A Map of Gender-Diverse Cultures," PBS, August 11, 2015, https://www.pbs.org/independent lens/content/two-spirits_map-html/.

38. Christine Helliwell, "'It's Only a Penis': Rape, Feminism, and Difference," *Signs* 25, no. 3 (2000): 806–7.

39. Susan Chira, "When Japan Had a Third Gender," *New York Times*, March 10, 2017, https://www .nytimes.com/2017/03/10/arts/design/when-japan -had-a-third-gender.html.

40. Christine Gailey, "Evolutionary Perspectives on Gender Hierarchy," in *Analyzing Gender: A Handbook of Social Science Research*, ed. Beth Hess and Myra Marx Ferree (Thousand Oaks, CA: Sage, 1987).

41. Ifi Amadiume, *Male Daughters, Female Husbands: Gender and Sex in an African Society* (London: Zed Books, 1987).

42. Nelly Oudshoorn, *Beyond the Natural Body: An Archeology of Sex Hormones* (New York: Routledge, 1994).

43. Ross Nehm and Rebecca Young, "'Sex Hormones' in Secondary School Biology Textbooks," *Science and Education* 17 (2008): 1175–90.

44. Jenny Nordberg, "Afghan Boys Are Prized, So Girls Live the Part," *New York Times*, September 20, 2010, https://www.nytimes.com/2010/09/21/world/asia/21gender.html.

45. René Grémaux, "Woman Becomes Man in the Balkans," in *Third Sex, Third Gender: Beyond Sexual Dimorphism in Culture and History*, ed. Gilbert Herdt (New York: Zone Books, 2020): 241–81; Antonia Young, *Women Who Become Men: Albanian Sworn Virgins* (New York: Berg, 2000); and Nanda, *Gender Diversity*.

46. Stanley B. Alpern, *Amazons of Black Sparta: The Women Warriors of Dahomey* (New York: New York University Press, 1998).

47. *The Sworn Virgins of Albania* (RT documentary), YouTube, uploaded December 18, 2016, https://www.youtube.com/watch?v=3UUikqpotiE.

48. Nicola Smith, "'Sworn Virgins' Dying Out as Albanian Girls Reject Manly Role," *Times of London*, January 6, 2008, https://www.thetimes.co.uk/article/sworn-virgins-dying-out-as-albanian-girls-reject-manly-role-v2ft3x82lz5.

49. Linton Weeks, "'Female Husbands' in the 19th Century," *NPR History Dept.* (blog), January 29, 2015, https://www.npr.org/sections/npr-history-dept/2015/01/29/382230187/-female-husbands-in-the-19th-century.

50. Gabrielle Bellot, "Think Being Trans Is a 'Trend'? Consider These 18th-Century 'Female Husbands,'" *Guardian*, September 10, 2021, https://www.theguardian.com/commentisfree/2021/sep/10/transgender-history-18th-century-female-husbands.

51. Peter L. Berger and Thomas Luckmann, *The Social Construction of Reality: A Treatise in the Sociology of Knowledge* (New York: Doubleday, 1966).

52. P. W. Hammond, *Food & Feast in Medieval England* (Gloucestershire, UK: Alan Sutton, 1993).

53. Malia Wollan, "Rise and Shine: What Kids around the World Eat for Breakfast," *New York Times Magazine*, August 10, 2014, https://www.nytimes.com/interactive/2014/10/08/magazine/eaters-all-over.html; and Pamela Goyan Kittler, Kathryn P. Sucher, and Marcia Nahikian-Nelms, *Food and Culture*, 7th ed. (Belmont, CA: Cengage Learning, 2017), chap. 13.

54. Douglas S. Massey, "A Brief History of Human Society: The Origin and Role of Emotion in Social Life," *American Sociological Review* 67 (2002): 1–29.

55. Cordelia Fine, *Delusions of Gender: How Our Minds, Society, and Neurosexism Create Difference* (New York: W. W. Norton, 2010), 229.

56. Daniel L. Schacter and Elaine Scarry, eds., *Memory Brain and Belief* (Cambridge, MA: Harvard University Press, 2001); and Steven B. Most, Anne Verbeck Sorber, and Joseph G. Cunningham, "Auditory Stroop Reveals Implicit Gender Associations in Adults and Children," *Journal of Experimental Social Psychology* 43, no. 2 (2007): 287–94.

57. Sandra Lipsitz Bem, "Androgyny and Gender Schema Theory: A Conceptual and Empirical Integration," in *Nebraska Symposium on Motivation 1984: Psychology and Gender*, ed. T. B. Sonderegger (Lincoln: University of Nebraska Press, 1985), 179–226.

58. Schacter and Scarry, *Memory Brain and Belief*; and Most, Sorber, and Cunningham, "Auditory Stroop," 287–94.

59. Sandra Lipsitz Bem, "Gender Schema Theory: A Cognitive Account of Sex Typing," *Psychological Review* 88, no. 4 (1981): 354–64.

60. Cecilia L. Ridgeway, "Framed by Gender: How Inequality Persists in the Modern World," *European Sociological Review* 29, no. 2 (2013): 408–10.

61. Alison P. Lenton, Irene V. Blair, and Reid Hastie, "Illusions of Gender: Stereotypes Evoke False Memories," *Journal of Experimental Social Psychology* 37, no. 1 (2001): 3–14; Lynn S. Liben and Margaret L. Signorella, "Gender-Related Schemata and Constructive Memory in Children," *Child Development* 51, no. 1 (1980): 11–18.

62. Martin and Ruble, "Children's Search for Gender Cues," 67–70; Timothy J. Frawley, "Gender Schema and Prejudicial Recall: How Children Misremember, Fabricate, and Distort Gendered Picture Book Information," *Journal of Research in Childhood Education* 22, no. 3 (2008): 291–303; Joshua E. Susskind, "Children's Perception of Gender-Based Illusory Correlations: Enhancing Preexisting Relationships between Gender and Behavior," *Sex Roles* 48, no. 11 (2003): 483–94; Lea Conkright, Dorothy Flannagan, and James Dykes, "Effects of Pronoun Type and

Gender Role Consistency on Children's Recall and Interpretation of Stories," *Sex Roles* 43, nos. 7/8 (2000): 481–97; Lenton, Blair, and Hastie, "Illusions of Gender," 3–14; and Eileen Wood, Alison Groves, Shirliana Bruce, Teena Willoughby, and Serge Desmarais, "Can Gender Stereotypes Facilitate Memory when Elaborative Strategies Are Used?" *Educational Psychology* 23, no. 2 (2003): 169–80.

63. Mahzarin Banaji and R. Bhaskar, "Implicit Stereotypes and Memory: The Bounded Rationality of Social Beliefs," in *Memory, Brain, and Belief*, ed. Daniel L. Schacter and Elaine Scarry (Cambridge, MA: Harvard University Press, 2000), 139–75; Heather M. Kleider, Kathy Pezdek, Stephen D. Goldinger, and Alice Kirk, "Schema-Driven Source Misattribution Errors: Remembering the Expected from a Witnessed Event," *Applied Cognitive Psychology* 22, no. 1 (2008): 1–20; Kimberly A. Quinn, C. Neil Macrae, and Galen V. Bodenhausen, "Stereotyping and Impression Formation: How Categorical Thinking Shapes Person Perceptions," in *The SAGE Handbook of Social Psychology: Concise Student Edition*, ed. Michael A. Hogg and Joel Cooper (London: Sage, 2007), 68–92.

64. Lauren R. Shapiro, "Eyewitness Testimony for a Simulated Juvenile Crime by Male and Female Criminals with Consistent or Inconsistent Gender-Role Characteristics," *Journal of Applied Developmental Psychology* 30, no. 6 (2009): 649–66.

65. Ibid., 651. See also *What Would You Do? Bike Theft (White Guy, Black Guy, Pretty Girl)*, YouTube, uploaded May 27, 2010, https://www.youtube.com/watch?v=ge7i60GuNRg.

66. Armand Chatard, Serge Guimond, and Leila Selimbegovic, "'How Good Are You in Math?' The Effect of Gender Stereotypes on Students' Recollection of Their School Marks," *Journal of Experimental Social Psychology* 43, no. 6 (2007): 1017–24.

Chapter 2: Bodies

1. Kathryn Dindia, "Men Are from North Dakota, Women Are from South Dakota," in *Sex Differences and Similarities in Communication*, 2nd ed., ed. Kathryn Dindia and Daniel J. Canary (Mahwah, NJ: Erlbaum, 2006), 3–18.

2. Kim Parker, Juliana Menasce Horowitz, and Renee Stepler, "On Gender Differences, No Consensus on Nature vs. Nurture," Pew Research Center, December 5, 2017, https://www.pewsocialtrends.org/2017/12/05/on-gender-differences-no-consensus-on-nature-vs-nurture/.

3. Ethan Zell, Zlatan Krizan, and Sabrina Teeter, "Evaluating Gender Similarities and Differences Using Metasynthesis," *American Psychologist* 70, no. 1 (2015): 10–20.

4. Mary Beth Oliver and Janet S. Hyde, "Gender Differences in Sexuality: A Meta-Analysis," *Psychological Bulletin* 114 (1993): 29–51.

5. Reviewed in Janet Hyde, "The Gender Similarities Hypothesis," *American Psychologist* 60, no. 6 (2005): 581–92.

6. Richard Joiner, Caroline Stewart, Chelsey Beaney, Amy Moon, Pam Maras, Jane Guiller, Helen Gregory, et al., "Publically Different, Privately the Same: Gender Differences and Similarities in Response to Facebook Status Updates," *Computers in Human Behavior* 39 (2014): 165–69.

7. Mark H. Davies and Linda A. Kraus, "Personality and Empathic Accuracy," in *Empathic Accuracy*, ed. William J. Ickes (New York: Guilford Press, 1997), 144–68; and Nancy Briton and Judith Hall, "Beliefs about Female and Male Non-Verbal Communication," *Sex Roles* 32 (1995): 79–90.

8. David M. Marx and Diederik A. Stapel, "It Depends on Your Perspective: The Role of Self-Relevance in Stereotype-Based Underperformance," *Journal of Experimental Social Psychology* 42 (2006): 768–75.

9. Krista J. K. Klein and Sara D. Hodges, "Gender Differences, Motivation, and Empathic Accuracy: When It Pays to Understand," *Personality and Social Psychology Bulletin* 27, no. 6 (2001): 720–30; and Michael J. Clarke, Anthony D. G. Marks, and Amy D. Lykins, "Bridging the Gap: The Effect of Gender Normativity on Differences in Empathy and Emotional Intelligence," *Journal of Gender Studies* 25, no. 5 (2016): 522–39.

10. Geoff Thomas and Gregory R. Maio, "Man, I Feel Like a Woman: When and How Gender-Role Motivation Helps Mind-Reading," *Journal of Personality and Social Psychology* 95, no. 5 (2008): 1165–79.

11. Anne Fausto-Sterling, Cynthia García Coll, and Meghan Lamarre, "Sexing the Baby: Part 1—What Do We Really Know about Sex Differentiation in the First Three Years of Life?" *Social Science & Medicine* 74, no. 11 (2012): 1684–92; Anne Fausto-Sterling, Cynthia Garcia Coll, and Meghan Lamarre, "Sexing the Baby: Part 2—Applying Dynamic Systems Theory to the Emergences of Sex-Related Differences in Infants and Toddlers," *Social Science & Medicine* 74, no. 11 (2012): 1693–17.

12. Joseph Henrich, Steven J. Heine, and Ara Norenzayan, "The Weirdest People in the World," *Behavioral and Brain Sciences* 33 (2010): 61–135.

13. Joan Chrisler and Donald McCreary, eds., *Handbook of Gender Research in Psychology* (New York: Springer, 2010).

14. Brian Nosek, Mahzarin Banaji, and Anthony Greenwald, "Math = Male, Me = Female, Therefore Math ≠ Me," *Journal of Personality and Social Psychology* 83, no. 1 (2002): 44–59.

15. Natalie Angier and Kenneth Chang, "Gray Matter and Sexes: A Gray Area Scientifically," *New York Times*, January 24, 2005, https://www.nytimes.com/2005/01/24/science/24women.html?_r=1.

16. Janet S. Hyde, Sara M. Lindberg, Marcia C. Linn, Amy B. Ellis, and Caroline C. Williams, "Gender Similarities Characterize Math Performance," *Science* 321 (2008): 494–95; Sara M. Lindberg, Janet Shibley Hyde, Jennifer L. Petersen, and Marcia C. Linn, "New Trends in Gender and Mathematics Performance: A Meta-Analysis," *Psychological Bulletin* 136, no. 6 (November 2010): 1123–35; and David I. Miller and Diane F. Halpern, "The New Science of Cognitive Sex Differences," *Trends in Cognitive Science* 18, no. 1 (2014): 37–45.

17. Natalie Angier and Kenneth Chang, "Gray Matter and Sexes: A Gray Area Scientifically," *New York Times*, January 24, 2005, https://www.ny times.com/2005/01/24/science/24women.html?_r=1.

18. Ibid.

19. David Reilly, David L. Neumann, and Glenda Andrews, "Sex Differences in Mathematics and Science Achievement: A Meta-Analysis of National Assessment of Educational Progress Assessments," *Journal of Educational Psychology* 107, no. 3 (2015): 645–62.

20. Angier and Chang, "Gray Matter and Sexes."

21. Hyde, Lindberg, Linn, Ellis, and Williams, "Gender Similarities Characterize Math Performance," 494–95; and Lindberg, Hyde, Petersen, and Linn, "New Trends in Gender and Mathematics Performance: A Meta-Analysis," 1123–35.

22. Jonathan Wai, Megan Cacchio, Martha Putallaz, and Matthew C. Makel, "Sex Differences in the Right Tail of Cognitive Abilities: A 30 Year Examination," *Intelligence* 38, no. 4 (2010): 412–23.

23. Elizabeth Spelke, "Sex Differences in Intrinsic Aptitude for Mathematics and Science? A Critical Review," *American Psychologist* 60, no. 9 (2005): 950–58.

24. Joan Burrelli, *Thirty-Three Years of Women in S&E Faculty Positions*, InfoBrief. Science Resources Statistics, NSF 08-308, National Science Foundation Directorate for Social, Behavioral, and Economic Sciences, 2008. Retrieved from https://wayback.archive-it.org/5902/20160210152800/http://www.nsf.gov/statistics/infbrief/nsf08308/. See also Robert J. Daverman, "Statistics on Women Mathematicians Compiled by the AMS," *Notices of the AMS* 58 (2011): 1310; and National Science Foundation, National Center for Science and Engineering Statistics, "Women, Minorities, and Persons with Disabilities in Science and Engineering: 2021" (Special Report NSF 21-321, Alexandria, VA, NSF), https://ncses.nsf.gov/pubs/nsf21321/.

25. Brian A. Nosek, Frederick L. Smyth, N. Sriram, Nicole M. Lindner, Thierry Devos, Alfonso Ayala, Yoav Bar-Anan, et al., "National Differences in Gender–Science Stereotypes Predict National Sex Differences in Science and Math Achievement," *Proceedings of the National Academy of Sciences* 106, no. 26 (June 30, 2009): 10593–97.

26. Luigi Guiso, Ferdinando Monte, Paola Sapienza, and Luigi Zingales, "Culture, Gender, and Math," *Science* 320, no. 5880 (May 30, 2008): 1164–65; Nicole Else-Quest, Janet Hyde, and Marcia Linn, "Cross-National Patterns of Gender Differences in Mathematics: A Meta-Analysis," *Psychological Bulletin* 136, no. 1 (2010): 103–27.

27. Diane Halpern, Camilla Benbow, David Geary, Ruben Gur, Janet Hyde, and Morton Gernsbacher, "The Science of Sex Differences in Science and Mathematics," *Psychological Science in the Public Interest* 8, no. 1 (2007): 1–51.

28. Ian Craig, Emma Harper, and Caroline Loat, "The Genetic Basis for Sex Differences in Human Behaviour: Role of the Sex Chromosomes," *Annals of Human Genetics* 68 (2004): 269–84.

29. R. Scott Hawley and Catherine A. Mori, *The Human Genome: A User's Guide* (San Diego: Academic Press, 1999).

30. Eric Turkheimer and Diane F. Halpern, "Sex Differences in Variability for Cognitive Measures: Do the Ends Justify the Genes?" *Perspectives on Psychological Science* 4 (2009): 612–14.

31. Rebecca Jordan-Young and Katrina Karkazis, *Testosterone: An Unauthorized Biography* (Cambridge, MA: Harvard University Press, 2019).

32. Ibid.

33. Ibid.

34. Roy Baumeister, Kathleen Catanese, and Kathleen Vohs, "Is There a Gender Difference in Strength of Sex Drive? Theoretical Views, Conceptual Distinctions, and a Review of Relevant Evidence," *Personality and Social Psychology Review* 5, no. 3 (2001): 242–73.

35. Diane Halpern, *Sex Differences in Cognitive Abilities*, 4th ed. (New York: Psychology Press, 2012).

36. Anthony Esgate and David Groome, *An Introduction to Applied Cognitive Psychology* (Hove, UK: Psychology Press, 2004).

37. Halpern, *Sex Differences in Cognitive Abilities*; and Kristin Oinonen and Dwight Mazmanian, "Effects of Oral Contraceptives on Daily Self-Ratings of Positive and Negative Affect," *Journal of Psychosomatic Research* 51, no. 5 (2001): 647–58.

38. Jessica McFarlane, Carol Martin, and Tannis Williams, "Mood Fluctuations: Women versus Men and Menstrual versus Other Cycles," *Psychology of Women Quarterly* 12 (1988): 201–24; Jessica McFarlane and Tannis Williams, "Placing Premenstrual Syndrome in Perspective," *Psychology of Women Quarterly* 18 (1994): 339–74; and Jordan-Young and Karkazis, *Testosterone*.

39. Anne Fausto-Sterling, *Myths of Gender: Biological Theories about Women and Men* (New York: Basic Books, 1992).

40. Peter H. Sönksen, Richard I. G. Holt, Walailuck Böhning, Nishan Guha, David A. Cowan, Christiaan Bartlett, and Dankmar Böhning, "Why Do Endocrine Profiles in Elite Athletes Differ between Sports?" *Clinical Diabetes and Endocrinology* 4, no. 3 (2018), https://clindiabetesendo.biomedcentral.com/articles/10.1186/s40842-017-0050-3.

41. Melissa Hines, "Sex-Related Variation in Human Behavior and the Brain," *Trends in Cognitive Science* 14, no. 10 (2010): 448–56; Yuan-shan Zhu and Li-qun Cai, "Effects of Male Sex Hormones on Gender Identity, Sexual Behavior, and Cognitive Function," *Zhong Nan Da Xue Bao Yi Xue Ban* 31, no. 2 (2006): 149–61; and Amber N. V. Ruigrok, Gholamreza Salimi-Khorshidi, Meng-Chuan Lai, Simon Baron-Cohen, Michael V. Lombardo, Roger J. Tait, and John Suckling, "A Meta-Analysis of Sex Differences in Human Brain Structure," *Neuroscience and Biobehavioral Reviews* 39, no. 100 (2014): 34–50.

42. Daphna Joel, Zohar Berman, Ido Tavor, Nadav Wexler, Olga Gaber, Yaniv Stein, Nisan Shefi, et al., "Sex Beyond the Genitalia: The Human Brain Mosaic," *Proceedings of the National Academy of Sciences* 112, no. 50 (2015): 15468–73.

43. Halpern, *Sex Differences in Cognitive Abilities*; and Melissa Hines, *Brain Gender* (New York: Oxford University Press, 2004).

44. Geert J. De Vries, "Sex Differences in Adult and Developing Brains: Compensation, Compensation, Compensation," *Endocrinology* 145, no. 3 (2004): 1063–68; Celia L. Moore, "Maternal Contributions to Mammalian Reproductive Development and the Divergence of Males and Females," *Advances in the Study of Behavior* 24 (1995): 47–118; Norbert Jauŝovec and Ksenija Jauŝovec, "Sex Differences in Mental Rotation and Cortical Activation Patterns: Can Training Change Them?" *Intelligence* 40 (2012): 151–62; and Rhoshel K. Lenroot and Jay N. Giedd, "Sex Differences in the Adolescent Brain," *Brain and Cognition* 72, no. 1 (2010): 48–55.

45. Jacques Balthazart, "Minireview: Hormones and Human Sexual Orientation," *Endocrinology* 152, no. 8 (2011): 2937–47; Elke Stefanie Smith, Jessica Junger, Birgit Derntl, and Ute Habel, "The Transsexual Brain—A Review of Findings on the Neural Basis of Transsexualism," *Neuroscience & Biobehavioral Reviews* 59 (2015): 251–66; Baudewijntje P. C. Kreukels and Peggy T. Cohen-Kettenis, "Male Gender Identity and Masculine Behavior: The Role of Sex Hormones in Brain Development," in *Hormonal Therapy for Male Sexual Dysfunction*, ed. Mario Maggi (Oxford: John Wiley, 2012): 1–10; Ai-Min Bao and Dick F. Swaab, "Sexual Differentiation of the Human Brain: Relation to Gender Identity, Sexual Orientation and Neuropsychiatric Disorders," *Frontiers in Neuroendocrinology* 32, no. 2 (2011): 214–26; Jacques Balthazart, "Brain Development and Sexual Orientation," *Colloquium Series on the Developing Brain* 3, no. 2 (2012): 1–134; Simon LeVay, *Gay, Straight, and the Reason Why: The Science of Sexual Orientation* (New York: Oxford University Press, 2017); Annelou L. C. de Vries, Baudewijntje P. C. Kreukels, Thomas D. Steensma, and Jenifer K. McGuire, "Gender Identity Development: A Biopsychosocial Perspective," in *Gender Dysphoria and Disorders of Sex Development: Progress in Care and Knowledge*, ed. Baudewijntje P. C. Kreukels, Thomas D. Steensma, and Annelou L. C. de Vries (New York: Springer, 2014), 53–80; and Brenda K. Todd, Rico A. Fischer, Steven Di Costa, Amanda Roestorf, Kate Harbour, Paul Hardiman, and John A. Barry, "Sex Differences in Children's Toy Preferences: A Systematic Review, Meta-Regression, and Meta-Analysis," *Infant and Child Development* 27, no. 2 (2018): e2064.

46. Jiska Ristori, Carlotta Cocchetti, Alessia Romani, Francesca Mazzoli, Linda Vignozzi, Mario Maggi,

and Alessandra Daphne Fisher, "Brain Sex Differences Related to Gender Identity Development: Genes or Hormones?" *International Journal of Molecular Sciences* 21, no. 6 (2020): 2123; Baudewijntje P. C. Kreukels and Antonio Guillamon, "Neuroimaging Studies in People with Gender Incongruence," *International Review of Psychiatry* 28, no. 1 (2016): 120–28; and Mikhail Votinov, Katharina S. Goerlich, Andrei A. Puiu, Elke Smith, Thomas Nickl-Jockschat, Birgit Derntl, and Ute Habel, "Brain Structure Changes Associated with Sexual Orientation," *Scientific Reports* 11, no. 5078 (2021): https://doi.org/10.1038/s41598-021-84496-z.

47. David H. Uttal, Nathaniel G. Meadow, Elizabeth Tipton, Linda L. Hand, Alison R. Alden, and Christopher Warren, "The Malleability of Spatial Skills: A Meta-Analysis of Training Studies," *Psychological Bulletin* 139, no. 2 (2013): 352–402.

48. Melissa S. Terlecki, Nora S. Newcombe, and Michelle Little, "Durable and Generalized Effects of Spatial Experience on Mental Rotation: Gender Differences in Growth Patterns," *Applied Cognitive Psychology* 22 (2007): 996–1013.

49. Jing Feng, Ian Spence, and Jay Pratt, "Playing an Action Video Game Reduces Gender Differences in Spatial Cognition," *Psychological Science* 18 (2007): 850–55.

50. Richard De Lisi and Jennifer Wolford, "Improving Children's Mental Rotation Accuracy with Computer Game Playing," *Journal of Genetic Psychology* 163, no. 3 (2002): 272–82.

51. Isabelle D. Cherney, Kavita Jagarlamudi, Erika Lawrence, and Nicole Shimabuku, "Experiential Factors on Sex Differences in Mental Rotation," *Perceptual and Motor Skills* 96 (July 2003): 1062–70.

52. Richard J. Haier, Sherif Karama, Leonard Leyba, and Rex E. Jung, "MRI Assessment of Cortical Thickness and Functional Activity Changes in Adolescent Girls Following Three Months of Practice on a Visual-Spatial Task," *BioMed Central Research Notes* 2 (2009): 174.

53. For a summary, see Isabelle D. Cherney, "Mom, Let Me Play More Computer Games: They Improve My Mental Rotation Skills," *Sex Roles* 59 (2008): 776–86.

54. Nora Newcombe, "Science Seriously: Straight Thinking about Spatial Sex Differences," in *Why Aren't More Women in Science? Top Researchers Debate the Evidence*, ed. Stephen Ceci and Wendy Williams (Washington, DC: American Psychological Association, 2007), 69–77.

55. Lise Eliot, *Pink Brain, Blue Brain* (New York: Houghton Mifflin Harcourt, 2009); Isabelle D. Cherney and Kamala L. London, "Gender-Linked Differences in the Toys, Television Shows, Computer Games, and Outdoor Activities of 5- to 13-Year-Old Children," *Sex Roles* 54 (2006): 717–26; and Joanne Kersh, Beth M. Casey, and Jessica Mercer Young, "Research on Spatial Skills and Block Building in Girls and Boys: The Relationship to Later Mathematics Learning," in *Mathematics, Science and Technology in Early Childhood Education: Contemporary Perspectives on Mathematics in Early Childhood Education*, ed. Olivia N. Saracho and Bernard Spodek (Charlotte, NC: Information Age, 2008), 233–53.

56. Susan C. Levine, Marina Vasilyeva, Stella F. Lourenco, Nora S. Newcombe, and Janellen Huttenlocher, "Socioeconomic Status Modifies the Sex Difference in Spatial Skill," *Psychological Science* 16, no. 11 (November 2005): 841–45; and Kimberly G. Noble, M. Frank Norman, and Martha J. Farah, "Neurocognitive Correlates of Socioeconomic Status in Kindergarten Children," *Developmental Science* 8 (2005): 74–87.

57. Stephen J. Ceci, Wendy Williams, and Susan Barnett, "Women's Underrepresentation in Science: Sociocultural and Biological Considerations," *Psychological Bulletin* 135, no. 2 (2009): 218–61.

58. Daniel Voyer, Susan Voyer, and Philip M. Bryden, "Magnitude of Sex Differences in Spatial Abilities: A Meta-analysis and Consideration of Critical Variables," *Psychological Bulletin* 117, no. 2 (March 1995): 250–70; Mary Soares Masters and Barbara Sanders, "Is the Gender Difference in Mental Rotation Disappearing?" *Behavior Genetics* 23, no. 4 (1993): 337–41; and Ceci, Williams, and Barnett, "Women's Underrepresentation in Science," 218–61.

59. Maryann Baenninger and Nora Newcombe, "Environmental Input to the Development of Sex-Related Differences in Spatial and Mathematical Ability," *Learning and Individual Differences* 7, no. 4 (1995): 363–79.

60. Eliot, *Pink Brain, Blue Brain*.

61. Mark Pagel, *Wired for Culture: Origins of the Human Social Mind* (New York: W. W. Norton, 2012); and Joseph Henrich and Rich McElreath, "The Evolution of Cultural Evolution," *Evolutionary Anthropology* 12, no. 3 (2003): 123–35.

62. Cordelia Fine, *Testosterone Rex: Myths of Sex, Science, and Society* (New York: W. W. Norton, 2017).

63. Frank Browning, *The Fate of Gender: Nature, Nurture and the Human Future* (New York: Bloomsbury, 2016); Fausto-Sterling, García Coll, and Lamarre, "Sexing the Baby: Part 2," 1693–17; and Anne Fausto-Sterling, "The Bare Bones of Sex: Part I—Sex and Gender," *Signs* 30, no. 2 (2005): 1510.

64. Described in Michael J. Meaney, "The Nature of Nurture: Maternal Effects and Chromatin Remodeling," in *Essays in Social Neuroscience*, ed. John T. Cacioppo and Gary G. Berntson (Cambridge, MA: MIT Press, 2004): 1–14.

65. Judith Lorber, *Paradoxes of Gender* (New Haven, CT: Yale University Press, 1993), x.

66. Charlie Lovett, *Olympic Marathon: A Centennial History of the Games' Most Storied Race* (Westport, CT: Praeger, 1997).

67. Halpern, *Sex Differences in Cognitive Abilities*; and Rebecca Jordan-Young, *Brain Storm: The Flaws in the Science of Sex Differences* (Cambridge, MA: Harvard University Press, 2010).

68. Marco Taubert, Bogdan Draganski, Alfred Anwander, Karsten Müller, Annette Horstmann, Arno Villringer, and Patrick Ragert, "Dynamic Properties of Human Brain Structure: Learning-Related Changes in Cortical Areas and Associated Fiber Connections," *Journal of Neuroscience* 30, no. 35 (September 1, 2010): 11670–77.

69. Sari M. van Anders and Neil V. Watson, "Social Neuroendocrinology: Effects of Social Contexts and Behaviors on Sex Steroids in Humans," *Human Nature* 17, no. 2 (2006): 212–37; and Rui F. Oliveira, "Social Behavior in Context: Hormonal Modulation of Behavioral Plasticity and Social Competence," *Integrative and Comparative Biology* 49, no. 4 (2009): 423–40.

70. David Edwards, "Competition and Testosterone," *Hormones and Behavior* 50 (2006): 682; Leander van der Meij, Abraham P. Buunk, Johannes P. van de Sande, and Alicia Salvador, "The Presence of a Woman Increases Testosterone in Aggressive Dominant Men," *Hormones and Behavior* 54, no. 5 (November 2008): 640–44; and Alicia Salvador, "Coping with Competitive Situations in Humans," *Neuroscience and Biobehavioral Reviews* 29, no.1 (2005): 195–205.

71. Allan Mazur, Elizabeth Susman, and Sandy Edelbrock, "Sex Difference in Testosterone Response to a Video Game Contest," *Evolution and Human Behavior* 18, no. 5 (1997): 317–26; Richard E. Nisbett and Dov Cohen, *Culture of Honor: The Psychology of Violence in the South* (Boulder, CO: Westview,

1996); Alan Booth, Greg Shelley, Allan Mazur, Gerry Tharp, and Roger Kittok, "Testosterone, and Winning and Losing in Human Competition," *Hormones and Behavior* 23, no. 4 (December 1989): 556–71; Alan Booth, David R. Johnson, and Douglas A. Granger, "Testosterone and Men's Depression: The Role of Social Behavior," *Journal of Health and Social Behavior* 40 (1999): 130–40; and Robert Sapolsky, *The Trouble with Testosterone and Other Essays on the Biology of the Human Predicament* (New York: Simon & Schuster, 1997).

72. Allan Mazur, Alan Booth, and James Dabbs Jr., "Testosterone and Chess Competition," *Social Psychology Quarterly* 55, no. 1 (1992): 70–77.

73. Paul C. Bernhardt, James M. Dabbs Jr., Julie A. Fielden, and Candice D. Lutter, "Testosterone Changes during Vicarious Experiences of Winning and Losing among Fans at Sporting Events," *Physiology and Behavior* 65, no. 1 (1998): 59–62.

74. Gad Saad and John Vongas, "The Effect of Conspicuous Consumption on Men's Testosterone Levels," *Organizational Behavior and Human Decision Processes* 110, no. 2 (2009): 80–92.

75. Steven J. Stanton, Jacinta C. Beehner, Ekjyot K. Saini, Cynthia M. Kuhn, and Kevin S. LaBar, "Dominance, Politics, and Physiology: Voters' Testosterone Changes on the Night of the 2008 United States Presidential Election," *PLoS ONE* 4, no. 10 (2009): 7543.

76. Kathleen V. Casto, David A. Edwards, Modupe Akinola, C. Davis, and Pranjal H. Mehta, "Testosterone Reactivity to Competition and Competitive Endurance in Men and Women," *Hormones and Behavior* 123 (July 2020), https://doi.org/10.1016/j.yhbeh.2019.104665; Kathleen V. Casto and Smrithi Prasad, "Recommendations for the Study of Women in Hormones and Competition Research," *Hormones and Behavior* 92 (2017): 190–94.

77. Sari M. van Anders, Jeffrey Steiger, and Katherine L. Goldey, "Effects of Gendered Behavior on Testosterone in Women and Men," *Proceedings of the National Academy of Sciences* 112, no. 45 (2015): 13805–10.

78. Fine, *Testosterone Rex*; and Jordan-Young and Karkazis, *Testosterone*.

79. Sapolsky, *Trouble with Testosterone*; and Jordan-Young and Karkazis, *Testosterone*.

80. "Men Also Wired for Childcare," National Science Foundation, September 13, 2011, https://www.nsf.gov/news/news_summ.jsp?cntn_id=121658;

Allan Mazur and Joel Michalek, "Marriage, Divorce, and Male Testosterone," *Social Forces* 77, no. 1 (1998): 315–30; Lee T. Gettler, Thomas W. McDade, Alan B. Feranil, and Christopher W. Kuzawa, "Longitudinal Evidence that Fatherhood Decreases Testosterone in Human Males," *Proceedings of the National Academy of Sciences* 108, no. 39 (2011): 16194–99.

81. Christopher W. Kuzawa, Lee T. Gettler, Martin N. Muller, Thomas W. McDade, and Alan B. Feranil, "Fatherhood, Pairbonding, and Testosterone in the Philippines," *Hormones and Behavior* 56, no. 4 (October 2009): 429–35; Gettler, McDade, Feranil, and Kuzawa, "Longitudinal Evidence that Fatherhood Decreases Testosterone in Human Males," 16194–99; and Sari M. van Anders, Richard M. Tolman, and Brenda L. Volling, "Baby Cries and Nurturance Affect Testosterone in Men," *Hormonal Behavior* 61, no. 1 (2012): 31–36.

82. Martin N. Muller, Frank W. Marlowe, Revocatus Bugumba, and Peter T. Ellison, "Testosterone and Paternal Care in East African Foragers and Pastoralists," *Proceedings of the Royal Society B: Biological Sciences* 276, no. 1655 (January 22, 2009): 347–54.

83. Jordan-Young, *Brain Storm*, 271; Michael Meaney, "Nature, Nurture, and the Disunity of Knowledge," *Annals New York Academy of Sciences* 935 (2001): 50–61; Alissa J. Mrazek, Joan Y. Chiao, Katherine D. Blizinksy, Janetta Lun, and Michele J. Gelfand, "The Role of Culture–Gene Coevolution in Morality Judgment: Examining the Interplay between Tightness–Looseness and Allelic Variation of the Serotonin Transporter Gene, *Culture and Brain* 1, no. 2–4 (2013): 100–117; and Helga Nowotny and Giuseppe Testa, *Naked Genes: Reinventing the Human in the Molecular Age*, (Cambridge, MA: MIT Press, 2010).

84. Genetic Science Learning Center, "Insights from Identical Twins," Learn.Genetics, January 5, 2014, https://learn.genetics.utah.edu/content/epigenetics /twins/.

85. Kristen Jacobson, "Considering Interactions between Genes, Environments, Biology, and Social Context," *Psychological Science Agenda*, April 2009, American Psychological Association, https://www .apa.org/science/about/psa/2009/04/sci-brief.aspx.

86. Remi J. Cadoret, William R. Yates, and Ellis Le Geyt Troughton, "Genetic-Environmental Interaction in the Genesis of Aggressivity and Conduct Disorders," *Archives of General Psychiatry* 52 (1995): 916–24.

87. Cynthia Fuchs Epstein, *Deceptive Distinctions: Sex, Gender, and the Social Order* (New Haven, CT: Yale University Press, 1988).

88. Pranjal H. Mehta, Keith M. Welker, Samuele Zilioli, and Justin M. Carré, "Testosterone and Cortisol Jointly Modulate Risk-Taking," *Psychoneuroendocrinology* 56 (2015): 88–99.

89. Gilbert Herdt, ed., *Third Sex, Third Gender: Beyond Sexual Dimorphism in Culture and History* (New York: Zone Books, 1994).

90. Lisa Selin Davis, *Tomboy: The Surprising History and Future of Girls Who Dare to Be Different* (New York: Hachette Book Group, 2020).

91. "Annual Bone Fracture Rate Almost 4 Percent and Double Previous Estimates," Medical Xpress, January 17, 2008, https://medicalxpress.com/news /2008-01-annual-bone-fracture-percent-previous .html.

92. Jordan-Young, *Brain Storm*, 285.

93. Fausto-Sterling, "Bare Bones of Sex: Part I," 1510.

94. Gloria Anzaldua, *Borderlands/La Frontera: The New Mestiza* (San Francisco: Aunt Lute Books, 1987); Kimberlé W. Crenshaw, "Mapping the Margins: Intersectionality, Identity Politics, and Violence against Women of Color," *Stanford Law Review* 43, no. 6 (1991): 1241–99; and Patricia Hill Collins, *Black Feminist Thought: Knowledge, Consciousness, and the Politics of Empowerment* (New York: Routledge, 1991).

95. David Riches, "Hunting and Gathering Societies," in *Encyclopedia of Social and Cultural Anthropology*, 2nd ed., ed. Alan Barnard and Jonathan Spencer (New York: Routledge, 2009).

96. V. Spike Peterson, "Sex Matters: A Queer History of Hierarchies," *International Feminist Journal of Politics* 16, no. 3 (2014): 389–409. Scholars also think that Christians of the fourth and fifth centuries shared this view of women as more carnal and sexually insatiable but viewed this as diabolic. See Sheila Briggs, "Women and Religion," in Beth H. Hess and Myra Marx Ferree, *Analyzing Gender* (Thousand Oaks, CA: Sage, 1987), 408–41.

97. Herdt, *Third Sex, Third Gender*.

98. Rob Craig Kirkpatrick, "The Evolution of Human Homosexual Behavior," *Current Anthropology* 41, no. 3 (2000): 385–413.

99. Joan Roughgarden, "Homosexuality and Evolution: A Critical Appraisal," in *On Human Nature*, ed. Michel Tibayrenc and Francisco J. Ayala (Cambridge, MA: Academic Press, 2017), 495–516.

100. Fine, *Testosterone Rex*.

101. Oyeronke Oyewumi, *What Gender Is Motherhood? Changing Yoruba Ideals of Power, Procreation, and Identity in the Age of Modernity* (New York: Palgrave Macmillan, 2016).

102. "Women in Construction," Mahila Housing Sewa Trust, accessed Nov. 11, 2021, https://www.mahilahousingtrust.org/our-work/women-in-construction/.

103. Christine W. Gailey, "Evolutionary Perspectives on Gender Hierarchy," in *Analyzing Gender*, ed. Beth H. Hess and Myra Marx Ferree (Thousand Oaks, CA: Sage, 1987), 32–67; and Peterson, "Sex Matters," 389–409.

104. H. L. Mencken, "The Divine Afflatus," *New York Evening Mail*, November 16, 1917.

Chapter 3: Performances

1. Spencer Kornhaber, "How Pop's Biggest Weirdo Swept the Grammys," *Atlantic*, January 27, 2020, https://www.theatlantic.com/culture/archive/2020/01/why-billie-eilish-swept-grammys/605587/.

2. Rob Haskell, "How Billie Eilish Is Reinventing Pop Stardom," *Vogue*, February 3, 2020, https://www.vogue.com/article/billie-eilish-cover-march-2020.

3. US Department of Education, National Center for Education Statistics, "Table 318.30: Bachelor's, Master's, and Doctor's Degrees Conferred by Postsecondary Institutions, by Sex of Student and Discipline Division: 2017–18," Digest of Education Statistics, September 2019, https://nces.ed.gov/programs/digest/d19/tables/dt19_318.30.asp.

4. Rose A. Woods, "Spotlight on Statistics: Sports and Exercise," US Bureau of Labor Statistics, May 2017, https://www.bls.gov/spotlight/2017/sports-and-exercise/pdf/sports-and-exercise.pdf.

5. "The Gender Gap in Religion around the World," Pew Research Center, March 22, 2016, https://www.pewforum.org/2016/03/22/the-gender-gap-in-religion-around-the-world/.

6. Sandra L. Bem, *The Lenses of Gender: Transforming the Debate on Sexual Inequality* (New Haven, CT: Yale University Press, 1993), 149.

7. Jessica Rose, Susan Mackey-Kallis, Len Shyles, Kelly Barry, Danielle Biagini, Colleen Hart, and Lauren Jack, "Face It: The Impact of Gender on Social Media Images," *Communication Quarterly* 60, no. 5 (2012): 588–607; Mike Thelwall and Farida Vis, "Gender and Image Sharing on Facebook, Twitter, Insta-gram, Snapchat and WhatsApp in the UK: Hobbying Alone or Filtering for Friends?" *Aslib Journal of Information Management* 69, no. 6 (2017): 702–20; Richard Joiner, Caroline Stewart, Chelsey Beaney, Amy Moon, Pam Maras, Jane Guiller, Helen Gregory, et al., "Publically Different, Privately the Same: Gender Differences and Similarities in Response to Facebook Status Updates," *Computers in Human Behavior* 39 (October 2014): 165–69; Sigal Tiffert and Iris Vilnai-Yavetz, "Gender Differences in Facebook Self-Presentation: An International Randomized Study," *Computers in Human Behavior* 35 (2014): 388–99; Francisco Rangel, Irazú Hernández, Paolo Rosso, and Antonio Reyes, "Emotions and Irony per Gender in Facebook," in *Proceedings of the 5th International Workshop on Emotion, Social Signals, Sentiment & Linked Open Data*, ed. Björn Schuller, Paul Buitelaar, Laurence Devillers, Catherine Pelachaud, Thierry Declerck, Anton Batliner, Paolo Rosso, et al. (Reykjavik, Iceland, May 26–31, 2014), 68–73, http://www.lrec-conf.org/proceedings/lrec2014/workshops/LREC2014Workshop-ES3LODProceedings.pdf; and Pin Luarn, Hsien-Chih Kuo, Yu-Ping Chiu, and Shu-Chen Chang, "Social Support on Facebook: The Influence of Tie Strength and Gender Differences," *International Journal of Electronic Commerce Studies* 6, no.1 (2015): 37–50.

8. L. Susan Williams, "Trying on Gender, Gender Regimes, and the Process of Becoming Women," *Gender & Society* 16, no. 1 (2002): 29–52.

9. Kathy Novak, "Why South Korea's Men Are Buying Tons of Cosmetics," CNN Money, October 4, 2015, https://money.cnn.com/2015/10/04/news/south-korea-men-cosmetics/index.html.

10. Lim Yun Suk, "Putting the Best Face Forward: How South Korean Men Are Shaping the Beauty Industry," CNA, July 31, 2019, https://www.channelnewsasia.com/news/asia/south-korea-mens-makeup-shaping-beauty-industry-11763050.

11. David Yi, "How K-Pop Changed the Meaning of Masculinity in South Korea," *Allure*, April 15, 2020, https://www.allure.com/story/k-pop-and-masculinity.

12. Ibid.

13. "Flowerboys and the Appeal of 'Soft Masculinity' in South Korea," BBC News, September 5, 2018, https://www.bbc.com/news/world-asia-42499809; Sun Jung, "Chogukjeok Pan-East Asian Soft Masculinity: Reading Boys over Flowers, Coffee Prince and Shinhwa Fan Fiction," in *Complicated Currents: Media Flows, Soft Power and East Asia*, ed. Daniel Black, Stephen Epstein, and Alison Tokita (Victoria, Australia: Monash University ePress), 1–17.

14. Miki Nakai, "Social Stratification and Consumption Patterns: Cultural Practices and Lifestyles in Japan," in *New Perspectives in Statistical Modeling and Data Analysis: Studies in Classification, Data Analysis, and Knowledge Organization*, ed. Salvatore Ingrassia, Roberto Rocci, and Maurizio Vichi (Berlin: Springer, 2011), 211–18.

15. Yumiko Iida, "Beyond the 'Feminization of Masculinity': Transforming Patriarchy with the 'Feminine' in Japanese Youth Culture," *Inter-Asia Cultural Studies* 6, no. 1 (2006): 56–74.

16. Jack Kilbride and Bang Xiao, "China's 'Sissy Pants Phenomenon': Beijing Fears Negative Impact of 'Sickly Culture' on Teenagers," ABC, September 14, 2018, https://www.abc.net.au/news/2018-09-15/male-beauty-in-china-does-not-fit-with-push-for-global-influence/10221984.

17. Elizabeth Dori Tunstall, "Un-designing Masculinities: K-Pop and the New Global Man?" *Conversation*, January 22, 2014, https://theconversation.com/un-designing-masculinities-k-pop-and-the-new-global-man-22335.

18. Margo DeMello, *Encyclopedia of Body Adornment* (Westport, CT: Greenwood Press, 2007).

19. Carla Pfeffer, *Queering Families: The Postmodern Partnerships of Cisgender Women and Transgender Men* (New York: Oxford University Press, 2017), 55.

20. For a review, see Carol Martin and Diane Ruble, "Children's Search for Gender Cues," *Current Directions in Psychological Science* 13, no. 2 (2004): 69.

21. Joan Roughgarden, *Evolution's Rainbow: Diversity, Gender and Sexuality in Nature and People* (Berkeley: University of California Press, 2004), 27.

22. Anne A. Fast, Kristina R. Olson, "Gender Development in Transgender Preschool Children," *Child Development* 89, no. 2 (2018): 620–37; Selin Gülgöz, Jessica J. Glazier, Elizabeth A. Enright, Daniel J. Alonso, Lily J. Durwood, Anne A. Fast, Riley Lowe, et al., "Similarity in Transgender and Cisgender Children's Gender Development," *Proceedings of the National Academy of Sciences* 116, no. 49 (December 2019): 24480–85.

23. Martin and Ruble, "Children's Search for Gender Cues," 67.

24. Ibid., 67.

25. David F. Bjorklund, *Children's Thinking: Developmental Function and Individual Differences* (Belmont, CA: Wadsworth, 2000); Barbara Martin, *Children at Play: Learning Gender in the Early Years* (Stoke-on-Trent, Staffordshire, UK: Trentham Books, 2011).

26. Emily Kane, *The Gender Trap* (New York: New York University Press, 2012).

27. Ibid.

28. Sara M. Moniuszko, "What Is Gender Creative Parenting? We Spoke to Parents Who Let Their Kids Explore Gender Freely," *USA Today*, October 21, 2021, https://www.usatoday.com/story/life/health-wellness/2021/10/21/gender-creative-parenting-what-it-tiktok-families-explain/8521720002/.

29. Kane, *Gender Trap*.

30. Ibid., 2.

31. Martin and Ruble, "Children's Search for Gender Cues," 67–70.

32. Hanns M. Trautner, Diane N. Ruble, Lisa Cyphers, Barbara Kirsten, Regina Behrendt, and Petra Hartmann, "Rigidity and Flexibility of Gender Stereotypes in Childhood: Developmental or Differential?" *Infant and Child Development* 14, no. 4 (October 2005): 365–81.

33. Tey Meadow, "Deep Down Where the Music Plays: Parents' Accounts of Their Child's Gender Variance," *Sexualities* 14, no. 6 (2011): 725–47; and "Boys in Quebec Are Wearing Skirts to School. Here's What a Girl Thinks," CBC Kids News, October 16, 2020, https://www.cbc.ca/kidsnews/post/boys-in-quebec-are-wearing-skirts-to-school.-heres-what-a-girl-thinks.

34. Lauren Spinner, Lindsey Cameron, and Rachel Calogero, "Peer Toy Play as a Gateway to Children's Gender Flexibility: The Effect of (Counter)Stereotypic Portrayals of Peers in Children's Magazines," *Sex Roles* (2018), https://link.springer.com/article/10.1007/s11199-017-0883-3.

35. Meadow, "Deep Down Where the Music Plays," 725–47; and Sara M. Moniuszko, "What Is Gender Creative Parenting? We Spoke to Parents Who Let Their Kids Explore Gender Freely," *USA Today*, November 2, 2021, https://www.usatoday.com/story/life/health-wellness/2021/10/21/gender-creative-parenting-what-it-tiktok-families-explain/8521720002/.

36. Cecilia L. Ridgeway, *Framed by Gender: How Gender Inequality Persists in the Modern World* (New York: Oxford University Press, 2011).

37. Laura Snapes, "'It's All about What Makes You Feel Good': Billie Eilish on New Music, Power Dynamics, and Her Internet-Breaking Transformation,"

Vogue, May 2, 2021, https://www.vogue.co.uk/news /article/billie-eilish-vogue-interview.

38. Martin Weinberg and Colin Williams, "Fecal Matters: Habitus, Embodiments, and Deviance," *Social Problems* 52, no. 3 (2005): 315–36.

39. Kate Handley, "The Unbearable Daintiness of Women Who Eat with Men," *Sociological Images*, December 27, 2015, https://www.thesocietypages.org /socimages/2015/12/27/the-unbearable-daintiness -of-women-who-eat-with-men/.

40. Arit John, "Go Natural, Try a New Style or Panic? How Black Women in the Coronavirus Era Deal with Their Hair," *Los Angeles Times*, April 11, 2020, https:// www.latimes.com/lifestyle/story/2020-04-11 /coronavirus-black-hair-care-natural-braiding.

41. See, for example, Kerry Pieri, "But Will We Ever Wear Bras Again?" *Harper's Bazaar*, April 8, 2020, https://www.harpersbazaar.com/fashion/trends /a32070316/bra-free-quarantine/.

42. Alex Marzano-Lesnevich, "How Do I Define My Gender If No One Is Watching Me?" *New York Times*, April 2, 2021, https://www.nytimes.com/2021 /04/02/opinion/transgender-nonbinary-pandemic -transition-.html.

43. Ibid.

44. Guy Trebay, "The Boys in Their Summer Dresses," *New York Times*, updated July 7, 2021, https://www .nytimes.com/2021/06/09/style/gender-the-boys-in -their-summer-dresses.html.

45. Ronan Farrow and Jia Tolentino, "Britney Spears's Conservatorship Nightmare," *New Yorker*, July 3, 2021, https://www.newyorker.com/news/american -chronicles/britney-spears-conservatorship -nightmare.

46. "2019 Hate Crime Statistics," Federal Bureau of Investigation, November 16, 2020, https://ucr.fbi.gov /hate-crime/2019/topic-pages/incidents-and -offenses.

47. Kristin Schilt and Danya Lagos, "The Development of Transgender Studies in Sociology," *Annual Review of Sociology* 43 (2017): 437; and Kristen Springer, "The Race and Class Privilege of Motherhood: The *New York Times* Presentations of Pregnant Drug-Using Women," *Sociological Forums* 25, no. 3 (2010): 476–99.

48. Laurel Westbrook and Kristin Schilt, "Doing Gender, Determining Gender: Transgender People, Gender Panics, and the Maintenance of the Sex/ Gender/Sexuality System," *Gender & Society* 28 no. 1 (2014): 32–57; Kristen Schilt and Laurel Westbrook, "Doing Gender, Doing Heteronormativity: 'Gender Normals,' Transgender People, and the Social Maintenance of Heterosexuality," *Gender & Society* 23, no. 4 (2009): 440–64; and Betsy Lucal, "What It Means to Be Gendered Me: Life on the Boundaries of a Dichotomous Gender System," *Gender & Society* 13, no. 6 (1999): 781–97.

49. Chioma Nnadi, "This Was the Decade That Hip-Hop Style Got Femme," *Vogue*, July 18, 2019, https:// www.vogue.com/article/young-thug-jeffrey-lil-uzi -vert-kanye-west-lil-nas-x-hip-hop-style; Brian "Z" Zisook, "Lil Uzi Vert on Why He Wears Women's Clothing: 'I Bought Everything in the Men's Section,'" *DJBooth*, updated October 23, 2018, https:// djbooth.net/features/2018-05-14-lil-uzi-vert -womens-clothing.

50. Oliver Grady, "*Pose* Star Billy Porter: 'Did I Ever Think I'd Be This Successful? No, because I'm Gay'" *Times*, October 17, 2021, https://www.thetimes.co .uk/article/pose-star-billy-porter-did-i-ever-think-id -be-this-successful-no-because-im-gay-k59wszd5p.

51. "'Harry Styles, I Apologize to You for Having Your Name in My Mouth'—Billy Porter," *The Late Show with Stephen Colbert*, YouTube, uploaded November 5, 2021, https://www.youtube.com/watch?v=YbD _LgHZoEI&ab_channel=TheLateShowwithStephen Colbert.

52. Harry Barbee and Douglas Schrock, "Un/gendering Social Selves: How Nonbinary People Navigate and Experience a Binarily Gendered World," *Sociological Forum* 34, no. 3 (2019): 572–93, 578.

53. Ibid.

54. Ibid., 579.

55. Ibid., 580.

56. Ibid.

57. Ibid., 582.

58. Erin Patricia Savoia, "'Neither of the Boxes': Accounting for Non-binary Gender Identities" (master's thesis, Portland State University, June 19, 2017), 40, https://doi.org/10.15760/etd.5900.

59. Helana Darwin, "Doing Gender beyond the Binary: A Virtual Ethnography," *Symbolic Interaction* 40, no. 3 (2017): 317–34, 10.

60. Barbee and Schrock, "Un/gendering Social Selves," 582.

61. Tey Meadow, *Trans Kids: Being Gendered in the Twenty-First Century* (Oakland: University of California Press, 2018), 20.

62. Cecilia L. Ridgeway, *Framed by Gender: How Gender Inequality Persists in the Modern World* (New York: Oxford University Press, 2011).

63. Lucal, "What It Means to Be Gendered Me," 781–97.

Chapter 4: Intersections

1. Fem Korsten, "Grappling with My Sexuality Now That I'm in a Wheelchair," *xoJane UK* (blog), September 19, 2012, https://www.xojane.co.uk/issues /disability-sexuality-street-harassment (content no longer available).

2. Henri Tajfel, *Human Groups and Social Categories: Studies in Social Psychology* (Cambridge: Cambridge University Press, 1981); and Peggy A. Thoits and Lauren K. Virshup, "Me's and We's: Forms and Functions of Social Identities," in *Self and Identity: Fundamental Issues*, ed. R. D. Ashmore and L. Jussim (New York: Oxford University Press, 1997), 106–33.

3. "Word We're Watching: Intersectionality," Merriam-Webster, accessed December 14, 2021, https://www.merriam-webster.com/words-at-play /intersectionality-meaning.

4. Patricia Madoo Lengermann and Gillian Niebrugge, *The Women Founders: Sociology and Social Theory 1830–1930* (Long Grove, IL: Waveland Press, 2006).

5. Rachel A. Feinstein, *When Rape Was Legal: The Untold History of Sexual Violence during Slavery* (New York: Routledge, 2018); and "Anna Julia Haywood Cooper, 1858–1964," *The Church Awakens: African Americans and the Struggle for Justice* (online exhibit), Archives of the Episcopal Church, accessed November 10, 2020, https://episcopal archives.org/church-awakens/exhibits/show/leader ship/lay/cooper.

6. Vivian M. May, *Anna Julia Cooper, Visionary Black Feminist: A Critical Introduction* (London: Routledge, 2007); and Anna Julia Cooper, *A Voice from the South* (Xenia, OH: Aldine Printing House, 1892; digitized in Documenting the American South, University of North Carolina–Chapel Hill, online ed., 2000), accessed November 28, 2020, https:// docsouth.unc.edu/church/cooper/cooper.html.

7. Akasha Gloria Hull, Patricia Bell Scott, and Barbara Smith (eds.), *All the Women Are White, All the Blacks Are Men, but Some of Us Are Brave: Black Women's Studies* (Westbury, NY: Feminist Press, 1982).

8. Kimberlé Crenshaw, "Mapping the Margins: Intersectionality, Identity Politics, and Violence against Women of Color," *Stanford Law Review* 43, no. 6 (1991): 1241–99. See also Gloria Anzaldúa, *Borderlands/La Frontera: The New Mestiza* (San Francisco, CA: Aunt Lute Books, 1987); Patricia Hill Collins, *Black Feminist Thought: Knowledge, Consciousness, and the Politics of Empowerment* (New York: Routledge, 1991); Angela Davis, *Women, Race and Class* (New York: Random House, 1983); Trinh Minh-ha, *Woman, Native, Other: Writing Postcoloniality and Feminism* (Bloomington: Indiana University Press, 1989); and Cherríe Moraga and Gloria Anzaldúa, *This Bridge Called My Back: Writings by Radical Women of Color* (New York: Kitchen Table, 1981).

9. Kimberlé Crenshaw, "Demarginalizing the Intersection of Race and Sex: A Black Feminist Critique of Antidiscrimination Doctrine, Feminist Theory and Antiracist Politics," *University of Chicago Legal Forum* 1, no. 8 (1989): 139–67.

10. Collins, *Black Feminist Thought*.

11. Arlie Hochschild, *The Second Shift* (New York: Viking, 1989).

12. Tara Bahrampour, "They Considered Themselves White, but DNA Tests Told a More Complex Story," *Washington Post*, February 6, 2018, https://www .washingtonpost.com/local/social-issues/they-con sidered-themselves-white-but-dna-tests-told-a-more -complex-story/2018/02/06/16215d1a-e181-11e7-8679 -a9728984779c_story.html; Ryan Brown and George Armelagos, "Apportionment of Racial Diversity: A Review," *Evolutionary Anthropology* 10 (2001): 34–40; Luigi Cavalli-Sforza, Paolo Menozzi, and Alberto Piazza, *The History and Geography of Human Genes* (Princeton, NJ: Princeton University Press, 2004); Lynn Jorde, "Genetic Variation and Human Evolution," American Society of Human Genetics, October 16, 2003, https://www.ashg.org/wp -content/uploads/2019/09/genetic-variation-essay .pdf; Lynn B. Jorde, W. Scott Watkins, Michael J. Bamshad, Mary E. Dixon, Chris E. Ricker, Mark T. Seielstad, et al., "The Distribution of Human Genetic Diversity: A Comparison of Mitochondrial, Autosomal, and Y-Chromosome Data," *American Journal of Human Genetics* 66 (2000): 979–88; Richard Lewontin, "Confusions about Human Races," Is Race "Real"? (Web forum), June 7, 2006, http://race andgenomics.ssrc.org/Lewontin/; David Serre and Svante Pääbo, "Evidence for Gradients of Human Genetic Diversity within and among Continents," *Genome Research* 14, no. 9 (2004): 1679–85; and Dalton Conley and Jason Fletcher, *The Genome Factor: What the Social Genomics Revolution Reveals about Ourselves, Our History, and the Future* (Princeton, NJ: Princeton University Press, 2017).

13. American Association of Physical Anthropologists, "AAPA Statement on Biological Aspects of Race," *American Journal of Physical Anthropology*, 101 (1996): 569–70.

14. Matthew Desmond, "In Order to Understand the Brutality of American Capitalism, You Have to Start on the Plantation," *New York Times*, August 14, 2019, https://www.nytimes.com/interactive/2019/08/14/magazine/slavery-capitalism.html.

15. Joane Nagel, *Race, Ethnicity, and Sexuality: Intimate Intersections, Forbidden Frontiers* (New York: Oxford University Press, 2003).

16. Ibid.

17. Yolanda F. Niemman, Leilani Jennings, Richard M. Rozelle, James C. Baxter, and Elroy Sullivan, "Use of Free Responses and Cluster Analysis to Determine Stereotypes of Eight Groups," *Personality and Social Psychology Bulletin* 20 (1994): 379–90; and John Wilson, Kurt Hugenberg, and Nicholas Rule, "Racial Bias in Judgments of Physical Size and Formidability: From Size to Threat," *Journal of Personality and Social Psychology* 113, no. 1 (March 2017): 59–80.

18. Adam D. Galinsky, Erika V. Hall, and Amy J. C. Cuddy, "Gendered Races: Implications for Interracial Marriage, Leadership Selection, and Athletic Participation," *Psychological Science* 24, no. 4 (2013): 498–506.

19. Ann Ferguson, *Bad Boys: Public Schools in the Making of Black Masculinity* (Ann Arbor: University of Michigan Press, 2001); and Walter S. Gilliam, Angela N. Maupin, Chin R. Reyes, Maria Accavitti, and Frederick Shic, "Do Early Educators' Implicit Biases Regarding Sex and Race Relate to Behavior Expectations and Recommendations of Preschool Expulsions and Suspensions?" Yale University Child Study Center, September 28, 2016, https://marylandfamiliesengage.org/wp-content/uploads/2019/07/Preschool-Implicit-Bias-Policy-Brief.pdf.

20. Cristobal de Brey, Lauren Musu, Joel McFarland, Sidney Wilkinson-Flicker, Melissa Diliberti, Anlan Zhang, et al., "Status and Trends in the Education of Racial and Ethnic Groups 2018," US Department of Education (NCES 2019-038), February 2019, https://eric.ed.gov/?id=ED592833.

21. Dawn Dow, "The Deadly Challenges of Raising African American Boys: Navigating the Controlling Image of the 'Thug,'" *Gender & Society* 30, no. 2 (2016): 161–88.

22. Ibid., 87; and Joe R. Feagin, "The Continuing Significance of Race: Antiblack Discrimination in Public Places," *American Sociological Review* 56, no. 1 (Feb., 1991): 101–16.

23. Rashawn Ray, "Black People Don't Exercise in My Neighborhood: Perceived Racial Composition and Leisure-Time Physical Activity among Middle Class Blacks and Whites," *Social Science Research* 66 (2017): 42–57.

24. Brent Staples, "Just Walk on By: A Black Man Ponders His Power to Alter Public Space," in *Reconstructing Gender: A Multicultural Anthology*, 5th ed., Estelle Disch (New York: McGraw Hill, 1997), 204.

25. Odis Johnson Jr., Keon Gilbert, and Habiba Ibrahim, "Race, Gender, and the Contexts of Unarmed Fatal Interactions with Police," Fatal Interactions with Police Study (FIPS), accessed Jan. 7, 2021, https://cpb-us-west-2-juc1ugur1qwqqqo4.stackpathdns.com/sites.wustl.edu/dist/b/1205/files/2018/02/Race-Gender-and-Unarmed-1y6zo9a.pdf; Ryan Gabrielson, Eric Sagara, and Ryan Grochowski Jones, "Deadly Force, in Black and White: A ProPublica Analysis of Killings by Police Shows Outsize Rise for Young Black Males," *ProPublica*, October 10, 2014, www.propublica.org/article/deadly-force-in-black-and-white; David D. Kirkpatrick, Steve Eder, Kim Barker, and Julie Tate, "Why Many Police Traffic Stops Turn Deadly," *New York Times*, October 31, 2021, https://www.nytimes.com/2021/10/31/us/police-traffic-stops-killings.html; Keon L. Gilbert and Rashawn Ray, "Why Police Kill Black Males with Impunity: Applying Public Health Critical Race Praxis (PHCRP) to Address the Determinants of Policing Behaviors and 'Justifiable' Homicides in the USA," *Journal of Urban Health* 9, Suppl. 1 (2016): 122–40; and Frank Edwards, Michael H. Esposito, and Hedwig Lee, "Risk of Police-Involved Death by Race/Ethnicity and Place, United States, 2012–2018," *American Journal of Public Health* 108 (2018): 1241–48.

26. Audra D. S. Burch, Weiyi Cai, Gabriel Gianordoli, Morrigan McCarthy, and Jugal K. Patel, "How Black Lives Matter Reached Every Corner of America," *New York Times*, June 13, 2020, https://www.nytimes.com/interactive/2020/06/13/us/george-floyd-protests-cities-photos.html.

27. Evelynn M. Hammonds, "Toward a Genealogy of Black Female Sexuality: The Problematic of Silence," in *Feminist Genealogies, Colonial Legacies, Democratic Futures*, ed. M. Jacqui Alexander and Chandra Talpade Mohanty (New York: Routledge, 1997), 170–82; Siobhan Somerville, *Queering*

the Color Line: Race and the Invention of Homosexuality in American Culture (Durham, NC: Duke University Press, 2000); Patricia Hill Collins, Black Sexual Politics: African Americans, Gender, and the New Racism (New York: Routledge, 2004); Deborah Gray White, Ar'n't I a Woman? Female Slaves in the Plantation South (New York: W. W. Norton, 1985); Robert Fogel, Without Consent or Contract: The Rise and Fall of American Slavery (New York: W. W. Norton, 1989); and Evelyn Brooks Higginbotham, "African American Women's History and the Metalanguage of Race" Signs 17, no. 2 (1992): 251–74.

28. Tamara Beauboeuf-Lafontant, Behind the Mask of the Strong Black Woman: Voice and the Embodiment of a Costly Performance (Philadelphia: Temple University Press, 2009); Collins, Black Sexual Politics; and bell hooks, Ain't I a Woman: Black Women and Feminism (New York: Routledge, 2015).

29. Bonnie Thornton Dill, "The Dialectics of Black Womanhood," Signs 4, no. 3 (1979): 543–55; and Gregory S. Parks, Shayne E. Jones, Rashawn Ray, Matthew W. Hughey, and Jonathan M. Cox, "White Boys Drink, Black Girls Yell? A Racialized and Gendered Analysis of Violent Hazing and the Law," Journal of Gender, Race, and Justice 18 (2015): 97–168.

30. John F. Dovidio, "Under the Radar: How Unexamined Biases in Decision-Making Processes in Clinical Interactions Can Contribute to Health Care Disparities," American Journal of Public Health 102, no. 5 (2012): 945–52; Elizabeth N. Chapman, Anna Kaatz, and Molly Carnes, "Physicians and Implicit Bias: How Doctors May Unwittingly Perpetuate Health Care Disparities," Journal of General Internal Medicine 28, no. 11 (2013): 1504–10; and Joe Feagin and Zinobia Bennefield, "Systemic Racism and U.S. Health Care," Social Science & Medicine 103 (2014): 7–14.

31. Lily D. McNair and Helen Neville, "African American Women Survivors of Sexual Assault: The Intersection of Race and Class," Women & Therapy 18, nos. 3–4 (1996): 107–18.

32. Monique W. Morris, Pushout: The Criminalization of Black Girls in Schools (New York: New Press, 2016).

33. Johnson, Gilbert, and Ibrahim, "Race, Gender, and the Contexts."

34. Kimberlé Williams Crenshaw and Andrea J. Ritchie, "Say Her Name: Resisting Police Brutality against Black Women" (New York: African American Policy Forum, 2015); and "Violence against the Transgender Community in 2017," Human Rights Campaign, 2018, accessed Jan. 7, 2021, https://www.hrc.org/resources/violence-against-the-transgender-community-in-2017.

35. Drucilla Cornell, "Las Grenudas: Recollections on Consciousness-Raising," Signs 25, no. 4 (2000): 1033–39; Collins, Black Sexual Politics; Charisse Jones and Kumea Shorter-Gooden, Shifting: The Double Lives of Black Women in America (New York: HarperCollins, 2003).

36. Shannon Malone Gonzalez, "Black Girls and the Talk? Policing, Parenting, and the Politics of Protection," Social Problems, September 8, 2020, https://doi.org/10.1093/socpro/spaa032.

37. Kim Parker, Juliana Menasce Horowitz, and Renee Stepler, "On Gender Differences, No Consensus on Nature vs. Nurture," Pew Research Center, December 5, 2017, https://www.pewresearch.org/social-trends/2017/12/05/on-gender-differences-no-consensus-on-nature-vs-nurture/; Elizabeth R. Cole and Alyssa N. Zuckerman, "Black and White Women's Perspectives on Femininity," Cultural Diversity and Ethnic Minority Psychology 13, no. 1 (2007): 1–9; and Roxanne Angela Donovan and Michelle Williams, "Living at the Intersection: The Effects of Racism and Sexism on Black Rape Survivors," Women & Therapy 25, nos. 3–4 (2002): 95–105.

38. Hannah Eko, "As a Black Woman, I'm Tired of Having to Prove My Womanhood," Buzzfeed News, February 27, 2018, https://www.buzzfeed.com/hannaheko/aint-i-a-woman.

39. Ingrid Banks, Hair Matters: Beauty, Power, and Black Women's Consciousness (New York: New York University Press, 2000): 45.

40. Niemman et al., "Use of Free Responses and Cluster Analysis," 379–90; and Galinsky, Hall, and Cuddy, "Gendered Races," 498–506.

41. Robert Lee, Orientals: Asian Americans in Popular Culture (Philadelphia: Temple University Press, 1999).

42. Anthony Chen, "Lives at the Center of the Periphery, Lives at the Periphery of the Center: Chinese American Masculinities and Bargaining with Hegemony," Gender & Society 13, no. 5 (1999): 584–607.

43. Karen Eng, "The Yellow Fever Pages," Bitch 12 (Summer 2000): 68–73, 69.

44. Ibid., 70.

45. Karen D. Pyke and Denise L. Johnson, "Asian American Women and Racialized Femininities:

'Doing' Gender across Cultural Worlds," *Gender & Society* 17, no. 1 (2003): 33–53, 46.

46. Ibid., 45.

47. Ronald Takaki, *Strangers from a Different Shore* (New York: Little, Brown, 1998).

48. Yen Le Espiritu, "'We Don't Sleep around like White Girls Do'": Family, Culture, and Gender in Filipina American Lives," *Signs* 26, no. 2 (2001): 415–40.

49. Amy Wilkins, *Wannabes, Goths, and Christians: The Boundaries of Sex, Style, and Status* (Chicago: University of Chicago Press, 2008), 52.

50. Ibid.

51. Maya Strong, "Every Day I Dress Up like a Girl," *Human Parts* (blog), February 13, 2019, https://humanparts.medium.com/its-easier-to-stay-in-a-closet-filled-with-girly-clothes-ccccf5081506.

52. Gerard Wright, "Gay Grief in Cowboy Country," *Guardian*, March 27, 1999, https://www.guardian.co.uk/books/1999/mar/27/books.guardianreview7?INTCMP=SRCH. See also Tony Silva, "Bud Sex: Constructing Normative Masculinity among Rural Straight Men That Have Sex with Men," *Gender & Society* 31, no. 1 (2016): 51–73; and Tony Silva, "Helpin' a Buddy Out": Perceptions of Identity and Behavior among Rural Straight Men That Have Sex with Each Other," *Sexualities* 21, nos. 1–2 (2017): 68–89.

53. Michelle A. Marzullo and Alyn J. Libman, "Hate Crimes and Violence against LGBTQ People," (Washington, DC: Human Rights Campaign Foundation, 2009); and Ilan H. Meyer, "Gender Nonconformity as a Target of Prejudice, Discrimination, and Violence against LGB Individuals," *Journal of LGBT Health Research* 3, no. 3 (2007): 55–71.

54. Laura Hamilton, "Trading on Heterosexuality: College Women's Gender Strategies and Homophobia," *Gender & Society* 21, no. 2 (2007): 145–72, 156.

55. Anthony Ocampo, "Making Masculinity: Negotiations of Gender Presentation among Latino Gay Men," *Latino Studies* 10, no. 4 (2012): 448–72, 465.

56. Nathan Shae Rodriguez, Jennifer Huemmer, and Lindsey Blumell, "Mobile Masculinities: An Investigation of Networked Masculinities in Gay Dating Apps," *Masculinities and Social Change* 5, no. 3 (2016), 241–67; and Brandon Miller, "Textually Presenting Masculinity and the Body on Mobile Dating Apps for Men Who Have Sex with Men," *Journal of Men's Studies* 26, no. 3 (2018): 305–26.

57. Kirsten Dellinger and Christine Williams, "Makeup at Work: Negotiating Appearance Rules in the Workplace," *Gender & Society* 11, no. 2 (1997): 162.

58. Michael Price, "Rugby as a Gay Men's Game" (PhD diss., University of Warwick, Coventry, UK, 2000).

59. Jennifer Taub, "Bisexual Women and Beauty Norms: A Qualitative Examination," in *Lesbians, Levis and Lipstick: The Meaning of Beauty in Our Lives*, ed. Joanie Erickson and Jeanine Cogan, Haworth Gay and Lesbian Studies (New York: Routledge, 1999), 27–36.

60. Lisa Duggan, *The Twilight of Equality? Neoliberalism, Cultural Politics, and the Attack on Democracy* (Boston: Beacon Press, 2003); and Mignon R. Moore, "Lipstick or Timberlands? Meanings of Gender Presentation in Black Lesbian Communities," *Signs* 32, no. 1 (2006): 113–39.

61. Taub, "Bisexual Women and Beauty Norms," 31.

62. Julie E. Hartman, "Creating a Bisexual Display: Making Bisexuality Visible," *Journal of Bisexuality* 13, no. 1 (2013): 39–62.

63. Mignon Moore, *Invisible Families: Gay Identities, Relationships, and Motherhood among Black Women* (Berkeley: University of California Press, 2011).

64. JeeYeun Lee, "Why Suzie Wong Is Not a Lesbian: Asian and Asian American Lesbian and Bisexual Women and Femme/Butch/Gender Identities," in *Queer Studies: A Lesbian, Gay, Bisexual and Transgender Anthology*, ed. Brett Beemyn and Mickey Eliason (New York: New York University Press, 1996), 123. See also Rosalind Chou, *Asian-American Sexual Politics: The Construction of Race, Gender and Sexuality* (New York: Rowman & Littlefield, 2021).

65. Collins, *Black Feminist Thought*.

66. Michael Stambolis-Ruhstorfer, "Labels of Love: How Migrants Negotiate (or Not) the Culture of Sexual Identity," *American Journal of Cultural Sociology* 1, no. 3 (2013): 321–45.

67. Ibid., 331.

68. Lesley Doyal, Sara Paparini, and Jane Anderson, "'Elvis Died and I Was Born': Black African Men Negotiating Same-Sex Desire in London," *Sexualities* 11, nos. 1–2 (2008): 171–92.

69. Ibid., 179–80.

70. Yen Le Espiritu, *Asian American Panethnicity: Bridging Institutions and Identities* (Philadelphia:

Temple University Press, 1992); Leah Schmalzbauer, "'Doing Gender,' Ensuring Survival: Mexican Migration and Economic Crisis in the Rural Mountain West," *Rural Sociology* 76, no. 4 (2011): 441–60; Lan Anh Hoang and Brenda Yeoh, "Breadwinning Wives and 'Left-Behind' Husbands: Men and Masculinities in the Vietnamese Transnational Family," *Gender & Society* 25, no. 6 (2011): 717–39; Deborah A. Boehm, "Intimate Migrations: Gender, Family, and Illegality among Transnational Mexicans" (New York: New York University Press: 2012); Hung Cam Thai, *For Better or for Worse: Vietnamese International Marriages in the New Global Economy* (New Brunswick, NJ: Rutgers University Press, 2008); Suzanne Y. P. Choi and Yinni Peng, *Masculine Compromise: Migration, Family, and Gender in China* (Berkeley: University of California Press, 2016).

71. Leisy Abrego and Ralph LaRossa, "Economic Well-Being in Salvadoran Transnational Families: How Gender Affects Remittance Practices," *Journal of Marriage and Family* 71, no. 4 (2009): 1070–85; and Anju Mary Paul, "Negotiating Migration, Performing Gender," *Social Forces* 94, no. 1 (2015): 271–93.

72. Deborah A. Boehm, "'Now I Am a Man *and* a Woman!' Gendered Moves and Migrations in a Transnational Mexican Community," *Latin American Perspectives* 35, no. 1 (2008): 16–30, 16.

73. Pierrette Hondagneu-Sotelo, "Overcoming Patriarchial Constraints: The Reconstruction of Gender Relations among Mexican Immigrant Women and Men," *Gender & Society* 6, no. 3 (1992): 393–415, 408.

74. Cecilia Menjivar, "The Intersection of Work and Gender: Central American Immigrant Women and Employment in California," *American Behavioral Scientist* 42, no. 4 (1999): 601–27, 609.

75. Ibid., 616.

76. Kris Paap, *Working Construction: Why White Working-Class Men Put Themselves—and the Labor Movement—in Harm's Way* (Ithaca, NY: IRL Press, 2006).

77. Ibid., 137.

78. Jo Little, *Gender and Rural Geography: Identity, Sexuality and Power in the Countryside* (London: Pearson, 2002); Jo Little and Ruth Panelli, "Gender Research in Rural Geography," *Gender, Place, and Culture* 10, no. 3 (2003): 281–89; Emily Kazyak, "Midwest or Lesbian? Gender, Rurality, and Sexuality," *Gender & Society* 26, no. 6 (2012): 825–48; Barbara Pini, "Farm Women: Driving Trac-

tors and Negotiating Gender," *International Journal of Sociology of Agriculture and Food* 13, no. 1 (2005): 1–18.

79. Kazyak, "Midwest or Lesbian?," 837.

80. Ibid.

81. Arlie Hochschild, *The Time Bind: When Work Becomes Home and Home Becomes Work* (New York: Metropolitan Books, 1997).

82. Ibid., 59.

83. Arlie Hochschild, *The Second Shift* (New York: Viking, 1989).

84. Thomas Gerschick and Adam Miller, "Coming to Terms: Masculinity and Physical Disability," in *Men's Health and Illness: Gender, Power, and the Body*, ed. Donald Sabo and David Frederick Gordon (Thousand Oaks, CA: Sage, 1995), 192.

85. Ibid.

86. R. Noam Ostrander, "When Identities Collide: Masculinity, Disability, and Race," *Disability & Society* 23, no. 6 (2008): 585–97.

87. Ibid., 594.

88. Gerschick and Miller, "Coming to Terms," 192.

89. Ingunn Moser, "Sociotechnical Practices and Difference: On the Interferences between Disability, Gender, and Class," *Science, Technology, and Human Values* 31, no. 5 (2006): 537–64.

90. Ibid., 538.

91. Tom Shakespeare, Kath Gillespie-Sells, and Dominic Davies, *The Sexual Politics of Disability: Untold Desires* (London: Cassell, 1996).

92. Ibid., 10.

93. Michelle Fine and Adrienne Asch, *Women with Disabilities: Essays in Psychology, Culture and Politics* (Philadelphia: Temple University Press, 1988), 29. See also Nancy A. Naples, Laura Mauldin, and Heather Dillaway, "From the Guest Editors: Gender, Disability, and Intersectionality," in "Gender, Disability, and Intersectionality," ed. Nancy A. Naples, Laura Mauldin, and Heather Dillaway, special issue, *Gender and Society* 33, no. 1 (2019): 5–18.

94. Harilyn Rousso, "Daughters with Disabilities: Defective Women or Minority Women?" in *Women with Disabilities: Essays in Psychology, Culture and Politics*, ed. Michelle Fine and Adrienne Asch (Philadelphia: Temple University Press, 1988), 139–71.

95. Nasa Begum, "Disabled Women and the Feminist Agenda," *Feminist Review* 40 (1992): 70–84.

96. Deborah Lisi, "Found Voices: Women, Disability and Cultural Transformation," *Women & Therapy* 14, nos. 3/4 (1994): 195–209.

97. Ibid.

98. Cheryl Laz, "Act Your Age," *Sociological Forum* 13, no. 1 (1998): 85–113.

99. Ibid., 86.

100. Barbro Johanssen, "Doing Age and Gender through Fashion," in *INTER: A European Cultural Studies Conference in Sweden, 11–13 June 2007*, ed. Johan Fornäs and Martin Fredriksson (Linköping, Sweden: Linköping University Electronic Press), 283–90, 285, ww.ep.liu.se/ecp/025/029/ecp072529.pdf.

101. Ibid.

102. Juliet Jacques, "What Sort of Woman Do I Want to Be?" *Guardian*, February 9, 2011, https://www.theguardian.com/lifeandstyle/2011/feb/09/transgender-women-femininity.

103. R. N. Butler, "Ageism: Another Form of Bigotry," *Gerontologist* 9 (1969): 243–46.

104. Susan Sontag, "The Double Standard of Aging," *Saturday Review*, September 23, 1972, 29–38.

105. Ibid., 36.

106. Ibid., 36.

107. Duncan Kennedy, *Sexy Dressing, Etc.: Essays on the Power and Politics of Cultural Identity* (Cambridge: Harvard University Press, 1993), 164.

108. Elizabeth A. Pascoe and Laura Smart Richman, "Perceived Discrimination and Health: A Meta-Analytic Review," *Psychological Bulletin* 135, no. 4 (2009): 531–54; NiCole R. Keith, Kimberly A. Hemmerlein, and Daniel O. Clark, "Weight Loss Attitudes and Social Forces in Urban Poor Black and White Women," *American Journal of Health Behavior* 39, no. 1 (2015): 34; and Ray, "Black People Don't Exercise in My Neighborhood," 42–57.

Chapter 5: Inequality: Masculinities

1. William Shakespeare, *Hamlet*, ed. Robert S. Miola (New York: W. W. Norton, 2019), 2.2.265.

2. Andrea Waling, " 'We Are So Pumped Full of Shit by the Media': Masculinity, Magazines, and the Lack of Self-Identification," *Men and Masculinities* 20, no. 4 (2016): 427–52, 44.

3. Quoted in Natalie Adams and Pamela Bettis, "Commanding the Room in Short Skirts: Cheering as the Embodiment of Ideal Girlhood," *Gender & Society* 17, no. 1 (2003): 73–91, 76.

4. Mary Ellen Hanson, *Go! Fight! Win! Cheerleading in American Culture* (Bowling Green, OH: Bowling Green State University Popular Press, 1995), 2.

5. Rebecca Boyce, "Cheerleading in the Context of Title IX and Gendering in Sport," *Sports Journal* 11, no. 3 (2008), https://thesportjournal.org/article/cheerleading-in-the-context-of-title-ix-and-gendering-in-sport/.

6. Hanson, *Go! Fight! Win!*, 17.

7. Quoted in Laurel Davis, "A Postmodern Paradox? Cheerleaders at Women's Sporting Events," in *Women, Sport, and Culture*, ed. Susan Birrell and Cheryl Cole (Champaign, IL: Human Kinetics Press, 1994), 149–58, 153.

8. Hanson, *Go! Fight! Win!*, 16.

9. James McElroy, *We've Got Spirit: The Life and Times of America's Greatest Cheerleading Team* (New York: Simon & Schuster, 1999), 15.

10. Ibid., 2–3.

11. Pamela Paxton, Sheri Kunovich, and Melanie Hughes, "Gender in Politics," *Annual Review of Sociology* 33 (2007): 263–84; and Law Library of Congress, State Suffrage Laws, https://guides.loc.gov/american-women-law/state-laws.

12. Jennifer R. Lambdin, Kristen M. Greer, Kari Selby Jibotian, Kelly Rice Wood, and Mykol C. Hamilton, "The Animal = Male Hypothesis: Children's and Adults' Beliefs about the Sex of Non-Sex-Specific Stuffed Animals," *Sex Roles* 48 (2003): 471–82.

13. Mary Beard, *Women and Power: A Manifesto* (New York: W. W. Norton, 2017).

14. *Thesaurus.com*, s.v. "power," accessed January 29, 2022, https://www.thesaurus.com/browse/power?s=t.

15. *Thesaurus.com*, s.v. "femininity," accessed January 29, 2022, https://www.thesaurus.com/browse/femininity?s=t.

16. Joan Wallace Scott, *Gender and the Politics of History* (New York: Columbia University Press, 1999), 44.

17. Karen Ross, *Gendered Media: Women, Men, and Identity Politics* (Lanham, MD: Rowman & Littlefield, 2010); and Rosalind Gill, *Gender and the Media* (Malden, MA: Polity Press, 2007).

18. Amanda Shendruk, "Analyzing the Gender Representation of 34,476 Comic Book Characters," *Pudding*, accessed January 29, 2022, https://pudding.cool/2017/07/comics/.

19. Janet Swim, Eugene Borgida, Geoffrey Maruyama, and David G. Myers, "Joan McKay versus John McKay: Do Gender Stereotypes Bias Evaluations?" *Psychological Bulletin* 105, no. 3 (1989): 409–29; and Pamela Paxton, Sheri Kunovich, and Melanie Hughes, "Gender in Politics," *Annual Review of Sociology* 33 (2007): 263–84.

20. Corinne Moss-Racusin, John F. Dovidio, Victoria L. Brescoll, Mark J. Graham, and Jo Handelsman, "Science Faculty's Subtle Gender Biases Favor Male Students," *Proceedings of the National Academy of Sciences* 109, no. 41 (2012): 16474–79.

21. Swim et al., "Joan McKay versus John McKay," 409–29.

22. Stanley Lieberson, Susan Dumais, and Shyon Baumann, "The Instability of Androgynous Names: The Symbolic Maintenance of Gender Boundaries," *American Journal of Sociology* 105, no. 5 (2000): 1249–87.

23. "Leslie," NameTrends.net, accessed January 29, 2022, https://nametrends.net/name.php?name=Leslie.

24. US Bureau of Labor Statistics, *Women in the Labor Force: A Databook*, BLS Reports, April 2021, https://www.bls.gov/opub/reports/womens-databook/2020/home.htm.

25. US Bureau of Labor Statistics, "Labor Force Statistics from the Current Population Survey," Table 11, "Employed Persons by Detailed Occupation and Sex, and Hispanic or Latino Ethnicity," BLS, accessed March 14, 2022, https://www.bls.gov/cps/cpsaat11.htm.

26. Patricia Yancey Martin, "'Said and Done' versus 'Saying and Doing'—Gendering Practices, Practicing Gender at Work," *Gender & Society* 17, no. 3 (2003): 342–66; Rosabeth Moss Kanter, *Men and Women of the Corporation* (New York: Basic Books, 1993); Joan C. Williams and Rachel Dempsey, *What Works for Women at Work: Four Patterns Working Women Need to Know* (New York: New York University Press, 2014); and Deborah L. Kidder, "The Influence of Gender on the Performance of Organizational Citizenship Behaviors," *Journal of Management* 28, no. 5 (2002): 629–48.

27. Martin, "'Said and Done' versus 'Saying and Doing,'" 342–66.

28. Emily Kane, "'No Way My Boys Are Going to Be Like That!' Parents' Responses to Children's Gender Nonconformity," *Gender & Society* 20, no. 2 (2006): 149–76.

29. Julia Menasce Horowitz, "Most Americans See Value in Steering Children toward Toys, Activities Associated with Opposite Gender," Pew Research Center, December 19, 2017, https://www.pewresearch.org/fact-tank/2017/12/19/most-americans-see-value-in-steering-children-toward-toys-activities-associated-with-opposite-gender/.

30. C. J. Pascoe, *Dude, You're a Fag* (Berkeley: University of California Press, 2011); E. Anderson, "'Being Masculine Is Not about Who You Sleep With . . .': Heterosexual Athletes Contesting Masculinity and the One-Time Rule of Homosexuality," *Sex Roles: A Journal of Research* 58, nos. 1–2 (2008): 104–15; and Tristan Bridges, "A Very 'Gay' Straight? Hybrid Masculinities, Sexual Aesthetics, and the Changing Relationship between Masculinity and Homophobia," *Gender & Society* 28, no. 1 (2014): 58–82.

31. Eric Anderson, "Open Gay Athletes: Contesting Hegemonic Masculinity in a Homophobic Environment," *Gender & Society* 16, no. 6 (2002): 860–77, 872.

32. Ibid.

33. Kim Parker, Juliana Menasce Horowitz, and Renee Stepler, "On Gender Differences, No Consensus on Nature vs. Nurture," Pew Research Center, December 5, 2017, https://www.pewsocialtrends.org/2017/12/05/on-gender-differences-no-consensus-on-nature-vs-nurture/.

34. Ibid.

35. Paula England and Su Li, "Desegregation Stalled: The Changing Gender Composition of College Majors, 1971–2002," *Gender & Society* 20, no. 5 (2006): 657–77.

36. Anne Lincoln, "The Shifting Supply of Men and Women to Occupation: Feminization in Veterinary Education," *Social Forces* 88, no. 5 (2010): 1969–98.

37. Jack Kahn, Benjamin Brett, and Jessica Holmes, "Concerns with Men's Academic Motivation in Higher Education: An Exploratory Investigation of the Role of Masculinity," *Journal of Men's Studies* 19, no. 1 (2011): 65–82.

38. Richard V. Reeves and Ember Smith, "The Male College Crisis Is Not Just in Enrollment, but Completion," Brookings, October 8, 2021, https://www.brookings.edu/blog/up-front/2021/10/08/the-male-college-crisis-is-not-just-in-enrollment-but-completion/.

39. Robert Stillwell and Jennifer Sable, "Public School Graduates and Dropouts from the Common Core of Data: School Year 2009–10: First Look (Provisional Data)" (NCES 2013-309rev, Washington, DC, National Center for Education Statistics), US

Department of Education, January 2013, https://nces.ed.gov/pubs2013/2013309rev.pdf; and Office for Civil Rights, "Gender Equity in Education: A Data Snapshot," US Department of Education, June 2012, https://www2.ed.gov/about/offices/list/ocr/docs/gender-equity-in-education.pdf.

40. "2016 College-Bound Seniors: Total Group Profile Report," College Board, https://reports.collegeboard.org/pdf/total-group-2016.pdf.

41. "Overview: Spring 2021 Enrollment Estimates," National Student Clearinghouse Research Center, Spring 2021, https://nscresearchcenter.org/wp-content/uploads/CTEE_Report_Spring_2021.pdf.

42. R. W. Connell, *Gender and Power: Society, the Person, and Sexual Politics* (Stanford, CA: Stanford University Press, 1987); and R. W. Connell and James Messerschmidt, "Hegemonic Masculinity: Rethinking the Concept," *Gender & Society* 19, no. 6 (2005): 829–59.

43. Peter Glick, Maria Lameiras, Susan T. Fiske, Thomas Eckes, Barbara Masser, Chiara Volpato, et al., "Bad but Bold: Ambivalent Attitudes toward Men Predict Gender Inequality in 16 Nations," *Journal of Personality and Social Psychology* 86, no. 5 (2004): 713–28.

44. "Men Will Never . . . Clean without Being Asked 'because It Sucks,'" *MetaFilter* (blog), May 16, 2013, https:///www.metafilter.com/128141/Men-will-never-clean-without-being-asked-because-it-sucks.

45. Elliot Liebow, Jessie S. Bernard, Philip M. Hauser, Preston Valien, Reynolds Farley, Edwin D. Driver, Paul R. Williams, et al. "Attitudes toward Marriage and Family among Black Males in Tally's Corner." *The Milbank Memorial Fund Quarterly* 48, no. 2 (1970): 151–80.

46. Lisa Wade crowdsourced this phrase on social media. Thanks to the whole team, especially Scott Knickelbine and Damian Tatum, who dropped "exculpatory" and "chauvinism," respectively, and Jay Livingston, who recommended Elliot Liebow's "theory of manly flaws" in *Tally's Corner: A Study of Negro Streetcorner Men, Legacies of Social Thought Series* (Lanham, MD: Rowman & Littlefield, 2003).

47. Glick et al., "Bad but Bold," 713.

48. Lily Liang, "Raising Upper-Middle-Class Children in China" (PhD diss., University of Wisconsin–Madison, 2020).

49. Sarah Grogan and Helen Richards, "Body Image: Focus Groups with Boys and Men," *Men and Masculinities* 4, no. 3 (2002): 219–32; Marissa E. Wagner Oehlhof, Dara R. Musher-Eizenman, Jennie M. Neufeld, Jessica C. Hauser, "Self-Objectification and Ideal Body Shape for Men and Women," *Body Image* 6, no. 4 (2009): 308–10; John F. Morgan, "Body Image in Gay and Straight Men: A Qualitative Study," *European Eating Disorders Review* 17, no. 6 (2009): 435–43; Marika Tiggemann, "Sociocultural Perspectives on Human Appearance and Body Image," in *Body Image: A Handbook of Science, Practice, and Prevention*, ed. Thomas F. Cash and Linda Smolak (New York: Guilford Press, 2011), 12–19; and Sarah Grogan, *Body Image: Understanding Body Dissatisfaction in Men, Women and Children* (New York: Routledge, 2016).

50. Shamus Rahman Khan, *Privilege: The Making of an Adolescent Elite at St. Paul's School* (Princeton, NJ: Princeton University Press, 2012); and Tiggemann, "Sociocultural Perspectives on Human Appearance and Body Image," 12–19.

51. Melanie A. Morrison, Todd G. Morrison, and Cheryl-Lee Sager, "Does Body Satisfaction Differ between Gay Men and Lesbian Women and Heterosexual Men and Women? A Meta-Analytic Review," *Body Image* 1, no. 2 (2004): 127–38.

52. Jay Prosser, *Second Skins: The Body Narratives of Transsexuality* (New York: Columbia University Press, 1998); and Jack Halberstam, *Trans*: A Quick and Quirky Account of Gender Variability* (Berkeley: University of California Press, 2018).

53. Torkild Thanem, "Embodying Transgender in Studies of Gender, Work, and Organization," in Emma L. Jeanes, David Knights, and Patricia Yancy Martin, eds., *Handbook of Gender, Work & Organization* (London: Wiley, 2011): 191–204; and T. J. Jourian, "Trans*forming College Masculinities: Carving Out Trans*masculine Pathways through the Threshold of Dominance," *International Journal of Qualitative Studies in Education* 30, no. 3 (2017): 245–65.

54. Raewyn W. Connell, *Masculinities*, 2nd ed. (Berkeley: University of California Press, 2005); Baker A. Rogers, "Trans Manhood: The Intersections of Masculinities, Queerness, and the South," *Men and Masculinities* 25, no. 1 (May 2020): 24–42; Megan Y. Phillips, "'That's a Man': How Trans Men in the South Bolster Their Claims to Manhood" (master's thesis, Georgia Southern University, Spring 2020), Digital Commons@Georgia Southern, https://digitalcommons.georgiasouthern.edu/etd/2045.

55. Emma Jeanes and Kirsty Janes, "Trans Men Doing Gender at Work," *Gender, Work & Organization* 28, no. 4 (2021): 1237–59.

56. Kristin Schilt and Catherine Connell, "Do Workplace Gender Transitions Make Gender Trouble?" *Gender, Work & Organization* 14, no. 6 (2007): 596–618.

57. Rogers, "Trans Manhood"; Tat Bellamy-Walker, "Not Manly Enough: Femmephobia's Stinging Impact on the Transmasculine Community" (master's thesis, City University of New York, December 13, 2019), CUNY Academic Works, https://academicworks.cuny.edu/gj_etds/411/.

58. Kristin Schilt, "Just One of the Guys?" *Gender & Society* 20, no. 4 (2006): 465–90; Miriam J. Abelson, "Dangerous Privilege: Trans Men, Masculinities, and Changing Perceptions of Safety," *Sociological Forum* 29, no. 3 (2014): 549–70; and Stephen Whittle, Lewis Turner, and Maryam Al-Alami, *Engendered Penalties: Transgender and Transsexual People's Experiences of Inequality and Discrimination*, Equalities Review, February 2007, https://www.researchgate.net/publication/265032393_Engendered_Penalties_Transgender_and_Transsexual_People%27s_Experiences_of_Inequality_and_Discrimination.

59. Waling, "'We Are So Pumped Full of Shit by the Media,'" 444.

60. Erving Goffman, *Stigma* (Englewood Cliffs, NJ: Prentice Hall, 1963).

61. Michael Kaufman, "Men, Feminism, and Men's Contradictory Experiences of Power," in *Theorizing Masculinities*, ed. Harry Brod and Michael Kaufman, Sage Series on Men and Masculinity (Newbury Park: Sage, 1994), 142–65, 148.

62. Ibid.

63. David Gal and James Wilkie, "Real Men Don't Eat Quiche: Regulation of Gender-Expressive Choices by Men," *Social Psychological and Personality Science* 1, no. 4 (2010): 291–301.

64. Joseph A. Vandello and Jennifer K. Bosson, "Hard Won and Easily Lost: A Review and Synthesis of Theory and Research on Precarious Manhood," *Psychology of Men & Masculinity* 14, no. 2 (2013): 101–13.

65. Jonathan R. Weaver, Joseph A. Vandello, Jennifer K. Bosson, and Rochelle M. Burnaford, "The Proof Is in the Punch: Gender Differences in Perceptions of Action and Aggression as Components of Manhood," *Sex Roles* 62, no. 3 (2010): 241–51.

66. Jennifer K. Bosson, Joseph A. Vandello, Rochelle M. Burnaford, Jonathan R. Weaver, and S. Arzu Wasti, "The Links between Precarious Manhood and Physical Aggression," *Personality and Social Psychology Bulletin* 35 (2009): 623–34.

67. Deborah Bach, "Manning Up: Men May Overcompensate when Their Masculinity Is Threatened," *UW News*, June 22, 2015, www.washington.edu/news/2015/06/22/manning-up-men-may-overcompensate-when-their-masculinity-is-threatened/; Robb Willer, Christabel L. Rogalin, Bridget Conlon, and Michael T. Wojnowicz, "Overdoing Gender: A Test of the Masculine Overcompensation Thesis," *American Journal of Sociology* 118, no. 4 (2013): 980–1022; Phillip Atiba Goff, Brooke Allison Lewis Di Leone, and Kimberly Barsamian Kahn, "Racism Leads to Pushups: How Racial Discrimination Threatens Subordinate Men's Masculinity," *Journal of Experimental Social Psychology* 48, no. 5 (2012): 1111–16; and Sherilyn MacGregor, *Routledge Handbook of Gender and Environment* (New York: Routledge, 2017).

68. Natasza Kosakowska-Berezecka, Tomasz Besta, Krystyna Adamska, Michał Jaśkiewicz, Paweł Jurek, and Joseph A. Vandello, "If My Masculinity Is Threatened I Won't Support Gender Equality? The Role of Agentic Self-Stereotyping in Restoration of Manhood and Perception of Gender Relations, *Psychology of Men & Masculinity* 17, no. 3 (2016): 274–84; Willer, Rogalin, Conlon, and Wojnowicz, "Overdoing Gender," 980–1022; Christin L. Munsch and Robb Willer, "The Role of Gender Identity Threat in Perceptions of Date Rape and Sexual Coercion," *Violence Women* 18, no. 10 (2012): 1125–46; Michael Schwalbe, *Manhood Acts: Gender and the Practices of Domination* (New York: Routledge, 2014); and Christin L. Munsch, "Her Support, His Support: Money, Masculinity, and Marital Infidelity," *American Sociological Review* 80, no. 3 (2015): 469–95.

69. Carl A. Kallgren, Raymond R. Reno, and Robert B. Cialdini, "A Focus Theory of Normative Conduct: When Norms Do and Do Not Affect Behavior," *Personality and Social Psychology Bulletin* 26, no. 8 (2000): 1002–12; Lynnette C. Zelezny, Poh-Pheng Chua, and Christina Aldrich, "New Ways of Thinking about Environmentalism: Elaborating on Gender Differences in Environmentalism," *Journal of Social Issues* 56, no. 3 (2002): 443–57; Riitta Räty and Annika Carlsson-Kanyama, "Energy Consumption by Gender in Some European Countries," *Energy Policy* 38, no. 1 (2010): 646–49; Jessica Greenebaum and Brandon Dexter, "Vegan Men and Hybrid Masculinity," *Journal of Gender Studies* 27, no. 6 (2017): 637–48; and Aaron R. Brough, James E. B. Wilkie, Jingjing Ma, Mathew S. Isaac, and David Gal, "Is

Eco-Friendly Unmanly? The Green-Feminine Stereotype and Its Effect on Sustainable Consumption," *Journal of Consumer Research* 43, no. 4 (2016): 567–82.

70. Keith Edwards and Susan Jones, "'Putting My Man Face On': A Grounded Theory of College Men's Gender Identity Development," *Journal of College Student Development* 50, no. 2 (2009): 210–28, 216.

71. Ibid., 219.

72. Ibid., 218.

73. Thomas B. Edsall, "'It's Become Increasingly Hard for Them to Feel Good about Themselves,'" *New York Times*, September 22, 2021, https://www.nytimes.com/2021/09/22/opinion/economy-education-women-men.html.

74. Michael J. Sandel, *The Tyranny of Merit: What's Become of the Common Good?* (New York: Farrar, Straus & Giroux, 2020). See, among other reviews, Julian Coman, "Michael Sandel: 'The Populist Backlash Has Been a Revolt against the Tyranny of Merit,'" *Guardian*, September 6, 2020, https://www.theguardian.com/books/2020/sep/06/michael-sandel-the-populist-backlash-has-been-a-revolt-against-the-tyranny-of-merit; and Michèle Lamont, *The Dignity of Working Men: Morality and the Boundaries of Race, Class, and Immigration* (Cambridge, MA: Harvard University Press, 2002).

75. Douglas Schrock and Michael Schwalbe, "Men, Masculinity, and Manhood Acts," *Annual Review of Sociology* 35 (2009): 277–95.

76. Emine Fidan Elcioglu, *Divided by the Wall: Progressive and Conservative Politics at the US-Mexico Border* (Oakland: University of California Press, 2020).

77. Judith Kegan Gardiner, "Masculinity, the Teening of America, and Empathic Targeting," *Signs* 25, no. 4 (2000): 1257–61.

78. Jeffrey Hall, "Sex Differences in Friendship Expectations: A Meta-Analysis," *Journal of Social and Personal Relationships* 28, no. 6 (2011): 723–47; Geoffrey Greif, *Buddy System: Understanding Male Friendships* (New York: Oxford University Press, 2008); and Peggy Orenstein, *Boys and Sex: Young Men on Hookups, Love, Porn, Consent, and Navigating the New Masculinity* (New York: Harper, 2020).

79. Niobe Way, *Deep Secrets* (Cambridge, MA: Harvard University Press, 2011), 2.

80. Miller McPherson, Lynn Smith-Lovin, and Matthew Brashears, "Social Isolation in America: Changes in Core Discussion Networks over Two Decades," *American Sociological Review* 71, no. 3 (2006): 353–75.

81. Lillian Rubin, *Just Friends: The Role of Friendship in Our Lives* (New York: Harper & Row, 1985); Gale Berkowitz, "UCLA Study on Friendship among Women: An Alternative to Fight or Flight," *Melissa Kaplan's Chronic Neuroimmune Diseases*, updated January 1, 2014, www.anapsid.org/cnd/gender/tendfend.html; Natasha Raymond, "The Hug Drug," *Psychology Today*, November 1, 1999, www.psychologytoday.com/articles/199911/the-hug-drug; and Tara Parker-Pope, "What Are Friends For? A Longer Life," *New York Times*, April 20, 2009, www.nytimes.com/2009/04/21/health/21well.html?_r=4&.

82. Schrock and Schwalbe, "Men, Masculinity, and Manhood Acts," 277–95; Jen'nan Ghazal Read and Bridget K. Gorman, "Gender and Health Inequality," *Annual Review of Sociology* 36 (2010): 371–86; US Federal Bureau of Investigation, Crime Data Explorer, Arrests in the United States by Offense, accessed December 20, 2021, https://crime-data-explorer.app.cloud.gov/pages/explorer/crime/arrest; James Byrnes, David Miller, and William Schafer, "Gender Differences in Risk Taking: A Meta-Analysis," *Psychological Bulletin* 125, no. 3 (1999): 367–83; and Bryan Denham, "Masculinities in Hardcore Bodybuilding," *Men and Masculinities* 11, no. 2 (2008): 234–42.

83. "Road Traffic Injuries," World Health Organization, June 21, 2021, www.who.int/news-room/fact-sheets/detail/road-traffic-injuries.

84. "Census of Fatal Occupational Injuries," US Bureau of Labor Statistics, accessed September 9, 2021, https://www.bls.gov/iif/oshcfoi1.htm#2019.

85. Deborah B. Reed, Steven R. Browning, Susan C. Westneat, and Pamela S. Kidd, "Personal Protective Equipment Use and Safety Behaviors among Farm Adolescents: Gender Differences and Predictors of Work Practices," *Journal of Rural Health* 22, no. 4 (2006): 314–20.

86. Will Courtenay, "Constructions of Masculinity and Their Influence on Men's Well-Being: A Theory of Gender and Health," *Social Science & Medicine* 50 (2000): 1385–401; and Schrock and Schwalbe, "Men, Masculinity, and Manhood Acts," 277–95.

87. For a review, see Courtenay, "Constructions of Masculinity and Their Influence on Men's Well-Being," 1385–401.

88. Nathan B. Warren and Troy H. Campbell, "The Sleep-Deprived Masculinity Stereotype," *Journal*

of the Association for Consumer Research 6, no. 2 (2021), https://doi.org/10.1086/711758.

89. Ibid.; and "Cancer Facts & Figures 2021," American Cancer Society, accessed Jan. 31, 2022, https://www.cancer.org/content/dam/cancer-org/research/cancer-facts-and-statistics/annual-cancer-facts-and-figures/2021/cancer-facts-and-figures-2021.pdf.

90. Zed Nelson, Love Me (Rome: Contrasto, 2009), www.zednelson.com/?LoveMe:31.

91. Kelly R. Moran and Sara Y. Del Valle, "A Meta-Analysis of the Association between Gender and Protective Behaviors in Response to Respiratory Epidemics and Pandemics," PLOS ONE 11, no. 10 (2016): e0164541, https://doi:10.1371/journal.pone.0164541.

92. Jennifer Steinhauer, "What Do Women Want? For Men to Get Covid Vaccines," New York Times, April 23, 2021, https://www.nytimes.com/2021/04/22/health/covid-vaccines-rates-men-and-women.html.

93. Richard V. Reeves and Beyond Deng, "At least 65,000 More Men than Women Have Died from COVID-19 in the US," Brookings, October 19, 2021, https://www.brookings.edu/blog/up-front/2021/10/19/at-least-65000-more-men-than-women-have-died-from-covid-19-in-the-us/.

94. "Suicide Statistics," American Foundation for Suicide Prevention, accessed January 29, 2022, https://afsp.org/suicide-statistics/; Michael E. Addis, "Gender and Depression in Men," Clinical Psychology: Science and Practice 15, no. 3 (2008): 153–68; and John L. Oliffe and Melanie J. Phillips, "Men, Depression and Masculinities: A Review and Recommendations," Journal of Men's Health 5, no. 3 (2008): 194–202.

95. US Federal Bureau of Investigation, Crime Data Explorer, https://crime-data-explorer.fr.cloud.gov/pages/explorer/crime/crime-trend, accessed December 20, 2021.

96. Mark Follman, Gavin Aronsen, and Deanna Pan, "US Mass Shootings, 1982–2021: Data from Mother Jones' Investigation," Mother Jones, November 20, 2021, https://www.motherjones.com/politics/2012/12/mass-shootings-mother-jones-full-data/.

97. Sarai B. Aharoni and Élise Féron, "National Populism and Gendered Vigilantism: The Case of the Soldiers of Odin in Finland," Cooperation and Conflict 55, no. 1 (2020): 86–106; and Alan Grieg, "Masculinities and the Far Right: Implications for Oxfam's Work on Gender Justice," October 30, 2019, https://www.oxfamamerica.org/explore/research-publications/masculinities-and-the-far-right/.

98. Michael Kimmel, Healing from Hate: How Young Men Get Into—and Out of—Violent Extremism (Berkeley: University of California Press, 2018).

99. Ibid., 10.

100. Ibid.

101. Deniz Kandiyoti, "Bargaining with Patriarchy," Gender & Society 2, no. 3 (1988): 274–90.

102. Michael Messner, "Becoming 100 Percent Straight," in Privilege, ed. Michael Kimmel and Abby Ferber (Boulder, CO: Westview Press, 2003), 184.

103. Kanter, Men and Women of the Corporation; Williams, Dempsey, and Slaughter, What Works for Women at Work; Kidder, "Influence of Gender on the Performance of Organizational Citizenship Behaviors," 629–48; Richard L. Zweigenhaft, "Diversity among Fortune 500 CEOs from 2000 to 2020: White Women, Hi-Tech South Asians, and Economically Privileged Multilingual Immigrants from around the World," Who Rules America, January 2021, https://whorulesamerica.ucsc.edu/power/diversity_update_2020.html.

104. Darrell J. Steffensmeier, Jennifer Schwartz, and Michael Roche, "Gender and Twenty-First-Century Corporate Crime: Female Involvement and the Gender Gap in Enron-Era Corporate Frauds," American Sociological Review 78, no. 3 (2013): 448–76.

105. Yeung King-To, Mindy Stombler, and Renee Wharton, "Making Men in Gay Fraternities: Resisting and Reproducing Multiple Dimensions of Hegemonic Masculinity," Gender & Society 20, no. 1 (2006): 5–31.

106. Ibid., 22.

107. Amanda C. Cote, Gaming Sexism: Gender and Identity in the Era of Casual Video Games (New York: New York University Press, 2020).

108. Lori Kendall, "'Oh No! I'm a Nerd!': Hegemonic Masculinity on an Online Forum," Gender & Society 14, no. 2 (2000): 256–74; and James S. Martin, Christian A. Vaccaro, D. Alex Heckert, and Robert Heasley, "Epic Glory and Manhood Acts in Fantasy Role-Playing Dagorhir as a Case Study," Journal of Men's Studies 23, no. 3 (2015): 293–314.

109. Cote, Gaming Sexism.

110. Michael M. Kasumovi and Jeffrey H. Kuzekoff, "Insights into Sexism: Male Status and Performance Moderates Female-Directed Hostile and Amicable Behaviour," PLOS ONE 10, no. 7 (2015): e0131613.

111. Andrea Braithwaite, "It's About Ethics in Games Journalism? Gamergaters and Geek Masculinity," *Social Media and Society* (October 2016), doi:10.11 77/2056305116672484.

112. Jackson Katz, "8 Reasons Why Eminem's Popularity Is a Disaster for Women," JacksonKatz.com (blog), 2002, www.jacksonkatz.com/pub-eminem2/.

113. Kasumovic and Kuznekoff, "Insights into Sexism"; and Michael Kimmel, *Angry White Men: American Masculinity at the End of an Era* (New York: Nation Books, 2013).

114. Jack Kilbride and Bang Xiao, "China's 'Sissy Pants Phenomenon': Beijing Fears Negative Impact of 'Sickly Culture' on Teenagers," ABC News, September 14, 2018, https://www.abc.net.au/news/2018 -09-15/male-beauty-in-china-does-not-fit-with-push -for-global-influence/10221984; "China's War on 'Sissy Pants' Men," Book of Man, accessed Jan. 29, 2022, https://thebookofman.com/mind/masculinity/mas culinity-in-china/.

115. Demetrakis Demetriou, "Connell's Concept of Hegemonic Masculinity: A Critique," *Theory and Society* 30 (2001): 337–61; and Tristan Bridges and C. J. Pascoe, "Hybrid Masculinities: New Directions in the Sociology of Men and Masculinities," *Sociology Compass* 8, no. 3 (2014): 246–58.

116. Eric Anderson, *Inclusive Masculinity: The Changing Nature of Masculinities* (New York: Routledge, 2009).

117. Michael Messner, "Changing Men' and Feminist Politics in the United States,' *Theory and Society* 22, no. 5 (1993): 723–37.

118. N. Tatiana Masters, "'My Strength Is Not for Hurting': Men's Anti-Rape Websites and Their Construction of Masculinity and Male Sexuality," *Sexualities* 13, no. 1 (2010): 33–46; and Michael Murphy, "Can 'Men' Stop Rape? Visualizing Gender in the 'My Strength Is Not for Hurting' Rape Prevention Campaign," *Men and Masculinities* 12, no. 1 (2009): 113–30.

119. Melanie Heath, "Soft-Boiled Masculinity," *Gender & Society* 17, no. 3 (2003): 423–44.

120. Jocelyn Hollander, "The Roots of Resistance to Women's Self-Defense," *Violence against Women* 15, no. 5 (2009): 574–94.

121. Jessica Pfaffendorf, "Sensitive Cowboys: Privileged Young Men and the Mobilization of Hybrid Masculinities in a Therapeutic Boarding School," *Gender & Society* 31, no. 2 (April 2017): 197–222.

122. Ibid., 215.

123. Lisa Wade, "The Big Picture: Confronting Manhood after Trump," Public Books, January 1, 2018, www.publicbooks.org/pb-staff-favorites-2017-big -picture-confronting-manhood-trump/.

124. Anderson, *Inclusive Masculinity*; Robert Jensen, *The End of Patriarchy: Radical Feminism for Men* (North Geelong, VIC, Australia: Spinifex Press, 2017); Jackson Katz, *The Macho Paradox: Why Some Men Hurt Women and How All Men Can Help* (Naperville, IL: Sourcebooks, 2006); Kimmel, *Healing from Hate*; John Stoltenberg, *Refusing to Be a Man: Essays on Sex and Justice* (Abingdon, Oxon, UK: Routledge, 2000); and Allan G. Johnson, *The Gender Knot: Unraveling Our Patriarchal Legacy* (Philadelphia: Temple University Press, 2014).

Chapter 6: Inequality: Femininities

1. Natalie Adams and Pamela Bettis, "Commanding the Room in Short Skirts: Cheering as the Embodiment of Ideal Girlhood," *Gender & Society* 17, no. 1 (2003): 73–91.

2. Nada Naiyer, Thiphalak Chounthirath, and Gary A. Smith, "Pediatric Cheerleading Injuries Treated in Emergency Departments in the United States," *Clinical Pediatrics* 56, no. 11 (2017): 985–92.

3. Eric Anderson, "'I Used to Think Women Were Weak': Orthodox Masculinity, Gender Segregation, and Sport," *Sociological Forum* 23, no. 2 (2008): 257–80, 270.

4. Ibid.

5. Laura Grindstaff and Emily West, "Cheerleading and the Gendered Politics of Sport," *Social Problems* 53, no. 4 (2006): 500–18, 500.

6. Ibid., 509–10.

7. Ibid., 510.

8. Rachel Greenspan, "*Cheer* Shows Competitive Cheerleading Is Almost as Dangerous as Football. So Why Isn't It Officially Considered a Sport?" *Time*, March 10, 2020, https://time.com/5782136/cheer-net flix-cheerleading-dangers/.

9. Kristen L. Kucera and Robert C. Cantu, "Catastrophic Sports Injury Research: Thirty-Sixth Annual Report," National Center for Catastrophic Sport Injury Research at the University of North Carolina at Chapel Hill, October 3, 2019, https://nccsir.unc .edu/wp-content/uploads/sites/5614/2019/10/2018 -Catastrophic-Report-AS-36th-AY2017-2018-FINAL .pdf.

10. Claire Cain Miller, "Americans Might No Longer Prefer Sons over Daughters," *New York Times*,

March 5, 2018, https://www.nytimes.com/2018/03/05/upshot/americans-might-no-longer-prefer-sons-over-daughters.html.

11. Emily Kane, "'No Way My Boys Are Going to Be Like That!' Parents' Responses to Children's Gender Nonconformity," *Gender & Society* 20, no. 2 (2006): 149–76.

12. Ibid., 156–57.

13. Tey Meadow, *Trans Kids: Being Gendered in the Twenty-First Century* (Berkeley: University of California Press, 2018).

14. Kim Parker, Juliana Menasce Horowitz, and Renee Stepler, "On Gender Differences, No Consensus on Nature vs. Nurture," Pew Research Center, December 5, 2017, https://www.pewsocialtrends.org/2017/12/05/on-gender-differences-no-consensus-on-nature-vs-nurture/.

15. Elizabeth Narins, "In Defense of Female Cross-Fit Competitors: Strong Women Aren't Just Meatheads," *Cosmopolitan*, August 13, 2015, https://www.cosmopolitan.com/health-fitness/a44819/christmas-abbott-crossfit-body-image/.

16. "Christmas Abbott," *Inked*, December 19, 2013.

17. "NASCAR's First Female Pit Crew Member," YouTube, uploaded March 14, 2013, https://www.youtube.com/watch?v=doZmQaJDkCc.

18. Mignon R. Moore, *Invisible Families: Gay Identities, Relationships, and Motherhood among Black Women* (Berkeley: University of California Press, 2011), 26; see also Mignon Moore, "Intersectionality and the Study of Black, Sexual Minority Women," *Gender & Society* 26, no. 1 (2012): 33–39; and Mignon R. Moore, "Lipstick or Timberlands? Meanings of Gender Presentation in Black Lesbian Communities," *Signs: Journal of Women in Culture and Society* 32, no. 1 (Autumn 2006): 113–39.

19. Ingrid Banks, *Hair Matters: Beauty, Power, and Black Women's Consciousness* (New York: New York University Press, 2000); Rose Weitz, *Rapunzel's Daughters: What Women's Hair Tells Us about Women's Lives* (New York: Farrar, Straus & Giroux, 2004); Nadia Brown, "'It's More than Hair . . . That's Why You Should Care': The Politics of Appearance for Black Women State Legislators," *Politics, Groups, and Identities* 2, no. 3 (2014): 295–312; Germine H. Awad, Carolette Norwood, Desire S. Taylor, Mercedes Martinez, Shannon McClain, Bianca Jones, et al., "Beauty and Body Image Concerns among African American College Women," *Journal of Black Psychology* 41, no. 6 (2014): 540–64; Althea Prince, *The Politics of Black Women's Hair* (London, ON, Canada: Insomnia Press, 2009); and Ayana Byrd and Lori Tharps, *Hair Story: Untangling the Roots of Black Hair in America* (New York: St. Martin's Press, 2001).

20. Weitz, *Rapunzel's Daughters*, 125.

21. Paulette M. Caldwell, "A Hair Piece: Perspectives on the Intersection of Race and Gender," *Duke Law Review* 1991, no. 2 (1991): 365–96.

22. Maya Rhodan, "U.S. Military Rolls Back Restrictions on Black Hairstyles," *Time*, August 13, 2014, https://time.com/3107647/military-black-hairstyles/.

23. Taryn Finley, "Appeals Court Rules Employers Can Ban Dreadlocks at Work," *Huffington Post*, September 20, 2016, https://www.huffingtonpost.com/entry/appeals-court-rules-dreadlocks-work_us_57e0252ae4b0071a6e08a7c3.

24. Cindy Boren, "'There's No Wrong Way to Be a Woman': Serena Williams Drops a Powerful Message in Nike Ad," *Washington Post*, March 5, 2018, https://www.washingtonpost.com/news/early-lead/wp/2018/03/05/theres-no-wrong-way-to-be-a-woman-serena-williams-drops-a-powerful-message-in-nike-ad/?utm_term=.1948a9dba615.

25. Mimi Schippers, "Recovering the Feminine Other: Masculinity, Femininity, and Gender Hegemony," *Theory and Society* 36 (2007): 85–102.

26. Claudia Goldin and Cecilia Rouse, "Orchestrating Impartiality: The Impact of 'Blind Auditions' on Female Musicians," *American Economic Review* 90, no. 4 (September 2000): 715–41.

27. Deborah Rhode, *Speaking of Sex: The Denial of Gender Inequality* (Cambridge, MA: Harvard University Press, 1997), 15; and Sandra Lee Bartky, "Foucault, Femininity, and the Modernization of Patriarchal Power," in *Writing on the Body: Female Embodiment and Feminist Theory*, ed. Katie Conboy, Nadia Medina, and Sarah Stanbury (New York: Columbia University Press, 1997) 129–54.

28. Peter Glick, Susan T. Fiske, Antonio Mladinic, José L. Saix, Dominic Abrams, Barbara Masser, et al., "Beyond Prejudice as Simple Antipathy: Hostile and Benevolent Sexism across Cultures," *Journal of Personality and Social Psychology* 79, no. 5 (2000): 763–75, 765.

29. Jodi Kantor and Jessica Silver-Greenberg, "Wall Street Mothers, Stay-Home Fathers," *New York Times*, December 7, 2013, https://www.nytimes.com/2013/12/08/us/wall-street-mothers-stay-home-fathers.html?searchResultPosition=1.

30. Bartky, "Foucault, Femininity, and the Modernization of Patriarchal Power," 132.

31. Karin Martin, "Giving Birth Like a Girl," *Gender and Society* 17, no. 1 (2003): 54–72.

32. Ibid., 62.

33. Bartky, "Foucault, Femininity, and the Modernization of Patriarchal Power," 141.

34. Ibid.

35. William M. O'Barr and Bowman K. Atkins, "'Women's Language' or 'Powerless Language'?," in *Language and Gender: A Reader*, 2nd ed., ed. Jennifer Coates (Malden, MA: Wiley-Blackwell, 2011), 451–60.

36. Nathan Ferguson, "Is This Assistant Bothering You?" *Cyborgology*, March 28, 2018, https://thesocietypages.org/cyborgology/2018/03/28/is-this-assistant-bothering-you/.

37. Michael Kimmel, *Angry White Men: American Masculinity at the End of an Era* (New York, Nation Books, 2013).

38. Glick et al., "Beyond Prejudice as Simple Antipathy," 765.

39. Amanda LeCouteur and Melissa Oxlad, "Managing Accountability for Domestic Violence: Identities, Membership Categories and Morality in Perpetrators' Talk" *Feminism & Psychology* 21, no. 1 (2011): 5–28.

40. Michele C. Black, Kathleen C. Basile, Matthew J. Breiding, Sharon G. Smith, Mikel L. Walters, Melissa T. Merrick, et al., *The National Intimate Partner and Sexual Violence Survey (NISVS): 2010 Summary Report* (National Center for Injury Prevention and Control, Centers for Disease Control and Prevention, Atlanta, GA: November 2011).

41. Megan Garvey, "Transcript of the Disturbing Video 'Elliot Rodger's Retribution,'" *Los Angeles Times*, May 24, 2014, https://latimes.com/local/lanow/la-me-ln-transcript-ucsb-shootings-video-20140524-story.html.

42. Nicole Chavez, "Toronto Van Attack Suspect's Facebook Post Linked to Anti-Women Ideology," CNN, April 25, 2018, https://www.cnn.com/2018/04/25/americas/toronto-van-attack/index.html; and Kelley Weill, Taylor Lorenz, Samantha Allen, and Kate Briquelet, "White Supremacists Claim Nikolas Cruz Trained with Them; Students Say He Wore Trump Hat in School," *Daily Beast*, February 15, 2018, https://www.thedailybeast.com/nikolas-cruz-trained-with-florida-white-supremacist-group-leader-says.

43. Madeline Holcombe, Holly Yan, and Amir Vera, "Victims of the Spa Shootings Highlight the Vulnerability of Working-Class Asian Women as More Asian Americans Get Attacked," CNN, March 19, 2021, https://www.cnn.com/2021/03/18/us/metro-atlanta-shootings-thursday/index.html.

44. "Mass Shootings in America," Everytown for Gun Safety, accessed December 8, 2021, https://everytownresearch.org/maps/mass-shootings-in-america-2009-2019/.

45. Ibid.

46. Sharon G. Smith, Xinjian Zhang, Kathleen C. Basile, Melissa T. Merrick, Jing Wang, Marcie-jo Kresnow, Jieru Chen, "National Intimate Partner and Sexual Violence Survey: 2015 Data Brief," Centers for Disease Control and Prevention, November 2018, https://www.cdc.gov/violenceprevention/pdf/2015data-brief508.pdf.

47. Susan B. Sorenson and Rebecca A. Schut, "Nonfatal Gun Use in Intimate Partner Violence: A Systematic Review of the Literature," *Trauma, Violence, and Abuse* 19, no. 4 (2018): 431–42.

48. Giulia Lausi, Alessandra Pizzo, Clarissa Cricenti, Michela Baldi, Rita Desiderio, Anna Maria Giannini, et al. "Intimate Partner Violence during the COVID-19 Pandemic: A Review of the Phenomenon from Victims' and Help Professionals' Perspectives," *International Journal of Environmental Research and Public Health* 18, no. 12 (2021): 6204.

49. Shannan Catalano, *Intimate Partner Violence; Attributes of Victimization, 1993–2011* (Special Report NCJ243300), Bureau of Justice Statistics, November 2013, www.bjs.gov/content/pub/pdf/ipvav9311.pdf.

50. *An Epidemic of Violence 2021: Fatal Violence Against Transgender and Gender Non-Confirming People in the United States in 2021* (report), Human Rights Campaign, updated October 2021, https://reports.hrc.org/an-epidemic-of-violence-fatal-violence-against-transgender-and-gender-non-confirming-people-in-the-united-states-in-2021.

51. Mark Lee, "A Time to Act: Fatal Violence against Transgender People in America 2017," Human Rights Campaign Foundation and Trans People of Color Coalition, November 2017, http://assets2.hrc.org/files/assets/resources/A_Time_To_Act_2017_REV3.pdf.

52. George Yancy, "James Bond Is a Wimp," *New York Times*, February 26, 2018, www.nytimes.com/2018/02/26/opinion/drucilla-cornell-misogyny-sex-gender.html.

53. Suruchi Thapar-Bjoerkert and Karen J. Morgan, "'But Sometimes I Think . . . They Put Themselves in the Situation': Exploring Blame and Responsibility in Interpersonal Violence," *Violence against Women* 16, no. 1 (2010): 32–59.

54. Elizabeth A. Armstrong and Laura T. Hamilton, *Paying for the Party: How College Maintains Inequality* (Cambridge, MA: Harvard University Press, 2013), 92.

55. Laurie Penny, "Who Does She Think She Is?," *Longreads*, March 2018, https://longreads.com/2018/03/28/who-does-she-think-she-is/.

56. Kate Manne, *Down Girl: The Logic of Misogyny* (New York: Oxford University Press, 2018), 197.

57. Kate Manne, "Brett Kavanaugh and America's 'Himpathy' Reckoning," *New York Times*, September 26, 2018, https://www.nytimes.com/2018/09/26/opinion/brett-kavanaugh-hearing-himpathy.html.

58. Quoted in ibid.

59. Sean Illing, "Brett Kavanaugh and the Problem of 'Himpathy,'" *Vox*, September 28, 2018, https://www.vox.com/2018/9/27/17887210/brett-kavanaugh-christine-blasey-ford-hearing-kate-manne.

60. Susan Bordo, *The Male Body: A New Look at Men in Public and Private* (New York: Farrar Straus & Giroux, 1999); Josep Armengol, ed., *Embodying Masculinities: Towards a History of the Male Body in U.S. Culture and Literature* (New York: Peter Lang, 2013); Robert Rushing, *Descended from Hercules: Biopolitics and the Muscled Male Body on Screen* (Bloomington: Indiana University Press, 2016); Iris Marion Young, *On Female Body Experience: "Throwing Like a Girl" and Other Essays* (New York: Oxford University Press, 2005); Jocelyn Hollander, "Vulnerability and Dangerousness: The Construction of Gender through Conversations about Violence," *Gender & Society* 15, no. 1 (2001): 83–109; Bartky, "Foucault, Femininity, and the Modernization of Patriarchal Power," 93–111; Susan Bordo, "Reading the Slender Body," in *Body/Politics: Women and the Discourses of Science*, ed. Mary Jacobus, Evelyn Fox Keller, and Sally Shuttleworth (New York: Routledge, 1990), 83–112.

61. Jill E. Yavorksy and Liana Sayer, "'Doing Fear': The Influence of Hetero-Femininity on (Trans)women's Fears of Victimization," *Sociological Quarterly* 54, no. 4 (2013): 511–33.

62. Ibid.

63. J. Clay-Warner, "Avoiding Rape: The Effects of Protective Actions and Situational Factors on Rape Outcome," *Violence and Victims* 17 (2002): 691–705;

S. E. Ullman, "Does Offender Violence Escalate when Women Fight Back?" *Journal of Interpersonal Violence* 13 (1998): 179–92; and S. E. Ullman, "A 10-Year Update of 'Review and Critique of Empirical Studies of Rape Avoidance,'" *Criminal Justice and Behavior* 34 (2007): 1–19.

64. Jocelyn Hollander, "Women's Self-Defense and Sexual Assault Resistance: The State of the Field," *Sociology Compass* 12, no. 8 (2018): e12597.

65. Ellen Barry, "In Sweden's Preschools, Boys Learn to Dance and Girls Learn to Yell," *New York Times*, March 24, 2018, https://www.nytimes.com/2018/03/24/world/europe/sweden-gender-neutral-preschools.html.

66. R. W. Connell, *Gender and Power: Society, the Person, and Sexual Politics* (Stanford, CA: Stanford University Press, 1987), 183.

67. Ashley Mears, "Girls as Elite Distinction: The Appropriation of Bodily Capital," *Poetics* 53 (2015): 22–37; and Kimberly Kay Hoang, *Dealing in Desire: Asian Ascendancy, Western Decline, and the Hidden Currencies of Global Sex Work* (Berkeley: University of California Press, 2015).

68. Hoang, *Dealing in Desire*.

69. Corey Seymour, "Meet Najiah Knight, the 13-Year-Old Girl Upending the World of Professional Bull Riding," *Vogue*, January 7, 2020, https://www.vogue.com/article/najiah-knight-interview-professional-bull-riders.

70. Ibid.

71. Jule Gilfillan, "Oregon Teen Sets Sights on Becoming First Female to Compete in Professional Bull Rider's Elite Circuit," *Oregon Field Guide*, Oregon Public Broadcasting, March 18, 2021, https://www.opb.org/article/2021/03/18/oregon-bull-riding-najiah-knight-professional-bull-riders-mini/.

72. Nikki Jones, "Working 'the Code': On Girls, Gender, and Inner-City Violence," *Australian & New Zealand Journal of Criminology* 41, no. 1 (2008): 63–83.

73. Nikki Jones, "'I Was Aggressive for the Streets, Pretty for the Pictures': Gender, Difference, and the Inner-City Girl," *Gender & Society* 23, no. 1 (2009): 89–93, 89.

74. Jeré Longman, "Track's Caster Semenya Loses Appeal to Defend 800-Meter Title," *New York Times*, September 8, 2020, https://www.nytimes.com/2020/09/08/sports/olympics/caster-semenya-court-ruling.html.

75. Barbara Lee Family Foundation and Center for American Women and Politics, *Finding Gender in*

Election 2016: Lessons from Presidential Gender Watch, Presidential Gender Watch, https://presidentialgenderwatch.org/report/.

76. Ju-Min Park, "Is South Korea Ready for 'Madam President'?," *Chicago Tribune*, December 11, 2012.

77. Ermine Saner, "Top 10 Sexist Moments in Politics: Julia Gillard, Hillary Clinton and More," *Guardian*, June 14, 2013.

78. Gina Serignese Woodall and Kim L. Fridkin, "Shaping Women's Chances: Stereotypes and the Media," in *Rethinking Madam President: Are We Ready for a Woman in the White House?*, ed. Lori Cox Han and Caroline Heldman (Boulder, CO: Lynne Rienner, 2007), 1–16.

79. Nathan Heflick and Jamie Goldenberg, "Sarah Palin, a Nation Object(ifie)s," *Sex Roles* 65 (2011): 156–64; and Jennifer L. Pozner, "Hot and Bothering: Media Treatment of Sarah Palin," NPR, July 8, 2009, https://www.npr.org/templates/story/story.php?storyId=106384060.

80. See, for example, Connell, *Gender and Power*.

81. Hamilton, Armstrong, Seeley, and Armstrong, "Hegemonic Femininities and Intersectional Domination, 315–41.

82. Patricia Hill Collins, *Black Feminist Thought: Knowledge, Consciousness, and the Politics of Empowerment* (Boston: Unwin Hyman, 1990); bell hooks, *Feminist Theory: From Margin to Center* (Cambridge, MA: South End Press, 1984); Gloria Anzaldúa, *Borderlands/La Frontera: The New Mestiza* (San Francisco: Aunt Lute Books, 1987); and Trinh T. Minh-Ha, *Woman, Native, Other: Writing Postcoloniality and Feminism* (Bloomington: Indiana University Press, 1989).

83. Collins, *Black Feminist Thought: Knowledge*.

84. Philip Cohen, "How Can We Jump-Start the Struggle for Gender Equality?" *New York Times*, November 23, 2013; Paula England, "The Gender Revolution: Uneven and Stalled," *Gender & Society* 24, no. 2 (2010): 149–66; Scott Jaschik, "Women Lead in Doctorates," *Inside Higher Ed*, September 14, 2010, https://www.insidehighered.com/news/2010/09/14/doctorates; David Cotter, Joan H. Hermsen, and Reeve Vanneman, "The End of the Gender Revolution? Gender Role Attitudes from 1977 to 2008," *American Journal of Sociology* 117, no. 1 (2011): 259–89; Sarah Friedman, "Still a 'Stalled Revolution'? Work/Family Experiences, Hegemonic Masculinity, and Moving toward Gender Equality," *Sociology Compass* 9, no. 2 (2015): 140–55; US Bureau of Labor Statistics, *Women in the Labor Force: A Databook*,

April 2021, https://www.bls.gov/opub/reports/womens-databook/2020/home.htm.

85. Arlie Russell Hochschild, with Anne Machung, *The Second Shift: Working Parents and the Revolution at Home* (New York: Penguin Books, 1989).

86. Jean Twenge, "Status and Gender: The Paradox of Progress in an Age of Narcissism," *Sex Roles* 61 (2009): 338–40.

87. Thomas F. Pettigrew, "School Desegregation and the Pipeline of Privilege," *Du Bois Review: Social Science Research on Race* 18, no. 1 (2021): 1–13.

88. Anne Case and Angus Deaton, *Deaths of Despair and the Future of Capitalism* (Princeton, NJ: Princeton University Press, 2020).

Chapter 7: Institutions

1. Strobe Talbott, "Monnet's Brandy and Europe's Fate," Brookings Essay, February 11, 2014, http://csweb.brookings.edu/content/research/essays/2014/monnets-brandy-and-europes-fate.html.

2. Juliet Lapidos, "Do Kids Need a Summer Vacation?" *Slate*, July 11, 2007, https://www.slate.com/articles/news_and_politics/explainer/2007/07/do_kids_need_a_summer_vacation.html.

3. Barrie Thorne, *Gender Play: Girls and Boys in School* (New Brunswick, NJ: Rutgers University Press, 1993).

4. Ibid, 44.

5. See "People Practicing Open Defecation (% of Population)," figure, World Bank, https://data.worldbank.org/indicator/SH.STA.ODFC.ZS. Numbers from the World Bank don't necessarily include people who live in countries with public sanitation but have little access to those facilities, such as people without homes in the United States.

6. Quoted in Terry Kogan, "Sex Separation: The Cure-All for Victorian Social Anxiety," in *Toilet: Public Restrooms and the Politics of Sharing*, ed. Harvey Molotch and Laura Norén (New York: New York University Press, 2010), 145–64, 157.

7. Ibid.

8. Ibid., 145–64.

9. Harvey Molotch and Laura Norén, *Toilet: Public Restrooms and the Politics of Sharing* (New York: New York University Press, 2010).

10. Betsy Lucal, "What It Means to Be Gendered Me: Life on the Boundaries of a Dichotomous Gender System," *Gender & Society* 13, no. 6 (1999): 787.

11. Ibid.

12. Daniel Greenberg, Maxine Najle, Natalie Jackson, Oyindamola Bola, and Robert P. Jones, "America's Growing Support for Transgender Rights," PPRI, June 11, 2019, https://www.prri.org/research/americas-growing-support-for-transgender-rights/.

13. "Know Your Rights: Public Accommodations," National Center for Transgender Equality, accessed December 1, 2021, https://transequality.org/know-your-rights/public-accommodations.

14. Ibid.

15. Eileen Boris, "'You Wouldn't Want One of 'Em Dancing with Your Wife': Racialized Bodies on the Job in World War II," *American Quarterly* 50, no. 1 (1998): 77–108.

16. Donald G. Mathews and Jane Sherron De Hart, *Sex, Gender, and the Politics of ERA: A State and the Nation* (New York: Oxford University Press, 1990).

17. "Manufacturers (Wholesale) Sales Sports Products Industry in the U.S. from 2008 to 2020," Statista, May 2021, https://www.statista.com/statistics/240946/sports-products-industry-wholesale-sales-in-the-us/.

18. Maury Brown, "MLB Sees Record $10.7 Billion in Revenues for 2019," *Forbes*, December 21, 2019, https://www.forbes.com/sites/maurybrown/2019/12/21/mlb-sees-record-107-billion-in-revenues-for-2019/?sh=1ec655935d78; and "Report: NFL Revenue Dropped by $4 Billion in 2020," *Reuters*, March 11, 2021, https://www.reuters.com/lifestyle/sports/report-nfl-revenue-dropped-by-4-billion-2020-2021-03-11/.

19. Amir Somoggi, "Coronavirus's Economic Impact on the Sports Industry," Sports Value, March 18, 2020, https://www.sportsvalue.com.br/en/coronaviruss-economic-impact-on-the-sports-industry/.

20. Sue Macy, *Wheels of Change: How Women Rode the Bicycle to Freedom (with a Few Flat Tires along the Way)* (Washington, DC: National Geographic Society, 2011).

21. Nellie Bly, "'Let Me Tell You What I Think of Bicycling': Nellie Bly Interviews Susan B. Anthony, 1896," Hairpin, April 28, 2014, https://thehairpin.com/let-me-tell-you-what-i-think-of-bicycling-nellie-bly-interviews-susan-b-anthony-1896-c2b15900a5a8.

22. Joseph Stromberg, "'Bicycle Face': A 19th-Century Health Problem Made Up to Scare Women Away from Biking," *Vox*, March 24, 2015, https://www.vox.com/2014/7/8/5880931/the-19th-century-health-scare-that-told-women-to-worry-about-bicycle.

23. Stephanie Apstein, "Women's Skateboarding Debut Exemplifies Progress in Sport: 'Girls Can Skateboard,'" *Sports Illustrated*, July 26, 2021, https://www.si.com/olympics/2021/07/26/womens-skateboarding-tokyo-olympics-debut-momiji-nishiya.

24. Jean Twenge, "Mapping Gender: The Multifactorial Approach and the Organization of Gender-Related Attributes," *Psychology of Women Quarterly* 23, no. 3 (1999): 485–502.

25. Rosalind Miles, *The Rites of Man: Love, Sex, and Death in the Making of the Male* (Hammersmith, UK: Paladin, 1992); and Michael Messner, *Power at Play: Sports and the Problem of Masculinity* (Boston: Beacon Press, 1992), 24.

26. R. W. Connell, *Which Way Is Up?* (North Sydney, NSW: George Unwin & Allen, 1983), 18; and Messner, *Power at Play*, 61.

27. Michael Messner, "Becoming 100% Straight," in *Privilege: A Reader*, ed. Michael Kimmel and Abby Ferber (Philadelphia: Westview Press, 2010), 87.

28. Messner, *Power at Play*, 33.

29. Quoted in Jennifer Hargreaves, *Sporting Females: Critical Issues in the History and Sociology of Women's Sports* (New York: Routledge, 1994), 38.

30. Todd W. Crosset, *Outsiders in the Clubhouse: The World of Women's Professional Golf* (Albany: State University of New York Press, 1995), 223–24.

31. Michael Messner, "Boys and Girls Together: The Promise and Limitations of Equal Opportunity in Sports," in *Sex, Violence, and Power in Sports: Rethinking Masculinity*, ed. Michael Messner and Donald Sabo (Freedom, CA: Crossing Press, 1994), 200.

32. Jane English, "Sex Equality in Sports," in *Femininity, Masculinity, and Androgyny*, ed. Mary Vetterling-Braggin (Boston: Littlefield, Adams, 1982).

33. Michael Messner, "Sports and Male Domination: The Female Athlete as Contested Ideological Terrain," in *Women, Sport and Culture*, ed. Susan Birrell and Cheryl L. Cole (Champaign, IL: Human Kinetics, 1994), 65–80.

34. Ibid., 71.

35. Ibid.

36. Trina Calderón, "Female Skateboarders Still Striving for Even Footing with Male Peers," Vice,

April 5, 2017, https://www.vice.com/en/article/4xz44d/female-skateboarders-still-striving-for-even-footing-with-male-peers.

37. "BMX Course Ready to Roll for Rio 2016," Olympic Games, September 9, 2015, https://www.olympic.org/news/bmx-course-ready-to-roll-for-rio-2016; and Ella Koeze, "What if Men and Women Skied against Each Other in the Olympics?" FiveThirtyEight, February 14, 2018, https://fivethirtyeight.com/features/what-if-men-and-women-skied-against-each-other-in-the-olympics/?src=obbottom=ar_5.

38. Abigail Feder, "'A Radiant Smile from the Lovely Lady': Overdetermined Femininity in 'Ladies' Figure Skating," in Women on Ice, ed. Cynthia Baughman (New York: Routledge, 1995), 24.

39. Lex Boyle, "Flexing the Tensions of Female Muscularity: How Female Bodybuilders Negotiate Normative Femininity in Competitive Bodybuilding," Women's Studies Quarterly 33, nos. 1/2 (2005): 134–49. See also Anne Bolin, "Vandalized Vanity: Feminine Physiques Betrayed and Portrayed," in Tattoo, Torture, Mutilation, and Adornment: The Denaturalization of the Body in Culture and Text, ed. Frances Mascia-Lees and Patricia Sharpe (Albany: State University of New York Press, 1992), 79–99.

40. "IFBB Rules," International Federation of Bodybuilding, accessed January 10, 2022, https://ifbb.com/rules-2/.

41. Susan Mitchell and Ken Dyer, Winning Women: Challenging the Norms in Australian Sport (Ringwood, Vic.: Penguin, 1985), 97.

42. Michael Messner, Power at Play, 1.

43. Jonathan Wall, "Girl Football Player Sits Out Game after Foe Threatens Forfeit," Prep Rally (Yahoo! Sports blog), October 13, 2011, https://ca.sports.yahoo.com/blogs/highschool-prep-rally/girl-football-player-sits-game-foe-threatens-forfeit-130942497.html.

44. "Lunenburg Girl Won a Boys' Golf Tournament but Was Denied the Trophy," Boston Globe, October 26, 2017, https://www.bostonglobe.com/sports/high-schools/2017/10/25/lunenberg-emily-nash-won-boys-golf-tournament-but-was-denied-winner-trophy-because-she-girl/WtZDRnhPDe8rd7Bv5vMJ5J/story.html.

45. Colleen O'Connor, "Girls Going to the Mat," Denver Post, December 23, 2007.

46. Eileen McDonagh and Laura Pappano, Playing with the Boys: Why Separate Is Not Equal in Sports (New York: Oxford University Press, 2008).

47. "Vision Quest: Alaskan Girl Wins State H.S. Wrestling Title Over Boys," Sports Illustrated, February 6, 2006.

48. Koeze, "What if Men and Women Skied against Each Other in the Olympics?"

49. Brett Knight and Justin Birnbaum, "Highest-Paid Athletes 2021: The Top 50 Sports Stars Combined to Make Nearly $2.8 Billion in a Year of Records," Forbes, accessed September 10, 2021, www.forbes.com/athletes/.

50. Crosset, Outsiders in the Clubhouse, 224.

51. Laura La Bella, Women in Sports (New York: Rosen, 2013).

52. Crosset, Outsiders in the Clubhouse, 225.

53. Harvey Molotch, "On Not Making History: What NYU Did with the Toilet and What It Means for the World," in Toilet: Public Restrooms and the Politics of Sharing, ed. Harvey Molotch and Laura Norén (New York: New York University Press, 2010), 255–72.

54. Ibid., 258.

55. Ibid., 261.

56. 20 U.S. Code § 1681—Sex, Legal Information Institute, accessed January 10, 2022, https://www.law.cornell.edu/uscode/20/1681.html.

57. NCAA Sports Sponsorship and Participation Rates Database, accessed January 10, 2022, https://www.ncaa.org/about/resources/research/ncaa-sports-sponsorship-and-participation-rates-database; "2018–19 High School Athletics Participation Survey" (table), National Federation of State High School Associations, accessed January 10, 2022, https://www.nfhs.org/media/1020412/2018-19_participation_survey.pdf; and "More College Students than Ever Before Are Student-Athletes," NCAA, November 19, 2021, https://www.ncaa.org/about/resources/media-center/news/more-college-students-ever-are-student-athletes.

58. StoryCorps, "A Little League of Her Own: The First Girl in Little League Baseball," NPR, March 20, 2018, https://www.npr.org/2018/03/30/597960442/a-little-league-of-her-own-the-first-girl-in-little-league-baseball.

59. Liz Roscher, "MLB Announces New Girls Baseball Camp, Plus the Return of the All-Girls Trailblazer Series," Yahoo! Sports, April 2, 2018, https://sports.yahoo.com/mlb-announces-new-girls-baseball-camp-plus-return-girls-trailblazer-series-162654801.html.

60. Raewyn Connell, *Gender and Power: Society, the Person, and Sexual Politics* (Stanford, CA: Stanford University Press, 1987), 139.

Chapter 8: Change

1. Octavia E. Butler, *Parable of the Sower* (New York: Hachette Book Group, 1993), 3.

2. Jaclyn Geller, *Here Comes the Bride: Women, Weddings, and the Marriage Mystique* (New York: Four Walls Eight Windows, 2001).

3. John D'Emilio and Estelle Freedman, *Intimate Matters: A History of Sexuality in America* (Chicago: University of Chicago Press, 1997), 28.

4. Ibid.

5. Quoted in Claude Lévi-Strauss, *The Elementary Structures of Kinship* (Boston: Beacon Press, [1949], 1969), 481.

6. Gregory D. Smithers, "Rethinking Genocide in North America," in *The Oxford Handbook of Genocide Studies*, ed. Donald Bloxham and A. Dirk Moses (Oxford: Oxford University Press, 2010), 322–44.

7. Francis J. Bremer and Tom Webster, *Puritans and Puritanism in Europe and America: A Comprehensive Encyclopedia*, vol. 2 (Santa Barbara: ABC-CLIO, Inc., 2006), 152.

8. Alan Taylor, *American Colonies* (New York: Viking, 2001).

9. Smithers, "Rethinking Genocide in North America," 322–44; Karen Ordahl Kupperman, *Pocahontas and the English Boys: Caught between Cultures in Early Virginia* (New York: New York University Press, 2019).

10. Robert Fogel, *Without Consent or Contract: The Rise and Fall of American Slavery* (New York: W. W. Norton and Company, 1989); Shirley Hill, "Class, Race, and Gender Dimensions of Child Rearing in African American Families," *Journal of Black Studies* 31, no. 4 (2001): 494–508.

11. Quoted in Fogel, *Without Consent or Contract*, 163.

12. Brown, Vincent, "The Eighteenth Century: Growth, Crisis, and Revolution," in *The Princeton Companion to Atlantic History*, ed. Vincent Brown et al., STU-Student edition (Princeton University Press, 2015), 36–45, http://www.jstor.org/stable/j.ctt18s30x4.11.

13. Estelle Freeman, "Sexuality in Nineteenth-Century America: Behavior, Ideology, and Politics," *Reviews in American History* 10, no. 4 (1982): 196–215.

14. Ibid; see also Robert Woods, *The Demography of Victorian England and Wales* (Cambridge: Cambridge University Press, 2000).

15. Freeman, "Sexuality in Nineteenth-Century America," 196–215.

16. Ibid.; see also Steven Seidman, "The Power of Desire and the Danger of Pleasure: Victorian Sexuality Reconsidered," *Journal of Social History* 24, no. 1 (1990): 47–67.

17. Francesca Cancian, "The Feminization of Love," *Signs* 11, no. 4 (1986): 692–709; Seidman, "The Power of Desire and the Danger of Pleasure," 47–67.

18. Seidman, "The Power of Desire and the Danger of Pleasure," 47–67; Freeman, "Sexuality in Nineteenth-Century America," 196–215.

19. Ibid.

20. Carroll Smith-Rosenberg, *Disorderly Conduct: Visions of Gender in Victorian America* (New York: Oxford University Press, 1985), 55–56.

21. Robert Long, "Sexuality in the Victorian Era," (lecture presented to Innominate Society), www.innominatesociety.com/Articles/Sexuality%20In%20The%20Victorian%20Era.htm.

22. Ibid.

23. William Acton, *Prostitution, Considered in Its Moral, Social, and Sanitary Aspects* (1870), Internet Archive, accessed June 8, 2022, http://archive.org/details/prostitutioncons00acto; Stephanie Coontz, "Blame Affairs on Evolution of Sex Roles," *CNN Opinion*, November 18, 2012, www.cnn.com/2012/11/17/opinion/coontz-powerful-men-affairs/index.html.

24. Freeman, "Sexuality in Nineteenth-Century America," 196–215; Joane Nagel, *Race, Ethnicity, and Sexuality: Intimate Intersections, Forbidden Frontiers* (New York: Oxford University Press, 2003).

25. Joy Hakim, *War, Peace, and All That Jazz* (New York: Oxford University Press, 1995).

26. Douglas Harper, *Online Etymology Dictionary*, s.v., "sexy (adj.)," 2014, www.etymonline.com/index.php?allowed_in_frame=0&search=sexy&searchmode=none.

27. Chad Heap, *Slumming: Sexual and Racial Encounters in American Nightlife, 1885–1940* (Chicago: University of Chicago Press, 2009).

28. John D'Emilio and Estelle Freedman, *Intimate Matters: A History of Sexuality in America* (Chicago: University of Chicago Press, 1997), 279.

29. Beth Bailey, *From Front Porch to Back Seat* (Baltimore: Johns Hopkins University, 1988).

30. Ibid., 20.

31. Ibid., 20.

32. Kathy Peiss, "'Charity Girls' and City Pleasures: Historical Notes on Working-Class Sexuality, 1880–1920," in *Passion and Power: Sexuality in History*, ed. Kathy Peiss and Christina Simmons, with Robert A. Padgug (Philadelphia: Temple University Press, 1989), 63.

33. Ibid., 61.

34. John McDonough and Karen Egolf (eds.), *The Advertising Age Encyclopedia of Advertising* (Chicago: Fitzroy Dearborn Publishers), 409.

35. D'Emilio and Freedman, *Intimate Matters*, 279.

36. Ibid., 199.

37. Planned Parenthood, "Historical Abortion Law Timeline: 1850 to Today," Accessed June 8, 2022, https://www.plannedparenthoodaction.org/issues/abortion/abortion-central-history-reproductive-health-care-america/historical-abortion-law-timeline-1850-today.

38. Amin Ghaziani, *Sex Cultures* (Malden, MA: Polity Press, 2017); Colin Spencer, *Homosexuality in History* (New York: Harcourt Brace, 1995); George Chauncey, *Gay New York: Gender, Urban Culture, and the Making of the Gay Male World, 1890–1940* (New York: Basic Books, 1994).

39. Quoted in D'Emilio and Freedman, *Intimate Matters*, 226–27.

40. John D'Emilio, "Capitalism and Gay Identity," in *Powers of Desire: The Politics of Sexuality*, ed. A. Snitow, C. Stansell, and S. Thompson (New York: Monthly Review Press, 1983), 100–113.

41. Bailey, *From Front Porch to Back Seat*; Lynn Peril, *College Girls: Bluestockings, Sex Kittens, and Coeds, Then and Now* (New York: W. W. Norton and Company, 2006).

42. D'Emilio and Freedman, *Intimate Matters*, citing a study by Katharine Davis, 193.

43. Natalie Zarrelli, "In the Early 20th Century, America Was Awash in Incredible Queer Nightlife," *Atlas Obscura*, April 14, 2016, https://www.atlasobscura.com/articles/in-the-early-20th-century-america-was-awash-in-incredible-queer-nightlife.

44. B. E. Wells and J. M. Twenge, "Changes in Young People's Sexual Behavior and Attitudes, 1943–1999: A Cross-Temporal Meta-Analysis," *Review of General Psychology* 9 (2005): 249–61; Jennifer L. Petersen and Janet Shilbey Hyde, "A Meta-Analytic Review of Research on Gender Differences in Sexuality, 1993–2007," *Psychological Bulletin* 136, no. 1 (2010): 21–38.

45. Stephanie Coontz, "The World Historical Transformation of Marriage," *Journal of Marriage and Family* 66, no. 4 (2004): 974–79, 977.

46. Ibid.

47. Linda Gordon, *Social Insurance and Public Assistance: The Influence of Gender in Welfare Thought in the United States, 1890–1935* (Madison: University of Wisconsin Press, 1992).

48. Michael H. Minton and Jean Libman Block, *What Is a Wife Worth: The Leading Expert Places a High Dollar Value on Homemaking* (New York: William Morrow & Co, 1983).

49. Stephanie Coontz, *The Way We Never Were: American Families and the Nostalgia Trap* (New York: Basic Books, 1992), 58.

50. Freeman, "Sexuality in Nineteenth-Century America"; Coontz, *The Way We Never Were*.

51. Coontz, *The Way We Never Were*, 25, 27.

52. Quoted in D'Emilio and Freedman, *Intimate Matters*, 283.

53. K. A. Cuordileone, "'Politics in an Age of Anxiety': Cold War Political Culture and the Crisis in American Masculinity, 1949–1960," *The Journal of American History* 87, no. 2 (2000): 515–45.

54. Francis J. Bremer and Tom Webster, *Puritans and Puritanism in Europe and America: A Comprehensive Encyclopedia*, vol. 2 (Santa Barbara: ABC-CLIO, Inc., 2006).

55. *US Selective Service and Victory* (Washington, D.C.: Government Printing Office, 1948), 91.

56. D'Emilio and Freedman, *Intimate Matters*, 290.

57. Ibid., 289.

58. For historical context, see the documentary *Before Stonewall*, directed by Greta Schiller and Robert Rosenberg (1984), www.imdb.com/title/tt0088782/.

59. K. A. Cuordileone, "'Politics in an Age of Anxiety': Cold War Political Culture and the Crisis in American Masculinity, 1949–1960," *The Journal of American History* 87, no. 2 (2000): 515–45.

60. Gwendolyn Mink, *The Wages of Motherhood: Inequality in the Welfare State 1917-1943* (Ithaca: Cornell University Press, 1996).

61. Fred Fejes, "Murder, Perversion, and Moral Panic: The 1954 Media Campaign against Miami's Homosexuals and the Discourse of Civic Betterment," *Journal of the History of Sexuality* 9, no. 3 (2000): 305–47.

62. Cuordileone, "'Politics in an Age of Anxiety'," 532.

63. Jessica Toops, "The Lavender Scare: Persecution of Lesbianism During the Cold War," *Western Illinois Historical Review* 5 (2013): 91–107.

64. Cuordileone, "'Politics in an Age of Anxiety'," 515–45.

65. Bailey, *From Front Porch to Back Seat*.

66. Ibid., 53.

67. D'Emilio and Freedman, *Intimate Matters*, 261.

68. Cited in Bailey, *From Front Porch to Back Seat*, 81.

69. Coontz, *The Way We Never Were*, 202.

70. US Census Bureau, "Historical Marital Status Tables," *Estimated Median Age of First Marriage, by Sex: 1890 to Present*, November 2021, www.census.gov/data/tables/time-series/demo/families/marital.html.

71. Alfred Kinsey, *Sexual Behavior of the Human Male* (Bloomington: Indiana University Press, 1948).

72. Betty Friedan, *The Feminine Mystique* (New York: W. W. Norton and Company, 1963), 15.

73. Louis Menand, "Books as Bombs: Why the Women's Movement Needed *The Feminine Mystique*," *New Yorker*, January 24, 2011, www.newyorker.com/arts/critics/books/2011/01/24/110124crbo_books_menand.

74. Stephanie Coontz, *A Strange Stirring: The Feminine Mystique and American Women at the Dawn of the 1960s* (Philadelphia: Basic Books, 2011).

75. Coontz, *The Way We Never Were*.

76. Ibid., 31.

77. Carol Warren, *Madwives: Schizophrenic Women in the 1950s* (New Brunswick: Rutgers University Press, 1987).

78. Coontz, *The Way We Never Were*, 37.

79. Quoted in ibid., 37.

80. Jennifer L. Reimer, "Psychiatric Drugs: A History in Ads," *Practical Madness*, March 2010, www.practiceofmadness.com/2010/03/psychiatric-drugs-a-history-in-ads/.

81. Coontz, *The Way We Never Were*, 36.

82. S. Straussner and P. Attia, "Women's Addiction and Treatment through a Historical Lens," in *The Handbook of Addiction Treatment for Women*, ed. S. Straussner and S. Brown (San Francisco: Jossey-Bass, 2002), 3–25.

83. Friedan, *The Feminine Mystique*, 15.

84. Barbara Ehrenreich, *The Hearts of Men: American Dreams and the Flight from Commitment* (New York: Anchor Books, 1987).

85. Ibid., 50.

86. Ibid., 50.

87. The Alliance for Metropolitan Stability, "The G.I. Bill: America's Largest Affirmative Action Program," accessed January 24, 2022, http://thealliancetc.org/wp-content/uploads/2016/08/AMS_Report1_GI_bill_Final2012-1.pdf.

88. Claudia Goldin, *Understanding the Gender Gap: An Economic History of American Women* (New York: Oxford University Press, 1990).

89. Judith Warner, *Perfect Madness: Motherhood in the Age of Anxiety* (New York: Riverhead Books, 2005), 138; D. A. Cotter, J. M. Hermsen, and P. England, "Moms and Jobs: Trends in Mothers' Employment and which Mothers Stay Home," in *American Families: A Multicultural Reader*, ed. S. Coontz, M. Parson, and G. Raley, 2nd. ed. (New York: Routledge, 2008), 379–86.

90. C. Wright Mills, *White Collar: The American Middle Classes* (New York: Oxford University Press, 1951).

91. Goldin, *Understanding the Gender Gap*; Coontz, *The Way We Never Were*.

92. Bailey, *From Front Porch to Back Seat*.

93. Goldin, *Understanding the Gender Gap*.

94. Ibid.

95. Susan Lehrer, *Origins of Protective Labor Legislation for Women* (Albany: State University of New York Press, 1987).

96. Ibid.

97. Ibid.

98. Cynthia Deitch, "Gender, Race, and Class Politics and the Inclusion of Women in the Title VII of the 1964 Civil Rights Act," *Gender & Society* 7, no. 2 (1993): 183–203.

99. Jo Freeman, *We Will Be Heard: Women's Struggles for Political Power in the United States* (New York: Rowman & Littlefield, 2008).

100. Lynn Weiner, *From Working Girl to Working Mother: The Female Labor Force in the United States 1820–1980* (Chapel Hill: University of North Carolina Press, 2016).

101. Myra Marx Ferree, "Beyond Separate Spheres: Feminism and Family Research," *Journal of Marriage and Family* 52, no. 4 (1990): 866–84.

102. US Department of Labor, Women's Bureau, "Labor force participation rate of mothers by age of youngest child," accessed January 24, 2022, https://www.dol.gov/agencies/wb/data/lfp/mother-age-youngestchild.

103. James Dobson, "Dr. James Dobson's Newsletter: Marriage on the Ropes?" *Focus on the Family Newsletter*, September 2003, www.catholicfamilycatalog.com/dr-james-dobson-on-marriage.htm.

104. Lenore Weitzman, *The Divorce Revolution: The Unexpected Social and Economic Consequences for Women and Children in America* (New York: The Free Press, 1985).

105. P. J. Smock, W. D. Manning, and S. Gupta, "The Effect of Marriage and Divorce on Women's Economic Well-Being," *American Sociological Review* 64, no. 6 (1999): 794–812; Michael J. Rosenfeld, "Who Wants the Breakup? Gender and Breakup in Heterosexual Couples," in *Social Networks and the Life Course: Integrating the Development of Human Lives and Social Relational Networks* ed. Duane F. Alwin, Diane H. Felmlee, and Derek A. Kreager (Cham, Switzerland: Springer International Publishing, 2018).

106. Jennifer Glass and Philip Levchak, "Red States, Blue States, and Divorce: Understanding the Impact of Conservative Protestantism on Regional Variation in Divorce Rates," *American Journal of Sociology* 119, no. 4 (2014): 1002–46.

107. Justin McCarthy, "Record-High 70% in U.S. Support Same-Sex Marriage," *Gallup*, June 8, 2021, https://news.gallup.com/poll/350486/record-high-support-same-sex-marriage.aspx.

108. Pew Research Social & Demographic Trends Project, "The Decline of Marriage and Rise of New Families," Pew Research Center, November 18, 2010, www.pewsocialtrends.org/2010/11/18/the-decline-of-marriage-and-rise-of-new-families/.

109. Kim Parker and Renee Stepler, "As U.S. Marriage Rate Hovers at 50%, Education Gap in Marital Status Widens," Pew Research Center, September 14, 2017, www.pewresearch.org/fact-tank/2017/09/14/as-u-s-marriage-rate-hovers-at-50-education-gap-in-marital-status-widens/; U.S. Census Bureau, "Historical Living Arrangements of Adults," Table AD-3: Living Arrangements of Adults 18 and Over, 1967 to Present, accessed November 22, 2021, www.census.gov/data/tables/time-series/demo/families/adults.html.

110. J. A. Martin, B. E. Hamilton, M. J. K. Osterman, A. K. Driscoll, and P. Drake, "Births: Final Data for 2016," *National Vital Statistics Reports* 67, no 1 (Hyattsville, MD: National Center for Health Statistics, 2018), www.cdc.gov/nchs/data/nvsr/nvsr67/nvsr67_01.pdf.

111. Ye Luo, Tracey A. LaPierre, Mary Elizabeth Hughes, and Linda J. Waite, "Grandparents Providing Care to Grandchildren: A Population-Based Study of Continuity and Change," *Journal of Family Issues* 33, no. 9 (2012): 1143–67.

112. Frank Newport, "Understanding the Increase in Moral Acceptability of Polygamy," *Gallup*, June 26, 2020, https://news.gallup.com/opinion/polling-matters/313112/understanding-increase-moral-acceptability-polygamy.aspx; Amy C. Moors, Amanda N. Gesselman, and Justin R. Garcia, "Desire, Familiarity, and Engagement in Polyamory: Results from a National Sample of Single Adults in the United States," *Frontiers in Psychology* 12, no. 619640, https://doi.org/10.3389/fpsyg.2021.619640.

113. For early feminist resistance to marriage and monogamy, see Leila J. Rupp, "Feminism and the Sexual Revolution in the Early Twentieth Century: The Case of Doris Stevens," *Feminist Studies* 15, no. 2 (1989): 289–309.

114. Coontz, "The World Historical Transformation of Marriage," 978.

115. Pew Research Center, "Parenting in America" December 17, 2015, https://www.pewresearch.org/social-trends/2015/12/17/1-the-american-family-today/#fnref-21321-12.

116. Coontz, "The World Historical Transformation of Marriage," 974.

117. Reprints of her more incendiary speeches from the 1970s are collected in Phyllis Schlafly, *Feminist Fantasies*, ed. Ann Coulter (Dallas: Spence Publishers, 2003).

118. Leslie Steiner, *Mommy Wars: Stay-at-Home and Career Moms Face Off about Their Choices, Their Lives, Their Families* (New York: Random House, 2006); Miriam Peskowitz, *The Truth Behind the Mommy Wars* (Boston: DaCapo Press, 2005).

119. Patrick Buchanan, "Homosexuals and Retribution," *New York Post*, May 24, 1983.

120. Molly Dragiewicz, *Equality with a Vengeance: Men's Rights Groups, Battered Women, and Anti-feminist Backlash* (Boston: Northeastern University Press, 2011).

121. Thomas Piketty, *Capital in the Twenty-First Century* (Cambridge, MA: Belknap Press of Harvard University, 2014).

122. Kathleen Gerson, "Moral Dilemmas, Moral Strategies, and the Transformation of Gender: Lessons from Two Generations of Work and Family Change," *Gender & Society* 16, no. 1 (2002): 8–28.

123. Myra Marx Ferree, "The View from Below: Women's Employment and Gender Equality in Working Class Families," *Marriage and Family Review* 7, no. 3/4 (1984): 57–75; Myra Marx Ferree, "Class, Housework, and Happiness," *Sex Roles* 11, no. 11/12 (1984): 1057–74.

Chapter 9: Sexualities

1. Leonore Tiefer, *Sex Is Not a Natural Act & Other Essays*, 2nd ed. (Boulder, CO: Westview Press, 1995).

2. Jess Butler, "Sexual Subjects: Hooking Up in the Age of Postfeminism" (PhD diss., University of Southern California, 2013), 74.

3. Jessie Ford, Paula England, and Jonathan Bearak, "The American College Hookup Scene: Findings from the Online College Social Life Survey" (paper, American Sociological Association Annual Meeting, Chicago, August 2015).

4. Zhana Vrangalova and Anthony Ong, "Who Benefits from Casual Sex? The Moderating Role of Sociosexuality," *Social Psychological and Personality Science* 5, no. 8 (2014): 883–91.

5. Angus McLaren, *Twentieth Century Sexuality: A History* (Oxford: Blackwell, 1999).

6. For a great overview, see Marion C. Willetts, Susan Sprecher, and Frank D. Beck, "Overview of Sexual Practices and Attitudes within Relational Contexts," in *The Handbook of Sexuality in Close Relationships*, ed. John H. Harvey, Amy Wenzel, and Susan Specher (Mahwah, NJ: Erlbaum, 2004), 57–85.

7. Steven Epstein, *Impure Science: AIDS, Activism, and the Politics of Knowledge* (Berkeley: University of California Press, 1998); and Benita Roth, *The Life and Death of ACT UP/LA: Anti-AIDS Activism in the Los Angeles from the 1980s to the 2000s* (New York: Cambridge University Press, 2017).

8. Martha E. Kempner, "A Controversial Decade: 10 Years of Tracking Debates around Sex Education," *SIECUS Report* 31, no. 6 (2003): 33–48.

9. "Federally Funded Abstinence-Only Programs: Harmful and Ineffective," Guttmacher Institute, May 2021, https://www.guttmacher.org/sites/default/files/factsheet/abstinence-only-programs-fact-sheet.pdf.

10. Darcy Cosper, "Shock Value," *Print* 51 (1997): 38–40; Anthony Vagnoni, "Something about This Advertising," *Advertising Age*, February 8, 1999, 30; and Sut Jhally, "Advertising and the End of the World" (transcript), Media Education Foundation, 1997, https://www.mediaed.org/transcripts/Advertising-and-the-End-of-the-World-Transcript.pdf.

11. Natalie Jarvey, "Sexual Assault Movement #MeToo Reaches Nearly 500,000 Tweets," *Hollywood Reporter*, October 16, 2017, https://www.hollywoodreporter.com/news/metoo-sexual-assault-movement-reaches-500000-tweets-1049235.

12. "For Women, It's Not Just the O'Reilly Problem" (editorial), *New York Times*, April 22, 2017, https://www.nytimes.com/2017/04/22/opinion/sunday/for-women-its-not-just-the-oreilly-problem.html; and Kathryn Casteel, "Sexual Harassment Isn't Just a Silicon Valley Problem," FiveThirtyEight, July 13, 2017, https://fivethirtyeight.com/features/sexual-harassment-isnt-just-a-silicon-valley-problem/.

13. HRC Foundation, "Sexual Assault and the LGBTQ Community," Human Rights Campaign, accessed Feb. 11, 2022, https://www.hrc.org/resources/sexual-assault-and-the-lgbt-community.

14. J. R. Thorpe, "This Is How Many People Have Posted #MeToo since October," Bustle, December 1, 2017, https://www.bustle.com/p/this-is-how-many-people-have-posted-me-too-since-october-according-to-new-data-6753697; Alka Kurian, "#MeToo Is Riding a New Wave of Feminism in India," Conversation, February 1, 2018, https://theconversation.com/metoo-is-riding-a-new-wave-of-feminism-in-india-89842; and Pardis Mahdavi, "How #MeToo Became a Global Movement," *Foreign Affairs*, March 6, 2018, https://www.foreignaffairs.com/articles/2018-03-06/how-metoo-became-global-movement.

15. Roee Levy and Martin Mattsson, "The Effects of Social Movements: Evidence from #MeToo," August 6, 2021, http://dx.doi.org/10.2139/ssrn.3496903.

16. Selina Noetzel, Mari F. Mussalem Gentile, Gianna Lowery, Sona Zemanova, Sophie Lecheler, and Christina Peter, "Social Campaigns to Social Change? Sexual Violence Framing in U.S. News before and

after #metoo," *Journalism*, January 3, 2022, https://doi.org/10.1177/14648849211056386; and "Sexual Violence, The #MeToo Movement, and Narrative Shift," Opportunity Agenda, accessed February 1, 2022, https://www.opportunityagenda.org/shifting-narrative/sexual-violence-metoo-movement-and-narrative-shift.

17. Hanna Szekeres, Eric Shuman, Tamar Saguy, "Views of Sexual Assault Following #MeToo: The Role of Gender and Individual Differences," *Personality and Individual Differences* 166 (November 1, 2020), https://doi.org/10.1016/j.paid.2020.110203; "Voters' Views toward Justice Kavanaugh, #MeToo, and the Supreme Court," PerryUndem Research/Communication, September 27, 2019, https://view.publitas.com/perryundem-research-communication/perryundem-kavanaugh-and-metoo-report/page/1; Chloe Grace Hart, "Has #MeToo Changed the Attitudes towards Women Who Complain of Sexual Harassment?" Conversation, May 24, 2019, https://scroll.in/article/924371/has-metoo-changed-the-attitudes-towards-woman-who-complain-of-sexual-harassment; and "Majority of Americans Favor #MeToo and Want More Done on Fighting Violence against Women," Harris Poll, accessed February 2, 2022, https://theharrispoll.com/majority-americans-favor-metoo-want-done-fighting-violence-women.

18. "Voters' Views toward Justice Kavanaugh, #MeToo, and the Supreme Court."

19. Ksenia Keplinger, Stefanie K. Johnson Jessica F. Kirk, and Liza Y. Barnes, "Women at Work: Changes in Sexual Harassment between September 2016 and September 2018," *PLOS ONE* 14, no. 7 (2019): e0218313, https://doi.org/10.1371/journal.pone.0218313.

20. Courtney Vinopal, "Coronavirus Has Changed Online Dating. Here's Why Some Say That's a Good Thing," PBS News Hour, May 15, 2020, https://www.pbs.org/newshour/nation/coronavirus-has-changed-online-dating-heres-why-some-say-thats-a-good-thing.

21. Carey M. Noland, "Negotiating Desire and Uncertainty on Tinder during the COVID-19 Pandemic: Implications for the Transformation of Sexual Health Communication," *Cyberpsychology, Behavior, and Social Networking* 24, no. 7 (2021): 488–92; and Lisa Wade, not yet published research, 150 in-depth semistructured interviews with Tulane undergraduates about social life on campus during the Covid-19 pandemic in the 2020/2021 academic year. Works are in progress.

22. "Singles in America," Match, accessed February 2, 2022, https://www.singlesinamerica.com/.

23. Rhonda N. Balzarini, Amy Muise, Giulia Zoppolat, Amanda N. Gesselman, Justin J. Lehmiller, Justin R. Garcia, et al., "Sexual Desire in the Time of COVID-19: How Covid-Related Stressors Are Associated with Sexual Desire in Romantic Relationships," PsyArXiv, March 26, 2021, https://doi.org/10.31234/osf.io/nxkgp.

24. Jennifer Scanlon, "Sexy from the Start: Anticipatory Elements of Second Wave Feminism," *Women's Studies* 38, no. 2 (2009): 127–50; Rosalind Gill, "Mediated Intimacy and Postfeminism: A Discourse Analytic Examination of Sex and Relationships Advice in a Women's Magazine," *Discourse & Communication* 3, no. 4 (2009): 345–69; and Jennifer Stevens Aubrey, Leah Dajches, and Larissa Terán, "Media as a Source of Sexual Socialization for Emerging Adults," in *Sexuality in Emerging Adulthood*, ed. Elizabeth M. Morgan and Manfred H. M. van Dulmen (New York: Oxford University Press, 2021), 312–32.

25. McLaren, *Twentieth Century Sexuality*.

26. Jean Twenge, "Status and Gender: The Paradox of Progress in an Age of Narcissism," *Sex Roles* 61 (2009): 338–40.

27. Lisa Wade, *American Hookup: The New Culture of Sex on Campus* (New York: W. W. Norton, 2017).

28. Brooke Wells and Jean Twenge, "Changes in Young People's Sexual Behavior and Attitudes, 1943–1999: A Cross-Temporal Meta-Analysis," *Review of General Psychology* 9 (2005): 249–61; Jennifer L. Petersen and Janet Shibley Hyde, "A Meta-Analytic Review of Research on Gender Differences in Sexuality, 1993–2007," *Psychological Bulletin* 136, no. 1 (2010): 21–38; Willetts, Sprecher, and Beck, "Overview of Sexual Practices and Attitudes within Relational Contexts," 57–85; Anjani Chandra, William D. Mosher, Casey Copen, and Catlainn Sionean, "Sexual Behavior, Sexual Attraction, and Sexual Identity in the United States: Data from the 2006–2008 National Survey of Family Growth," *National Health Statistics Reports*, no. 36 (March 3, 2011), https://www.cdc.gov/nchs/data/nhsr/nhsr036.pdf; and Megan Brenan, "Changing One's Gender Is Sharply Contentious Moral Issue," Gallup, June 11, 2021, https://news.gallup.com/poll/351020/changing-one-gender-sharply-contentious-moral-issue.aspx.

29. Wade, *American Hookup*, 120.

30. Ann Ferguson, "Sex War: The Debate between Radical and Libertarian Feminists," *Signs* 10, no. 1

(Autumn 1984): 108; Ilene Philipson, "The Repression of History and Gender: A Critical Perspective on the Feminist Sexuality Debate," *Signs* 10, no. 1 (Autumn 1984): 113–14; and Carole S. Vance and Ann Barr Snitow, "Toward a Conversation about Sex in Feminism: A Modest Proposal," *Signs* 10, no. 1 (Autumn 1984): 129–30.

31. Carole S. Vance, ed., *Pleasure and Danger: Exploring Female Sexuality* (Boston: Routledge, 1984).

32. Lynn Comella, "Revisiting the Feminist Sex Wars," *Feminist Studies* 41, no. 2 (2015): 437–62.

33. Gail Dines, "Don't Be Fooled by *Fifty Shades of Grey*—Christian Grey Is No Heartthrob," *Guardian*, October 25, 2013, https://www.theguardian.com /commentisfree/2013/oct/25/fifty-shades-of-grey -christian-jamie-dornan-fall.

34. McLaren, *Twentieth Century Sexuality*.

35. Ana J. Bridges, Robert Wosnitzer, Erica Scharrer, Chyng Sun, and Rachael Liberman, "Aggression and Sexual Behavior in Best-Selling Pornography Videos: A Content Analysis Update," *Violence against Women* 16, no. 10 (2010): 1065–85; Martin Barron and Michael Kimmel, "Sexual Violence in Three Pornographic Media: Toward a Sociological Explanation," *Journal of Sex Research* 37 (2010): 161–69; Chyng Sun, Robert Wosnitzer, Ana J. Bridges, Erica Scharrer, and Rachael Liberman, "Harder and Harder: The Content of Popular Pornographic Movies," in *Victims of Sexual Assault and Abuse: Resources and Responses for Individuals and Families*, ed. Michele A. Paludi and Florence L. Denmark (Santa Barbara, CA: Praeger, 2010).

36. Niki Fritz, Vincent Malic, Bryant Paul, and Yanyan Zhou, "A Descriptive Analysis of the Types, Targets, and Relative Frequency of Aggression in Mainstream Pornography," *Archives of Sexual Behavior* 49, no. 4 (2020): 3041–52, https://doi.org/10.1007 /s10508-020-01773-0.

37. Niki Fritz, Vincent Malic, Bryant Paul, and Yanyan Zhou, "Worse Than Objects: The Depiction of Black Women and Men and Their Sexual Relationship in Pornography," *Gender Issues* 38 (2020): 100–120.

38. Andrew Dugan, "More Americans Say Pornography Is Morally Acceptable," Gallup, June 5, 2018, https://news.gallup.com/poll/235280/americans -say-pornography-morally-acceptable.aspx.

39. "Prostitution: Opinion Polls/Surveys 1978–2016," ProCon.org., updated March 29, 2018, https://pros titution.procon.org/opinion-polls-surveys/; and Nina Luo, "Decriminalizing Survival: Policy Platform and Polling on the Decriminalization of Sex Work," Data for Progress, accessed February 2, 2022, https:// www.filesforprogress.org/memos/decriminalizing -sex-work.pdf.

40. Jason D. Hans, Martie Gillen, and Katrina Akande, "Sex Redefined: The Reclassification of Oral-Genital Contact," Guttmacher Institute, March 30, 2010, https://doi.org/10.1363/420 7410; Lisa Remez, "Oral Sex among Adolescents: Is It Sex or Is It Abstinence?" *Family Planning Perspectives* 32, no. 6 (2000): 298–304; Stephanie A. Sanders and June Machover Reinisch, "Would You Say You 'Had Sex' If . . . ?" *JAMA* 281, no. 3 (1999): 257–77; Melina M. Bersamin, Deborah A. Fisher, Samantha Walker, Douglas L. Hill, and Joel W. Grube, "Defining Virginity and Abstinence: Adolescents' Interpretations of Sexual Behaviors," *Journal of Adolescent Health* 41, no. 2 (2007): 182–88.

41. Janelle M. Pham, "The Limits of Heteronormative Sexual Scripting: College Student Development of Individual Sexual Scripts and Descriptions of Lesbian Sexual Behavior," *Frontiers in Sociology* 1, no. 7 (2016), https://doi.org/10.3389/fsoc.2016.00007.

42. Ibid.

43. Ibid.

44. Kathryn McPhillips, Virginia Braun, and Nicola Gavey, "Defining Heterosex: How Imperative Is the 'Coital imperative'?" *Women's Studies International Forum* 24 (2001): 229–40.

45. Tiefer, *Sex Is Not a Natural Act*.

46. Elisabeth A. Lloyd, *The Case of the Female Orgasm: Bias in the Science of Evolution* (Boston: Harvard University Press, 2005); and Shere Hite, *The Hite Report: A Nationwide Study of Female Sexuality* (New York: Seven Stories Press, 1977).

47. Debby Herbenick, Michael Reece, Vanessa Schick, Stephanie Sanders, Brian Dodge, and J. Dennis Fortenberry, "An Event-Level Analysis of the Sexual Characteristics and Composition among Adults Ages 18 to 59: Results from a National Probability Sample in the United States," *Journal of Sexual Medicine* 7, no. 5 (2010): 346–61; and David A. Frederick, H. Kate St. John, Justin R. Garcia, and Elisabeth A. Lloyd, "Differences in Orgasm Frequency among Gay, Lesbian, Bisexual, and Heterosexual Men and Women in a U.S. National Sample," *Archives of Sexual Behavior* 47 (2018): 273–88.

48. Butler, "Sexual Subjects"; Léa Jeanne Séguin and Martin Blais, "The Development and Validation

of the Orgasm Beliefs Inventory," *Archives of Sexual Behavior* 50 (2021): 2543–61; and Barry McCarthy and Lana M. Wald, "Mindfulness and Good Enough Sex," *Sexual Relationship Therapy* 28 (2013): 37–47.

49. Zach Beauchamp, "6 Maps and Charts that Explain Sex around the World," *Vox*, May 26, 2015.

50. Frederick, St. John, Garcia, and Lloyd, "Differences in Orgasm Frequency," 273–88; Heather Armstrong and Elke Reissing, "Women Who Have Sex with Women: A Comprehensive Review of the Literature and Conceptual Model of Sexual Function," *Sexual and Relationship Therapy* 28, no. 4 (2013): 364–99; Justin Garcia, Elisabeth A. Lloyd, Kim Wallen, and Helen E. Fisher, "Variation in Orgasm Occurrence by Sexual Orientation in a Sample of U.S. Singles," *International Society for Sexual Medicine* 11, no. 11 (2014): 2645–52.

51. M. Douglass and L. Douglass, *Are We Having Fun Yet?* (New York: Hyperion, 1997); and Alfred Kinsey, Wardell Pomeroy, Clyde Martin, and Paul Gebhard, *Sexual Behavior in the Human Female* (Philadelphia: Saunders, 1953). See also Sharon Thompson, "Search for Tomorrow: On Feminism and the Reconstruction of Teen Romance," in *Pleasure and Danger: Exploring Female Sexuality*, ed. Carole S. Vance (London: Pandora, 1989); and John Harvey, Amy Wenzel, and Susan Sprecher, *The Handbook of Sexuality in Close Relationships* (Mahwah, NJ: Lawrence Erlbaum, 2004).

52. Lisa Wade and Gwen Sharp, "Selling Sex," in *Images That Injure: Pictorial Stereotypes in the Media*, ed. Lester Paul and Susan Ross (Westport, CT: Praeger, 2011), 165.

53. Janet Holland, Caroline Ramazanoglu, Sue Sharpe, and Rachel Thomson, *The Male in the Head: Young People, Heterosexuality and Power*, 2nd ed. (London: Tufnell Press, 2004).

54. Laura Mulvey, "Visual Pleasure and Narrative Cinema," *Screen* 16, no. 3 (1975): 6–18.

55. See, for example, Erin Hatton and Mary Nell Trautner, "Equal Opportunity Objectification? The Sexualization of Men and Women on the Cover of *Rolling Stone*," *Sexuality & Culture* 15, no. 3 (2011): 256–78.

56. Michelle R. Hebl, Eden B. King, and Jean Lin, "The Swimsuit Becomes Us All: Ethnicity, Gender, and Vulnerability to Self-Objectification," *Personality and Social Psychology Bulletin* 30 (2004): 1322–31; Shelly Grabe and Janet Shibley Hyde, "Body Objectification, MTV, and Psychological Outcomes among Female Adolescents," *Journal of Applied Psychology* 39, no. 12 (2009): 2840–58; and Shelly Grabe, Janet Shibley Hyde, and Sara M. Lindberg, "Body Objectification and Depression in Adolescents: The Role of Gender, Shame, and Rumination," *Psychology of Women Quarterly* 31, no. 2 (2007): 164–75.

57. Lisa M. Diamond, "'I'm Straight, but I Kissed a Girl': The Trouble with American Media Representations of Female-Female Sexuality," *Feminism & Psychology* 15 (2005): 104–11; and Sue Jackson and Tamsyn Gilbertson, "'Hot Lesbians': Young People's Talk about Representations of Lesbianism," *Sexualities* 12 (2019): 199–224.

58. Melanie S. Hill and Ann R. Fischer, "Examining Objectification Theory: Lesbian and Heterosexual Women's Experiences with Sexual-and Self-Objectification," *Counseling Psychologist* 36, no. 5 (2008): 745–76.

59. Barbara L. Fredrickson and Tomi-Ann Roberts, "Objectification Theory: Toward Understanding Women's Lived Experiences and Mental Health Risks," *Psychology of Women Quarterly* 21, no. 2 (1997): 173–206.

60. Rachel M. Calogero and J. Kevin Thompson, "Potential Implications of the Objectification of Women's Bodies and Sexual Satisfaction," *Body Image* 6, no. 2 (2009): 145–48; Amy Steer and Marika Tiggemann, "The Role of Self-Objectification in Women's Sexual Functioning," *Journal of Social and Clinical Psychology* 27, no. 3 (2008): 205–25; and Virginia Ramseyer Winter, Elizabeth A. O'Neill, Mackenzie Cook, Kelsey L. Rose, Amanda Hood, "Sexual Function in Hook-Up Culture: The Role of Body Image," *Body Image* 34 (2020): 135–44.

61. Catherine Hakim, "Erotic Capital," *European Sociological Review* 26, no. 5 (October 2010): 499–518; and Adam Green, "The Social Organization of Desire: The Sexual Fields Approach," *Sociological Theory* 26, no. 1 (2008): 25–50.

62. Christine A. Smith and Shannon Stillman, "Butch/Femme in the Personal Advertisements of Lesbians," *Journal of Lesbian Studies* 6, no. 1 (2002): 45–51; and Michael J. Bailey, Peggy Y. Kim, Alex Hills, and Joan A. W. Linsenmeier, "Butch, Femme, or Straight Acting? Partner Preferences of Gay Men and Lesbians," *Journal of Personality and Social Psychology* 73, no. 5 (November 1997): 960–73.

63. Chelsea Reynolds, "'I Am Super Straight and I Prefer You Be Too': Constructions of Heterosexual Masculinity in Online Personal Ads for 'Straight' Men Seeking Sex with Men," *Journal of Communi-*

cation Inquiry 39, no. 3 (2015): 213–31; Cory J. Cas-calheira and Brandt A. Smith, "Hierarchy of Desire: Partner Preferences and Social Identities of Men Who Have Sex with Men on Geosocial Networks," Sexuality & Culture 24 (2020): 630–48; Tony Silva, "Bud-Sex: Constructing Normative Masculinity among Rural Straight Men That Have Sex with Men," Gender & Society 31, no. 1 (2016): 51–73, 64; and Martin J. Downing Jr. and Eric W Schrimshaw, "Self-Presentation, Desired Partner Characteristics, and Sexual Behavior Preferences in Online Personal Advertisements of Men Seeking Non-Gay-Identified Men," Psychology of Sexual Orientation and Gender Diversity 1, no. 1 (2014): 30–39.

64. Nathan S. Rodriguez, Jennifer Huemmer, and Lindsey E. Blumell, "Mobile Masculinities: An Investigation of Networked Masculinities in Gay Dating Apps," Masculinities & Social Change 5, no. 3 (2016): 241–67.

65. Christian Rudder, "Your Looks and Your Inbox," OkTrends (blog), November 17, 2009, https://www.gwern.net/docs/psychology/okcupid/yourlooksandyourinbox.html.

66. Ibid.

67. Leonardo Bursztyn, Thomas Fujiwara, and Amanda Pallais, "'Acting Wife': Marriage Market Incentives and Labor Market Investments," American Economic Review 107, no. 11 (2017): 3288–319.

68. Norman K. Denzin, "Selling Images of Inequality: Hollywood Cinema and the Reproduction of Racial and Gender Stereotypes," in The Blackwell Companion to Social Inequalities, ed. Mary Romero and Eric Margolis (Malden, MA: Blackwell, 2005), 469–501; Charles Ramirez Berg, Latino Images in Film: Stereotypes, Subversion and Resistance (Austin: University of Texas Press, 2002); Stephanie Greco Larson, Media & Minorities: The Politics of Race in News and Entertainment (Lanham, MA: Rowman & Littlefield, 2006); and Scott Poulson-Bryant, Hung: A Meditation on the Measure of Black Men in America (New York: Harlem Moon, 2005).

69. Green, "The Social Organization of Desire," 25–50; Lawrence Stacey and TehQuin D. Forbes, "Feeling Like a Fetish: Racialized Feelings, Fetishization, and the Contours of Sexual Racism on Gay Dating Apps," Journal of Sex Research (September 2021), https://doi.org/10.1080/00224499.2021.1979455.

70. John Sides and Kimberly Gross, "Stereotypes of Muslims and Support for the War on Terror," Journal of Politics 75, no. 3 (2013): 583–98; Iris Wigger, "Anti-Muslim Racism and the Racification of Sex-ual Violence: 'Intersectional Stereotyping' in Mass Media Representations of Male Muslim Migrants in Germany," Culture and Religion 20, no. 3 (2019): 248–71; and Laura Navarro, "Islamophobia and Sexism: Muslim Women in the Western Mass Media," Human Architecture: A Journal of the Sociology of Self-Knowledge 8, no. 2 (2010): 95–114.

71. Robert G. Lee, Orientals: Asian Americans in Popular Culture (Philadelphia: Temple University Press, 1999); Anthony Chen, "Lives at the Center of the Periphery, Lives at the Periphery of the Center: Chinese American Masculinities and Bargaining with Hegemony," Gender & Society 13, no. 5 (1999): 584–607; Y. Joel Wong, Jesse Owen, Kimberly K. Tran, Dana L. Collins, and Claire E. Higgins, "Asian American Male College Students' Perceptions of People's Stereotypes about Asian American Men," Psychology of Men & Masculinity 13, no. 1 (2012): 75–88.

72. Kevin K. Kumashiro, "Supplementing Normalcy and Otherness: Queer Asian American Men Reflect on Stereotypes, Identity, and Oppression," International Journal of Qualitative Studies in Education 12, no. 5 (1999): 491–508, 501.

73. Yen Le Espiritu, Asian American Women and Men: Labor, Laws, and Love (Lanham, MD: Rowman & Littlefield, 2008), 110.

74. Kevin K. Kumashiro, "Supplementing Normalcy and Otherness: Queer Asian American Men Reflect on Stereotypes, Identity, and Oppression," International Journal of Qualitative Studies in Education 12, no. 5 (1999): 491–508, 503.

75. Celeste Vaughan Curington, Jennifer Hickes Lundquist, and Ken-Hou Lin, The Dating Divide: Race and Desire in the Era of Online Romance (Oakland: University of California Press, 2021).

76. Ken-Hou Lin and Jennifer Lundquist, "Mate Selection in Cyberspace: The Intersection of Race, Gender, and Education," American Journal of Sociology 119, no. 1 (2013): 183–215.

77. Courtney Weaver, "Tiny, Flat-Chested, and Hairless!," Salon, May 6, 1998, https://www.salon.com/1998/05/06/weav_22/.

78. Jerry A. Jacobs and Teresa G. Labov, "Gender Differentials in Intermarriage among Sixteen Race and Ethnic Groups," Sociological Forum 17 (2002): 621–46; and "America's Families and Living Arrangements," (Table FG-3, 2021), US Census Bureau, Nov. 29, 2021, https://www.census.gov/data/tables/2021/demo/families/cps-2021.html.

79. Zhenchao Qian and Daniel T. Lichter, "Social Boundaries and Marital Assimilation: Interpreting Trends in Racial and Ethnic Intermarriage," *American Sociological Review* 72, no. 1 (2007): 68–94; and Zhenchao Qian and Daniel T. Lichter, "Changing Patterns of Interracial Marriage in a Multiracial Society," *Journal of Marriage and Family* 73, no. 5 (2011): 1065–84.

80. Debbie Lum, dir., *Seeking Asian Female* (documentary), May 6, 2013, https://www.pbs.org/inde pendentlens/documentaries/seeking-asian-female/; and Pei-Chia Lan, "New Global Politics of Reproductive Labor: Gendered Labor and Marriage Migration," *Sociological Compass* 2, no. 6 (2008): 1801–15.

81. "Singles in America."

82. "2019 Statistics," Women and Hollywood, accessed Feb. 11, 2022, https://womenandhollywood .com/resources/statistics/2019-statistics/.

83. John Gagnon and William Simon, *Sexual Conduct: The Social Sources of Human Sexuality* (Chicago: Aldine, 1973); and Michael W. Wiederman, "Sexual Script Theory: Past, Present, and Future," in *Handbook of the Sociology of Sexualities*, ed. John DeLamater and Rebecca F. Plante (Cham, Switzerland: Springer, 2015).

84. Joyce Endendijk, Anneloes van Baar, and Maja Deković, "He Is a Stud, She Is a Slut! A Meta-analysis of the Continued Existence of Sexual Double Standards," *Personality and Social Psychology Review* 24, no. 2 (2020): 163–90; and Aubrey, Dajches, and Terán, "Media as a Source of Sexual Socialization for Emerging Adults," 312–32.

85. Nicola Gavey, *Just Sex? The Cultural Scaffolding of Rape* (London: Routledge, 2005).

86. David A. Moskowitz and Michael E. Roloff, "Recognition and Construction of Top, Bottom, and Versatile Orientations in Gay/Bisexual Men," *Archives of Sexual Behavior* 46 (2017): 273–85; David A. Moskowitz, Andrés Alvarado Avila, Ashley Kraus, Jeremy Birnholtz, and Kathryn Macapagal, "Top, Bottom, and Versatile Orientations among Adolescent Sexual Minority Men," *Journal of Sex Research* (2021): 1–9.

87. Michelle Marie Johns, Emily Pingel, Anna Eisenberg, Matthew Leslie Santana, and José Bauermeister, "Butch Tops and Femme Bottoms? Sexual Positioning, Sexual Decision Making, and Gender Roles among Young Gay Men," *American Journal of Men's Health* 6, no. 6 (2012): 505–18; and Susan Kippax and Gary Smith, "Anal Intercourse and Power in Sex between Men," *Sexualities* 4, no. 4 (2001): 413–34.

88. James P. Ravenhill and Richard O. de Visser, "'It Takes a Man to Put Me on the Bottom': Gay Men's Experiences of Masculinity and Anal Intercourse," *Journal of Sex Research* 55, no. 8 (2018): 1033–47.

89. Ibid.

90. David J. Lick and Kerri J. Johnson, "Intersecting Race and Gender Cues Are Associated with Perceptions of Gay Men's Preferred Sexual Roles," *Archives of Sexual Behavior* 44, no. 5 (2015): 1471–81.

91. Niels Teunis, "Sexual Objectification and the Construction of Whiteness in the Gay Male Community," *Culture, Health & Sexuality* 9, no. 3 (2007): 263–275.

92. Ibid.

93. Maria K. Walsey, "Sexual Ad-Lib? Sexual Scripts and the Negotiation of Sexual Boundaries when Women Have Sex with Women" (master's thesis, Texas State University, 2013), https://digital.library .txstate.edu/bitstream/handle/10877/4877/WASLEY -THESIS-2013.pdf?isAllowed=y&sequence=1.

94. Kelsey K. Sewell, Larissa A. McGarrity, and Donald S. Strassberg, "Sexual Behavior, Definitions of Sex, and the Role of Self-Partner Context Among Lesbian, Gay, and Bisexual Adults," *Journal of Sex Research* 54, no. 7 (2017): 825–31.

95. Jacqui Gabb, "The Relationship Work of Sexual Intimacy in Long-Term Heterosexual and LGBTQ Partnerships," *Current Sociology* 70, no. 1 (2022): 24–41.

96. Margaret Campbell, "Disabilities and Sexual Expression: A Review of the Literature," *Sociology Compass* 11, no. 9 (2017): e12508.

97. Tom Shakespeare, "Disabled Sexuality: Toward Rights and Recognition," *Sexuality and Disability* 18, no. 3 (2000): 159–166, 163.

98. Sharon Block, *Rape and Sexual Power in Early America* (Chapel Hill: University of North Carolina Press, 2006); Elizabeth Fox-Genovese, *Within the Plantation Household: Black and White Women of the Old South* (Chapel Hill: University of North Carolina Press, 1988); Thomas A. Foster, "The Sexual Abuse of Black Men under American Slavery," *Journal of the History of Sexuality* 20, no. 3 (2011): 445–64.

99. Antonia I. Castañeda, "Sexual Violence in the Politics and Policies of Conquest: Amerindian Women and the Spanish Conquest of Alta California," in *Building with Our Hands: New Directions in*

Chicana Studies, ed. Adela de la Torre, Beatríz M. Pesquera (Berkeley: University of California Press, 1993), 15–33.

100. Carole Pateman, *The Sexual Contract* (Cambridge: Polity, 1988); and Myra Marx Ferree, "The Crisis of Masculinity for Gendered Democracies: Before, during, and after Trump," *Sociological Forum* 35, no. 1 (2020): 898–917.

101. Kathrin Zippel, *The Politics of Sexual Harassment: A Comparative Study of the United States, the European Union and Germany* (Cambridge: Cambridge University Press, 2006); and Abigail Saguy, *Sexual Harassment in France: From Capitol Hill to the Sorbonne* (Los Angeles: University of California Press, 2003).

102. US Federal Bureau of Investigation, "Crime in the United States, 2013," accessed Feb. 11, 2022, https://ucr.fbi.gov/crime-in-the-u.s/2013/crime-in-the-u.s.-2013/violent-crime/rape.

103. Susan Estrich, *Real Rape* (Cambridge, MA: Harvard University Press, 1987); Susan Brownmiller, *Against Our Will: Men, Women, and Rape* (New York: Simon & Schuster, 1975); Cassia Spohn and Julie Horney, *Rape Law Reform: A Grassroots Revolution and Its Impact* (New York: Plenum Press, 1992); Diana E. H. Russell, *Rape in Marriage* (Bloomington: Indiana University Press, 1990); Kristin Bumiller, *The Civil Rights Society: The Social Construction of Victims* (Baltimore, MD: Johns Hopkins University Press, 1988).

104. Amy Elman, "Gender Violence," in *The Oxford Handbook of Gender and Politics*, ed. Georgina Waylen, Karen Celis, Johanna Kantola, and S. Laurel Weldon (New York: Oxford University Press, 2013); and S. Laurel Weldon, *Protest, Policy, and the Problem of Violence against Women: A Cross-National Comparison* (Pittsburgh: University of Pittsburgh Press, 2002).

105. Jessica L. Wheeler, "Revisit: A Review of National Crime Victim Victimization Findings on Rape and Sexual Assault" (briefing paper), Council on Contemporary Families, Nov. 21, 2017, https://thesocietypages.org/ccf/2017/11/21/revisit-a-review-of-national-crime-victim-victimization-findings-on-rape-and-sexual-assault/; and Michael Planty, Lynn Langton, Christopher Krebs, Marcus Berzofsky, and Hope Smiley-McDonald, *Female Victims of Sexual Violence, 1994–2010* (Special Report NCJ 240655, Washington, DC, Bureau of Justice Statistics, revised May 31, 2016), https://bjs.ojp.gov/content/pub/pdf/fvsv9410.pdf.

106. Colleen Cleere and Steven J. Lynn, "Acknowledged versus Unacknowledged Sexual Assault among College Women," *Journal of Interpersonal Violence* 28, no. 12 (2013): 2593–611; Courtney E. Ahrens, "Being Silenced: The Impact of Negative Social Reactions on the Disclosure of Rape," *American Journal of Community Psychology* 38, nos. 3–4 (2006): 263–74; and Lynn M. Phillips, *Flirting with Danger: Young Women's Reflections on Sexuality and Domination* (New York: New York University Press, 2000).

107. Rebecca M. Hayes, Rebecca L. Abbott, and Savannah Cook, "It's Her Fault: Student Acceptance of Rape Myths on Two College Campuses," *Violence Against Women* 22, no. 13 (2016): 1540–55.

108. "The Criminal Justice System: Statistics," RAINN, accessed Feb. 11, 2022, https://www.rainn.org/statistics/criminal-justice-system; and Rachel E. Morgan and Grace Kena, Criminal Victimization, 2016: Revised (NCJ 252121, Washington, DC, Bureau of Justice Statistics, revised October 2018), https://www.bjs.gov/content/pub/pdf/cv16.pdf.

109. Jamie L. Small, "Trying Male Rape: Legal Renderings of Masculinity, Vulnerability, and Sexual Violence" (PhD diss., University of Michigan, 2015); Rose Corrigan, *Up against a Wall: Rape Reform and the Failure of Success* (New York: New York University Press, 2013); Xavier L. Guadalupe-Diaz and Jana Jasinski,"'I Wasn't a Priority, I Wasn't a Victim': Challenges in Help Seeking for Transgender Survivors of Intimate Partner Violence," *Violence against Women* 23, no. 6 (2016): 772–92; Megan R. Greeson, Rebecca Campbell, and Giannina Fehler-Cabral, "'Nobody Deserves This': Adolescent Sexual Assault Victims' Perceptions of Disbelief and Victim Blame from Police," *Journal of Community Psychology* 44, no. 1 (2016): 90–110; Jennifer Christine Nash, "Black Women and Rape: A Review of the Literature" (Feminist Sexual Ethics Project, Brandeis University, June 12, 2009); and Helen A. Neville, Mary J. Heppner, Euna Oh, Lisa B. Spanierman, and Mary Clark, "General and Culturally Specific Factors Influencing Black and White Rape Survivors' Self-Esteem," *Psychology of Women Quarterly* 28, no. 1 (2004): 83–94.

110. Katie J. M. Baker, "Here's the Powerful Letter the Stanford Victim Read to Her Attacker," BuzzFeed News, June 3, 2016, https://www.buzzfeednews.com/article/katiejmbaker/heres-the-powerful-letter-the-stanford-victim-read-to-her-ra.

111. Jessica Shaw, Rebecca Campbell, Debi Cain, and Hannah Feeney, "Beyond Surveys and Scales:

How Rape Myths Manifest in Sexual Assault Police Records," *Psychology of Violence* 7, no. 4 (2017): 602–14; Kimberly A. Lonsway, Joanne Archambault, and David Lisak, "False Reports: Moving beyond the Issue to Successfully Investigate and Prosecute Non-Stranger Sexual Assault," *Voice* 3, no. 1 (2009), 1–11; Sokratis Dinos, Nina Burrowes, Karen Hammond, and Christina Cunliffe, "A Systematic Review of Juries' Assessment of Rape Victims: Do Rape Myths Impact on Juror Decision-Making?" *International Journal of Law, Crime, and Justice* 43, no. 1 (2015): 36–49; Jon Krakauer, *Missoula: Rape and the Justice System in a College Town* (New York: Doubleday, 2015); and Sameena Mulla, *The Violence of Care: Rape Victims, Forensic Nurses, and Sexual Assault Intervention* (New York: New York University Press, 2014).

112. "False Reporting," National Sexual Violence Resource Reporting, 2012, https://www.nsvrc.org/sites/default/files/Publications_NSVRC_Overview_False-Reporting.pdf; and David Lisak, Lori Gardinier, Sarah C. Nicksa, and Ashley M. Cote, "False Allegations of Sexual Assault: An Analysis of Ten Years of Reported Cases," *Violence Against Women* 16 (2010): 1318–34.

113. Peggy Reeves Sanday, "The Socio-Cultural Context of Rape: A Cross-Cultural Study," *Journal of Social Issues* 37, no. 4 (1981), https://doi.org/10.1111/j.1540-4560.1981.tb01068.x; Christine Helliwell, "'It's Only a Penis': Rape, Feminism, and Difference," *Signs* 25, no. 3 (2000): 789–816; and Maria-Barbara Watson-Franke, "A World in which Women Move Freely without Fear of Men: An Anthropological Perspective on Rape," *Women's Studies International Forum* 25, no. 6 (2002): 599–606.

114. Catharine MacKinnon, *Toward a Feminist Theory of the State* (Cambridge, MA: Harvard University Press, 1989); Sharon Marcus, "Fighting Bodies, Fighting Words: A Theory and Politics of Rape Prevention," in *Feminists Theorize the Political*, ed. Judith Butler and Joan W. Scott (New York: Routledge, 1992), 385–403; Valerie Jenness and Sarah Fenstermaker, "Forty Years after Brownmiller: Prisons for Men, Transgender Inmates, and the Rape of the Feminine," *Gender & Society* 30, no. 1 (2016): 14–29; C. J. Pascoe and Jocelyn A. Hollander, "Good Guys Don't Rape: Gender, Domination, and Mobilizing Rape," *Gender & Society* 3, no. 1 (2016): 67–79; and Small, "Trying Male Rape."

115. Virginia Braun and Sue Wilkinson, "Socio-cultural Representations of the Vagina," *Journal of Reproductive and Infant Psychology* 19, no. 1 (2001): 17–32; and Anna Chave, "O'Keefe and the Masculine Gaze," in *Reading American Art*, ed. Marianne Doezema and Elizabeth Milroy (New Haven, CT: Yale University Press, 1998), 350–70.

116. Poulson-Bryant, *Hung*; and David Friedman, *A Mind of Its Own: A Cultural History of the Penis* (New York: Penguin Books, 2001).

117. Elwin Verrier, "The Vagina Dentata Legend," *British Journal of Medical Psychology* 19, nos. 3–4 (1943): 439–53; and Benjamin Beit-Hallahmi, "Dangers of the Vagina," *British Journal of Medical Psychology* 58, no. 4 (1985): 351–56.

118. Kate Harding, *Asking for It: The Alarming Rise of Rape Culture—and What We Can Do about It* (Boston: Da Capo Press, 2015).

119. Tafkarfanfic, "Rape in ASOIAF vs. Game of Thrones: A Statistical Analysis," Tumblr, May 24, 2015, https://tafkarfanfic.tumblr.com/post/119770640640/rape-in-asoiaf-vs-game-of-thrones-a-statistical.

120. Tanya Serisier, "Sex Crimes and the Media," Oxford Research Encyclopedias, Criminology and Criminal Justice, January 25, 2017, https://criminology.oxfordre.com/view/10.1093/acrefore/9780190264079.001.0001/acrefore-9780190264079-e-118.

121. Elizabeth A. Armstrong, Laura Hamilton, and Brian Sweeney, "Sexual Assault on Campus: A Multilevel, Integrative Approach to Party Rape," *Social Problems* 53 (2006): 483–99.

122. Jessie V. Ford, "Unwanted Sex on Campus: The Overlooked Role of Interactional Pressures and Gendered Sexual Scripts," *Qualitative Sociology* 44 (2020): 31–53.

123. Robert Jensen, "Rape, Rape Culture and the Problem of Patriarchy," *Waging Nonviolence*, April 29, 2014, https://wagingnonviolence.org/feature/rape-rape-culture-problem-patriarchy/. See also Philip Kavanaugh, "The Continuum of Sexual Violence: Women's Accounts of Victimization in Urban Nightlife," *Feminist Criminology* 8, no. 1 (2013): 20–39.

124. CBS/AP, "More than 12M 'Me Too' Facebook Posts, Comments, Reactions in 24 Hours," CBS News, October 17, 2017, https://www.cbsnews.com/news/metoo-more-than-12-million-facebook-posts-comments-reactions-24-hours/.

125. Elizabeth A. Armstrong, Miriam Gleckman-Krut, and Lanora Johnson, "Silence, Power, and Inequality: An Intersectional Approach to Sexual Violence," *Annual Review of Sociology* 44 (2018): 99–122; Adam M. Messinger, *LGBTQ Intimate Partner Violence: Lessons for Policy, Practice, and Research* (Berkeley: University of California Press, 2017); Stéphanie Wahab and Lenora Olson, "Intimate Partner

Violence and Sexual Assault in Native American Communities," *Trauma Violence Abuse* 5, no. 4 (2004): 353–66; David Finkelhor, Anne Shattuck, Heather Turner, and Sherry Hamby, "The Lifetime Prevalence of Child Sexual Abuse and Sexual Assault in Late Adolescence," *Journal of Adolescent Health* 55, no. 3 (2014): 329–33; William George Axinn, Maura Elaine Bardos, and Brady Thomas West, "General Population Estimates of the Association between College Experience and the Odds of Forced Intercourse," *Social Science Research* 70 (2017): 131–43; Jennifer Barber, Yasamin Kusunoki, and Jamie Budnick, "Women Not Enrolled in Four-Year Universities and Colleges Have Higher Risk of Sexual Assault" (briefing paper), Council on Contemporary Families, April 20, 2015, https://sites .utexas.edu/contemporaryfamilies/2015/04/20/not -enrolled-brief-report/; and Sharon G. Smith, Xinjian Zhang, Kathleen C. Basile, Melissa T. Merrick, Jing Wang, Marcie-jo Kresnow, et al., "The National Intimate Partner and Sexual Violence Survey (NISVS): 2015 Data Brief–Updated Release," Centers for Disease Control and Prevention, National Center for Injury Prevention and Control, Atlanta, GA, 2018.

126. US Federal Bureau of Investigation, Crime Data Explorer, "Arrests in the United States by Offense," accessed February 11, 2022, https://crime-data -explorer.app.cloud.gov/pages/explorer/crime/arrest.

127. Thomas Vander Ven, *Getting Wasted: Why College Students Drink Too Much and Party Too Hard* (New York: New York University Press, 2011), 2.

128. Ibid., 75.

129. Lynn Peril, *College Girls: Bluestockings, Sex Kittens, and Coeds, Then and Now* (New York: W. W. Norton, 2006); and Brian J. Willoughby, Jason S. Carroll, William J. Marshall, and Caitlin Clark, "The Decline of In Loco Parentis and the Shift to Coed Housing on College Campuses," *Journal of Adolescent Research* 24, no. 1 (2009): 21–36.

130. Michael Moffett, *Coming of Age in New Jersey: College and American Culture* (New Brunswick, NJ: Rutgers University Press, 1898).

131. Murray Sperber, *Beer and Circus: How Big-Time College Sport Is Crippling Undergraduate Education* (New York: Henry Holt, 2000); and Henry Wechsler and Bernice Wuethrich, *Dying to Drink: Confronting Binge Drinking on College Campuses* (Emmaus, PA: Rodale Books, 2002).

132. Elizabeth A. Armstrong and Laura T. Hamilton, *Paying for the Party: How College Maintains Inequality* (Cambridge, MA: Harvard University Press, 2013); Jill Russett, "Women's Perceptions of High-Risk Drinking: Understanding Binge Drinking in a Gender Biased Setting," (PhD diss., College of William and Mary, 2008); and Wade, *American Hookup*.

133. Clare Hollowell, "The Subject of Fun: Young Women, Freedom and Feminism," (PhD diss., Centre for Gender and Women's Studies, Lancaster University, 2010).

134. Ford, England, and Bearak, "American College Hookup Scene"; Jeremy Uecker, Lisa Pearce, and Brita Andercheck, "The Four U's: Latent Classes of Hookup Motivations among College Students," *Social Currents* 2, no. 2 (2015): 163–81; Rachel Kalish, "Sexual Decision Making in the Context of Hookup Culture: A Mixed-Method Examination" (PhD diss., Stony Brook University, 2014); and Arielle Kuperberg and Joseph E. Padgett, "The Role of Culture in Explaining College Students' Selection into Hookups, Dates, and Long-Term Romantic Relationships," *Journal of Social and Personal Relationships* 33, no. 8 (2016): 1070–96.

135. American College Health Association, *American College Health Association–National College Health Assessment II: Reference Group Executive Summary Spring 2013* (Hanover, MD: American College Health Association, 2013), https://www.acha .org/documents/ncha/ACHA-NCHA-II_Reference Group_ExecutiveSummary_Spring2013.pdf.

136. Kathleen A. Bogle, *Hooking Up: Sex, Dating, and Relationships on Campus* (New York: New York University Press, 2008); Elizabeth L. Paul, "Beer Goggles, Catching Feelings, and the Walk of Shame: Myths and Realities of the Hookup Experience," in *Relating Difficulty: The Processes of Constructing and Managing Difficult Interaction*, ed. D. Charles Kirkpatrick, Steve Duck, and Megan K. Foley (Mahwah, NJ: Lawrence Erlbaum, 2006), 141–60; and Tracy A. Lambert, Arnold S. Kahn, and Kevin J. Apple, "Pluralistic Ignorance and Hooking Up," *Journal of Sex Research* 40 (2003): 129–33.

137. Lisa Wade and Joseph Padgett, "Hookup Culture and Higher Education," in *Handbook of Contemporary Feminism*, ed. Andrea Press and Tasha Oren (New York: Routledge, 2019), 162–76.

138. Kuperberg and Padgett, "Role of Culture," 1070–96; and Ryan J. Watson, Yousef M. Hahin, Miriam R. Arbeit, "Hookup Initiation and Emotional Outcomes Differ across LGB Young Men and Women," *Sexualities* 22, no. 5-6 (2018): 932–50.

139. Watson, Hahin, and Arbeit, "Hookup Initiation and Emotional Outcomes," 932–50; and Janelle M. Pham, "Queer Space and Alternate Queer Geographies: LGB Women and the Search for Sexual Partners at Two LGBTQ-Friendly U.S. Universities," *Journal of Lesbian Studies* 24, no. 3 (2020): 227–39.

140. Laura Hamilton, "Trading on Heterosexuality: College Women's Gender Strategies and Homophobia," *Gender & Society* 21, no. 2 (2007): 145–72; Kate M. Esterline and Charlene L. Muehlenhard, "Wanting to Be Seen: Young People's Experiences of Performative Making Out," *Journal of Sex Research* 54 (2017): 1051–63; and Janelle M. Pham, "Institutional, Subcultural and Individual Determinants of Same-Sex Sexual Contact among College Women," *Journal of Sex Research* 56, no. 8 (2019): 1031–44.

141. Personal communication with sociologist Paula England; Rachel Allison and Barbara Risman, "'It Goes Hand in Hand with the Parties': Race, Class, and Residence in College Negotiations of Hooking Up," *Sociological Perspectives* 57, no. 1 (2014): 102–23.

142. Wade and Padgett, "Hookup Culture and Higher Education," 162–76.

143. Butler, "Sexual Subjects"; and Kristine J. Ajrouch, "Gender, Race, and Symbolic Boundaries: Contested Spaces of Identity among Arab American Adolescents," *Sociological Perspectives* 47, no. 4 (2004): 371–91.

144. Yen Le Espiritu, "'We Don't Sleep around like White Girls Do': Family, Culture, and Gender in Filipina American Lives," *Journal of Women in Culture and Society* 26, no. 2 (Winter 2001): 415–40, 415, https://doi.org/10.1086/495599.

145. Michael Kimmel, *Guyland: The Perilous World Where Boys Become Men* (New York: HarperCollins, 2008), 204.

146. Kristine Wang, Jessie Ford, and Paula England, "What Does Studying College Sex Tell Us about Immigrant Assimilation?" *Contexts* (blog), August 18, 2017, https://contexts.org/blog/what-does-studying-college-sex-tell-us-about-immigrant-assimilation/.

147. Allison and Risman, "'It Goes Hand in Hand with the Parties,'" 102–23; Laura Hamilton and Elizabeth A. Armstrong, "Gendered Sexuality in Young Adulthood: Double Binds and Flawed Options," *Gender & Society* 23, no. 5 (2009): 589–616; Hamilton, "Trading on Heterosexuality," 145–72; and Armstrong and Hamilton, *Paying for the Party*.

148. Elizabeth A. Armstrong, Laura T. Hamilton, Elizabeth M. Armstrong, and J. Lotus Seeley, "'Good Girls': Gender, Social Class, and Slut Discourse on Campus," *Social Psychology Quarterly* 77, no. 2 (2014): 100–122.

149. Hamilton and Armstrong, "Gendered Sexuality in Young Adulthood," 589–616.

150. Armstrong and Hamilton, *Paying for the Party*.

151. Melina M. Bersamin, Byron L. Zamboanga, Seth J. Schwartz, M. Brent Donnellan, Monika Hudson, Robert S. Weisskirch, et al., "Risky Business: Is There an Association between Casual Sex and Mental Health among Emerging Adults?" *Journal of Sex Research* 51, no. 1 (2013): 43–51; Kevin Eagan, Jennifer B. Lozano, Sylvia Hurtado, and Matthew H. Case, *The American Freshman: National Norms Fall 2013* (Los Angeles: Higher Education Research Institute, UCLA, 2013); Maryanne L. Fisher, Kerry Worth, Justin R. Garcia, and Tami Meredith, "Feelings of Regret Following Uncommitted Sexual Encounters in Canadian University Students," *Culture, Health & Sexuality* 14 (2012): 45–57; Donna Freitas, *The End of Sex: How Hookup Culture Is Leaving a Generation Unhappy, Sexually Unfulfilled, and Confused about Intimacy* (New York: Basic Books, 2013); Melissa A. Lewis, David C. Atkins, Jessica A. Blayney, David V. Dent, and Debra L. Kaysen, "What Is Hooking Up? Examining Definitions of Hooking Up in Relation to Behavior and Normative Perceptions," *Journal of Sex Research* 50, no. 8 (2012): 757–66; Melissa A. Lewis, Hollie Granato, Jessica A. Blayney, Ty W. Lostutter, and Jason R. Kilmer, "Predictors of Hooking Up Sexual Behaviors and Emotional Reactions among U.S. College Students," *Archives of Sexual Behavior* 41 (2012): 1219–29; and Jesse Owen, Frank D. Fincham, and Jon Moore, "Short-Term Prospective Study of Hooking Up among College Students," *Archives of Sexual Behavior* 40 (2011): 331–41.

152. Ford, England, and Bearak, "American College Hookup Scene"; Uecker, Pearce, and Andercheck, "Four U's," 163–81; Justin R. Garcia, Chris Reiber, Sean G. Massey, and Ann M. Merriwether, "Sexual Hookup Culture: A Review," *Review of General Psychology* 16, no. 2 (2012): 161–76; and "Singles in America."

153. Wade, *American Hookup*, 141.

154. Ibid.

155. Ibid.

156. Brian Sweeney, "Masculine Status, Sexual Performance, and the Sexual Stigmatization of Women," *Symbolic Interaction* 37, no. 3 (2014): 369–90, 380–381.

157. Wade, *American Hookup*, 160.

158. Peggy Orenstein, *Girls and Sex: Navigating the Complicated New Landscape* (New York: Harper, 2016); and Ruth Lewis and Cicely Marston, "Oral Sex, Young People, and Gendered Narratives of Reciprocity," *Journal of Sex Research* 53, no. 7 (2016): 776–87.

159. Laina, Bay-Cheng, Adjoa Robinson, and Alyssa Zucker, "Behavioral and Relational Contexts of Adolescent Desire, Wanting, and Pleasure: Undergraduate Women's Retrospective Accounts," *Journal of Sex Research* 46, no. 6 (2009): 511–24.

160. Ford, England, and Bearak, "American College Hookup Scene."

161. Ibid.; and Laura Backstrom, Elizabeth Armstrong, and Jennifer Puentes, "Women's Negotiation of Cunnilingus in College Hookups and Relationships," *Journal of Sex Research* 49, 1 (2012): 1–12.

162. Elizabeth Armstrong, Paula England, and Alison Fogarty, "Accounting for Women's Orgasm and Sexual Enjoyment in College Hookups and Relationships," *American Sociological Review* 77, no. 3 (2012): 435–62.

163. Elizabeth Armstrong, Paula England, and Alison Fogarty, "Orgasm in College Hookups and Relationships," in *Families as They Really Are*, 2nd ed., ed. Barbara Risman and Virginia Rutter (New York: W. W. Norton and Company, 2015): 280–96.

164. Armstrong, England, and Fogarty, "Accounting for Women's Orgasm and Sexual Enjoyment," 456.

165. Ibid.

166. Wade, *American Hookup*.

167. David Cantor, Bonnie Fisher, Susan Chibnall, Reanne Townsend, Hyunshik Lee, Carol Bruce, et al., *Report on the AAU Campus Climate Survey on Sexual Assault and Misconduct* (Rockville, MD: Westat, 2020), https://www.aau.edu/sites/default/files /AAU-Files/Key-Issues/Campus-Safety/Revised%20 Aggregate%20report%20%20and%20appendices %201-7_(01-16-2020_FINAL).pdf.

168. Kevin M. Swartout, Mary P. Koss, Jacquelyn W. White, Martie P. Thompson, Antonia Abbey, and Alexandra L. Bellis, "Trajectory Analysis of the Campus Serial Rapist Assumption," *JAMA Pediatrics* 169, no. 12 (2015): 1148–54. See also Claude A. Mellins, Kate Walsh, Aaron L. Sarvet, Melanie Wall, and Louisa Gilbert, John S. Santelli, et al., "Sexual Assault Incidents among College Undergraduates: Prevalence and Factors Associated with Risk," *PLOS ONE* 13, no. 1 (2008): e0192129.

169. Elizabeth Armstrong and Jamie Budnick, "Sexual Assault on Campus" (briefing paper), Council on Contemporary Families, April 20, 2015, https://sites .utexas.edu/contemporaryfamilies/2015/04/20 /assault-on-campus-brief-report/; Armstrong, Hamilton, and Sweeney, "Sexual Assault on Campus," 483–99; Heather Littleton, Holly Tabernik, Erika J. Canales, and Tamika Backstrom, "Risky Situation or Harmless Fun? A Qualitative Examination of College Women's Bad Hook-Up and Rape Scripts," *Sex Roles* 60, nos. 11/12 (2009): 793–804; Paul, "Beer Goggles, Catching Feelings, and the Walk of Shame," 141–60.

170. Swartout et al., "Trajectory Analysis of the Campus Serial Rapist Assumption," *JAMA Pediatrics* 169, no. 12 (2015): 1148–54.

171. Christian Alexandersen, "Terrible Revelations of Penn State Frat Pledge's Death Detailed in Report," *Pennsylvania Real-Time News*, January 5, 2019, https://www.pennlive.com/news/2017/05/terrible _revelations_of_penn_s.html.

172. Caitlin Flanagan, "Death at a Penn State Fraternity," *Atlantic*, November 2017, https://www.the atlantic.com/magazine/archive/2017/11/a-death-at -penn-state/540657/.

173. US Department of Education, "Dear Colleague Letter: Office of the Assistant Secretary," April 4, 2011, www2.ed.gov/about/offices/list/ocr/letters/col league-201104.html.

174. End Rape on Campus (@endrapeoncampus), "Since the #DoubleRedZone begin [sic] in August, 100+ demonstrations, protests, rallies, vigils and walkouts have occurred across the country," Instagram, October 25, 2021, https://www.instagram.com /p/CVeBjmJMms-/.

175. Helen Bovill, Sarah McMahon, Jennifer Demers, Victoria Banyard, Vlad Carrasco, and Louise Keep, "How Does Student Activism Divide Cultural Campus Change in the UK and US regarding Sexual Violence on Campus?" *Critical Social Policy* 41, no. 2 (2020): 165–87.

176. US Bureau of Labor Statistics, "60 Percent of College Graduates Born from 1980 to 1984 Were Married at Age 33," *Economics Daily*, June 30, 2020, https://www.bls.gov/opub/ted/2020/60-percent-of -college-graduates-born-from-1980-to-1984-were -married-at-age-33.htm.

177. Betsey Stevenson and Justin Wolfers, "The Paradox of Declining Female Happiness, 2009," *American Economic Journal: Economic Policy*, American Economic Association 1, no. 2 (2009): 190–225,

https://www.nber.org/system/files/working_papers/w14969/w14969.pdf; Michelle Frisco and Kristi Williams, "Perceived Housework Equity, Marital Happiness, and Divorce in Dual-Earner Households," *Journal of Family Issues* 24, no. 1 (2003): 51–73; Mamadi Corra, Shannon K. Carter, J. Scott Carter, and David Knox, "Trends in Marital Happiness by Gender and Race, 1973 to 2006," *Journal of Family Issues* 30, no. 10 (2009): 1379–1404; Paul R. Amato, David R. Johnson, Alan Booth, and Stacy J. Rogers, "Continuity and Change in Marital Quality between 1980 and 2000," *Journal of Marriage and Family* 65, no. 1 (2003): 1–22; Rhonda A. Faulkner, Maureen Davey, and Adam Davey, "Gender-Related Predictors of Change in Marital Satisfaction and Marital Conflict," *American Journal of Family Therapy* 33, no. 1 (2005): 61–83; Ryan G. Henry, Richard B. Miller, and Roseann Giarrusso, "Difficulties, Disagreements, and Disappointments in Late-Life Marriages," *International Journal of Aging & Human Development* 61, no. 3 (2005): 243–65; Gayle Kaufman and Hiromi Taniguchi, "Gender and Marital Happiness in Later Life," *Journal of Family Issues* 27, no. 6 (2006): 735–57; Laura Lo Wa Tsang, Carol D. H. Harvey, Karen A. Duncan, and Reena Sommer, "The Effects of Children, Dual Earner Status, Sex Role Traditionalism, and Marital Structure on Marital Happiness over Time," *Journal of Family and Economic Issues* 24, no. 1 (2003): 5–26.

Chapter 10: Families

1. Quoted in Anne Helen Petersen, "'Other Countries Have Social Safety Nets. The U.S. Has Women,'" *Culture Study* (blog), Substack, November 11, 2020, https://annehelen.substack.com/p/other-countries-have-social-safety.

2. Mamadi Corra, Shannon K. Carter, J. Scott Carter, and David Knox, "Trends in Marital Happiness by Gender and Race, 1973–2006," *Journal of Family Issues* 30, no. 10 (2009): 1379–404; Paul R. Amato, David R. Johnson, Alan Booth, and Stacy J. Rogers, "Continuity and Change in Marital Quality between 1980 and 2000," *Journal of Marriage and Family* 65 (2003): 1–22; Gayle Kaufman and Hiromi Taniguchi, "Gender and Marital Happiness in Later Life," *Journal of Family Issues* 27 (2006): 735–57; and Betsey Stevenson and Justin Wolfers, "The Paradox of Declining Female Happiness," *American Economic Journal: Economic Policy* 1, no. 2 (2009): 190–225, https://www.aeaweb.org/articles?id=10.1257/pol.1.2.190.

3. Kimberly F. Balsam, Theodore P. Beauchaine, Esther D. Rothblum, and Sondra E. Soloman, "Three-Year Follow-Up of Same-Sex Couples Who Had Civil Unions in Vermont, Same-Sex Couples Not in Civil Unions, and Heterosexual Married Couples," *Developmental Psychology* 44, no. 1 (2008): 102–16; John Mordechai Gottman, Robert W. Levenson, James Gross, Barbara L. Frederickson, Kim McCoy, Leah Rosenthal, et al., "Correlates of Gay and Lesbian Couples Relationship Satisfaction and Relationship Dissolution," *Journal of Homosexuality* 45, no. 1 (2003): 22–43; Francisco Perales and Janeen Baxter, "Sexual Identity and Relationship Quality in Australia and the United Kingdom," *Family Relations: Interdisciplinary Journal of Applied Family Science* 67, no. 1 (2018): 55–69; and Claire Kimberly and Amanda Williams, "Decade Review of Research on Lesbian Romantic Relationship Satisfaction," *Journal of LGBT Issues in Counseling* 11, no. 2 (2017): 119–35.

4. Belinda Hewitt, Mark Western, and Janeen Baxter, "Who Decides? The Social Characteristics of Who Initiates Divorce," *Journal of Marriage and Family* 68, no. 5 (2006): 1165–77; and Paula England, Paul D. Allison, and Liana C. Sayer, "When One Spouse Has an Affair, Who Is More Likely to Leave?" *Demographic Research* 30 (2014): 535–46.

5. US Census Bureau, "America's Families and Living Arrangements: 2021," accessed February 9, 2022, https://www.census.gov/data/tables/2021/demo/families/cps-2021.html.

6. Arlie Hochschild, *The Second Shift* (New York: Penguin, 1989).

7. Susan Walzer, "Thinking about the Baby: Gender and the Division of Infant Care," *Social Problems* 43, no. 2 (1996): 219–34, 219; Allison Daminger, "The Cognitive Dimension of Household Labor," *American Sociological Review* 84, no. 4 (2019): 609–33; and Liz Dean, Brendan Churchill, and Leah Ruppanner, "The Mental Load: Building a Deeper Theoretical Understanding of How Cognitive and Emotional Labor Overload Women and Mothers," *Community, Work & Family* 25, no. 1 (2021): 13–29.

8. Annette Lareau, "Invisible Inequality: Social Class and Childrearing in Black Families and White Families," *American Sociological Review* 67, no. 5 (2002): 747–76.

9. Lily Liang, "Raising Upper-Middle-Class Children in China" (PhD diss., University of Wisconsin-Madison, 2020).

10. Garey Ramey and Valerie A. Ramey, "The Rug Rat Race," *Brookings Papers on Economic Activity* 41, no. 1 (Spring 2010): 129–99.

11. Dawn Marie Dow, *Mothering while Black* (Berkeley: University of California Press, 2019); Mary Patillo, *Black Picket Fences: Privilege and Peril in the Black Middle Class*, 2nd ed. (Chicago: University of Chicago Press, 2013); and Debbie Irving, *Waking Up White and Finding Myself in the Story of Race* (Cambridge, MA: Elephant Room Press, 2016).

12. "American Time Use Survey—2016 Results," US Bureau of Labor Statistics, June 27, 2017, https://www.bls.gov/tus/home.htm#data.

13. Peter Stearns, *Anxious Parents: A History of Modern Childrearing in America* (New York: New York University Press, 2004), 3.

14. L. Emmett Holt, *The Care and Feeding of Children: A Catechism for the Use of Mothers and Children's Nurses*, 2005, Project Gutenberg, www.gutenberg.org/ebooks/15484

15. John Watson, *Psychological Care of Infant and Child* (New York: W. W. Norton, 1928), 87.

16. Ibid., 81–82.

17. Harry F. Harlow, Robert O. Dodsworth, and Margaret K. Harlow, "Total Social Isolation in Monkeys," *Proceedings of the National Academy of Sciences of the United States of America* 54 (1965): 90–97, https://www.ncbi.nlm.nih.gov/pmc/articles/PMC285801/pdf/pnas00159-0105.pdf.

18. Sharon Hays, *The Cultural Contradictions of Motherhood* (New Haven, CT: Yale University Press, 1996), 159.

19. Ibid., 8. See also Cameron MacDonald, *Shadow Mothers: Nannies, Au Pairs, and the Micropolitics of Mothering* (Berkeley: University of California Press, 2011).

20. Don Feder, "Feminists to Women: Shut Up and Do as You're Told," *Human Events* 62, no. 9 (2006): 15.

21. Patrick Ishizuka, "Social Class, Gender, and Contemporary Parenting Standards in the United States: Evidence from a National Survey Experiment," *Social Forces* 98, no. 1 (2019): 31–58.

22. Suzanne M. Bianchi, John P. Robinson, and Melissa A. Milkie, *Changing Rhythms of American Family Life* (New York: Russell Sage Foundation, 2006).

23. Carol J. Auster and Lisa A. Auster-Gussman, "Contemporary Mother's Day and Father's Day Greeting Cards: A Reflection of Traditional Ideologies of Motherhood and Fatherhood?" *Journal of Family Issues* 37, no. 9 (2016): 1294–326.

24. Erica Scharrer, Stephen Warren, Eean Grimshaw, Gichuhi Kamau, Sarah Cho, Menno Reijven, et al. "Disparaged Dads? A Content Analysis of Depictions of Fathers in U.S. Sitcoms over Time," *Psychology of Popular Media* 10, no. 2 (2021): 275–87.

25. Jessica Troilo, "Stay Tuned: Portrayals of Fatherhood to Come," *Psychology of Popular Media Culture* 6, no. 1 (2017): 82–94.

26. Gareth M. Thomas, Deborah Lupton, and Sarah Pedersen, "'The Appy for a Happy Pappy': Expectant Fatherhood and Pregnancy Apps," *Journal of Gender Studies* 27, no. 7 (2018): 759–70.

27. Jane Sunderland, "'Parenting' or 'Mothering'? The Case of Modern Child Care Magazines," *Discourse and Society* 17, no. 4 (2006): 503–27; Glenda Wall and Stephanie Arnold, "How Involved Is Involved Fathering?: An Exploration of the Contemporary Culture of Fatherhood," *Gender & Society* 21, no. 4 (2007): 508–27; Jennifer Krafchick, Toni Schindler Zimmerman, Shelley A. Haddock, and James H. Banning, "Best Selling Books Advising Parents about Gender: A Feminist Analysis," *Family Relations* 54 (2005): 84–100; Lisa Rashley, "'Work It Out with Your Wife': Gendered Expectations and Parenting Rhetoric Online," *Feminist Formations* 17, no. 1 (2005): 58–92; and Katherine M. Johnson, "Single, Straight, Wants Kids: Media Framing of Single, Heterosexual Fatherhood via Assisted Reproduction," *Journal of Gender Studies* 26, no. 4 (2017): 387–401.

28. Kristin Natalier, "'I'm Not His Wife': Doing Gender and Doing Housework in the Absence of Women," *Journal of Sociology* 39, no. 3 (2003): 253–69.

29. Carla Pfeffer, "'Women's Work'? Women Partners of Transgender Men Doing Housework and Emotion Work," *Journal of Marriage and Family* 72 (2010): 165–83.

30. Ibid., 172.

31. Dana Berkowitz, "Maternal Instincts, Biological Clocks, and Soccer Moms: Gay Men's Parenting and Family Narratives," *Symbolic Interaction* 34, no. 4 (2011): 514–35.

32. Ibid., 518.

33. Brad Harrington, Fred Van Deusen, and Iyar Mazar, "The New Dad: Right at Home," Boston College Center for Work & Family, 2012, https://www.bc.edu/content/dam/files/centers/cwf/research/publications/researchreports/The%20New%20Dad%202012_Right%20at%20Home; Catherine Solomon, "'I Feel Like a Rock Star': Fatherhood for Stay-at-Home Fathers," *Fathering* 12, no. 1 (2014): 52–70;

Joyce Y. Lee and Shawna J. Lee, "Caring Is Masculine: Stay-at-Home Fathers and Masculine Identity," *Psychology of Men & Masculinity* 19, no. 1 (2018): 47–58; Richard J. Petts, Kevin M. Shafer, and Lee Essig, "Does Adherence to Masculine Norms Shape Fathering Behavior?" *Journal of Marriage and Family* 80, no. 3 (2018): 704–20.

34. Harrington, Van Deusen, and Mazar, "The New Dad."

35. Brian D. Doss, Galena K. Rhoades, Scott M. Stanley, and Howard J. Markman, "Marital Therapy, Retreats, and Books: The Who, What, When and Why of Relationship Help-Seeking Behaviors," *Journal of Marital and Family Therapy* 35, 18–29 (2009); S. Katherine Nelson, Kostadin Kushlev, and Sonja Lyubomirsky, "The Pains and Pleasures of Parenting: When, Why, and How Is Parenthood Associated with More or Less Well-Being?" *Psychological Bulletin* 140, no. 3 (2014): 846–95; and Debra Umberson, Tetyana Pudrovska, and Corinne Reczek, "Parenthood, Childlessness, and Well-Being: A Life Course Perspective," *Journal of Marriage and Family* 72 (2010): 612–29.

36. William J. Scarborough, Saray Sin, Barbara Risman, "Attitudes and the Stalled Gender Revolution: Egalitarianism, Traditionalism, and Ambivalence from 1977 through 2016," *Gender & Society* 33, no. 2 (2019): 173–200; Sarah Thebaud and Laura Halcomb, "One Step Forward? Advances and Setbacks on the Path toward Gender Equality in Families and Work," *Sociological Compass* 13, no. 6 (2019): e12700, https://doi.org/10.1111/soc4.12700.

37. Claire Cain Miller, "Americans Value Equality at Work More than Equality at Home," *New York Times*, December 3, 2018, https://www.nytimes.com/2018/12/03/upshot/americans-value-equality-at-work-more-than-equality-at-home.html; Claire Cain Miller, "Millennial Men Aren't the Dads They Thought They'd Be," *New York Times*, July 30, 2015, https://www.nytimes.com/2015/07/31/upshot/millennial-men-find-work-and-family-hard-to-balance.html; Patricia Hill Collins, *Black Feminist Thought* (New York: Routledge, 2015); Shannon N. Davis and Theodore N. Greenstein, "Gender Ideology: Components, Predictors, and Consequences," *Annual Review of Sociology 2009* 35 no. 1 (2009): 87–105; and Jonathan Vespa, "Gender Ideology Construction: A Life Course and Intersectional Approach," *Gender & Society* 23, no. 3 (June 2009): 363–87.

38. Shira Offer and Danny Kaplan, "The 'New Father' between Ideals and Practices: New Masculinity Ideology, Gender Role Attitudes, and Fathers'

Involvement in Childcare," *Social Problems* 68, no. 4 (2021): 986–1009; Scott J. Carter, Mamadi Corra, and Shannon K. Carter, "The Interaction of Race and Gender: Changing Gender-Role Attitudes, 1974–2006," *Social Science Quarterly* 90, no. 1 (2009): 196–211; and Sandra Hofferth, "Race/Ethnic Differences in Father Involvement in Two-Parent Families: Culture, Context, or Economy?" *Journal of Family Issues* 24, no. 2 (2003): 185–216.

39. Samantha L. Tornello, Bettina N. Sonnenberg, and Charlotte J. Patterson, "Division of Labor among Gay Fathers: Associations with Parent, Couple, and Child Adjustment," *Psychology of Sexual Orientation and Gender Diversity* 2, no. 4 (2015): 365–75; Melanie E. Brewster, "Lesbian Women and Household Labor Division: A Systematic Review of Scholarly Research from 2000 to 2015," *Journal of Lesbian Studies* 21, no. 1 (2017): 47–69; and Gabrielle Gotta, Robert-Jay Green, Esther Rothblum, Sondra Solomon, Kimberly Balsam, and Pepper Schwartz, "Heterosexual, Lesbian, and Gay Male Relationships: A Comparison of Couples in 1975 and 2000," *Family Process* 50, no. 3 (2011): 353–76.

40. Jill E. Yavorsky, Yue Qian, and Amanda C. Sargent, "The Gendered Pandemic: The Implications of Covid-19 for Work and Family," *Sociology Compass*, April 9, 2021, https://doi.org/10.1111/soc4.12881.

41. Eunsil Oh, "Who Deserves to Work? How Women Develop Expectations of Childcare Support in Korea," *Gender & Society* 32, no. 4 (2018): 493–515; and Michael Enku Ide, Blair Harrington, Yolanda Wiggins, Tanya Rouleau Whitworth, Naomi Gerstel, "Emerging Adult Sons and Their Fathers: Race and the Construction of Masculinity," *Gender & Society* 32, no. 1 (2018): 5–33.

42. Kathleen Gerson, *The Unfinished Revolution: Coming of Age in a New Era of Gender, Work, and Family* (New York: Oxford University Press, 2010). See also Scarborough, Sin, and Risman, "Attitudes and the Stalled Gender Revolution," 173–200; "CCF Press Advisory: Gender and Millennials Online Symposium," Council on Contemporary Families, March 30, 2017, https://contemporaryfamilies.org/ccf-gender-and-millennials-online-symposium/; Barbara Risman, *Where the Millennials Will Take Us* (New York: Oxford University Press, 2018); David S. Pedulla and Sarah Thébaud, "Can We Finish the Revolution? Gender, Work-Family Ideals, and Institutional Constraint," *American Sociological Review* 80, no. 1 (February 2015): 116–39; and Miller, "Americans Value Equality at Work More than Equality at Home."

43. Lewis A. Coser, *Greedy Institutions: Patterns of Undivided Commitment* (New York: Free Press, 1974).

44. Mary Blair-Loy, *Competing Devotions: Career and Family among Women Executives* (Cambridge, MA: Harvard University Press, 2005).

45. Barbara Risman, *Gender Vertigo: American Families in Transition* (New Haven, CT: Yale University Press, 1999).

46. Naomi Gerstel and Daniel Clawson, "Class Advantage and the Gender Divide: Flexibility on the Job and at Home," *American Journal of Sociology* 120, no. 2 (2014): 395–431.

47. Risman, *Gender Vertigo.*

48. Perales and Baxter, "Sexual Identity and Relationship Quality in Australia and the United Kingdom," 55–69; John Mordechai Gottman, Robert Wayne Levenson, Catherine Swanson, Kristin Swanson, Rebecca Tyson, et al., "Observing Gay, Lesbian, and Heterosexual Couples' Relationships: Mathematical Modeling of Conflict Interaction," *Journal of Homosexuality* 45, no. 1 (2003): 65–91

49. Lynn Cooke, "'Traditional' Marriages Now Less Stable than Ones Where Couples Share Work and Household Chores," in *Families as They Really Are*, ed. Barbara Risman (New York: W. W. Norton, 2010), 431–432; and Pilar Gonalons-Pons and Marcus Gangl, "Marriage and Masculinity: Male-Breadwinner Culture, Unemployment, and Separation Risk in 29 Countries" *American Sociological Review* 86, no. 3 (2021): 465–502.

50. Social Security Administration, "Maximum Taxable Income," accessed February 24, 2022, https://www.ssa.gov/benefits/retirement/planner/maxtax.html. This doesn't apply if both earners are above the Social Security tax cap of $147,000 in 2022.

51. Shelly Lundberg and Elaina Rose, "Parenthood and the Earnings of Married Men and Women," *Labour Economics* 7, no. 6 (2000): 689–710.

52. Bianchi, Robinson, and Milkie, *Changing Rhythms of American Family Life*; and Suzanne Bianchi, "Demographic Perspectives on Family Change" *Journal of Family Theory and Review* 6, no. 1 (2014): 35–44.

53. Blair-Loy, *Competing Devotions.*

54. Claire Cain Miller, "Women Did Everything Right. Then Work Got 'Greedy,'" *New York Times*, April 26, 2019, https://www.nytimes.com/2019/04/26/upshot/women-long-hours-greedy-professions.html

55. Kim A. Weeden, Youngjoo Cha, and Mauricio Bucca, "Long Work Hours, Part-Time Work, and Trends in the Gender Gap in Pay, the Motherhood Wage Penalty, and the Fatherhood Wage Premium," *RSF: The Russell Sage Foundation Journal of the Social Sciences* 2, no. 4 (2016): 71–102.

56. Miller, "Women Did Everything Right."

57. Youngjoo Cha and Kim A. Weeden, "Overwork and the Slow Convergence in the Gender Gap in Wages," *American Sociological Review* 79, no. 3 (2014): 457–84.

58. Mignon Moore, "Gendered Power Relations among Women: A Study of Household Decision Making in Black, Lesbian Stepfamilies," *American Sociological Review* 73, no. 2 (2008): 335–56; Tornello, Sonnenberg, and Patterson, "Division of Labor among Gay Fathers," 365–75; and Brewster, "Lesbian Women and Household Labor Division," 47–69.

59. Quoted in Claire Cain Miller, "How Same-Sex Couples Divide Chores, and What It Reveals about Modern Parenting," *New York Times*, May 16, 2018, https://www.nytimes.com/2018/05/16/upshot/same-sex-couples-divide-chores-much-more-evenly-until-they-become-parents.html.

60. Daniel Schneider and Orestes P. Hastings, "Income Inequality and Household Labor," *Social Forces* 96, no. 2 (2017): 162.

61. Ibid., 167.

62. Petts, Shafer, and Essig, "Does Adherence to Masculine Norms Shape Fathering Behavior?," 704–20.

63. Roland E. Buland, "Paternal Involvement with Children: The Influence of Gender Ideologies," *Journal of Marriage and Family* 66, no. 1 (2004): 40–45; and Petts, Shafer, and Essig, "Does Adherence to Masculine Norms Shape Fathering Behavior?," 704–20.

64. Lyn Craig and Janeen Baxter, "Domestic Outsourcing, Housework Shares and Subjective Time Pressure: Gender Differences in the Correlates of Hiring Help," *Social Indicators Research* 125 (2016): 271–88; and Alexandra Killewald and Margaret Gough, "Money Isn't Everything: Wives' Earnings and Housework Time," *Social Science Research* 39, no. 6 (2010): 987–1003.

65. Rhacel S. Parreñas, *Servants of Globalization: Women, Migration and Domestic Work* (Stanford: Stanford University Press, 2001); and MacDonald, *Shadow Mothers.*

66. "Economic Policy Institute (EPI) Analysis of Current Population Survey Basic Monthly Microdata,"

EPI Current Population Survey Extracts, Version 1.0.2, 2020, https://microdata.epi.org.

67. Parreñas, *Servants of Globalization*; and MacDonald, *Shadow Mothers*.

68. Parreñas, *Servants of Globalization*.

69. Arlie Hochschild, "The Nanny Chain," *The American Prospect*, December 19, 2001, https://prospect.org/article/nanny-chain.

70. MacDonald, *Shadow Mothers*.

71. Parreñas, *Servants of Globalization, 58*.

72. Bart Landry, *Black Working Wives: Pioneers of the American Family Revolution* (Berkeley, University of California Press, 2000).

73. Dow, *Mothering while Black*.

74. Stanlie M. James, "Mothering: A Possible Black Feminist Link to Social Transformation," in *Theorizing Black Feminisms: The Visionary Pragmatism of Black Women*, ed. Stanlie M. James and Abena P. A. Busia (London: Routledge, 1993), 45; Linda M. Chatters, Robert Joseph Taylor, and Rukmailie Jayakody, "Fictive Kinship Relations in Black Extended Families," *Journal of Comparative Family Studies* 25, no. 3 (Autumn 1994): 297–312; and Patricia Hill Collins, "Black Women and Motherhood," in *Motherhood and Space: Configurations of the Maternal through Politics, Home, and the Body*, ed. Sarah Hardy and Caroline Wiedmer (New York: Palgrave Macmillan, 2005).

75. Dawn Marie Dow, "Integrated Motherhood: Beyond Hegemonic Ideologies of Motherhood," *Journal of Marriage and Family* 78, no. 1 (2016): 180–96.

76. Lynne Haney and Miranda March, "Married Fathers and Caring Daddies: Welfare Reform and the Discursive Politics of Paternity," *Social Problems* 50, no. 4 (2003): 478; K. Roy and J. Smith, "Nonresident Fathers and Intergenerational Parenting in Kin Networks," in *Handbook of Father Involvement: Multidisciplinary Perspectives*, 2nd ed., ed. Natasha Cabrera and Catherine S. Tamis-LeMonda (New York: Routledge, 2012), 320–37; and Sangeetha Madhavan and Kevin Roy, "Securing Fatherhood through Kin Work: A Comparison of Black Low Income Fathers and Families in South Africa and the U.S.," *Journal of Family Issues* 33 (2012): 801–22.

77. Christina J. Cross, "Racial/Ethnic Differences in the Association between Family Structure and Children's Education," *Journal of Marriage and Family* 82, no. 2 (2020): 691–712.

78. "World Family Map 2015: Mapping Family Change and Child Well-Being Outcomes," Institute for Family Studies, https://ifstudies.org/ifs-admin/resources/reports/wfm-2015-forweb.pdf.

79. Natalia Sarkisian and Naomi N. Gerstel, *Nuclear Family Values, Extended Family Lives: The Power of Race, Class, and Gender* (New York: Routledge, 2012).

80. Choo WaiHong, *The Kingdom of Women: Life, Love and Death in China's Hidden Mountains* (New York: I.B. Tauris, 2017).

81. Christopher Carrington, *No Place Like Home: Relationships and Family Life among Lesbians and Gay Men* (Chicago: University of Chicago Press, 1999).

82. Elisabeth Sheff, *The Polyamorists Next Door: Inside Multiple-Partner Relationships and Families* (Lanham, MD: Rowman & Littlefield, 2014).

83. "Marriage, Family, & Stepfamily Statistics," Smart Stepfamilies, updated 2021, https://www.smartstepfamilies.com/smart-help/marriage-family-stepfamily-statistics.

84. Emily E. Wiemers, Judith A. Seltzer, Robert F. Schoeni, V. Joseph Hotz, and Suzanne M. Bianchi, "Stepfamily Structure and Transfers between Generations in U.S. Families," *Demography* 56, no. 1 (2019): 229–60.

85. Arlie Hochschild, *The Second Shift* (New York: Penguin, 1989), 62.

86. Ibid., 68.

87. Robert VerBruggen and Wendy Wang, "The Real Housewives of America: Dad's Income and Mom's Work," January 2019, https://ifstudies.org/ifs-admin/resources/newfinalifsresearchbrief-verbruggen wang-realhousewives.pdf.

88. Ibid.

89. Caitlyn Collins, *Making Motherhood Work: How Women Manage Careers and Caregiving* (Princeton, NJ: Princeton University Press, 2019).

90. Simon Workman, "The True Cost of High-Quality Child Care across the United States," Center for American Progress, June 28, 2021, https://www.americanprogress.org/article/true-cost-high-quality-child-care-across-united.states/.

91. Gretchen Livingston, "Stay-at-Home Moms and Dads Account for about One-in-Five U.S. Parents," Pew Research Center, September 24, 2018, https://www.pewresearch.org/fact-tank/2018/09/24/stay-at-home-moms-and-dads-account-for-about-one-in-five-u-s-parents/.

92. Noelle Chesley and Sarah Flood, "Signs of Change? At-Home and Breadwinner Parents' Housework and Child-Care Time," *Journal of Marriage and Family* 79, no. 2 (2017): 511–34.

93. Karen Z. Kramer, "At-Home Father Families in the United States: Gender Ideology, Human Capital, and Unemployment," *Journal of Marriage and Family* 78, no. 5 (2016): 1315–31; and Caryn E. Medved, "Stay-at-Home Fathering as a Feminist Opportunity: Perpetuating, Resisting and Transforming Gender Relations of Caring and Earning," *Journal of Family Communication* 16, no. 1 (2016): 16–31.

94. Gerson, *The Unfinished Revolution*, 176.

95. "American Time Use Survey—2016 Results," US Bureau of Labor Statistics, June 27, 2017, https://www.bls.gov/tus/home.htm#data.

96. Shira Offer and Barbara Schneider, "Revisiting the Gender Gap in Time-Use Patterns: Multitasking and Well-Being among Mothers and Fathers in Dual-Earner Families," *American Sociological Review* 76, no. 6 (2011): 809–33.

97. Allison Daminger, "De-Gendered Processes, Gendered Outcomes: How Egalitarian Couples Make Sense of Non-Egalitarian Household Practices," *American Sociological Review* 85, no. 5 (October 2020): 806–29.

98. Sunderland, "'Parenting' or 'Mothering'?," 521.

99. Carla Pfeffer, "'Women's Work'?," 174.

100. Walzer, "Thinking about the Baby," 219–34.

101. Carrington, *No Place Like Home*, 79.

102. Ibid., 79–80.

103. Myra Marx Ferree, "The Emerging Constituency: Feminism, Employment and the Working Class" (PhD diss., Harvard University, 1976).

104. Gerson, *The Unfinished Revolution*, 172.

105. Carrington, *No Place Like Home*, 54.

106. Walzer, "Thinking about the Baby."

107. Harrington, Van Deusen, and Mazar, "The New Dad."

108. Susan Dalton and Denise Bielby, "'That's Our Kind of Constellation': Lesbian Mothers Negotiate Institutionalized Understandings of Gender within the Family," *Gender & Society* 14, no. 1 (2000): 36–61; Maureen Sullivan, "Rozzie and Harriet? Gender and Family Patterns of Lesbian Coparents," *Gender & Society* 10 (1996): 747–67; Elizabeth Sheff, "Gender, Family, and Sexuality: Exploring Polyamorous Community" (PhD diss, University of Colorado, 2005); and Anisa Zvonkovic, Kathleen M. Greaves, Cynthia J. Schmiege, and Leslie D. Hall, "The Marital Construction of Gender through Work and Family Decisions: A Qualitative Analysis," *Journal of Marriage and the Family* 58, no. 1 (1996): 91–100.

109. Ann Crittenden, *The Price of Motherhood: Why the Most Important Job in the World Is Still the Least Valued* (New York: Henry Holt, 2001), 88.

110. $1,350,000, according to Crittenden, *Price of Motherhood*, 2001. Adjusted for inflation.

111. Sylvia Ann Hewlett, *Off-Ramps and On-Ramps* (Cambridge, MA: Harvard Business School Press, 2007), 46; and Jennifer Glass, "Blessing or Curse? Work-Family Policies and Mothers' Wage Growth over Time," *Work and Occupations* 31 (2004): 367–94.

112. Paul Hemez and Chanell Washington, "Percentage and Number of Children Living with Two Parents Has Dropped since 1968," April 12, 2021, US Census Bureau, https://www.census.gov/library/stories/2021/04/number-of-children-living-only-with-their-mothers-has-doubled-in-past-50-years.html.

113. Kathleen Gerson, *No Man's Land: Men's Changing Commitments to Family and Work* (New York: Basic Books, 1993); Kathleen Gerson, *Hard Choices: How Women Decide about Work, Career, and Motherhood* (Berkeley: University of California Press, 1986); and Risman, *Gender Vertigo*.

114. Kathryn Edin and Maria Kefalas, *Why Poor Women Put Motherhood before Marriage* (Berkeley: University of California Press, 2011).

115. Kathryn Edin and Maria Kefalas, "Unmarried with Children," *Contexts* 4, no. 2 (2005): 16–22; and Liana C. Landivar, "How the Timing of Children Affects Earnings in 20 Occupations," SocArXiv, April 10, 2018, https://doi.org/10.31235/osf.io/vn7zt.

116. Amanda Riley-Jones, "Mothers without Men," *Guardian*, June 9, 2000, https://www.guardian.co.uk/theguardian/2000/jun/10/weekend7.weekend2.

117. Sally C. Curtin, Stephanie J. Ventura, and Gladys M. Martinez, "Recent Declines in Nonmarital Childbearing in the United States," *NCHS Data Brief*, no. 162 (Hyattsville, MD: National Center for Health Statistics, 2014); "Percent of Births to Unmarried Mothers by Education, 1970–2012," Hamilton Project, June 19, 2014, www.hamiltonproject.org/charts/percent_of_births_to_unmarried_mothers_by_education_1970-2012; and Livingston, "They're Waiting Longer."

118. Joyce A. Martin, Brady E. Hamilton, Michelle J. K. Osterman, and Anne K. Driscoll, "Births: Final Data for 2019," *National Vital Statistics Reports*, 70,

no. 2 (March 23, 2021): 1–50, https://www.cdc.gov/nchs/data/nvsr/nvsr70/nvsr70-02-508.pdf.

119. Susanna Graham, "Choosing Single Motherhood? Single Women Negotiating the Nuclear Family Ideal," in *Families—Beyond the Nuclear Ideal*, ed. Daniela Cutas and Sarah Chan (New York: Bloomsbury Academic, 2012), 97–109, 101.

120. "Characteristics of Children's Families," National Center for Education Statistics, May 2021, https://nces.ed.gov/programs/coe/indicator/cce.

121. Single Mother Guide, "Single Mother Statistics," May 17, 2021. https://singlemotherguide.com/single-mother-statistics/.

122. Karen Schulman, "On the Precipice: State Child Care Assistance Policies 2020," National Women's Law Center, May 2021, https://nwlc.org/wp-content/uploads/2021/05/NWLC-State-Child-Care-Assistance-Policies-2020.pdf.

123. "Employment Characteristics of Families—2020," US Bureau of Labor Statistics, April 21, 2021, https://www.bls.gov/news.release/pdf/famee.pdf.

124. "HHS Poverty Guidelines for 2022," Office of the Assistant Secretary for Planning and Evaluation, February 11, 2022, https://aspe.hhs.gov/topics/poverty-economic-mobility/poverty-guidelines.

125. "A Profile of the Working Poor, 2019," US Bureau of Labor Statistics, May 2021, https://www.bls.gov/opub/reports/working-poor/2019/home.htm.

126. Crittenden, *The Price of Motherhood*; and Elizabeth Warren and Amelia Tyagi, *The Two-Income Trap: Why Middle-Class Parents Are Going Broke* (New York: Basic Books, 2003).

127. Martin et al., "Births: Final Data for 2019."

128. Michelle J. K. Osterman, Claudia P. Valenzuela, and Joyce A. Martin, "Provisional Estimates for Selected Maternal and Infant Outcomes by Month, 2018–2021," National Center for Health Statistics, National Vital Statistics System, December 2021, https://www.cdc.gov/nchs/data/vsrr/vsrr-17.pdf.

129. "First-Ever Census Bureau Report Highlights Growing Childless Older Adult Population," US Census Bureau, August 31, 2021, https://www.census.gov/newsroom/press-releases/2021/childless-older-adult-population.html.

130. Anna Brown, "Growing Share of Childless Adults in U.S. Don't Expect to Ever Have Children," Pew Research Center, November 19, 2021, https://www.pewresearch.org/fact-tank/2021/11/19/growing-share-of-childless-adults-in-u-s-dont-expect-to-ever-have-children/.

131. Nelson, Kushlev, and Lyubomirsky, "The Pains and Pleasures of Parenting," 846–95; Thomas Hansen, "Parenthood and Happiness: A Review of Folk Theories versus Empirical Evidence," *Social Indicators Research* 108, no. 1 (2012): 1–36; Jean M. Twenge, W. Keither Campbell, and Craig A. Foster, "Parenthood and Marital Satisfaction: A Meta-Analytic Review," *Journal of Marriage and Family* 65, no. 3 (2004): 574–83; Umberson, Pudrovska, and Reczek, "Parenthood, Childlessness, and Well-Being," 612–29; and Daniel Gilbert, *Stumbling on Happiness* (New York: Random House, 2007).

132. Melissa A. Milkie, Alex Bierman, and Scott Schieman, "How Adult Children Influence Older Parents' Mental Health: Integrating Stress-Process and Life-Course Perspectives," *Social Psychology Quarterly* 71 (2008): 86–105; and Tetyana Pudrovska, "Psychological Implications of Motherhood and Fatherhood in Mid Life: Evidence from Siblings Models," *Journal of Marriage and the Family* 70 (2008): 168–81.

133. Jennifer Glass, Robin W. Simon, and Matthew A. Anderson, "Parenthood and Happiness: Effects of Work-Family Reconciliation Policies in 22 OECD Countries," *American Journal of Sociology* 122, no. 3 (November 2016): 886–929, https://doi.org/10.1086/688892; Hiroshi Ono and Kristen Schultz Lee, "Welfare States and the Redistribution of Happiness," *Social Forces* 92 (2013): 789–814; and Luca Stanca, "Suffer the Little Children: Measuring the Effects of Parenthood on Well-Being Worldwide," *Journal of Economic Behavior and Organization* 81 (2012): 742–50.

134. Glass, Simon, and Anderson, "Parenthood and Happiness," 886–929; and Ono and Lee, "Welfare States and the Redistribution of Happiness," 789–814.

135. Beth Turnbull, Melissa L. Graham, and Ann R. Taket, "Social Exclusion of Australian Childless Women in Their Reproductive Years," *Social Inclusion* 4, no. 1 (2016): 102–15; Gilla Shapiro, "Voluntary Childlessness: A Critical Review of the Literature," *Studies in the Maternal* 6 (2014): 1–15; Leslie Ashburn-Nardo, "Parenthood as a Moral Imperative? Moral Outrage and the Stigmatization of Voluntarily Childfree Women and Men," *Sex Roles* 76 (2017): 393–401; and Rebecca Harrington, "Childfree by Choice," *Studies in Gender and Sexuality* 20, no. 1 (2019): 22–35.

136. Alicia Sasser Modestino, Alisa Lincoln, and Jamie Ladge, "The Importance of Childcare in Reopening the Economy," EconoFact, July 29, 2020, https://econofact.org/the-importance-of-childcare-in-reopening-the-economy.

137. Matt Krentz, Emily Kos, Anna Green, and Jennifer Garcia-Alonso, "Easing the COVID-19 Burden on Working Parents," BCG Global, May 21, 2020, https://www.bcg.com/publications/2020/helping-working-parents-ease-the-burden-of-covid-19.

138. International Labour Organization, "Impact of the COVID-19 Crisis on Loss of Jobs and Hours among Domestic Workers," June 15, 2020, https://www.ilo.org/wcmsp5/groups/public/---ed_protect/---protrav/---travail/documents/publication/wcms_747961.pdf.

139. Franca van Hooren, "Covid-19, Migrant Workers and the Resilience of Social Care in Europe," Migration Policy Centre, MigResHub, Think Pieces, April 2020, Cadmus, European University Institute, https://cadmus.eui.eu/handle/1814/70318; Rocío de Diego-Cordero, Lorena Tarriño-Concejero, María Ángeles Lato-Molina, and Maria Ángeles García-Carpintero Muñoz, "COVID-19 and Female Immigrant Caregivers in Spain: Cohabiting during Lockdown," European Journal of Women's Studies, June 2021, https://doi.org/10.1177/13505068211017577.

140. Smriti Rao, Sarah Gammage, Julia Arnold, and Elizabeth Anderson, "Human Mobility, COVID-19, and Policy Responses: The Rights and Claims-Making of Migrant Domestic Workers," Feminist Economics 27 (2021): 254–70.

141. Anna North, "The Problem Is Work," Vox, March 15, 2021, https://www.vox.com/22321909/covid-19-pandemic-school-work-parents-remote.

142. Alexandra Topping and Pamela Duncan, "Lockdown-Fuelled Novelty of Domestic Chores Wanes for Men," Guardian, December 9, 2020, https://www.theguardian.com/inequality/2020/dec/09/lockdown-fuelled-novelty-of-domestic-chores-wanes-for-men; Misty Heggeness, "Why Is Mommy So Stressed? Estimating the Immediate Impact of the COVID-19 Shock on Parental Attachment to the Labor Market and the Double-Bind of Mothers" (Institute Working Paper No. 33, Opportunity and Inclusive Growth Institute, Federal Reserve Bank of Minneapolis, Minneapolis, MN, revised October 26, 2020), https://www.minneapolisfed.org/research/institute-working-papers/why-is-mommy-so-stressed-estimating-the-immediate-impact-of-the-covid-19-shock-on-parental-attach-ment-to-the-labor-market-and-the-double-bind-of-mothers; Claire Cain Miller, "Nearly Half of Men Say They Do Most of the Home Schooling. 3 Percent of Women Agree," New York Times, May 6, 2020, https://www.nytimes.com/2020/05/06/upshot/pandemic-chores-homeschooling-gender.html.

143. Daniel L. Carlson, Richard Petts, and Joanna R. Pepin, "Changes in Parents' Domestic Labor during the COVID-19 Pandemic," SocArXiv, May 6, 2020, https://doi.org/10.1111/soin.12459; and Thomas Lyttelton, Kelly Musick, and Emma Zang, "Before and during COVID-19: Telecommuting, Work-Family Conflict, and Gender Equality," Council on Contemporary Families, August 2020, https://sites.utexas.edu/contemporaryfamilies/2020/08/03/covid-19-telecommuting-work-family-conflict-and-gender-equality/.

144. Matt Krentz, Emily Kos, Anna Green, and Jennifer Garcia-Alonso, "Easing the COVID-19 Burden on Working Parents," BCG, May 21, 2020, https://www.bcg.com/publications/2020/helping-working-parents-ease-the-burden-of-covid-19.

145. Jessica M. Calarco, Emily V. Meanwell, Elizabeth Anderson, and Amelia Knopf, "'My Husband Thinks I'm Crazy': Covid-19-Related Conflict in Couples with Young Children," SocArXiv, October 9, 2020, https://doi.org/10.31235/osf.io/cpkj6.

146. Lyttelton, Musick, and Zang, "Before and during COVID-19."

147. Jessica M. Calarco, Elizabeth M. Anderson, Emily V. Meanwell, and Amelia Knopf, "'Let's Not Pretend It's Fun': How Covid-19-Related School and Childcare Closures Are Damaging Mothers' Well-being," SocArXiv, October 4, 2020, https://doi.org/10.31235/osf.io/jyvk4; and Thomas Lyttelton, Emma Zang, and Kelly Musick, "Gender Differences in Telecommuting and Implications for Inequality at Home and Work," July 8, 2020, https://papers.ssrn.com/sol3/papers.cfm?abstract_id=3645561.

148. May Friedman, Kori Kostka Lichtfuss, Lucas Martignetti, and Jacqui Gingras, "'It Feels a Bit Like Drowning': Expectations and Experiences of Motherhood during COVID-19," Atlantis 42, no. 1 (2021): 47–57, 51.

149. Michael Barabo, "The Agony of Pandemic Parenting," The Daily (podcast), New York Times, April 16, 2021, https://www.nytimes.com/2021/04/16/podcasts/the-daily/parenting-covid-pandemic.html?showTranscript=1.

150. UOregon CTN, "Home Alone: The Pandemic Is Overloading Single-Parent Families," RAPID-EC

Project, Medium, November 11, 2020, https://medium.com/rapid-ec-project/home-alone-the-pandemic-is-overloading-single-parent-families-c13d48d86f9e.

151. Caitlyn Collins, Liana Christin Landivar, Leah Ruppanner, and William J. Scarborough, "Covid-19 and the Gender Gap in Work Hours," *Gender, Work & Organization* 28, no. S1 (2020): 101–12; and Liana Christin Landivar, Leah Ruppanner, William J. Scarborough, and Caitlyn Collins, "Early Signs Indicate that COVID-19 Is Exacerbating Gender Inequality in the Labor Force," *Socius: Sociological Research for a Dynamic World*, January 2020, https://doi.org/10.1177/2378023120947997.

152. Scott Horsley, "'My Family Needs Me': Latinas Drop out of Workforce at Alarming Rates," NPR, October 27, 2020, https://www.npr.org/2020/10/27/927793195/something-has-to-give-latinas-leaving-workforce-at-faster-rate-than-other-groups.

153. Zack Stanton, "How the Child Care Crisis Will Distort the Economy for a Generation," Politico, August 20, 2020, https://www.politico.com/news/magazine/2020/07/23/child-care-crisis-pandemic-economy-impact-women-380412.

154. Van Hooren, "Covid-19, Migrant Workers and the Resilience of Social Care in Europe."

155. Simon Workman and Steven Jessen Howard, "The True Cost of Providing Safe Child Care during the Coronavirus Pandemic," Center for American Progress, November 9, 2021, https://www.americanprogress.org/article/true-cost-providing-safe-child-care-coronavirus-pandemic/.

156. EJ Dickson, "Coronavirus Is Killing the Working Mother," *Rolling Stone*, July 8, 2020, https://www.rollingstone.com/culture/culture-features/working-motherhood-covid-19-coronavirus-1023609/.

157. Stanton, "How the Child Care Crisis Will Distort the Economy for a Generation."

158. Quoted in Petersen, "'Other Countries Have Social Safety Nets.'"

159. Daniel L. Carlson, Amanda J. Miller, Sharon Sassler, and Sarah Hanson, "The Gendered Division of Housework and Couples' Sexual Relationships: A Reexamination," *Journal of Marriage and Family* 78, no. 4 (2016): 975–95; "Couples That Split Childcare Duties Have Higher-Quality Relationships and Sex Lives," American Sociological Association, August 23, 2015, https://www.asanet.org/press-center/press-releases/couples-split-childcare-duties-have-higher-quality-relationships-and-sex-lives; Neil Chethik, *VoiceMale: What Husbands Really Think about Their Marriages, Their Wives, Sex, Housework, and Commitment* (New York: Simon & Schuster, 2006); Michelle L. Frisco and Kristi Williams, "Perceived Housework Equity, Marital Happiness, and Divorce in Dual-Earner Households," *Journal of Family Issues* 24 (2003): 51–73; Pepper Schwartz, *What Sexual Scientists Know about . . . Sexual Satisfaction in Committed Relationships* (Allentown, PA: Society for the Scientific Study of Sexuality, 2007); Lynn Cooke, "'Traditional' Marriages Now Less Stable," 431–432.

160. "Labor Force Statistics from the Current Population Survey," Table 3, "Employment Status of the Civilian Noninstitutional Population by Age, Sex, and Race," US Bureau of Labor Statistics, accessed February 2, 2022, https://www.bls.gov/cps/cpsaat03.htm.

Chapter 11: Work

1. Drew Whitelegg, *Working the Skies: The Fast-Paced, Disorienting World of the Flight Attendant* (New York: New York University Press, 2007), 1.

2. Logan L. Watts, Mark C. Frame, Richard G. Moffett, Judith L. Van Hein, and Michael Hein, "Gender, Perceived Career Barriers, and Aspirations," *Journal of Applied Social Psychology* 45 (2015): 10–22; and Kimberly A. S. Howard, Aaron H. Carlstrom, Andrew D. Katz, Aaronson Y. Chew, G. Christopher Ray, Lia Laine, et al., "Career Aspirations of Youth: Untangling Race/Ethnicity, SES, and Gender," *Journal of Vocational Behavior* 79, no. 1 (2011): 98–109.

3. Eileen Patten and Kim Parker, "A Gender Reversal on Career Aspirations: Young Women Now Top Young Men in Valuing a High-Paying Career," Pew Research Center, April 19, 2012, https://www.pewsocialtrends.org/2012/04/19/a-gender-reversal-on-career-aspirations.

4. Abigail Johnson Hess, "Survey of 563,000 Recent College Grads Finds Gender Pay Gap Already Impacting Class of 2020," CNBC, January 20, 2022, https://www.cnbc.com/2022/01/20/gender-pay-gap-for-class-of-2020-starting-salaries-shown-in-new-report.html.

5. Julie Zauzmer, "Where We Stand: The Class of 2013 Senior Survey," *Harvard Crimson*, May 28, 2013, https://www.thecrimson.com/article/2013/5/28/senior-survey-2013/?page=single.

6. "Highlights of Women's Earnings in 2020," US Bureau of Labor Statistics, September 2021, https://www.bls.gov/opub/reports/womens-earnings/2020/home.htm.

7. Kathleen Barry, "'Too Glamorous to Be Considered Workers': Flight Attendants and Pink-Collar Activism in Mid-Twentieth-Century America," *Labor: Studies in Working-Class History of the Americas* 3, no. 3 (2006): 119–38, 119.

8. Kathleen Barry, *Femininity in Flight: A History of Flight Attendants* (Durham: Duke University Press, 2007), 98.

9. Ibid., 62.

10. Linda Mizejewski, *Ziegfield Girl: Image and Icon in Culture and Cinema* (Durham, NC: Duke University Press, 1999), 12.

11. Barry, *Femininity in Flight*.

12. Barry, "'Too Glamorous to Be Considered Workers,'" 135; and Whitelegg, *Working the Skies*, 47, 133.

13. Barry, *Femininity in Flight*; Arlie Hochschild, *The Managed Heart: Commercialization of Human Feeling* (Berkeley: University of California Press, 1983); and Melissa Tyler and Pamela Abbott, "Chocs Away: Weight Watching in the Contemporary Airline Industry," *Sociology* 32, no. 3 (1998): 433–50.

14. Victoria Vantoch, *The Jet Sex: Airline Stewardesses and the Making of an American Icon* (Philadelphia: University of Pennsylvania Press, 2013).

15. Whitelegg, *Working the Skies*, 58.

16. Barry, *Femininity in Flight*, 26.

17. Claire Williams, "Sky Service: The Demands of Emotional Labour in the Airline Industry," *Gender, Work and Organization* 10, no. 5 (2003): 513–50.

18. Whitelegg, *Working the Skies*, 48.

19. Barry, *Femininity in Flight*, 119.

20. Ibid.

21. "Pyramid: Women in the United States Workforce (Infographic)," Catalyst, February 9, 2022, https://www.catalyst.org/research/women-in-the-united-states-workforce/; "Historical Women CEOs of the Fortune Lists: 1972–2021 (List)," Catalyst, June 4, 2021, https://www.catalyst.org/research/historical-list-of-women-ceos-of-the-fortune-lists-1972-2021/; and Tiffany Burns, Jess Huang, Alexis Krivkovich, Ishanaa Rambachan, Tijana Trkulja, and Lareina Yee, "Women in the Workplace 2021," McKinsey & Company, September 27, 2021, https://www.mckinsey.com/featured-insights/diversity-and-inclusion/women-in-the-workplace.

22. US Bureau of Labor Statistics, "Median earnings for women in 2021 were 83.1 percent of the median for men," Jan. 24, 2022, https://www.bls.gov/opub/ted/2022/median-earnings-for-women

-in-2021-were-83-1-percent-of-the-median-for-men .htm.

23. Congressional Research Service, "Real Wage Trends, 1979 to 2019," updated December 28, 2020, 1–30, https://sgp.fas.org/crs/misc/R45090.pdf; Heidi Shierholz, "The Wrong Route to Equality: Men's Declining Wages," Council for Contemporary Families, Equal Pay Symposium 2013, https://contemporaryfamilies.org/wp-content/uploads/2014/06/2013_Symposium_Equal-Pay.pdf; John Schmitt, Elise Gould, and Josh Bivens, "America's Slow-Motion Wage Crisis," Economic Policy Institute, September 13, 2018, https://www.epi.org/publication/americas-slow-motion-wage-crisis-four-decades-of-slow-and-unequal-growth-2/.

24. Lynn Prince Cooke, "Pathology of Patriarchy and Family Inequalities," in *Family Inequalities in Europe and the Americas: Causes and Consequences*, ed. Naomi Cahn, June Carbone, W. Bradford Wilcox, and Laurie DeRose (Cambridge: Cambridge University Press, 2017), 237–60.

25. "The Simple Truth about the Gender Pay Gap: 2021 Update," American Association of University Women, September 2021, https://www.aauw.org/resources/research/simple-truth/.

26. Janet Adamy and Paul Overberg, "Women in Elite Jobs Face Stubborn Pay Gap," *Wall Street Journal*, May 17, 2016, https://www.wsj.com/articles/women-in-elite-jobs-face-stubborn-pay-gap-1463502938?tesla=y.

27. "2021 Physician Compensation Report: Fifth Annual Study, Doximity," December 2021, https://c8y.doxcdn.com/image/upload/v1/Press%20Blog/Research%20Reports/Doximity-Compensation-Report-2021.pdf.

28. Amanda Fins, "Women and the Lifetime Wage Gap: How Many Woman Years Does It Take to Equal 40 Man Years?," Fact Sheet, National Women's Law Center, March 2020, https://nwlc.org/wp-content/uploads/2019/03/Women-and-the-Lifetime-Wage-Gap-v2.pdf.

29. Juliette Cubanski, Wyatt Koma, Anthony Damico, and Tricia Neuman, "How Many Seniors Live in Poverty?" Kaiser Family Foundation, November 19, 2018, https://www.kff.org/medicare/issue-brief/how-many-seniors-live-in-poverty/.

30. "Labor Force Statistics from the Current Population Survey," "Employed Persons by Detailed Occupation, Sex, Race, and Hispanic or Latino Ethnicity" (Table 11), US Bureau of Labor Statistics, accessed

February 23, 2022, https://www.bls.gov/cps/cpsaat11.htm.

31. Lynn Carlisle, "The Gender Shift, the Demographics of Women in Dentistry: What Impact Will It Have?" In a Spirit of Caring, October 2, 2007, https://www.inaspiritofcaring.com/public/The_Gender_Shift_the_demographics_of_women_in_dentistry_.cfm?sd=75.

32. Hasmik Gharibyan and Stephan Gunsaulus, "Gender Gap in Computer Science Does Not Exist in One Former Soviet Republic: Results of a Study," *Proceedings of the 11th Annual SIGCSE Conference on Innovation and Technology in Computer Science Education*, June 2006, 222–26, https://doi.org/10.1145/1140124.1140184.

33. Vivian Anette Lagesen, "Extreme Make-Over? The Making of Gender and Computer Science" (PhD diss., STS report 71, Norwegian University of Science and Technology, Trondheim, 2005).

34. Annette Barnabas, D. Joseph Anbarasu, and Paul S. Clifford, "Prospects of Women Construction Workers in Tamil Nadu, South India," *Indian Journal of Gender Studies* 18, no. 2 (June 2011): 217–35.

35. Hegewisch and Mefferd, "Gender Wage Gap by Occupation, Race and Ethnicity 2020."

36. Joyce Jacobsen, *The Economics of Gender* (Malden, MA: Wiley-Blackwell, 2007), data from International Labour Organization, *Yearbook of Labour Statistics* (1985–2004), 2007.

37. E. J. Hall, "Waitering/Waitressing: Engendering the Work of Table Servers," *Gender & Society* 7, no. 3 (1993): 329–46; and Anna Haley-Lock & Stephanie Ewert, "Serving Men and Mothers: Workplace Practices and Workforce Composition in Two US Restaurant Chains and States," *Community, Work & Family* 14, no. 4 (2011), 387–404.

38. "2019 Physicians Specialty Data Book," Association of American Medical College, December 2019, https://www.aamc.org/data-reports/workforce/interactive-data/active-physicians-sex-and-specialty-2019.

39. "Labor Force Statistics from the Current Population Survey," Table 11.

40. Eileen Patten and Kim Parker, "Women in the U.S. Military: Growing Share, Distinctive Profile," Pew Research Center, www.pewsocialtrends.org/files/2011/12/women-in-the-military.pdf.

41. "2020 TLC Factbook," New York City Taxi and Limousine Commission, accessed February 22, 2022, https://www1.nyc.gov/site/tlc/about/fact-book.page.

42. Ryan Finnigan, "Rainbow-Collar Jobs? Occupational Segregation by Sexual Orientation in the United States," *Socius*, January 2020, https://doi.org/10.1177/2378023120954795.

43. Phil Tiemeyer, *Plane Queer: Labor, Sexuality, and AIDS in the History of Men Flight Attendants* (Berkeley: University of California Press, 2013); and Finnigan, "Rainbow-Collar Jobs?"

44. Maria Charles, "A World of Difference: International Trends in Women's Economic Status," *Annual Review of Sociology* 37 (2011): 355–71; and Robin Ely, "Effects of Organizational Demographics and Social Identity on Relationships among Professional Women," *Administrative Science Quarterly* 39, no. 2 (1994): 203–38.

45. Sapna Cheryan, Victoria C. Plaut, Paul G. Davies, and Claude M. Steele, "Ambient Belonging: How Stereotypical Cues Impact Gender Participation in Computer Science," *Journal of Personality and Social Psychology* 97, no. 6 (2009): 1045–60.

46. Emily Chang, *Brotopia: Breaking Up the Boys' Club of Silicon Valley* (New York: Portfolio, 2018); Amy M. Denissen, "The Right Tools for the Job: Constructing Gender Meanings and Identities in the Men-Dominated Building Trades," *Human Relations* 63, no. 7 (2010): 1051–69.

47. Karen Hossfeld, "Hiring Immigrant Women: Silicon Valley's Simple Formula," in *Women of Color in U.S. Society*, ed. Maxine Baca Zinn and Bonnie Thornton Dill (Philadelphia: Temple University Press, 1994), 765–93, 65.

48. Emily Chang, "Women Once Ruled the Computer World. When Did Silicon Valley Become Brotopia?" *Bloomberg*, February 1, 2018, https://www.bloomberg.com/news/features/2018-02-01/women-once-ruled-computers-when-did-the-valley-become-brotopia.

49. Stefanie K. Johnson, David R. Hekman, and Elsa T. Chan, "If There's Only One Woman in Your Candidate Pool, There's Statistically No Chance She'll Be Hired," *Harvard Business Review*, April 26, 2016, https://hbr.org/2016/04/if-theres-only-one-woman-in-your-candidate-pool-theres-statistically-no-chance-shell-be-hired.

50. David J. Maume, "Occupational Segregation and the Career Mobility of White Men and Women," *Social Forces* 77, no. 4 (1999): 1449. See also "Why Engineering, Science Gender Gap Persists," *PBS News Hour*, April 25, 2012, https://www.pbs.org

/newshour/rundown/science-engineering-and-the
-gender-gap/.

51. Molly Connell, "Lack of Women Role Models Undermining STEM Career Paths," Business Women Media, April 15, 2017, https://www.thebusiness womanmedia.com/women-undermining-career -paths/.

52. Susan Chira, "The 'Manly' Jobs Problem," *New York Times*, February 8, 2018, https://www.nytimes .com/2018/02/08/sunday-review/sexual-harass ment-masculine-jobs.html.

53. Tiemeyer, *Plane Queer*, 93.

54. Ibid., 91.

55. Ibid., 102.

56. Ibid., 113.

57. Ibid.

58. Tyler and Abbott, "Chocs Away," 440.

59. LeAnn Erickson, dir., *Top Secret Rosies: The Women Computers of World War II* (documentary, 2010), http://www.topsecretrosies.com/; and Thomas Misa, ed., *Gender Codes: Why Women Are Leaving Computing* (Hoboken, NJ: John Wiley, 2010).

60. Anna Lewis, "Girls Go Geek . . . Again!" *Switch* (blog), July 28, 2011, https://switchthefuture.com /2011/07/28/20110728girls-go-geek-again-fog-creek -software-blog-new-york/.

61. Elizabeth Blair, "'Hidden Figures' No More: Meet the Black Women Who Helped Send America to Space," NPR, December 16, 2016, https://www .npr.org/2016/12/16/505569187/hidden-figures-no -more-meet-the-black-women-who-helped-send -america-to-space.

62. Karen Beyard-Tyler and Marilyn Haring, "Gender-Related Aspects of Occupational Prestige," *Vocational Behavior* 24, no. 2 (1984): 194–203; Katie Burns, "At Veterinary Colleges, Men Students Are in the Minority," *JAVMA*, February 1, 2010, https:// www.avma.org/javma-news/2010-02-15/veterinary -colleges-male-students-are-minority; Philip Cohen and Matt L. Huffman, "Individuals, Jobs, and Labor Markets: The Devaluation of Women's Work," *American Sociological Review* 68, no. 3 (2007): 443–63; Asaf Levanon, Paula England, and Paul Allison, "Occupational Feminization and Pay: Assessing Causal Dynamics Using 1950–2000 U.S. Census Data," *Social Forces* 88, no. 2 (December 2009): 865–91; and Harry Parker, Fong Chan, and Bernard Saper, "Occupational Representativeness and Prestige Rating: Some Observations," *Journal of Employment Counseling* 26, no. 3 (1989): 117–31.

63. Claudia Goldin, *Understanding the Gender Gap: An Economic History of American Women* (New York: Oxford University Press, 1990), 204.

64. Margery Davies, *Woman's Place Is at the Typewriter: Office Work and Office Workers, 1870–1930* (Philadelphia: Temple University Press, 1984); and Goldin, *Understanding the Gender Gap*.

65. For a review, see Cohen and Huffman, "Individuals, Jobs, and Labor Markets," 443–63.

66. Paula England, "Gender Inequality in Labor Markets: The Role of Motherhood and Segregation," *Social Politics: International Studies in Gender, State and Society* 12, no. 2 (2005): 264–88; Thomas S. Moore, "Occupational Career Change and Gender Wage Inequality," *Work and Occupations* 45, no. 1 (2018): 82–121; Tali Kristal, Yinon Cohen, Edo Navot, "Benefit Inequality among American Workers by Gender, Race, and Ethnicity, 1982–2015," *Sociological Science* 5 (2018): 461–88; Joan Llull, "Immigration and Gender Differences in the Labor Market," *Journal of Human Capital* 15, no. 1 (2021): 174–203; and Cohen and Huffman, "Individuals, Jobs, and Labor Markets," 443–63.

67. For a review, see Cohen and Huffman, "Individuals, Jobs, and Labor Markets," 443–63; and Stephanie Boraas and William M. Rodgers III, "How Does Gender Play a Role in the Earnings Gap? An Update," *Monthly Labor Review* (March 2003), https://www.bls.gov/opub/mlr/2003/03/art2full .pdf.

68. "May 2020 National Occupational Employment and Wage Estimates," US Bureau of Labor Statistics, accessed February 23, 2022, https://www.bls.gov /oes/current/oes_nat.htm.

69. Michael S. Kimmel, "Why Men Should Support Gender Equity," *Women's Studies Review* (Fall 2005): 102–14, 108, https://www.lehman.edu/academics /inter/women-studies/documents/why-men.pdf.

70. Soraya Chemaly, "What's Your Kids' Wage Gap? Boys Paid More, More Profitably," Huffington Post, updated March 24, 2015, https://www.huffpost.com /soraya-chemaly/whats-your-kids-wage-gap_b _6518772.

71. Nadine Kalinauskas, "Heroic Asiana Flight Attendant Carried Passengers to Safety on Her Back," Yahoo! News, July 13, 2013, https://ca.news.yahoo .com/blogs/good-news/heroic-asiana-flight-atten dant-carried-passengers-safety-her-183216700.html ?guccounter=1.

72. Lisa Wade, "The Unsung Heroes of the Crash Landing in San Francisco," *Sociological Images*,

December 26, 2013, https://thesocietypages.org/soc images/2013/12/26/working-through-the-crash -landing-in-san-francisco/.

73. Quoted in Barry, "'Too Glamorous to Be Considered Workers,'" 135.

74. Hochschild, *Managed Heart*, 107.

75. Ramsey Qubein, "The Rigors of Flight Attendant Training During COVID," *CN Traveler*, January 7, 2022, https://www.cntraveler.com/story/the-rigors-of -flight-attendant-training-during-covid; Rachel Gillett, "Inside the Intensive, Two-Month Training All Delta Flight Attendants Must Attend That's Harder to Get into Than Harvard," *Business Insider*, March 10, 2018, https://www.businessinsider.com/delta-airlines -flight-attendant-training-school-inside-look-2018-3 #not-being-able-to-swim-could-mean-its-the-end-of -the-road-for-flight-attendant-trainees-7; and Whitelegg, *Working the Skies*.

76. Hochschild, *Managed Heart*, 96.

77. T. J. Ballard, L. Corradi, L. Lauria, C. Mazzanti, G. Scaravelli, F. Sgorbissa, et al., "Integrating Qualitative Methods into Occupational Health Research: A Study of Women Flight Attendants," *Occupational and Environmental Medicine* 61 (2004): 163–66.

78. Sandee LaMotte, "What Flight Attendants Want You to Know about Traveling Right Now," CNN, November 23, 2021, https://www.cnn.com/travel /article/flight-attendants-holiday-travel-wellness /index.html.

79. "Unruly Passenger Survey Results," Association of Flight Attendants–CWA, July 30, 2021, https:// www.afacwa.org/unruly_passenger_survey _results.

80. Kelli María Korducki, "'Nobody Ever Put Hands on Me Before': Flight Attendants on the Air Rage Epidemic," *Guardian,* October 17, 2021, https://www .theguardian.com/us-news/2021/oct/17/flight-atten dants-air-rage-epidemic-coronavirus-covid.

81. "Unruly Passenger Survey Results."

82. Francesca Street, "Dread at 30,000 Feet: Inside the Increasingly Violent World of US Flight Attendants," CNN, September 6, 2021, https://www.cnn .com/travel/article/flight-attendants-unruly-pas sengers-covid/index.html.

83. Ibid.

84. Barry, *Femininity in Flight*, 27.

85. Chloe Grace Hart, "Trajectory Guarding: Managing Unwanted, Ambiguously Sexual Interactions

at Work," *American Sociological Review* 86, no. 2 (April 2021): 256–78.

86. Liza Mundy, "Why Is Silicon Valley So Awful to Women?" *Atlantic*, April 2017, https://www.the atlantic.com/magazine/archive/2017/04/why-is -silicon-valley-so-awful-to-women/517788/.

87. "May 2020 National Occupational Employment and Wage Estimates," US Bureau of Labor Statistics, accessed February 23, 2022, https://www.bls.gov /oes/current/oes_nat.htm.

88. Jill E. Yavorsky, Philip N. Cohen, and Yue Qian, "MAN UP, MAN DOWN: Race-Ethnicity and the Hierarchy of Men in Women-Dominated Work," *Sociological Quarterly* 57 (2016): 733–58.

89. Michele Lamont, *The Dignity of Working Men: Morality and the Boundaries of Race, Class, and Immigration* (New York: Russell Sage Foundation, 2000).

90. England, "Gender Inequality in Labor Markets"; Paula England, Michelle Budig, and Nancy Folbre, "Wages of Virtue: The Relative Pay of Care Work," *Social Problems* 49, no. 4 (2002): 455–73; and Elise Gould, Marokey Sawo, and Asha Banerjee, "Care Workers Are Deeply Undervalued and Underpaid," Economic Policy Institute, July 16, 2021, https:// www.epi.org/blog/care-workers-are-deeply-under valued-and-underpaid-estimating-fair-and-equitable -wages-in-the-care-sectors/.

91. "May 2020 National Occupational Employment and Wage Estimates," US Bureau of Labor Statistics, accessed February 23, 2022, https://www.bls.gov /oes/current/oes_nat.htm.

92. Boraas and Rodgers, "How Does Gender Play a Role in the Earnings Gap?"; and Margarita Torre, "Stopgappers? The Occupational Trajectories of Men in Female-Dominated Occupations," *Work and Occupations* 45, 3 (August 2018): 283–312.

93. Finnigan, "Rainbow-Collar Jobs?" M. V. Lee Badgett, Christopher S. Carpenter, and Dario Sansone, "LGBTQ Economics," *Journal of Economic Perspectives* 35, no. 2 (2021): 141–70; John Blandford, "The Nexus of Sexual Orientation and Gender in the Determination of Earnings," *Industrial and Labor Relations Review* 56, no. 4 (2003): 622–42.

94. Rakesh Kochhar and Jesse Bennett, "U.S. Labor Market Inches Back from the COVID-19 Shock, but Recovery Is Far from Complete," Pew Research Center, April 14, 2021, https://www.pewresearch.org /fact-tank/2021/04/14/u-s-labor-market-inches-back

-from-the-covid-19-shock-but-recovery-is-far-from-complete/.

95. Claire Ewing Nelson, "Another 275,000 Women Left the Labor Force in January," National Women's Law Center, February 2021, https://nwlc.org/wp-content/uploads/2021/02/January-Jobs-Day-FS.pdf.

96. Kristen Broady and Anthony Barr, "December's Jobs Report Reveals a Growing Racial Employment Gap, Especially for Black Women," Brookings, January 11, 2022, https://www.brookings.edu/blog/the-avenue/2022/01/11/decembers-jobs-report-reveals-a-growing-racial-employment-gap-especially-for-black-women/; and "The Employment Situation: April 2020," US Bureau of Labor Statistics, May 8, 2020, https://www.bls.gov/news.release/archives/empsit_05082020.pdf.

97. Gabriela Lotta, Michelle Fernandez, Denise Pimenta, Clare Wenham, "Gender, Race, and Health Workers in the COVID-19 Pandemic," Lancet 397, no. 10281 (April 3, 2021): 1264, https://www.thelancet.com/journals/lancet/article/PIIS0140-6736(21)00530-4/fulltext; and Inez Miyamoto, "Covid-19 Healthcare Workers: 70% Are Women," Daniel K. Inouye Asia-Pacific Center for Security Studies, May 13, 2020, http://www.jstor.org/stable/resrep24863.

98. "Labor Force Statistics from the Current Population Survey," Table 11.

99. Maryam Vizheh, Mostafa Qorbani, Seyed Masoud Arzaghi, Salut Muhidin, Zohreh Javanmard, and Marzieh Esmaeili, "The Mental Health of Healthcare Workers in the COVID-19 Pandemic: A Systematic Review," Journal of Diabetes and Metabolic Disorders 19, no. 2 (2020): 1–12.

100. Soham Bandyopadhyay, Ronnie E. Baticulon, Murtaza Kadhum, Muath Alser, Daniel K. Ojuka, Yara Badereddin, et al., "Infection and Mortality of Healthcare Workers Worldwide from COVID-19: A Systematic Review," BMJ Global Health 5 (2020), https://doi.org/10.1136/ bmjgh-2020-003097.

101. "Healthcare Workers 7 Times as Likely to Have Severe COVID-19 as Other Workers," BMJ, August 12, 2020, https://www.bmj.com/company/newsroom/healthcare-workers-7-times-as-likely-to-have-severe-covid-19-as-other-workers/.

102. "Sins of Omission: How Government Failures to Track Covid-19 Data Have Led to More Than 3,200 Health Care Worker Deaths and Jeopardize Public Health," National Nurses United, March 2021, https://www.nationalnursesunited.org/sites/default/files/nnu/documents/0321_Covid19_SinsOfOmission_Data_Report.pdf.

103. Catherine E. Shoichet," Covid-19 Is Taking a Devastating Toll on Filipino American Nurses," CNN, December 11, 2020, https://www.cnn.com/2020/11/24/health/filipino-nurse-deaths/index.html.

104. Catherine Ceniza Choy, Empire of Care: Nursing and Migration in Filipino American History (Durham, NC: Duke University Press).

105. "How Filipino Nurses Propped Up America's Medical System," Time, May 30, 2021, https://time.com/6051754/history-filipino-nurses-us/.

106. Benjamin Freedman, "Health Professions, Codes, and the Right to Refuse HIV-Infectious Patients," Hastings Center Report 18, no. 2 (1988): S20-5.

107. Shoichet, "Covid-19 Is Taking a Devastating Toll on Filipino American Nurses."

108. Jennifer Cheeseman Day and Cheridan Christnacht, "Women Hold 76% of All Health Care Jobs, Gaining in Higher-Paying Occupations," US Census Bureau, August 14, 2019, https://www.census.gov/library/stories/2019/08/your-health-care-in-womens-hands.html; and Peter I. Buerhaus, Douglas O. Staiger, David I. Auerbach, Max C. Yates, and Karen Donelan, "Nurse Employment during the First Fifteen Months of the COVID-19 Pandemic," Health Affairs 41, no. 1 (January 2022), https://www.healthaffairs.org/doi/abs/10.1377/hlthaff.2021.01289?journalCode=hlthaff .

109. Tyler and Abbott, "Chocs Away," 433–50; and Goldin, Understanding the Gender Gap.

110. Paul Overberg and Janet Adamy, "What's Your Pay Gap?" Wall Street Journal, May 17, 2016, graphics.wsj.com/gender-pay-gap/.

111. Eric Uhlmann and Geoffrey Cohen, "Constructed Criteria: Redefining Merit to Justify Discrimination," Psychological Science 16, no. 6 (2005): 474–80.

112. Kristen Schilt, "Just One of the Guys? How Transmen Make Gender Visible at Work," Gender & Society 20, no. 4 (2006): 465–90, 483.

113. Ibid., 477.

114. Ibid., 476.

115. Catherine Connell, "Doing, Undoing, or Redoing Gender? Learning from the Workplace Experiences of Transpeople," Gender and Society 24, no. 1 (2010): 31–55, 48.

116. Ibid.

117. Ibid.

118. Arlie Hochschild, *The Time Bind: When Work Becomes Home and Home Becomes Work* (New York: Henry Holt, 2001), 108–9; Sreedhari Desai, Dolly Chugh, and Arthur Brief, "Marriage Structure and Resistance to the Gender Revolution in the Workplace," Social Science Research Network, March 2012, http://papers.ssrn.com/sol3/papers.cfm?abstract_id=2018259; Sreedhari Desai, Dolly Chugh, and Arthur Brief, "The Organizational Implications of a Traditional Marriage: Can a Domestic Traditionalist by Night Be an Organizational Egalitarian by Day?" (UNC Kenn-Flagler Research Paper No. 2013–19), Social Science Research Network, updated August 20, 2014, https://papers.ssrn.com/sol3/papers.cfm?abstract_id=2018259; and M. Ena Inesi and Daniel M. Cable, "When Accomplishments Come Back to Haunt You: The Negative Effect of Competence Signals on Women's Performance Evaluations," *Personnel Psychology* 68 (2015): 615–57.

119. Laurel Smith-Doerr, Sharla Alegria, Kaye Husbands Fealing, Debra Fitzpatrick, and Donald Tomaskovic-Devey, "Gender Pay Gaps in U.S. Federal Science Agencies: An Organizational Approach," *American Journal of Sociology* 125, no. 2 (2019), https://www.journals.uchicago.edu/doi/full/10.1086/705514; Kim Parker, "Women in Majority-Men Workplaces Report Higher Rates of Gender Discrimination," Pew Research Center, March 7, 2018, www.pewresearch.org/fact-tank/2018/03/07/women-in-majority-men-workplaces-report-higher-rates-of-gender-discrimination/; and Kim Parker and Cary Funk, "Gender Discrimination Comes in Many Forms for Today's Working Women," Pew Research Center, December 14, 2017, www.pewresearch.org/fact-tank/2017/12/14/gender-discrimination-comes-in-many-forms-for-todays-working-women/. See also Chai R. Feldblum and Victoria A. Lipnic, *Select Task Force on the Study of Harassment in the Workplace*, US Equal Employment Opportunity Commission, June 2016, https://www.eeoc.gov/eeoc/task_force/harassment/report.cfm; and Rachel Thomas, Marianne Cooper, Ellen Konar, Megan Rooney, Ashley Finc, Lareina Yee, et al., *Women in the Workplace, 2021*, LeanIn.Org and McKinsey & Company, 2021, https://womenintheworkplace.com/.

120. Denissen, "Right Tools for the Job," 1061–62.

121. Shelley Correll and Caroline Simard, "Research: Vague Feedback Is Holding Women Back," *Harvard Business Review*, April 29, 2016, https://hbr.org/2016/04/research-vague-feedback-is-holding-women-back.

122. Denissen, "Right Tools for the Job," 1051–69.

123. Angus Chen, "Invisibilia: How Learning to Be Vulnerable Can Make Life Safer," NPR, June 17, 2016, https://www.npr.org/sections/health-shots/2016/06/17/482203447/invisibilia-how-learning-to-be-vulnerable-can-make-life-safer.

124. Robin J. Ely and Debra Meyerson, "Unmasking Manly Men," *Harvard Business Review*, July–August 2008, https://hbr.org/2008/07/unmasking-manly-men.

125. Jessica Smith Rolston, *Mining Coal and Undermining Gender: Rhythms of Work and Family in the American West* (New Brunswick, NJ: Rutgers University Press, 2014).

126. Robin J. Ely, "The Power in Demography: Women's Social Constructions of Gender Identity at Work," *Academy of Management Journal* 38 (1995): 589–634.

127. Philip Cohen and Matt Huffman, "Working for the Woman? Women Managers and the Gender Wage Gap," *American Sociological Review* 72, no. 5 (2007): 681–704.

128. Burns et al., "Women in the Workplace 2021."

129. Ibid.

130. Catherine Connell, *School's Out: Gay and Lesbian Teachers in the Classroom* (Oakland: University of California Press, 2015).

131. Rachael Bade and Ryan Lizza, "POLITICO Playbook: Republicans Can't Agree on a SCOTUS Strategy," *Playbook*, February 2, 2022, https://www.politico.com/newsletters/playbook/2022/02/02/republicans-cant-agree-on-a-scotus-strategy-00004536.

132. "Women of Color in the United States (Quick Take)," Catalyst, January 31, 2022, https://www.catalyst.org/research/women-of-color-in-the-united-states/; and Marlese Durr and Adia M. Harvey Wingfield, "Keep Your 'N' in Check: Black Women and the Interactive Effects of Etiquette and Emotional Labor," *Critical Sociology* 37, no. 5 (March 2011): 557–71.

133. Kimberly Atkins Stohr, "The Extra Unseen Talent of Biden's Supreme Court Nominee and All Black Women in Law," *Boston Globe*, February 3, 2022, https://www.bostonglobe.com/2022/02/03/opinion/extra-unseen-talent-bidens-supreme-court-nom

inee-all-black-women-law/; and Tsedale M. Melaku, *You Don't Look Like a Lawyer: Black Women and Systemic Gendered Racism* (New York: Rowman & Littlefield, 2019).

134. Michelle K. Ryan and S. Alexander Haslam, "The Glass Cliff: Evidence That Women Are Overrepresented in Precarious Leadership Positions," *British Journal of Management* 16 (2005): 81–90; and Michelle Ryan and S. Alexander Haslam, "The Glass Cliff: Exploring the Dynamics Surrounding the Appointment of Women to Precarious Leadership Positions," *Academy of Management Review* 32, no. 2 (2007): 549–72.

135. Emily Stewart, "Why Struggling Companies Promote Women: The Glass Cliff, Explained," *Vox*, October 31, 2018, https://www.vox.com/2018/10/31/17960156/what-is-the-glass-cliff-women-ceos.

136. Alison Cook and Christy Glass, "Glass Cliffs and Organizational Saviors: Barriers to Minority Leadership in Work Organizations," *Social Problems* 60, no. 2 (2013): 168–87.

137. Amy Nesbitt, "The Glass Ceiling Effect and Its Impact on Mid-Level Women Officer Career Progression in the United States Marine Corps and Air Force" (MA thesis, Naval Postgraduate School, 2004), 78, http://calhoun.nps.edu/public/handle/10945/1711.

138. Burns et al., "Women in the Workplace 2021"; Sylvia A. Hewlett and Carolyn Buck Luce, "Off-Ramps and On-Ramps: Keeping Talented Women on the Road to Success," *Harvard Business Review*, March 2005, 43–54; Nancy M. Carter and Christine Silva, *Pipeline's Broken Promise* (Catalyst, 2010); Linda K. Stroh, Jeanne M. Brett, and Anne H. Reilly, "Family Structure, Glass Ceiling, and Traditional Explanations for the Differential Rate of Turnover of Women and Men Managers," *Journal of Vocational Behavior* 49 (1996): 99–118; and Lauren Noel and Christie Hunter Arscott, "Millennial Women: What Executives Need to Know about Millennial Women," International Consortium for Executive Development Research, April 2016, www.icedr.org/research/documents/15_millennial_women.pdf.

139. Rosabeth Moss Kanter, "The Impact of Hierarchical Structures on the Work Behavior of Women and Men," *Social Problems* 23, no. 4 (1976): 415–30.

140. Donald Tomaskovic-Devey and Dustin Avent-Holt, *Relational Inequalities: An Organizational Approach* (New York: Oxford University Press, 2019); and Steven Ruggles, "Patriarchy, Power, and

Pay: The Transformation of American Families, 1800–2015," *Demography* 52, no. 6 (2015): 1797–823.

141. Margarita Torre, "Stopgappers? The Occupational Trajectories of Men in Female-Dominated Occupations," *Work and Occupations* 45, 3 (August 2018): 283–312.

142. Christine Williams, "Crossing Over: Interdisciplinary Research on 'Men Who Do Women's Work,'" *Sex Roles* 72, no. 7–8: 390–95; Christine Williams, *Still a Man's World: Men Who Do Women's Work* (Berkeley: University of California Press, 1995); Matt Huffman, "Gender Inequality across Wage Hierarchies," *Work and Occupations* 31, no. 3 (2004): 323–44; Mia Hultin, "Some Take the Glass Escalator, Some Hit the Glass Ceiling: Career Consequences of Occupational Sex Segregation," *Work and Occupations* 30 (2003): 30–61; David J. Maume, "Is the Glass Ceiling a Unique Form of Inequality? Evidence from a Random Effects Model of Managerial Attainment," *Work and Occupations* 31, no. 2 (2004): 250–74; and Deborah A. Harris and Patti Giuffre, *Taking the Heat: Women Chefs and Gender Inequality in the Professional Kitchen* (New Brunswick, NJ: Rutgers University Press, 2015).

143. Andrew Cognard-Black, "Will They Stay, or Will They Go? Sex-Atypical Work among Token Men Who Teach," *Sociological Quarterly* 45, no. 1 (2004): 113–39.

144. Allyson Stokes, "The Glass Runway: How Gender and Sexuality Shape the Spotlight in Fashion Design," *Gender & Society* 29, no. 2 (2015): 219–43.

145. Adia Wingfield, "Racializing the Glass Escalator: Reconsidering Men's Experiences with Women's Work," *Gender & Society* 23, no. 1 (2009): 5–26; Ryan Smith, "Money, Benefits, and Power: A Test of the Glass Ceiling and Glass Escalator Hypotheses," *Annals of the American Academy of Political and Social Science* 639, no. 1 (2012): 149–72; Catherine Connell, "Dangerous Disclosures," *Sexuality Research and Social Policy* 9 (2012): 168–77; Kristen Schilt, *Just One of the Guys?* (Chicago: University of Chicago Press, 2011); and Michelle Budig, "Men Advantage and the Gender Composition of Jobs: Who Rides the Glass Escalator?" *Social Problems* 49, no. 2 (2002): 258–77.

146. Williams, *Still a Man's World*, 88.

147. Laura Stokowski, "Just Call Us Nurses: Men in Nursing," *MedScape*, August 16, 2012.

148. Joan Acker, "Hierarchies, Jobs, Bodies: A Theory of Gendered Organizations," *Gender & Society* 4, no. 2 (1990); Barbara Risman, *Gender Vertigo:*

American Families in Transition (New Haven, CT: Yale University Press, 1999); and Phyllis Moen and Patricia Roehling, *The Career Mystique: Cracks in the American Dream* (Lanham, MD: Rowan & Littlefield, 2005).

149. Hochschild, *Time Bind*, 56.

150. Quoted in ibid., xix.

151. Youngjoo Cha, "Reinforcing Separate Spheres: The Effect of Spousal Overwork on Men's and Women's Employment in Dual-Earner Households," *American Sociological Review* 75, no. 2 (2010): 303–29.

152. Youngjoo Cha and Kim A. Weeden, "Overwork and the Slow Convergence in the Gender Gap in Wages," *American Sociological Review* 79, no. 3 (2014): 457–84; and Youngjoo Cha, "Overwork and the Persistence of Gender Segregation in Occupations," *Gender & Society* 27, no. 2 (2013): 158–84.

153. Melanie Wasserman, "Hours Constraints, Occupational Choice, and Gender: Evidence from Medical Residents," March 19, 2019, https://ssrn.com /abstract=3371100.

154. Arlie Hochschild, *The Second Shift* (New York: Penguin, 1989).

155. Richard J. Petts, Chris Knoester, and Qi Li, "Paid Paternity Leave-Taking in the United States," *Community, Work and Family* 23, no. 2 (2020): 162–83; and Kevin Miller, "The Simple Truth about the Gender Pay Gap," AAUW, Spring 2018, https:// www.aauw.org/resources/research/simple-truth/.

156. Kelly Musick, Megan Doherty Bea, and Pilar Gonalons-Pons, "His and Her Earnings Following Parenthood in the United States, Germany, and the United Kingdom," *American Sociological Review*, 85, no. 4 (2020): 639–74; Melissa Hogenboom, "The Corporate Ideals Driving 'Secret Parenting'" BBC, November 22, 2020, https://www.bbc.com/worklife /article/20201113-the-corporate-ideals-driving-secret -parenting.

157. Joan C. Williams, "The Maternal Wall," *Harvard Business Review*, October 2004, https://hbr .org/2004/10/the-maternal-wall.

158. Kevin Leicht, "Broken Down by Race and Gender? Sociological Explanations of New Sources of Earnings Inequality," *Annual Review of Sociology* 34 (2008): 237–55.

159. Denise D. Bielby and William T. Bielby, "She Works Hard for the Money: Household Responsibilities and the Allocation of Work Effort," *American Journal of Sociology* 93, no. 5 (1998): 1031–59; Peter Marsden, Arne Kalleberg, and Cynthia Cook, "Gender Differences in Organizational Commitment: Influences of Work Positions and Family Roles," *Work and Occupations* 20, no. 3 (1993): 368–90; William T. Bielby and Denise D. Bielby, "Family Ties: Balancing Commitments to Work and Family in Dual Earner Households," *American Sociological Review* 5, no. 4 (1989): 776–89; William T. Bielby and Denise D. Bielby, "Telling Stories about Gender and Effort: Social Science Narratives about Who Works Hard for the Money," in *New Economic Sociology: Developments in an Emerging Field*, ed. Mauro F. Guillén, Randall Collins, Paula England, and Marshall Meyer (New York: Russell Sage Foundation, 2002), 193–217; Denise D. Bielby and William T. Bielby, "Work Commitment, Sex-Role Attitudes, and Women's Employment," *American Sociological Review* 49 (1984): 234–47; Jenny Anderson, "The Ultimate Efficiency Hack: Have Kids," *Quartz*, October 11, 2016; Ylan Q. Mui, "Study: Women with More Children Are More Productive at Work," *Washington Post*, October 30, 2014; Julie Kmec, "Are Motherhood Penalties and Fatherhood Bonuses Warranted? Comparing Pro-Work Behaviors and Conditions of Mothers, Fathers, and Non-Parents," *Social Science Research* 40, no. 2 (2010): 444–59.

160. Michelle Budig, "The Fatherhood Bonus and the Motherhood Penalty: Parenthood and the Gender Gap in Pay," *Third Way*, September 2, 2017; Shelley Correll, Stephen Benard, and In Paik, "Getting a Job: Is There a Motherhood Penalty?" *American Journal of Sociology* 112, no. 5 (2007): 1297–339; Jessi Smith, Kristin Hawkinson, and Kelli Paull, "Spoiled Milk: An Experimental Examination of Bias Against Mothers Who Breastfeed," *Personality and Social Psychology Bulletin* 37, no. 7 (2011): 867–78; Madeline E. Heilman and Tyler G. Okimoto, "Motherhood: A Potential Source of Bias in Employment Decisions," *Journal of Applied Psychology* 93, no.1 (2008): 189–98; Sophie-Claire Valiquette-Tessier, Julie Gosselin, Marta Young, and Kristel Thomassin, "A Literature Review of Cultural Stereotypes Associated with Motherhood and Fatherhood," *Marriage & Family Review* 55, no. 4 (2019): 299–329; M. José González, Clara Cortina, Jorge Rodríguez, "The Role of Gender Stereotypes in Hiring: A Field Experiment," *European Sociological Review* 35, no. 2 (2019): 187–204.

161. Williams, "Maternal Wall."

162. Ivy Kennelly, "'That Single Mother Element': How White Employers Typify Black Women," *Gender & Society* 13, no. 2 (1999): 168–92.

163. Jessi Smith, Kristin Hawkinson, and Kelli Paull, "Spoiled Milk: An Experimental Examination of Bias Against Mothers who Breastfeed," *Person-*

ality and Social Psychology Bulletin 37, no. 7 (2011): 867–78.

164. Williams, "Maternal Wall."

165. Correll, Benard, and Paik, "Getting a Job," 1297–339; dollars converted from 2007 to 2022 dollars.

166. Jonathan Marc Bearak, Anna Popinchalk, Kristen Lagasse Burke, and Selena Anjur-Dietrich, "Does the Impact of Motherhood on Women's Employment and Wages Differ for Women Who Plan Their Transition into Motherhood?" Demography 58, no. 4 (2021): 1301–25; and Ewa Cukrowska-Torzewska and Anna Matysiak, "The Motherhood Wage Penalty: A Meta-Analysis," Social Science Research 88–89 (May–July 2020): 102416.

167. Paula England, Jonathan Bearak, Michelle J. Budig, and Melissa J. Hodges, "Do Highly Paid, Highly Skilled Women Experience the Largest Motherhood Penalty?" American Sociological Review 81, no. 6 (December 2016): 1161–89; Zachary Van Winkle and Anette Eva Fasang, "Parenthood Wage Gaps across the Life Course: A Comparison by Gender and Race," Journal of Marriage and Family 82, no. 5 (2020): 1515–33; Wei-hsin Yu and Janet Chen-Lan Kuo, "The Motherhood Wage Penalty by Work Conditions: How Do Occupational Characteristics Hinder or Empower Mothers?" American Sociological Review 82, no. 4 (August 2017): 744–69; Eunjung Jee, Joya Misra, and Marta Murray-Close, "Motherhood Penalties in the U.S., 1986–2014," Journal of Marriage and Family 81, no. 2 (2019): 434–49; Megan de Linde Leonard and Tom Stanley, "Married with Children: What Remains when Observable Biases Are Removed from the Reported Male Marriage Wage Premium," Labor Economics 33 (2015): 72–80; and Michelle Budig and Paula England, "The Wage Penalty for Motherhood," American Sociological Review 66, no. 2 (2001): 204–25.

168. Ilyana Kuziemko, Jessica Pan, Jenny Shen, and Ebonya Washington, "The Mommy Effect: Do Women Anticipate the Employment Effects of Motherhood?" National Bureau of Economic Research, December 2020, https://www.nber.org/papers/w24740; Amanda Baumle, "The Cost of Parenthood: Unraveling the Effects of Sexual Orientation and Gender on Income," Social Science Quarterly 90, no. 4 (2009): 983–1002; Koji Ueno, Teresa Roach, and Abráham E. Peña-Talamantes, "Sexual Orientation and Gender Typicality of the Occupation in Young Adulthood," Social Forces 92, no. 1 (2013): 81–108; Coral del Río and Olga Alonso-Villar, "Occupational Segregation by Sexual Orientation in the U.S.: Exploring Its Economic Effects on Same-Sex Couples,"

Review of Economics of the Household 17, no. 2 (2019): 439–67; and Pilar Gonalons-Pons, Christine R. Schwartz, and Kelly Musick, "Changes in Couples' Earnings following Parenthood and Trends in Family Earnings Inequality," Demography 58, no. 3 (June 2021): 1093–117.

169. De Linde Leonard and Stanley, "Married with Children," 72–80. See also Alexandra Killewald, "A Reconsideration of the Fatherhood Premium: Marriage, Coresidence, Biology, and Fathers' Wages," American Sociological Review 78, no. 1 (2013): 96–116; Rebecca Glauber, "Race and Gender in Families at Work: The Fatherhood Wage Premium," Gender & Society 22, no. 1 (2008): 8–30; Melissa Hodges and Michelle Budig, "Who Gets the Daddy Bonus? Organizational Hegemonic Masculinity and the Impact of Fatherhood on Earnings," Gender & Society 24, no. 6 (2010): 717–45; Renske Keizer, Pearl Dykstra, and Anne-Rigt Poortman, "Life Outcomes of Childless Men and Fathers," European Sociological Review 26, no. 1 (2010): 1–15; Emma Williams-Baron, Julie Anderson, and Ariane Hegewisch, "Mothers Earn Just 71 Percent of What Fathers Earn," Institute for Public Policy Research, May 23, 2017, https://iwpr.org/iwpr-general/mothers-earn-just-71-percent-of-what-fathers-earn/; and Charlotta Magnusson and Magnus Nermo, "Gender, Parenthood and Wage Differences: The Importance of Time-Consuming Job Characteristics," Social Indicators Research 131 (2017): 797–816.

170. Killewald, "Reconsideration of the Fatherhood Premium," 96–116.

171. YoonKyung Chung, Barbara Downs, Danielle H. Sandler, Robert Sienkiewicz, "The Parental Gender Earnings Gap in the United States," US Census Bureau, November 2017, https://www2.census.gov/ces/wp/2017/CES-WP-17-68.pdf; and Gonalons-Pons, Schwartz, and Musick, "Changes in Couples' Earnings following Parenthood," 1093–117.

172. US Bureau of Labor Statistics, "Median earnings for women in 2021 were 83.1 percent of the median for men," Jan. 24, 2022, https://www.bls.gov/opub/ted/2022/median-earnings-for-women-in-2021-were-83-1-percent-of-the-median-for-men.htm.

173. Ben Rogers, "Not in the Same Boat: Career Progression in the Pandemic," Qualtrics, August 26, 2020, https://www.qualtrics.com/blog/inequitable-effects-of-pandemic-on-careers/.

174. Felipe A. Dias, Joseph Chance, and Arianna Buchanan, "The Motherhood Penalty and the Fatherhood Premium in Employment During Covid-19: Evidence from the United States," Research in Social

Stratification and Mobility 69 (2020), https://doi
.org/10.1016/j.rssm.2020.100542.

175. Claire Pendergrast, "Women Report Worse
Employment Impacts from Family Caregiving"
(Research Brief #57, Lerner Center for Public Health
Promotion, Syracuse University), November 2, 2021,
https://surface.syr.edu/cgi/viewcontent.cgi?article
=1157&context=lerner.

176. Ann Bergman and Gunnar Gillberg, "The Cabin
Crew Blues: Middle-Aged Cabin Attendants and
Their Working Conditions," *Nordic Journal of Work-
ing Life Studies* 5, no. 4 (December 2015): 23–39.

177. Barry, *Femininity in Flight.*

178. Frédéric Dobruszkes, "An Analysis of European
Low-Cost Airlines and Their Networks," *Journal of
Transport Geography* 14, no. 4 (2006): 249–64; and
Bergman and Gillberg, "Cabin Crew Blues," 23–39.

179. Cited in Barry, *Femininity in Flight.*

180. "Union Members—2021," US Bureau of Labor
Statistics, January 20, 2022, https://www.bls.gov
/news.release/pdf/union2.pdf.

181. Kristen Harknett, Daniel Schneider, and Sigrid
Luhr, "Who Cares if Parents Have Unpredictable
Work Schedules? Just-in-Time Work Schedules and
Child Care Arrangements," *Social Problems* 69,
no. 1 (2022): 164–83.

182. Lonnie Golden, *Still Falling Short on Hours and
Pay: Part-Time Work Becoming New Normal*, Economic Policy Institute, December 5, 2016, https://
www.epi.org/publication/still-falling-short-on-hours
-and-pay-part-time-work-becoming-new-normal/;
and "Characteristics of Minimum Wage Workers,
2016" (Report 1067), *BLS Reports*, US Bureau of
Labor Statistics, April 2017, https://www.bls.gov
/opub/reports/minimum-wage/2016/home.htm.

183. Keith A. Bailey and James R. Spletzer, "Using
Administrative Data, Census Bureau Can Now Track
the Rise in Multiple Jobholders," US Census Bureau,
February 3, 2021, https://www.census.gov/library
/stories/2021/02/new-way-to-measure-how-many
-americans-work-more-than-one-job.html.

184. Risa Gelles-Watnick and Monica Anderson,
"Racial and Ethnic Differences Stand Out in the
U.S. Gig Workforce," Pew Research Center, December 15, 2021, https://www.pewresearch.org/fact-tank
/2021/12/15/racial-andethnic-differences-stand-out
-in-the-u-s-gif-workforce/; "How Many Gig Workers Are There?" Gig Economy Data Hub, accessed
February 28, 2022, https://www.gigeconomydata.
org/basics/how-many-gig-workers-are-there; and
Gerald Friedman, "Workers without Employers:

Shadow Corporations and the Rise of the Gig Economy," *Review of Keynesian Economics* 2, no. 2 (2014):
171–88.

185. "What Is the Future of Gig Work?" Gig Economy
Data Hub, accessed February 28, 2022, https://www
.gigeconomydata.org/basics/what-future-gig-work.

186. Thomas Piketty, *Capital in the Twenty-First Century* (Cambridge, MA: Harvard University Press,
2014); and Emmanuel Saez and Gabriel Zucman,
"Wealth Inequality in the United States Since 1913:
Evidence from Capitalized Income Tax Data," *Quarterly Journal of Economics* 131, no. 2 (May 2016):
519–78.

187. Andrew Van Dam, "Fewer Americans Are Earning Less than $15 an Hour, but Black and Hispanic
Women Make Up a Bigger Share of Them," *Washington Post*, March 3, 2021, https://www.washing
tonpost.com/business/2021/03/03/15-minimum
-wage-black-hispanic-women/.

188. Monique Morrissey, "The State of American
Retirement: How 401(k)s Have Failed Most American Workers," Economic Policy Institute, March 3,
2016, www.epi.org/publication/retirement-in-america/.

189. National Law Center on Homelessness & Pov-
erty, U.S. Human Rights Network, and UPR Housing
Working Group, *Housing and Homelessness in the
United States of America*, October 3, 2019, https://
homelesslaw.org/wp-content/uploads/2019/10
/Housing-Homelessness-US-UPR-2019.pdf; Sarah
Damaske, "Single Mother Families and Employ-
ment, Race, and Poverty in Changing Economic
Times," *Social Science Research* 62 (2017): 120–33.

190. Francine Blau and Lawrence Kahn, "The Gender Pay Gap: Have Women Gone as Far as They
Can?" *Academy of Management Perspectives* 21
(2007): 7–23.

191. US Bureau of Labor Statistics, Labor Force Statistics from the Current Population Survey, Median
weekly earnings of full-time wage and salary workers by selected characteristics, Jan. 20, 2022, https://
www.bls.gov/cps/cpsaat37.htm.

Chapter 12: Politics

1. Fannie Lou Hamer, speech, Founding of the
National Women's Political Caucus, Washington,
DC, July 10, 1971.

2. *First Convention Ever Called to Discuss the Civil
and Political Rights of Women* (pamphlet), Seneca
Falls, NY, July 19, 20, 1848, https://www.loc.gov
/item/rbcmiller001107/.

3. Corey Wrenn, "Woman-as-Cat in Anti-Suffrage Propaganda," *Sociological Images*, December 4, 2013, https://thesocietypages.org/socimages/2013/12/04/the-feminization-of-the-cat-in-anti-suffrage-propaganda/.

4. Quoted in Hilda Kean, *Animal Rights: Political and Social Change in Britain since 1800* (London: Reaktion Books, 1998), 146.

5. June Purvis, "The Prison Experiences of the Suffragettes in Edwardian Britain," *Women's History Review* 4, no. 1 (1995): 103–33.

6. Janice Tyrwhitt, "Why the Lady Horsewhipped Winston Churchill," *Montreal Gazette*, October 16, 1965, 6–9, https://www.newspapers.com/clip/46042214/why-the-lady-horsewhipped-winston/ https://news.google.com/newspapers?id=C5QtAAAAIBAJ&sjid=Yp8FAAAAIBAJ&pg=6699,4358424&dq=suffragist+mrs+pankhurst+bodyguards&hl=en%20%20; and John S. Nash, "The Martial Chronicles: Fighting Like a Girl 2," *Bloody Elbow* (blog), updated October 11, 2015, https://www.bloodyelbow.com/2013/2/23/4007176/the-martial-chronicles-fighting-like-a-girl-2-the-ju-jutsuffragists.

7. Sojourner Truth, Address to the First Annual Meeting of the American Equal Rights Association, New York City, May 9, 1867.

8. Paula Giddings, *When and Where I Enter: The Impact of Black Women on Race and Sex in America* (New York: Bantam, 1984); Glenda Elizabeth Gilmore, *Gender and Jim Crow: Women and the Politics of White Supremacy in North Carolina, 1896–1920*, 2nd ed., (Chapel Hill: University of North Carolina Press, 2019).

9. Myra Marx Ferree, "Resonance and Radicalism: Feminist Framing in the Abortion Debates of the United States and Germany," *American Journal of Sociology* 109, no. 2 (2003): 304–44.

10. Asma Alsharif, "Update 2-Saudi King Gives Women Right to Vote," *Reuters*, September 25, 2011, https://www.reuters.com/article/saudi-king-women/update-2-saudi-king-gives-women-right-to-vote-idUSL5E7KP0IB20110925.

11. Shelley J. Correll, "SWS 2016 Feminist Lecture: Reducing Gender Biases in Modern Workplaces: A Small Wins Approach to Organizational Change," *Gender & Society* 31, no. 6 (2017): 725–50.

12. Lisa D. Brush, *Gender and Governance* (Walnut Creek, CA: AltaMira Press, 2003); and Louise Chappell, "The State and Governance," in *The Oxford Handbook of Gender and Politics*, ed. Georgina Waylen, Karen Celis, Johanna Kantola, and S. Laurel Weldon (New York: Oxford University Press, 2013), 603–25.

13. Donald G. Mathews and Jane Sherron De Hart, *Sex, Gender, and the Politics of ERA: A State and the Nation* (New York: Oxford University Press on Demand, 1992); and Andrew R. Lewis, *The Rights Turn in Conservative Christian Politics: How Abortion Transformed the Culture Wars* (New York: Cambridge University Press, 2017).

14. "Statistical Handbook of Japan 2021," Statistics Japan, accessed March 21, 2022, https://www.stat.go.jp/english/data/handbook/index.html.

15. Simon Denyer and Annie Gowen, "Too Many Men," *Washington Post*, April 18, 2018, https://www.washingtonpost.com/graphics/2018/world/too-many-men/?utm_term=.7a0a0c72fbf9.

16. Ming-Hsuan Lee, "The One-Child Policy and Gender Equality in Education in China: Evidence from Household Data," *Journal of Family and Economic Issues* 33 (2012): 41–52.

17. Miriam Barcus, "The Gendered Impact of Employer-Provided Work-Family Policies" (PhD diss., University of Wisconsin, 2021).

18. "Access to Paid and Unpaid Family Leave in 2018," US Bureau of Labor Statistics, February 27, 2019, https://www.bls.gov/opub/ted/2019/access-to-paid-and-unpaid-family-leave-in-2018.htm.

19. Marre Karu and Diane-Gabrielle Tremblay, "Fathers on Parental Leave: An Analysis of Rights and Take-Up in 29 Countries," *Community, Work & Family* 21, no. 3 (2018): 344–62.

20. Marcus Tamm, "Fathers' Parental Leave-Taking, Childcare Involvement and Mothers' Labor Market Participation," *Labour Economics* 59 (2019): 184–97. Elin Kvande and Berit Brandth, "Designing Parental Leave for Fathers—Promoting Gender Equality in Working Life," *International Journal of Sociology and Social Policy* 40, no. 5/6 (2020): 465–77.

21. Nathaniel Popper, "Paternity Leave Has Long-Lasting Benefits. So Why Don't More American Men Take It?" *New York Times*, April 17, 2020, https://www.nytimes.com/2020/04/17/parenting/paternity-leave.html; and Richard Petts, Chris Knoester, and Jane Waldfogel, "Fathers' Paternity Leave-Taking and Children's Perceptions of Father-Child Relationships in the United States," *Sex Roles* 82 (2020): 173–88.

22. Joe Soss, Richard C. Fording, and Sanford Schram, *Disciplining the Poor: Neoliberal Paternalism and the Persistent Power of Race* (Chicago: University of Chicago Press, 2011).

23. Samantha Artiga, Olivia Pham, Kendal Orgera, and Usha Ranji, "Racial Disparities in Maternal and Infant Health: An Overview," Kaiser Family Foundation, November 10, 2020, https://www.kff.org/racial-equity-and-health-policy/issue-brief/racial-disparities-maternal-infant-health-overview/.

24. Iris Lopez, "Agency and Constraint: Sterilization and Reproductive Freedom among Puerto-Rican Women in New York City," in *Situated Lives: Gender and Culture in Everyday Life*, ed. Louise Lamphere, Helena Ragoné, and Patricia Zavella (New York: Routledge, 1997), 157–71. Also, Patricia Zavella, *The Reproductive Justice Movement* (New York: New York University Press, 2020).

25. Clare Foran, "How to Design a City for Women," CityLab, *Atlantic*, September 16, 2013.

26. Judith Lorber, "Gender Equality: Utopian and Realistic" (plenary address, American Sociological Association Annual Meetings, Denver, CO, August 16, 2012); Barbara Risman, Judith Lorber, and Jessica Sherwood, "Toward a World beyond Gender: A Utopian Vision" (revised version of remarks presented at American Sociological Association Annual Meetings, Denver, CO, August 16, 2012); and Michael Kimmel, "Comments on Risman, Lorber, and Sherwood" (American Sociological Association Annual Meetings, Denver, CO, August 16, 2012).

27. Kathleen Dolan, *Voting for Women: How the Public Evaluates Women Candidates* (Boulder, CO: Westview Press, 2004); Pamela Paxton, Sheri Kunovich, and Melanie Hughes, "Gender and Politics," *Annual Review of Sociology* 33 (2007): 263–84; Richard L. Fox, "Congressional Elections: Women's Candidacies and the Road to Gender Parity," in *Gender and Elections: Shaping the Future of American Politics*, 5th ed., ed. Susan J. Carroll and Richard L. Fox (New York: Cambridge University Press, 2018): 198–219; Jennifer L. Lawless and Kathryn Pearson, "The Primary Reason for Women's Under-Representation: Re-Evaluating the Conventional Wisdom," *Journal of Politics* 70, no. 1 (2008): 67–82; Sarah Anzia and Christopher Berry, "The Jackie (and Jill) Robinson Effect: Why Do Congresswomen Out-perform Congressmen?" *American Journal of Political Science* 55, no. 3 (2011): 478–93; and Richard Selzer, Jody Newman, and Melissa Leighton, *Sex as a Political Variable: Women as Candidates and Voters in U.S. Elections* (Boulder, CO: Lynne Rienner, 1997); Morgan Matthews, "Gender Polarization: The Institutional and Discursive Roots of Gendered Partisanship in U.S. State Legislatures, 1975–2020," (PhD diss., University of Wisconsin–Madison, 2022).

28. Robert Darcy, Janet Clark, and Susan Welch, *Women, Elections, and Representation* (Lincoln: University of Nebraska Press, 1994); and Eric Smith and Richard Fox, "The Electoral Fortunes of Women Candidates for Congress," *Political Research Quarterly* 54, no. 1 (2001): 205–21.

29. "Monthly Ranking of Women in National Parliaments," *IPU Parline*, accessed March 3, 2022, https://data.ipu.org/women-ranking?month=2&year=2022.

30. Melanie M. Hughes, Pamela Paxton, Mona Lena Krook, "Gender Quotas for Legislatures and Corporate Boards," *Annual Review of Sociology* 43, no. 1 (2017): 331–52; International Institute for Democracy and Electoral Assistance, "Gender Quotas Database," accessed March 17, 2022, https://www.idea.int/data-tools/data/gender-quotas/legislative-overview.

31. Aili Mari Tripp, *Women and Power in Post-Conflict Africa* (New York: Cambridge University Press, 2015).

32. Sarah Childs, "Political Representation," in *The Oxford Handbook of Gender and Politics*, ed. Georgina Waylen, Karen Celis, Johanna Kantola, and S. Laurel Weldon (New York: Oxford University Press, 2013), 489–513; Aili Tripp, "Political Systems and Gender," in *The Oxford Handbook of Gender and Politics*, ed. Georgina Waylen, Karen Celis, Johanna Kantola, and S. Laurel Weldon (New York: Oxford University Press, 2013), 514–35; Aili Tripp and Alice Kang, "The Global Impact of Quotas: On the Fast Track to Increased Female Legislative Representation," *Comparative Political Studies* 41, no. 3 (2008): 338–61; Mona Tajali, "Gender Quota Adoption in Postconflict Contexts: An Analysis of Actors and Factors Involved," *Journal of Women, Politics & Policy* 34, no. 3 (2013): 261–85; Mona Krook, "Women's Representation in Parliament: A Qualitative Comparative Analysis," *Political Studies* 58, no. 5 (2010): 886–908; and Tripp, *Women and Power in Postconflict Africa*.

33. "Women in Elective Office 2022," Center for American Women and Politics, accessed March 3, 2022, https://cawp.rutgers.edu/facts/current-numbers/women-elective-office-2022.

34. "Monthly Ranking of Women in National Parliaments."

35. "Women in the U.S. Congress 2022," Center for American Women and Politics, accessed March 3,

2022, https://cawp.rutgers.edu/facts/levels-office/congress/women-us-congress-2022.

36. Sheryl Gay Stolberg, "'It's about Time': A Baby Comes to the Senate Floor," *New York Times*, April 19, 2018, https://www.nytimes.com/2018/04/19/us/politics/baby-duckworth-senate-floor.html; and Laurie Kellman, "Senate Allows Babies in Chamber despite Concerns from Older, Male Senators," *Chicago Tribune*, April 18, 2018, https://www.chicagotribune.com/news/nationworld/ct-senate-babies-chamber-duckworth-20180418-story.html.

37. Karen Celis and Sarah Childs, *Feminist Democratic Representation* (New York: Oxford University Press, 2020); Caroline Tolbert and Gertrude Steuernagel, "Women Lawmakers, State Mandates and Women's Health," *Women & Politics* 22, no. 1 (2001): 1–39; and Pippa Norris and Jovi Lovenduski, "Westminster Women: The Politics of Presence," *Political Studies* 51, no. 1 (2003): 84–102.

38. Norris and Lovenduski, "Westminster Women," 84–102; Kathleen Bratton and Kerry Haynie, "Agenda Setting and Legislative Success in State Legislatures: The Effects of Gender and Race," *Journal of Politics* 61, no. 3 (1999): 658–79; Edith Barrett, "The Policy Priorities of African American Women in State Legislatures," *Legislative Studies Quarterly* 20, no. 2 (1995): 223–47; Sarah Gershon, "Communicating Female and Minority Interests Online: A Study of Web Site Issue Discussion among Female, Latino, and African American Members of Congress," *International Journal of Press/Politics* 13, no. 2 (2008): 120–40; and Karen Kaufmann and John Petrocik, "The Changing Politics of American Men: Understanding the Sources of the Gender Gap," *American Journal of Political Science* 43, no. 3 (1999): 864–87.

39. Amanda Clayton, "How Do Electoral Gender Quotas Affect Policy?" *Annual Review of Political Science* 24 (2021): 235–52; Dorothy McBride and Amy Mazur, "Women's Policy Agencies and State Feminism," in *The Oxford Handbook of Gender and Politics*, ed. Georgina Wayne, Karen Celis, Johanna Kantola, and S. Laurel Weldon (New York: Oxford University Press, 2013), 654–78; Thomas Little, Dana Dunn, and Rebecca Deen, "A View from the Top: Gender Differences in Legislative Priorities among State Legislative Leaders," *Women & Politics* 22, no. 4 (2001): 29–50; Leslie Schwindt-Bayer, "Still Supermadres? Gender and the Policy Priorities of Latin American Legislators," *American Journal of Political Science* 50, no. 3 (2006): 570–85; Bratton and Haynie, "Agenda Setting and Legislative Success in State Legislatures," 658–79; Kathleen Bratton, "Critical Mass Theory Revisited: The Behavior and Success of Token Women in State Legislatures," *Politics & Gender* 1, no. 1 (2005): 97–125; Christina Wolbrecht, *The Politics of Women's Rights: Parties, Positions and Change* (Princeton, NJ: Princeton University Press, 2000); and Laurel Weldon, *When Protest Makes Policy: How Social Movements Represent Disadvantaged Groups* (Ann Arbor: University of Michigan Press, 2014).

40. Beth Reingold, Kerry Haynie, and Kirsten Widner, "Women of Color Won Congressional Seats in Record Numbers. How Will They Legislate?" *Washington Post*, November 24, 2020, https://www.washingtonpost.com/politics/2020/11/24/women-color-won-congressional-seats-record-numbers-how-will-they-legislate/.

41. Debra Dodson, *The Impact of Women in Congress* (New York: Oxford University Press, 2006); Norris and Lovenduski, "Westminster Women," 84–102; "Finding Gender in Election 2016: Lessons from Presidential Gender Watch," Presidential Gender Watch 2016 (2017), http://presidentialgenderwatch.org/wp-content/uploads/2017/05/Finding-Gender-in-Election-2016_Highlights.pdf; and Per G. Fredriksson and Le Wang, "Sex and Environmental Policy in the U.S. House of Representatives," *Economics Letters* 113 (2011): 228–30.

42. Kathleen Ahrens, ed., *Politics, Gender and Conceptual Metaphors* (New York: Palgrave, 2009); Maureen Molloy, "Imagining (the) Difference: Gender, Ethnicity and Metaphors of Nation," *Feminist Review* 51 (Autumn 1995): 94–112; Julie Mostov and Rada Ivekovic, eds., *From Gender to Nation* (New Delhi: Zubaan Books, 2006); Joane Nagel, *Race, Ethnicity, and Sexuality* (New York: Oxford University Press, 2003); and George Lakoff, *The ALL NEW Don't Think of an Elephant!: Know Your Values and Frame the Debate* (White River Junction, VT: Chelsea Green Publishing, 2014).

43. Jackson Katz, *Leading Men: Presidential Campaigns and the Politics of Manhood* (Northampton, MA: Interlink Publishing, 2013); Meredith Conroy, *Masculinity, Media, and the American Presidency* (New York: Palgrave Macmillan, 2015); Kristin L. Hoganson, *Fighting for American Manhood: How Gender Politics Provoked the Spanish-American and Philippine-American Wars* (New Haven, CT: Yale University Press, 1998); and Wendy M. Christensen and Myra Marx Ferree, "Cowboy of the World? Gender Discourse and the Iraq War Debate," *Qualitative Sociology* 31, no. 3 (2008): 287–306.

44. Jackson Katz, *Man Enough?: Donald Trump, Hillary Clinton, and the Politics of Presidential Masculinity* (Northampton, MA: Interlink, 2016).

45. C. J. Pascoe, "Homophobia Linked to Definition of Masculinity," *The Register-Guard*, May 23, 2017, https://www.registerguard.com/story/opinion/2017/05/24/homophobia-linked-to-definition-masculinity/11708172007/; C. J. Pascoe, "Who Is a Real Man? The Gender of Trumpism," *Masculinities and Social Change* 6, no. 2 (2017): 119–41.

46. Luke Mogelson, "The Recent History of Bombing the Shit Out of 'Em," *The New Yorker*, April 20, 2017, https://www.newyorker.com/news/news-desk/the-recent-history-of-bombing-the-shit-out-of-em.

47. Pascoe, "Who Is a Real Man?," 119–41; Myra Marx Ferree, "The Crisis of Masculinity for Gendered Democracies: Before, During, and After Trump," *Sociological Forum* 35, no. S1 (2020): 898–917.

48. Hillary Clinton, Democratic National Convention acceptance speech, July 28, 2016, transcript and video, "Hillary Clinton's DNC Speech: Full Text," https://www.politico.com/story/2016/07/full-text-hillary-clintons-dnc-speech-226410.

49. James W. Messerschmidt, "Donald Trump, Dominating Masculine Necropolitics, and COVID-19," *Men and Masculinities* 24, no. 1 (2021): 189–94.

50. Caitlin Oprysko and Susannah Luthi, "Trump Labels Himself 'a Wartime President' Combating Coronavirus," Politico, updated March 18, 2020, https://www.politico.com/news/2020/03/18/trump-administration-self-swab-coronavirus-tests-135590.

51. Danielle Kurtzleben, "Trump Has Weaponized Masculinity as President. Here's Why It Matters," NPR, October 28, 2020, https://www.npr.org/2020/10/28/928336749/trump-has-weaponized-masculinity-as-president-heres-why-it-matters; Myra Marx Ferree, "After Trump? Radical Selfishness versus the Ethic of Care," *Sociological Forum* 36, no. 2 (2021): 546–47.

52. Quoted in Matt Viser, "Trump, Biden, and Masculinity in the Age of Coronavirus," *Washington Post*, October 15, 2020, https://www.washingtonpost.com/politics/masculinity-trump-biden/2020/10/15/e0646bf0-ff6d-11ea-9ceb-061d646d9c67_story.html.

53. Quoted in Rondell Pettus, "Beck: Trump Deserves Medal for Facing Down Coronavirus," *Business Standard News*, October 6, 2020, https://thebiznews.org/2020/10/06/beck-trump-deserves-medal-for-facing-down-coronavirus/.

54. Quoted in Asawin Suebsaeng, Sam Stein, Lachlan Markay, "Trump Actually Believes He Can Sell Himself to America as a COVID-Conquering Hero," Daily Beast, October 5, 2020, https://www.thedailybeast.com/trump-actually-believes-he-can-sell-himself-to-america-as-a-covid-conquering-hero.

55. Messerschmidt, "Donald Trump, Dominating Masculine Necropolitics, and COVID-19," 192.

56. Erna Solberg, "Norwegian Prime Minister Erna Solberg's Introduction at Press Conference for Children," March 23, 2020, https://www.regjeringen.no/en/aktuelt/norwegian-prime-minister-erna-solbergs-introductionat-press-conference-for-children/id2693742.

57. Jacinda Ardern, Facebook Live, March 25, 2020, https://www.facebook.com/jacindaardern/videos/evening-everyone-thought-id-jump-online-and-answer-a-few-questions-as-we-all-pre/147109069954329/.

58. Carol Johnson and Blair Williams, "Gender and Political Leadership in a Time of COVID," *Politics & Gender* 16, no. 4 (2020): 943–50.

59. Ibid.

60. Jessica Bennett, "Trump, Biden and the Tough Guy, Nice Guy Politics of 2020," *New York Times*, November 2, 2020, https://www.nytimes.com/2020/11/01/us/politics/trump-biden-masculinity-2020.html.

61. David Collinson and Jeff Hearn, "Trump v Biden: A Duel of Contrasting Masculinities," Conversation, October 23, 2020, https://theconversation.com/trump-v-biden-a-duel-of-contrasting-masculinities-148300.

62. Viser, "Trump, Biden, and Masculinity in the Age of Coronavirus."

63. Veronica Stracqualursi, "Biden Says He Would 'Beat the Hell' out of Trump if in High School," CNN, March 21, 2018, https://www.cnn.com/2018/03/21/politics/joe-biden-donald-trump/index.html.

64. Johnson and Williams, "Gender and Political Leadership in a Time of COVID," 943–50.

65. Kjersten Nelson, "You Seem Like a Great Candidate, but . . . : Race and Gender Attitudes and the 2020 Democratic Primary," *Journal of Race, Ethnicity, and Politics* 6, no. 3 (2021): 642–66; Ella Nilsen and Li Zhou, "Why Women Are Feeling So Defeated after Elizabeth Warren's Loss," *Vox*, March 6, 2020, https://www.vox.com/2020/3/6/21166338/elizabeth-warren-loss-2020-primary-sexism; and Ste-

phen M. Utych, "Sexism Predicts Favorability of Women in the 2020 Democratic Primary . . . and Men?" *Electoral Politics* 71 (2021): 102184, https://doi.org/10.1016/j.electstud.2020.102184.

66. Bennett, "Trump, Biden and the Tough Guy, Nice Guy Politics of 2020."

67. Gary N. Powell, D. Anthony Butterfield, Xueting Jiang, "Gender, Diversity and the 2020 US Presidential Election: Towards an Androgynous Presidential Profile?" *Gender in Management*, February 17, 2020, https://doi.org/10.1108/GM-06-2021-0182.

68. Alec Tyson and Shiva Maniam, "Behind Trump's Victory: Divisions by Race, Gender, Education," Pew Research Center, November 9, 2016, www.pew research.org/fact-tank/2016/11/09/behind-trumps -victory-divisions-by-race-gender-education/; Richa Chaturvedi, "A Closer Look at the Gender Gap in Presidential Voting," Pew Research Center, July 28, 2016, https://www.pewresearch.org/fact -tank/2016/07/28/a-closer-look-at-the-gender-gap-in -presidential-voting/; and Kei Kawashima-Ginsberg, "How Gender Mattered to Millennials in the 2016 Election and Beyond" (briefing paper prepared for the Council on Contemporary Families Online Symposium on Gender and Millennials, March 31, 2017), Society Pages, https://thesocietypages.org/ccf/2017 /05/23/how-gender-mattered-to-millennials-in-the -2016-election-and-beyond/.

69. Ruth Igielnik, Scott Keeter, and Hannah Hartig, "Behind Biden's 2020 Victory," Pew Research Center, June 30, 2021, https://www.pewresearch.org /politics/2021/06/30/behind-bidens-2020-victory/.

70. Daniel Q. Gillion, Jonathan M. Ladd, and Marc Meredith, "Party Polarization, Ideological Sorting and the Emergence of the US Partisan Gender Gap," *British Journal of Political Science* 50, no. 4 (2020): 1217–43.

71. Morgan Matthews, "Gender Polarization: The Institutional and Discursive Roots of Gendered Partisanship in U.S. State Legislatures, 1975–2020," (PhD diss., University of Wisconsin–Madison, 2022).

72. Katz, *Man Enough?*

73. Jean M. Twenge, *Generation Me: Why Today's Young Americans Are More Confident, Assertive, Entitled—and More Miserable than Ever Before* (New York: Simon & Schuster, 2006); and Jo Reger, *Everywhere and Nowhere: Contemporary Feminism in the United States* (New York: Oxford University Press, 2012).

74. Nicholas J. G. Winter, "Masculine Republicans and Feminine Democrats: Gender and Americans' Explicit and Implicit Images of the Political Parties," *Political Behavior* 32, no. 4 (2010): 587–618.

75. Quoted in Claire Cain Miller and Alisha Haridasani Gupta, "What Makes a Man Manly? Trump and Biden Offer Competing Answers," *New York Times*, October 30, 2020, https://www.nytimes.com /2020/10/30/upshot/trump-biden-masculinity-father hood.html; Nicholas J. G. Winter, "Masculine Republicans and Feminine Democrats: Gender and Americans' Explicit and Implicit Images of the Political Parties," *Political Behavior* 32, no. 4 (2010): 587–618.

76. "History of Women in the US Congress," Center for American Women in Politics, accessed March 4, 2022, https://cawp.rutgers.edu/facts/levels-office /congress/history-women-us-congress.

77. Tracy Osborn, Rebecca J. Kreitzer, Emily U. Schilling, and Jennifer Hayes Clark, "Ideology and Polarization among Women State Legislators," *Legislative Studies Quarterly* 44, no. 4 (2019): 647–80; Sarah Poggione, "Exploring Gender Differences in State Legislators' Policy Preferences," *Political Research Quarterly* 57 (2004): 305–14; Dennis M. Simon and Barbara Palmer, "The Roll Call Behavior of Men and Women in the US House of Representatives, 1937–2008," *Politics & Gender* 6, no. 2 (2010): 225–46; and Michele Swers, "Are Congresswomen More Likely to Vote for Women's Issue Bills than Their Male Colleagues?" *Legislative Studies Quarterly* 23 (1998): 435–48.

78. Danielle Kurtzleben, "CHARTS: White Voters Without College Degrees Are Feeling the Democratic Party," NPR, September 13, 2016, https://www .npr.org/2016/09/13/493763493/charts-see-how -quickly-white-non-college-voters-have-fled-the -democratic-party

79. Myra Marx Ferree, "Under Different Umbrellas: Intersectionality and Alliances in U.S. Feminist Politics," *European Journal of Politics and Gender* 4, no. 2 (2021): 199–216.

80. "Voters' Attitudes about Race and Gender Are Even More Divided than in 2016," Pew Research Center, September 10, 2020, https://www.pew research.org/politics/2020/09/10/voters-attitudes -about-race-and-gender-are-even-more-divided -than-in-2016.

81. Ibid.

82. Matthew J. Streb, Barbara Burrell, Brian Frederick, and Michael A. Genovese, "Social Desirability

Effects and Support for a Female American President," *Public Opinion Quarterly* 72, no. 1 (2008): 76–89; and Clare Malone, "From 1937 to Hillary Clinton, How Americans Have Felt about a Woman President," *FiveThirtyEight*, June 9, 2016. See also Myra Marx Ferree, "A Woman for President? Changing Responses 1958–1972," *Public Opinion Quarterly* 38, no. 3 (1974): 390–99; "Finding Gender in Election 2016"; and "Madame President: Changing Attitudes about a Woman President," *Roper Center for Public Opinion Research, Cornell University*, https://roper center.cornell.edu/madame-president-changing -attitudes-about-woman-president-0.

83. Deja Thomas, "In 2018, Two-Thirds of Democratic Women Hoped to See a Woman President in Their Lifetime," Pew Research Center, July 26, 2019, https://www.pewresearch.org/fact-tank/2019 /07/26/in-2018-two-thirds-of-democratic-women -hoped-to-see-a-woman-president-in-their-lifetime/.

84. Igielnik, Keeter, and Hartig, "Behind Biden's 2020 Victory."

85. Theresa K. Vescioa and Nathaniel E. C. Schermerhorn, "Hegemonic Masculinity Predicts 2016 and 2020 Voting and Candidate Evaluations," *Proceedings of the National Academy of Sciences*, 118, no. 2 (2021): e2020589118, https://doi.org/10.1073 /pnas.2020589118.

86. Karen Blair, "Did Secretary Clinton Lose to a 'Basket of Deplorables'? An Examination of Islamophobia, Homophobia, Sexism and Conservative Ideology in the 2016 US Presidential Election," *Psychology & Sexuality* 8, no. 4 (2017): 334–55; Jarrod Bock, Jennifer Byrd-Craven, and Melissa Burkley, "The Role of Sexism in Voting in the 2016 Presidential Election," *Personality and Individual Differences* 119 (2017): 189–93; Ana Bracic, Mackenzie Israel-Trummel and Allyson F. Shortle, "Is Sexism for White People? Gender Stereotypes, Race, and the 2016 Presidential Election," *Political Behavior* 41 (2019): 281–307; Peter Glick, "Gender, Sexism, and the Election: Did Sexism Help Trump More than It Hurt Clinton?" *Politics, Groups, and Identities*, 7, no. 3 (2019): 713–23; Margo J. Monteith, Laura K. Hildebrand, "Sexism, Perceived Discrimination, and System Justification in the 2016 US Presidential Election Context," *Group Processes & Intergroup Relations* 23, no. 2 (2020): 163–78; Kate A. Ratliff, Liz Redford, John Conway, and Colin Tucker Smith, "Engendering Support: Hostile Sexism Predicts Voting for Donald Trump over Hillary Clinton in the 2016 U.S. Presidential Election," *Group Processes & Intergroup Relations* 22, no. 4 (2019):

578–93; Valerie Rothwell, Gordon Hodson, and Elvira Prusaczyk, "Why Pillory Hillary? Testing the Endemic Sexism Hypothesis regarding the 2016 U.S. Election," *Perspectives on Individual Difference* 138 (2019): 106–8; Mark Setzler and Alixandra B. Yanus, "Why Did Women Vote for Donald Trump?" *PS: Political Science and Politics* 51, no. 3 (2018): 523–27; Lawrence D. Bobo, "Racism in Trump's America: Reflections on Culture, Sociology, and the 2016 US Presidential Election," *British Journal of Sociology* 68, suppl. 1 (2017): S85–S104; Randall D. Swain, "Negative Black Stereotypes, Support for Excessive Use of Force by Police, and Voter Preference for Donald Trump During the 2016 Presidential Primary Election Cycle," *Journal of African American Studies* 22, no. 1 (2018): 109–24.

87. Carrie Rentschler, "Doing Feminism in the Network: Networked Laughter and the 'Binders Full of Women' Meme," *Feminist Theory* 16, no. 3 (2015): 329–59.

88. Sikata Banerjee, "Gender and Nationalism: The Masculinization of Hinduism and Female Political Participation in India," *Women's Studies International Forum* 26 no. 2 (2003): 167–79; Nira Yuval-Davis, *Gender & Nation* (Thousand Oaks, CA: Sage, 1997); and Mieke Verloo, ed., *Varieties of Opposition to Gender Equality in Europe* (New York: Routledge, 2018).

89. Lena Surzhko Harned and Luis Jimenez, "President Trump's Use of the Authoritarian Playbook Will Have Lasting Consequences," Conversation, December 17, 2020, https://theconversation.com /president-trumps-use-of-the-authoritarian-play book-will-have-lasting-consequences-150895.

90. "A New Low for Global Democracy," *Economist*, February 9, 2022, https://www.economist.com /graphic-detail/2022/02/09/a-new-low-for-global -democracy.

91. Yuval-Davis, *Gender & Nation*; Verloo, *Varieties of Opposition to Gender Equality in Europe*; and Pankaj Mishra, "The Crisis in Modern Masculinity," *Guardian*, March 17, 2018, https://www.theguard ian.com/books/2018/mar/17/the-crisis-in-modern -masculinity.

92. "A New Low for Global Democracy."

93. Scott Sumner, "The Authoritarian Nationalist Playbook," Econlib, August 8, 2021, https://www .econlib.org/the-authoritarian-nationalist-play book/.

94. Roman Kuhar and David Paternotte, eds., *Anti-Gender Campaigns in Europe* (New York: Rowman

& Littlefield, 2017); and *Religion & Gender* 6, no. 2 (2016).

95. Erica Chenoweth and Zoe Marks, "Revenge of the Patriarchs," *Foreign Affairs*, March/April 2022, https://www.foreignaffairs.com/articles/china/2022 -02-08/women-rights-revenge-patriarchs.

96. Aili Mari Tripp, *Women and Power in Post-Conflict Africa*; Erica Chenoweth, "Women's Participation and the Fate of Nonviolent Campaigns," International Center on Nonviolent Conflict, October 2019, https://www.nonviolent-conflict.org/resource/wom ens-participation-and-the-fate-of-nonviolent-cam paigns-english_page/; and Erica Chenoweth and Maria J. Stephan, *Why Civil Resistance Works: The Strategic Logic of Nonviolent Conflict* (New York: Columbia University Press, 2011).

97. "Russian Feminists Stage Anti-War Protests in 100 Cities," March 9, 2022, the *Moscow Times*, https://www.themoscowtimes.com/2022/03/09 /russian-feminists-stage-anti-war-protests-in-100 -cities-a76832.

98. Feminist Anti-War Resistance, "Russia's Feminists Are in the Streets Protesting Putin's War," *Jacobin*, February 27, 2022, https://jacobinmag .com/2022/02/russian-feminist-antiwar-resis tance-ukraine-putin.

99. Independent Women's Democratic Initiative (NEZHDI) and Linda Edmondson, "Feminist Manifesto: 'Democracy without Women Is No Democracy!'" *Feminist Review* 39 (1991): 127–32.

100. Some feminist activists point out that the necessary three more states have ratified it now, but since other states have rescinded their ratification, it will fall on the Supreme Court to decide if ratification has or hasn't taken effect. See Carrie N. Baker, "The Equal Rights Amendment Is Ratified— Now What?" *Ms.* magazine, February 10, 2022, https://msmagazine.com/2022/02/10/equal -rights-amendment-ratified/.

101. "State Policies on Abortion," Guttmacher Institute, accessed May 11, 2017, www.guttmacher.org /united-states/abortion/state-policies-abortion; and Rachel K. Jones and Jenna Jerman, "Abortion Incidence and Service Availability in the United States, 2014," *Perspectives on Sexual and Reproductive Health* 49, no. 1 (2017): 17–27.

102. Isabella Grullón Paz, "Colorado Baker Fined for Refusing to Make Cake for Transgender Woman," *New York Times*, June 18, 2021, https://www.ny times.com/2021/06/18/us/wedding-cake-colorado -jack-phillips.html; and Nina Totenberg, "Supreme Court Undercuts Access to Birth Control under Obamacare," NPR, July 8, 2020, https://www.npr .org/2020/07/08/884104509/supreme-court-under cuts-access-to-birth-control-under-obamacare.

103. "An Overview of Abortion Laws," Guttmacher Institute, accessed March 4, 2022, https://www .guttmacher.org/state-policy/explore/overview -abortion-laws.

104. Lynn M. Paltrow, "Pregnant Drug Users, Fetal Persons, and the Threat to Roe v. Wade," *Albany Law Review* 62, no. 3 (1999): 999; and "About Us," National Advocates for Pregnant Women, accessed March 4, 2022, https://www.nationaladvocatesfor pregnantwomen.org/about-us/.

105. Elisabeth Clemons, *The People's Lobby* (Chicago: University of Chicago Press, 1997); and Kristen Goss, *The Paradox of Gender Equality: How American Women's Groups Gained and Lost their Public Voice* (Ann Arbor: University of Michigan Press, 2013).

106. Goss, *Paradox of Gender Equality*; and Nancy Cott, *The Grounding of Modern Feminism* (New Haven, CT: Yale University Press, 1989).

107. Benita Roth, *Separate Roads to Feminism: Black, Chicana, and White Feminist Movements in America's Second Wave* (New York: Cambridge University Press, 2004).

108. Jo Freeman, *The Politics of Women's Liberation* (Chicago: University of Chicago Press, 1976); and Myra Marx Ferree and Beth B. Hess, *Controversy and Coalition: The New Feminist Movement across Three Decades of Change*, 3rd ed. (New York: Routledge, 2000).

109. Harry Boyte and Sara Evans, *Free Spaces: The Sources of Democratic Change in America* (Chicago: Chicago University Press, 1986); and Jane J. Mansbridge and Aldon Morris, eds., *Oppositional Consciousness: The Subjective Roots of Social Problems* (Chicago: Chicago University Press, 2001).

110. Roth, *Separate Roads to Feminism*,

111. Marjorie J. Spruill, "Gender Roles, Women's Rights, and the Polarization of American Politics in the Late 20th Century," Oxford Research Encyclopedias: American History, January 25, 2019, https:// doi.org/10.1093/acrefore/9780199329175.013.66.

112. Jane J. Mansbridge, *Why We Lost the ERA* (Chicago: University of Chicago Press, 2015); and Donald G. Mathews and Jane Sherron De Hart, *Sex, Gender, and the Politics of ERA*.

113. "The United Nations Fourth World Conference on Women: Platform for Action," United Nations Entity for Gender Equality and the Empowerment of Women, September 1995, https://www.un.org/womenwatch/daw/beijing/platform/plat1.htm; and Jocelyn Olcutt, *International Women's Year: The Greatest Consciousness-Raising Event in History* (New York: Oxford University Press, 2017).

114. Douglas Frantz and Sam Fulwood III, "Senators' Private Deal Kept '2nd Woman' off TV: Thomas: Democrats Feared Republican Attacks on Angela Wright's Public Testimony. Biden's Handling of the Hearing Is Criticized," *Los Angeles Times*, October 17, 1991, https://www.latimes.com/archives/la-xpm-1991-10-17-mn-911-story.html.

115. Patricia Zavella, *The Reproductive Justice Movement* (New York: New York University Press, 2020); and Reger, *Everywhere and Nowhere*.

116. Banu Gökarıksel and Sara Smith, "Intersectional Feminism beyond U.S. Flag Hijab and Pussy Hats in Trump's America," *Gender, Place & Culture* 24, no. 5 (2017): 628–44; and Myra Marx Ferree, "Under Different Umbrellas: Intersectionality and Alliances in U.S. Feminist Politics," *European Journal of Politics and Gender* 4, no. 2 (2021): 199–216.

117. "Our Vision," Women's March, May 11, 2017, https://www.womensmarch.com/about-us.

118. Conor Friedersdorf, "The Significance of Millions in the Streets," *Atlantic*, January 23, 2017, https://www.theatlantic.com/politics/archive/2017/01/the-significance-of-millions-in-the-streets/514091/.

119. Julia Reinstein, "45 Clever Signs from the 2018 Women's March," *BuzzFeed*, January 20, 2018, https://www.buzzfeednews.com/article/julia reinstein/womens-march-2018-signs.

120. Alanna Vagianos and Damon Dahlen, "89 Badass Feminist Signs from the Women's March on Washington," *HuffPost*, January 21, 2017, https://www.huffingtonpost.com/entry/89-badass-feminist-signs-from-the-womens-march-on-washington_us_5883ea28e4b070d8cad310cd; Sebastian Murdock, "Signs for the 2018 Women's March Prove the Movement Is Here to Stay," *HuffPost*, January 20, 2018, https://www.huffingtonpost.com/entry/signs-2018-womens-march-movement_us_5a6371d9e4b0e56 300701d7c.

121. Greta J., "10+ Nasty Grandmas Who Can't Believe They Still Have to March for Women's Rights," *Bored Panda*, https://www.boredpanda.com/grandmas-still-fighting-women-rights-marching-donald-trump/.

122. "Signposts from the Women's March—Angry, Ironic and Sometimes Really Funny," *Los Angeles Times*, January 20, 2018, https://www.latimes.com/nation/la-na-womens-march-signs-20180120-story.html.

123. Calculated from data at the Center for American Women in Politics on women and minority women and Katherine Schaeffer, "Racial, Ethnic Diversity Increases Yet Again with the 117th Congress," Pew Research Center, January 28, 2021, https://www.pewresearch.org/fact-tank/2021/01/28/racial-ethnic-diversity-increases-yet-again-with-the-117th-congress/.

124. Jo Reger, "Debating US Contemporary Feminism," *Sociology Compass* 8, no. 1 (2014): 43–51; Jennifer Baumgardner and Amy Richards, *Manifesta: Young Women, Feminism and the Future* (New York: Farrar, Straus & Giroux, 2000); and Astrid Henry, *Not My Mother's Sister: Generational Conflict and Third Wave Feminism* (Bloomington: Indiana University Press, 2004).

125. Christina Ewig and Myra Marx Ferree, "Feminist Organizing: What's Old, What's New? History, Trends, and Issues," in *The Oxford Handbook of Gender and Politics*, ed. Georgina Waylen, Karen Celis, Johanna Kantola, and S. Laurel Weldon (New York: Oxford University Press, 2013), 437–61; Reger, *Everywhere and Nowhere*; Barbara Risman, *Where the Millennials Will Take Us* (New York: Oxford University Press, 2018); Rebecca Walker, ed., *To Be Real: Telling the Truth and Changing the Face of Feminism* (New York: Anchor, 1995); Leslie Heywood and Jennifer Drake, *Third Wave Agenda: Being Feminist, Doing Feminism* (Minneapolis: University of Minnesota Press, 1997); Clare Snyder, "What Is Third-Wave Feminism? A New Directions Essay," *Signs* 34, no. 1 (2008): 175–96; Charlotte Kroløkke and Anne Scott Sørensen, "Three Waves of Feminism: From Suffragettes to Grrls," in *Gender Communication Theories & Analyses: From Silence to Performance* (Thousand Oaks, CA: Sage, 2006), 1–25.

126. Myra Marx Ferree and Patricia Yancey Martin, eds., *Feminist Organizations: Harvest of the New Women's Movement* (Philadelphia: Temple University Press, 1995).

127. Dodson, *Impact of Women in Congress*; Weldon, *When Protest Makes Policy*; and Laurel Weldon, *Pro-*

test, Policy, and the Problem of Violence against Women: A Cross-National Comparison (Pittsburgh: University of Pittsburgh Press, 2002).

Conclusion

1. James Baldwin, "As Much Truth as One Can Bear," *New York Times*, January 14, 1962, Section T, Page 11, https://www.nytimes.com/1962/01/14/archives/as-much-truth-as-one-can-bear-to-speak-out-about-the-world-as-it-is.html.

2. Scott Richardson, "Blurred Lines of a Different Kind: Sexism, Sex, Media and Kids," in *Gender and Pop Culture: A Text-Reader*, ed. Adrienne Trier-Bieniek and Patricia Leavy (Rotterdam, Netherlands: Sense, 2014), 27–52.

3. C. Wright Mills, *The Sociological Imagination* (New York: Oxford University Press, 1959).

4. Kathleen Gerson, *Hard Choices: How Women Decide about Work, Career, and Motherhood* (Berkeley: University of California Press, 1986); Barbara Risman, *Gender Vertigo: American Families in Transition* (New Haven, CT: Yale University Press, 1998); and Christopher Carrington, *No Place like Home: Relationships and Family Life among Lesbians and Gay Men* (Chicago: University of Chicago Press, 1999), 32.

5. Gloria Steinem, *Outrageous Acts and Everyday Rebellions* (New York: Henry Holt, 1995).

6. Heather Karjane, Bonnie Fisher, and Francis Cullen, *Sexual Assault on Campus: What Colleges and Universities Are Doing about It* (US Department of Justice, Washington, DC, December 2005), https://www.ncjrs.gov/pdffiles1/nij/205521.pdf.

7. Quoted in Frank Sommers and Tana Dineen, *Curing Nuclear Madness: A New Age Prescription for Personal Action* (Toronto: Methuen, 1984), 158.

8. Joan Williams, *Unbending Gender: Why Family and Work Conflict and What to Do about It* (New York: Oxford University Press, 2000), 242.

9. Risman, *Gender Vertigo*.

CREDITS

INDEX